HOW TO EAT
THE PLEASURES AND PRINCIPLES OF GOOD FOOD

HOW TO EAT

THE PLEASURES AND PRINCIPLES OF GOOD FOOD

NIGELLA LAWSON

WILEY

Published by John Wiley & Sons, Inc., Hoboken, New Jersey
Published simultaneously in Canada

For general information on our other products and services or for technical support, please contact our Customer Care Department within the United States at (800) 762-2974, outside the United States at (317) 572-3993 or fax (317) 572-4002.

Wiley also publishes its books in a variety of electronic formats. Some content that appears in print may not be available in electronic books.

Library of Congress Cataloging-in-Publication Data:

ISBN: 0-471-25750-8

Printed in the United States of America

10 9 8 7 6 5 4 3 2 1

In memory of my Mother, Vanessa (1936 –1985)
and my sister Thomasina (1961 –1993)

and for John, Cosima, and Bruno

with love

CONTENTS

RECIPE CONTENTS

WEEKEND LUNCH

PREFACE

Cooking is not about just joining the dots, following one recipe slavishly and then moving on to the next. It's about developing an understanding of food, a sense of assurance in the kitchen, about the simple desire to make yourself something to eat. And in cooking, as in writing, you must please yourself to please others. Strangely, it can take enormous confidence to trust your own palate, follow your own instincts. Without habit, which itself is just trial and error, this can be harder than following the most elaborate of recipes. But it's what works, what's important.

There is a reason why this book is called *How to Eat* rather than *How to Cook*. It's a simple one: although it's possible to love eating without being able to cook, I don't believe you can ever really cook unless you love eating. Such love, of course, is not something that can be taught, but it can be conveyed—and maybe that's the point. In writing this book, I wanted to make food and my slavering passion for it the starting point; indeed, for me it was the starting point. I have nothing to declare but my greed.

The French, who've lost something of their culinary confidence in recent years, remain solid on this front. Some years ago in France, in response to the gastronomic apathy and consequent lowering of standards nationally—what is known as *la crise*—Jack Lang, then Minister of Culture, initiated *la semaine du goût*. He set up a body expressly to go into schools and other institutions not to teach anyone how to cook, but how to eat. This group might take with it a perfect baguette, an exquisite cheese, some local speciality cooked *comme il faut*, some fruit and vegetables grown properly and picked when ripe, in the belief that if the pupils, if people generally, tasted what was good, what was right, they would respect these traditions; by eating good food, they would want to cook it. And so the cycle continues.

I suppose you could say that we have had our own unofficial version of this. Our gastronomic awakening—or however, and with whatever degree of irony, you want to describe it—has been, to a huge extent, restaurant-led. It is, you might argue, by tasting food that we have become interested in cooking it. I do not necessarily disparage the influence of the restaurant; I spent twelve years as a restaurant critic, after all. But restaurant food and home food are not the same thing. Or, more accurately, eating in restaurants is not the same thing as eating at home. Which is not to say, of course, that you can't borrow from restaurant menus and adapt their chefs' recipes—and I do. This leads me to the other reason this book is called *How to Eat*.

I am not a chef. I am not even a trained or professional cook. My qualification is as an eater. I cook what I want to eat—within limits. I have a job—another job, that is, as an ordinary working journalist—and two children, one of whom was born during the writing of this book. And during the book's gestation, I would sometimes plan to cook some wonderful something or other, then work out a recipe, apply myself in anticipatory fantasy to it, write out the shopping list, plan the dinner—and then find that, when it came down to it, I just didn't have the energy. Anything that was too hard, too fussy, filled me with dread and panic, or, even if attempted, didn't work or was unreasonably demanding, has not found its way in here. And the recipes I do include have all been cooked in what television people call Real Time: menus have been made with all their component parts, together; that way, I know whether the oven settings correspond, whether you'll have enough burner space, how to make the timings work, and how not to have a nervous breakdown about it. I wanted food that can be made and eaten in a real life, not in perfect, isolated laboratory conditions.

Much of this is touched upon throughout the book, but I want to make it clear, here and now, that you need to acquire your own individual sense of what food is about, rather than just a vast collection of recipes.

What I am not talking about, however, is strenuous originality. The innovative in cooking all too often turns out to be inedible. The great modernist dictum, Make It New, is not a helpful precept in the kitchen. "Too often," wrote the great society hostess and arch food writer Ruth Lowinsky, as early as 1935, "the inexperienced think that if food is odd it must be a success. An indifferently roasted leg of mutton is not transformed by a sauce of hot raspberry jam, nor a plate of watery consommé improved by the addition of three glacé cherries." With food, authenticity is not the same thing as originality; indeed, they are often at odds. So while much is my own here—insofar as anything can be—many of the recipes included are derived from other writers. From the outset I wanted this book to be, in part, an anthology of the food I love eating and a way of paying my respects to the food writers I've loved reading. Throughout I've wanted, on principle as well as to show my gratitude, to credit honestly wherever appropriate, but I certainly wish to signal my thanks here as well. And if, at any time, a recipe has found its way onto these pages without having its source properly documented, I assure you and the putative unnamed originator that this is due to ignorance rather than villainy.

But if I question the tyranny of the recipe, that isn't to say I take a cavalier attitude. A recipe has to work. Even the great abstract painters have first to learn figure drawing. If many of my recipes seem to stretch out for a daunting number of pages, it is because brevity is no guarantee of simplicity. The easiest way to learn how to cook is by watching; bearing that in mind, I have tried more to talk you through a recipe than bark out instructions. As much as possible, I have wanted to make you feel that I'm there with you, in the kitchen, as you cook. The book that follows is the conversation we might be having.

EDITOR'S NOTE

The great success of *How to Eat* in its own land isn't hard to fathom. Rooted firmly in the pleasures of home cooking, the book also encourages readers to be themselves in the kitchen—to trust and nurture their own relationship to food and the pleasures of the table. It's a message people relish.

In "translating" *How to Eat* for American cooks, I've tried, whenever possible, to remain faithful to the book's spirit of spontaneity. The author's intention was to make the recipes easy to follow and reliable—they are—and also to allow cooks the freedom needed to gain pleasure and confidence in the kitchen. Thus, bossing and too much quantifying have been avoided; dish yields, for example, are given where necessary, but left otherwise to the judgment of the cook.

British readers have found *How to Eat* a new kitchen staple. I know its American audience will, too.

CHARTS AND MEASURES

OVEN TEMPERATURES

°F	*descriptionn*	°F	*description*
275	very cool	425	hot
300	cool	450 }	very hot
325	warm	475 }	
350	moderate		
375 }	fairly hot		
400 }			

ROASTING CHART

	Starting temperature, °F	After 15 minutes, °F	Approximate minutes per pound
Beef	475	350	Rare: 15
			Medium: 18
			Well done: 25
Chicken	400	400	15+10 overall
Duck	425	350	20
Goose	400	400	15+30 overall
Lamb and venison	425	400	Rare: 12
			Medium: 16
			Well done: 20
Pork	400	350	30
Veal	425	350	20
Turkey	See page 56		

There is more than one way to skin a cat; you may well find that, throughout this book, instructions are given for cooking various meats in the oven at temperatures or for times that differ from those given in the chart. There are many variables in roasting, as in cooking generally, but the chart, drawn up with my butcher, David Lidgate, should provide a clear and reliable guide to roasting times. An important factor in following these timings is the temperature of the meat before it goes into the oven. If it's fridge-cold the guidelines are irrelevant, inadequate; all bets are off. Let the meat stand, out of the fridge, to get to room temperature before you cook it as instructed. After the meat has had its advised cooking time, test it; either press it (if it feels soft, it's rare; bouncy, it's medium; hard, it's well done) or pierce with a knife to see. With chicken, stick a knife in between the thigh and the body; if the juices run clear, it's cooked. And always let meat rest out of the oven for at least 10 minutes before carving.

FISH

Go to a fish seller, while they still exist, to get good advice and wise information and to ensure, please, their continuing existence. Going to a fish seller, like going to a butcher, makes life easier where it matters—in the kitchen. I go for good fish, good meat, no funny stuff. But once there, I make the most of it; butchers and fish sellers have skills that we don't. Don't feel apologetic about asking a fish seller to fillet or a butcher to bone. When I order fish or meat, I practically hold a conference to discuss every possibility, every eventuality; I pick brains, ask for advice on cooking, and relentlessly exploit the expertise on offer. So should you.

For those times you can't get to a fish seller, I suggest you check the advice offered by the Canadian Department of Fisheries concerning cooking times: for every 1 inch of thickness, cook the fish, by whatever means—frying, grilling, poaching, baking—for 10 minutes; for a whole fish, measure at its thickest point and multiply accordingly. I heed this advice, but I alter it; I reckon that 8–9 minutes per inch will do, so I recommend changing the 1-inch rule to 1¼ inches, thus giving myself an extra quarter-inch for the Canadians' 10 minutes. When baking fish, whether wrapped in buttered foil or not, I use a 375° F oven. Obviously, there are exceptions. (See pages 289–290 for notes on cooking a whole salmon.) And there are times when I ignore these rules altogether.

SOME USEFUL WEIGHTS
AND MEASURES

garlic	1 minced medium clove = 1 teaspoon
onion	1 average onion = ¼ pound
citrus fruits	Using a zester and an electric juicer, you should find, give or take, that you get the following amounts:
1 lime	1 teaspoon zest 2 tablespoons juice
1 lemon	2 teaspoons zest 8 tablespoons juice
1 orange	1 tablespoon zest 10 tablespoons juice
nuts	Figure on nuts weighing twice as much in their shells as shelled, and adapt shopping lists accordingly.

peas and beans	Peas in the pod weigh about 3 times as much as they do shelled; the weight of shelled fava beans is about a third of the weight in the pod. Again, adapt shopping lists accordingly.
shellfish	8 small clams (about 2 inches across) = about 1 pound 24 mussels = about 1 pound
rhubarb	There are a lot of rhubarb recipes in this book, so it may be useful to know that when cooked in the oven with sugar, as on page 107, but with no liquid added, about 2 pounds untrimmed rhubarb = about 1 pound trimmed = about ½ pound or 1⅔ cups puréed (i.e., cooked and drained of excess juice)— producing, on average, 1 cup juice.

Throughout this book:

- All eggs are large (and see below).

- Olive oil is usually extra virgin; if "olive oil" is called for, you may use a lesser type, provided it's high quality.

- When "a drop of oil" or "oil" is called for, use any vegetable oil or ordinary olive oil, if the dish is Western. The drop of oil is usually mixed with butter to help prevent its burning.

- Flour is often Italian 00 (*farina dopia zero*; see page 458); all-purpose flour can easily be used in its place. All flour is measured by spooning it gently into a measuring cup, then leveling the top with the back of a knife or spatula.

- Brown sugar, light and dark, is often muscovado sugar (see page 460).

- All parsley is flat-leaf.

- A bouquet garni is an herb bunch that consists of 4–5 parsley sprigs, 2–3 thyme sprigs, and a bay leaf tied together or enclosed in a small cheesecloth or muslin bag. Used to flavor soups and stews, from which it's easily removable, it can also be bought in ready-prepared, dried form, in little bags.

I always use organic eggs from hens that are checked regularly for salmonella. I thus have no anxieties about raw eggs, but you should know that because of possible infection from salmonella, the old, the ill, the vulnerable, the pregnant, babies, and children are advised not to eat anything with uncooked egg in it.

See page 249 for a fuller discussion of beef, but as with the eggs, so with any foodstuff. Buy from shops where the produce is traceable; that's to say, you can find out where it comes from and what's happened to it along the way.

HOW TO EAT
THE PLEASURES AND PRINCIPLES OF GOOD FOOD

BASICS, ETC.

The Great Culinary Renaissance we have heard so much about has done many things—given us extra virgin olive oil, better restaurants, and gastroporn—but it hasn't taught us how to cook.

Of course, standards have improved. Better ingredients are available to us now, and more people know about them. Food and cooking have become more than respectable—they are fashionable. But the cooking renaissance, so relentlessly talked up in the 1980s, started in restaurants and newspapers and filtered its way into the home. This is the wrong way round. Cooking is best learned at your own stove; you learn by watching and by doing.

Chefs themselves know this. The great chefs of France and Italy learn about food at home; what they do later, in the restaurants that make them famous, is use what they have learned. They build on it, they start elaborating. They take home cooking to the restaurant, not the restaurant school of cooking to the home. Inverting the process is like learning a vocabulary without any grammar. The analogy is pertinent. In years as a restaurant critic, I couldn't help noticing that however fine the menu, some chefs, for all that they seem to have mastered the idiom, have no authentic language of their own. We are at risk, here, of becoming not cooks but culinary mimics. There are some things you just cannot learn from a professional chef. I am not talking of home economics—the rules that govern what food does when you apply heat or introduce air or whatever—but of home cooking, and of how experience builds organically. For there is more to cooking than being able to put on a good show. Of course, there are advantages in an increased awareness of and enthusiasm for food, but the danger is that it excites an appetite for new recipes, new ingredients: follow a recipe once and then—on to the next. Cooking isn't like that. The point about real-life cooking is that your proficiency grows exponentially. You cook something once, then again, and again. Each time you add something different (leftovers from the fridge, whatever might be in the kitchen or in season) and what you end up with differs also.

You can learn how to cook fancy food from the glossy magazines, but you need the basics. And anyway, it is better to be able to roast a chicken than to be a dab hand with focaccia. I would be exhausted if the cooking I did every day was recipe-index food. I don't want to cook like that all the time, and I certainly don't want to eat like that.

Nor do I want to go back to some notional golden age of nursery food. I wasn't brought up on shepherd's pie and bread pudding and I'm not going to start living on them now. It is interesting, though, that these homey foods were not revived in our homes so much as they were rediscovered by restaurants. And, even if I don't wish to eat this sort of thing all the time, isn't it more appropriate to learn how to cook it at home than to have to go to a restaurant to eat it?

By invoking the basics, I certainly don't mean to evoke a grim, puritanical self-sufficiency, with austere recipes for homemade bread and stern admonishments against buying any form of food already cooked. I have no wish to go on a crusade. I doubt I will ever become someone who habitually bakes her own bread—after all, shopping for good food is just as much of a pleasure as cooking it can be. But there is something between grinding your own flour and cooking only for special occasions. Cooking has become too much of a device by which to impress people rather than simply to feed them pleasurably.

In literature, teachers talk about key texts; they exist, too, in cooking. That's what I mean by basics.

Everyone's list of basics is, of course, different. Your idea of home cooking, your whole experience of eating, colors your sense of what foods should be included in the culinary canon. Cooking, indeed, is not so very different from literature; what you have read previously shapes how you read now. And so we eat; and so we cook.

If I don't include your nostalgic favorite in this chapter, you may find a recipe for it elsewhere in the book (see Index). And it is impossible to write a list without being painfully aware of what has been left out; cooking is not an exclusive art, whatever its grander exponents might lead you to think. Being familiar with making certain dishes—so familiar that you don't need to look in a book to make them (and much of this chapter should eventually make itself redundant)—doesn't preclude your cooking other things.

So what are basic dishes? Everyone has to know how to roast chicken and other birds, pork, beef, and lamb, and what to do with slabs of meat (turn to the roasting chart on page xviii). This is not abstruse knowledge, but general information so basic that many books don't bother to mention it. I am often telephoned by friends at whose houses I have eaten something more elaborate than I would ever cook, to be asked how long their leg of lamb needs to be in the oven, and at what temperature.

The key texts constitute the framework of your repertoire—stews, roasts, white sauce, mayonnaise, stocks, soups. You might also think of tackling pastry.

Lacking a firmly based culinary tradition with the range and variation of, say, regional French cooking, we in Britain and America tend to lack an enduring respect for particular dishes. It's not so much that we hunger to eat whatever is fashionable as that we drop anything that is no longer of the moment. The tendency is not exclusively Anglo-American—if you were to go to a grand dinner party in France or Italy, you might be served whatever was considered the culinary *dernier cri*—but what makes our behavior more emphatic, more ultimately sterile, is that, when we cook for company, we are inclined to try to reproduce style-conscious menu-fodder—dinner-party food with a vengeance.

I think it is true, too, that we are quick to despise what once we looked at so breathlessly in magazines and gourmet food shops. Just because a food is no longer flavor-of-the-month, it shouldn't follow that it is evermore to be spoken of as a shameful aberration. It is important always to judge honestly and independently. This can be harder than it sounds. Fashion has a curious but compelling urgency. Even those of us who feel we are free of fashion's diktats are, despite ourselves, influenced by them. As what is seemingly desirable changes, so our eye changes. It doesn't have to be wholesale conversion for this effect to take place; we just begin to look at things differently.

Of course, fashion may lead us to excesses. It is easy to ascribe the one-time popularity of nouvelle cuisine—which fashion decrees we must now treat as hootingly risible—to just such an excess. And to some extent that would be correct. But what some people forget is that the most ludicrous excesses of nouvelle cuisine were not follies committed by its most talented exponents but by the second and third rank. It is important to distinguish between what is fashionable and good and what is fashionable and bad.

With food, it should be easier to maintain your integrity; you must, after all, always know whether you enjoy the taste of something or not. And in cooking, as in eating, you just have to let your real likes and desires guide you.

My list of basics—and the recipes that constitute it—are dotted throughout this book. The list is eclectic. And in this chapter I have tried, in the main, to stay with the sort of food most of us anyway presume we can cook; it's only when we get started that we realize we need to look something up, check times, remind ourselves of the quantities. I want to satisfy those very basic demands without in any way wishing to make you feel as if there were some actual list of recipes you needed to master before acquiring some notional and wholly goal-oriented culinary expertise. My aim is not to promote notions of uniformity or consistency—or even to imply that either might be desirable—but to suggest a way of cooking that isn't simply notching up recipes. In short, cooking in context.

First, you have to know how to do certain things, things that years ago it was taken for granted would be learned at home. These are ordinary kitchen skills, such as how to make pastry or a white sauce.

I learned some of these things with my mother in the kitchen when I was a child, but not all of them. So I understand the fearfulness that grips you just as you anticipate rolling out some pastry dough, say. We ate no desserts at home; my mother didn't bake, nor did my grandmothers. I didn't acquire early in life that lazy confidence, that instinct. When I cook a stew I have a sense, automatically, of whether I want to use red or white wine, of what will happen if I add thyme or bacon lardons. But when I bake, I feel I lack that instinct, though I hope I am beginning to acquire it.

And of course I have faltered, made mistakes, cooked disasters. I know what it's like to panic in the kitchen, to feel flustered by a recipe that lists too many ingredients or takes for granted too much expertise or dexterity.

I don't think the answer, though, is to avoid anything that seems, on first view, complicated or involves elaborate procedures. That just makes you feel more fearful. But what is extraordinarily liberating is trying something—say, pastry—and finding out that, left quietly to your own devices, you can actually do it. What once seemed an arcane skill becomes second nature. It does happen.

And how it happens is by repetition. If you haven't made pastry before, follow the recipe for pastry dough on page 37. Make a tart. Don't wait too long to make another one. Or a pie or a savory tart. The point is to get used gradually to cooking something in the ordinary run of things. I concede that it might mean having to make more of a conscious effort in the beginning, but the time and concentration needed will recede naturally and the effort will soon cease altogether to be conscious. It will just become part of what you do.

You could probably get through life without knowing how to roast a chicken, but the question is, would you want to?

BASIC ROAST CHICKEN

When I was a child, we had roast chicken at Saturday lunch and probably one evening a week, too. Even when there were only a few of us, my mother never roasted just one chicken; she cooked two, one to keep in the fridge, cold and whole, for picking at during the week. It's partly for that reason that a roast chicken, to me, smells of home, of family, of food that carries some important, extra-culinary weight.

My basic roast chicken is the same as my mother's: I stick half a lemon up its bottom, smear some oil or butter on its breast, sprinkle it with a little salt, and put it in a 400°F oven for about 15 minutes per pound plus 10 minutes.

My mother could make the stringiest, toughest flesh—a bird that had been intensively farmed and frozen since the last Ice Age—taste as if it were a lovingly reared poulet de Bresse. She, you see, was a product of her age, which believed that cooking lay in what you did to inferior products (and I expect she did no more in this case than use much more butter than anyone would now); I, however, am a product of mine, which believes that you always use the best, the freshest produce of the highest quality you can afford—and then do as little as possible to it. So I buy organic free-range chickens and anoint them with the tiniest amount of extra virgin olive oil or butter—as if I were putting on very expensive hand cream—before putting them in the oven. I retain the lemon out of habit—and to make my kitchen smell like my mother's, with its aromatic, oily-sharp fog.

I can't honestly say that my roast chicken tastes better than hers, but I don't like eating intensively farmed, industrially reared meat. However, if you know you've got an inferior bird in front of you, cook it for the first hour breast-side down. This means you don't, at the end, have quite that glorious effect of the swelling, burnished breast—the chicken will have more of a flapper's bosom, flat but fleshy—but the white meat will be more tender because all the fats and juices will have oozed their way into it.

If you want to make a good gravy—and I use the term to indicate a meat-thick golden juice or, risking pretentiousness here, jus—then put 1 tablespoon of olive oil in the roasting dish when you anoint the bird before putting it in the oven; about half an hour before the end, add another tablespoon of oil and a spritz from the lemon half that isn't stuffed up the chicken. By all means, use butter if you prefer, but make sure there's some oil in the pan, too, to stop the butter from burning.

When you remove the chicken, let it stand for 5 or 10 minutes before carving it, and make gravy by putting the roasting dish on the burner (remove, if you want, any excess fat with a spoon, though I tend to leave it as it is). Add a little white wine and boiling water or chicken stock, letting it all bubble away till it's syrupy and chickeny. If you don't have at hand any homemade stock, a good-quality chicken bouillon cube, or portion thereof, would be fine. In fact, Italians sometimes put a bouillon cube inside the chicken along with or instead of the lemon half before roasting it.

My basic chicken recipe also includes garlic and shallots; this is the easy way to have dinner on the table without doing much. About 50 minutes before the end of the cooking time, pour 2 tablespoons olive oil either into the same pan or another one and add, per 4-pound chicken (which is for 4 people), the unpeeled cloves of 2 heads of garlic and about 20 unpeeled shallots. They don't roast, really, but steam inside their skins. Eat them by pressing on them with a fork and letting the soft, mild—that's to say intensely flavored and yet wholly without pungency—creamy interior squeeze out on to your plate. Put some plates on the table for the discarded skins and, if not finger bowls, then napkins or a roll of paper towels. My children adore garlic and shallots cooked like this and sometimes, when I don't want to cook a whole chicken for them, I roast a poussin instead and put the shallots and garlic and poussin in all at the same time. And if you want to make this basic recipe feel a little less basic, then you can sprinkle some toasted pine nuts and flat-leaf parsley, chopped at the last minute, over the food before serving.

If you've managed to fit the garlic and shallots in the pan with the chicken, you can roast a pan of potatoes in the same oven at the same time. Dice the potatoes, also unpeeled, into approximately ½-inch cubes, or just cut new potatoes in half lengthways and anoint them with oil (or melted lard, which fries them fabulously crisp). Sprinkle them with a little dried thyme (or freshly chopped rosemary) before cooking them for about 1 hour.

All of which leads us to the next basic recipe:

STOCK

Do not throw away the chicken carcass after eating the chicken. Go so far, I'd say, as to scavenge from everyone's plate, picking up the bones they've left. I'm afraid I even do this in other people's houses. You don't need to make stock now—and indeed you couldn't make anything very useful from the amount of bones from one bird—but freeze them. Indeed, freeze whatever bones you can, whenever you can, in order to make stock at some later date (see page 69 for further, passionate, adumbration of this thesis).

An actual recipe for stock would be hard to give with a straight face; boiling remains to make stock is as far from being a precise art as you can get. Look at the recipes for broth and consommé (see pages 83–84) if you want something highfalutin', but if you're looking for what I call chicken stock (but which classi-cally trained French chefs, who would use fresh meat and raw bones, boiled up specifically to make stock, would most definitely not), then follow my general instructions. At home, I would use the carcasses of 3 medium, cooked chickens.

Break or cut the bones up roughly and put them in a big pot. Add a stalk of celery broken in two or a few lovage leaves, 1 or 2 carrots, depending on size, peeled and halved, 1 onion stuck with a clove, 5 peppercorns, a bouquet garni (see page xx), some parsley stalks, and the white of a leek. Often I have more or less everything at hand without trying, except for that leek; in which case I just leave it out. (I sometimes add a couple of discs of veal shin if I want a deeper-toned broth of almost unctuous mellowness.) Cover with cold water, add 1 tea-spoon of salt, and bring to the boil, skimming off the froth and scum that rises to the surface. Lower the heat and let the stock bubble very, very gently, uncovered, for about 3 hours. Allow to cool a little, then strain into a wide, large bowl or another pot. When cold, put in the fridge without decanting. I like to let it chill in the fridge so that I can remove any fat that rises to the surface, and the wider that surface is, the easier.

When I've removed the fat, I taste the stock and consider whether I'd prefer it more strongly flavored. If so, I put it back in a pan on the burner and boil it down till I've got a smaller amount of rich, intensely flavored stock.

I then store it in differing quantities in the freezer. On the whole, I find pack-ages of ½ cup and 1 cup the most useful. For the smaller amount, I just ladle 8 tablespoons into a freezer bag or small tub with a lid; for the larger, I line a mea-suring cup with a freezer bag and pour it in till I've got, give or take, 1 cup (it's difficult, because of the baggy lining, to judge with super-calibrated accuracy). I then close the bag and put the whole thing, cup and all, into the freezer. This is why I own so many plastic measuring cups. I am constantly forgetting about them once they're buried in the freezer. But, in principle, what you should do is leave the stock till solid, then whisk away the cup, leaving the cup-shaped cylin-der of frozen liquid, which you slot back into the freezer. You may need to run hot water over the cup for a minute in order to let the stock in its bag just slip out. This is a useful way to freeze any liquid. Although it's a bore, it pays to mea-sure accurately and to label clearly at the time of freezing. Later you can take out exactly the quantity you need.

Poussins make wonderful, strong, easily jellied stock; it must be the amount of zip and gelatin in their poor young bones. So if ever you need to make a stock from scratch, with fresh meat, not cooked bones (in other words, the way you're supposed to), and you can't find a boiling fowl, then buy some poussins, about

4, cut each in half, use vegetables as above, cover with cold water, and proceed as normal.

I do not disapprove of bouillon cubes or other commercial stocks if they're good, not overly salty, and, of course, leave no chemical aftertaste.

One of the most useful things an Italian friend once showed me was how important even half a stalk of celery is in providing basenote flavor not just to stocks but to tomato and meat sauces, to pies—in fact, to almost anything savory. The taste is not boorishly celerylike; it just provides an essential floor of flavor.

In Italy, when you buy vegetables from the greengrocer, you can ask for a bunch of odori, which is a bunch of those herbs that breathe their essential scent into sauces and is given, gratis. Included in it will be one stick of celery. And I wish we could buy the same in our markets, let alone get it for free. You need so little of it when cooking—still, I'm gratified to know that a reliable product is in the market year-round.

In summer or even from spring onward, if you've got a garden or bit of yard, you can grow some lovage, the leaves and stalks of which fabulously impart the scent of a grassy, slightly more aromatic celery. You just pick a bit as you need it. I often use lovage as a replacement for celery; if I'm chopping some onion, carrot, and garlic to make a base for a shepherd's pie or a thick soup, I chop in some lovage leaves at the same time.

Naturally, you can use more if you want the lovage to be the subject, the actual focus. To make a lettuce and lovage soup, soften a handful of finely chopped lovage leaves along with 4 finely chopped scallions in about 2 tablespoons of butter, then add 2 shredded heads of romaine and let them wilt in the buttery heat. Stir in ½ teaspoon sugar and some salt, if the stock you're using is not very salty itself. Add about 4 cups of stock—a light chicken stock, possibly from your freezer, or vegetable stock, homemade or prepared from best-quality cubes—or half stock and the rest milk. Gently simmer, uncovered, for about 10 to 15 minutes, then either blend in a blender or food processor or push through a strainer or a food mill. Taste again for seasoning. Add a good grating of fresh nutmeg. If you want a velvety cream rather than a light, pale broth, stir an egg yolk beaten with ½ cup cream, heavy or light, into the soup over the heat, but make sure it doesn't boil. Remove from the heat and serve, sprinkling over some more chopped lovage leaves.

You can grow lovage from seed, but I bought a little pot from a garden center some years back and planted it; now each spring it grows back huge, its bushy, long-stalked arms outstretched, magnificently architectural.

You should grow your own herbs if you can and want to, but don't spread yourself, or your plants, too thin. It is counterproductive if you have so little of each herb that you never pick much of it for fear of totally denuding your stock. In my own garden, I stick to rosemary, flat-leaf parsley, arugula, and sorrel. I like to grow lots of parsley—at least two rows, the length of the whole bed—and even more arugula. Some years I've planted garlic so that I can use the gloriously infused leaves, as they grow, cut up freshly in a salad. In pots I keep bay, marjoram, and mint. This year I'm going to try some angelica—to flavor custards—and Thai basil, so that I don't have to go to the Thai shop to buy huge bunches of the stuff, wonderfully aromatic though it is, only to see it go bad before I've had a chance to use it all. I have never had any success with coriander (from seed). I can manage basil easily, but then I suddenly feel overrun. And I have to say, I find watering pots excruciatingly effortful.

As with so much to do with food, a lot of a little rather than a little of a lot is the best, most comforting, and most useful rule. You can always buy herbs growing in pots, in season, at good supermarkets and garden centers, and herbs cut in big bunches in specialist shops and at good greengrocers.

MAYONNAISE

Stock is what you may make out of the bones of your roasted chicken, but mayonnaise, real mayonnaise, is what you might make to eat with the cold, leftover meat. There is one drawback: when you actually make mayonnaise you realize, beyond the point of insistent denial, how much oil goes into it. But because even the best bottled mayonnaise—and I don't mean the one you think I mean, Hellman's, but one manufactured by a company called Cottage Delight (see page 461)—bears little or no relation to real mayonnaise, you may as well know how to make it.

When I was in my teens, I loved Henry James. I read him with uncorrupted pleasure. Then, when I was eighteen or so and had just started *The Golden Bowl,* someone—older, cleverer, whose opinions were offered gravely—asked me whether I didn't find James very difficult, as she always did. Until then, I had no idea that I might, and I didn't. From that moment, I couldn't read him but self-consciously; from then on, I did find him difficult. I do not wish to insult by the comparison, but I had a similar, Jamesian mayonnaise experience. My mother used to make mayonnaise weekly, twice weekly; we children would help. I had no idea it was meant to be difficult, or that it was thought to be such a nerve-racking ordeal. Then someone asked how I managed to be so breezy about it, how I stopped it from curdling. From then on, I scarcely made a mayonnaise that didn't break. It's not surprising; when confidence is undermined or ruptured, it can be difficult to do the simplest things, or to take any enjoyment even in trying.

I don't deny that mayonnaises can break, but please don't jinx yourself. Anyway, it's not a catastrophe if it does. A small drop of boiling water can fix things and, if it doesn't, you can start again with an egg yolk in a bowl. Beat it and slowly beat in the curdled mess of mayo you were previously working on. Later, add more oil and a little lemon juice. You should, this way, end up with the smoothly amalgamated yellow ointment you were after in the first place. I hate to say it, but you may have to do this twice. You may end up with rather more mayonnaise than you need, but getting it right in the end restores your confidence, and this is the important thing.

I make mayonnaise the way my mother did—I warm the eggs in the bowl (as explained more fully later), then beat and add oil just from the bottle, not measuring, until the texture feels right, feels like mayonnaise. I squeeze in lemon juice, also freehand, until the look and taste feel right. If you make a habit of making mayonnaise, you will inevitably come to judge it instinctively too. I don't like too much olive oil in it; if it's too strong, it rasps the back of the throat, becomes too invasive. I use a little over two-thirds peanut oil and a little under one-third olive oil, preferably that lovely mild stuff from Liguria. If you prefer, do use half and half and a mild French olive oil, which is probably more correct, anyway, than the Italian variety.

By habit and maternal instruction, I always used to use an ordinary whisk. This takes a long time (and I can see why my mother used us, her children, as *commis* chefs). Now I use my KitchenAid mixer with the wire whip in place. You can equally well use one of those hand-held beaters, which are cheap and useful. Please, whatever you do, don't use a food processor; if you do, your finished product tastes just like the gluey bought stuff. And then, hell, you might as well just go out and buy it.

2 egg yolks (but wait to separate the eggs, and see below)	**⅓ cup extra-virgin olive oil**
pinch salt	**juice of ½ lemon or more, to taste**
1 cup peanut or sunflower oil	**salt and freshly milled white pepper**

Put the eggs, in their shells, in a large bowl. Fill the bowl with warm water from the tap and leave for 10 minutes. (This brings eggs and bowl comfortably to room temperature, which will help stop the eggs from curdling, but is optional, as long as you remember to take the eggs out of the fridge well before you need them.) Then remove the eggs, get rid of the water, and dry the bowl thoroughly. Wet and then wring out a kitchen towel and set the bowl on it; this stops it slipping and jumping about on the work surface.

Separate the eggs. Put aside the whites and freeze them for another use (see page 17), and let the yolks plop into the dried bowl. Start whisking the yolks with the salt. After a few minutes, very, very gradually and drop by mean drop, add the peanut oil. You must not rush this. It's easier to let the oil seep in gradually if you pour from a height, holding the measuring cup (or bottle with a spout, if you're not actually using measured quantities) well above the bowl. Keep going until you see a thick mayonnaise form, about 2–3 tablespoons' worth; then you can relax and let the oil drip in small glugs. When both oils have been incorporated (first the peanut, then the olive oil) and you have a thick, smooth, firm mayonnaise, add the lemon juice, whisking all the time. Taste to see if you need to add more. Add salt and pepper as you like; my mother used white pepper, so she didn't end up with black specks, and so, generally, do I.

SAUCE VERT If you want a sharper, more vinegary taste, you can add ½–1 teaspoon Dijon mustard to the egg yolks in the beginning. A touch of mustard is fabulous in a sauce verte, or green mayonnaise, which is made by adding 2 tablespoons or so of chopped herbs—sorrel, tarragon, parsley, whatever—and, classically, a handful of spinach, blanched (dunked for a few seconds in boiling water), superefficiently drained, then minutely chopped into the mayonnaise at the end. Otherwise, a little watercress or arugula, chopped with the unblanched herbs, in place of the spinach, is fine. And if you're in the mood, you can add some chopped capers and gherkins (about 2 teaspoons of each) as well. In other words, treat this as what it is in Italian—salsa verde (page 181)—only hanging in an egg and oil emulsion rather than just bound in the oil; you can stir in some minced anchovy if you like too.

EGGS WITH MAYONNAISE I love sauce verte, especially with cold pork, but I have to say that every time I eat real mayonnaise, in its bleached-yolk yellow and unmodified state, I am freshly surprised how good it is. And eggs with mayonnaise—hard-boiled eggs, sliced and masked with light mayonnaise, with or without a criss-crossing of anchovies on top—has to be one of the most fashionably underrated of dishes.

HOLLANDAISE

Hollandaise is really a kind of hot mayonnaise. As children, we all took turns standing on the chair, pushed up against the stove, to stir the butter we'd conscientiously cut into cubes before starting into the swell of eggs in the pudding basin, suspended above a saucepan of boiling water. But you needn't worry about equipment; a double boiler is all you need. I'm glad, however, for my early training in making hollandaise (and béarnaise, see below) because it preempted any fear about how difficult saucemaking might be. Even my brother, who scarcely cooks anything other than pasta, can make hollandaise.

It's true, we didn't make it according to the classical canon. Most French textbooks instruct you to make a fierce reduction to whisk into the yolks at the beginning. I think—and, as my pared-down attitude is one also sanctioned by Carême, there's no need to apologize for it—that a simple, gentler hollandaise, just eggs and butter emulsified and spruced with lemon juice, is best. If you want to try the ur-recipe, then boil down 2 tablespoons of white wine vinegar, 1 of water, a good grating of fresh pepper, and the smallest pinch of salt until the liquid is reduced to about 1 tablespoon, then whisk that into the yolks at the very beginning, before you get on to adding any of the butter.

3 egg yolks	juice of ½–1 lemon
16 tablespoons (2 sticks) unsalted butter, soft, cut into ½-inch cubes	salt and freshly milled white or black pepper

Put the yolks in the top of a double boiler. Fill the bottom with cold water, which should not touch the top pan when it is inserted. Fit the pans together, put on high heat, and whisk the yolks while the water comes to the boil. When it does, reduce to a steady simmer and start whisking in the cubes of butter. As one piece of butter is absorbed, whisk in the next and, by the time they have all been added, you should have a bowlful of thick sauce. If you feel it's reached that stage before you've finished all the butter, don't worry—just stop. And throw in extra if you feel it could take it. Still whisking, squeeze in the juice of half a lemon—I love watching the yolk-yellow goo suddenly lighten—and add the salt, pepper (grinding in white pepper, if you've got it), and more lemon juice to taste.

When the sauce is ready, you can fill a saucepan with tepid water and suspend the top of the double boiler over that (this time with the base of the top submerged) to keep it warm for about 20 minutes, but beat it firmly again before serving. If the sauce looks as if it might curdle while you are making it, you can quickly whisk in an ice cube (to bring the temperature down) or stand the top of the double boiler in a saucepan of cold water and whisk well.

Hollandaise is not an essential accompaniment for asparagus, but a pretty divine one. I love it, too, made with saffron threads—a large pinch or ¼ teaspoon, however you prefer to measure it—softened in and added with the lemon juice.

You should know that sauce maltaise is a hollandaise with blood-orange juice. I don't go for it; I prefer, if I want that particular realm of flavor, to substitute Seville orange juice for the lemon juice. This means (if you don't freeze your Seville oranges) you can make it only in January or February (see Foods in Season, page 42). As a once-a-year accompaniment to plain, baked, or grilled white fish and broccoli, it might be a treat, but proceed—as with all deviations from the classical—with caution.

BÉARNAISE
for Dominic

I grew up believing, erroneously, that sauce béarnaise was just a hollandaise with chopped tarragon in it. Up to a point, it is. And if you want to make a quick almost-béarnaise, use my mother's method, which is to say follow the recipe for hollandaise above, adding 1 teaspoon dried tarragon to the egg yolks and then stirring in some freshly chopped tarragon at the end. Use a little lemon only, and lots of pepper. Be careful: too much tarragon can evoke that manure-underfoot, farmhouse scent, although I don't know why. When I was a child and dried herbs weren't considered as ignominious as they are today, we made béarnaise without any fresh tarragon, though with a drip of tarragon vinegar along with the squeeze of lemon juice. Unless you are trying to create the great classic in its purest form, be kind to yourself. If you can't get chervil, be assured that the sauce will still taste fabulous with just tarragon. Equally, you can use 4 tablespoons of vinegar and omit the wine.

This is my desert island sauce; there's little better in the world to eat than steak béarnaise. (It's also very good with salmon.) If you substitute mint for the tarragon, you have a sauce that goes very well with lamb, especially steaks cut off the leg and plain grilled.

1 tablespoon minced shallots	3 egg yolks
2 tablespoons fresh tarragon leaves, chopped, and their stalks, chopped roughly and bruised	1 tablespoon water
	16 tablespoons (2 sticks) unsalted butter, soft, cut into ½-inch dice
1 tablespoon chopped chervil (optional)	salt and freshly milled white or black
2 tablespoons wine or tarragon vinegar	pepper
2 tablespoons white wine	juice of ¼ – ½ lemon
1 teaspoon peppercorns (preferably white), crushed or bruised	

Put the shallot, tarragon stalks, 1 tablespoon of the chopped tarragon, and the chervil, if using, and the vinegar, wine, and peppercorns in a heavy-bottomed saucepan and boil until reduced to about 1 tablespoon. Don't move from the stove; this doesn't take long.

Press the reduced liquid through a regular or tea strainer and leave to cool. Put egg yolks and water in the top of a double boiler. Set over the bottom, in which water has come to a simmer. Add the reduced and strained liquid and whisk well. Keep whisking as you add the butter, cube by cube, until it is all absorbed. Taste, season as you wish with the salt and pepper, and add lemon juice as you wish. Treat it as the hollandaise to keep it warm and avert curdling. Stir in the remaining tablespoon of fresh chopped tarragon as you're about to serve it.

For each of the three sauces above, you need to separate the egg yolks from the albumen. Everyone always tells you that the best way to do this is by cracking open the egg and, using the broken half-shells to cup the yolk, passing it from one to the other and back again until all the white has dropped in the bowl or cup you've placed beneath and the perfect, naked round of yolk remains in the shell. I don't think so. All you need is for a little sharp bit of the cracked-open shell to pierce the yolk and the deal's off. It is easier and less fussy altogether just to crack the egg over a bowl and slip the insides from their shell into the palm of your hand near the bottoms of your fingers. Then splay your fingers a fraction. The egg white will run out and drip through the cracks between your fingers into the bowl, and the yolk will remain in the palm of your hand ready to be slipped into a different bowl.

I cannot bring myself to throw away the whites. Occasionally, when things threaten to get seriously out of hand, I just separate the eggs over the sink, not even giving myself the agony of choice. But otherwise I freeze the rejected whites, either singly or in multiples, marking clearly how many are in each freezer bag. Just in case you forget to label them or the bag's gone wrinkly and you can't read what's written on it, you should know that a frozen large egg white weighs about 1½ ounces. From that, you can work out how many you've got stashed away in any particular unmarked bag just by weighing it.

The obvious thing to make with egg white is meringue. For each egg white you need ⅓ cup sugar; the whites should be at room temperature before you start. I use superfine sugar, but you can substitute soft brown sugar to make beautiful ivory-colored, almost toffee-ish meringues, golden caster sugar (see page 460) if you want the ivory color but not such a pronounced taste, or maple sugar for the most fabulous, smoky, gleaming, elegant meringue of all time, the color of expensive oyster-satin underwear. The brown or maple sugar variants are worth bearing in mind to go with ice cream or fruit compotes of any sort or just with coffee after dinner. I wouldn't necessarily sandwich the meringues together with whipped cream, but a bowl of raspberries, another of thick cream, and a plate of sugary, creamy, soft-centered, buff-colored meringues is easy to get together and pretty damn fabulous—children's tea-party food with an edge.

To make about 40 meringues about 1 inch in diameter, or 20 about 2 inches, you need:

2 egg whites   **⅔ cup sugar**

Preheat the oven to a very low heat: 275°F. Whisk the egg whites until stiff. For this, I always use my free-standing mixer with the wire whip attached, but a hand-held electric beater or whisk will do. When you lift the beaters or whisk out of the mixture and firm peaks retain their shape, it's stiff enough. Gradually whisk in half the sugar. The meringue will take on a wonderful satiny gleam. Then fold in the remaining sugar with a metal spoon.

Line 1 or 2 baking sheets with parchment paper or, better still, a fabulous creation called, just as fabulously, Cook-Eze. This is some sort of nonstick flexible fiberglass sheet that you can reuse more or less indefinitely (until you lose it, in my case) to line cake and roasting pans. Mail-order kitchen equipment places and some baking goods shops stock it (see page 462 for a source). Another such item is called Silpat.

I am not dextrous, but I enjoy a bit of squeezing through piping bags. It makes me feel brisk and accomplished without having to be either. Remember to fold back the hem end of the piping bag by about half its whole length as you fill it. I stand the piping bags in a straight glass to do this. Once the piping bag is half full of the meringue mixture, you can unfold the bag's skirt and twist the ends together to put pressure on the meringue within, keeping one hand near the (plain) nozzle. Squeeze out individual meringues to your desired size on the lined sheets. Refill the piping bag and continue until all the mixture is used up. Don't worry if you haven't got a piping bag; just use teaspoons, or tablespoons if you're making the larger size, to deposit and shape them into neat piles, one by one.

Put the sheets of meringues in the oven for about 40 minutes for the smaller size, about 70 minutes for the larger. When they feel firm (and you can lift one up to check that the underside's cooked), turn the oven off, but keep the meringues in there until completely cold. If you take them out too soon, the abrupt change in temperature will make them hard and dry or even crack, and they're best with a hint of chewiness within. Once they are cold, you can keep them for a long time in an airtight tin.

And here are a couple of other recipes for which I use my egg whites (neither requires whisking).

Mix 1½ cups ground almonds with 1 cup superfine sugar and stir in 2 egg whites. Combine well into a thick cream, then add 2 tablespoons of Italian 00 flour (see page 458) or all-purpose flour and 1 teaspoon of almond extract. Pipe—through a plain tip—into rounds about 2 inches in diameter, leaving space between each, onto baking sheets lined with parchment paper or Cook-Eze. Traditionally, you should press a split almond into the center of each, but I don't always bother. Cook in a preheated 325°F oven for about 20 minutes. The macaroons will harden slightly as they cool, so be careful to time them to be softish in the center, and chewy. Don't panic at their cracked surface; macaroons are meant to look like that.

This amount should make about 15 macaroons.

Langue de chat are the sort of cookies that are wonderful with any dessert you eat with a small spoon. You take 4 tablespoons each of butter and vanilla sugar (see page 72) or superfine sugar and cream them until light and fluffy. To cream, simply put the ingredients in a large bowl and beat with a wooden spoon until soft and pale. (It helps if you beat the butter first, till it's really soft, and then beat in the sugar gradually, handful by sprinkled-in handful.) Add 2 egg whites, stirring until you have a curdy mass, add ½ teaspoon of vanilla extract and then ½ cup flour, preferably Italian 00 but otherwise all-purpose, and beat or stir till you have a stiffish cream. Pipe through a plain small-sized tip to form small strips like squeezed-out toothpaste, 2½–3 inches long, on a lined—or greased and then floured—baking sheet. These spread enormously, so leave a clear 2 inches between each. Bake in a preheated 400°F oven for about 8 minutes, until they're pale gold in the center, darker gold at the edges. These quantities make about 30.

For other ways to use up egg whites, see the hazelnut cake recipe on page 324 (substituting other nuts if you prefer), the pavlova on page 336, and the potato pancakes on page 220.

BÉCHAMEL

Béarnaise may be my favourite sauce, but béchamel is unquestionably the most useful.

All it is is a roux, which is to say a mixture of equal amounts of butter and flour (although I sometimes use a little more butter), cooked for a few minutes, to which you add, gradually, milk, and then cook until thickened.

I always use Italian 00 flour. The difference lies in the milling; these flours are finer-milled than all-purpose flour and they cook faster, so the flouriness cooks out more quickly. Undeniably, this is useful, but ordinary all-purpose flour has been used perfectly well to make béchamel for eons, so don't agonize over it. I find, though, that I keep no ordinary all-purpose flour in the house—just Italian 00 (superior for pastry, too; see page 458) and self-raising, which cuts down on clutter and lots of half-used packages in the cupboard.

1½ tablespoons unsalted butter	salt and freshly milled white or black
1½ tablespoons Italian 00 or all-purpose	pepper
flour	whole nutmeg
1 cup milk	

Melt the butter in a heavy-bottomed saucepan and then stir in the flour, cooking for 2–3 minutes until you have a walnut (sized and colored) paste. Meanwhile, heat the milk (I do this in a measuring cup in the microwave—very *moderne*) and take the pan with the roux off the heat. Gradually, using a whisk, beat the warm milk into it. Proceed slowly and cautiously to avoid lumps. Keep stirring and adding, adding and stirring, and when all the milk is smoothly incorporated, season with salt, pepper, and a grating of the nutmeg. If it does go lumpy, blitz it in your blender or with a hand-held equivalent.

Return to the heat and cook, at a lowish simmer, stirring all the time, for about 5 minutes (at least twice that if you're using ordinary all-purpose flour) until the sauce has thickened and has no taste of flouriness. Add some more nutmeg before using. And if you want to make your béchamel in advance, you can stop a skin forming by pouring a thin layer of milk or melted butter on top. Makes about 1 cup.

If you want a more intensely flavored sauce, heat 1 cup of milk first with 1 onion, ½ white part of a leek, sliced, or some sliced scallion whites, and 2 bay leaves or some mace (or whatever flavor it is you wish to intensify). Let it infuse, lid on, off the heat for 20 minutes or so before proceeding with the sauce.

CHEESE SAUCE To make cheese sauce, add a pinch of English mustard powder or cayenne along with the flour and about ½–1 cup (depending on how you want to use your cheese sauce) grated cheddar or Gruyère, or half Gruyère, half Parmesan, at the end.

PARSLEY SAUCE For parsley sauce—heavenly with cooked ham or to blanket fava beans—just infuse the milk with the stalks from a decent bunch of parsley. Then blanch the parsley leaves (although I have to say I don't always bother), dry them thoroughly, chop them finely, and add them when stirring in the milk, sprinkling over a little more parsley at the end. And you can chop up leftover ham and mix it with the cold sauce, together with some dry mashed potatoes and possibly chopped gherkins or capers, to make parsley and ham patties. I sometimes add 1 egg yolk and 2–3 tablespoons heavy cream to make a more voluptuous parsley sauce—especially good with poached smoked fish and mashed potato. (And you can make patties out of these, too.)

This is the way I make béchamel sauce most of the time. My mother's method was the same as above, except she put a little nut of a chicken bouillon cube— a quarter to a third of a cube—in the pan along with the butter and flour and made roux of them all together. This makes a good savory sauce; the stock isn't very pronounced, it just gives a more flavorful saltiness. So make really sure you don't season without thinking.

I use this method to make a white sauce to coat leeks or onions, using half milk and half the water the onions or leeks have been cooking in. Sometimes, even better, I use half light cream and half the vegetable cooking water. If no cream's available, I beat in an extra nut of butter at the end.

VEGETABLE SOUP

A vegetable soup doesn't really require a recipe, and I certainly don't want to suggest you get out your measuring cups to make it with mechanical accuracy. But it's helpful to have a working model for a plain but infinitely variable soup. This one is not exactly the mix of carrot, parsnip, and turnip my mother used to make, and which we knew as nip soup, but is based on its memory.

I use vegetable bouillon cubes to make the stock for this most of the time, but if I've got some good organic vegetables for the soup that taste properly and vigorously of themselves, I use water. A friend of mine swears that if you use Evian or other bottled still water it makes all the difference, but I haven't quite got round to that yet.

There are two ways to go about preparing the vegetables for this. For a chunkier soup, chop them roughly (with the exception of the leek, which is sliced), as I indicate below, or put the whole lot in a food processor and pulse it briefly until chopped medium-fine. This will give you a soup with a finer texture. If it's a smooth, velvety texture you're after, follow the directions about puréeing the soup.

Although my hand is pretty well permanently stuck, culinarily speaking, around the neck of a bottle of Marsala, I admit that there isn't a vegetable soup in the land that doesn't benefit from the addition of a little dry sherry.

3 tablespoons olive oil, or 3 tablespoons butter and a drop of oil

1 medium onion, roughly chopped

2 medium carrots, peeled and roughly chopped

1 turnip, peeled and roughly chopped

1 parsnip, peeled and roughly chopped

1 floury potato, peeled and roughly chopped

1 celery stalk, roughly chopped

1 medium leek, white part only, sliced thickly

salt

4 cups vegetable stock

1 bouquet garni (see page xx)

freshly milled black pepper

whole nutmeg (optional)

1–2 tablespoons dry sherry

2–3 tablespoons fresh parsley, chives, or chervil, for serving

Heat the oil, or butter with its drop of oil, in a large, wide saucepan (one which has a lid, preferably) and then add the chopped vegetables and the leek to it, turning all over a few times so they all have a slight slick of fat. Sprinkle with salt, cover, and, on a low heat, let them half-fry, half-braise until softened, 10–15 minutes, shaking the pan from time to time and occasionally opening the lid to stir (making sure nothing's sticking or burning at the bottom) before putting the lid back on again. Pour in the stock, adding the bouquet garni and a good grind of pepper, and bring, uncovered, to a simmer, then cook for 20–40 minutes (exactly how long depends on the age of the vegetables, the size you've chopped them, the dimensions of the pan, and the material of which the pan's made).

Serve as is or, for a finer texture, blend or process the cooked soup or push it through a food mill. Alternatively, if you've got one of those stick blenders, you can do an agreeably rough purée in the saucepan. Sometimes I take out a couple of ladlefuls, blend or process them, and put them back into the soup to thicken it without turning it all to mush. Season to taste with salt and pepper and, optionally, a bit of grated nutmeg at the end, and stir in the sherry before serving, sprinkling over fresh herbs as you wish. Serves 4–6.

BREAD CRUMBS

These are a regular and very ordinary kitchen requirement, but because we are all out of the habit of using up leftovers, few of us are clear on how to go about making that misnomer, fresh bread crumbs. I say misnomer, because you really want them stale.

I don't bother with drying out bread in the oven. I just take the crusts off some slices of stale-ish (but not bone dry) good white bread, cut the bread into chunks, and lacerate them into crumbs in the processor. I then leave the crumbs in a shallow bowl or spread them out on a plate to dry and get staler naturally. If you want to make the sort of bread crumbs that you can buy, those very dry, very small crumbs that could coat, say, a *scaloppina Milanese,* then just leave the bread till it's utterly dried out and cardboardy beyond belief before blitzing it in the processor. You can keep breadcrumbs in a freezer bag in the freezer and use them straight from frozen. I reckon an average slice of good bread, without crusts, weighs about an ounce; this in turn yields approximately 6 tablespoons bread crumbs.

VINAIGRETTE

One of the holdovers of the hostess-trolley age is the idea that the clever cook has a secret vinaigrette recipe that can transform the dullest lettuce into a Sensational Salad. I'm not sure I even have a regular vinaigrette recipe, let alone one with a winning, magic ingredient. But we all panic in the kitchen from time to time, so here is a useful, broad-brush reminder of desirable proportions for various dressings.

PLAIN SALAD DRESSING

I sometimes think the best way of dressing salad is to use just oil and lemon juice. The trick is to use the best possible olive oil—and as little of it as possible—and toss it far longer than you'd believe possible. Use your hands for this. Start off with 1 tablespoon of oil for a whole bowl of lettuce and keep tossing, adding more oil only when you are convinced the leaves need it. When all the leaves are barely covered with the thinnest film of oil, sprinkle over a scant ½ teaspoon sea salt. Toss again. Then squeeze over some lemon juice. Give a final fillip, then taste and adjust as necessary. Instead of lemon juice, you can substitute wine vinegar (and I use red wine vinegar rather than white, generally), but be sparing. Just as the perfect martini, it was always said, was made merely by tilting the vermouth bottle in the direction of the gin, so when making the perfect dressing you should merely point the cork of the vinegar bottle toward the oil.

As important is the composition of the salad itself. Keep it simple: there's a green salad, which is green; or there's a red salad, of tomatoes (and maybe onions). First-course salads may be granted a little extra leeway—the addition of something warm and sautéed—but I would never let a tomato find its way into anything leafy. For more detailed explanations (genetic as much as aesthetic) of this prejudice, please see page 197. When you're using those already mixed packets of designer leaves, you should add one crunchy lettuce like romaine, which you buy, radically and separately, as a lettuce and then tear up yourself at the last minute. Herbs—parsley, chives, chervil, lovage—are a good idea in a green salad (and you can add them either to the salad or the dressing) but, except on certain rare occasions, I think garlic is better left out.

BASIC FRENCH DRESSING

If you want to change oils for this, use part walnut or hazelnut oil, part olive oil. Don't replace the olive oil totally. Just a tablespoon of the nut oil plus olive oil should achieve the variation in flavor that you are after. If you want to change vinegars, do so uninhibitedly, but taste first to check the level of acidity and adjust the other components correspondingly.

scant ½ teaspoon Dijon mustard (optional)	I teaspoon sea salt
2 teaspoons red wine vinegar	good grinding black pepper
	6–8 tablespoons extra-virgin olive oil

If you're using the mustard (and I sometimes use a tarragon mustard—feltily green and lightly, rather than effusively, fragrant—and sometimes none at all), mix it in a bowl with the vinegar, the salt and pepper, and a drop or two of cold water, then whisk or fork in the oil (I often use Ligurian, which is sweet and mild). Or you can put all the ingredients for the dressing in an old jam jar, screw on the lid, and shake.

Put most—but not all—of your salad leaves in your salad bowl and add the dressing. Toss. Taste. If you find you have sloshed on too much dressing, add the spare leaves and toss again.

CAKES

We no longer live in a world where baking a cake is considered a basic skill. That, one could argue, is reason enough to include a recipe here. And I don't mean a fancy cake, but just a plain, ordinary sponge.

VICTORIA SPONGE

A traditional Victoria sponge is made in two halves that are sandwiched together with jam or crushed fresh raspberries and cream (and don't forget to sprinkle the top of the cake with superfine sugar later).

I make this cake in the processor. Realizing you can make a cake without all that creaming first is a revelation. Without the beating, however, you don't get all that air into it, so you have to add some extra baking powder. I don't always sift the flour, but I probably ought to. I have found that the addition of cornstarch gives the cake an almost feathery lightness. The butter must be very, very soft or it won't all blend together. I always use organic eggs.

1½ cups all-purpose flour	2 teaspoons baking powder
¼ cup cornstarch	1½ teaspoons vanilla extract or zest of
1 cup plus 2 tablespoons superfine	½ lemon or orange
sugar	4 eggs
16 tablespoons (2 sticks) very soft	2 tablespoons milk
unsalted butter	

Preheat the oven to 350°F. Butter two 8-inch round cake pans.

Put all the ingredients, except the milk, into the processor and process to mix. Check that everything has mixed all right, and then process some more while pouring the milk through the funnel. You want a batter of a soft, dropping consistency. Add more milk if necessary. Pour into the buttered pans and bake in the oven for about 25 minutes. When ready, the tops should spring back when pressed and a cake tester or fine skewer should come out clean.

Let the cakes stand in their pans for a minute or so and then turn onto a wire rack to cool. Sandwich together with cream, jam, raspberries, or whatever you like.

Obviously, you can make the cake the oldfangled way. Cream the butter and sugar till pale and soft, then add the eggs, alternating each egg with 1 tablespoon or so of the flour, cornstarch, and baking powder, sifted together. When the eggs are beaten in, add the milk and vanilla, then fold in the rest of the flour mixture.

You can also make the sponge in a single 8-inch layer. Halve all the ingredients except the vanilla—use 1 teaspoon—and keep the full amount of zest, if you're adding it. You'll have to make this the traditional way; there's too little batter for a processor to do the job properly.

BIRTHDAY CAKE

It's wise to have in your repertoire a pretty fail-safe chocolate cake. I call this birthday cake because that's what it seems to get made for mostly. It's plain but good, and the chocolate ganache with which it's draped is gleamingly spectacular and ideal for bearing birthday candles. With this recipe, you don't need to be dextrous or artistic—and any other form of icing for a birthday cake requires you to be both. But if you want to make the sort of cake you actually write Happy Birthday on, make a Victoria sponge and look at the children's party food on page 450 for additional ideas.

So many chocolate cakes now are luscious, rich, and resolutely uncakey—rather like my chocolate pudding cake with raspberries on page 316—that I feel nostalgically drawn to this solid offering. And—this is the best bit—it is ridiculously easy to make. No creaming or beating or whisking. Stirring is about the extent of it. I know condensed milk looks like a spooky ingredient, but trust me.

A note on the chocolate: I like to make the cake with bittersweet chocolate (average 60 percent cocoa solids in best-quality brands) but the ganache with a mixture of bittersweet and milk chocolate. The light chocolate I use is Valrhona Lacte (which I think has about 35 percent cocoa solids), but most supermarkets sell a good-quality continental chocolate, which is comparable. As to what proportions to use, that really is up to you. I change them depending on who's eating the cake, but it's likely to be half dark, half milk, or sometimes two-thirds dark to one-third milk.

FOR THE CAKE

1¾ cups all-purpose flour

⅓ cup best-quality unsweetened cocoa powder

2 teaspoons baking powder

pinch salt

1 cup superfine sugar

8 tablespoons (1 stick) unsalted butter

⅔ cup evaporated milk

3½ ounces best-quality bittersweet chocolate, broken into small pieces

2 eggs, beaten

FOR THE CHOCOLATE GANACHE

8 ounces best-quality bittersweet and milk chocolates (see above)

1 cup heavy cream

Preheat the oven to 350°F. Put the kettle on. Butter an 8-inch springform cake pan (or two 8-inch round cake pans) and line the base with baking parchment. This last is not crucial if you're using nonstick pans, but even so, it removes all worries about turning out the cake later.

Sift the flour, cocoa, baking powder, and salt together into a large bowl and set aside.

Put the sugar, butter, evaporated milk, ½ cup just-boiled water, and the chocolate in a saucepan and heat until melted and smooth. Then, using a wooden spoon, stir this robustly but not excitedly into the flour mixture and, when all is glossily amalgamated, beat in the eggs.

Pour into the springform pan and bake for 35–45 minutes, less if you're using the shallower cake pans. When it's ready, the top will feel firm. Don't expect a skewer to come out clean; indeed, you wouldn't want it to. And don't worry about any cracking on the surface; the ganache will cover it later.

Leave the cake to cool in the pan for 10 minutes and then turn out onto a rack.

When completely cool, split in half horizontally; if this sort of thing spooks you, you should certainly use 2 cake pans and stick the 2 layers together—though remember, even if the cake breaks while you divide it, you can stick it together with the ganache.

To make the ganache, chop the chocolate (I put it in the processor until reduced to rubble) and put it in a medium-sized bowl, preferably a wide, shallow one rather than a deep basin shape. Heat the cream to boiling (but do not let it boil) and pour it over the chocolate. Leave for 5 minutes and then, by choice with an electric mixer, beat until combined, coolish, thickish, and glossy. You want it thin enough to pour but thick enough to stay put. At this stage, think of the ganache as somewhere between a sauce and an icing; later, it will set hard and Sacher-torte shiny. Pour some over the cut side of one half of the cake, using a metal spatula to spread, and then plank the other half of the cake on top. Pour the rest of the chocolate ganache over the top of the cake, letting it drape over, swirling this overspill with your spatula to coat the sides. Leave for a couple of hours or till set. You can make the cake the day before and then make the ganache the next morning before you set off for work. You can then get back in the evening to your gleaming masterpiece with nothing to do save puncture its flawlessly smooth surface with candleholders.

FANCY CAKE

Well, this is not so much a fancy cake as a plain one that looks partyish. It is just an almond sponge leavened with whisked egg whites and baked in a brioche or bundt mold. It looks wonderful, intrinsically celebratory, which is why I do it. Added to any plate of fruit—fresh or thawed frozen—it can be served after dinner or lunch. It's no harder to make than a round cake; it's just that the fancy mold (and try to find a nonstick one) makes it, illogically, look as if you've made about ten thousand times the effort. The brioche mold won't work for a Victoria sponge because you need the whoosh of air supplied here by the whisked egg whites.

6 eggs, separated	2 cups ground blanched almonds
1 cup superfine sugar	zest of 1 lemon

Preheat the oven to 325°F. Butter an 8-cup brioche or bundt mold (you can use a standard 10-cup bundt pan, but if you do, reduce the baking time by about 7 minutes).

Whisk the egg yolks and sugar until you have a pale, creamy mass. It's easier to use electrical equipment for this but not impossible with an ordinary, hand-held whisk.

Fold in the ground almonds and zest. In another bowl, whisk the egg whites until stiff. Add a dollop of egg white to the cake batter to lighten it and make it easier to fold the remaining whites in gently, which you should proceed to do with a metal spoon. When the whites are all folded in, pour the batter into the brioche or bundt mold and bake for 1 hour. The cake will rise and grow golden, but will deflate on cooling; that's fine. When you take it out, give it a prod. If you feel it needs another 10 minutes or so (ovens do differ so radically from one another, it's always a possibility), just put it back and don't worry about the cake sinking. Think of it as accounted for.

Let the cake cool in the pan for about 10 minutes, then unmold onto a wire rack, immediately turn to stand the right way up, and leave to cool.

A MOORISH CAKE

I ate a cake rather like this once at Moro, a wonderful London restaurant with—as the name suggests—a Moorish menu. The proportions of the cake were slightly different (2⅓ cups ground almonds, 2 cups plus 2 tablespoons confectioners' sugar, 8 eggs, the zest of 2½ oranges), but the method was the same. (Because of the increase in the batter's volume, however, bake this in a 10-cup mold.) The real difference in the cake was the syrup, which was spooned over it as it cooled, leaving some more to be handed round on serving.

THE SYRUP

To make the syrup, combine the juice of 10 oranges, ½ cup sugar, and a cinnamon stick in a saucepan and bring to the boil. Let it bubble away for about 10 minutes or until the liquid is syrupy. Exactly how long this takes depends on the width of the pan and how it conducts the heat. Remove from the heat and allow to cool. If you need to cool the syrup quickly, stand the pan in a sink of cold water. And when it's cool, taste, and add the juice of 1–2 lemons, depending on how sweet it is. Bear in mind that the cake will be very sweet, so it is important to keep a sour edge to the syrup for balance.

Blood oranges, available at the end of winter/beginning of spring, make a spectacular, impossibly scarlet, syrup.

BREAD

Bread is basic in the staff-of-life sense, but making it is hardly a fundamental activity for most of us. I don't get the urge that often, but every time I have, and have consulted a suitable book, I have been directed to make whole-wheat bread. You may as well bake burlap. Why should it be thought that only those who want whole-wheat bread are the sort to bake their own? Good whole-wheat bread is very hard to make, and I suspect it needs heavy machinery or enormous practice and muscularity.

Anyway, I give you this recipe for old-fashioned white bread, really good white bread, the sort you eat with unsalted butter and jam—one loaf in a sitting, no trouble. The recipe found its way to me at a breadmaking workshop given at the Flour Advisory Board in London by John Foster. He was an exceptional teacher, and completely turned me, a lifelong skeptic of the breadmaking tendency, into a would-be baker.

BASIC WHITE LOAF

Buy the best flour you can and use compressed fresh yeast, not dried, if at all possible. Before you get put off, you should know two things. The first is that fresh yeast is available at many supermarkets; the second is that you use the fresh yeast here as you would easy-blend or instant yeast—there's no frothing or blending or anything, you just add it to the mound of flour. Be aware, however, that fresh yeast is extremely perishable; always check package expiration dates before buying it, and use it promptly—within two weeks if stored in the fridge. If you do want to use dry yeast, make sure it is easy-blend or instant.

For a good white loaf such as even I can make convincingly—a small one, so double the quantities if you want a big loaf or a couple—you need:

2¼ cups bread flour

2½ teaspoons compressed fresh yeast, or 2 teaspoons easy-blend or instant dry yeast

1 teaspoon salt

½ teaspoon sugar

¾ cup tepid water

1 tablespoon lard, vegetable shortening, or oil

So—tip the flour onto a worktop and add the yeast of whichever type, salt, and sugar. Pour over the water and bring together, working with one hand, clawing at the floury mess rather as if your hand were a spider and your fingers the spider's legs. The spider analogy is apposite; you do have to be a bit "If at first you don't succeed, try, try again" about bread making. As the dough starts to come together, add the fat and keep squishing with your hands. When the dough has come together, begin kneading. Do this by stretching the dough away from you and working it into the worktop. Rub a little flour into your hands to remove any bits of dough that stick.

Keep kneading, pressing the heel of your hand into the dough, pushing the dough away, and bringing it back and down against the work surface, for at least 10 minutes. John Foster warns that after 5 minutes you'll want to give up, and he's right. He suggests singing a song to keep yourself going; I prefer listening to the radio or talking to someone.

When the dough's properly mixed—after about 10 minutes—you can tell the difference; it suddenly feels smoother and less sticky. Bring it to a ball, flour it and the worktop lightly, and cover with a plastic bag or sheet of plastic film and a kitchen towel. Leave it for 30 minutes.

Then knead again for 3 minutes. Flour the worktop and dough ball again, cover as before, and leave for another 30 minutes.

Flatten the dough to expel the gas bubbles. Fold it in half, then in half again, and again, and keep folding the dough over itself until it feels as if you can fold no longer, as if the dough itself resists it (rather than you can't bear it), and then shape it into a ball again. Flour the worktop and so forth, cover the dough, and leave it, this time for 10 minutes.

Then shape the dough as you want: either round or oval and smooth, or you can slash the top with a knife, or put it in a greased 9-inch loaf pan. Now, place on a baking sheet (or in its pan) and put it in a warm place, under a plastic bag, for 1 hour, before baking for about 35 minutes in a preheated 450°F oven. The trick is to lift the bread up and knock the base; if it sounds hollow, it's cooked. Try to let the bread cool before eating it.

IMPORTANT VARIANT You can do the final proofing in the fridge overnight (technically, this is known as *retarding*). This doesn't cut out any work, but I find it makes things easier because I can do all the kneading when the children are in bed and before I go to bed (incidentally, it is, if not exactly calming, certainly very stress-relieving) and then bake the bread when I get up.

You do, however, need to increase the amount of yeast for this. Exactly how much you need to increase it by will depend on your fridge and the nature of your yeast. This may not be helpful, but it's true. Try increasing the yeast to 3 teaspoons if fresh and 2½ teaspoons if instant; then, if the bread over-rises when it's in the oven, you'll know to use less next time. When you get up in the morning, preheat the oven, taking the bread out of the fridge on its baking sheet as you do so. Leave it for about 30 minutes and then bake as above, maybe giving it an extra couple of minutes.

If you're going to start baking your own bread, what's to stop you making something to go on it?

LEMON CURD

I must admit that I don't use a double boiler, as commonly instructed, to make lemon curd. It isn't because I'm brilliant and know how to stop it from curdling, or because I like living dangerously, but just because I'm impatient.

Fill up the sink with cold water before you start—so you can plunge the pan in it if the mixture looks like it may be curdling—and just use a heavy-bottomed saucepan (with a heat diffuser beneath it as another safety measure, if you like) and keep stirring at all times. I use an electric citrus juicer; if you're squeezing by hand, you'll get less juice, so use 3 eggs and 3 yolks. The best way of zesting the lemons is with a zester, not a grater. If you use a grater, you spend hours with a knife trying to chisel out the stuck bits later.

4 eggs	14 tablespoons (1¾ sticks) unsalted
4 egg yolks	butter
1½ cups superfine sugar	4 organic lemons, zested and juiced

Beat the eggs, yolks, and sugar together until the sugar's dissolved. Add the butter, lemon juice, and zest and heat gently in a pan on a low heat, stirring constantly, until the mixture thickens and grows smooth and looks, in fact, like lemon curd. If it's in danger of curdling, dunk the pan into the icy water in the sink and beat like fury.

Strain, if desired, and put into sterilized jars—if I'm in the mood, I boil the jars in water for 10 minutes before using them, though really I think the dishwasher sanitizes them perfectly adequately—seal, and keep in the fridge. This fills about two 8-ounce jars.

Passion fruit curd may as well be made in half quantities (use 7 tablespoons unsalted butter, ¾ cups sugar, 2 eggs, and 2 egg yolks), just because the amount of juice you get from each fruit is small, especially after you've removed the seeds. So, remove the inner pulp from 10 passion fruits and blitz it in the food processor for a minute before straining; this helps the seeds to separate from the pulp. Proceed as for lemon curd. Stir in the fresh pulp, including seeds of an eleventh passion fruit, before the end.

See, too, the recipe for Seville orange curd on page 246.

CUSTARD

In many ways, curd is just custard made using juice in place of cream. And I mean cream; I take the view that when custard originated, the milk used would have been much richer, much fattier, rather like light cream. So I use light cream or half milk, half cream.

As when making curd, I fill the sink with icy water and am prepared to plunge the pan in and start beating like mad if the custard looks like it's breaking. And I don't even keep the heat all that low underneath the pan. If I do that, I lose patience and then suddenly turn it up in a fury—and then, of course, it does curdle.

Better to keep the heat middling and stir all the time. With the quantities below, if I'm using my widest saucepan (8 inches in diameter), I find this takes 10 minutes. It's always hard to explain when exactly custard becomes custard. I don't find it particularly helpful to be told that it's cooked when it coats the back of a wooden spoon, because it does that at the beginning. Think rather of aiming for it to be the texture and smooth thickness of good heavy cream. But you should, anyway, turn to page 339 to see my remarks about a revolutionary method for cooking pouring custard in advance in the oven, without stirring.

REAL CUSTARD

You may as well go the whole hog and use a vanilla bean. Otherwise, use vanilla sugar and/or stir in 1 teaspoon of good vanilla extract at the end. Or you can add 1 tablespoon of rum to the cream when heating it at the beginning.

It is helpful to know, when making custard, that you need 1 egg yolk for each ½ cup of milk or cream. It's harder to be precise about the sugar, as that really depends on your taste, what you're eating the custard with, and whether it's going to be hot or cold, but I should say 1 heaping teaspoon of sugar per yolk should be fine.

2 cups plus 2 tablespoons light cream or half milk, half cream	5 egg yolks
I vanilla bean	¼ cup sugar

Half fill the sink with cold water.

Pour the cream into your widest saucepan and add to it the vanilla bean, split lengthways. Heat, and when it's about to come to the boil but isn't boiling, remove from the heat and leave to infuse for 20–30 minutes.

Whisk the egg yolks with the sugar until thick and creamy and then strain the cream onto them, beating all the while, having swapped the whisk for a wooden spoon or spatula. To be frank, I find it easier just to fish out the 2 strands of vanilla; I don't lose any sleep over the speckles of vanilla finding their way into the custard. But there is something to be said (for ease of pouring alone) for straining the vanilla cream into a wide measuring cup before adding it to the yolks and sugar. Whichever way you do it, wash out the saucepan and dry it well, then pour in the beaten-together yolks, sugar, and cream and, on a low to medium heat, stir unceasingly for 8–10 minutes.

When the custard is cooked, even if it isn't breaking, dunk the saucepan quickly in the cold water in the sink and beat well with a wooden spoon. If it looks as if it is curdling, then use a whisk or, better still, an immersion blender (or keep a blender jar in the fridge for just such eventualities) for some frenzied, violent beating here.

Pour into a bowl to cool (you can reheat it over a saucepan of simmering water later if you like) or serve as is. Enough for 4.

There is another way, and it's adapted from British restaurateur Tessa Bramley's book, *The Instinctive Cook*.

2½ cups heavy cream

I vanilla bean

5 egg yolks

I level teaspoon cornstarch

I–2 tablespoons superfine sugar

Put the cream into a saucepan. Split the vanilla bean in half lengthways and scrape out seeds into the cream, then bung in the bean, too. In a bowl, whisk together the yolks, cornstarch, and sugar. Bring the vanilla cream to boiling point. Remove the bean, allow the cream to rise in the pan, and then quickly pour it onto the egg mixture, whisking continuously until the mixture thickens. This takes about 10 minutes with an electric mixer, so do it with a hand whisk only if you're feeling strong.

Strain the custard and pour. That's it. You can reheat it later, and if the custard looks like curdling during the reheating, then you can save it by quickly whisking in 1 tablespoon heavy cream. Serves 4–6.

ICE CREAM

Frankly, if you've made a custard, you've made (bar the freezing) your ice cream; this asks no more of you, just of your kitchen. All that's needed is an ice cream maker that slots into the freezer rather than a big expensive one that you plug in. Of course, you can just pour the mixture into a Tupperware bowl to freeze and keep taking it out of the freezer to beat the mixture and break up the crystals, but not only is this a bore, the ice cream just won't be as voluptuously smooth as if it had been churned. Though in fact, the vanilla ice cream below is more doable than most without special equipment—one of the reasons I include it.

BASIC VANILLA ICE CREAM

The difference between custard and ice cream—the temperature at which it's eaten—makes a difference to the amount of sugar you need; generally speaking, the colder you eat something, the sweeter it needs to be. All flavors, indeed, need to be intense when icy, which is why it drives me so mad when a dessert—or indeed any food—is kept in the fridge until the moment at which it's served. The cold kills the taste.

So—make the real custard above, only using ⅔ cup sugar in place of the ¼ cup stipulated, and using light cream. And I certainly wouldn't worry here about the specks of vanilla; on the contrary, I'd welcome them. Indeed, scrape the seeds into the cream before adding the bean strips and don't bother to strain the cream when you pour it over the egg yolks and sugar; you want maximum flavor.

When the custard's made and you've plunged the hot pan into the cold water in the sink, beating well, then you can remove the bean. Let the custard cool (if you keep it in the sinkful of water, beating every now and again, it doesn't take long) and then freeze in the ice cream maker according to its manufacturer's instructions.

If you want to make a creamier ice cream, you can stir 1¼ cups heavy cream into the cooled custard before freezing it, in which case use about another ½ cup sugar. And taste for sweetness once the cream's in: if you think you need more, sifted confectioners' sugar stirred in will dissolve easily enough.

You can flavor this ice cream to make the flavor the Italians, who know about such matters, call crema. In place of the vanilla pod, infuse the cream with lemon zest and strain as above. I like lemon custard, too, and also custard made with cream infused with the zest of an orange.

THE WORLD'S BEST CHOCOLATE ICE CREAM

If you were only ever going to make one ice cream, it would have to be vanilla. But once you've lost your ice cream–making virginity, you have to allow yourself to be seduced by the world's best chocolate ice cream. Marcella Hazan managed to procure the recipe for the Cipriani's dark and smokily voluptuous chocolate ice cream for *Marcella's Italian Kitchen,* and it is from that book that I reproduce it.

4 egg yolks	3½ ounces semisweet chocolate
⅔ cup plus 2 tablespoons sugar	½ cup unsweetened cocoa powder, best
2 cups milk	available

Whisk the yolks and ⅔ cup of the sugar in a bowl until thick and creamy, forming pale ribbons when you lift the beaters or whisk. Bring the milk to the boil and add it to the beaten yolks, pouring slowly and beating all the while.

Melt the chocolate by breaking it up into small squares or pieces and putting it in the top of a double boiler above (but not touching) some simmering water in the below pan. Then whisk this, followed by the cocoa, into the eggs and milk. Now pour the chocolate mixture into a pan and cook on low to medium heat, stirring with a wooden spoon, until everything's smooth and amalgamated and beginning to thicken. You don't need to cook this until it is really custardlike, which makes life easier. Now for the bit that gives this ice cream its essential smoky bitterness. Put 2 tablespoons of sugar with 2 teaspoons water into a heavy-bottomed saucepan and turn the heat to high. Make a caramel; in other words, heat this until it's dark brown and molten. Live dangerously here; you are after the taste of burnt sugar. As it browns, whisk it into the chocolate custard; don't worry if it crystallizes on contact, as the whisking will dissolve it.

Turn into a bowl or wide measuring cup and cool. Plunging the pan into cold water and beating, as usual, will do the trick. Then chill in the fridge for about 20 minutes (or longer, if that's more convenient) before churning it in your ice cream maker according to instructions. Serves 4–6.

CRÊPES

At some time in your life, you might want to make crêpes. Obviously, a batter is a batter is a batter; you could easily consult the recipe for Yorkshire Pudding. But it is surprising how useful it is just to know what the proportions of a regular batter are, especially because the Yorkshire pudding recipe I give (see page 253) isn't the traditional one.

I cup Italian 00 or all-purpose flour	2–4 tablespoons melted and cooled
pinch salt	unsweetened butter (optional)
I egg	vegetable oil, for the pan
I ¼ cups milk	

The way I remember crêpes being made when I was a child is as follows.

Make a mound of the flour in a bowl, add the salt, then make a dip in the top. Crack open the egg and let it slip into this hole at the top of the hill and, with a wooden spoon, beat well, gradually incorporating the flour from the sides and beating in the milk to make a smooth batter. Stop when the batter's creamy, change to a whisk, and then whisk in the melted butter if you like (ordinary, as opposed to fancy, crêpes don't need butter). Leave the batter to stand for at least half an hour; overnight wouldn't matter. The batter might thicken in the meantime, in which case add milk or water (or possibly a little rum, if you're making fancy crêpes) to get the batter back to the right, thickish light-cream consistency.

The trick of crêpes is not so much in the batter, though, as in the frying: use very little oil and very little batter. The pan must be hot, and what I do is heat oil in it, then empty the oil down the sink before putting in the batter. Use less batter than you would imagine you need—you want just to line the pan. When bubbles come to the surface, the crêpe is ready to flip. You should be prepared to throw away (and by that I mean eat yourself standing up at the stove) the first crêpe. It never works. Re-oil every 4 crêpes or so. Using an 8-inch crêpe pan, you should get about 12 pancakes out of the above quantities. You don't need a special pan, but you must use a well-seasoned frying pan. Nonstick pans are hopeless here, as the crêpes they make are blond and pallid and rubbery; the batter seems steamed rather than seared.

There is nothing better on a crêpe than a thick sprinkling of sugar (I keep only superfine in the house now, but granulated is the gritty taste I remember from my childhood) and a good squeeze of lemon juice.

If you want to make breakfast pancakes—to be eaten, preferably, with maple syrup and maybe even some crisp shards of bacon—you should alter the balance of the ingredients. Obviously you want a thicker batter, so add another egg, double the flour, and to that flour add 1 teaspoon sugar and 1 teaspoon baking powder and regard the melted butter later as obligatory. Cook them, in about 3-inch rounds, on a hot griddle or pan. Makes about 22.

PASTRY

On the subject of pastry, I am positively evangelical. Until fairly recently, I practiced heavy avoidance techniques, hastily, anxiously turning away from any recipe that included pastry, as if the cookbook's pages themselves were burning—I was hot with fear, could feel the flush rise in my panicky cheeks. I take strength from that, and so should you. Because if I can do the culinary equivalent, for me, of Learning to Love the Bomb, so can you.

It came upon me gradually. I made some plain pastry dough, alone and in silence, apart from the comforting wall of voices emanating from Radio 4, the BBC talk station. It worked; I made some more. Then I tried some pâte sucrée. It worked; I made some more; it didn't. But the next time, it did—or rather, I dealt better with its difficulties.

But pastry dough, or even rich pastry dough, is really easy, and that's all you need to know. If you want something a little more exalted, you can make almond pastry (see page 264); this is as simple as the plainest pastry dough, tastes rich, and rolls out like Play-Doh; the ground almonds seem to make it stretchy and extra-pliable.

PLAIN PASTRY DOUGH

At its simplest, pastry is just a quantity of flour mixed with half its weight in fat and bound with water.

So, to make enough plain pastry dough to line and cover a 9-inch pie dish (in other words, for a double-crust pie), you would mix 1¾ cups flour with ½ cup cold, diced fat (half lard or vegetable shortening and half butter for preference), rubbing the fat in with your fingertips until you have a bowl of floury bread crumbs or oatmeal-sized flakes. Then you add iced water until the flour and fat turn into a ball of dough; a few tablespoons should do it. But as simple as that is, I can make it simpler—or rather, I can make it easier, as easy as it can be.

The first way to do this is to use not ordinary all-purpose flour but Italian 00 flour (see page 458). This is the flour Italians at home, rather than in factories, use for pasta, and it's certainly true that it seems to give pastry an almost pastalike elasticity.

The second part of my facilitation program is as follows.

Measure the flour into a bowl and add the cold fat, cut into ½-inch dice. You then put this, as is, in the freezer for 10 minutes. Then you put it in the food processor with the metal blade attached or into a food mixer with the paddle attached, and switch on (at slow to medium speed, if you're using the mixer) until the mixture resembles oatmeal. Then you add, tablespoon by cautious tablespoon, the ice water, to which you've added a squeeze of lemon and a pinch of salt. I find you need a little more liquid when making pastry by this method than you do when the flour and fat haven't had that chilling burst in the deep freeze.

When the dough looks as if it's about to come together, but just before it actually does, you turn off all machinery, remove the dough, divide into two, and form each half into a ball; flatten the balls into fat discs and cover these discs with plastic film or put them each inside a freezer bag and shove them in the fridge for 20 minutes. This makes pastry anyone could roll out, even if you add too much liquid by mistake.

Now, this method relies on a machine to make the pastry. To tell the truth, I culled and simplified the technique from a fascinating book, *Cookwise,* by food scientist Shirley O. Corriher, and she does all sorts of strenuous things, including making the pastry by tipping out the freezer-chilled flour and fat onto a cold surface and battering it with a rolling pin until it looks like "paint-flakes that have fallen off a wall." She does, however, sanction the use of a mixer bowl (well chilled) and paddle (set on slowest speed) and I have found it works well in the processor too. I know that I am not up to her hand-rolling method—or not yet, at any rate.

RICH PASTRY DOUGH

"Rich," in terms of pastry dough, normally implies an egg to bind and more than half fat to flour, but I find my method makes the pastry taste both more tender and more buttery anyway, so I don't change the basic dough. In all cases, I prefer half lard, half butter. Lard is unfashionable these days, but it is seriously underrated both as a frying medium and, here, as a pastry shortener; it helps the crust get wonderfully flaky.

Since learning from *Cookwise* that a slightly acidic liquid makes the pastry more tender (the freezing of the flour and fat, which makes for flattened crumbs rather than beady ones, contributes to its desirable flakiness), I have taken to using lemon or orange juice instead of, or as well as, an egg yolk and water to bind. And sometimes I just add a little sour cream, yogurt, or crème fraîche, whatever's at hand. For instance, when I make an onion tart (see page 353), I use some of the crème fraîche I've got in for the onion-covering custard. I always use just the yolk, not the whole egg, when making rich pastry dough.

Anyway, to make rich pastry dough to line a deep 8-inch or shallow 9-inch tart pan, you need:

1 cup Italian 00 or all-purpose flour	pinch salt
4 tablespoons (½ stick) unsalted butter, cold and cut into ½-inch dice	1 teaspoon yogurt or crème fraîche or sour cream or orange or lemon juice
1 egg yolk	

Measure the flour into a bowl, add the butter, and put in the freezer for 10 minutes. Beat the egg yolk with the salt and whatever acidic ingredient you choose and put it in the fridge. Keep a few tablespoons of ice water in a measuring cup or bowl in the fridge in case you need them, too.

As above, you can make this in either a food processor or a mixer. Put the flour and butter in the processor with the metal blade fitted or in a mixer with the flat paddle on slow and turn on. After barely a minute, the mixture will begin to resemble oatmeal or flattened bread crumbs, and this is when you add the yolk mixture. Add, and process or mix. If you need more liquid, add a little ice water, but go slowly and carefully; you need to stop just as the dough looks like it's about to clump, not once it has.

When it looks right, take it out and form into a fat disc, then put the dough disc into a freezer bag or cover with plastic film and put into the fridge to rest for 20 minutes.

SWEET PASTRY DOUGH

I have to say, I mostly use unsweetened rich pastry dough for sweet pies and tarts—in the first instance, because making pâte sucrée can give me a nervous breakdown at the best of times; in the second, because I nearly always think that a plain, sugarless, neutral base is best. There are some pies or tarts though—the custard tart on page 287 for example, or any French fruit tart—that do need a crisp and sweet crust. This is it. It is as easy as the pastry recipes above, but it has the sweet, rich, tart-base delicacy of far more complicated pastries. Just use it whenever you see pâte sucrée stipulated. I can't guarantee your sanity otherwise.

1 cup Italian 00 or all-purpose flour	1 egg yolk
¼ cup confectioners' sugar	½ teaspoon pure vanilla extract
6 tablespoons (¾ stick) unsalted butter	pinch salt

Sift the flour and confectioners' sugar into a dish and add the cold butter, cut into small cubes (and here I always use just butter). Put this dish, just as it is, in the freezer for 10 minutes. In a small bowl, beat the egg yolk with the vanilla extract, a tablespoon of ice water, and the salt. Put this bowl in the fridge. Then, when the 10 minutes are up, proceed with the flour and butter as above (i.e., in processor or mixer) and, when you reach oatmeal stage, add the egg mixture to bind. Be prepared to add more ice water, drop by cautious drop, until you have a nearly coherent dough. Then scoop it out, still just crumbly, push it into a fat disc, cover with plastic film, and stick in the fridge for 20 minutes. Enough to line a deep 8-inch or shallow 9-inch tart pan.

BLIND
BAKING

If you're going to fill the pastry case with anything creamy or liquid, you should blind bake first. This simply means covering the pastry with foil, covering that with beans, and baking it. The beans can be ceramic, especially bought for the purpose, or you can use any old dried beans as long as you remember not to cook them later to eat by mistake. I remember reading in a magazine that a metal dog leash (a relatively fine one) is useful here, as the metal conducts the heat well and you don't have to worry about dropping all the beads on the kitchen floor (apparently there are those who worry about just this); I'm longing to try it.

I like to bake blind at a slightly higher temperature than many people do. The drawback is that the pastry sides can burn, so I keep the edges covered with foil strips for the final bit of baking.

Take the pastry disc out of the fridge and unwrap it. Flour a work surface, put the pastry on it, and sprinkle the pastry and the rolling pin with flour. An ordinary wooden rolling pin will do; those beautiful stainless steel ones sold in some modish kitchen shops are not a good idea except for rolling out fondant icing, which needs heavy battering.

Roll out the pastry fairly thinly. I can't see the point of giving measurements here, as you are hardly going to get your ruler out to check, are you? Anyway, in all recipes I've given specific quantities for the pastry to make exactly the right amount for the stipulated tart shell, so once you've rolled it in a circle to fit, the thickness should be right too.

You can lift the pastry over to the tart pan by carrying it on the rolling pin or you can fold it in quarters and carry the pastry over, place the corner of the dough in the center of the pan, and open it out to cover. Or just lift it up. One of the benefits of pastry made by the blitz-freezing method is that it travels, as it handles, well.

Now you have a choice. You can either line the pan with the pastry, letting it hang slightly over at the rim—use a metal tart pan with a removable bottom, not one of the ceramic tart dishes that make the soggiest pastry—and then roll the pin over the edges to cut off the pastry at the top, which looks neat and clean and smart. Or you can keep the overhang so that if it shrinks (which it can) as it cooks, you won't find you've got a truncated and filling-leaking pastry case. (I never prick the base, as I think it just makes holes for the filling to seep through later.) Whichever you decide—and I veer toward the latter—put the pastry-lined pan back in the fridge for 20 minutes or longer. Indeed, you can make the pastry and line the tart pan the day before you bake it; if so, keep it covered with plastic film.

When you want to bake, preheat the oven to 400°F, put a baking sheet in it, and line the pastry with foil. Then fill with the beans of your choice and bake on the hot sheet for 15 minutes. Take out of the oven and remove the beans and foil. Cut out a long strip or a couple of strips of foil and fold over the edges so they don't burn. Put the foil-rimmed but bare-bottomed pastry case back in the oven and give it another 10–12 minutes or until it is beginning to color lightly. Sweet pastry burns more easily, so turn down the oven to 350°F for the second bout in the oven.

I used to bake blind and then fill the tart shell as soon as it cooled a little, but my friend Tracey Scoffield, one of the best cooks I know and the daughter of a wonderful pastry maker, has taught me that you can bake blind a day in advance as long as, when the case is cool, you slip it into a freezer bag and seal and keep it in the fridge. It must be wrapped airtight—plastic film would do—or it will go soggy. The advantage of staggering the work—making the pastry, rolling it out, and blind baking it on three different days if you really want to—is that you never need to spend more than a few minutes on it each evening. But even in one go, this method is relatively painless.

CRUMBLE

I can't say I don't ever use machinery to make crumble, but there is something peculiarly relaxing about rubbing the cool, smooth butter through the cool, smooth flour with your fingers. It also makes for a more gratifyingly nubbly crumble; the processor can make the crumbs so fine you end up, when cooked, with a cakey rather than crumbly texture. So just remember, if you aren't making this by hand, to go cautiously.

In either case, the texture is improved by a quick blast in the freezer, but rather than freezing the flour and butter mixture before working on it, as with the pastry recipes above, I plonk it in the freezer for 10 minutes or so after it's been rubbed together. And, if you want, you can just leave it there, in an airtight container, on standby for when you get home from work and want to make something sweet and comforting quickly.

I find this mixture makes enough to cover about 2 pounds of fruit in a 4-cup pie dish, which should easily be enough to feed 4–6 people. To make plain apple crumble (though see also the recipe on page 156), peel, core, and segment the apples and toss them for a minute or so in a pan, on the heat, with 1 tablespoon of butter, 3–4 tablespoons of sugar (to taste), and a good squeeze of orange juice, before transferring to the pie pan and topping with the crumble. In fact, I use orange with most fruits; it seems to bring out their flavor rather than striking an intrusive note of its own. Make a blueberry or blackberry crumble by tossing the fruit in a buttered pie pan with 1 tablespoon each of all-purpose flour and sugar for the blueberries, 2 each for the blackberries, and the juice of ½ orange. For rhubarb crumble, trim 1 pound of the fruit, cut it into 2-inch lengths, and toss, again in a buttered pan, with a couple of tablespoons each (or more to taste) of superfine and light muscovado sugar (see page 460), or light brown sugar, the zest of 1 orange, and the merest spritz of the juice.

PLAIN APPLE
CRUMBLE

BLUEBERRY,
BLACKBERRY,
OR RHUBARB

I tend to add a bit of baking powder to the flour for the topping—it's unorthodox, but gives a desirable lightness to the mixture, which can otherwise tend to heaviness. Add spices—ground ginger, cinnamon, nutmeg, even a pinch of ground cardamom—as you like to the crumble recipe below; treat it merely as a blueprint.

1 cup flour	3 tablespoons light muscovado sugar
1 teaspoon baking powder	(see page 460) or light brown sugar
pinch salt	3 tablespoons vanilla sugar or regular
6 tablespoons (¾ stick) unsalted butter,	sugar
cold and cut into about ½-inch cubes	

Put the flour in a bowl with the baking powder and salt. Add the cold cubes of butter and, using the tips of your fingers—index and middle flutteringly stroking the fleshy pads of your thumbs—rub it into the flour. Stop when you have a mixture that resembles oatmeal. Stir in the sugars. I love the combination of muscovado and vanilla sugars, but if you haven't got round to making vanilla sugar yet (see page 72), then don't worry about what white sugar you use; any will do.

Keep the mixture in the fridge until you need it or put the bowl, as is, in the freezer for 10 minutes. Preheat the oven to 375°F and, when ready to cook, sprinkle the crumble over the prepared fruit in the pie dish and cook for 25–35 minutes.

FOODS IN SEASON

Don't believe everything you're told about the greater good of eating foods only when they are in season. The purists may be right, but being right isn't everything. If you live in the Tuscan hills, you may find different lovely things to eat every month of the year, but for us it would mean having to subsist half the time on a diet of tubers and cabbage, so why shouldn't we be grateful that we live in the age of jet transport and extensive culinary imports? More smug guff is spoken on this subject than almost anything else.

There is no doubt that there are concomitant drawbacks: the food is out of kilter with the climate in which it is eaten; it's picked underripe and transported in the wrong conditions; the intense pleasure of eating something when it comes into its own season is lost; the relative merits, the particular properties of individual fruits and vegetables are submerged in the greedy zeal of the tantrumming adult who must Have It Now. There's no point in eating out-of-season asparagus that tastes of nothing (though not all of it does), or peaches in December, ripe-looking but jade-fleshed. But my life is improved considerably by the fact that I can go to my greengrocer's and routinely buy stuff I used to have to go to Italy to find.

I love fresh peas, but they aren't the high point of our culinary year for me. Once they get to the shops, all that pearly sugariness has pretty well turned to starch anyway. As far as I'm concerned, the foods whose short season it would be criminal to ignore are:

rhubarb: May–June; hothouse, which is superior, January–February

Seville oranges: January–February

asparagus: height of season, May–June

gooseberries: domestic, July–August; imported, November–January

grouse: imported marketed, October–November

damson plums: August–September

quinces: October–November

white truffles: November–January

RHUBARB

Rhubarb is amply covered in this book. I know many people are put off because of vile experiences in childhood. I have faith, however, or rather passionate hope, that I can overcome this prejudice. And as my own childhood contained little traditional nursery food, it takes on, for me, something of the exotic. My adult love affair with rhubarb is heady illustration of this (see Index).

SEVILLE ORANGES

Seville oranges are regarded almost exclusively as for making marmalade. This is such a waste. Seville oranges have the fragrance and taste of oranges but the sourness of lemons. Try them, then, wherever you'd use lemons—to squirt over fish, to squeeze into salad dressings, to use in a buttery hollandaise-like sauce or in mayonnaise to eat with cold duck. A squeeze of Seville orange is pretty divine in black tea, too. And although you can only buy them in January or early February, they freeze well. See, also, the recipe for Seville orange curd tart on page 246.

Traditionally, oranges go with duck. Real *canard à l'orange* should be made with bitter and not sweet oranges; you shouldn't end up with jam. Put half a Seville orange up the bottom of a duck (a mallard, preferably, if you have access to wild game, or see page 458) and squeeze the other half, mixed with 1 teaspoon honey or sesame oil, as you wish, over the breast before you cook it. Roast a domestic 4–5 pound duck in a 450°F oven for 15 minutes, reduce the heat to 400°, and cook 1¼–1½ hours, draining the rendered fat periodically. (Don't throw this away; spoon it into a bowl, put it in the fridge, and use it to make the best, wonderfully crisp fried or roast potatoes.) Roast a mallard at 425° for 40 minutes.

If preparing the dish with a domestic duck, remove all visible fat from the pan and deglaze it with some stock and additional Seville orange juice. Stir in a teaspoon or so of honey, or to taste, and there's your sauce. For a mallard, you won't even need to deglaze the pan to make a sauce; the juices there will be

CANARD À
L'ORANGE

good enough just as they are, though if you wish, you can add more orange juice, sweetened with honey to taste or left sharp. If you want something more sauce-like, thicken with 1 teaspoon cornstarch, made first into a paste with some of the juice.

SCALLOPS WITH BITTER ORANGES

Scallops have been cooked with bitter oranges since the eighteenth century. You can do a modern turn on the same theme simply by sautéing the glorious white discs—whole bay scallops or sea scallops halved—in bacon fat, butter, or olive oil, 1 minute or so each side, before removing and deglazing the pan with a good squirt of Seville orange juice. Make sure you've also got enough juices in the pan to make a dressing for the watercress with which you're going to line the plate.

If they make up supper in its entirety, I'd get about 5 scallops of either kind per head. Should you find scallops with coral, fry the coral for about 30 seconds or freeze it to fry up later with a lot of minced garlic to eat, alone and greedily, spread on toast.

SEVILLE ORANGE MARMALADE

I confess I have never made marmalade. The nearest I've got is buying a box of oranges that then, reproachfully, went moldy in my pantry. I have since never even pretended to myself that I'm the sort of person who's about to turn into a bottler and canner and storer of good things, though I live in hope. A friend, however, swears it's easy—you cook the fruit whole—and it doesn't produce so much that you feel like you're starting a marmalade-making factory.

| 1½ pounds Seville oranges | 7 cups sugar |
| juice of 2 lemons | |

Put the oranges in a saucepan with water to cover by a few inches, bring to the boil, and then simmer robustly until the oranges are soft, about 2 hours. Remove the oranges, keeping the water in the saucepan. Cut the oranges up, pulp and all, into whatever size peel you prefer.

Remove the seeds and put them in a small saucepan, with a small amount of water to cover, and boil for 5 minutes. In the meantime, put the chopped oranges and the lemon juice into a bowl. Strain out the seeds and add their cooking water to the lemon juice and chopped oranges.

Return this mixture to the first saucepan, put over a low heat, add sugar, and stir until dissolved. Then bring to boil and cook till set. To establish this, put a small amount, 1 scant teaspoon, on a cold saucer. Let it cool and then prod or stroke it with a fingertip. The marmalade's set if the surface wrinkles. You should remove the saucepan of marmalade from the heat while you test just in case the setting point has been reached. About 15 minutes is usually fine for a softish set.

Take off the heat and put in jars, after removing any scum and stirring to make sure the peel is mixed through. This should fill about six 8-ounce warm, cleaned jam jars. Leave to cool a little more before screwing on the lids.

ASPARAGUS

Asparagus is easy to cook well. Don't worry about special asparagus pans; just trim the butt ends and cook the asparagus in abundant boiling salted water in a pan or couple of pans that are wide and big enough for the whole spears, stem, tip and all, to be submerged. Cook for 3–5 minutes (test and taste regularly—it's better to waste some spears than for them to be either woody or soggy) and drain thoroughly, first in a colander and then flat on a paper towel–lined surface, but do it gently, too; you want the spears to stay beautiful and remain intact.

The usual accompaniment, and always a successful one, is hollandaise (see page 14), but often I like to do something more homey and give each person a boiled egg in an egg cup for them to dip their asparagus into, like the bread and butter fingers British children dip into soft-boiled eggs. The eggs have to be perfectly soft-boiled; there is no room whatsoever for error. I don't wish to frighten you, but it's the truth. Provide two per person and smash or cut the tops off each as soon as they're cooked.

If you feel safer with a nontraditional method, then roll the asparagus in a little olive oil, then roast them, laid out on a pan, in a seriously preheated 450°F oven for 15–20 minutes. When cooked, the spears should be wilted and turning sweet and brown at the tips. Sprinkle over some coarse salt, arrange on a big plate, and line another big plate with thin slices of prosciutto imported from Italy, if possible. Let people pick up the hot, soft, blistered spears and use the ham to wrap around the asparagus like the finest rosy silk-damask napkins.

GOOSEBERRIES

SCENTED PANNA COTTA WITH GOOSEBERRY COMPOTE

I don't normally go in for individual puddings, each precious darling to be ceremoniously unmolded from its ramekin. But I make an exception here, would have to. As with the Italian dessert for which it is named, this fragrant cream, accompanied by a gooseberry compote, needs to be set with as little gelatin as possible. I've tried with big molds and just can't set it enough without turning it halfway into rubber. These are perfection as they are, and anyway, I use a mixture of teacups, dariole molds, and ramekins, feeling that the pleasurable lack of uniformity makes up for any potential dinkiness. Line whichever molds you choose (you can, of course, use custard cups) with plastic film, pushing it well against the sides and over the rim so you've got a tuggable edge; it may make for the odd wrinkle or crease on the surface of the set cream, but that doesn't matter; what does is that you will be able to unmold them easily.

Note that here and elsewhere throughout the book I call for leaf gelatin, which works best for me and produces the most delicate result. I cannot use granulated gelatin for the life of me, but I have to accept that others can and am prepared, grudgingly, to accommodate them.

¾ cup heavy cream	6 tablespoons superfine sugar, plus
2 teaspoons orange-flower water	more, if needed
I teaspoon vanilla	3 leaves gelatin or I envelope
¼ teaspoon grated nutmeg	granulated gelatin

Heat the cream over low heat in saucepan with the orange-flower water, vanilla, and nutmeg. When it comes bubbling to a simmering near-boil, turn it off; remove from the heat. Then stir in the sugar and bring back to boiling point. Taste to see if more sugar is needed and then strain into a large measuring cup. Soak the leaves of gelatin in cold water to cover until softened, or sprinkle the granulated gelatin over ¼ cup cold water to soften, about 5 minutes in either case. Transfer softened granulated gelatin to a double boiler and heat it over simmering water until the granules have dissolved completely and the mixture is clear, about I minute, or dissolve the gelatin in a microwave at high power, about I minute. Squeeze the leaves out if using, and then beat them into the warm cream in the cup, or add the dissolved granulated gelatin to the cream and blend well. Make sure the leaves are dissolved, if using, and dispersed, then pour the cream into the film-lined molds. Cool and then put in the fridge overnight.

I originally used elderflowers to flavor the panna cotta; with it I served this contrastingly lumpy gooseberry compote. (The Victorians knew well and invoked often the muscatty aptness of the combination of elderflowers and gooseberry. About many things they were wrong; about this they were right.) The compote, however, is wonderful with the orange-flower-water-scented version.

To make it, put 5 cups gooseberries in a pan with 1½ cups water and 6 tablespoons of sugar. Bring it all to the boil and simmer for a couple of minutes. Drain, reserving syrup, then put the fruit in a bowl and return the lightly syrupy juices to the pan. Bring it to the boil again and let boil for 5 minutes. Pour it into a bowl or jug to cool while the fruit cools separately in its bowl. Then, when you're about it eat, put the gooseberries in a shallow dish and cover with the syrup.

GROUSE

Grouse (see page 459 for information about its availability) should be roasted plain, first smeared thickly with butter, in a 400°F oven for 30–45 minutes (the size of the birds varies, but you want the flesh to be rubied and juicy, but not underdone to the point of tough quiveriness). Eat the grouse with bread sauce (see page 58) or stuffed with thyme and mascarpone (yes, really), as on page 151.

DAMSONS

Damsons are a glorious fruit. They can't be eaten raw and are a chore to prepare and cook, but it's only once a year. . . .

I sometimes make damson ice cream, but damson fool is the recipe for which I wait most greedily. This fool is not difficult to make, but it is stunning, utterly distinctive; you can taste in it both the almost metallic depth of the sour fruit and billowy sweetness of the bulky cream. And it's wonderful after grouse.

DAMSON FOOL

I pound damsons

2 teaspoons each dark and light muscovado sugar (see page 460), or dark and light brown sugar, and superfine sugar, plus more, if desired

¼ teaspoon allspice

I cup heavy cream, whipped with 2 tablespoons confectioners' sugar

Put the whole damsons (try to stone them now and you'll go really mad) in a saucepan with ½ cup water and the sugars, bring to the boil, and cook till soft. Push through a strainer or food mill to get rid of the stones and add the spice and more sugar to taste if you think they need it.

When cool, stir into the sugar-whipped cream and pour either into individual pots or into a bowl. This will also fill 6 glasses of the sort you'd eat pudding from, but if you're putting the fool in a bowl, then count on feeding only 4.

QUINCES

Quince, the apple that Paris presented to Helen and maybe even the one that grew in the garden of Eden (although there is, it's argued, a more convincing academic case to be made for the pomegranate here), is a ravishing mixture of One Thousand and One Nights exotic and Victorian kitchen homeliness. It looks like a mixture between apple and pear but tastes like neither. And actually the taste is not the point; what this fruit is all about is heady, perfect fragrance. I have something of an obsession for quinces, although they are in the shops only for a scant eight weeks, aren't at all easy to deal with, and can't be eaten raw. In the old days, quinces were kept in airing cupboards to perfume the linen, pervading the house with their honeyed but sharp aroma, so you needn't feel bad if you buy a bowlful and then just watch them rot in a kitchen or wherever.

As for cooking with quinces, what you should know is that for all their hardness, they bruise very easily. Whenever I have a batch of quinces, at least a third of them have been riddled within with speckles, or worse, what looks like rust. I just ignore it, unless of course it's obviously rotten. Anyway, quinces darken as they cook, going from glassy yellow to coral to deepest, burnt terracotta; the odd bit of bruising really won't show.

You should add a quince, peeled, cored, and sliced or chunked, to apple pie or crumble. Poach them as you might pears (only longer, and see the recipe for quinces in muscat wine on page 329) or make mostarda. Although I am not someone who goes in for preserve making, I do make mostarda.

MOSTARDA DI VENEZIA

There's mostarda di Cremona, which has become modishly familiar in Britain, those stained-glass-window-colored gleaming pots of fruits glossily preserved in mustard oil; no one, even in Italy, apparently, makes their own. But mostarda di Venezia is different. You can't buy it and it's easy to make. It's just quinces boiled up with white wine, with the addition of sugar, candied peel, and mustard powder. It's wonderful with any cold meat (which makes it very useful for Christmas and, as you have to leave it a month or so before eating, rather well timed for it, too). I risk a culinary culture clash by eating it alongside couscous and curries and to pad out the sort of low-fat, highly flavored food on pages 366–383. Or you can eat it with a dollop of mascarpone, sweetened (and perhaps bolstered with egg, as on page 107) and flavored with rum, as dessert.

This recipe is adapted from the one in *Classic Food of Northern Italy* by Italian food writer Anna del Conte; the recipe, as these things do, has a mixed parentage of its own. I have changed it a little. I simplify the procedure (see below) and also make it hotter and with almost double the amount of candied fruit. Now, I loathe and detest most commercial candied fruit, but it's different here, not least because you must not use the already diced, bitter and oversweet at the same time, vile stuff from the supermarket. Search out the good imported candied fruit in whole pieces.

The second time I made mostarda di Venezia, I didn't peel and core the quinces. It's such hard work. Instead I just roughly chopped the fruit and then pushed the lot through a fine food mill. Laziness prompted this modification, but as the peel and core help the set and intensify the flavor, you should have no qualms. If you don't own a food mill, I suppose you could just push the fruit through a strainer, but that's strenuous too. So if you don't own this cheap and useful piece of equipment, it would be easier to peel, quarter, and core to start with.

4 pounds quinces, roughly chopped	**8 tablespoons English mustard powder**
I bottle white wine	**I teaspoon salt**
grated rind and juice of I lemon	**8–9 ounces candied fruit, cut into small**
5½ cups sugar	**cubes**

Put the quinces in a saucepan and cover them with the wine. Add the lemon rind and juice and cook until soft, about 40 minutes. Purée the mixture by pushing it through a food mill and add the sugar. Return to the pan. Dissolve the mustard powder in a little hot water and add to the purée with the salt and the candied fruit. Cook gently until the liquid is reduced and the mostarda becomes dense and, normally, deeper-colored, 20–30 minutes.

Sterilize five I-pint jars (I find the dishwasher's performance on this adequate) and fill with the mostarda. When it is cool, cover, seal, and store away. Keep for about a month before you use it.

WHITE TRUFFLES

No greedy person's mention of foods in season could ignore the white truffle. I don't really understand the fuss about black truffles, but a white truffle—called by Rossini the Mozart of *funghi*—is something else. And you don't do anything to it. You just shave it. And if you're buying a truffle, you may as well go the whole hog and buy the thing with which to shave it over a plate of buttery egg pasta or into an equally rich risotto made with good broth. It is instant culinary nirvana. And although expensive, so much less so, unbelievably less so, than eating it in a restaurant.

CHRISTMAS

Seasonal food doesn't come much more seasonal than at Christmas; this is not exactly to do with what's in season, but with what's expected of it—and you. If, like the majority of British, you are going to be cooking multiple meals at this time, or even just one, for upward of six people, you will need to be organized.

It is hard not to feel swamped by food and food preparation during the holidays, and even if you like cooking, Christmas can induce panic and depression. And the quantity of food involved can also begin to instill a sense of unease; so much excess is unsettling, and it feels decadent to be the creator of it in the first place.

This isn't, of course, purely a moral distaste—after all, food is celebratory and it's perfectly respectable to choose to appreciate its plentifulness—but, rather, a narcissistic anxiety. We feel uncomfortable with the prospect of overeating. But just as we fear it, we court it, because the truth is that we don't have to plow our way through seasonal cakes and chocolates and nuts and pies. We feel we have an excuse, and so we plunge into an orgy of overindulgence that is utterly unnecessary and that makes us feel both guilty and resentful at the same time.

For me, an urban person, Christmas is rather like being in the country: not much to do apart from eat and drink. I end up suffering from boredom-induced bloat. But cooking itself can make a difference. It's the amount of packaged and processed food around at Christmas that makes us feel truly bad. Not all Christmas food has to be the sort that leaves us stultified and slumped over the table for hours after we've eaten it.

Christmas Day itself is, in my view, nonnegotiable. It's fashionable to decry the traditional English Christmas lunch as boring and the turkey invariably served as dry, but I love it all and on December 26 start longing for next year's lunch. My great-grandmother was so keen on Christmas lunch, and felt it was such a waste to eat it only once a year, that she had a second one each Midsummer's Day in celebration of the summer solstice. This was the first sign of great-grandmother's eccentricity.

Some British argue for a Christmas lunch goose; I've eaten it, and have no fierce objections, but I don't think I would like to see my turkey ousted by it. Cooking a goose for a Christmas Eve or Day dinner seems to me the best idea, as one can then make sure at least of getting some excellent leftovers. Goose is anyway much better cold than hot.

What I really object to are the bright magazine alternatives to traditional Christmas dining—medallions of pheasant in Armagnac sauce, guinea fowl with grapes and sweet potato galettes, rolled breast of turkey with chestnut and pine nut stuffing and celeriac rösti. I do see that if you're a vegetarian, some alternative is required. But, frankly, I would still avoid the nut-roast route. Forget the whole thing and eat as normal on Christmas Day—even consider a simplified menu. I would be happier with this than with some jaunty ersatz number.

But even if you've got Christmas Day dining figured out, there is still the other holiday-time to think of. Remember that anything you serve for Christmas Eve or Day can be devised for enjoyment after. I am a huge fan of cold leftovers. Resist, please, the tendency to camouflage, to go in for makeovers. Cold beef, as long as it hasn't been overcooked, is wonderful, as is cold ham, cold duck, maybe even some cold lamb.

The best sorts of leftover meals are those that are glorified picnics. Alongside the cold meats, you need a good purchased pâté en croûte—one made with veal or duck would be just the thing. Also put on the table some salad and bread. I occasionally add cheese to this board, sometimes serve the cheese after the meat has been eaten and cleared away. And at Christmas, not unreasonably, I have at hand some good English cheeses—an excellent Stilton, naturally, but some Cheddar and possibly some Cheshire, too. These British cheeses seem right for American holiday tables, too.

You need some sort of mayonnaise (page 12), if only for sandwiches. And sandwiches, especially for eating television-side, are an essential part of Christmas food.

But other sauces are important for leftovers, too. Cranberry sauce (see page 59) is an obvious poultry accompaniment, but I also have to have mustard. I have a painful Christmas memory of lunch at a friend's house where everything was perfect, only there was no English mustard. Mustard is especially good with cold stuffing. Mango chutney is fundamental to cold meat sandwiches, and if you are eating cold goose, you should make sure you have some horseradish. You should try here, too, that Jewish mix of horseradish and beetroot called *chrain.* And while we're on this particular culture clash, potato latkes (see page 63) are wonderful with cold fowl.

I think it's all right to give people leftovers if they're coming for dinner around Christmas, but in that case, make a hot dessert. It needn't be complicated, but it looks as if you've made some effort. Soup, too, not out of a can, gives a hospitable uplift to the inevitable leftover offerings.

However much you like cold cuts and leftovers, you can't eat them for every meal. Christmas food divides into food that is seasonal and food that is deliberately not. By this latter category, I don't mean you should be serving strawberries flown in from distant hemispheres, but that it can be a relief to eat food that is innocent of any seasonal connotation. So much Christmas food, too, is so palate-stickingly luxy; instead, keep it simple, make it fresh. Avoid the slavish overprovision of rich food that turns eating into a burdensome duty rather than a pleasure and turns cooking into an entirely out-of-character exercise.

A CHRISTMAS GOOSE

Years ago, I cut out this recipe for goose stuffed with mashed potato from one of British food writer Simon Hopkinson's columns in the *Independent*. The recipe comes via restaurateur Peter Langan and was his grandmother Callinan's. It must represent a curious axis, where Irish and Polish culinary practices meet, for I've only come across something similar in a book on Polish-Jewish cooking.

Simon Hopkinson, no namby-pamby when it comes to food, says this recipe feeds six and I believe him (normally I treat printed portion sizes with distrust), so if you're having more than six guests, cook a couple of geese, eat all the unctuous stuffing, and have the cold meat later on in the week. Because you need to dry out the skin well before you start, you have to get cracking early.

I goose, about 10 pounds, with giblets

2 tablespoons vegetable oil

1½ pounds potatoes, peeled, cut into
    large chunks and rinsed thoroughly

4 medium onions, chopped coarsely

2 garlic cloves, peeled and minced

I heaping tablespoon fresh sage leaves,
    chopped

grated rind of 2 lemons

freshly milled black pepper

salt

FOR THE GRAVY

4 strips bacon, chopped

I goose neck, chopped coarsely

I goose gizzard, cleaned (ask your
    butcher to do this) and chopped
    coarsely

I medium onion, chopped

I medium carrot, peeled and chopped

2 celery stalks, chopped

2 tablespoons Calvados

½ cup Madeira

1¼ cups strong chicken stock

I scant tablespoon red currant jelly

I heaping teaspoon arrowroot, mixed
    with a little water

First prepare the goose and render some lovely goose fat. Remove all the lumps of pale fat that lie just inside the goose's cavity, attached to the skin. Put them in a saucepan with the oil and place on a very low heat and let the fat melt. Render it all down, pour it into a bowl, and add to this, later, the great glorious amounts of fat that drip off the goose into the pan as it roasts. The goose fat will be wonderful for roast potatoes on Christmas Day—or any day.

Now, get to work on the goose's skin, so that it crisps up in the oven like Peking duck. Put the goose on a rack in a roasting pan, puncture the skin several times with the point of a thin skewer or very sharp knife, then pour over boiling water. Tip all the water out of the pan and let the goose dry. The brave or rural can do this by placing it by an open window—at this time of year, I think you can count on a fair breeze—and leave for hours, preferably overnight. Otherwise, and even better, direct an electric fan toward the bird for a few hours. Remember to turn it regularly so that all sides get dried. You are often advised to hang the bird up, but this is hard enough to do with a duck and a coat hanger, and a duck is very much lighter than a goose. But if you've got a butcher's hook handy, and somewhere to hang it, why not give it a try?

Your goose is prepared; now preheat the oven to 425°F. Boil the potatoes in salted water until tender, drain well, and mash coarsely. Fry the onions in the recently rendered goose fat until golden brown. Add the garlic and stir them both into the mashed potato, along with the sage and lemon rind. Season with the pepper, rub a generous amount of salt over the goose, and put a good grinding of pepper inside the cavity. Then pack the mashed potato mixture into the cavity and put the goose back on its wire rack in the largest possible roasting pan and place in the oven.

Roast for 30 minutes, then turn the temperature down to 350°F. Cook the goose for a further 2½ hours or so. Don't baste—you want the fat to run off the goose, the more the better—but do remember to remove fat regularly during the goose's cooking or you might have a messy and dangerous accident.

Make the gravy while the goose is cooking. Fry the bacon in 2 tablespoons of the goose fat in a heavy-bottomed pan until crisp and brown. Add the neck and gizzard and cook until well colored, then do the same with the vegetables. Pour off any excess fat and add the Calvados and Madeira (I'd also be happy using my usual Marsala here). Bring to the boil and reduce until syrupy. Pour in the chicken stock and red currant jelly and simmer for 30 minutes. Strain through a fine sieve into a clean saucepan. Allow to settle and, with some paper towels, lift off any fat that is floating on the surface. Whisk in the arrowroot and bring the gravy back to a simmer until clear and slightly thickened. Make sure you don't let it boil or the arrowroot can break down and thin the gravy. Keep warm. Just putting the lid on a good saucepan should do this, or use a heat diffuser and keep the flame low.

When your goose is cooked—the drumstick will be soft when squeezed—remove it from the oven and let it rest for 15 minutes or so before carving. Simon Hopkinson suggests serving some extra potatoes (in addition to the potato stuffing—now you see why I trust him on portion size), fried with garlic in some of the goose fat you've collected and sprinkled with parsley, and some big bunches of watercress. You certainly don't need sophisticated vegetables—frozen peas, good and buttery, with some blanched and buttered snow peas stirred in would be good.

After eating the goose, I'd just make sure there were big bowls of lychees, clementines, and some nuts on the table.

I think for Christmas lunch it has to be turkey; furthermore, this turkey has to be fresh, free-range turkey. A good bird. My mother did a splendid job, though, with a lesser bird, by soaking some clean reusable kitchen wipes in melted butter, then bandaging the turkey's breast with them for the first part of the roasting, first on one side, then on the other. But a good turkey, carefully cooked, removes instantly all association with dryness forever.

Though traditional for British Christmas lunch, there is no reason, of course, why this recipe can't be drafted to fit in with Thanksgiving plans. If serving it for a Christmas lunch, however, forgo any starters. I can't see the point of blunting your appetite before you even get to the main event.

The turkey needs to be stuffed, and I should, in all honesty, own that I get my butcher, Mr. Lidgate, to do that for me. I couldn't improve on his recipes, and so I've got them for you—one for chestnut stuffing, the other for cranberry and orange. This is the perfect pair—the one sweet and mealy, the other sharp and fruited; the quantities in both are enough to stuff, one at each end, a 12–14 pound bird, with some stuffing left over to cook in a separate dish; adjust quantities accordingly for larger or smaller birds, and remember—if you don't make extra stuffing, you can run out before second helpings, which is a grave error.

LIDGATE'S CHESTNUT STUFFING

½ pound shallots, minced

5 tablespoons unsalted butter

¼ pound piece slab bacon, chopped (any
    rind removed and reserved for
    making the gravy, page 461)

2 eggs

1 can (16 ounces) unsweetened
    chestnut purée

8 ounces canned whole chestnuts,
    roughly chopped

2 cups fresh bread crumbs (see page 22)

1 bunch parsley, chopped

salt and freshly milled black pepper

whole nutmeg

Cook the shallots in the butter, melted in a heavy-bottomed frying pan, with the bacon for about 10 minutes on a lowish heat or until soft and beginning to color. Beat the eggs and add to the chestnut purée to help thin it, or it will be hard to mix everything together later (unless you've got one of those sturdy free-standing mixers). Add the chestnuts to the eggy purée, along with the bread crumbs, parsley, and buttery shallots and bacon. Season with the salt and pepper and a good grating of the nutmeg.

LIDGATE'S CRANBERRY AND ORANGE STUFFING

4½ cups fresh or thawed cranberries

zest and juice of I large orange

8 tablespoons (I stick) unsalted butter, cut in slices

4½ cups fresh bread crumbs (see page 22)

2 eggs, beaten

salt and freshly milled black pepper

whole nutmeg

Put the cranberries into a heavy-bottomed saucepan with the orange juice and zest. Bring to simmering point on a moderate to high heat, then cover, turn down the heat slightly, and simmer for about 5 minutes. Add the butter gradually and stir, off the heat, until it melts, then add the bread crumbs and the eggs. Season with salt and pepper and a good grating of fresh nutmeg.

If you have a kitchen scale, weigh the stuffings before adding them to the turkey because you'll need to count that weight in the total cooking time. Otherwise, know that 2 cups of stuffing equal about 10 ounces, and estimate stuffing weights accordingly.

Neither stuffing here uses sausage meat; if you think you'll miss it, just get a pile of sausages to cook alongside.

To cook the turkey, proceed as follows.

Remove the giblets (though you should have done this when you first got the bird home). Reserve them for the gravy. Wash the inside of the bird with cold running water. Drain well and blot dry with a few paper towels.

Fill the neck end with the chestnut stuffing; you want to fill it firmly, but don't pack it in. Cover the stuffing with the neck skin when you've done. Use the wing tips rather like pincers—or paper clips—to keep the neck skin in place while it's cooking. Now, fill the body cavity with the cranberry and orange stuffing. Melt some goose fat (if you've got any) or some butter (if you haven't) and brush over the turkey breast.

I don't understand why people make such a song and dance about the length of time a turkey needs to be cooked. My mother made a great point of getting up at the crack of dawn to put the turkey in the oven. But one of the things that I discovered the first time I actually cooked turkey myself is that it doesn't need that much cooking.

I have always followed the instructions given to me by my butcher, and the turkey's been cooked perfectly. So don't be alarmed by the shortness of the cooking times, below. And do remember to take the turkey out of the fridge in good time—it should be at room temperature when it goes in the oven. Also, take into account the additional stuffing weight when figuring the cooking time.

Put the turkey breast down in the roasting tray; the only fat deposits in a turkey are in the back, and this allows them to percolate through the breast meat as it cooks; this makes for the tenderest possible, succulent meat.

Preheat the oven to 400°F and keep it at this temperature for the first 30 minutes. Then turn it down to 350°F.

For the following weights of turkey (stuffing included, remember) you need to cook it for about these times:

Weight	Time
5 pounds	1½ hours
10 pounds	2 hours
15 pounds	2¾ hours
20 pounds	3½ hours
25 pounds	4½ hours

It is not possible to give one serve-all timing based on minutes per pound; this time decreases as the weight of the bird increases. For such information, you should consult those who are selling your bird to you.

Baste regularly throughout the cooking time and turn the bird the right way up for the last half hour of cooking to brown. I use no foil, as some do, to retard browning or retain moisture, but if you want to use it, add an hour onto cooking time—and still remove it for the last, breast-burnishing half-hour.

To see for yourself that the turkey is ready, poke a skewer or fork where the thigh meets the breast, and if it is cooked the juices will run clear. Or use an instant-read thermometer, in which case the bird is done when the thermometer, plunged into the thickest part of the thigh, registers 175°F–180°F.

GRAVY

Now for the gravy. I am not one of life's gravy makers. I make disgusting coffee, too; obviously, brown liquids are not my thing. This one works, though.

Make the giblet stock well in advance. Keep the liver covered with milk in a dish in the fridge till you need it.

giblets from the turkey

1 bouquet garni (see page xx)

4 peppercorns

1 medium onion, halved

1 medium carrot, peeled and quartered

1 celery stalk, roughly chopped

bacon rind (reserved from making the chestnut stuffing), if available

| 1 teaspoon salt | 1 tablespoon unsalted butter |
| 1 tablespoon Italian 00 or all-purpose flour | 1 tablespoon Marsala |

Put the giblets, except for the liver, in a saucepan (that's to say the heart, neck, and gizzard), add the bouquet garni, the peppercorns, onion, carrot, and celery, and bacon rind, if using, and cover with 4 cups water, sprinkling over the salt. Bring to the boil, cover, lower the heat, and simmer for about 2 hours. Strain into a measuring cup. Set it aside if you're doing this stage in advance, or else get on with the next stage, which takes place when the turkey's cooked and sitting, resting, on its carving board.

Pour off most of the fat from the roasting pan, leaving behind about 2 tablespoons plus all the usual sticky and burnt bits. Put the pan back on the burner at a low heat and, in a separate little bowl, mix together the flour with, gradually, 3–4 tablespoons of the liquid from the saucepan. When you have a smooth, runny paste, stir it back into the pan. Cook for a couple of minutes, scraping up any bits from the bottom and incorporating them, but make sure the pan's not so hot it burns. Still stirring, gradually pour in 2 cups of the giblet stock, or more if the mixture seems too thick, bearing in mind you're adding the liver later.

While the gravy's cooking gently, leave it for a moment (though keep stirring every now and again) to fry the liver. To do so, melt the butter in a small pan and toss the liver in it for 1–2 minutes, then remove to a board and chop finely.

Add the liver to the gravy. Add the Marsala and stir well, cooking for another few minutes, before pouring into a couple of gravy boats. Since first making this gravy, I have bought a blender and would now add a little more of the giblet stock, say 2½ cups, and blend the gravy after the liver has been chopped and added.

POTATOES

You should parboil and roast the potatoes as instructed on page 253, and use goose fat if you have any (it can now be bought from some specialty markets, especially at Christmas). Otherwise, vegetable oil will do. The oven the turkey is in is not hot enough for the potatoes. If you don't have a double oven, you can leave the turkey to sit while you're blasting the potatoes.

BRUSSELS SPROUTS AND CHESTNUTS

I know there are chestnuts in the stuffing, but I'd put still more of them in with the brussels sprouts. I don't suggest you peel your own; buy them in cans or jars. What makes a difference in preparing this is the butter you add after cooking;

don't refrain from using the whole quantity. And season well with pepper and fresh nutmeg.

For 10 people, buy about 1 pound sprouts and ½ pound canned whole chestnuts. Roughly chop the chestnuts so that some are cut in 2, some in 3; that's to say, you don't need them whole, but nor do you want mealy rubble. After you've cooked the sprouts—lightly—drain them and melt about 8 tablespoons (1 stick) of unsalted butter in a large saucepan. Toss the chestnuts in the butter and then add the sprouts. Add salt, pepper, and fresh nutmeg and coat well with the butter in the pan before turning into a couple of warmed bowls.

You need other vegetables too, but if you're a large group of people, it cuts down the possibilities of what can be done easily. Delicious though a bowl of sharp-edged-tasting shredded cabbage would be (see page 335), you hardly want to stir-fry a large amount at the last minute. But you do want crunch. Barely blanch a bowl of sugar snap peas. Or buy some already prepared broccoli florets and toss them, just cooked, in butter to which you've added a little sesame oil. And I know it's untraditional, but green beans are not a bad idea. I wouldn't mind one puréed vegetable as well, though it's not crucial. You could prepare it much earlier, even the day before, so it doesn't add too much horror. Puréed Jerusalem artichokes would be my choice.

BREAD SAUCE

This is essential for a true English Christmas lunch. For 10 people you need:

2 small onions, each stuck with 3 cloves	salt
I bay leaf	1½ cups fresh bread crumbs (see page
4 peppercorns	22)
blade of mace or ¼ teaspoon ground	2 tablespoons (¼ stick) unsalted butter
mace	2 tablespoons heavy cream
3½ cups milk	whole nutmeg

Put the clove-stuck onions, bay leaf, peppercorns, and the blade of mace (or sprinkle the ground mace over) into a saucepan with the milk. Add a good pinch of salt and bring to the boil, but do not actually let boil. Remove from the heat, cover the pan, and infuse. I tend to do this first thing in the morning when I get up, but if you forget or can't, then just make sure you get the infusion done about an hour before eating.

Back on a very low heat, sprinkle over and stir in the bread crumbs and cook for about 15 minutes, by which time the sauce should be thick and warm. I have to say I don't bother with removing any of the bits—the onions, the peppercorns, and so on—

but you can strain the milk before adding the bread crumbs if you want to. Just before serving, melt the butter and heat up the cream together in another saucepan, grate over quite a bit of nutmeg, and stir into the bread sauce. Taste to see if it needs any more salt or, indeed, anything else.

CRANBERRY SAUCE

We always had cranberry sauce out of a jar at home, which is why I'm fond of it, as I am of horseradish sauce out of a bottle, too. But both, truly, are better freshly made. Cranberry sauce is so easy as not to be worth even hesitating about.

I pound cranberries

I cup sugar, plus more, if desired

2 tablespoons (¼ stick) unsalted butter

zest and juice of I orange

I tablespoon Grand Marnier (optional)

Put the cranberries, sugar, butter, juice and zest of the orange, and Grand Marnier, if using, in a saucepan. Add ½ cup water and bring to the boil. After a minute or so's fierce bubbling, lower to a simmer and cook for about 10 minutes, until the berries have popped and you have a thick, fruity sauce. Taste to see if you want more sugar, then decant into a bowl and let cool before serving. Don't panic if it's still fairly runny, though, as it solidifies on cooling.

I have to say I have never yet made my own Christmas pudding, the traditional Christmas lunch finale. I will, I will. One day. But buying one seems an entirely sensible thing to do (see page 462). And I pass on a tip I've learned from Coping with Christmas, coauthored by Fanny Craddock, the renowned British TV cook: use vodka in place of the brandy for flaming the pudding. Apparently it burns for much longer. Fanny boasts of keeping the flame alive for 11 minutes on a TV spectacular she did at the Albert Hall.

But I do make my own brandy butter, the usual pudding accompaniment, to go with my unashamedly bought one, the brandy butter of my childhood. I have recently taken to making an odd sort of semifrozen rum sauce, too, which is a variant of the eggy, brandy-spiked cream a friend of mine makes.

BRANDY BUTTER

This is what was always traditionally called hard sauce, but somehow it looks affected and quaint to call it that now. I add ground almonds—because my mother did, so it's the taste I know, and because they give it a glorious marzipanny depth and velvetiness.

You need the butter to be as soft as possible before you start, but not at all oily. Obviously, it makes life easier if you can make this in a machine, either a mixer or processor; I prefer the former.

10 tablespoons (1¼ sticks) unsalted butter, soft	½ cup ground almonds
2 cups confectioners' sugar, sifted	3 tablespoons brandy, or to taste

Beat the butter until creamy, then add the sugar and beat them together till pale. Mix in the ground almonds and, when all is smooth, add the brandy. Add a tablespoon at first, then taste, then another and see if you want more. You may find that the suggested 3 tablespoons is far from enough; it is a question of taste, and what is lethally strong for one person seems insipid to another. You must please yourself, as you can't please everyone.

ICED RUM SAUCE

This is a sort of rum-sodden and syrupy egg nog with cream that's kept in the freezer until about an hour before eating. You put it on the searing hot pudding and it melts on impact. It's odd, but it works.

¼ cup heavy cream	2 tablespoons dark rum
2 egg yolks	
2 tablespoons golden syrup (see page 460) or light corn syrup	

Beat the cream until stiff. In another bowl, beat the yolks until extremely frothy. Add the syrup and rum to eggs, still beating. Then fold this egg mixture into the cream. You could serve it straightaway, as it is, un-iced; the plan, though, is to put it in the freezer to set hard and then transfer it to the fridge, allowing it to ripen for about an hour so that it's frozen but beginning to flop by the time you add it to the hot pudding.

MINCEMEAT

Mince pies, I feel, are a bit like Christmas pudding: you may as well buy one. I once made my own mincemeat—adding quince in place of the more usual apple, and eau de vie de Coings instead of the brandy—but it was years ago and I've still got most of it lying about. I am not, therefore, inspired to repeat the experience just yet.

What you can always do, if you want to go one step further than getting bought pies, is use about 1½ cups of the best commercial mincemeat you can buy and, a couple of weeks before Christmas, grate into it a cooking apple or a quince, stir in 3 tablespoons of rum, Grand Marnier, or eau de vie de Coings, add some chopped flaked almonds (about ½ cup) and the juice of half a lemon and half an orange each, and a bit of the grated zest of both. Then you'll almost feel you have made your own mincemeat.

There are two ways of approaching the making of the pastry for your mince pies: either make tiny pies of about 2 inches in diameter (which I think I like best) and use a plain pastry dough (see page 37), binding the dough with iced, salted orange juice in place of water, or make them the usual size, 8–9 inches in diameter, but out of almond pastry (see page 264). For the small pies, cut out circles of dough, put in tartlet tins, add a scant 1 teaspoon of mincemeat to each, and top, not with a round pastry lid, but with a star stamped out with a specially shaped cutter. About quarter of an hour in a 400°F oven should be fine. For the bigger pies, use an almond pastry base and top with a dollop of frangipane. Cook at 400°F for about 10 minutes, then at 350°F for another 15–20 minutes.

LEFTOVERS

BUBBLE AND SQUEAK

This dish, which consists of fried mashed potatoes and cabbage, has an unexpected buttery and nutty resonance when made with brussels sprouts. Though the sprouts have become something of a byword for the culinary awfulness of a British Christmas, my absolute favorite Christmas Day or Boxing Day supper is a bubble and squeak made by frying leftover, roughly chopped sprouts with an onion and some mashed potatoes in a pan, then topping it with a fried or poached egg, and maybe some crisp, salty bacon.

And I know I said that leftovers must not be reformulated in any way, but here is the exception.

ED VICTOR'S
TURKEY HASH

Obviously, one can't be specific about amounts; who knows how much you've got left or how many people you are trying to feed? I give you this recipe, then, just as my literary agent, Ed Victor, gave it to me. Use whatever quantities and proportions feel right, taste good, to you.

Sauté chopped onions and green peppers in a mixture of butter and olive oil in a large saucepan. Add diced turkey (white and dark meat) plus any leftover stuffing to the cooked onion and peppers mixture, and cook till warmed through. You can season it at this stage with salt and pepper.

Then stir in pitted ripe black olives and toasted almonds. Finally, drizzle over the top some beaten eggs mixed with heavy cream, and stir till set.

Optionally, you can finish the hash off with some grated Parmesan on top and brown it under the grill.

Voilà! It's usually much, much better than the turkey itself. In fact, it's the only reason to eat turkey on Christmas Day!

I don't concede that last point, but we should allow a man his prejudices.

POTATOES You don't need to do very much to make cold cuts interesting, as long as the meat's good to start off with. I suggest serving alongside potatoes, cut small and roasted till crisp. Cut them into about ½-inch dice, toss in a freezer bag with garlic-infused oil (see page 459) and dried thyme, and then turn into a baking pan, or just sprinkle with the thyme and drop in a roasting pan with 2–3 tablespoons hot goose fat. Roast for about an hour at 400°F. When the potatoes are done, remove to a plate and sprinkle with coarse sea salt. Work on rations of about ⅓ pound potatoes per person. And serve with two salads: one green, another of tomatoes.

ROASTED WHOLE GARLIC CLOVES AND SHALLOTS My other regular standby is a plate, a huge plate, of roasted whole garlic cloves and shallots. When I'm eating hot meat alongside (as with the chicken on page 7), I don't peel them, but with cold cuts I do. This is made easier if you blanch them first. So, preheat the oven to 325°F. And, figuring on half a head of garlic and ¼ pound of shallots per person, peel the shallots and put them in a baking pan in the oven, coated with some olive oil. They'll need about 45 minutes and the garlic will need about 25, so give the shallots a 20-minute head start. Meanwhile, separate the garlic cloves, put them in a saucepan of cold water, bring to the boil and let boil for 2 minutes. Drain and peel the garlic; the blanching will have made it very easy. Just exert pressure on one end of the clove and it will pop out of its skin at the other. Put the garlic in its own baking pan, with some olive oil, too, and roast.

When both garlic and shallots are cooked, mix on a large plate and sprinkle salt and chopped parsley over them. I know half a head of garlic each and all those shallots sounds a lot, but people always seem to eat incredible amounts of this. You can also eat them cold, with a little more olive oil and a drop or two of balsamic vinegar poured over them, along with a load of fresh chopped parsley and maybe some toasted pine nuts. The vegetables reheat well, too, if you stir them over a low heat in a heavy-bottomed saucepan on the burner, so don't skimp.

If you want to make latkes to eat with the cold meats, then—for six or so peo-ple—push about 4½ pounds of peeled potatoes through the grater disc of the food processor. Remove and drain in a strainer, pushing well to extract all excess liq-uid. Then fit the metal blade in the processor and put a peeled medium onion, coarsely chopped, 3 eggs, 1 teaspoon salt, some pepper, ¼ cup flour, plus a scant ¼ teaspoon baking powder or fine matzo meal in the processor and process briefly. Add the grated potatoes and give a quick pulse till the mixture is pulpy but not totally puréed. You should have a thick mass; add more flour if it's at all runny.

Fry the latkes in lumps of about 1 tablespoon each in a heavy-bottomed fry-ing pan with hot oil bubbling away in it to a depth of about 1 inch. About 5 min-utes a side should do it, maybe even less. Drain on paper towels. These are not great if they are left lying around to cool off, but you can fry them earlier, then reheat in a very hot oven, about 450°F, for 5–10 minutes. You can even fry them, freeze them, defrost, and reheat them—or so I'm told—but I am not the freeze-ahead type.

And while we're mixing culinary cultures, I should mention that cookbook writer Sameen Rushdie's potatoes with whole spices are wonderful with the Christmas cold cuts. I don't include the recipe here just because it includes nigella seeds, but I admit that I was inspired to cook this for the first time by just such embar-rassingly egomaniac promptings. You might need to go to a specialty store for them; you should know, then, that their Indian name is kalonji; or you can buy the particular spices listed below—called panchphoran—ready mixed.

PANCHPHORAN ALOO
(POTATOES IN WHOLE SPICES)

½ teaspoon fenugreek seeds

½ teaspoon nigella seeds

½ teaspoon black mustard seeds

½ teaspoon white cumin seeds

½ teaspoon fennel seeds

about 2 tablespoons vegetable oil

2 pounds potatoes, peeled and cut into
  small dice

½ teaspoon turmeric

½ teaspoon ground red chili pepper

salt

3–4 tablespoons freshly chopped
  coriander

Mix together the whole spices. Using a wok or other nonstick pan, take the mini-mum amount of oil needed to fry the potatoes and fry them over high heat to start with, then turn the heat down and cover. When the potatoes are a little more than half done, add the turmeric, red chili powder, and some salt, closely followed by the mixed-together whole spices. Stir to combine and put the lid back on once again. When the potatoes are nearly ready (and you will have to be vigilant to ensure they don't get too soft), take the lid off, turn the heat up, and stir-fry to enable any excess liquid to evaporate.

Garnish with the coriander and serve.

LENTIL AND CHESTNUT SOUP

Another way of adding zip to cold leftovers is to serve hot soup first.

I first had this aromatic, velvety, buff-colored soup at Le Caprice, a fashionable London restaurant, about ten years ago, and still hanker after it. This is, with some help from the restaurant, my interpretation of it.

I have specified vegetable stock, and I tend to use vegetable bouillon cubes, but obviously you can use chicken stock if you prefer.

Peeling chestnuts gives me a nervous breakdown, so for this, I use the commercially packed whole chestnuts (and so, I have since found out, does Le Caprice).

2 tablespoons olive oil, goose fat, or butter	1 cup red lentils
1 small onion, minced	6⅓ cups vegetable stock
½ leek, minced	8 ounces canned chestnuts
1 medium carrot, minced	2–3 tablespoons chopped parsley
1 celery stalk, minced	heavy cream, for serving

Heat the oil in the pan, add the minced vegetables, and let sweat and soften. Add the lentils and stir, then add the stock. Bring to the boil and simmer until the lentils are very soft, about 40 minutes. Add the chestnuts and simmer for a further 20 minutes or so. Purée in a blender or food processor until smooth, adding water as you need. When you want to serve it, reheat and, at the table, sprinkle each full bowl of soup with the parsley and lace with the cream. Serves 4–6.

You can otherwise make any old supper, whether of cold meats or whatever's lying around, seem a little more effortful (and indeed it will be a little more effortful) by making a dessert to have after. A hot dessert, I mean. And my favorite for this time of year is one of the recipes I did for my first piece as food writer for *Vogue*. It's a version of the rightly named queen of puddings, which has mystifyingly never come into fashionable focus like bread pudding, to which it is grandly, indubitably, superior.

CHRISTMAS QUEEN
OF PUDDINGS

The only things that are remotely Christmassy about this are that I use marmalade (sweetened with golden syrup) in place of the more usual jam, replace the lemon zest with orange zest (the smell of oranges, see also clementine cake below, always feels Christmassy to me), and I make the crumbs (in the processor as normal) not out of bread but out of pandoro, one of those yeasty cakes (this one's unfruited; see page 461) that Italians eat in significant numbers at this time of year. You don't need to get pandoro; you could just as easily use brioche or, indeed, the normal white bread crumbs.

And as Christmas is very much the season for déclassé liqueurs, I would serve this with heavy cream with a hint of Grand Marnier or Cointreau whipped up into it.

1½ cups pandoro bread crumbs or brioche or plain white bread crumbs
1½ teaspoons superfine sugar
zest of 1 orange
orange-flower water (optional)
2½ cups milk
2 tablespoons unsalted butter, plus more

5 eggs, separated
3–5 tablespoons good-quality marmalade
1–2 teaspoons golden syrup or light corn syrup, to taste
½ cup superfine sugar, plus more for sprinkling

Put the pandoro crumbs, sugar, and the zest of the orange with 1–2 drops orange-flower water, if you are using it, in a bowl. Heat the milk and 2 tablespoons butter in a saucepan until hot but just not boiling, and then stir into the bowl of flavored crumbs. Leave to steep for about 10 minutes, and then thoroughly beat in the egg yolks.

Grease a shallow dish (I use a round dish about 4 inches deep, 10 inches in diameter, because that's what I've got, but an oval dish is traditional) with butter and pour in the crumb custard. Bake at 325°F for 20–30 minutes, depending on depth of dish.

When it's ready, the custard should be set on top but may still be runny underneath. Let it stand out of the oven for a few minutes so that the top of the custard gets a bit harder while you turn your attention to the marmalade and egg whites. Heat the marmalade in a saucepan. Add the golden syrup to taste to the hot marmalade and then pour it over the surface of the custard. Meanwhile, whisk the egg whites until stiff and then whisk in half the sugar. In a few seconds the egg whites will become smooth and gleaming; then fold in the remaining sugar with a metal spoon.

Cover your pudding with the meringue mixture, sprinkle with sugar, and then put it back in the oven for about 20 minutes or until the meringue is browned and crispish. Serves 4–6.

CLEMENTINE CAKE

Another fixed item in my Christmas repertoire is my clementine cake. This is suitable for any number of reasons. First, it's made of clementines, which are seasonal. Then there's the fact that you need to cook them for 2 hours; you're more likely to be hanging around the house and to feel in the mood for this sort of thing during the Christmas period. It's incredibly easy to make; even if you're stressed out, it won't topple you over into nervous collapse. And, finally, it's such an accommodating kind of cake; it keeps well, indeed it gets better after a few days, and it is perfect either as a dessert with some crème fraîche or as cake to be eaten with seasonally sociable visitors in the midmorning or afternoon. What more do you want?

It was only after I did this a few times—the route it took to get to me was circuituous, as these things can be—that I realized it was more or less food writer Claudia Roden's orange and almond cake.

It is a wonderfully damp and aromatic flourless cake; it tastes like one of those sponges you drench, while cooling, with syrup, only you don't have to. This is the easiest cake I know.

4–5 clementines (about 1 pound total weight)	2⅓ cups ground almonds
6 eggs	1 heaping teaspoon baking powder
1 cup plus 2 tablespoons sugar	

Put the clementines in a pot with cold water to cover, bring to the boil, and cook for 2 hours. Drain and, when cool, cut each clementine in half and remove the seeds. Then chop everything finely—skins, pith, fruit—in the processor (or by hand, of course). Preheat the oven to 375°F. Butter and line an 8-inch springform pan.

Beat the eggs. Add the sugar, almonds, and baking powder. Mix well, adding the chopped clementines. I don't like using the processor for this, and frankly, you can't balk at a little light stirring.

Pour the cake mixture into the prepared pan and bake for an hour, when a skewer will come out clean; you'll probably have to cover the cake with foil after about 40 minutes to stop the top burning. Remove from the oven and leave to cool, on a rack, but in the pan. When the cake's cold, you can take it out of the pan. I think this is better a day after it's made, but I don't complain about eating it any time.

I've also made this with an equal weight of oranges, and with lemons, in which case I increase the sugar to 1¼ cups and slightly anglicize it, too, by adding a glaze made of confectioners' sugar mixed to a paste with lemon juice and a little water.

FREEZER

I lived for years without a freezer without ever minding very much. Certainly this allowed me the luxury of dreaming of all the good things I would cook and put by should I ever have one; I imagined with pleasure the efficient domestic angel I would then become. Now that I do have a freezer, it is indeed full. And, yet, I feel faintly resentful of its fullness.

The difficulty I find with stuffing a freezer full of food to eat at some future date is that when that future date comes I probably won't want to eat it. This is not because the food will spoil or disappoint, but because every time I open my freezer I see the same efficiently stowed-away packages of coq au vin or beef stew or whatever it may be, and I get bored with them. I begin to feel as if I've eaten them as many times as I've opened the freezer door.

The freezer can easily become a culinary graveyard, a place where good food goes to die.

If you're someone who is meticulous about cooking, freezing, filing, and then thawing in an orderly fashion, you need no advice from me as to how best to use your freezer. But you must be honest with yourself. There is no point in stowing away stews and soups if you are going to let them linger so long in its depths that finally all you can do is chuck them out. You'll probably find you stand more chance of eating the food you cook in advance if—when you put it in the freezer—you do so with some particular occasion in mind rather than just stashing it away for some unspecified future time. Obviously, if you know people are coming for dinner on Friday but the only time you can get any cooking done is on the weekend before, then the freezer will be useful (see Cooking in Advance, page 75). But unless you have an astonishingly capacious freezer and a mania for planning in advance, I wouldn't advise stocking up for more than one or two such occasions at any one time. However, there are two areas in which even I am ruthlessly efficient about freezing and then using food: cooking for children and dieting are both unimaginably easier if you create a form of culinary database in the deep freeze (see Feeding Babies and Small Children, page 405, and Low Fat, page 365).

Leftovers are obviously better put away in the freezer if the alternative destination is several days lingering in the fridge and then the trash can. On the other hand, beware of using the freezer as a less guilt-inducing way of chucking food you know you don't want. If no one, including you, liked the soup the first time round (and that's why you've got so much left over), there is no point in freezing it for some hopeful future date when, miraculously, it will taste delicious. But bagging leftovers—say, stews—in single portions can be useful for those evenings when you're eating alone. Take the little package out of the freezer before you go to work in the morning and heat it up for supper when you get back at night. Immensely cheering.

The freezer really comes into its own not so much when you don't have time for cooking as when you don't have time for shopping. In other words, the best use for the freezer is as a pantry.

As with a pantry, you must be on your guard against overstocking. In fact, having far too much in the freezer can be very much worse than a moldering pantry, because food so easily gets buried and really forgotten about rather than simply ignored. But a solid supply of ingredients with which to cook, rather than just wholly prepared dishes, can really help you make good simple things to eat without exhausting last-minute trawls around the supermarket.

SHRIMP
You should always have in your freezer some raw shrimp. Most shrimp available to us has been frozen at some point on their way to the market, then defrosted. Therefore, if you buy shrimp to store in the freezer, it's best to get them in still-frozen form rather than refreezing already frozen and defrosted specimens. Speak to your fish seller about the availability of these "fresh" still-frozen shrimp.

You can cook frozen shrimp without having to defrost them in advance; just plunge them, unthawed, into boiling water, salted and maybe spiked with a little vinegar. Peel them and pile them on top of garlicky puy lentils or mix them, cooled, into a fennel salad.

MASHED POTATOES, TRUFFLE OIL, AND WARM SANTA BARBARA SHRIMP
When I was in Los Angeles some years back, I ate at Joachim Splichal's Patina the most wonderful starter of mashed potatoes and truffles with warm Santa Barbara shrimp on top. The combination works. Purée some potatoes (they need to be whipped as well as mashed) with butter and white pepper, put a small, or maybe not so small, mound on a plate, add some barely cooked shrimp, then drizzle over some truffle oil if you have some, or some Ligurian olive oil if you haven't.

BACON
Bacon is another ingredient any cook should keep in the freezer. (And I like to keep some pancetta there too.) I always freeze bacon in pairs of slices so that

they defrost in minutes. The point about bacon is that it's sold everywhere, even the corner convenience store, but the good stuff is hard to find. I get my bacon from my butcher, and I know when I cook it that (1) white froth won't seep out of it, and (2) it will taste of bacon. If your butcher doesn't have excellent bacon (and very few do), I really wouldn't turn to the supermarket, however upmarket its reputation; find instead a mail-order supplier (see page 461) and get some sent to you.

Nothing is as good as a bacon sandwich made with white bread. There are times when you just need to have that salty-sweet curl of seared flesh pressed between fat-softened, lean-stained, spongy supermarket-white-bread slices. My guiding rule is that I always have the wherewithal for a bacon sandwich in the house. I aim to keep all the ingredients for spaghetti carbonara at hand, too.

Bread is worth keeping in the freezer. It freezes well, and I keep good bread in loaves and plastic white bread (such as is needed for bacon sandwiches) in pairs of slices. It's when I have to go shopping for basics such as bread and milk that I come back having spent far too much on absolute unnecessities. BREAD

Most varieties of milk freeze all right, too. For various reasons, all of them good ones, I try to keep visits to a supermarket to a minimum; I use my freezer to help keep me away. MILK

You must keep stock in your freezer, and also the bones you have saved to make it. Turn your freezer into your very own Golgotha by throwing in lamb bones, chicken carcasses, and any other bones at hand. I have been known to take home the carcasses with me after a dinner party once I've found out that (a) they have come from my butcher and (b) they were going to be thrown away. Keep ham bones or leftover trimmings from cooked hams, too, to flavor pea and bean soups at some later date. STOCK

Freeze your own, consequent, homemade stock in manageable portions (see page 9). I also keep a couple of tubs of good commercial stock or demi-glace in my freezer. Certainly, good commercial fish stock is very useful to have on hand; making a good fish fumet is rather more serious work than making a chicken stock, and I feel guiltless about having someone else do it for me, especially if it's done better than I would myself.

Parmesan rinds can be stowed away for future use. Every time you come to the end of a wedge of Parmesan, or if you've left it out unwrapped for so long that it has become rebarbatively hard, don't throw the piece away but chuck it in the freezer (preferably in a marked bag) to use whenever you make a minestrone or other soup which would benefit from that smoky, salty depth of flavoring. PARMESAN

As for desserts, other than the obvious ones that are meant to be frozen, such FRUITS as ice cream, you don't need to do more than keep a package or so of frozen fruits, which can be made to serve in most eventualities. Remember that defrosted strawberries take on the texture of soft, cold slugs. Remove them from the packages of mixed fruits, and chuck them out.

WINE

If, like me, you're not much of a drinker, then you can stop yourself from wasting leftover wine after dinner parties by measuring out glassfuls and freez-

EGG WHITES

ing them, well labeled (or you'll mistake white wine for egg whites, and see below) to use for cooking later on. And as for egg whites, I've got so many frozen my freezer is beginning to look like a sperm bank.

PANTRY

Unless you want to spend your every waking free hour buying food, you need to have at home basic ingredients that you can use to make something good when you haven't had time to shop or plan for a particular meal. But don't believe what you are told about essentials; all it means is that you'll have a pantry full of lost bottles of Indonesian soy sauce with a use-by date of November 1994. There is a compromise. Buy those few ingredients that really do provide a meal quickly and easily, and don't weigh yourself down with various tempting bits and pieces that you think you may get round to using one day.

I don't want to be too dictatorial, though. Apart from anything else, so much depends on the amount of space you've got. I am the Imelda Marcos—she who had a cushion with "Nouveau Riche Is Better than No Riche at All" embroidered on it—of the food shop world. I am not safe in food stores. No wonder I can't move on account of food I've bankrupted myself to buy. You have to avoid finding yourself in the same position. For there is no such thing as having food to cover most eventualities that doesn't also involve regularly throwing away food that goes bad before you eat it.

It's not easy to hold back. Nothing is as good as buying food. Buying pantry food is highly seductive because it doesn't go bad and you don't have the stress of actual, imminent here-and-now cooking. It's fantasy shopping—and that's why it gets out of hand. Food bought on these expeditions lingers on for years, untouched. Partly this is because items you buy to store away are so often expensive, rarefied delicacies that having been bought, you then feel you have to save for something special. If you can get out of that frame of mind—which is the same mindset that leads you to buy an extremely expensive piece of cloth-ing that you then leave hanging in the closet rather than allow it to be sullied by being worn around the house—then food shopping isn't quite such a dangerous pastime.

But it isn't the pattern of extravagance followed by austerity, nor the habit of saving things for best, that argues against intensive stockpiling. There is a hard-headed, practical reason for being modest in your supplies: the food that people buy bags and bags of—flour, spices, rice, lentils—doesn't actually keep forever. The chances are that you will end up with a pantry full of stale beans. It's not that this food goes bad, necessarily, but it becomes less good to eat. It's comforting to know that you've got a bag of chickpeas, but you must be strict with yourself and use it, not just keep it there for some rainy day when you fondly think you'll stay in and cook *pasta e ceci*. After a few years, they won't be dried, they'll be fossilized—and tasteless.

Anyway, unless you live in very remote parts, the chances are that it won't be too difficult to go shopping for any special items you need for a specific recipe. A pantry is much more useful for keeping stuff in that you know you'll want regularly. This sort of food is likely to be the food you eat alone or with your family. You want to be able to cook something in the evening after work without having to go shopping, and you don't want to have to start thinking about it before you get home. (I always want to think about what I'm going to eat, not in any elaborate organizational way, but because the speculation gives me pleasure. But there are many times when idly, greedily speculating is indeed the most energetic thing I can manage to do in advance. So what I need to know is that I have some food at home that won't take long to cook and won't demand too much of me.)

The most important ingredient to keep in your larder, or food cupboard, or whatever it might be, is pasta. Stick to a few different shapes only; if you try to cover too many bases, you will simply end up with about ten opened, almost finished, packages and you will never be able to make a decent plateful of any of them. It's useful to have rather a lot of spaghetti so that you can suddenly cook a huge plateful of something for a kitchen load of people if need be. Linguine is sufficiently different to be worth having as well. Short pasta is quick and easier to cook for children; choose fusilli or penne, for example. Some kinds of eggy pasta need little cooking and are therefore wonderful for when you feel like Elizabeth Taylor shouting "Hurry!" to the microwave, as Joan Rivers's cruel joke had it.

You need some pasta sauces in your pantry too. A good tomato sauce is indispensable. What you want to avoid is having your fridge full of large opened jars and bottles that have been half used up. I buy a whole case of smallish bottles of tomato sauce at a time, so that I know there's always some on hand. With jars and cans, it is worth getting as much as you have room for, as anything heavy is a nightmare to buy; better to get it over and done with in one exhausting go. (For this reason, I also buy baked beans, the 8-ounce size, in bulk.) I would never be without two containers of good commercial pesto—one in use, the other in the pantry. If you can have pasta with tomato sauce or pasta with pesto in an everyday emergency, then you have all you need in your larder.

I do keep, though, a mixture of canned foods (soup, baked beans) so that there's something there for when I don't want to cook at all.

I know I said that flour and so forth doesn't keep forever, but I do keep a modest and restrained selection, including flours, especially Italian 00, sugars, salt, spices, oil, vinegar, canned tomatoes, vanilla extract, and meat and vegetable bouillon cubes. I also make up a jar of vanilla sugar—simply by filling a screw-top jar with superfine sugar and chopping a couple of vanilla beans into about 2-inch lengths to go in it. This takes very little effort, makes one feel positively holy, and also gives one gloriously scented sugar to use in cakes, puddings, custards, and so forth whenever needed. The beans give out their sweet and fleshy scent for ages; just pour over fresh sugar as you use it.

VANILLA SUGAR

Naturally, what I want to keep in my kitchen cupboards might not be what you want to have in yours. But I couldn't live without Marsala, Noilly Prat (or Chambéry vermouth), dry sherry, and sake pretty close at hand. I don't drink much and so don't tend to have bottles of wine open; if I need alcohol for cooking, I need to have it in the sort of bottles that come with a screw top. Most often, I use Marsala in recipes that specify red wine, vermouth where white's required. Other drinks have their part to play. As ever, follow your own impulses; go with your own palate.

MARSALA, NOILLY PRAT

CHAMBÉRY, DRY SHERRY, AND SAKE

Anytime I let myself run out of garlic or onions, I curse. These base-note ingredients should be a given in your kitchen, or you always feel you're scrabbling around before you can make anything. And for me, whole nutmeg is crucial, too. You don't have to get a special little nutmeg grater (you could just shave off bits with a sharp knife), but it's not expensive and it is useful.

GARLIC

ONIONS

WHOLE NUTMEG

FRIDGE

I keep a modest but restrained selection in my fridge, including butter, eggs, milk, salad leaves, some herbs, and blocks of Parmesan cheese. That's in theory;

in reality, it's a constant culinary clutter. I have either too much or not enough. But that's life.

Not everything in my kitchen is organic, but it seems to be going that way. Eggs, I've already mentioned, though make sure the box says organic. I can't buy meat any longer from a supermarket. I want it best quality, and I want to be able to talk with someone knowledgeable about where it comes from. I want it traceable, if at all possible, and not pumped full of revolting things. And now that supermarkets have got wise to the ever-more-widespread lure of organic produce, it's easier to find vegetables from organic farms that aren't utterly covered in mud just to show their virtuous credentials. I worry about the chemicals in nonorganic-reared fruit and vegetables, but to tell the truth, it's the taste of the organic stuff that often seems to me better—that's the clincher. And it's worth buying organic oranges and lemons whose skins are free from chemicals. Because I use the zests of these fruit so often in my cooking, using these is only common sense.

COOKING
IN ADVANCE

Quick cooking has become so implanted in people's minds as the way to eat well without having a nervous breakdown that everyone ignores the real way to make life easier for yourself: cooking in advance. Knocking out a meal in fifteen minutes is good for everyday cooking, when there's just one or two of you, or if you're one of those people who feels uncomfortable with too much planning. But when you're having people to dinner, life is made so much simpler if you don't have to do everything at the last minute. If you feel flustered at the very idea of cooking, indeed hate it, doing it in advance takes away some of the stress; if you enjoy it, you'll enjoy it more if you don't put yourself under pressure—that's for the professionals, who thrive on it. I love the feeling of puttering about the kitchen, cooking slowly, stirring and chopping and getting everything done when I'm feeling well disposed and not utterly exhausted. When I cook with too much of an audience, I immediately worry about what'll happen if something goes wrong—and then, of course, something does.

Cook in advance and, if the worse comes to the worst, you can ditch it. No one but you will know that it tasted disgusting, or failed to set, or curdled, or whatever. That may sound a rather negative approach, but in fact it's liberating; moreover, because you're not stressed out or desperately working against the clock, there's less chance of disaster. And if something does go wrong, you have the time calmly to find a way of rectifying it.

And things do go wrong in cooking. Indeed, it's one of the ways you learn and eventually find your own style. Some of the best food I've cooked has been as a result of trying to make up for some fault, some blip. It's when you're exploring and trying out, not simply following a recipe, that you feel what the food needs, what will make it taste how you want it to taste. Without the pressure of having to perform, you can concentrate on the food. This is not to say that cooking has to be a solitary pursuit. In a way, there's nothing better than cooking with someone to talk to while you do it. But I am someone who panics if there's too much commotion or if I've got too little time to think.

Perhaps this is a temperamental thing, but cooking is about temperament, and so, I think, is eating. You have to find a way of cooking that suits you, and that isn't just about your life, your working hours, your environment—though these, of course, matter. But what counts, too, is whether you're the sort of person who's soothed or cramped by list making, whether you're impatient or tidy, whether spontaneity makes you feel creative or panic-stricken. Most of us like eating, but many people feel flustered and a sense of panic and, frankly, boredom when it comes to cooking. It's difficult to be good at something you aren't really interested in. But some people don't like cooking simply because they've never given themselves the chance to do it calmly and quietly and in the right mood. Obligation can be a useful prompt to activity, but it can be a terrible blight, too. Cooking in advance is a good way to learn confidence, to learn what works and why and how, and from that you can then teach yourself to trust your intuition, to be spontaneous—in short, to cook.

Cooking is about working toward a goal, toward something you have decided upon in advance. But any creative work (however cringe-makingly pretentious it sounds, cooking is creative, has to be) needs to liberate itself from the end product during the act of producing. This can be very difficult. There are practical constraints, which are what make the form, in cooking as in poetry. You have to learn to use these constraints to your advantage. Get over economic constraints by buying ingredients you can afford rather than making do with inferior versions of expensive produce. Make the best of the equipment you happen to have in your kitchen. Be ready to adapt to what you've got. But some other constraints—such as lack of time—merely add to your obstacles and to the risk that if your dinner is inedible, you and your guests will just have to live with it.

Some food actually benefits from being cooked in advance. Stews, for example, are always best cooked, left to get cold and hang around for a while, and then reheated. Desserts can need time to set or for their flavors to settle and deepen. Soups mellow. That's why I love this sort of cooking; the rhythms are so reassuring, I no longer feel I'm snatching at food, at life. It's not exactly that I'm constructing a domestic idyll, but as I work in the kitchen at night, or on the weekend, filling the house with the smells of baking and roasting and filling the fridge with good things to eat, it feels, corny as it sounds, as if I'm making a home.

SOUP

Soups are the obvious place to start for those thus in domestic-goddess mode. Soups, of course, are some of the quickest meals that you can make. Somehow the homemade soup, lovingly prepared in advance, is no longer popular. I think it comes down to making stock, our disinclination to make it from scratch, together with our disdain for bouillon or stock cubes. It is important to stress that even though the better a stock, the better a soup, it does not follow that no good soup, no superlatively good soup, can be made with bouillon cubes. Naturally, it depends on the kind of soup—no consommé or delicate broth should be made with anything but homemade stock—but a hearty vegetable soup can, frankly, be made with water, and in between these two extremes, use bouillon cubes. But, for making your own stock, see page 9.

If you haven't already got a supply of homemade stock in the freezer, you'll need a good day's grace—time to make the stock, to cool it, to skim the fat off it. A ham stock (just the liquid in which a ham's been cooked) makes all the difference to a pea soup; a chicken stock, light though it may be, gives instant depth and velvety swell to a very basic parsnip soup. Grate fresh Parmesan over the pea soup; drop chili oil into the pale sweetness of the parsnip soup to add a probing fierceness. To both you could add some bacon, fried, grilled, or baked in a hot oven, and crumbled into salty shards; marjoram, too, would work equally well with either.

Both these soups can be made in advance and kept in the fridge for reheating throughout the week, whether on the burner or in the microwave.

CHICKPEAS   The soups that you really have to cook in advance are the ones made from dried peas, beans, and other legumes. Most of these need a good day's soaking. I tend to put beans in to soak as I go to bed even if I won't actually be cooking with them until the next evening. Chickpeas need 24 hours, and I don't mind if I give them 36. And they need a lot of cooking, much longer than you are usually told. There seems to be a conspiracy to misinform you about chickpeas; I cannot believe the number of times I've read that 45 minutes will do, when it takes double that time to cook them. Anna del Conte is realistic about this, admitting that some chickpeas can take as long as 4 hours. I use her technique for preparing chickpeas. Put them in a bowl and cover them with cold water. Then mix together 1 teaspoon baking soda and 1 tablespoon each of salt and flour—or those ingredients in that ratio; a very large quantity of peas will need more of this tenderizing mixture—add water to form a runny paste, and stir this paste into the soaking chickpeas. Leave for a good 24 hours. Then, when cooking the chickpeas (drained and rinsed), don't lift the lid off the pan for the first hour or so, or the peas will harden. (Curiosity often gets the better of me.) Fava beans similarly need longer soaking than, say, cannellini or cranberry (both of which are fine with 12 hours), and all are better if you leave the salting till the last moments of the cooking time. If you're cooking in advance, it doesn't matter how long it all takes, and good though canned chickpeas are, dried, soaked, and cooked ones are so much better. You can taste the full, grainy, chestnutty roundness of them.

Chickpea and pasta soup is my favorite soup of all. You can cook it days before you actually want to eat it. Obviously it can't all be done in advance because the pasta must be cooked at the last minute, but as you have to reheat the soup anyway, what does it matter to you if, when reheating, you keep it simmering for 20 minutes or so extra while the ditalini swell and soften.

I cook this soup so often—just for us, at home, for supper, in great big greedy bowlfuls; for a first course when I've got people coming for dinner; or, if they're coming for lunch, for a main course, with a salad and cheese after—that I don't follow a recipe any more. But this is the recipe that started me off. It is Anna del Conte's, adapted from her *Entertaining All'Italiana*. I have several copies of this book; one in the kitchen—where, eccentrically perhaps, I tend not to keep my cook books—one in my study, where all books on food notionally live (in practice they are dotted on floors, in bathrooms, throughout the house), and one in the bedroom, for late-night soothing reading and midnight feast fantasizing.

ANNA'S CHICKPEA AND PASTA SOUP

This will make enough soup for 8. I sometimes add a glass of white wine or any stock at hand, from whatever animal it emanates, to it, but the soup has quite enough taste with simply water. Use the best vegetable stock you can make or buy. You can prepare the soup (bar the pasta) up to 3 days in advance, or longer if you freeze it.

2 cups dried chickpeas	1 pound tomatoes, skinned and seeded
2 teaspoons baking soda	salt and freshly milled black pepper
2 tablespoons all-purpose flour	8 ounces small tubular pasta such as
2 tablespoons salt	ditalini
3 quarts vegetable stock, meat stock,	2–3 tablespoons chopped parsley
white wine and water, or water	(optional)
3 rosemary sprigs	chili oil, for serving (optional)
8 garlic cloves, peeled and bruised	piece of Parmesan, for grating over
½ cup extra-virgin olive oil, plus more	
for serving (optional)	

Put the chickpeas in a bowl and cover with plenty of water. Mix together the baking soda, flour, and salt and add enough water to make a thin paste. Stir this mixture into the bowl with the chickpeas and leave to soak for at least 12 hours, and preferably 24.

When the chickpeas have doubled in size (you don't have to get your ruler out; trust your eyes), they are ready to be cooked. Drain and then rinse them. Put them in a large pot and add the vegetable stock.

Tie the rosemary sprigs in cheesecloth and add to the pot. This will make it possible to remove the rosemary without leaving any needles to float in the soup. This might sound persnickety, but when I ignored the advice, I found the sharp and, by now, bitter needles an unpleasant intrusion. If you feel intimidated by the idea of cheesecloth then use, disgusting though it sounds, an old clean knee-high stocking and tie a knot at the open end, or use a tea infuser. Frankly, it doesn't matter what you use providing it does the job, although I imagine untreated cheesecloth is better. You can get cheesecloth in most kitchen shops or hardware stores.

Add the garlic to the chickpea mixture and pour in half the oil. Cover the pot tightly and bring to the boil. You will have to gauge this by ear without peeping in. Lower the heat and cook over the lowest simmer until the chickpeas are tender, 2–4 hours. Take a look after 1½ hours.

When the chickpeas are tender, remove the garlic and the rosemary bundle, which should be floating on the surface. Purée the tomatoes in a food mill or in a food processor and add to the soup with their juice. Stir well, add salt and pepper to taste, and cook for 10 minutes further or so. This is the point at which you should stop when you're cooking the soup in advance.

When you want to eat it, put the soup back on the burner and reheat it, so that you can proceed to the final step, which is to cook the pasta. Before you add the pasta to the soup, check that there is enough liquid in the pot. If not, add some boiling water. Now, to the boiling soup, add the pasta and cook till al dente. At this point, I like to add chopped parsley, but the glory of this soup will be undiminished if you prefer not to. But do pour some of the remaining olive oil into the pot of soup, and drizzle some more into each bowl after you've ladled the soup in. Or just pour some into the big pot and let people add what they want as they eat. I put good extra-virgin olive oil on the table as well as a bottle of chili oil for those who like some heat—and it does work. Serve, too, the Parmesan, on a plate with a grater, so people can add their own.

SPLIT PEA SOUPS

Split pea soups don't need to be cooked in advance, since the peas don't need soaking, but it is a rare soup—or stew, for that matter—that doesn't improve with a few days' hanging around. The only thing to remember is that you will need to add more liquid when you reheat it, as legumes seem to drink up their cooking liquid for ages. I love all split pea soups and remember wonderful grainy, tobacco-tinted purées eaten in Amsterdam—thick, puddingy soups, smelling of sausage. But green split peas are the ones I tend to cook the most. Whenever I've boiled a ham, I save the salty stock. Into this I throw some green split peas and sliced leeks, maybe a potato or two, for a near-enough instant supper. When the weather is relentlessly, intrusively windy and cold, then a thick, pale green sludge of split peas is perfect. Recently, though, I've begun to think that the ham stock is even better used as a base for a pea soup with fresh (or frozen) peas on a spring or summer's day.

Cooking ahead is the only way to keep sane when you're cooking for a lot of people. Thick soups will do, as you don't need to add too much to fill people up: good bread, good cheese, good wine. I was never particularly keen on black bean soup till I had a bowlful in a small Cuban place in South Beach, Miami; I loved its spice-foggy muddiness. The recipe that follows attempts to evoke it. It serves about 8 people, but obviously the quantities can be boosted without requiring a doctorate in higher mathematics on the part of the cook.

SOUTH BEACH BLACK BEAN SOUP

2⅓ cups dried black beans

2 bay leaves

I cup extra-virgin olive oil

2 large red peppers, cored, seeded, and
   chopped

2 shallots, chopped

2 medium onions, chopped

8 garlic cloves, minced

I tablespoon ground cumin

2 tablespoons ground dried oregano

zest of I lime, plus 4 limes, quartered,
   for serving

½ tablespoon light or dark muscovado
   sugar, or light or dark brown sugar

I tablespoon salt, or to taste

2 tablespoons dry sherry

2–3 tablespoons chopped fresh
   coriander

I medium red onion, diced, for serving

I cup sour cream, for serving (optional)

Tabasco sauce, for serving

Place the beans in a large pot and cover with 2 quarts water. There is no need to soak. Add the bay leaves and bring to the boil. Reduce the heat and simmer the beans for 1½–2 hours till soft but not squishy, stirring frequently and adding more water if necessary to keep them well covered.

Meanwhile, heat the olive oil in a large, deep frying pan and sauté the peppers, shallots, and onions over medium heat until the onions are translucent, about 15 minutes. Add the garlic, cumin, oregano, and lime zest and sauté for an additional 5 minutes. Transfer to a blender and purée until smooth.

When the beans are almost tender, add the puréed mixture, sugar, and salt, or salt to taste, to the beans and cook until just tender, 20–30 minutes. Adjust the seasonings and add the sherry if you're serving straightaway, but otherwise season and sherry the soup when you're reheating it later, and you will also need to add water as the soup thickens on cooling. Put the coriander, red onion, quartered limes, and sour cream, if using, in separate bowls and bring these to the table with the Tabasco so that people can add as much of each as they want.

But *the* soup you have to make in advance, and a soup unjustifiably ignored today, is consommé. There is, for most people, a ring of *bon viveur* about the word consommé; it conjures up a world of napkin-arranged gentility and brisk effortfulness. Well, then, call it *brodo.* A beautiful, clear, flavor-infused liquid that is unsurpassable. And it's strange that, in our gush and lust for all things Italian, that amber broth, which is such an ordinary and integral part of the Italian diet, gets routinely ignored.

I've come to the conclusion that our disdain is twofold. It is fueled in the first part by fear and the second by insecurity. The fear is culinary, the insecurity social. There are certain words that immediately make people feel the recipe they are reading is not for them. Stock, pestle and mortar, bain marie are just some such. And stock is, I think, the most terror-laden. But more than that, people are afraid that a plain consommé will be boring. For all our modern talk about valuing simplicity, we balk when faced with something truly, perfectly simple. We want the vibrant, the robust, the instant, the simplified—that's different. A consommé strikes us—correctly—as a dish that belongs to a formal dinner. We are afraid that borrowing from the earlier canon of the elaborately arranged dinner party will mark us out as infra dig, out of touch, or just plain suburban.

A clear soup, made properly, is not at all without personality. It is uplifting, delicately but insistently flavored. But even chefs, with their splendid stockpots, are rarely sufficiently confident to serve an unadorned broth. Too often, these days, it comes fashionably spiked with lemongrass or pebbled with beans. I love all variations—and I do willingly admit that the point of a good broth is that it is a wonderfully deep-toned base for the bits you can float in it—and am happy with just about any innovation that has integrity, but an ordinary, straightforward consommé or *brodo,* golden poolfuls of the stuff, is a joy and a restorative— bracingly elegant.

It is time-consuming to make but not difficult, and a wonderfully mood-enhancing way of putskying around in a kitchen. You need to get started a good day before you're planning to eat it—in order to let it cool and skim off the fat—but you can leave it in the fridge for 3 or so days and not worry.

The recipe here is from a book that should never have been allowed to go out of print: Arabella Boxer's *Book of English Food*—subtitled *A Rediscovery of British Food from Before the War*—which was published in 1991. You don't read cookbooks just for culinary instruction—I don't—but also for comment, for history, for talk. And it is for all these that I want Arabella Boxer's literary company. Here she is on the fashionable emergence of the consommé in the 1920s:

> *Roughly speaking, the more elegant the occasion, the smoother, or clearer, the soup. A consommé was considered the ultimate test of a good cook, and the ideal start to an exquisite meal. It might be served quite plain, or with some small garnish floating in it: small vegetable dice, a few grains of rice, or minuscule soup pasta. In a less conventional household a more elaborate garnish might be served separately: round croûtons piled high with whipped cream, or a bowl of saffron-flavoured rice, or even a jug of beetroot juice for adding, with cream, to a consommé made with duck and beef stock. This practice of handing round a number of elaborate garnishes separately amused the English. Part of its appeal was that by enabling the guests to assemble their own dishes it pandered to their distrust of what they described as "mucky food."*

CONSOMMÉ

Arabella Boxer adapted this recipe from June Platt's *Vogue* column in the 1930s and prefaces it with the remark—pertinent here—that it is best made over 2 days, adding that "the original recipe calls for 12 pints of water, but few of us have pans that large. I use half that amount, filling up the pan from time to time with more cold water." Stewing hens, which are most desirable for making the consommé, are difficult to come by but not impossible to find. Kosher or halal butchers usually sell them, or you may find frozen stewing hens. I don't want to be too prissy, but I like to feel confident about the origin of the birds. I don't want to eat some miserable fowl raised on fish pellets in squalor somewhere. Poussins can also provide wonderful stock, as I've found (see page 10).

The idea of cooking anything for 7 hours seems incredible these days. Consider using a heat diffuser—you want a gentle simmer, the odd bubble rising up. Avoid, at all costs, all the precious liquid's ungovernable evaporation.

1 stewing hen or large chicken (about
　　6 pounds)

2½ pounds beef stew meat, cubed

2 large carrots, peeled and sliced thickly

2 medium onions, sliced thickly

2 leeks, sliced thickly

3 parsley sprigs

3 thyme sprigs

1 large garlic clove, peeled

salt and freshly milled black pepper

2 cloves

Wash the hen and put it in a large soup pot, add the beef, and cover well with 4 quarts cold water. Let stand for ½ hour, then put on the heat and bring slowly to the boil. Remove the scum, add ½ cup cold water, and bring to the boil again. Repeat this process twice. (The added water stops the boiling; each time it recommences, the action draws more flavor from the hen and beef.) Simmer very slowly for 1 hour, then add the carrots, onions, leeks, parsley sprigs, thyme, and garlic. Season with the salt and pepper, add the cloves, and let simmer for 7 hours.

Strain through a fine sieve, then through wet cheesecloth. You can also use a clean reusable kitchen wipe or a paper funnel-shaped coffee filter. Paper towels won't work; they're too absorbent and end up not straining anything.

Chill overnight and, when cold, carefully remove grease. Makes 3–4 quarts; serves 12.

A basic *brodo* of an Italian sort provides a fragrant liquid base for tortellini or gnocchetti di semolino (see below) or any other manner of culinary punctuation. This broth is cooked for less time than the one above and so one would expect it to be lighter, more delicate, and less suited to being served just as it is. It is also, preeminently, designed to make divine risotti.

ITALIAN BROTH

1 pound piece of beef flank

2 pieces veal shank cut 1–1½ inches
　　thick

1 pound chicken wings, 1 chicken
　　carcass, or 1 poussin

1 medium onion, halved, each half stuck
　　with 1 clove

2 medium carrots, peeled and sliced
　　chunkily

2 celery stalks, sliced chunkily

2 leeks, white part only, sliced

1 ripe tomato, halved, or 1 canned plum
　　tomato, drained of juice

1 garlic clove, peeled

1 bay leaf

6 parsley sprigs

6 black peppercorns

1 teaspoon salt

Put all the ingredients into a stockpot or large saucepan and cover with water by about 2 inches. Bring to the boil slowly—over medium heat—then turn down the heat so that it simmers gently. Skim the scum from the surface and keep an eye on it so that you can see when more scum rises to the surface and needs to be skimmed off again. Do this about 3 times in quick succession, then every hour. Let simmer—always very gently, and you may well need a heat diffuser if even at the lowest heat the broth bubbles overexuberantly—for 3 hours.

Remove the large pieces of meat and vegetable with a slotted spoon and then pour the broth into a large bowl (a wide one makes it easier to remove the fat later) through a sieve lined with cheesecloth or a clean, single-thickness reusable kitchen wipe. When cool, put in the fridge. When it's set (overnight or after about 8 hours), skim the fat off the surface. I find wiping the top, firmly but not so brutally you break into the jelly below, with paper towels the easiest way of degreasing it. It keeps in the fridge for up to 3 days. Makes about 3 quarts.

GNOCCHETTI DI SEMOLINO

Somehow these sound rather better in Italian than they do in English—semolina dumplings have a heavy, puddingy ring to them and these are light, puffy things.

I cup milk	I egg, separated
½ cup semolina flour	4 tablespoons grated Parmesan
4 tablespoons (½ stick) unsalted butter, softened	whole nutmeg
	salt

Bring the milk just to the boil. Off the heat, add the semolina. Whisking constantly, hold the semolina in your fist and let a light rain of grain fall into the pan as you beat. Keep beating till you have a thick paste and then let the mixture cool.

Mix the butter with the egg yolk, the cheese, a good grating of the nutmeg, and a pinch of salt. Mash this mixture into the semolina paste to combine. Whisk the egg white with a good pinch of salt till stiff, and then fold in; you may find this easiest if you stir in a tablespoonful of whites quite briskly first to loosen the semolina. If it helps, too, do everything a few hours in advance up to the whisking and incorporating of the egg white. (Don't keep the dough in the fridge.)

When the broth's boiling, form little oval balls by scooping out bits with a teaspoon and drop them in. Cook until they swell and rise to the surface, about 10 minutes. Enough for 4–6 servings.

Some food won't suffer if allowed a little resting time. By all means, parboil potatoes before you need to roast them. I have eaten for Sunday lunch roast potatoes that were parboiled on Friday evening. My one proviso here is that they shouldn't be put in the fridge in the interim. I find potatoes go slightly powdery and heavy after they've been put in the fridge, even leftover mashed potato. Just leave them out somewhere cold, like a pantry.

If you are boiling the potatoes in advance, before roasting, rub over their surfaces (though gently—you're not trying to make rösti) with the coarse side of a grater, just to rough them up before putting them in the hot fat. Cook in a hot oven.

SKINNING
PEPPERS
Skinning peppers a day or so before you want to eat them is sensible even when you're not planning anything elaborate. They're better the longer they sit in their oily juices. So—blister them under the grill or in the oven and while they are still very hot, put them either in a plastic bag, which you tie tightly at the neck, or in a bowl, which you seal quickly with plastic film. The peppers then steam, and this enables the skins to be removed more easily. Skin them, seed them, and cut them into strips, being sure to catch the juice to add to the dressing. Make them glisten with some peppery glass-green olive oil. You can pound some anchovies into a paste and mix that with the olive oil now, or, just before you want to eat the peppers, arrange them on a plate, criss-cross them with the best anchovy fillets you can find, and dot here and there (not too neatly) with some stoned black olives, halved to form shiny little squished black rounds, like a teddy bear's nose. Pour over some fresh olive oil and eat. I like the anchovies striating the glossy, flat mass of peppers rather than being actually part of the dressing, just because that can make the whole look rather muddy. Garlic and rosemary, added at any and all stages, are also to be welcomed. With food like this, you should just relax and do what tastes best to you. Peppers and anchovies are an incomparable mix and, pertinently, one that has consistently found favor, regardless of fashion, from the age of the hors d'oeuvres trolley to the balsamic-soaked present.

Some sauces can be cooked a day ahead and left in the fridge until you need them. If you don't want a skin to form, then cover them flush with plastic film or a thin film of milk, if it's a milk-based sauce. Obviously those egg-butter liaisons—hollandaise, béarnaise, and so on—need to be done at the lastish minute but a white sauce, béchamel, anything with a roux base, can be cooked and then forgotten for a while. Just reheat slowly and be prepared to add more liquid.

Pasta sauces can be made up to 3 days before you need them. At least, those pasta sauces that are not predominantly cream or butter can. Any vegetable-based sauce, even if it does contain cream, can be made when it suits you, which may well not be at the same time as cooking the pasta. Pasta itself obviously needs to be cooked at the last moment—unless, that is, it's baked pasta. This is incredibly useful if you've invited quite a lot of people for lunch or supper when you're not going to be at home very long before you want to eat. You can cook the pasta, the sauces, assemble everything a couple of days or so in advance, refrigerate and then give the whole thing about 40 minutes in a hottish oven when you want to eat it.

This is the only baked pasta dish I go in for much—it's mellow, comforting, but resonantly flavored as well; you're not swamped in puddingy béchamel, as you can be. My children love it, incidentally, and as you can feed a good 8 people (more if children are included in the numbers), this makes it a good filler for one of those low-key mixed-generation meals, when you're too busy with everything else you have to do to be absolutely attentive in the kitchen before you eat.

BAKED VEAL AND HAM PASTA

The name I give it evokes, and is meant to, the old-fashioned flavors of those British hot-water-crust veal-and-ham pies: picnic food to be eaten on scratchy rugs; this is the winter, indoors variety. But it's very garlicky, too, so it's not a complete transposition of those pies' mild, sausagy taste. Boiling the garlic not only makes it easier to peel but reduces any latent acridness, producing, later, warmth rather than smoky heat. The ham in question is pancetta (or chopped bacon, if you prefer) but if you've got some cold cooked ham in the fridge, do use that. Cut it into small cubes and stir it into the quantity of béchamel the pasta is coated in later.

6 garlic cloves	8 tablespoons (1 stick) unsalted butter,
3 ounces pancetta, chopped roughly	plus more for greasing and dotting
2 celery stalks, chopped roughly	⅔ cup Italian 00 or all-purpose flour
1 medium onion, quartered	pinch mace, plus ¼ teaspoon
1 carrot, peeled and cut into chunks	salt and freshly milled white or
good handful fresh parsley	black pepper
2 heaping tablespoons lard or	6 cups milk
2 tablespoons olive oil	5 bay leaves
¼ teaspoon paprika	whole nutmeg
¼ teaspoon ground mace	4 ounces Parmesan, freshly grated, plus
3 tablespoons Marsala	more for grating over later
¾ pound veal, ground	1 pound penne or rigatoni

Put the garlic cloves in a small saucepan, cover with cold water, bring to the boil, and boil for 7 minutes. Drain. Put the pancetta into a food processor. Peel the garlic (just press them and the cloves will pop out of their skins) and throw into the processor with the celery, onion, carrot, and parsley, and pulse until finely chopped. Melt the lard or oil in a heavy-bottomed frying pan and then, when it's hot, add the vegetable mixture. Stir well over highish heat for a minute or so, adding the paprika, mace, and Marsala, then turn the heat down to low and cook, stirring regularly to make sure it doesn't stick, for 15 minutes.

While this is happening, put copious water on to boil for the pasta.

When the 15 minutes are up, briefly turn the heat back to high, add the ground veal, and turn well for a minute or so before, again, turning down to low for 15 minutes. While this is cooking, get on with the béchamel. Melt the butter in a large saucepan, stir in the flour and pinch of mace, and cook for a couple of minutes, still stirring, adding a fat pinch of salt and some pepper. Off the heat, slowly stir in the milk. I don't bother to heat the milk up; there's too much of it.

When all the milk's smoothly amalgamated, add the bay leaves and put back on a medium heat, stirring, until the sauce cooks and thickens, then reduce the heat to low. Although you want to cook this for a good long time—about 20 minutes—so it's velvety, bear in mind that this is meant to be a thin, runny sauce. Toward the end of cooking time, taste for salt (though remember, you will be adding quite a bit of salty Parmesan later) and pepper and add, too, the remaining mace and grate in some nutmeg. When the sauce is cooked and the flouriness gone—taste after 12 minutes if you're using 00 flour—turn off the heat and stir in the Parmesan, beating well with your wooden spoon to make sure all is smoothly incorporated. You should by now have started cooking the pasta. You want it slightly undercooked, as it will be cooked again in the oven. On the packages of penne I have at home, the instructions are to cook for 13 minutes; for this recipe, I drain them after 10.

Butter a lasagne dish or any form of shallowish casserole and pour in about a third of the béchamel; don't bother to measure, just make a rough estimate by eye. Add the drained pasta and turn well to coat. Add the veal and toss well again, then another third of the béchamel and give a good final mix, adding more salt and pepper, if necessary. Level the pasta in the pan and pour over the last third of béchamel. Let cool, then put, covered, in the fridge for a couple of days or so before baking, though of course you can put it straightaway in the oven to bake if you want (in which case it will need less time than otherwise mentioned).

If you've fridged it, take it out and make sure it's at room temperature before you bake it. Sprinkle with more Parmesan and dot with butter and bake in a preheated 375°F oven until golden and bubbly, about 40 minutes.

KAFKAESQUE OR SOFT AND CRISPY DUCK

You'd think, wouldn't you, that a roast could never ever be done in advance. Yes, we all know that any roast needs to rest after it's come out of the oven and before it goes on the table, but I now do a roast duck—the best roast duck I have ever eaten, let alone cooked—that can be started a good few days before you want to eat it. This is semi-cooking in advance and I'm blazingly evangelical about it. A method of doing the perfect roast duck that leaves you with just three-quarters of an hour's cooking on the night—and all in the oven, no basting, no fiddling, nothing—has to be a good thing. I let the duck sit around in the fridge in a state of semi-cookedness for up to 3 days, but if you feel at all nervous about this, don't leave it as long. But actually, before we get on to it, it isn't that new an idea: Apicius—he of the first cookery book—likewise instructed his readers, "lavas, ornas et in olla elixabis cum acqua, sale et aneto dimidia coctura." Admittedly, even if he, to translate, suggested boiling the duck in water (with dill as well as salt) until half cooked, the second half's cooking would not be exactly by roasting; it would have been more like pot roasting. Nevertheless, it reminds us pointedly that there is nothing new in cooking. That's if it's to taste good.

But this is the story: when I was last in New York, I bought a copy of Barbara Kafka's *Roasting*, the premise of which is that roasting at very high temperatures makes for the most succulent, fleshily yielding, and crispy-skinned birds and roasts. The drawback is that you need a clean oven, otherwise all that roasting at very high temperatures gives you a smoky kitchen, burning eyes, and an acrid glaze on the putative pièce de résistance. I noticed that there was a recipe for roast duck that involved poaching the bird first in stock for about three-quarters of an hour and then blitzing it in the oven for half an hour. The result: tender flesh and crisp skin. And it's true, if you're not careful when you roast a duck in the more usual way, you often find that the desirably crunchy carapace comes at the cost of overcooked and thus stringy meat. Everyone has an answer to this one—covering the bird with boiling water, hanging it up on a clothesline on a blustery (but dry) day, suspending it on high by means of a clothes hanger and then getting a stiff wrist by aiming a hair dryer, at full though icy blast, at it for hours.

The *echt* Kafkaesque technique involves poaching the duck, upright, in a thin, tall pot in duck stock. I couldn't quite see why you needed to poach the bird in stock, as the flesh is rich itself. More to the point, I had none. So the first time I tried it, I put the water into the requisite tall, thin pot (the bottom half of my couscoussier), added the giblets, brought it to the boil, added salt, and lowered in the duck. Then, as directed, I made sure the bird was submerged for the whole 40 minutes. I did this in the morning, let the duck get cool, put it in the fridge, and then brought it out in the evening, letting it get to room temperature before roasting it for the 30 minutes as recommended. The meat was wonderfully tender, but I wanted a crisper skin.

So, the next time I tried it, I made some changes. For one thing, duck doesn't yield much flesh, and cooking a single, lone duck is no use unless there are only two or three of you eating. But I couldn't get two ducks into my couscoussier, and getting even one out, from an upright position, tore its skin. So I decided to be even more disobedient. Figuring that the ducks would stay moist if they were steamed, not necessarily submerged, I put one duck, breast down, in a large, oblong casserole and the other in a large, deep, all-purpose frying pan. Both pans were filled with boiling salted water. The casserole had its own lid, and for the frying pan I made a tent of foil. I wasn't sure it would work, but there's only ever one way of finding out.

I had decided anyway—on the evidence produced by my first stab—to swap around cooking times—that's to say, poach the birds for the half-hour and roast them for 1 hour. The ducks weren't exactly the same size, but I didn't alter the poaching times to suit—I merely took the lighter one out of its water first. And it is very much easier taking the ducks out when they are flat rather than upright. Use wooden paddle-spoons or rubber spatulas to make sure you don't rip the flesh. It would be even easier to steam the birds breast up, and frankly I doubt it matters which way up they are. I noticed some slight scalding on both ducks where the breast had come into contact with the hot base of the pan, but this didn't seem to make any difference either.

Boiling ducks produces a rather gamey fog that can linger in the kitchen, so open a window—but I was going away for the weekend and had promised to cook something. I knew I wouldn't have time to poach the birds on the Friday so did them on Thursday at about six in the evening, let them cool on a baking pan with a wire-mesh grill set over it, and then put them in the fridge before going to bed.

For traveling on Friday evening, I just put them in a plastic bag and put that plastic bag in a picnic bag with frozen gel packs. On arrival, I put the ducks, uncovered, on a large plate in my friends' fridge. When I got around to cooking them—which turned out to be Sunday lunch—it transpired that the stove had died. I put the birds, anyway, into the supposedly hot oven, which turned out to be a rapidly cooling sooty box, and left them there for a hopeless 20 minutes.

The ducks just got greasy, not even hot, and I got more teary and mutinous by the minute. But someone living in a neighboring farm set her oven to high for me (she was doubtful about having ducks at top heat so we compromised on 450°F); the ducks were driven over to her, roasted for 45 minutes, and came back, after the brief car journey, bronze and crisp and perfect.

I don't think it is possible to try out a recipe more conclusively than that.

I love having someone in the kitchen just to talk to as I chop, measure, and stir, and generally get things ready. I love cooking with other people, too. I do it rarely, though used to often with my sister Thomasina. There's something about that industrious intimacy that is both cushioning and comforting, but also hugely confidence building. I love that sense of companionable bustle, of linked activity and joint enterprise. It makes it easier to attempt food that normally you would shrink from, not because you rely on another's superior capabilities or experience necessarily, but because you aren't isolated in the attempt. Everything doesn't feel geared toward the end product because it is a shared activity—and that itself is pleasurable. You feel a sense of satisfaction about the process. It isn't drudgery.

Claudia Roden, recounting her memories of childhood in Egypt, recollected kitchenfuls of women kneading and pummeling pastries, stuffing them, wrapping them, baking them together. But I suppose those Middle Eastern delicacies, meticulous confections with their elaborate farces, could have sprung only from a culture in which the cooking was carried out by posses, by armies, of sisters and female relatives. It doesn't do to get too lyrical about this culinary companionship, though; which of us now would want our lives to be spent in such service, companionable though it might have been?

Still, it's a pity to lose all of it, never to become immersed in that female kitchen bustle. For me, so much of cooking in advance is tied up with that image, that idea; that's when cooking feels like the making of provisions, the bolstering up of a life. I don't see it as a form of subjection (unless the position is a forced one) and I don't see it as a secondary role, either. Some people hate domesticity, I know. I'm glad I don't; I love the absorbing satisfactions of the kitchen. For me, the pleasure to be got from cooking, from food—in the shop, on the chopping board, on the plate, or in the pan—is aesthetic. I think it's that I find food beautiful, intensely so.

Not that I need to be tackling hideously complicated recipes. I feel just as caught up with the domestic spirit when I'm making a very basic stew. I love the reminder that good food is simple food. It's as if there's a sort of alchemy about a stew; what do you put in it? Onions, carrots, meat, wine or beer, stock or water. And you don't even do anything to it; it just cooks, slowly, and turns, untouched, into something restorative, comforting, toothsome and wonderful.

STEWS

I love oxtail stew. Oxtail has to be cooked at least a day ahead because you'll need to let the stew get cold so that you can degrease it properly. To tell the truth, I'm happy with the fat left in; I love the artery-thickening deep and unctu-ous sauce it provides. But oxtail always makes for a good gravy, always gratify-ingly thickens the liquid in which it cooks. What I don't like is oxtail that has been boned, chopped, piled into darioles or ramekins, and then unmolded artis-tically on the plate, surrounded by its sauce-soaked vegetables. In a restaurant, that's fine. In the home, I like food to be less messed around with. Sprinkling with parsley is one thing, sculpture is quite another. My grandfather—and mother after him—used to speak disparagingly about landscape cookery.

I have a rather wonderful book, published by W. H. Allen in 1960 at the cost of 25 shillings, that I picked up in a secondhand bookshop. It is Rupert Croft-Cooke's deliciously camp, charmingly authoritative *English Cooking: A New Approach,* dedicated to Noël Coward—who, one hopes, appreciated it. Regard-ing oxtail, Mr Croft-Cooke advises, "If you like producing meat moulds with sub-tle decorations, an oxtail is a splendid thing to work on for the stock from it will set hard and firm. You boil till you can remove the meat from the bones and putting this aside with fresh seasoning, herbs and spices, you boil the bones for another hour or two then mix the stock and meat and pour into a mould. It looks," he concludes devastatingly, "what cook used to call 'a picture.' "

Oxtail can be cooked in any beer or wine. I like to use Sam Smith's Imper-ial Stout, which has a smoky licoriceness, or Young's Oatmeal Stout, both of which are increasingly available in America. Of course you can use red wine if you prefer, in which case just substitute it for the stout, below.

OXTAIL WITH STOUT
AND MARJORAM

I buy oxtail only from a butcher, in which case you can get him to disjoint it for you. What you want are rounds of oxtail that are nice and chunky (not little and scrawny, though these you can profitably use for soup) and as near to the same size as is possible. As for the stock: if you can, use any homemade you may have stowed away in the freezer or else use the best-quality commercial beef stock available. Otherwise, to be frank, you could use water.

⅓ cup vegetable oil

4 medium onions, sliced finely

2 garlic cloves, minced

1 teaspoon dried marjoram

1 tablespoon chopped parsley, plus more, for serving

½ cup all-purpose flour

1 teaspoon mustard powder

½ teaspoon powdered mace

½ teaspoon ground cloves

salt and freshly milled black pepper

5½ pounds oxtail, disjointed

4 medium carrots, peeled and cut into slim sticks about 1½ inches long

1 small can (14.5 ounces) plum tomatoes, drained, juice reserved to use, if needed

2 celery stalks

2 bay leaves

1⅔ cups stout (see above)

1¼ cups beef stock or water

Preheat the oven to 300°F.

Heat half the oil in a large casserole (I use a big cast-iron rectangular one measuring 14½ by 10 inches, which goes across 2 burners and in the oven) and fry the onions over a gentle heat until they are translucent (not brown), about 15 minutes. About 2 minutes before you think they're done, add the garlic, marjoram, and 1 tablespoon of the parsley. Remove to a plate.

Spread the flour on a large plate or, better still, a chopping board and mix in the mustard powder, mace and cloves, and some salt and pepper. Dredge the oxtail in this, heat the remaining oil in the casserole, and brown the meat well on both sides. Top with the already softened, garlicky, and marjoram-flecked onions, then pile on the carrots, the canned tomatoes, the celery, and the bay leaves. Pour over the stout and stock and bring to the boil. If the liquid looks too sparse—you want to have a decent amount covering the oxtail—throw in the reserved juice from the tomatoes. Put the lid on the casserole and transfer to the oven.

Cook for 3–4 hours or until unctuous and tender. Remove the celery and cool before putting in the fridge. The next day, remove the fat that has risen to the surface. And when you want to eat it, taste for seasoning (you may well need to add a pinch or so of salt) and then reheat, either over gentle heat on the stove for about 1 hour or in the oven at 350°F for about ¾ hour. Before serving, sprinkle with chopped parsley. And I think the parsley necessary, not an effete optional extra; without the bright, jewel-vivid flecks of green, the meat can look rather sludgy. This final touch somehow brings it to life, seems to give it the gloss of a seventeenth-century Dutch painting.

Mashed potatoes are traditional with oxtail stew, and I wouldn't offer a dissenting voice. But rice (I like basmati) works as well.

The rediscovery in Britain of traditional cooking over the past few years has tended to overlook the Welsh contribution. Part of this is, perhaps, due to the fact that for the non-Welsh British person, the experience of Welsh food will probably be limited to pubs or restaurants. In other words, the food will be poor—and probably little of it will be specifically Welsh. I had much the same experience in Spain. After a week of eating indifferent food in public places, I had to be stopped from ringing the doorbells of private houses and begging, pleading, to be allowed to go in for supper and to eat some real Spanish food cooked at home.

Good peasant cooking needs a rural society, and it is true that Wales is not quite that any more. Good bourgeois cooking needs a large and successful middle class, and Wales doesn't seem to have that either. But I feel affectionately drawn toward Welsh food. I first had the stew known as cawl (pronounced "cowl") when I was staying with my sister Thomasina, who lived in Wales. Her neighbor, Dai, would make it and bring pots of it over.

There is no one set of rules for making cawl any more than there is for pot au feu or any of those other soupy stews—cockaleekie, Scotch broth, Irish stew—that change from region to region, from household to household. Cawl just means stew, and it is made with beef just as often as with lamb. That's in theory—in practice it has always been lamb, as is the one that follows.

CAWL

Obviously the quantities are variable, but the amounts given will be enough for about 6 people. It's not necessary to finish it all at one sitting. Traditionally in Wales cawl was always eaten over a couple of days; the broth and vegetables on the first day, the meat the next, and both with a great deal of bread and butter. Now people eat it all together, but it is still important to have lots of bread and butter.

1⅔ pounds lamb neck pieces	1 rutabaga, chunked
2 large onions, sliced	3 large carrots, peeled and chunked
6 medium or 3 large potatoes, chunked	2 leeks, sliced
2 parsnips, chunked	2–3 tablespoons parsley, chopped

Put the lamb in a large saucepan and fill with cold water to cover. Bring to the boil, add salt, and then cook gently for about 1½ hours. Remove from the heat, let it get cold, and leave somewhere cool overnight.

The next day, or when you want to eat, skim the fat off. Put it back on the heat, bring it back to the boil, and then throw in the onions, potatoes, parsnips, rutabaga, and carrots. Cook for about ½ hour or until the vegetables are nearly tender. I would test the carrots, as they seem to take the longest, but check the potatoes, too; obviously, the relative size of the vegetables will determine how long they take to cook, so use your judgment. About 10 minutes before you think everything's ready, add the leeks. Sprinkle the parsley on top when you serve the cawl.

Giving actual recipes for stews always sounds inappropriately bossy. All you ever need to do is fry some onions and carrots, brown (or not) the meat, and add seasoning, wine, or other liquid, and that's it. Once you get in the habit of making stews, you won't even think of measuring this or that. You'll be comfortable building around what you've got in the kitchen, accommodating the odd bottle of wine left without a cork or half-empty can of anchovies. But even so, a recipe can be a prompt to action, a reminder of possibilities.

One of the advantages of cooking lamb stews in advance is that you can use shoulder rather than leg and just remove the fat when it's cold. I love the oozy, sticky juice you get from shoulder, and the extra fat keeps the meat tender.

GREEK LAMB STEW

Meats such as lamb and venison you'd presume would be best stewed with red wine. I love them cooked with white. When you cook this Greek lamb stew, please don't do what I did and use retsina. It wasn't a good idea. Failing homemade stock, you can use a good commercial beef stock—even water is fine—and you can always ask the butcher for the shoulder bone, chopped, and throw it in while the stew's cooking.

If you don't have a pan that will accommodate all the meat and all the pasta and is heatproof, then you will just have to cook the pasta completely separately and find some other cavernous vessel (remember to warm it first, even if it's just by filling it with some hot water in the sink) and mix the lot together in that. You'll lose something, I know; the pasta won't suck in any of the sweet, tomatoey, winy juices, but it won't be the end of the world. Obviously, as the stew has pasta in it, it can't be cooked entirely in advance. But just add the pasta when you reheat.

What is so useful about this stew is that you certainly don't need vegetables. Just make a salad to serve after. The addition, when you eat, of crumbled feta and oregano (or basil, if you like) may not be exactly authentic, but it tastes wonderful.

4 tablespoons olive oil, plus more,
    if needed
5½ pounds boned shoulder of lamb,
    trimmed of excess fat and cut
    into cubes about 1½ by 2½ inches
5 medium onions, sliced finely
salt
4 garlic cloves, minced
2 celery stalks, minced
leaves from 4 thyme sprigs
1 teaspoon dried oregano
3 bay leaves

2 carrots, peeled, halved lengthways,
    and then halved across
3 cans (14.5 ounces) diced tomatoes
1¼ cups lamb or beef stock or water
1 bottle dry white wine
freshly milled black pepper
1 pound ditalini or other smallish
    tubular pasta
⅔ pound feta
2–3 tablespoons finely chopped parsley,
    oregano or basil

Preheat the oven to 325°F.

Into the largest saucepan or casserole you have that will go in the oven, pour 3 tablespoons of the oil. Brown the meat in batches over high heat and remove with a slotted spoon to a plate nearby. You may need to add more oil as you do this. The onions will certainly need it, so pour in the remaining oil or add more, add the onions, sprinkling a little salt over them, and cook them until soft and translucent. Add the garlic, celery, thyme, and oregano. After a couple of minutes or so, when the smell of garlic wafts up, remove half the mixture. Add the meat to the mixture in the pan, cover with the remaining half, add the bay leaves, carrots, tomatoes, stock, and wine. I use a big but flattish casserole and this amount of liquid covers the meat, but if you find you need more liquid, add water—you want a lot of liquid, because you will, eventually, be cooking some pasta in it. Bring to the boil, remove scum, and let bubble for about 3 minutes. Then cover, transfer to the oven, and bake for about 2–2½ hours, or cook on a very low heat. The meat should be tender and yielding. Remove the carrots (and eat, cook's treat) and bay leaves, too, if you want, and season to taste with the salt and pepper.

Of course you can proceed to the final stage now, but I am presuming you're not going to. In which case, let the stew cool and keep it in the fridge until you want it. Skim the fat off the top, and do remember to take it out of the fridge a good 1–2 hours before you cook it again. You can reheat this in the oven, but because the pasta will be put in it on the stove, I tend to heat it there. Make sure the stew is piping hot. Meanwhile, bring a large pot of water to the boil. When it boils, add salt and then the pasta. Cook this till it's nearly but not quite cooked; it should have a couple of minutes still to go.

Then drain the pasta and add it quickly to the bubbling juices in the casserole, making sure first that there are enough bubbling juices. You don't want the meat to be drowned, but you want enough for the pasta to be covered. The pasta will absorb some of the liquid as it finishes cooking, of course.

In a couple of minutes, the pasta should be cooked. Crumble some feta and put in a bowl with the chopped parsley, oregano, or basil. Stir to combine and then leave the spoon with it, so that people can sprinkle the herb-spiked cheese over the stew as they wish. Ladle the stew into shallow soup bowls. This should be plenty for about 10.

One of the advantages of the following stew—apart from its honeyed and luscious taste—is that it can be done seriously in advance: that's to say, you can leave the venison in its marinade for 2–3 days in the fridge and then put the cooked casserole back in the fridge when it's cold, where it can stay for another 2–3 days.

I don't necessarily scale down the quantities if I'm cooking for fewer people (these quantities are enough for about 8) because the oniony juices, with or without the leftover meat, make the most fabulous pasta sauce the next day.

VENISON IN WHITE WINE

FOR THE MARINADE

1 bottle dry white wine

2 tablespoons olive oil

2 bay leaves

2 medium carrots, sliced finely

1 large onion, sliced finely

2 celery stalks, sliced finely

2 garlic cloves, squashed with flat
of knife

10 juniper berries, crushed slightly

10 black peppercorns, crushed slightly

3⅓ pounds venison stew meat, cut into
chunks about 1½ by 2½ inches

¼ cup dried porcini

½ cup goose or duck fat or
8 tablespoons (1 stick) unsalted
butter plus a drop olive oil

6 medium onions, very finely sliced

1 tablespoon sugar

3 sage leaves

½ teaspoon ground cinnamon

½ teaspoon ground cloves

½ teaspoon grated nutmeg

salt and freshly milled black pepper

3 tablespoons all-purpose flour

1¼ cups beef stock, plus more, if needed

⅔ pounds mushrooms, preferably
cremini

1–2 tablespoons chopped parsley

Put the marinade ingredients into a bowl and add the venison. Give a good stir, cover with plastic film, and leave overnight somewhere cool. If the weather's warm (though you are unlikely to be wanting to eat this in summer) or you just want to stow this away for a few days, then put it to marinate in the fridge, but make sure you take it out and get it back to room temperature before you want to cook it.

When you do, preheat the oven to 300°F and, at the same time, cover the porcini with hot water. Then put ⅓ cup of the goose or duck fat or 5 tablespoons of the butter and the drop of oil in a large casserole and, when it's melted, add the onions and cook for 10–15 minutes or until the onions are soft and translucent. Strain the dried mushrooms, reserving the water, and then chop them very small. Add these to the onion and give a good stir. Cook gently for another minute or so, stir again, then sprinkle with the sugar. Turn up the heat and caramelize slightly and then add the sage and spices. Tear a piece of foil about the same measurements as the casserole and place it just above the onions. Turn the heat to low—you may need to use a heat diffuser—and cook for 30–40 minutes, lifting up the foil every now and again to give a gentle prod and stir. You want a brown, sweet mess under there.

Pour the venison into a colander or strainer placed over a saucepan. Then pick out the marinade ingredients or meat (whichever is easier). Remove half the onions from the pan and cover the half still in it with the venison. Season with the salt and pepper, sprinkle with the flour, and cover with the rest of the onions. Heat up the marinade liquid in its pan, add the stock and reserved, strained mushroom-soaking liquid, and pour over the venison. If the meat isn't covered, you can add some more stock (though heat it up first) or wine (ditto). Put in the preheated oven and cook for about 2½ hours or until very tender indeed.

You can now let this cool and keep it in the fridge for 2–3 days. Forty minutes at 350°F or on the stove, should be enough to reheat it, but do remember it should be brought back to room temperature first. About 15 minutes before the stew is hot again, wipe the mushrooms, cut them into quarters, heat the remaining fat or butter in a small frying pan, and cook the mushrooms in it, sprinkling with salt and pepper. After about 5 minutes, add the mushrooms to the stew in the oven. Let the stew cook for another 10 minutes.

Sprinkle the stew with the parsley when you serve it. I always have this with mashed potatoes and I like sliced green beans with it, too.

Cooking chicken in white wine is hardly revolutionary, but then the point of cooking is not to surprise but, gratifyingly, to satisfy. Chicken doesn't benefit from sitting around in its cooking juices for as long as meat does—you want the meat to be tender rather than sodden—but a day or two definitely helps with brown meat.

CHICKEN AND CHICKPEA TAGINE

I have done this stew with dried, soaked, and cooked chickpeas and with canned, and it is, I have to tell you, better with dried. I cook them till more or less tender first. If you want to substitute canned ones, add 2 or 3 cans of them, drained, on reheating.

You can choose whether or not you want to keep the skin on your chicken thighs, but make certain they have not been boned.

½ pound dried chickpeas	½ teaspoon ground cinnamon
I large onion	I teaspoon each ground cumin and
5 garlic cloves	turmeric
I celery stalk	1⅔ cups white wine
3 tablespoons olive oil	1¼ cups light chicken stock
10 chicken thighs	salt and freshly milled black pepper
2 carrots, peeled and cut into French	2–3 tablespoons fresh coriander,
fry–like sticks	for serving
I tablespoon Italian 00 or all-purpose	
flour	

Soak and cook the chickpeas, following instructions on page 78 but removing them from the pot slightly before they're soft. Drain and reserve.

Put the onion, garlic, and celery in a processor and pulse till chopped. Put the oil in a casserole or tagine, put it on the stove, and, when hot, brown the chicken thighs; remove to a plate. Now add the onion mixture to the casserole and cook till soft—about 5 minutes—then add the carrots and cook for another 5 minutes. Mix the flour with the spices and stir in, cooking for a couple of minutes. Put the chicken pieces back in, add the chickpeas, and pour over the wine and stock. Season and cook on a low heat, covered, for about I hour. Let cool and then stick in the fridge for up to 3 days.

Sprinkle the coriander on top. I love eating this with a pile of pinenut-sprinkled couscous to the side. Serves 4–5.

This next stew resolutely uses red wine, and makes the most of it, too. I think it is a waste, almost, if you don't cook it in advance, as the anchovies seem to get mellower after a day or two's soaking. It's delicious straight off, too, but you get its full, deep-bellied roundness when it's given time to rest and wallow between cooking and reheating. I don't think you should necessarily tell people about the anchovies. In my experience, many people who claim not to be able to stomach them love this stew.

BEEF STEW WITH ANCHOVIES
AND THYME

I love this with mashed or baked potatoes (with sour cream) and some cold-sour fat gerkins, sliced, or little cornichons just as they are. I sometimes make (and see Weekend Lunch, page 193) a horseradish–yogurt sauce to go with it, too. It doesn't need anything to spruce it up in itself, but stews are useful in this way: what you do to them, with them, when you eat, entirely changes the mood of the meal. You could just as easily use lamb here, by the way.

3 tablespoons olive oil, plus more, if needed

3⅓ pounds beef stew meat, cut into chunky strips about 1½ by 2½ inches

1 large onion, halved lengthwise and finely sliced

5 cloves garlic, minced

3 medium carrots, peeled and cut in fat matchstick-sized pieces

4 inner stalks celery, finely sliced

6 anchovy fillets, well drained and minced

2 tablespoons dried thyme or 1½ tablespoons fresh

2 tablespoons Marsala

2 cups robust red wine

1¼ cups beef stock

2 heaping tablespoons all-purpose flour

1 tablespoon tomato paste

½ teaspoon mace

freshly milled black pepper

salt, if necessary

Preheat the oven to 300°F. Put a casserole on the stove with oil. Heat and then brown the meat briskly in batches; do not overcrowd the casserole or the meat will steam rather than sear. Remove the meat to a plate and then, first adding more oil if necessary, toss in the vegetables, anchovies, and thyme. Cook, turning frequently, on medium heat for about 10 minutes or until the mixture is beginning to soften. While this is going on, heat the Marsala, wine, and stock in a saucepan and remove when it reaches boiling point.

Return the beef to the pan and then stir in the flour. After a couple of minutes or so, pour in the wine mixture and stir well, then stir in the tomato paste and then the mace and some pepper. Taste and add salt, if you want.

Put on a lid and then cook in the preheated oven for 3 hours. Remove, cool, and then keep in the fridge until needed. I tend to reheat in the casserole on the stove. Serves 6–8.

I love game birds roasted; I like them plain, with bread sauce, a port-fortified gravy perhaps, some salty bacon fried to a bronzy puce, with English mustard and nutty fried bread crumbs. But a girl's got to have a casserole under her belt, too, if only because game birds tend quite often to be beyond roasting. This way of casseroling pheasant is a recipe—unfancy, reliable, and just what you need—of the estimable Anne Willan's (from *Real Food: Fifty Years of Good Eating*) and is great with birds that have dwindled into toughness.

Ask the butcher to cut up the pheasants for you and try to get the bacon or pancetta from him at the same time. I like using half veal and half chicken stock (I tend to buy my veal stock), but if I've got some game stock in the freezer, I'll use that. You will have lots of little bits of bird here, so each portion will be very small, of course; you should get enough for about 8 people out of 3 birds. If you want, substitute guinea fowl for the pheasant and white wine for the red.

BRAISED PHEASANT WITH MUSHROOMS AND BACON

1 tablespoon vegetable oil	¼ cup all-purpose flour
2 tablespoons (¼ stick) unsalted butter	2½ cups red wine
3 pheasants, about 1 pound each, cut into 6 pieces each	2½ cups veal or chicken stock, or more if needed
1 pound mushrooms, quartered	2 garlic cloves, crushed
20–24 baby onions, peeled	bouquet garni (see page xx)
½-pound piece pancetta, cut into lardons	salt and freshly milled black pepper

Heat the oil and butter in a casserole and brown the pheasant pieces, a few at a time. Take them out, add the mushrooms, and cook until tender, about 5 minutes. Remove them with a slotted spoon, add the onions, and cook until brown, shaking the casserole so that they color evenly. Remove the onions, add the pancetta, and brown it too.

Discard all but 2 tablespoons fat, stir the flour into the pancetta, and cook gently, stirring until brown. Stir in the wine, bring to the boil, and simmer for 5 minutes. Add the stock, garlic, bouquet garni, and salt and pepper to taste, and return the mushrooms, onion, and the pheasant pieces to the casserole. Cover and simmer on the stove or cook in a 350°F oven until the meat is very tender when pierced with a fork. Cooking time varies from 1 to 2 hours, depending on the age of the pheasants. Stir from time to time, especially if cooking on the stove, and add more stock if the meat begins to stick. The wing and breast pieces may finish cooking before the legs; if so, take them out first.

Discard the bouquet garni and taste the sauce for seasoning. Now, you can let the casserole cool, then put it in the fridge and take it out when you need it, up to 3 days later. Reheat it on top of the stove or in a 350°F oven for about 30 minutes.

Instead of the usual mashed potatoes, this stew—and, indeed, any of them—is wonderful with bulghur, or cracked wheat, however you like to call it. This has the advantage of being quicker and much less laborious to make than mashed potatoes, too; you can get on with it while you reheat the stew.

For 8 people, you need 4 cups of bulghur and 4 cups of water. Melt 3 table-spoons of butter in a heavy-bottomed saucepan (which has a lid that fits) and stir in the bulghur till all coated. Then add the water, bring to the boil, add a good pinch of salt, cover, and turn down the heat to the absolute minimum. Use a heat diffuser, preferably. Cook for about 30 minutes or until all the water is absorbed and the bulghur is cooked but not soft; it should still be nutty in texture. You can leave the bulghur, when it's cooked, with the lid on but the pan off the heat, for 10 minutes or so without harm.

VEGETABLES

One could go on forever with stews, braises, casseroles; the permutations are enormous, and I can't think of one that couldn't be cooked in advance. Vegetables are a different matter. Few vegetables take long to cook, and now you can get most ready trimmed, chopped, even utterly prepared for you at many supermarkets. I make three exceptions to the "quickly cooked" list: ratatouille, moussaka, and petits pois à la française. Of course there are other vegetable braises that you could add to this list—fava beans with bacon, certainly, and stewed artichokes—but most vegetable dishes that can be left sitting around to be reheated later are variations (technically, at any rate) on this theme.

I know some would argue that you can't cook and then reheat ratatouille, that it will go mushy and lose its vibrant, just-cooked freshness. But I like it soft-ened slightly in the pan, the flavors still discrete but mingling into one another, everything sweet and steeped. But perhaps that's because my mother always had a bowl of ratatouille in the fridge; I remember it beginning to go soggy in its gar-licky syrup.

RATATOUILLE

I couldn't remember exactly how my mother made ratatouille and didn't know if she used 2 zucchini or 3, or how many minutes she fried them. Pinpoint accuracy disappears with recipes you do often, but somehow I felt even more at a loss in transcribing this one from memory. And so, working on the principle that my mother would have consulted her, I turned to Elizabeth David. I'm not sure what follows is something Mrs. David would be pleased with, if only because I have ignored something she is very firm about indeed: I never bother with salting and draining eggplant, and am not now going to start degorging zucchini, either. Neglecting this stage hasn't resulted in a hopelessly soggy mess, otherwise I'm sure we, *mère et fille,* would have done as we were told in the first place. But if you feel it's important, then by all means cut the eggplant and zucchini into unpeeled ¼-inch-thick rounds, sprinkle with salt, and put in a colander with a plate on top of them, a weight on top of the plate, and leave all that in place for an hour or so, then rinse the vegetables and wipe them dry with kitchen paper.

I have also boosted the number of zucchini in Elizabeth David's recipe and decreased the amount of eggplant, simply because I like zucchini more than I like eggplant. She suggests 2 coffee cups of olive oil, which I reckon is about 10 tablespoons.

The vegetables in a ratatouille are cooked in this order—onions first, then eggplant, zucchini, garlic and peppers, and lastly tomatoes. You can either prepare all the vegetables before you start, as the recipe indicates, or one at a time, chucking them into the pan in the right order.

4 large flavorful tomatoes or 1 small can (14.5 ounces) plum tomatoes	**3 large red bell peppers, cored, seeded, and cut into thin strips or chunks**
6 tablespoons olive oil	**2 garlic cloves, minced**
2 medium onions, halved lengthwise and finely sliced	**1 generous teaspoon coriander seed, pounded, or ½–1 teaspoon ground coriander**
1 eggplant, halved lengthwise and thinly sliced	**salt and freshly milled black pepper**
5 smallish zucchini, halved lengthwise and sliced ¼-inch thick	**2–3 tablespoons basil or parsley, chopped**

Skin the tomatoes: plunge them into boiling water for a few minutes and slip the skins off. Then halve them, scoop out the seeds, and cut each hollowed half in two crosswise. Or if you're using canned, just squeeze the seeds out of the tomatoes.

Heat the olive oil in a heavy-bottomed wide pot—a round Le Creuset casserole is good here, or I use my deep Calphalon frying pan as, even though it isn't heavy-bottomed, it doesn't stick on a low heat. Earthenware dishes look authentic—the perfect Sunday supplement picture—but they do tend to stick.

Put the onions into this pot, whichever one you're using, and cook until they're soft but not brown. Then add the eggplant, cook for a minute or so, then add the zucchini,

stirring them into the oil for a few minutes. Carry on like this with the peppers and garlic. If you feel you need more oil, pour it in.

Cover the pot and cook gently for 40 minutes. Make sure, though, that it *is* gently.
You don't want the bottom burning and the top steaming. Now add the tomatoes and
coriander and season with the salt and pepper. Cook for another 30–40 minutes until
all the vegetables are soft but not mushy. Stir in the basil or parsley and eat hot or cold.
I think that cold it is rather good with chopped fresh coriander, too. And it's excellent
as a side dish, served tepid, with cold roast chicken or pork, or hot roast lamb. It keeps
in the fridge for 5 days, but remember to take it out of the fridge well before you eat it.

MOUSSAKA

Turning back to Elizabeth David reminded me of the smoky, satiny wonderful-
ness of eggplant stews.

This is a Lebanese recipe, very different from the traditional Greek one of the
same name. Boldly, strongly flavored, but mellow, the spices and seasoning
dovetail into a perfect, aromatic whole. The recipe is adapted from a wonderful
book of Lebanese home cooking by Nada Saleh, called, evocatively enough,
Fragrance of the Earth. The pomegranate molasses (or syrup) stipulated here is
found in Middle-Eastern or specialty food stores. If you can't get baby eggplant,
use large ones, cut into ½-inch cubes.

1 pound baby eggplants	1 pound tomatoes, rinsed, peeled,
5 tablespoons olive oil	seeded, and quartered
1 medium onion, sliced thinly	1½ teaspoons salt, or to taste
10–12 small garlic cloves, peeled and	½ teaspoon cinnamon
left whole or sliced thickly	½ teaspoon allspice
¾ cup chickpeas, soaked, rinsed,	¼ teaspoon freshly milled black pepper
drained, and precooked (see	1 cup water
page 78)	2–3 tablespoons parsley, coriander, or
1½ tablespoons pomegranate molasses	mint, chopped
(optional)	

Trim the eggplant stems. Peel the eggplants partially to look like old-fashioned hot-
air balloons, leaving alternating lengthwise strips of peel and flesh each about ½ inch
wide. In a saucepan, heat 3 tablespoons of the oil over medium heat and sauté the eggplant for a few minutes or until golden brown. With a slotted spoon, remove to a side
dish lined with paper towels and reserve. To the saucepan add the remaining oil, the
onions, and the garlic and sauté, stirring constantly, until pale in color and soft, about

5 minutes, adding more oil if necessary. Add the chickpeas and stir occasionally for 5 minutes, then add the pomegranate molasses, if using. Return the reserved eggplant to the saucepan and add the tomatoes, sprinkle with the salt, cinnamon, allspice, and black pepper, and add the water; bring to the boil and quickly reduce the heat to moderately low. Cover and simmer for about an hour. If you're using a large, shallow saucepan, you may find they are ready after 45 minutes.

Serve warm or cold, but either way, sprinkle with the parsley, coriander, or mint, even if Nada Saleh issues no such command. Eat with lots of bread. It keeps in the fridge easily for 3–5 days.

Cooking this sort of thing in advance enables you to make more of it later. You could cook this moussaka on the weekend and stash it away for a quick midweek supper by pairing it with some noisettes of lamb, cooked for a few minutes on each side. For vegetarians, sprinkle with feta cheese when reheating.

These dishes can be meals in themselves or served as a vegetable accompaniment alongside meat. But if you want to do an all-purpose vegetable accompaniment to meat or fish, plain or fancy, petits pois à la française are useful. Everyone loves peas cooked like this, fragrant with the lettuce and syrupy with the butter.

PETITS POIS À LA FRANÇAISE

For the lettuce, I use part of a head of romaine, if I'm shopping specially for it, but otherwise I'm happy to make do with whatever I've got at hand. I use fresh peas when I'm in the mood to shell them and when they're available; otherwise, I use a package of frozen young peas. Don't bother to buy fresh peas ready shelled; there's no advantage here over frozen. If you are using frozen peas, you won't have to cook them for so long. I tend to thaw them first and cook them for about 10 minutes. I like using chicken stock in place of the water, but this is not classic.

3 tablespoons butter	6 scallions, white and green parts,
3⅓ pounds peas, in the pod, or 3 cups	chopped
frozen young peas	salt and freshly milled black pepper
I small lettuce or 8–10 leaves of a	I teaspoon sugar
larger lettuce, shredded roughly	

Melt the butter in a saucepan and stir in the peas, lettuce, and scallions. Let everything become glossy and buttery and then add ¼ cup of boiling water, season with the salt and pepper, and add the sugar; remember that the liquid will boil down, so the seasoning will taste more acute in the finished dish. You can always add more salt or sugar later, anyway. And you may need to add more water if you're using fresh peas. Put a lid on the pan and stew gently for about 20 minutes. The peas should be tender and the juices scarce but thick. Taste for seasoning. Let cool, put in the fridge—for a couple of days at most—and reheat on the stove when you want to eat them. You may need to add a little butter and water when you reheat.

When serving, I like sometimes to strike an unorthodox note by sprinkling them with some freshly chopped mint. Basil is wonderful, too—to me it always smells of summer. Chopped parsley is always good.

The next recipe isn't exactly a vegetable course, but it is such a perfect example of the cooking-in-advance principle that I don't want to leave it out. Actually, you can eat it as a vegetable, but it has wider uses and applications, as you'll see.

ONION MUSH

This may not be a very attractive-sounding name for anything, but what it aims to describe is wonderful, a kind of savory honey. Indeed, this sort of thing often goes, in restaurants, by the name of onion jam. What it is, simply, is onion cooked slowly and at a very low heat till it turns golden and soft, a mellow, caramelized gloop to be stirred into anything when you want depth and flavor. It does take a long time to make (but with a food processor requires hardly any effort to prepare), but you need to do pretty well nothing while it's cooking—the odd peek, the odd prod. I make up a lot of this, then freeze it in quantity-labeled bags to be brought out when needed. You need to bear in mind that every ⅓ cup of the mush is roughly equal to 1 onion in seasoning power. Freeze the mush in ⅓-cup quantities and use each in place of an onion whenever a recipe stipulates one. In practice, I like this so much I use much more than any recipe calls for; 1 pound of ground meat, cooked with even 1 cup of this, is out-of-this-world wonderful: sweet, creamy, deep-toned, and softly hearty. And I love it plain, too, on sandwiches, with steak, with anything. It's OK for 2 weeks in the fridge, or I find it so, but it does make life easier to make a lot and then freeze it in those small, recommended portions.

1 heaping teaspoon lard or butter and	2 pounds onions, very thinly sliced
3 tablespoons olive oil, or	salt
4–5 tablespoons olive oil	½ cup Marsala

Put a very large, heavy-bottomed frying pan over low heat, using a heat diffuser if you've got one. You may need a couple of pans. Put in the lard or butter and oil or olive oil and, when it starts melting and warming up but before any heat emanates or any siz-zles can be heard, add the onions, press down with a wooden spoon, then sprinkle some salt over. Add to the Marsala in its measuring cup enough boiling water to bring the liquid up to the ¾-cup mark and pour over the onions. Cut out some foil and press it down over the onions, shiny side down, to form a tight, low lid. Then put on the pan's real lid and cook, over very low heat, for a good 2 hours. Check after an hour; the mix-ture shouldn't be hot enough for any burning or sticking. If using a heat diffuser and a sound heavy-bottomed pan, you may want to give it a third hour. When the onion tastes completely cooked, very soft, take the lid and foil off and turn the heat up high to let all liquid bubble and burn off. When it's reduced and evaporated, you should have a soft, thick, caramel-colored mush. That's it.

DESSERTS

It is perfectly honorable to buy a tart from a pâtisserie. But I have discovered that I love making desserts, provided I can do them in advance. What I hate is having to get up from the dinner table to start fiddling with a dessert just as the evening is getting underway and I'm beginning to relax. Anyway, most of the sweet things I like need to be made a good day or so before they're eaten.

Any trifle needs a day to sit in the fridge or a cool place, everything meld-ing, setting, the component parts becoming this one glorious whole. Here are three such.

RHUBARB, MUSCAT, AND MASCARPONE TRIFLE

I first made this, like so many good things, by accident. I'd cooked some rhubarb and had some juice left over and turned it into jelly (and see page 312). I then thought that the jelly itself would be mysterious and wonderful as part of a toned-down but at the same time expanded trifle. I had some mascarpone in the fridge, so used that in place of the custard and cream of an English trifle. The result is more of a dinner-party trifle, but not affectedly so.

If you've got a suitable glass bowl or dish, use that, as the colors are ravish-ing—the dusty carmine of the rhubarb, the soft green of the pistachios, the soft squish of cream between. I find that the proportions are best if you use a rela-tively wide and shallow dish, but if a bowl-shaped bowl is all you've got, then just prepare for deeper layers. It's best when you use hothouse rhubarb, but I make it just as often with the coarser stuff. And as for the pistachios, you can sometimes buy them ready-chopped. If you do, keep a stash in a jar with a lid in the fridge; 2 or 3 tablespoons sprinkled over the top should be fine.

The first time I put this together, I made my own cake for the base, but I've since moved on to bought sponge layers. Feel free to use a purchased 8-inch sponge layer (you may not need it all), although I'll give the recipe for the home-made version just in case.

The mascarpone layer in this contains raw egg; assure yourself that the eggs you'll use are wholesome and remember that the old, ill, vulnerable, pregnant, babies, and children are advised not to eat anything with uncooked eggs in it.

FOR THE SPONGE
2 eggs, separated
⅓ cup superfine sugar
pinch salt
½ cup Italian 00 or all-purpose flour

Preheat the oven to 350°F. Butter a small (2-cup) loaf pan well, then dust with flour, tapping to shake off excess.

Whisk the egg yolks with the sugar (preferably with an electric mixer) until pale and thick and creamy. The mixture should have the texture of extraordinarily aerated mayonnaise. Add the salt to the flour and then sift it (sift it twice if you're using all-purpose flour), holding the sifter high above the bowl so you get maximum lightness later.

Whisk the egg whites with another pinch of salt until stiff, then add a dollop to the egg yolk mixture and sprinkle over a couple of tablespoons of flour. Fold in with a metal spoon. Then carry on, gradually and with a gossamer touch, using up all the egg whites and all the flour until you have a creamily combined mixture.

Pour the cake batter into the prepared pan and bake for half an hour or until the surface is springy and the sides have shrunk a little away from the pan. Gently unmold onto a rack and leave to cool. You can, of course, make this even further in advance and either freeze it, wrapped tightly, or keep it in the fridge for a day or so.

FOR THE REST OF THE TRIFLE
2¼ pounds rhubarb, trimmed and cut
    into 1½-inch slices
juice of 2 blood oranges or 1 large
    ordinary orange
1½ cups sugar
about ¾ cup sweet muscat wine (see
    page 459)
6 leaves gelatin or 1 envelope plus
    2 teaspoons granulated gelatin
2 egg yolks
½ cup superfine sugar
3 cups mascarpone
1 egg white
½ cup peeled pistachios (about ¾ cup in
    the shell), chopped very fine

Preheat the oven to 375°F. Put the rhubarb into an ovenproof dish, squeeze over the orange juice, spoon over the sugar, and then either put the lid on or cover tightly with foil. Cook in the oven for an hour—opening oven and lifting up lid to give a good, sugar-dissolving stir after 30 minutes—until the rhubarb's soft and floating in a pool of pink liquid. Remove from oven and let cool a little before straining into a 4-cup measuring cup. Reserve the rhubarb pulp for the time being. You should have around 3 cups. Add ¾ cup of the muscat—or however much you need—to take the liquid up to the 3¾ cups mark. If using granulated gelatin, remove ½ cup of the liquid, sprinkle over the gelatin, and allow to soften. Transfer the mixture to the top of a double boiler, and heat over simmering water until the gelatin has dissolved, about 1 minute. Otherwise, soften the leaf gelatin in cold water till soft, about 5 minutes. Heat 1 cup of the rhubarby liquid in a saucepan until boiling point, then remove from heat. Squeeze out the gelatin leaves, if using, whisk them into the hot liquid, and stir. Then pour that hot liquid into the rest of the juice, or add the dissolved granulated gelatin, and taste to see if you want more sugar or, to sharpen, a squeeze of lemon. Leave to cool.

Now get your dish: I find this amount does enough for an oblong shallow container measuring 12 × 8 × 2 inches, which would feed 12–14 people, though I'd use the same quantities for 8 and up; for 6–8, I do half measurements and use a bowl 8 inches in diameter and with a capacity of about 5 cups.

Cut the sponge cake into very thin slices or split bought sponge horizontally, and line the bottom of the dish with the slices. Next, spread over the rhubarb pulp, but if it is very green and stringy, then leave this step out. Now, pour over the jelly and put in the fridge to set for 6 hours or so—poke and see, but I am happy to do this over a few days, and indeed I prefer it.

To make the cream to go on top, whisk the egg yolks with the sugar and, when pale and moussy (though it doesn't have to be quite as moussy as for the sponge, above), mix it into the mascarpone. When all's combined, whisk the egg white till stiff and then fold it into the mascarpone mixture. Spoon over the jellied sponge and put back in the fridge for 12–24 hours. An hour or so before you want to eat this, take it out of the fridge and, before serving, sprinkle with the pistachios.

PROPER ENGLISH TRIFLE

When I say proper, I mean proper: lots of sponge, lots of jam, lots of custard, and lots of cream. This is not a timid construction, nor should it be. Of course, the ingredients must be good, but you don't want to end up with a trifle so upmarket it's inappropriately, posturingly elegant. A degree of vulgarity is requisite.

I soak the sponge in orange-flavored alcohol (I loathe the acrid dustiness of standard-issue sherry), infuse the custard with orange, and make an orange caramel to sprinkle over the top; this seems to bring out the fruity egginess of it all, even if you are reduced to using frozen fruit. I've specified raspberries, but you could substitute blackberries (maybe sprinkling with a little sugar and using blackberry jam with the sponge), and I have used, too, those packages of frozen mixed berries. They're fine, but they definitely bring a sponge-soaked reminder of summer pudding, the classic English berry dessert, with them. You can use a purchased 8-inch sponge layer here, as I do, but for those who cannot countenance such an unchic thing, I suggest some brioche or challah, sliced; indeed, loaf-shaped brioche or challah, both of which have a denser crumb than the boulangerie-edition or *echt* article, are both perfect here.

In a way it is meaningless, or certainly unhelpful, to give exact measurements; as ever, it so depends on the bowl you're using. Think rather of layers: one of jam-sandwiched sponge, one of custard, one of cream, and then the nutty, toffee-ish topping. So use the quantities below—which will fill a bowl of 10-cup capacity or a 9 × 13-inch rectangular dish—as a guide only.

2½ cups light cream	4 cups raspberries
zest and juice of I orange	8 egg yolks
½ cup Grand Marnier	½ cup superfine sugar
¼ cup Marsala	2 cups heavy cream
I 8-inch purchased sponge layer or	½ cup flaked almonds
4–5 slices of brioche or challah	I orange
about 10 heaping teaspoons best-	about ½ cup sugar
quality raspberry or boysenberry	
jam	

Pour the light cream into a wide, heavy-bottomed saucepan, add the orange zest—reserving the juice, separately, for the moment—and bring just to the boil. Take off the heat and set aside for the orange flavor to infuse while you get on with the bottom layer of the trifle.

Mix together the Grand Marnier, Marsala, and the reserved orange juice and pour about half of it into a shallow soup bowl, keeping the rest for replenishing halfway through. If you're using bought sponges, split them horizontally; if the challah or brioche slices, take the crusts off and cut them each into two equal slices. Make little sandwiches of the sponge or bread with the jam and dunk each sandwich, first one side, then the other, into the booze in the bowl. Arrange the alcohol-saturated sandwiches at the bottom of the trifle bowl. If you're using the challah or brioche, you might need to make up more of your alcoholic mixture, as the bread seems to soak it all in much more quickly and thirstily.

When the bottom of the bowl's covered, top with the fruit and put in the fridge to settle while you get on with the custard. Bring the orange-zested cream back to the boil while you whisk together the egg yolks and sugar in a bowl large enough to take the cream, too, in a moment. When the yolks and sugar are thick and frothy, pour the about-to-bubble cream into them, whisking as you do so. Wash out the saucepan, dry it well, and return the custard mixture, making sure you disentangle every whisk-attached string of orange zest; you will be straining this later, but for now you want to hold on to all of it.

Fill the sink with enough cold water to come about halfway up the custard pan. On medium to low heat cook the custard, stirring all the time with a wooden spoon or spatula. With so many egg yolks, the custard should take hardly any time to thicken (and remember, it will continue to thicken further as it cools), so don't overcook it. If it looks as if it might be about to boil or break, quickly plunge the pan into the sink of cold water, beating furiously until danger is averted. But I find this yolk-rich custard uneventful to make—about 7 minutes, if that, does it; it's unlikely to need cooking for more than 10. When it's cooked and thickened, take the pan over to the sink of cold water and beat robustly but calmly for a minute or so. When the custard's smooth and cooled, strain it over the fruit-topped sponge and put the bowl back in the fridge for 24 hours.

Not long before you want to eat it, whip the heavy cream till thick and, preferably with one of those bendy rubber spatulas, smear it thickly over the top of the custard. Put it back in the fridge. Toast the flaked almonds by tossing them in a hot, dry frying pan for a couple of minutes and then remove to a plate till cool. Squeeze the orange, pour the juice into a measuring cup, and then measure out an equal quantity of sugar; I reckon on getting ½ cup of juice out of the average orange. Pour the orange juice into a saucepan and stir in sugar to help it dissolve. Bring to the boil and let bubble away until you have a thick but still runny caramel; if you let it boil too much until you have, almost, toffee (and I often do), it's not the end of the world, but you're aiming for a densely syrupy, sticky caramel. Remove from heat and, when cooled slightly, dribble over the whipped cream; you may find this easier to do teaspoon by slow-drizzling tea-spoon. You can do this an hour or so before you want to eat it. Scatter the toasted almonds over before serving.

This is certainly enough for 10, and maybe even more, though it certainly wouldn't swamp 8.

WHITE TIRAMISU

I wouldn't suggest a tiramisu, ubiquitous in the 1990s, in the normal run of things, but this coffeeless, chocolateless, all-white confection is a rather chic take on it; it evokes, just by virtue of its name, the cliché and the overfamiliar, but elegantly, rather grandly, overturns that presumption, which I quite like. But even if it were to become the tackiest, most overfamiliar, and thus generally downgraded and despised dolce ever constructed, I would still stand by it; you'll see. . . .

This dessert is always a success; it always works, and everyone always loves it. It is, once again, a recipe that bears the mark of Anna del Conte. I have made one slight alteration, which is to increase the liquid in which the biscuits are soaked. You must use the Italian *savoiardi,* crisp sponge fingers, not our regular lady fingers. To get these, you need to go to a good Italian food shop, or see page 461 for sources. If you can't be bothered to make your own meringues, crumble some bought meringue nests.

20 small meringues, about 1 inch in diameter, made with 2 egg whites and ⅔ cup sugar (see recipe on page 17)	½ cup superfine sugar
	3 cups mascarpone
	⅔ cup white rum, such as Bacardi
	1 cup milk
2 eggs, separated	18 savoiardi

Choose a dish about 4 inches deep, suitable for holding 9 savoiardi.

Heat the oven to 275°F. Then make the meringues. Set aside 10 of them and crumble the others.

Beat the egg yolks with the sugar until pale and mousse like. Fold in the mascarpone gradually and then beat until incorporated. Whisk 1 egg white (you don't need the second) until firm and fold into the mascarpone mixture.

Mix the rum and milk in a soup plate and dip the savoiardi in the mixture just long enough for them to soften. Lay about 9 moistened biscuits in the dish and spread over about a third of the mascarpone mixture. Sprinkle with the meringue crumbs. Dip another 9 biscuits into the rum and milk as before and then arrange them on top of the meringue crumbs. Spread over about half the remaining cream, cover with plastic film, and refrigerate. Put the remaining cream in a closed container and refrigerate also. Leave for a day. (I have left it for 2 days without any problem.)

Before serving, smooth the remaining cream all over the tiramisu and decorate with the whole meringue coins. I would offer a bowl of raspberries alongside.

Serves 6.

The white tiramisu is far less effort in the kitchen than it looks on the page. Another standby of mine is syllabub. You hardly have to do anything, although that isn't my prime motivation; it tastes fabulous, all that softly piled-up whiteness infused with nutmeg, the sort of dessert you imagine eating in heaven.

QUINCE SYLLABUB

This version is particularly fragrant, as the name suggests. The quince in question is not the actual fruit but the peachy-peppery breath of an eau de vie de Coings (quince liqueur or quince brandy). Instead of the sherry, you could use white wine, and instead of the quince liqueur, you could use ordinary brandy. The dessert might look rather lovely—to amplify the coral tones of the quince liqueur—if you chose one of those French dry rosés in place of the sherry. And if you want to play on the Arabian Nights feel of the creamy, quince-fragrant confection, then add a drop of rosewater (only a drop, or it'll smell like bath lotion). I think I'd stop short of decorating with rose petals, though.

I normally hate things in individual portions, restaurant-style, but with a syllabub, there's no getting round it. You have to eat it with a teaspoon. So, I pile it into separate glasses.

As the alcohol, lemon juice, and zest have to sit and steep overnight, you need to do this a little in advance, but I have happily done it rather a lot in advance and left the syllabub, made up and spooned into its glasses, on the bottom shelf of the fridge for a couple of days before eating it. This amount makes enough to fit into 6 small glasses or 4 wineglasses—the syllabub looks best piled right up to the top and swelling bulkily beyond.

8 tablespoons dry sherry or dry rosé	4 tablespoons superfine sugar
2 tablespoons eau de vie de Coings	1¼ cups heavy cream
or brandy	drop rosewater (optional)
juice and grated zest of 1 lemon	whole nutmeg

Put the sherry, eau de vie de Coings, lemon zest, and juice in a bowl, cover with plastic film, and leave overnight; the mixture does not have to be refrigerated. The next day, strain the liquid into another bowl, stir in the sugar, and keep stirring until it's dissolved. Keep on stirring as you gradually pour in the cream. Add the drop of rosewater and a grating of nutmeg; I once tried cinnamon instead and, although I prefer the nutmeg, the cinnamon variant was well liked, so you may want to give it a whirl yourself.

Now whip the syllabub until it is about to form soft peaks. It should occupy some territory between solid and liquid, rather like the cool, buttery flesh of a newborn baby does when, touching it, you can't tell where the skin stops and the air begins. You don't want the cream to become too thick or, indeed, to go further and curdle. The answer is probably to use a wire whisk, but if you promise to keep the beaters going at the lowest possible speed and to be vigilant, then you can use an electric hand-held whisk.

Cookbook author Jane Grigson, in her St. Valentine's Syllabub (white wine and brandy, flavored with honey and sprinkled with toasted nuts), talks of its "bulky whiteness"; that seems the perfect, poetic, description of the point at which you should stop whisking.

Spoon the syllabub into the glasses and set aside in a cold place or the fridge for 2–3 days. Sometimes I grate some more nutmeg over the syllabubs just before eating. And serve with cookies, delicate, thin, light ones—tuiles, langue de chat (see page 19), or pistachio-studded Middle Eastern pastry curls.

STEM GINGER GINGERBREAD

Gingerbread is perhaps more of a tea bread than a dessert, but, with some sharp, damp, but crumbly Caerphilly, Wensleydale, or Lancashire cheese, or a sourish American cheddar, it makes a stylish ending to an informal meal. I include the recipe under cooking in advance because—to get the seductive, highly scented stickiness—the gingerbread must be wrapped in foil and kept for a day or so before being eaten. It is also good—if eccentric—in plain unbuttered slices with the aromatic spiced baked plums on page 116. And I love gingerbread with ice cream; all you need is good vanilla ice cream sprinkled with a little cinnamon, but if you really want to go for it you could serve, along with the ice cream and gingerbread, some more stem ginger in its pungent syrup.

The recipe comes from *The Baking Book* by Linda Collister and Anthony Blake. I use a drum grater to prepare the ginger for this.

2 cups all-purpose flour
½ teaspoon baking soda
pinch salt
1 tablespoon ground ginger
1 teaspoon ground cinnamon
1 teaspoon pumpkin-pie spice
8 tablespoons (1 stick) unsalted
   butter, diced
⅓ cup molasses

⅓ cup golden syrup or light corn syrup
½ cup light or dark muscovado sugar
   or light or dark brown sugar
1 cup milk
¼ cup stem ginger (preserved ginger in
   syrup), drained
   and grated
1 egg, beaten

Grease a 10 × 4 × 3-inch loaf tin and line the bottom with parchment paper. Preheat the oven to 350°F.

Sift the flour, baking soda, salt, and all the spices into a large mixing bowl. Add the diced butter and rub in with your fingers until the mixture resembles fine crumbs. (I use my freestanding mixer, with the flat beater in place.)

In a small saucepan, melt the molasses with the corn syrup, then leave to cool to tepid. Meanwhile, in another saucepan, dissolve the sugar in the milk over low heat, stirring occasionally.

Add the ginger to the flour mixture. Then whisk or beat the milk mixture into the flour mixture and next whisk in the molasses mixture, followed by the egg. When thoroughly blended, the mixture should be a thin batter.

Pour the batter into the prepared pan and bake for 1–1¼ hours or until a skewer inserted into the center comes out clean. Start checking after 45 minutes. But be warned: the mixture goes very runny before it is ready. Don't panic. The gingerbread will rise during baking and then fall and shrink slightly as it cools. Leave to cool completely in the pan, then turn out and wrap first in wax paper and then in foil. Keep for a day before slicing thickly, then eat hungrily.

Serves 6–8.

ALMOND AND ORANGE-BLOSSOM CAKE

For no real reason, I think of this as a summer version of the sticky gingerbread. It is wonderfully fragrant, dense with almonds, and gently scented with oranges and orange-flower water. It is wonderful served with a compote of cherries, or indeed with any fruit. I rely on cakes with berries for a dinner-party dessert and I'm particularly pleased with this one. Like the gingerbread, this almond cake has to be wrapped in foil (without the wax paper layer) for a day or so before being eaten.

16 tablespoons (2 sticks) unsalted butter, softened	1 scant teaspoon almond essence
1 cup superfine sugar	zest of 1 medium orange
4 eggs	juice of ½ medium orange
½ cup Italian 00 or all-purpose flour	2 tablespoons orange-flower water
1¼ cups ground almonds	confectioners' sugar, for dusting

Grease an 8-inch springform cake pan (if the only one you've got measures 9 inches then that'll do, or anything between these figures, but no bigger) and cut out a circle of parchment paper to line the bottom. I lay the paper out on the table, put the tin on top, press down heavily on it with one hand and, using the other, tear the paper away from the base of the tin. What you end up with is a circle of the right size with maybe a few fuzzy edges, but what does it matter?

Preheat the oven to 350°F. Then cream together the butter and sugar until almost white. (Again, I use a freestanding mixer, with the flat paddle beater, for the entire operation.) Beat the eggs and add them gradually to the creamed butter and sugar, beating all the while. I put in a couple of tablespoons at a time and, with each addition, sprinkle on some flour. When all the eggs and flour have been incorporated, gently stir in the ground almonds, then the almond essence, grated orange zest, orange juice, and orange-flower water.

Pour the mixture into the cake pan and bake for about 1 hour. After about 40 minutes, you may well find you have to cover it, loosely, with foil; you don't want the top of the cake to burn. The cake is ready when the top is firm and a skewer, inserted in the center, comes out clean. Take it out and let it stand for 5 minutes or so in the pan. Then turn it out on to a rack and leave till cool. Wrap it well in foil and leave for a day or two. Shake some confectioners' through a fine or tea strainer over the cake when serving.

Serves 8.

BAKED SPICED AROMATIC PLUMS

I am not normally the sort of person who bakes, bottles, or otherwise prepares or preserves fruit; I like it ripe, fresh, as it is. I make a couple of exceptions: one for quinces, about which I can grow somewhat obsessive during November, the other for plums. We have a few trees in the garden and from them more fruit than we can eat. Even in a bad year, when the dusty blue, grape-black skins enclose disappointingly unyielding Pucci-green fruit, baking them like this transforms them. You can bake the plums a few days in advance, and they freeze very well in their aromatic syrup. This is a favorite dessert in my house.

2 pounds plums, halved and pitted	1 star anise
1 cup red wine	seeds from 4 cardomom pods or scant
2 bay leaves	¼ teaspoon ground cardomom
½ teaspoon ground cinnamon	½ cup honey
2 cloves	

Set oven to 325°F. Choose a baking dish that will hold the plums, halved, in one layer; if you haven't got one big enough you could use a couple, but make sure you fill whichever dishes you're using or there won't be enough syrup.

Put the plums in the dish, cut side down. Then put all the other ingredients into a saucepan and bring to the boil. Pour over the plums, cover the dish tightly with foil (or a lid, of course, if you've got one that fits), and bake for about 1 hour or until the plums are tender.

Keep the cooled, covered fruit in the fridge for 3 or so days or freeze them with impunity until you need them. I find them easier to reheat, gently, on the stove.

Serves 6–8.

Opinions are divided in my household as to what goes best with these spicy, wine-dark plums. There is a custard contingent, but I veer more toward ice cream or crème fraîche. But what I really love—and not just with this but with plain, uncooked blueberries (which you can now get all the year round, it seems) and most other berries—is something my grandmother used to make, called Barbados cream.

BARBADOS CREAM

It's difficult to be precise about measurements here; the idea is to stir together more or less equal quantities of yogurt and heavy cream and then sprinkle over a good covering of brown sugar.

These are the quantities I use to fill a shallow bowl (and it must be a shallow bowl) measuring about 8 inches in diameter. If you're having the Barbados cream as an accompaniment to fruit, then this will provide enough for about 6, maybe more; it is delectably rich.

1¼ cups heavy cream   about ⅓ cup light brown sugar
1⅓ cup plain yogurt

Mix everything together and beat till fairly but not too stiffly thick. Pour into the bowl. Sprinkle over it a thick carpet of brown sugar, cover with plastic, and leave somewhere cool for at least 12 hours or, better still, 24 hours.

ONE AND TWO

"Don't knock masturbation," Woody Allen once said: "it's sex with someone I love." Most people can't help finding something embarrassingly onanistic about taking pleasure in eating alone. Even those who claim to love food think that cooking just for yourself is either extravagantly self-indulgent or a plain waste of time and effort. But you don't have to belong to the drearily narcissistic learn-to-love-yourself school of thought to grasp that it might be a good thing to consider yourself worth cooking for. And the sort of food you cook for yourself will be different from the food you might lay on for tablefuls of people: it will be better.

I don't say that for effect. You'll feel less nervous about cooking it and that translates to the food itself. It'll be simpler, more straightforward, the sort of food you want to eat.

I don't deny that food, its preparation as much as its consumption, is about sharing, about connectedness. But that's not all that it's about. There seems to me to be something robustly affirmative about taking trouble to feed yourself— enjoying life on purpose rather than by default.

Even in culinary terms alone there are grounds for satisfaction. Real cooking, if it is to have any authenticity, any integrity, has to be part of how you are, a function of your personality, your temperament. There's too much culinary ventriloquism about as it is; cooking for yourself is a way of countering that. It's how you're going to find your own voice.

One of the greatest hindrances to enjoying cooking is that tense-necked desire to impress others. It's virtually impossible to be innocent of this. Even if this is not your motivation, it's hard, if you're being honest, to be insensible to the reactions of others. As cooking for other people is about trying to please them, it would be strange to be indifferent to their pleasure, and I don't think you should be. But you can try too hard. When you're cooking for yourself, the stakes simply aren't as high. You don't mind as much. Consequently, it's much less likely to go wrong. And the process is more enjoyable in itself.

When I cook for myself, I find it easier to trust my instinct—I am sufficiently relaxed to listen to it in the first place—and, contrariwise, I feel freer to overturn a judgment, to take a risk. If I want to see what will happen if I add yogurt or stir in some chopped tarragon instead of parsley, I can do so without worrying that

I am about to ruin everything. If the sauce breaks or the tarragon infuses everything with an invasive farmyard grassiness, I can live with it. I might feel cross with myself, but I won't be panicked. It could be that the yogurt makes the sauce or that the tarragon revitalizes it. I'm not saying that cooking for seven other people would make it impossible for me to respond spontaneously, but I do think it's cooking for myself that has made it possible.

Far too much cooking now is about the tyranny of the recipe on the one hand and the absence of slowly acquired experience on the other. Cooking for yourself is a way of finding out what you want to cook and eat, rather than simply joining up the dots. Crucially, it's a way of seeing which things work, which don't, and how ingredients, heat, implements, vessels, all have their part to play. When I feel like a bowl of thick, jellied white rice noodles, not soupy but barely bound in a sweet and salty sauce, I'm not going to look up a recipe for them. I know that if I soak the noodles in boiling water until they dislodge themselves from the solid clump I've bought them in, fry 2 cloves of garlic with some knife-flattened scallions and tiny square beads of chopped red chili in a pan before wilting some greens and adding the noodles with a steam-provoking gush of soy and mirin, with maybe a teaspoon of black bean sauce grittily dissolved in it, it will taste wonderful, comforting, with or without chopped coriander or a slow-oozing drop or two of sesame oil. I can pay attention to texture and to taste. I know what sort of thing I'm going to end up with, but I'm not aiming to replicate any particular dish. Sometimes it goes wrong: I'm too heavy-handed with the soy and drench everything in brown brine, so that the sweet stickiness of the rice sticks is done for, and there's no contrast; I might feel, when eating, that the chili interrupts too much when I'm in the mood to eat something altogether gentler. These aren't tragedies, however. And, frankly, most often I get satisfaction simply from the quiet putting together of a meal. It calms me, which in turn makes me enjoy eating it more.

But cooking for yourself isn't simply therapy and training. It also happens to be a pleasure in itself. As most women don't have lives now whereby we're plunged into three family meals a day from the age of nineteen, we're not forced to learn how to cook from the ground up. I don't complain. Nor do I wish to make it sound as if cooking for yourself were some sort of checklisted culinary foundation course. The reason why you learn so much from the sort of food you casually throw together for yourself is that you're learning by accident, by osmosis. This has nothing to do with the culinary supremacism of the great chefs or those who'd ape them. Too many people cook only when they're giving a din-

NOODLES

GARLIC
SCALLIONS
CHILI
SOY

SESAME OIL

ner party. And it's very hard to go from zero to a hundred miles an hour. How can you learn to feel at ease around food, relaxed about cooking, if every time you go into the kitchen it's to cook at competition level?

I love the open-ended freedom of just puttering about in the kitchen, of opening the fridge door and deciding what to cook. But I like, too, the smaller special project, the sort of indulgent eating that has something almost ceremonial about it when done alone. I'm not saying I don't often end up with the au pair special, a bowl of cereal, or its street-princess equivalent, the phone-in pizza. But I believe in the rule of "Tonight Lucullus is dining with Lucullus."

BREAD AND CHEESE

Eating alone, for me, is most often a prompt to shop. This is where self-absorption and consumerism meet—a rapt, satisfyingly convoluted pleasure. The food I want most to buy is the food I most often try not to eat—a swollen-bellied tranche of cheese, a loaf of bread. These constitute the perfect meal. A slither of gorgonzola or coulommiers sacrificed on the intrusive and unyielding surface of a cracker at the end of dinner is food out of kilter. Just bread and cheese is fine to give others if you've shown the consideration of providing variety. But I want for myself the obsessive focus of the one huge, heady *baveuse* soft cheese, or else a wedge of the palate-burning hard stuff, a vintage Cheddar or strong blue—too much, too strong. If I'm eating a salty blue cheese, its texture somewhere between creamy and crumbly, I want baguette or a bitter, fudge-colored *pain au levain;* with Cheddar, real Cheddar, I want doughier white bread—whichever, it must be a whole loaf. I might eat tomatoes with the bread and cheese, but the tomatoes mustn't be in a salad, but left whole on the plate, to be sliced or chopped, *à la minute*. But, then, I love the takeout-shop equivalent of the TV dinner.

MUSHROOM SANDWICH

I am pretty keen on the culinary ethos of the Greasy Spoon, too—bacon sandwiches, fried-egg sandwiches, egg and bacon sandwiches, sausage sandwiches; none requires much in the way of attention and certainly nothing in the way of expertise. Even easier is a sandwich that on paper sounds fancier, a fab merging of diner and gourmet-store cultures. Get a large portobello mushroom, put it in a preheated 400°F oven stemmed and covered with softened butter, chopped garlic, and parsley for about 20 minutes; when ready, and garlicky, buttery juices are oozing with black, cut open a soft roll, small ciabatta, or chunk of baguette even, and wipe the cut side all over the pan to soak up the pungent juices. Smear with Dijon mustard, top with the mushroom, squeeze with lemon juice, sprinkle some salt, and add some chopped lettuce or parsley as you like; think of this as a fungoid—but, strangely, hardly less meaty—version of a steak sandwich. Bite in, with the juices dripping down your arm as you eat.

There are other memorable, more or less noncooking solitary suppers: one is a bowl of good canned tomato soup with some pale, undercooked, but overbuttered toast (crusts off for full nostalgic effect); another, microwave-zapped, mustard-dunked frankfurters (proper frankfurters, from a delicatessen, not those flabby, adulterated things from the supermarket). The difficulty is that if I have them in the house, I end up eating them while I wait for whatever I'm actually cooking for dinner to be ready. And my portions are not small to start off with. Two defenses, other than pure greed: I hate meagerness, the scant, sensible serving, and if I long to eat a particular thing, I want lots of it. I don't want course upon course, and I don't want excess every day. But when it comes to a feast, I don't know the meaning of enough.

Cooking for two is just an amplification of cooking for one (rather than the former being a diminution of the latter). To tell the truth, with my cooking and portion sizes, there isn't often a lot to choose between them. Many of the impulses that inform or inspire this sort of cooking are the same: the desire to eat food that is relaxed but at times culinarily elevated without loss of spontaneity; the pleasures of fiddling about with what happens to be in the fridge; and, as with any form of eating, the need to make food part of the civilized context in which we live.

LINGUINE WITH CLAMS

My absolutely favorite dinner to cook for myself is linguine with clams. I have a purely personal reason for thinking of fish, of any sort, as the ideal solitary food because I live with someone who's allergic to it. But my principle has wider application: fish doesn't take long to cook and tastes best dealt with simply, but because it has to be bought fresh needs enough planning to have something of the ceremonial about it. I don't know why *spaghetti alle vongole* (I use linguine because I prefer, here, the more substantial, more resistant, and, at the same time, more sauce-absorbent tangle they make in the mouth) is thought of as restaurant food, especially as so many restaurants ruin it by adding tomatoes. I have to have my sauce bianco.

The whole dish is easy to make. It is, for me, along with a steak béarnaise, unchallengeable contender for that great, fantasy Last Meal on Earth.

15 littleneck clams, well rinsed and scrubbed	2 tablespoons olive oil
⅓ pound linguine	½ dried red chili pepper or pinch dried red pepper flakes
salt	⅓ cup white wine or vermouth
1 garlic clove, minced or finely sliced	1–2 tablespoons chopped parsley

To further cleanse the clams of their sand, put them to soak in a sinkful of cold water to which you've added 1 tablespoon of baking soda. Allow to soak 1 hour.

Heat water for the pasta. When the water comes to the boil, add salt and then the linguine. Cook the linguine until nearly but not quite ready; you're going to give them a fractional amount more cooking with the clams and their winy juices. Try to time this so that the pasta's ready at the time you want to plunge it into the clams. Otherwise drain and douse with a few drops of olive oil.

In a frying pan with a lid, into which you can fit the pasta later, fry the garlic gently (it mustn't burn) in the olive oil and then crumble in the red chili pepper or add the pepper flakes. Add the clams to the pan. Pour the wine or vermouth over and cover. In 2 minutes, the clams should be open. Add the pasta, put the lid on again, and swirl about. In another minute or so, everything should have finished cooking and come together; the pasta will have cooked to the requisite tough tenderness, absorbed the salty, garlicky, winy clam juices, and be bound in a wonderful, almost pungent sea syrup. But if the pasta needs more cooking, clamp on the lid and give it more time. Chuck out any clams that have failed to open.

Add half the parsley, shake the pan to distribute evenly, and turn into a plate or bowl and sprinkle over the rest of the parsley. Cheese is not grated over any pasta with fish in it in Italy (nor indeed where garlic is the predominant ingredient, either) and the rule holds good. You need add nothing. It's perfect already. Serves 1.

COD WITH CLAMS

If you are afraid of tackling fish in general and of cooking seafood in particular, just reading this recipe will show you how easy it is, but doing it is even better. Ease of execution is not the same as ease of attainment, of course; as with all fish, cod is ruined by overcooking. This is one of those simple but essentially last-minute recipes that is easier to cook for one or two (or, at a pinch, four) than a huge tableful of waiting people. But if you want to turn this into dinner-party food, choose a firmer (and more expensive) fish such as monkfish and strain the sauce to get rid of the stray bits of fishy detritus. I have nothing against cod, but it can disintegrate a little when it sits around.

10 littleneck clams, well scrubbed
    and rinsed
pinch cayenne pepper
½ pound cod fillet with skin, cut
    from the top end of the fish,
    ¾–1¼ inches thick
scant tablespoon cornstarch
1 tablespoon unsalted butter plus
    1 teaspoon, cold (optional)

drop of oil
1 fat clove or 2 smaller garlic cloves,
    minced or sliced
4 tablespoons dry sherry
2 tablespoons water
1 tablespoon chopped chives
1 tablespoon chopped parsley

Throw out any clams that have remained open after cleaning. Put the clams to soak in a sinkful of cold water to which you've added 1 tablespoon of baking soda (this will help them disgorge sand) for 1 hour. Mix the cornstarch and the cayenne and dredge the cod lightly with it. You'll have some flour left over; just chuck it out.

In a wide, heavy-bottomed pan into which the cod will fit flat, melt the tablespoon of butter and the drop of oil. Add the garlic and cook for a bare minute, stirring all the time; above all, you don't want the garlic to burn or even burnish. Put the cod in, skin side down (I don't eat the skin; it's just that I find the cod is more likely to stay in one piece if I cook it like this) and cook for 2 minutes, then turn and cook on the other side. Flip back to its skin side and throw in the clams, then add the sherry and water and put the lid on. Cook for about 3 minutes. Take out the cod, remove or keep the skin, as you wish, and put the gaping-shelled clams around it on your plate; discard any that stay shut. Then let the juices left in the pan reduce by bubbling away for 2–3 minutes. If you want—and I do—whisk in the teaspoon of butter, divided into 2 or 3 tiny bits. Pour the juices over the fish on your plate. Throw over the chopped herbs. Eat with thickly cut bread that's good enough to be dunked without turning to pap.

Serves 1.

If you've never cooked moules marinière, you might balk at the thought—too fiddly, too unknown, too intimidating. But cook them once and you'll see that actually this is scarcely cooking at all. It is easy to buy cultivated mussels that don't require cleaning; then there's just shallots to chop, with some parsley and garlic, and the rest is about applying heat and liquid. Try this once and you won't need me to persuade you that it's easy. After that you will automatically start thinking of this as something you can cook quickly, with little effort and to great effect.

MOULES MARINIÈRE

I like a lot of winy mussel liquor here, so use more wine to start off with than you might find elsewhere. Traditionally, the onion or shallot, garlic, and parsley are just simmered in the wine at first; then, after the mussels are in and steamed open, everything's removed to the bowls, the liquid strained, and the butter whisked in. Do it that way, by all means, if you want to. More often I tend to do it as follows.

4½ pounds mussels, preferably cultivated	2 garlic cloves, minced or thinly sliced
4 tablespoons (½ stick) unsalted butter	5 tablespoons chopped parsley
2 shallots or 1 small onion, minced	1¼ cups white wine

If using uncultivated mussels, wash them well. Scrape off any barnacles and pull off any beards. Throw away the cracked mussels or those that stay open after you've rapped rudely and insistently on their shells. (And when cooked, throw away any mussel that has stayed closed.)

On medium heat, in a pot that will take all the mussels later and that has a lid, put in the butter with the shallots, the garlic, and about 1 tablespoon of the parsley. Stir about for a minute till the smell of the garlic rises and that particular, familiar fragrance wafts gloriously out of the pan. Add the wine; cook for another minute or so, with the lid on, but with the heat lowish. Then turn the heat up up up, throw in the cleaned mussels, and clamp the lid back on. Give the pot a shake occasionally. Look after 3 minutes and remove all the opened mussels you see, then put the lid on again and give them another 2 minutes. As you've got time while waiting for the rest of the mussels to open, I'd remove the empty shells of the already cooked mussels; it'll just make the plates a little less crowded, but it's hardly crucial. When the rest of the mussels are steamed open, remove them to your bowls (and you'll need huge ones). Take the pot off the heat; let the juices settle for a moment so any grit that might be in the mussels sits at the bottom. Then pour the juices carefully over each bowl of waiting, gaping shells, leaving the gritty bits at the bottom. Sprinkle over the remaining parsley. On the table put another couple of bowls or plates for the empty shells and a baguette or other good white bread.

Serves 2.

As I say, I do think it's a good idea to get into the swing of cooking fish. When I've got a lot of people eating, I might cook a fish pie (see pages 242 and 357), but when there's just me, or two of us, I don't mind a bit of the necessary last-minute flash in the pan. Fish, I think, is best fried in bacon fat, which you can't easily buy. If the bacon you get is good enough, you can provide the where-withal easily enough. I always mean to keep the fat left in the pan after frying bacon (I've given up grilling it; apart from anything else, I can't wait that long for the grill to heat up), but the immediate pleasure of dunking a piece of bread in the pan to soak up the salty juices, the delectable grease, often prevents me.

To cook exceptional but unfancy salmon for your supper, fry 2 slices of bacon, chopped fairly small (pancetta, cubed, would do as well), in a frying pan you've sprinkled with a little oil and then heated. When they're beginning to go from crisp to hard brown, remove the bacon to a waiting paper towel. Immediately put a piece of salmon in the pan, sear on each side, then cook for a minute or so, depending on the thickness of the fillet, at a lower heat. Put together some green leaves—just lettuce, or varieties of, and some scallions cut into rings—and leave them be for a moment while you transfer the fish to a plate. Then squeeze some lemon juice into the frying pan and pour the juices over the waiting undressed salad. Toss the salad, add the bacon bits and toss again, and add to the plate with the salmon. Sometimes I leave the salad in a bowl, cut the salmon into pieces, and add it, tossing, with the bacon.

EXCEPTIONAL SALMON

If I'm feeling in the mood for excess, I boil 2 eggs for about 6 minutes (some-where between soft and hard, yolk still oily but dense), peel and halve, and add them to the bowl of bacon and salmon salad. Or I take 2–3 tomatoes, briefly cover them in boiling water, then peel and seed them and add them in fat strips to the salad. This is one of the few times I'd consider eating tomatoes with fish. The following suggestion is another.

The world doesn't need another recipe for seared tuna. But the only way I like salade niçoise is inauthentically—that's to say, with fresh, not canned, tuna. This makes for good solitary eating; there's also enough cooking to make you feel that you're actually making something.

SALADE NIÇOISE

First, you have to see to your potatoes. What you want are boiled or steamed small waxy potatoes, about 6, cut into thick coins while still warm, then dribbled over with olive oil and given a good grinding of pepper, preferably white, but the color is no big deal. Meanwhile you should have put your 6–8-ounce piece of tuna, cut into thick short strips, to marinate in a tablespoonful of olive oil, a good squeeze of lemon juice or red wine vinegar, and a sprinkling of soy sauce. At the same time, put 1 tablespoon of capers, which, preferably, have been packed in salt rather than brine, to soak. Cook some trimmed and halved green beans, drain, plunge into cold water, and drain again. Put about 4 cherry tomatoes in a bowl, pour over some boiling water from a kettle and leave for a few minutes, then peel. Leave till cool, then quarter.

So—to the oil-drizzled potatoes in your bowl (I like a big shallow one, all to myself), add the tomatoes, green beans, some fresh marinated anchovies (the sort that lie in bowls in the slope-windowed fridge case at the specialty food shop), the capers, rinsed and drained well, and some torn-up bits of lettuce or baby spinach. Make a garlicky dressing, strong and astringent, pour over, and toss the salad gently. If you want eggs, boil for 6 minutes. I like them still oily-yolked, a good dripping gold, not dusty yellow. And if you're in fancy mode and are up to all that fiddly peeling, quails' eggs work well.

Meanwhile, heat your pan to seething, add oil, if you need it, then the tuna pieces; cook briefly but intensely on all sides. Throw in the marinade and let it bubble up, clinging stickily to the pieces of fish. Add the fish to the salad, toss, and eat. And d'you know, if you can get those silver-skinned, ivory-fleshed, fresh filleted anchovies, you don't even need to bother with the tuna.

SCALLOPS AND BACON

This is one of my favorites; it has just the right balance between nursery comfort and dining room elegance and takes hardly any time to cook—and thus is just what you need after a hard day's work. Properly speaking, it is more of a starter, but when there's just two of you eating, it makes a perfect supper almost in its entirety; all I'd add is a dark and leafy salad, dressed with walnut oil and lemon juice.

Always buy your scallops from a fishseller, never in a supermarket.

I teaspoon oil	freshly milled black pepper
4 slices bacon, halved lengthwise	I tablespoon unsalted butter
I0 bay or sea scallops	¼ cup dry sherry
I tablespoon all-purpose flour	I tablespoon chopped parsley

Put the oil in a heavy-bottomed frying pan and, when hot, add the bacon. Cook until crisp and remove. If using sea scallops, cut in half horizontally. Season the flour with the pepper and dredge the scallops all over in the flour. Add the butter to the pan and over a low to medium heat, fry the floury scallops, turning once, for 2–3 minutes or until they are just cooked through. Put the scallops and the bacon on a plate. Over the heat, add the sherry to the pan and pour it over the scallops and bacon. Sprinkle with the parsley and there you have it.

Serves 2.

When I'm in Italy, I love eating those small, fleshy shrimp that are scarcely cooked, but just turned with garlic, chili pepper, wine, and oil in a hot pan until they lose their gray transparency, becoming suddenly, shinily coral. You can make a variation of this at home with ingredients that can be kept easily at hand.

SHRIMP WITH GARLIC AND CHILI PEPPER

2 tablespoons olive oil	½ pound unshelled medium shrimp
½–1 fresh red chili, according to size and taste, minced	½ cup white wine
	salt, if needed
2 garlic cloves, chopped	1 tablespoon chopped parsley

Pour the olive oil into a wide, heavy-bottomed frying pan. Then add the chili and garlic and, over moderate to low heat, to infuse rather than to color, fry for 2 minutes, stirring all the time. Then turn the heat to high, add the shrimp, and stir-fry them for another 2 minutes or until they turn pink and are just, delicately, cooked; you want the flesh to stay tender. Pour in the white wine and let it bubble up. You don't want a liquid puddle around the shrimp, just enough wine to let the juices ooze into a winy sauce. Another minute or so should do it. Season with the salt, if necessary, and then turn into your bowl and sprinkle with the parsley. Eat with some good hunks of baguette. I eat these carapace, head, and all: one of the reasons I designate them for solitary dinner.

If you want, and you keep some to hand anyway, you can add a tablespoonful or so of brandy before throwing in the wine.

Serves 1.

I have a growing collection of Australian cookery books. The following recipe—for shrimp again—comes from Leonie Palmer's *Noosa Cook Book,* which is by way of being the food eaten at a small, paradisiacal-looking resort village on Australia's Queensland coast. The chief drawback to anything deep fried is that it has to be eaten right away. If there's you at the stove cooking, sending plate by plate out to your friends waiting at the table, then life's not going to be much fun. If there are only two of you, you can both stand by the stove and eat as the food comes hot and crunchy out of the pan. The quantities below make about 12 little patties.

FRIED SHRIMP CAKES

½ pound shrimp, minced

1 garlic clove, minced

2 scallions (white and green parts), minced

½ teaspoon salt

½ cup all-purpose flour

4 teaspoons sherry

olive oil

Process or blend the shrimp with the garlic, scallions, salt, flour, sherry, and enough water to make a thick batter. Let stand, covered with plastic film, for 1 hour. Then fry, in drops of 1 teaspoon, in the oil poured to a depth of 2 inches in a pan, for about a minute each side, or until golden brown. Drain on paper towels.

These are delicious with a fierce mayonnaise (see page 12 for method) made by substituting lime juice for the lemon, and with a handful of fresh chopped coriander added at the end. But if the shrimp cakes have exhausted your cooking capacity, then add some lime juice and chopped coriander to a bowlful of Hellman's. (Normally, I can't see why everyone is so keen on the stuff, but it lends itself well to this kind of adulteration; anyway, fried fish cakes of this sort seem to be able to handle the peculiar emulsification of factory-made mayo.) Or just squeeze the shrimp patties with fresh lime as you eat them.

One of the great advantages of eating alone or with one other person is that you don't have to take into account the squeamishness of the average, unknown eater. By this I don't mean that you might otherwise be inviting strangers to dinner, but that there are always going to be some people (someone's boyfriend, a newish friend) whose tastes you can't test with strange bits of internal organs or the spookier meats. The fewer people you're cooking for, the more permissive and inclusive you can be.

Ever since a friend of mine told me about a wittily conceived warm rabbit salad with baby radishes and carrots she'd eaten at The French House restaurant in London's Soho, I've wanted to appropriate it. I've made up my own version here. If you know someone who likes rabbit and who will appreciate the joke, you're lucky.

Have your butcher cut up a rabbit and bone two pieces; save the remaining for another use. Yes, this is very much an arranged salad, and normally I shun such restauranty displays of food. But when eating *à deux*, or indeed solo, you can generally get away with a greater level of cheffiness, if that's your secret desire, without losing your culinary integrity. Indeed, it's probably the best way to get it out of your system.

If you put the rabbit in the fridge to marinate when you get up in the morning, you won't have much to do when you get back from work in the evening.

PETER RABBIT IN MR. McGREGOR'S SALAD

½ cup yogurt

1 teaspoon extra-virgin olive oil

2 tablespoons wine vinegar

1 tablespoon Dijon mustard

4 garlic cloves, crushed with flat of knife

½ teaspoon dried thyme

2 pieces boned rabbit (about ⅔ pound
   meat)

2 tablespoons olive oil, for frying

1 package (5 ounces) mixed
   lettuce leaves

1 handful radishes, whole, quartered, or
   halved, depending on size, or sliced

1 handful baby carrots, halved
   lengthwise and across

FOR THE DRESSING

½ teaspoon Dijon mustard

scant tablespoon wine vinegar

salt and freshly milled black pepper

4 tablespoons extra-virgin olive oil

Make the marinade by mixing together the yogurt, oil, vinegar, mustard, garlic, and thyme. Add the rabbit meat, turn to make sure it's marinated on all sides, cover, and leave for 12 hours, or thereabouts, in the fridge.

At about the time you want to eat, preheat the oven to 400°F. Take the rabbit out of its marinade and wipe it dry with paper towels. On the stove, in a frying pan (preferably one that will go in the oven), pour the oil for frying and, when hot, sear the rabbit a minute or so each side till golden, then transfer the pan to the oven and bake for 25 minutes or until tender. Remove and let cool a bit; you want this to remain warm.

Divide the lettuce between the two plates. Arrange the radishes and carrots over the lettuces in any way that gives you pleasure. Make an emulsified dressing by putting the mustard and vinegar in a bowl, seasoning with the salt and pepper, and whisking. Continue whisking while you add the oil. Dribble over the salad. Put the warm rabbit pieces in the middle of each plate and serve. Serves 2.

LIVER WITH
MARSALA

Liver in general, and calves' liver in hands-up-in-horror particular, also belong to that genre of foodstuffs that cannot be served up confidently to a tableful of average eaters. But as I eat, so I write, and we often eat liver for lunch or dinner. To fry liver, melt a knob of butter in a frying pan with a drop of oil in it and fry 2–3 pieces of thinly sliced calves' liver (I estimate just over ¼ pound per person) in it, a minute or so a side, till still pink within, then remove to a plate, throw 2 tablespoons Marsala into the pan, let it bubble away until syrupy, and pour over the liver. The mashed potatoes we eat with this need more planning, but if I'm feeling lazy—and have the time—I just put 3 large baking potatoes in a 425°F oven for about 1½ hours before we count on eating and then, when they're thoroughly cooked inside, I scrape out the flesh and mash it with some butter and warmed milk to which I've added a good grating of fresh nutmeg and some salt and pepper.

The last time we ate this, I see from my notebooks, we had some damson plum purée (made with ½ pound damsons, cooked with ½ cup sugar and ¼ cup water) and custard afterwards—just perfect.

LIVER WITH SWEET ONIONS

I can't remember what I'd been reading—some Italian recipe for duck, I think, with a sauce of pomegranate juice thickened with the mashed liver from the duck. But it made me want to try to use pomegranate in a low-key way in my cooking. You get pomegranate juice the same way you get orange or lemon juice—use a juicer. I use one pomegranate here with an electric juicer, but I suspect if I were using a normal hand juicer, I'd need a couple to provide the same amount of juice. In place of fresh pomegranates, which have a short season, you could get some of the divinely, darkly syrupy Middle Eastern pomegranate molasses—which is sold in Middle Eastern and Greek shops and at some specialty food stores (or see page 459)—in which case, I'd dilute a tablespoon of the molasses in the same amount of wine or vermouth and add a bit of water (to taste), otherwise you'll have something much too sticky and strong. The extraordinary thing about the fresh pomegranate juice is how delicate and modestly fragrant it is.

2 tablespoons unsalted butter	1 tablespoon all-purpose flour
2 tablespoons olive oil	salt and freshly milled black pepper
1 medium onion, sliced very finely	½ pound calves' liver
juice from 1 pomegranate	

In a heavy-bottomed frying pan over medium to low heat, heat 1 tablespoon each of the butter and oil. Add the onions and cook until they're soft, about 10 minutes. Pour over half the pomegranate juice and a little water, 1–2 tablespoons, and cook for another 10 minutes or so until the liquid's absorbed and you have a soft, sweet, and bronzy-puce tangle of onions in the pan. Remove to warmed plates and tent over with foil to stop them cooling.

Add the remaining tablespoons of butter and oil to the frying pan. Mix the flour with the salt and pepper to taste and dredge the liver lightly in this mixture, and fry in the butter and oil for a minute or so on each side. Remove from the pan and put on the waiting plates with the onions. To the remaining pomegranate juice, add half its volume in water. Add this to the hot pan and deglaze. Correct the seasoning, if necessary, and pour over the liver and onions. I like this with plain boiled potatoes.

Serves 2.

Roast a duck and baste it with reduced pomegranate juice. To make the sauce, sauté and purée the duck liver with 1 teaspoon rosemary leaves sautéed with 1 minced onion in 1–2 teaspoons butter until soft and fragrant, some more pomegranate juice, and the well-skimmed juices from the pan. And duck is perfect for two; there just isn't enough meat to feed four, as is often, shockingly, recommended. Magrets (duck breasts), fried and with a bare sauce made from the pan juices deglazed with pomegranate juice and sprinkled with a few pomegranate seeds, is a lower-effort take on the same theme.

The difficulty with giving quail to large numbers of people is that the scale's wrong—too many little bits. When there's just two of you, it suits somehow; less itsy-bitsy and failed nouvelle. I have a special fondness for the marinated quail below because I remember cooking it with my sister Thomasina. Not that the cooking is so involved that it needs two people, but chopping and cooking, the companionability of the kitchen, is always sustaining. She adored this, and I suppose it just became incorporated into our comfortingly repetitive, private culinary repertoire. Together, we ate bowls of chicken broth with leeks and boiled potatoes; roast chicken and leeks in white sauce with boiled potatoes; spaghettini with tomato sauce and lots of fresh basil on top. On the evening of her arrival, at the beginning of any weekend she stayed with me, we always shared taramasalata eaten with warm pita with, alongside on the table, a plate of hot crisp grilled bacon and a bunch of scallions.

You can use good-quality beef and chicken bouillon to make the stock for this.

MARINATED, FLATTENED QUAIL

4 quails

1 tablespoon olive oil

½ tablespoon fresh rosemary leaves, minced

2 bay leaves, crumbled

1 fat garlic clove, minced

salt and freshly milled black pepper

2 tablespoons red wine or Marsala

½ cup meat or chicken stock or water

You have to start this well before you want to eat. If you don't mind fiddling about with meat first thing in the morning (and I don't), do it before going to work; otherwise, do it before you go to bed the previous night. With kitchen shears or any good scissors, trim the wing tips from the quails. Then cut along both sides of the backbone and remove the backbone, so the quails lie flat, or flattish. I do love a bit of surgery. Give the quails a wipe all over with paper towels. Mix together the oil, rosemary, bay leaves, and garlic. Sprinkle the quails, both sides, with the salt and pepper, then rub the herb mixture into the flesh. It looks as if there's not a lot of the herb mixture, I know, but what you have is enough. Remember, I said rub, not smear. Arrange in a single layer in a baking pan or something flat that will fit in the fridge, cover with foil or plastic film, and leave in the fridge for at least 6 hours, preferably twice as long.

When you want to eat, heat a large, heavy-bottomed frying pan (if you've got the wrists for it, a cast iron affair is ideal here)—or two if you don't think you can fit all four quail, flat out as they are, in one. If you don't feel safe using the pans you've got without adding oil first, then do so, otherwise just wipe off the marinade and put the quails, skin side down, in the hot pan for about 5 minutes. Prod or move with a spatula every now and again to make sure they don't stick; you may want to turn the heat down after the first searing minute. When the skin's dark and meat juices start appearing on the upper side of the quails, turn them over for a moment, just to sear the bone side. Remove to a large warmed plate and cover with foil.

Turn the heat back to high and to the pan with its meat juices add the red wine or Marsala, let half of it bubble away, and then pour in the stock or water. Let the stock bubble away in the pan until it is greatly reduced, becoming thick and syrupy. Pour these juices over the quail and eat. I like to eat this with my fingers, with bread, salad, tomatoes, scallions, ham or bacon, maybe some beans, elsewhere on the table. This is picnic food. And obviously, you can alter the marinade: try chili pepper, sesame oil, coriander, Thai basil, soy, the usual suspects, deglazing with sake and/or mirin.

Serves 2.

The fact that there might be only two of us eating would never prevent my roasting and eating a chicken (see page 7). Cold chicken sandwiches—bread cut thick, chicken, mango chutney, just possibly mayonnaise, and lettuce—are the dinner I dream of, for myself, the next day, or any time. I might want a bag of potato chips with it.

LEFTOVERS Leftovers come into their own when you're eating alone; I love a really fruitful mopping-up exercise. The fabulousness of leftovers is their randomness. I'm the sort of person who can't throw away half a cold cooked potato or a tablespoon of yesterday's gravy. But, of course, it's impossible to know what might be lurking in anyone else's fridge. If you have leftover potatoes, slice and fry them up. Or mash them into a patty with some pan-softened onions, some chopped cooked greens, maybe an egg yolk, then fry and pour the heated, slightly diluted, leftover gravy over them. Or bind the potatoes with the gravy and top with the egg, poached. Or cut a slice of leftover meat into strips and make a salad with warm potatoes, gherkins, chives, lettuce, and chopped hard-boiled egg. Whatever you have, eat it. Somehow, however lovingly I've done my shopping, it's the food I haven't planned on cooking that I want most to eat.

Other times, when there are two of you, you might want something not exactly fussier but more elegantly composed, dinner rather than supper. Actually, I'd have no compunction about making this chicken with morels just for me; it's hardly difficult, and I don't know what there is about it—maybe the creamy old-fashionedness—that makes me sometimes, definitely and distinctly, yearn for it. I have a feeling, which memory doesn't actually ratify, that my mother or grandmother must have cooked something similar. Anyway, this is what I do.

CHICKEN WITH MORELS

¼ cup dried morels

I tablespoon unsalted butter

I teaspoon garlic-infused olive oil (see
    page 459) or ordinary olive oil

4 chicken thighs

I small onion, minced

I garlic clove, minced, if not using
    garlic-infused oil

2 tablespoons Marsala

⅓ chicken bouillon cube

1–2 tablespoons mascarpone

salt and freshly milled black pepper

1–2 tablespoons chopped parsley

Put the morels into a measuring cup and pour over hot (but not boiling) water to reach the I-cup mark. Leave for at least 30 minutes.

Put the butter and oil into a frying pan that has a lid and in which the 4 chicken thighs will fit snugly enough, and, when hot, put the chicken pieces in, skin side down. Cook for about 10 minutes, maybe slightly less, until the skin has lost its goose-pimply pallor and has become a warm golden brown. Remove to a plate, skin side up.

Into the pan now put the onion and garlic, too, if you haven't used that incredibly useful standby, the garlic-infused oil, and cook at a low to medium heat until soft.

Drain the morels, reserving the soaking liquid. Strain this brown and aromatic water

(I use a tea strainer) into a small saucepan and heat. Inspect the morels (you can do this by feel, using fingers), remove any grit or gravel, and add the morels to the pan with the onion. Put back the chicken pieces, this time skin side up, and add the Marsala. To the mushroom-soaking liquid, add the ⅓ bouillon cube and dissolve. Pour this into the pan too and put the lid on. Let it bubble away, but not vociferously so, for 20–25 minutes, by which time the chicken should be cooked through. Remove the chicken thighs to a plate while you reduce the sauce. You needn't remove the morels (though you can), but do push them to the edges of the pan so they don't get hit by the full blast of the fire. Using an ordinary tablespoon, ladle out any fat you might see collecting about the edges of this still-fluid sauce; some chicken pieces can give off a lot of watery fat.

Turn the heat up high and let the mushroomy, chickeny, Marsala-deepened sauce thicken; depending on the dimensions of your pan, the material it is made of, and the burner you're using, this could take 5 minutes or it could take 15. And it depends on how much sauce you want at the end. I stop when the sauce in the pan looks as if it could be generously spooned over and around the chicken pieces without turning it into soup. When the sauce is the right consistency to your mind (and this isn't a crucial decision: it will taste delicious whatever), add the mascarpone. One heaping tablespoon should be enough, but add more if you want a paler, richer, more buttery sauce. Sometimes I add a glug more Marsala too. Taste and season with the salt and pepper.

Put the chicken pieces back in the pan, spooning the oaky-brown sauce over them. Sprinkle with the freshly chopped parsley and serve—with plain boiled or steamed waxy potatoes or a floury mound of absorbent mashed potatoes, or just plain boiled rice—and eat a pale, crisp, and astringent green salad after.

Serves 2.

STEAK
BÉARNAISE

The essence of cooking for two exists in just one word: steak. I'm not saying I wouldn't cook it just for me, but there's something solid, old-fashioned, and comforting about the two of you sitting down and eating steak. Too often, when I'm at home alone, I waft along, as you do, in a tangle of noodles, lemongrass, and suchlike. Steak béarnaise is my dream. Fry a steak as a steak is meant to be fried, in a hot pan and for a short time. Turn to page 16 for a recipe for béarnaise. I don't do frites. Green salad made bloody with the steak's juices and some real baguette more than make up, in my book, for my french-fry deficiency. Just as I think that roast chicken is so good that I need a lot of persuading to cook a chicken any other way, so I feel about steak that it is perfect simply grilled or fried. But steak au poivre, aux poivres, peppered steak, whichever handle you like to put on it, is, in shorn form, a forceful contender. For me, it's better without the addition of cream; I like my steak butch, brown and meaty. This is hardly the orthodox approach, and I can see that you might feel a culinary classic ought to be respected. Sometimes I'd even agree. Just go cautiously. You don't want to feel you're having dessert at the same time.

I use either black peppercorns, half black, half white or, more often, a many-berried pepper mixture; some of the mixture isn't strictly speaking pepper at all, but I like its warm aromatic quality, rather mellower than the heat of pepper alone. I have been meaning for years now to buy a coffee grinder especially for spices, but still haven't managed to do so, and use a pestle and mortar.

STEAK AU POIVRE

2 boneless strip steaks (12–14 ounces
    each), about 1½ inches thick
scant tablespoon olive oil
3 tablespoons peppercorns, coarsely
    ground (see above)

3 tablespoons unsalted butter, plus
    more if desired
3 tablespoons brandy
salt, if needed

Using a pastry brush, if you've got one, paint the steaks on both sides with oil; you should need not more than a teaspoon on each side. Then dredge the oily steaks in the ground peppercorns—you want a good, crusty coat. If the peppercorns are too coarse, they'll just fall off; if they're too fine, you won't stop coughing when you eat them.

In a heavy-bottomed frying pan, put the remaining oil to heat up. Add the steaks and sear over high heat on each side; then, over moderate heat, add the butter and another drop of olive oil and cook the steaks for about another 3 minutes a side or to requisite bloodiness. Remove to warmed plates. Turn the heat up to high again, then pour in the brandy, stirring well all the time to deglaze the pan. When you've got a thick syrupy glaze, taste it; you may want to add salt, and you may want to whisk in a little butter just to help it all taste and look smooth and amalgamated. This, too, is where you could add your dollop of cream if you wanted. I've also, instead of the brandy, used Marsala, without which I'm pathologically incapable of existing, and it was dee-licious.

Serves 2.

Real carpaccio, as invented by Harry's Bar and served up in modish joints all over the northern and southern hemispheres, really is restaurant food—though for mechanical rather than culinary reasons. If you've got a slicer or can otherwise be sure of producing the correct, tissue-paper-thin slices, by all means try it. Otherwise, do what any sensible, greedy person would do and work along the lines of the recipe in Richard Whittington and chef Alastair Little's seminal cookbook, *Keep It Simple*. This is my adaptation; some quantities are changed, ingredients modified. I don't use the truffle oil the authors specify because the first time I did this, I didn't have any. Now I feel that it might interfere, so I use olive oil to dress the salad and replace their specified balsamic vinegar with lemon juice. And I use less cheese. But that's what you should do when cooking—you draw on your own tastes and adapt according to your personality. I wouldn't suggest substituting like for unlike, or not paying respect to the natural lie of a dish, but lemon, vinegar, oil, schmoil—don't get het up.

HOME CARPACCIO OF BEEF

½ pound beef fillet, cut from the tail end

vegetable oil

4 tablespoons peppercorns, coarsely
   ground

3 cups trimmed arugula (or other soft
   leafy salad green)

2–3 tablespoons olive oil

salt

½ lemon

2–3 ounce piece Parmesan

If the meat's been in the fridge, take it out a good 30 minutes before cooking. Put a griddle or cast-iron frying pan over high heat to get really hot. Brush the fillet all over with a little oil, then dredge to coat with the peppercorns.

Fill a bowl with ice water. Put the fillet to sear in the hot pan, and give it 60 seconds on each side—and that's all six sides, the ends as well as the top and bottom, so that it's encased in searedness. Use tongs, ones that won't pierce the meat, to turn and hold the meat in place as you sear. Plunge the seared meat into the ice water, then take out, pat dry with paper towels, and leave to cool. You can do this in advance and put it in the fridge for a few days.

When you're ready to eat, take the meat out of the fridge and let it get to room temperature. Strew the arugula on 2 plates. I never wash salad greens if I can get away with not, but arugula can be sandy, so wash it. Dribble the olive oil over the salad, sprinkle some salt and squeeze some lemon juice on, and, using your hands, turn to coat well but lightly.

Carve—cutting slightly on the diagonal—the fillet into thinnish but not waferlike slices, but you can go chunkier if you want, and divide between the plates. Using a vegetable peeler, shave the cheese into thin curls and let them fall over the top of the steak and salad. I rather like this with some steamed waxy potatoes that, when cooked, are peeled and sliced into thick coins and laid, warm, on the plate with the salad, under the cold dull-ruby slices of fillet.

Serves 2.

Man cannot live on steak alone. Anyone who really likes eating likes stew. This one, which comes via English food journalist Nigel Slater's *Real Cooking,* is as wonderful as you'd expect anything of his to be. I love his writing and his food, both of which inspire and comfort—and at the same time, which is more than most of us deserve. This particular recipe has another virtue—it's the perfect amount for two slathering, stew-deprived people or even one, as I can testify.

LAMB AND BEAN BRAISE

Apart from some initial rough chopping, this is an almost hands-free exercise— low effort, high yield. You do need to soak the beans and steep the lamb, but if you do them before you leave for work in the morning, you'll be ready to go when you get back in the evening. I suppose you could always use canned beans, but I can't honestly say that turning on the tap, and later the stove, are either of them fearsome strains.

1½ cups dried cannellini beans	5 peppercorns
2 shoulder lamb chops, each about 2½ inches thick	1 large dried chili, or 2 small
	1 orange
1 medium onion, cut into wedges	1 bottle red wine
2 bay leaves	3 tablespoons olive oil
few thyme springs	2 portobello mushrooms, quartered or
2 celery stalks, sliced	cut into eighths, depending on size
2 medium carrots, peeled and sliced	1 tablespoon balsamic vinegar
3 garlic cloves, squashed with the flat of a knife	salt and freshly milled black pepper

Soak the beans in cold water for a day or overnight. Put the lamb, onion, herbs, celery, carrots, garlic, peppercorns, and chili in a large bowl. Shave off some orange peel— 2½ inches or so, it isn't crucial—with a vegetable peeler and add it to the dish of meat and vegetables, along with the rest of the orange, pith, peel, and all, sliced thickly. Pour over the wine to cover. If you want to drink wine with the stew, get two bottles (or indeed more). Put the bowl of meat and vegetables somewhere cool or in the fridge.

When the beans have soaked and the meat steeped, drain the beans, put them in a saucepan, cover by about 4 inches with cold water, bring to the boil, and then let boil for about 20 minutes. Put the lid on and remove from the heat.

Strain the meat and vegetables over another bowl; in other words, reserve the wine. Throw out the orange slices, but keep the strip of peel; I get rid of the chili at this stage, too.

Now get a heavy-bottomed casserole with a lid that goes with it and heat the oil in it. Pick out the bits of lamb from the sieve or colander and brown on all sides. Remove to a plate and put the rest of the stuff that you had marinating in the casserole to soften, adding the mushrooms. Cook for 10 minutes or so and then pour in the wine from the marinade (and the rest of the bottle, if you didn't use it all earlier). Add the drained beans.

Bring to the boil over medium heat, but turn it down just before it actually boils. Add the balsamic vinegar (though it's wonderful without, too) and put the lamb back in. Cover the pot with foil. Stick on the lid tightly. This is to help stop the liquid evaporating.

Leave to simmer gently for about 1½ hours. The meat should be tender enough to come away from the bone and the beans soft enough to squish, at the push of a wooden spoon, against the side of the dish. Prod both meat and beans to check.

Turn up the heat and cook, uncovered, at a vigorous bubble until all of a sudden the juices thicken. This may take about 10 minutes, but be vigilant; it may not need to be much more concentrated than it is already. Season with the salt and pepper. I eat this in a shallow soup bowl, with a hunk or three of good bread, buttered or not, as I feel.

Serves 2.

PEAS

Every day I thank God, or his supermarket stand-in, for frozen peas. For me, they are a leading ingredient, a green meat, almost. I don't eat them that much straight as a vegetable, but I'd hate to have to cook without them. The almost instant soup—a handful of peas, some stock, a rind of cheese, whatever's to hand—that I make for a sweetly restoring supper is itemized in Fast Food on page 159. The pea risotto that follows is another regular. Risotto is best suited to two. I like relative peace in which to cook it, and I prefer handling small quantities. It is also the world's best comfort food.

The quantities I use might be nearer those ordinarily specified for four, but when I cook risotto I don't want to eat anything else after. And I feel a pang if there's only enough for one middling-sized flat puddle of the stuff.

PEA RISOTTO

I specify frozen young peas, simply because that's what I always use. I have used real peas, just shelled, to make *risi e bisi,* the fabulously named Venetian slurpily soft risotto, or thick rice soup, however you like to think of it, complete with pea-pod stock. But to be frank, if you don't grow peas yourself, then there is not a huge advantage in using fresh ones. By the time they're in the market, they're big and starchy and without that extraordinary, almost floral, scent, that heady but contained sweetness of peas just picked from the garden.

On the whole, I take the peas out and let them thaw before using them. But I don't see that it makes much difference.

As for stock: I haven't specified any in particular. When I can, I use ham stock—which, because of my stock-making obsession, I usually have in the freezer; otherwise I make up some using vegetable bouillon cubes. I wouldn't use a dark beef stock here, but any chicken, veal, or light broth would be fine.

4 tablespoons (½ stick) unsalted butter	whole nutmeg
	drop of oil
1 cup frozen young peas	2 shallots or 1 small onion, minced
4 cups stock (see headnote), hot	1 cup arborio or Canaroli rice
2 tablespoons freshly grated Parmesan, plus more for the table	⅓ cup white wine or vermouth
	salt and freshly milled black pepper
freshly milled black pepper	

Put about 1 tablespoon of the butter in a saucepan and, when it's melted, add the peas and cook, stirring every now and again, for 2 minutes. Remove half the peas and to the remaining half in the pan add a ladleful of the stock. Put a lid on the pan and let cook gently for about 5 minutes or so till soft. Purée this mixture—I use the miniprocessor I used to use for baby food—with 1 tablespoon each of the grated Parmesan and remaining butter and a grating each of pepper and nutmeg.

Melt another tablespoon of the butter, with the drop of oil in it, in a pan. Cook the shallots, stirring with a wooden spoon, for about 4 minutes, then add the rice and stir till every grain glistens with the oniony fat. Pour in the wine or vermouth (last time I did this I used Chambéry and it was fabulous; it seemed to add to the grassy freshness of the peas) and let it bubble away and absorb. Then add a ladleful of the hot stock (I keep it on low on the neighboring burner) and stir until this too is absorbed. Carry on in this vein, patiently, for another 10 minutes, then add the whole, just sautéed peas, and then start again, a ladleful of stock at a time. In about another 8 minutes or so, the rice should be cooked and the risotto creamy. Taste to see if it needs any more cooking or liquid. It's hard to be precise; sometimes you'll find you have stock left over, at others you'll need to add water from the kettle.

When you're happy with it, add the buttery pea and Parmesan purée and beat it in well. Taste, season with the salt and pepper as needed, then beat in the remaining Parmesan and butter. You can sprinkle over some chopped parsley (and as I've got it growing in the garden I have no reason not to), but the lack of it won't give you any grief.

Serves 2.

The first time I made pea soufflé (in response to an urgent request), I had no cheese in the house other than some processed Gruyère and Emmental slices, and so had to chop those up small in place of the real grated stuff—and may I tell you they were absolutely delicious. I now keep them in the fridge and I always have egg whites in the freezer. Making a soufflé is no longer a kitchen requirement for the aspiring hostess, but it's always worth tackling recipes that scare you with their attendant mythologies, just so that you're no longer cramped by that lurking fear. Read carefully and you'll see that absolutely no culinary pyrotechnics are called for.

PEA SOUFFLÉ

2 tablespoons unsalted butter	½ cup milk
I cup frozen young peas	2 eggs plus I extra egg white
4 ounces Gruyère, grated	salt and freshly milled black pepper
2 tablespoons Italian 00 or all-purpose flour	pinch ground mace or freshly grated nutmeg

Preheat the oven to 400°F and put a baking pan in it to heat up. Butter a soufflé dish with about a 2-cup capacity, if you've got one. Otherwise, any same-sized casserole or container, preferably round, should do. If you've got any Parmesan at hand, then you could grate some over the buttered soufflé dish, tapping the dish so that it's lightly covered with it, much as you would when flouring a greased cake pan.

Put I tablespoon of the butter in a saucepan and cook the peas in it till soft. Purée them with the grated cheese and set this aside while you make the paste-thick white sauce. Melt the remaining butter in a heavy-bottomed saucepan and stir in the flour. Cook, still stirring, for 2–3 minutes, then, off the heat, very gradually whisk in the milk. When all is smoothly amalgamated, put back over low heat and cook, stirring frequently, for about 5 minutes or until the sauce is thick and all flouriness gone; if you're using all-purpose flour, you may find that you need another 5 minutes. Let the white sauce cool slightly.

Separate the eggs and put the yolks aside. If you've got a lemon in the house, slice it in half and wipe its cut side around the interior of a bowl—preferably copper or else other metal. Put in all the egg whites and a pinch of salt and whisk until they stand in soft peaks. You want the whites firm, but not dry or stiff.

Leave the whites for a moment and add I yolk to the white sauce, beating well, then add the other and beat that in. Then beat in the cheese and pea purée. Taste and season with the salt and pepper and sprinkle on the mace or add the nutmeg. Remember the egg whites will damp down the flavor. Take a clean spoon and add a big dollop of the whisked whites to the now pea-green sauce. Beat this in as roughly as you like; you could use an electric whisk and it wouldn't matter. The idea is just to lighten the mixture to make it easier to fold the remaining egg whites in gently, which you should now do.

When the whites have been serenely and lightly folded in, pour the mixture into the prepared dish—it should be about three quarters full—and put it on the baking sheet in the oven. Immediately turn the heat down to 350°F and cook for about 30 minutes or until the soufflé is risen to well above the rim of the dish. I'm presuming you've got an oven with a glass door and a light that works so that you can see the action inside.

Take out of the oven and eat immediately. This is intended to be supper in its entirety; it's not a delicate item before something more substantial. Mind you, some prosciutto eaten alongside is not a bad idea.

Serves 2.

In theory, at least, I prefer meatier, chunkier soups (preferably with pasta in, too), but when I need soothing rather than bolstering, this nostalgic chicken soup is unparalleled.

CREAM OF CHICKEN SOUP

Use slender leeks for this, if you can find them. Discard most of the green part— you want this creamily white, not a pale, lurid lime green. I happily use chicken bouillon cubes in place of the stock here; half of one in 1¼ cups water will be fine.

4 tablespoons (½ stick) unsalted butter	1 tablespoon Italian 00 or all-purpose flour
3 slender leeks (white part only) or 1 regular, sliced very finely	pinch salt
1¼ cups chicken stock	pinch ground mace
1¼ cups milk	1 egg yolk
2 bay leaves	3–4 tablespoons heavy cream to taste
1 garlic clove, peeled	
1 free-range chicken cutlet (½ whole breast; about 6 ounces)	

Put 2 tablespoons of the butter in a heavy-bottomed saucepan, melt it, and in it cook the leeks gently until soft. Meanwhile, put the stock and milk in a saucepan with the bay leaves, garlic, and chicken. Bring to the boil, turn down the heat, and simmer until the chicken is just tender. I know it sounds not very long, but about another 5 minutes should do it. A couple or so minutes before the chicken's ready, the leeks should be soft and cooked enough. Into the leek mixture stir the flour and cook on a low heat, stirring, for a couple of minutes.

By this time the chicken should be ready to come out, so remove it and pour the milk mixture into the floury leeks, stirring while you do so. Bring this to just below the boil, stirring occasionally. While you're not stirring, shred or finely chop the chicken and return it to the saucepan. Add the salt and mace and keep cooking over a lowish heat, stirring occasionally, for 5 minutes. Add the remaining butter and cook in the same way for another 5 minutes. If the soup looks as if it's getting too thick and white-saucy, just add a glug of milk or as much as you feel you need.

Pour into a blender in batches of about 1 cup of liquid at a time and whizz and then push through a strainer back into the rinsed-out saucepan.

Put back on the heat, stirring until warm enough to eat. Mix the egg yolk and cream together and, off the heat, stir into the soup.

Serves 1–2.

BUTTERNUT SQUASH AND PASTA SOUP

This is robuster stuff altogether. I make it for lunch when it's cold and I want to cook something easy but with some distracting chopping involved. You can use best-quality vegetable bouillon cubes to make the stock for this.

½ tablespoon olive oil	2½ cups vegetable stock
½ small onion, minced	1 bay leaf
8–9 ounces butternut squash, peeled and cut into ½-inch dice	2 ounces ditalini or other soup pasta
	salt, if needed
¼ cup white wine or vermouth	Parmesan, for grating at table

Put the oil in a biggish, heavy-bottomed pan on the stove and, when hot, add the onion. Cook for about 10 minutes, stirring frequently, until soft, then add the squash and turn well in the pan for 2 minutes. Pour in the wine, let it bubble up, then add the stock and bay leaf. Bring to the simmering point, then leave to simmer away for about 10 minutes. Take out a ladleful, purée it, then put it back in the pan. Turn up the heat and add the ditalini. Cook for 10–12 minutes until the pasta is cooked. Taste and add salt, if needed, remembering that Parmesan will be added to each serving, then ladle this thick, sweet stew of a soup into your bowl. Grate the Parmesan over as you eat.

Serves 2.

I see in my notes I've called this Sunday Night Chicken Noodle, and it's true I do often cook this, or a version of it, on Sunday nights. But if I do, I almost certainly have to have a rerun of it on Monday evening. You can use chicken bouillon cubes, the best you can buy, to make the stock for this.

SUNDAY NIGHT CHICKEN NOODLE

4 tablespoons sake

3 tablespoons mirin

I tablespoon soy sauce

I fat garlic clove crushed with flat
   of knife

I dried red chili pepper

I chicken cutlet (about 6 ounces), cut
   diagonally into ¼-inch strips

4 ounces fresh noodles

handful choi sum or other Asian green

2 cups chicken stock

I tablespoon vegetable oil plus few
   drops sesame oil

I tablespoon chopped coriander

Mix the sake, mirin, soy sauce, garlic, and chili in a bowl. Add the chicken and coat with this marinade. Leave for an hour.

Cook the noodles in boiling salted water and throw in the choi sum during the last 2 minutes of cooking. Drain. Heat up the stock.

Into a hot wok or frying pan pour the oils and, when they in turn are hot, throw in the pieces of chicken and toss about till cooked, about 3 minutes. Pour over the marinade and, when it's bubbled nearly away and the chicken is glossy and dark, put the noodles in a bowl, pour the stock over them, and top with the pieces of wok-bronzed chicken. Sprinkle over the coriander and eat.

Serves 1.

Pasta is inevitably, these days, what one eats just in the normal run of things in the evening. You don't need a recipe for this any more than you do for bacon, lettuce, and tomato sandwiches, but this is not meant to be a manual to cook from so much as a prompt or companion guide to eating. These, then, are suggestions based on a presumption of interest rather than barked instructions to be carried out to the patronizing letter. At home, alone, especially if I've been working late, I make a vast bowl of spaghetti aglio olio (sometimes, peperoncino): just spaghetti, or spaghettini, turned in some olive oil, in which some fat cloves of garlic have been turned till golden and then discarded, with maybe a sprinkling of dried red chili pepper. A glass of cold beer is wonderful with it. If you are so exhausted you want an even easier version, then I suggest you buy a bottle of garlic-infused olive oil and use it to make the dish.

LINGUINE
WITH BACON This is a particularly good, particularly low-effort supper. Get in from work. Run your bath. Preheat the oven to 350°F. Put some bacon slices cut into ¼-inch strips on a baking tray with a few cloves of garlic, peeled and minced, thrown over. Drizzle with about 1 tablespoon olive oil. Put the water for the pasta on to boil and put the tray of garlic-strewn bacon in the oven. When the water's boiling, add salt and throw in the pasta—linguine or spaghetti—and run up to your bath, taking with you the timer, set for 10 minutes (the pasta should take about 12 minutes). When the timer goes off, rush down in your towel, taste the pasta and, when it's ready, drain it, reserving a cup of the water. Take the cooked bacon out of the oven and toss with the pasta, adding a drop or two of the cooking water if you think it needs lubrication. Decant into a bowl and, if you like, take it back up to the bath with you.

SPAGHETTI
CARBONARA This is my favorite—along with all my other favorites. I love the buttery, eggy creaminess of the sauce, saltily spiked with hot cubed pancetta—it's comforting, but not in a sofa-bound kind of way. It feels like proper dinner, only it takes hardly any time to cook. This is my most regular dinner for two; I keep, at all times, the wherewithal to make it in the house. You can add heavy cream to the egg-and-cheese mixture if you want—a couple of tablespoons, but then use 2 yolks only, rather than one yolk and one whole egg—but this takes it away from being something one can get together with ingredients at hand. On this ease-of-assembly principle, do by all means substitute 3 or 4 slices of bacon, cut into strips, for the pancetta. But it's not so hard to buy several 4-ounce chunks of pancetta at one time and just bag them up and freeze them separately; this, really, is what I'd advise.

½ pound spaghetti	I whole egg
4 ounces pancetta, cut into ¼-inch dice	¼ cup freshly grated Parmesan
or in ¼-inch strips	freshly milled black pepper
2 teaspoons olive oil	whole nutmeg
4 tablespoons vermouth or white wine	I generous tablespoon unsalted butter
I egg yolk	

Put some water on and, when it's boiling, add a decent amount of salt and then, when it's boiling again, the pasta. Italians say the water pasta cooks in should be as salty as the Mediterranean. Put the pancetta in a frying pan with the oil on medium to high and fry for about 5 minutes, maybe more, until it is beginning to crisp. Throw in the vermouth and let it bubble away for about 3 minutes until you have about 2 teaspoons or so of syrupy wine-infested bacon fat. Remove from the heat, unless you have so brilliantly timed it that the egg mixture is prepared and the pasta cooked.

For the egg mixture, simply beat the yolk, the whole egg, and cheese. Season with the pepper, grate in some nutmeg to taste (the pancetta or bacon and the cheese should provide enough salt), and mix with a fork. When the pasta's ready, quickly put the pancetta pan back on the heat, adding the butter as you do so. Give the pasta a good shake in the colander (but mind it isn't too drained) and then turn it into the hot pan. Turn it with a spatula and a wooden spoon, or whatever works for you, and then when it's all covered and any excess liquid absorbed, turn off the heat (take the pan away from the burner if your stove's electric), pour the egg mixture over the bacony pasta, and quickly and thoroughly turn the pasta so that it's all covered in the sauce. Be patient; whatever you do, don't turn the heat back on or you'll have scrambled eggs. In time, the hot pasta along with the residual heat of the pan will set the eggs to form a thickly creamy sauce that binds and clings lightly to each strand of pasta.

This makes two platefuls; it's up to you whether you conclude this is enough for one or two of you. I incline toward two for lunch and one for dinner.

The Italians do a wonderful pasta sauce that is really just the meat juices left in the roasting pan after their particularly flavorsome way of cooking what they call *rosbif*. They make it with the rosemary-spiked juices left from a roast chicken, too, and you can adapt this to the last-minute, pantry school of cookery by melting part of a crumbled bouillon cube in some rosemary-flecked butter. Again, I like linguine here, but spaghetti's good, too.

While about ¼ pound of pasta is cooking—I'm taking it you're eating this alone, but just double for two of you—melt 2 tablespoons butter in a saucepan and add 1 teaspoon olive oil and 2 peeled garlic cloves, crushed with the flat of a knife. When the butter starts fizzing, throw in the very finely chopped leaves from a finger-length sprig of rosemary. When the cloves of garlic turn brown, remove them and in their place crumble in about half a meat or chicken bouillon cube, preferably Italian. Turn in the pan, adding another dollop of butter, and then add 1 tablespoon white wine or vermouth and 1 tablespoon water and carry on cooking for a minute or so before spooning in another nut of butter.

When the pasta's ready, drain it, reserving a small cupful of water. Toss the pasta in the stock sauce, adding some of the water if the pasta absorbs too much of the liquid too fast. Grate over some Parmesan and eat.

PASTA WITH
UNPESTOED
PESTO

In summer, when you might consider eating outside, make a large bowl, just for the two of you, of linguine with what I think of as pesto in its discrete parts: we're talking culinary deconstruction here. While the pasta's cooking, pour some preferably Ligurian olive oil into a large frying pan and throw in some peeled cloves of garlic. Cook over gentle heat until the garlic colors and its scent wafts upward. Remove the cloves from the pan and the pan from the heat. Roughly tear up or shred a mound of basil leaves, set aside, and, in a second dry frying pan, toast a handful or so of pine nuts. When the pasta's ready, drain it, toss it in the garlic-infused olive oil, then transfer to a warm bowl. Grate over some Parmesan, then, using a vegetable peeler, shave in some pecorino (and, frankly, it doesn't matter if you use Parmesan for both grating and shaving; who wouldn't, really?) and sprinkle with the toasted pine nuts. Toss well, throw over all but a small handful of the basil leaves, and turn again. Grate a little more cheese over and sprinkle with the remaining shredded basil leaves. Leave the bottle of oil within reach.

Mostly, when I'm cooking some pasta for myself I want it to take as little time as possible. But I don't mind that the recipe that follows is, well, not laborious, but time-consuming. I just love it. It's a version of the Venetian bigoli in salsa, the salsa in question being a pungent, long-cooked, almost emulsified sauce of onions and anchovies. Bigoli are the only pasta with an excuse for being whole wheat—that's how they are traditionally made. I made this the first time, though, to use up some spelt pasta—pasta made with farro—I had. I'd been writing a piece for *Vogue* on farro and had been sent, as part of the requested consignment, some pasta made with this grain. I tried it once and loathed it. Then it occurred to me that with a heartier sauce, something with real depth to it, it might work. I tried this and was transported, converted. I've made it since many times with ordinary spaghetti—which works fine—and you can use any whole-wheat version of pasta. And any long, hollow pasta, such as perciatelli or bucatini (in effect, non-wholewheat bigoli) is wonderful here. If you're intent on locating spaghetti di farro, turn to page 461 for a source.

PASTA WITH ANCHOVY SAUCE

My mother always soaked anchovies in milk, just as she did kidneys and chicken livers; therefore, so do I. The inclusion of Marsala is a non-Venetian innovation, but its dry, deep mellowness works well with the fierce saltiness of the anchovies.

What makes this ideal for me for eating alone is that I don't need to worry about any other person's tiresomeness about anchovies.

6 anchovy fillets in olive oil

4 tablespoons milk plus more,
   if needed

2 tablespoons olive oil

1 medium onion, sliced very finely (use
   a processor, if possible)

2 tablespoons Marsala

4 ounces regular or whole-wheat long
   or shaped dry pasta (see above)

2 heaping tablespoons chopped parsley

Wipe the anchovies with a paper towel, put them in a small dish—a ramekin, say—and cover with some of the milk; about 2 tablespoons should do it. In a heavy-bottomed frying pan, heat 1 tablespoon of the oil and then add the onion. Cook uncovered over low heat for about 5 minutes, then add the Marsala and cook for about 30 minutes, till you have a soft, golden, oniony mush. You may need to sprinkle in some water while it's cooking to keep it from drying up or sticking to the pan. If you make a lid out of foil and press down on the top of the onions (rather than the pan), this will help. Then turn up the heat and cook uncovered for 1–2 minutes, stirring to prevent sticking. While all this is going on, put on some water for the pasta.

Remove the anchovies from the milk and chop them finely. Add them to the onion mixture, stir well, pour in the milk in which they'd been soaking, and keep stirring. When the anchovies have been incorporated into the purée, add the remaining milk, the remaining oil, and about half the parsley. Stir well and remove from the heat. Taste to see if you'd like some more milk; it will soften the taste and loosen the texture. When the pasta's cooked, drain it, and then quickly but thoroughly turn it in the warm anchovy and onion sauce. Transfer to your bowl or plate and sprinkle over the remaining parsley.

Serves 1.

When I'm cooking for myself, as you see, I want strong tastes. This kale with chorizo is one of my regular fast hot lunches.

KALE WITH CHORIZO AND POACHED EGG

Make sure you can get proper chorizo, and I mean here the fresh (or semi-dried, rather) sausages, not the larger salami-like kinds. Sometimes fresh chorizo come in horseshoe-shaped linked sausage loops; in which case use half. If you don't like kale or it's not around, then a package of baby spinach salad, just wilted in the pan in which the chorizo's been cooking, will do—indeed more than do. It's a pleasurable variant rather than forced substitution.

6 ounces kale, stemmed and torn in small pieces	I chorizo (about 4 ounces), sliced ¼–½-inch thick and the slices quartered
I tablespoon vegetable oil	I egg

Put some water on to boil and when it boils, add salt.

Put the kale into the water and cook till tenderish (kale is never going to be that tender and certainly shouldn't be floppy), which will take 5–7 minutes, depending on its age.

Put the oil in a heavy-bottomed, deepish frying pan and cook the chorizo pieces for a few minutes, stirring and pressing with a wooden spoon or spatula so that the paprika-red fat oozes out as the sausage cooks, 3 or so minutes. While all this is going on you should, as well as keeping an eye on the kale, be putting a small frying pan of water on to poach the egg. I use that much despised thing, a store-bought egg poaching pan with molds. Drain the kale well and then stir into the chorizo. Put the egg in to poach and when it is ready, turn the orange-spliced kale onto a plate and turn out the poached egg on top.

Serves I.

CHICKPEAS WITH SORREL
A comparable, desirable pungency is evoked by this bowl of chickpeas and sorrel. If I've got some dried, cooked, and soaked chickpeas in a container in the fridge (and I might have), I use them, but canned, preferably organic (better textured) ones are fine. I first did this for the age-old reason that I needed to use something up, in this case some sorrel. There's a Middle Eastern way with chickpeas that I like, sour with lemon juice and thick with spinach. It occurred to me that using sorrel would provide the leafiness and the acidity—it does. For a can (about 14 ounces) of chickpeas, drained, put 1 tablespoon olive oil in a pan and fry in it a small chopped onion with 2 finely sliced garlic cloves and a good pinch of dried cumin. Crumble in ½ dried red chili pepper, sprinkle over a pinch of salt, and cook over medium heat for about 5 minutes. Shred or chop a good handful, about ⅔ cup, of sorrel and throw into the onion pan. Throw in the drained chickpeas after it and stir well till the sorrel's wilted and the chickpeas are warm. I eat this from a large bowl with some more oil drizzled over it and warmed pita. If this is supper, not lunch, I might make a cold plate of tomato salad to eat alongside, too.

I wouldn't want to suggest all cooking for one or two must necessarily be of the impromptu, quickly-thrown-together kind (and I say this as someone who is eating a Laughing Cow cheese and plastic bread sandwich as she writes; very delicious it is, too). I don't mean it should be elaborate and minutely organized, but that cooking for two can be out of the ordinary in a way that a dinner party, unless you really are fabulously extravagant or very rich, just can't. The solitary diner can sometimes, if not often, eat lobster alone. I buy it cooked and cold and I fry some bacon to eat with it. I might make mayonnaise. I don't mind what I have to do to it or how I eat my lobster—salad, club sandwich (toast some brioche, just see), as it is in my fingers. The pleasure lies in the solitary indulgence.

My most intense solitary indulgence, without question, is grouse; its season figures strongly in my diary (see page 459). Plain roast grouse is wonderful enough; this is dreamlike. I'd never have thought of messing about with the perfect simplicity of the bird, but when we all went to the River Café, London's hottest Italian restaurant, on the eve of my sister Horatia and Inigo's wedding, we ate quail stuffed with mascarpone and thyme, and it was so deeply fabulous that I thought I'd try it with grouse. The rest is culinary history—or it is in my house. As good as this is, don't turn the page if you can't manage grouse; try it instead with squab, poussin, or small cornish hens.

GROUSE WITH MASCARPONE AND THYME

1 grouse (12–14 ounces)	3 tablespoons red wine
2 slices bacon or 1 tablespoon unsalted butter	zest of ¼ lemon
	salt and freshly milled black pepper
1 tablespoon olive oil	10 sprigs fresh thyme
About ¼ cup mascarpone	

Wrap the grouse in the bacon or smear the breast thickly with butter to keep it from drying out.

Heat the oven to 400°F. Put in a small roasting pan with the oil in it to heat. Remove the innards from the grouse and chop finely (I use my mezzaluna). Put the offally mess into a small bowl. Add 3 heaping tablespoons of the mascarpone, 1 tablespoon of the wine, the zest of lemon, and a vigorous amount of salt and pepper; mix well. You should now have a bowl of divinely pungent dusty-pink cream. Remove the thyme leaves from the sprigs—you want a good tablespoonful—and chop them finely. Again, I use my mezzaluna, but whatever you use make sure the thyme is well chopped—otherwise it will be woody and ruin the smooth aromatic creaminess of the sauce-stuffing.

Put the mascarpone mixture into the cavity of the grouse and put it in the roasting pan in the oven. Cook for 30–45 minutes; you want the breast to be medium-rare and the legs done through.

When it's ready, remove the grouse to a plate and put the roasting pan on a burner. Some of the mascarpone stuffing will have oozed out into the pan. This will form the basis for your sauce. Add to this grunge another tablespoon of mascarpone and the remaining wine, and stir well, scraping it all up. Let it bubble and then pour the sauce onto a warmed plate. Put the grouse on top and dive in. (If you're going to share the grouse with someone else, you will need to double the final bit of wine and mascarpone to make enough sauce for the two of you.) I eat this with a big bowl of tender young kale with some butter stirred in and some nutmeg grated; mashed potatoes—for obvious reasons—are a pretty wonderful accompaniment, too.

Serves 1.

What, though, is in the back of my mind when I talk about the allowable and elegant excesses of eating for two is caviar. It would head my list of perfect dinners *à deux*. And this brings me to the subject of the seduction dinner. I am at the stage in my life when cooking for two is just about the shape of every day rather than the occasional lusty stab at culinary and extraculinary conquest. But the seduction dinner is just a dinner party in miniature; the same constraints apply, and I advise those interested to turn to the Dinner chapter (page 297) with their calculator for ease of downsizing. For what it's worth, I still think (as I always do) that you can't go wrong with roast chicken. And I would be predisposed to respond warmly to anyone who had the cool grace to give me caviar to start. But, of course, I would prefer to buy my own caviar rather than be given it as part of the trade off for a wearyingly unwelcome lunge.

And if a girl wants to eat caviar, a girl's got to know how to make blini. Sister, read on.

BLINI

SMOKED SALMON, CURED HERRING

Though you can use a griddle to make these, it's best to acquire a blini pan or platar, a flat pan with seven 3-inch circular indentations. In the context of caviar, this is not a big expense. I use my blini pan for much else besides; it happens to be the perfect size for a single, Cyclopean fried egg. Anyway, proper caviar is not obligatory with blini; I'm not sure they're not actually better with smoked salmon and salmon roe, pickled or cured herring, sour cream and a makeshift salsa of red onions chopped with capers. Really good caviar—and I like osetra much better than beluga—needs nothing else but good, lightly toasted, heavily buttered sandwich bread. But if you're going with the blini, provide some butter (unsalted, of course, and either soft enough to be spread or, as the Russians do, poured in a little jug already melted) and either crème fraîche or sour cream; whichever you choose, use it in the blini batter.

The one difficulty with blini is not the yeast (though everyone seems phobically obsessed with that). Now that we have instant or easy-blend yeast, all you need to do is add it to the flour and proceed as normal—no proofing or any of that. And as all batters need to stand for a while, what does it matter that there's some yeast in it? I have tried, in the pursuit of science and reader-friendliness, to substitute baking powder, but without the yeast you lose that moussy lightness. You just have buckwheat pancakes, which are fine enough, but they're not blini.

The real awkwardness is, I admit, to do with the yeast factor; you don't necessarily have a couple of hours to let the batter rise. So I tried making up the batter in the morning and left it, not in a warm place for 2 hours, but in my fridge all day. It rose beautifully; they were the best blini ever. Which means that you can get back from work and take the batter out of the fridge, whisk up and add the egg white, and you're ready to roll.

Before you start, preheat the oven to 300°F and put in a large ovenproof plate. I like to make these when I've got a friend over. I make him or her sit on some steps near my stove, talking to me with a drink while I fry the blini and stash them, one by one, under a foil tent on the plate in the oven. I may throw one to my friend while I'm making them, but the rest we eat at the table later—the perfect, companiable dinner.

This amount makes about 12 blini, which in my book (as this is) is just right for an entire meal, with additions, admittedly, for two; you need to feel at the end that you couldn't eat another. Remember that, as with all pancakes, the first one is often a complete disaster. Once you've got the heat right and the feel of the pan, the rest will follow perfectly.

⅔ cup buckwheat flour	2 tablespoons crème fraîche or sour cream
½ cup all-purpose flour	
2 teaspoons instant or easy-blend yeast	1 tablespoon butter, plus more, for frying
½ teaspoon salt	
½ teaspoon sugar	1 egg, separated
½ cup milk	drop oil

Mix the flours, yeast, salt, and sugar in a warm bowl (I let it sit, empty, in a sink of hottish water for a few minutes first). Pour the milk into a measuring cup and add the crème fraîche. Stir with a fork to combine well and then add water so that the liquid comes up to the 1-cup mark. Pour this liquid into a saucepan, add the tablespoon of butter, and warm up till the butter melts. You don't want this actually hot, so leave it to cool slightly if, when you dip a finger in, it feels more than about blood heat.

Beat the egg yolk into the liquid and then pour this liquid into the flours and leave in a warmish place, covered with a damp tea-towel, for 2 hours (or all day in the fridge). Whisk the egg white till stiff but not dry and fold into the batter.

Preheat the oven (and see above). Melt a dab of butter and the drop oil in a 4-inch blini pan and, when hot, pour the butter mixture out. For each blini you'll need a couple of tablespoonfuls or so of batter. I dunk in my ¼-cup measure, fill it about halfway, and transfer the batter evenly to the pan. Fry each blini on the first side for a minute or two, until the batter starts bubbling on top, then flip it over with a spatula or palette knife and give about another minute. Don't, whatever you do, press down on the blini while it cooks. You want maximum fluffage here.

Of course, you can, without loss, make these in advance and keep them in fridge or freezer before reheating wrapped in foil in a 325°F oven, but nothing feels quite the same as making or eating blini hot from the pan.

If I had to choose a perfect, dream dessert, after the caviar and the roast chicken, it would have to be zabaglione. It's not comfortable to make for any number larger than two.

Celestial though it is, it is not suitable for a seduction dinner. You don't want to have to stand up and start whirring away at a double boiler on the stove for a quarter of an hour at the end of dinner. Those of us who don't have such nervily romantic considerations to constrain us can plug ourselves into our electric mixers without embarrassment and for as long as it takes.

ZABAGLIONE

I use a stainless-steel, round-bottomed bowl that I suspend over (without touching) bubbling water in a saucepan, but a double boiler will be fine. If you haven't got a hand-held electric beater, then just use a whisk; zabaglione does, after all, predate the invention of mixers, and I dare say it predates the discovery of electricity.

2 egg yolks   **4 tablespoons Marsala**
2 tablespoons superfine sugar

Put warm water in the bottom of a double boiler to heat, insert the top, and into it put the egg yolks and sugar. Start whisking them and continue whisking while the water heats up and starts to simmer. The egg mixture should become as thick as heavy cream and pale as butter; by the very end it should have tripled in volume. Continue whisking and slowly, slowly add the Marsala as you do so. When you have a soft, foaming, bulkily billowing mass—in short, when you have zabaglione—you can stop whisking and spoon into a couple of glasses. This may be after a good quarter-hour's pneumatic whisking. Langue de chat are the cookies to serve with it or, failing that, savoiardi.

Serves 2.

COMFORT FOOD

If you've got that lust for something soft and sweet, for babyfied comfort food, you might as well go flat out for it. Eating alone, I make what I remember my mother making for herself, bread and milk, in a large, cream china pudding basin. Put some torn-up pieces of white bread in a bowl, sprinkle over some sugar, and then pour in some hot milk. Eat, in an armchair, bowl on lap. If you keep vanilla sugar in the house, use that, but fiddle no further; this is not a dish that lends itself to great refinements.

BAKED SEMOLINA

For all the fashionable enthusiasm for polenta, one related product tends to be snubbed, if not forgotten: semolina. With its comforting wheaty taste, its ability to warm and fill, it deserves to be better known. I like to heat the semolina with vanilla and milk, adding sugar after it's thick and grainy and set, and dollop in jam once it's in the bowl.

For some reason, I don't eat jam with this version of semolina, but drizzle from a gummy teaspoon a glowing, teak-colored, dripping bead of honey.

1 vanilla bean or 1 teaspoon pure vanilla extract or 2 tablespoons vanilla sugar	3 tablespoons semolina
	1 egg, separated
	2 tablespoons sugar if not using vanilla
2 cups milk	sugar

Preheat the oven to 350°F and butter a dish with a 2-cup capacity.

If you're using a vanilla bean, heat the milk in a saucepan and infuse it with the bean for 15 minutes. Otherwise, just heat the milk and sprinkle in the semolina, stirring all the time to prevent lumps. After about 10 minutes the semolina should be cooked, swollen, and thick. Leave to cool for about 10 minutes. Whisk the egg white till stiff; you may find this easier if you first wipe the bowl with the cut side of a lemon and sprinkle a little sugar into the whites.

Stir the yolk into the semolina and then the vanilla sugar, if you're using it; otherwise, add the plain sugar and/or the vanilla extract, if you're using that. Add a good dollop of the whisked white, just to loosen the mixture, then fold the rest in gently. Pour into the waiting dish and bake for 35–45 minutes; the pudding will be risen, the top golden and blistered.

Serves 2.

I don't make desserts very often when there's just the two of us. I might do something with the plums or apples from the garden, maybe put together a crumble. The amount of actual crumble needed for a little pie dish is so small as not to be worth worrying about. You don't need to go dragging a machine into it.

APPLE AND WALNUT CRUMBLE

Crumble is a good way to start fiddling about with the idea of a crust; it's pastry, really, only without the fear factor. Just plain, it's wonderful enough, especially on those grim days with saucepan-lid skies in late November and early February, but it's truly good as expanded here, with the nubbliness of the nuts and the almost honeyed crunchiness of the brown sugar. For two people who are wisely eating this with custard (see page 32 if you intend to make your own), ice cream, crème fraîche, or just old-fashioned cream in a pitcher (check where applicable) but with nothing else before or after at all, use a pie dish of any sort with a capacity of about 2 cups. Though I call for Marsala here, dark rum works well too; once it's cooked, the rumminess ripens into something more aromatic than boozy.

2 tablespoons raisins or sultanas

3 tablespoons Marsala or dark rum, warmed

¾ cup all-purpose flour

4 tablespoons (½ stick) unsalted butter, cold and cut into small dice

½ cup walnuts, chopped finely

¼ cup light brown sugar plus I heaping tablespoon

I very large or 2 medium cooking apples

Heat oven to 375°F. Grease a pie pan with butter. Cover the raisins or sultanas with the warmed Marsala.

Sift the flour into a bowl and rub in the butter with your fingertips; the crumble should look like rubbly meal. Stir the walnuts into the mixture, then stir in the sugar.

Set aside in a cool place—even stash in the freezer. Peel and core the apples and cut them into 1-inch chunks. Put them in a heavy saucepan with the tablespoon of sugar and the Marsala and raisins. Put the lid on and cook for 5 minutes to soften, giving the pan a good shake once or twice in that time. Then put the fruit into the pie pan, cover with the crumble mixture, and cook for about 25 minutes or until the top is golden brown.

There are times when real rice pudding is what's wanted, but it can take a good 3 hours to make one. It occurred to me that you could proceed along the lines of a risotto—turn the rice in butter and then add hot liquid, ladleful by ladleful, until it's creamily absorbed. I did, and it worked—the perfect rice pudding for one. And all the stirring kept me occupied (without eating) until it was ready. This takes about half an hour. You need to give it about 10 minutes longer than the usual risotto, as you want the rice rather less al dente.

RISOTTO-INSPIRED RICE PUDDING

3 cups milk	2 tablespoons superfine sugar if not
½ teaspoon pure vanilla extract or 2	using vanilla sugar
tablespoons vanilla sugar	¼ cup arborio rice
1 heaping tablespoon unsalted butter	2–3 tablespoons heavy cream

Heat the milk in a saucepan that, preferably, has a lip. When it's about to boil (but don't let it), turn off the heat. (Or give the milk 4 minutes or so in a wide-topped plastic measuring cup in the microwave.) If you're using the vanilla extract, add it to the milk now. Melt the butter and 1 tablespoon of the plain or vanilla sugar, if using, in a heavy-bottomed saucepan. When hissing away in a glorious pale caramelly pool, add the rice and stir to coat stickily. Slowly add the milk, stirring the rice all the time, letting each quantity of milk—about ½ cup at a time—get absorbed into the consequently swelling rice before adding the next. Start tasting at 20 minutes but be prepared to go on for 35. You may want to add more milk, too. (And if the rice tastes cooked before all the milk's absorbed, don't carry on adding it.)

When the rice feels as it should, thick and sticky and creamy, take it off the heat and beat in the remaining sugar (taste and see if you want yet more) and as much of the cream as you like. Think of this as the *mantecatura,* the final addition to a risotto, to thicken and add fat-globular volume of butter and grated Parmesan; indeed, just add butter if you haven't got any cream in the house.

Eat as is: no jam, no syrup, no honey, no nothing. Serves 1.

FAST FOOD

For the past few years I have written an annual roundup of cookery books and, putting aside fashions and fads, it is the subject of fast food that has recently begun to dominate. The reasons are understandable enough—we seem to have less time for cooking as we have more interest in food. Women have been traditionally the producers and providers of food in the home, but now that we go out to work, there's no one to spend all afternoon making tonight's supper. But the disinclination to spend hour upon hour in the kitchen every night is not sex-specific. No one would want, after a long day in the office, to come back and start on some elaborate culinary masterpiece. Cooking can be relaxing (although it's interesting that it's men rather than women who tend more often to cite its therapeutic properties), but not if you are already exhausted. And as the working day seems to get ever longer, why would you want to be cooking a meal that isn't going to be ready for two and a half hours? What we all want is to eat something good and simple and soon.

POINTS TO REMEMBER

- Don't take shortcuts with dishes that ought to be cooked slowly, to infuse and blend, to be cooled and added to. Choose instead food that is meant to be, has to be, cooked quickly, such as liver, fish, or meat scallops.

- Remember to think not just in terms of actual cooking time in the oven but of the amount of effort it will take you to put dinner together. I like shopping for food and I don't work in an office; but on days when I'm really fraught, it's the shopping, not the cooking, that finishes me off. And when you're really exhausted, the easiest thing to cook is a roast chicken; it takes a while in the oven (see page xviii) but demands a minimum of interference and energy from you.

- Quick, last-minute-assembly food can be the most stressful cooking of all. Its popularity is in part due to the influence of restaurants on our culinary imagination and repertoires. Restaurant cooking has to be quick; food has to be made fast, to order; chefs and their minions have to conjure up the finished dish within minutes. The constraints of cooking at home are entirely different—what makes life easier for a chef can make life hell for the domestic cook.

- I shy away from recipes that, however quick they may be to cook, require too much detailed attention in the preparation. Stir-frys are an example. In delicate moods, the idea of having to shred finely, dice, mince, and slice into julienne seven different sorts of vegetable—even if the dish takes a mere three minutes to cook—could reduce me to tears.

- If you hate cooking, don't do it. You can certainly eat well enough just by learning how to shop. You can buy food that you don't need to cook—picnic food, cold food, things to heat up. Of course, trimmed vegetables and packaged salads are pandering to laziness and inviting extravagance on a ludicrous scale, but be grateful for them. If they taste good, don't worry about it. No one has to be made miserable over cooking.

- Make use of your pantry and fridge. You can rely on bought pasta sauces, on cans of white beans, anchovies, and good tuna (in olive oil only) as well as small glass bottles of tapenade, green olive paste, and goat cheese in oil. Bacon is the easiest thing for the quick cook; grilling a piece of bacon is hardly cooking, and a few salty shards crumbled over or chopped into a pile of mashed potato, or mixed with beans and spinach or chickpeas and chili-fried tomatoes and topped with a poached egg, make a better dinner than anything more elaborate and expensive from the freezer case.

REMINDERS OF AND IDEAS FOR
HASTY IMPROVISATIONS

SALAD

You don't need to be reminded how to open a package of designer lettuce leaves. But if you're in a hurry, salad can be useful, either as a starter to keep people quiet while you get other things ready, or as a main course if you are putting together a bought picnic supper (fruit, as well as cheese, good bread, pâtisserie). However, some lettuce leaves can be just a little too flabby; you need texture, too. So get a romaine lettuce, tear it into large, crisp chunks, and add it to any bought salad package (or mixture of packages). The quickest way of making a dressing is, at the last minute, to grind some salt over and then to drizzle some good olive oil and add the scarcest spritz of lemon (see also page 23).

To frisée or escarole, add hot, fried, diced pancetta or bacon lardons. Make a dressing by adding Dijon mustard, more oil, and some red wine vinegar to the bacony juices in the pan. Then, onto the warm tossed salad, shave some Parmesan or other hard cheese and toss very lightly again. The Chestnut and Pancetta Salad on page 326 is a slightly more solid variant. And you can substitute warm, just-cooked chicken livers, too.

To packages of baby spinach, add hot bacon and raw sliced mushrooms. Or make a spinach, gorgonzola, and pine nut salad. Cut the gorgonzola (or whichever blue cheese you happen to like best) into crumbly cubes (don't worry about uniformity, size, or even shape, or you really will have a nervous breakdown) and toast the pine nuts in a hot dry pan until they begin to turn gold and fragrant.

To watercress and mâche—arranged on a plate, not in a bowl—add some sliced, just-cooked-through scallops. Better still, fry some bacon first, then fry the scallops in the bacon fat. Chop the bacon finely and sprinkle over the scallop salad.

If you're in Germanic mood, then make a mustardy dressing for chicory—adding a stiff spoonful of crème fraîche—and buy thick slices of good ham, cut them into thick strips, and mix into the salad. You could do the same with warm potatoes, too, in which case you should really go whole hog and add, instead of the ham, thickly sliced frankfurters, though please don't even think of using the flabby adulterated sort too often available.

A huge green salad, no funny stuff, with a walnut oil dressing and a good cheese selection, is one of the loveliest dinners I can think of. Have a tumbling mass of grapes, too, plus good bread, thin and thick crackers, and, if you can ever find ripe pears, then make sure you have a dish of those, too.

SOUPS

PEA SOUP The quickest and best soup you can make is to cook 3 cups of frozen peas in 2 cups of vegetable stock made with a good-quality bouillon cube. When the peas are tender, purée in the food processor or blender. Add some olive oil (preferably basil-infused, see below) and season to taste. Serve Parmesan to sprinkle over.

You can improve on this; if you've boiled a ham previously, then freeze the ham stock it's made and use that here. Also, if you've stashed any hard, unyielding rinds of finished Parmesan in the freezer as you go along, then salvage one now and throw that into the soup as it's cooking.

Just as easy is a tomato and rice soup (see page 422, too), which you can make by adding water to a good, bought tomato sauce to make it liquid enough for rice to cook in. Bring to the boil. Throw in some basmati rice and 10 minutes later you've got soup.

TOMATO AND RICE

Spinach, because you can buy it frozen and ready chopped, makes a good basis for a quick soup. Chop and fry an onion first, then add the spinach and, when it has more or less thawed, add 2 cups or so of chicken or vegetable stock made from cubes. After about 5 minutes, add a good squeeze of lemon and, if you want to make it richer when it's off the heat, whisk in some light cream beaten with an egg yolk.

SPINACH

PASTA

You need to wait for the water to boil, but you can lessen the overall time for cooking pasta by buying fine egg pasta, which doesn't take very long to cook. Some butter, cream, Parmesan, and a few drops of white truffle oil make a wonderful sauce. Or don't even bother about the truffle oil. People shy away from cream and butter so much that, when they taste them, just as they are, warmed by a tangle of slippery-soft pasta, it comes as a surprise how transportingly good they are. And don't get anxious about the artery-thickening properties of such a sauce: you don't want to drench the pasta, just lightly cover it. I sometimes think that butter alone, with a grating of fresh nutmeg, is the best dressing for pasta.

BUTTER

CREAM

PARMESAN

TRUFFLE OIL

NUTMEG

And, finally, bear in mind Chinese egg noodles. They need a scant 5 minutes cooking, and a sprinkling of sesame oil.

FLAVORED AND INFUSED OILS

I have come to the conclusion, having abominated them for ages, that infused oils, purchased or homemade, are among the most important allies of the quick cook. I use basil oil mixed with lemon juice to make a quick, scented dressing for salads, or just as it is to anoint waxy boiled potatoes or peas or poached or fried meats. I have made a basil-rich version of the pea soup above by frying a chopped onion first in basil-infused oil, then adding some more of the basil oil at the end.

I habitually have an effort-free spaghetti aglio olio by just dousing the cooked pasta in 2 tablespoons of garlic-infused oil. I use it for frying and marinating chicken pieces and coat diced potatoes with it before roasting them. I use it to warm through cans of cannellini beans, which I then let steep so the garlicky oil penetrates the soft interior of the grainy beans, before sprinkling the beans with chopped sage or parsley or both. In short, I have become a complete flavored-oil convert, with all the evangelical zeal that implies.

CANNED BEANS

Canned beans and other legumes are obviously useful for fast-food preparation. You can just heat them up, but they will need some help. Just put onion, garlic, a stalk of celery, parsley (I don't even bother to remove the stems), and some bacon or pancetta in the food processor, blitz, and throw the green-flecked, fragrant mound into a pan with 1–2 tablespoons olive oil.

When this mixture is really soft (remember you're not going to cook the legumes, just heat them up), stir in white or cranberry beans, lentils or chickpeas. If I'm using lentils (which aren't quite as satisfactory as other canned beans) I add a carrot to the pulped mixture; chickpeas can take the fierce rasp of a dried or fresh red chili. And if you have lying around herbs other than parsley, then use them; rosemary and sage work particularly well with cannellini and cranberry beans, but you will need, especially with the rosemary, to make sure the herbs are well minced.

When the beans are warmed through, add more chopped fresh parsley and olive oil and, having tasted, probably quite a bit of salt. Beans and other legumes are best at room temperature and taste all the better having sat around with the herbs and garlic and olive oil seeping stickily into them, so do them first thing when you come in from work and leave them, reheating as necessary later.

MEAT AND FISH

Providing you don't leave them lying around to dry up and curl at the edges, scallops—thin slices of meat or fish—are probably the best bet for the quick cook. They need about 2 minutes each side in a buttery frying pan (add a drop of oil first to stop the butter burning).

You have several options for finishing them: you can deglaze the pan with lemon juice, red or white wine vinegar, or a teaspoon or two of soy sauce to which you've added twice the amount of water and a pinch of sugar, and pour this over, or simply squeeze over lemon or lime juice and serve. Salmon and other fish scallops are perhaps at their best treated this way, but pork and veal benefit from this approach, too. For pork or veal try also a final deglazing with a glug of Marsala, white wine, vermouth, or sherry, with or without a dollop of cream.

Calves' liver scallops taste wonderful in a buttery Marsala puddle. Dredge the slices first in some flour into which you've grated some nutmeg. This makes the

SALMON
PORK
VEAL
SCALLOPS

sauce more velvety. Breaded slices are also worth remembering. If you're in a hurry, you might not want to bother with bread crumbs, however. And I wouldn't get the boxed ones; buy instead some matzo meal. Dip the slices in egg, then in matzo meal, let them stand for a while to dry, and fry each one for 2 minutes or so in sizzling butter with the customary drop of oil.

If you're cooking these for more than two, leave meat slices as they are; otherwise, snip each into three 1½-by-2½-inch pieces before serving. These will look better, more inviting, piled on a big plate.

CHICKEN

Chicken, especially the breast, needs to be paid quite lavish attention to keep it interesting, and I speak as someone whose favorite food is roast chicken. But when you're trying to get something together quickly, be careful. Everyone likes the idea of breast portions, but they can easily be bland or desiccated. If possible, let chicken breasts marinate for as long as you can, but at least 20 minutes, in olive oil and lemon juice and some peeled, knife-flattened garlic cloves. For each portion of chicken breast, work along the lines of 3 tablespoons olive oil, 2 tablespoons lemon juice, and 1 garlic clove. But this is just the loosest of guides.

OLIVE OIL
LEMON
GARLIC

Lay the chicken in the lemony oil, cover with plastic film, and turn at half-time. To broil the chicken, preheat the broiler while the chicken's steeping. The cooking itself is quick enough, about 6 minutes under the broiler each side; sautéing is even quicker, about 4 minutes a side. Let stand at the end to allow the heat to seep through. Sprinkle with herbs, adding more lemon juice and some sea salt.

If you don't want to bother with marinating, then consider adding fat while the chicken's cooking. Make any mixture of herbs and butter and, having slashed the chicken cutlets with a knife, smear this over. Or, very easy, mix some good bottled pesto with some softened butter (about 5 tablespoons of butter and 3 tablespoons pesto should do for about 4 chicken cutlets) and dollop this over both sides, making sure you press well over the slashed skin so the mixture permeates. Cook for 10 minutes a side, but you may find you need a bit longer; you don't want the pesto mixture to burn too quickly (it will blacken slightly; that is part of the plan, so don't panic), so cook with a less fierce heat.

PESTO

Leg and thigh portions take longer than breast, and for that reason are perhaps not ideal for the quickest of quick cooking. The answer is just to get the butcher to cut up the meat into smaller portions. Chicken cut up already and swathed in plastic wrap from the supermarket is tasteless. It annoys me that so many people prefer the white meat. The dark meat is better, and particularly so when cooked in portions.

You can make bland chicken pieces more memorable by serving them with salsa verde. It doesn't take long to poach chicken pieces. Take some skinned and boned chicken breasts, preferably free-range, and poach them in some stock (and I feel relaxed about some liberally diluted cubes here) mixed with white wine or vermouth, into which you put some parsley sprigs, a drop of soy sauce if the stock isn't already salty enough, some celery, and 2 bay leaves. Poach gently till just done—10 minutes or so should do it. Serve with the salsa verde on page 181, a spoonful or so drizzled over, the rest in a jug or bowl with a ladle, to the side.

WITH
VERMOUTH
PARSLEY

DUCK

Duck breasts are always worth bearing in mind when you have to get something together quickly. Follow a proper recipe, as below, or just slash the skin side diagonally at about ½-inch intervals, douse with strained ginger marmalade that you've made runnier with soy sauce, or honey mixed with orange juice (the sharper the better, and if you cook this in January or February, you should try to get hold of Seville oranges), or grainy mustard mixed with a drop or two of pineapple juice and a pinch of brown sugar. Roast, skin side up, in a hot oven (450°F for about 20 minutes). I work on an allowance of 1 (½ whole breast) per person if I'm slicing them up. The meat is rich and you somehow taste the duck better, get the sense of its flavor and feathery-velvety texture, when it is sliced. I'd just carve the breasts into diagonal, thin but not wafer-thin slices and spread them out on a large plate for people to take what they want themselves. I wouldn't give people their own little portion of fanned-out slices on an individual plate. Of course, you can just serve the duck breasts whole, as they are, in which case it might be safer to cook 2 extra per 4 people in case some want seconds; overcatering is always better than not accommodating people's greed.

GINGER AND
SOY
HONEY AND
ORANGE

Don't worry about having leftovers. What could be nicer the next day than cold duck, thinly sliced, stirred into warm rice, doused with soy sauce, and studded with just-hot sugar snaps? Or just eat it as it is, with a fat clump of Japanese pickled ginger and waxy, warm new potatoes.

DESSERTS

The first thing the quick cook can dispense with is cooking the last course. No French person would consider apologizing for buying something from a good pâtisserie, and neither should you.

Otherwise, think along the lines of good, bought ice cream eaten with good, bought cookies or splodged with easily-thrown-together sauces. Warm some honey, pour it over, then sprinkle with toasted flaked almonds, or substitute maple syrup and pecans or walnuts. Throw over a cup of espresso to make what the Italians call an *affoggato* (or use rum). Spoon over stem ginger in its oozing, golden, throat-catchingly hot and sweet syrup. Or, as in one of the suggested menus below, just grind some good dark chocolate to powdery grains in the food processor and sprinkle over the ice cream.

And, as mentioned in Basics, Etc., in regard to the freezer and how it may usefully be stocked, keep a ready supply of frozen berries—raspberries, black- berries, mixed. Use as they are—removing all strawberries from the mixed bag— only add sugar. You can also add some glugs of liqueur, some finely grated orange zest, a few mint leaves, or some orange-flower water. Serve with crème fraîche or ice cream, as you like. Just before serving, sprinkle with confectioners' sugar or ground pistachios. You can make a creamy, red-splodged mess by whip- ping up some heavy cream, crumbling some store-bought meringues, and stirring in a package of thawed, sweetened berries. I think this is much better than using the meringues whole and going in for nest-like effects.

It is worth always bearing in mind the confectioners'-sugar-and-strainer trick. Somehow, giving any bought or hastily-thrown-together dessert a smart dusting of the sugar makes it automatically look like the loving product of hours-long labor in the kitchen. I don't suggest you ever pretend something bought is home- made. Nor do I advise forays into cheffy fiddling in general—I am not a garnish girl—but this small degree of finish pleases me.

A BRIEF NOTE ON EQUIPMENT

The microwave is the usually cited without-which tool for the time-pressed kitchen survivor. But consider, rather, the pressure cooker. Newfangled models don't explode, don't hiss or honk or emit clouds of threatening steam, and they cut cooking time, on average, by a third. And—by way of even more dramatic example—you can cook dried, unsoaked chickpeas in them in 35 minutes. Another very useful piece of gadgetry, if you're going to be having people round for supper often when you haven't really got the time to cook for them, is an electric rice cooker. You'd be surprised how much food can be eaten with rice; and the whole after-work kitchen flurry is much reduced when you're not deal- ing with potatoes, too.

QUICK AFTER-WORK SUPPERS
FOR FOUR

Individual recipes that take under 30 minutes to cook are dotted throughout the book (and are listed as such in the Index; after all, in the normal course of cooking we all mix food that can be rustled together quickly with that which takes longer or needs more care or attention. But there are times when anything that can't be done fast and without fussing is out of the culinary question. If you don't get back from work till seven and have got people coming over at eight, you need to get moving. And bearing in mind that planning—the sheer effort of exhausted thought required—can sometimes feel just as burdensome as the preparation, I've drawn up a list of quick and easy two-course after-work suppers.

Nothing here takes more than half an hour to cook; most dishes don't even take 10 minutes. And all recipes feed four.

RED MULLET WITH GARLIC AND ROSEMARY
GOOEY CHOCOLATE PUDDINGS

This menu exemplifies my ideas for fast food: the fish itself takes a bare few minutes; the puddings you mix together when you get in and then just leave until the moment, more or less, you want to eat. You can thus appear the very model of serenity in the kitchen, however late or in whatever stressed state you actually got back.

The red mullet—sometimes referred to by its French name, *rouget*—is fragrant, light, beautiful. (You can substitute baby trout fillets if you can't get red mullet.) The chocolate puddings, which are really Patricia Wells' recipe for chocolate gourmandise in *At Home in Provence,* provide a harmoniously voluptuous counterpoint: chewy and cracked like macaroons on top and on the base, with a thick, glossy goo of chocolate sauce in the middle.

RED MULLET WITH GARLIC
AND ROSEMARY

Ask the fish seller to leave the pearly-pink, crimson-beaded skin on the fish but to remove the scales. For mincing the garlic, rosemary, and orange zest, I pile everything onto the chopping board and use my mezzaluna.

4 garlic cloves, minced

1 teaspoon fresh rosemary leaves,
   minced

zest of 2 oranges, minced

6 tablespoons olive oil

10 red mullet fillets with skin (about
   3 ounces each)

¾ cup vermouth or white wine

Combine the garlic, rosemary, and orange zest and put half of this mixture into a large frying pan with 3 tablespoons of the oil. Heat, bring up to sizzling point, then add half the fish fillets, skin side down. Give them a couple of minutes a side or until you can see that the flesh has lost its raw transparency. Remove the fish fillets to a warmed plate big enough to take everything later and repeat the whole process with the remaining garlic mixture and fillets. Add these fillets to the warmed plate. Deglaze the pan with vermouth, let it bubble up, and, when syrupy, pour this, scraping up the chopped bits as you do so, over the fish. If you want a noodle accompaniment—and they do go well with it—then look at the noodle and snow pea stir-fry on page 178, eliminating, I'd think, the mushrooms. The mullet is wonderful without noodles, too, just with some grilled tomatoes and good bread.

GOOEY CHOCOLATE PUDDINGS

4½ ounces best-quality bittersweet
   chocolate, finely chopped

8 tablespoons (1 stick) unsalted
   butter

3 large eggs

¾ cup sugar

¼ cup Italian 00 or all-purpose flour

Before you've even taken your coat off, put the chocolate and butter in the top of a double boiler above simmering water. Whisk every now and again until melted. In a bowl, whisk together the eggs, sugar, and flour until just blended. Gradually whisk in the melted chocolate mixture. Set aside.

Grease 4 1-cup ramekins with butter and add flour to cover the butter, tapping the ramekins to get rid of excess. Preheat the oven to 400°F about half an hour before you want to eat the puddings. And I'd leave cooking them until you've finished the main course. It doesn't matter if there's no food on the table for 10 minutes; and these do have to be done at the last minute.

So, pour the mixture into the ramekins and put them on a baking sheet in the oven for 10–12 minutes, until the tops are firm and cracking slightly and the edges set. Serve immediately and consider providing a pitcher of cold, cold cream for people to pour into their pudding's hotly deliquescing interior as they eat.

Although beef stroganoff has to be cooked at the very last minute—which can often be the quickest route to a nervous breakdown in the kitchen—you can fry the onions and butter as soon as you get in. Then all you need to do once you're on the verge of sitting down is reheat them gently for a couple of minutes in a little butter, remove them again from the pan and then proceed with the meat. From that stage you're not more than about 3 minutes away from being able to eat, so this is worth bearing in mind for friends you just know are going to be late.

BEEF STROGANOFF

Most butchers can get you tail bits of fillet, which will cost less and which you won't mind so much tearing into raggedy scraps. Cook a buttery mound of basmati rice to eat with it.

6 tablespoons (¾ stick) unsalted butter	salt and freshly milled black pepper
a few drops oil	2 pounds beef fillet, cut into thin strips
I large onion, minced	scant ½ teaspoon Dijon mustard
½ pound button mushrooms, sliced	I cup crème fraîche
whole nutmeg	a few pinches ground paprika

Put 2 tablespoons of the butter in a frying pan with a drop of the oil. Put on the heat, add the onion, and sauté gently, stirring frequently, until soft and beginning to color. Add 2 tablespoons more of the butter and, when melted, toss in the mushrooms and cook for another 4–5 minutes. Grate some nutmeg over the onions and mushrooms in the pan and season with the salt and pepper. Stir well and remove to a plate. Add the remaining butter to the pan with a drop or two more of the oil and turn the heat to high. When the butter's hot, stir-fry the fillet for a couple of minutes, until it's seared on the outside but still pinkly tender within. Return the onions and mushrooms to the pan; stir well. Grate over some more nutmeg and stir in the Dijon mustard, then the crème fraîche. Sprinkle in a pinch of paprika, add more salt, if needed, then pour onto a warmed plate. If you want, you can put the rice on the same plate, in a circle with the beef stroganoff in the middle (which is very much in keeping with the period in which this dish found most fashionable favor) or pile onto separate plates. Either way, dust a little more paprika over it once it's served up.

ROAST SUGAR-SPRINKLED PEACHES

This is scarcely a recipe: get 5–6 peaches (enough for 2 halves each and then a little more), split them in half, remove the stones, and put them, cut-side up, in a buttered ovenproof dish in which they fit snugly. Into each cavity add a dot of butter and a tablespoon of sugar—vanilla, brown, or ordinary white, as you like—then another few dots of butter, and roast in a preheated 400°F oven for about 20 minutes. Think about providing some good bought ice cream to go with. And you can substitute apricots or, of course, nectarines.

SQUID WITH CHILI AND CLAMS

RICOTTA WITH HONEY AND TOASTED PINE NUTS

This is the sort of dinner I cook when I've got girlfriends coming over, chapter meetings of the martyred sisterhood. Even though quantities are enough for four, for some reason there are always only three of us, and I don't reduce amounts of ingredients correspondingly.

I'm not saying that this menu is necessarily unsuitable for mixed company, but my experience teaches me that this is more naturally girlfood. Your experience may be fortunate enough to make you feel otherwise.

SQUID WITH CHILI AND CLAMS

I tend to get my fish from the fish seller and get him to clean the squid, but you can sometimes buy it ready-cleaned at the supermarket. If you don't have any sake at hand, then use dry sherry.

32 cherrystone clams, well scrubbed and rinsed	4 large squid (about ½ pound each), cleaned and the bodies cut into rings
5 tablespoons olive oil	I cup sake or dry sherry
4 garlic cloves, squished with flat of knife	2–3 tablespoons chopped parsley or
I dried red chili pepper	Thai basil

Rinse and scrub the clams under cold running water, throwing out any that are cracked, damaged, or stay open. Put the oil in a wide saucepan (which has a lid, though you don't need it yet) on a high heat. When hot, add the garlic and crumble in the dried, whole chili pepper. Stir well, then add the squid and fry, stirring, for about a minute, until the glassy flesh turns a denser white. Add the clams, the sake, and I cup water, and then clamp on the lid and turn the heat down a little. Cook for 4–5 minutes, shaking the pan a bit every now and again, or until the clams are all steamed open, then pour into a large bowl and cover with the parsley or Thai basil.

It's idiosyncratic, perhaps, but I find a bowl of plain basmati rice the perfect accompaniment. You might think of adding a couple of cardamom pods to infuse the rice while cooking, but no butter or oil at the end—that's the point.

RICOTTA
WITH HONEY
AND
TOASTED
PINE NUTS

This doesn't really count as a recipe; it's more a suggestion.

Mound about 12 ounces of fresh ricotta in a pretty bowl (fresh, unsalty goat's cheese, sliced and arranged on a plate, works just as well). Dribble a couple of tablespoons of good, clear honey over and then sprinkle on about ⅓ cup pine nuts, which you've first toasted till golden and waxily fragrant in a hot, oil-less pan.

SOLE WITH CHANTERELLES

MASCARPONE, RUM, AND LIME CREAM

What I generally do here is complete the first part of the mascarpone cream when I get in (that's to say, everything up to the egg whites) and then whisk and fold in the egg whites just before I get started on the fish. It all depends on how early you get in from work; if it's a bare half hour before you're expecting everyone else, just make up the dessert, egg whites and all, in its entirety.

SOLE WITH CHANTERELLES

I love the ecstatic saffron intensity of the chanterelles against the fine whiteness of the sole, but don't feel obliged to use them. I often substitute those surreally tinted pieds bleues mushrooms, available sometimes in gourmet markets, and oyster mushrooms should be just as good. If you can't get your hands on garlic-infused oil to make this, add 1 teaspoon of chopped garlic to the butter with 1 tablespoon of olive oil; allow the butter mixture to heat and the garlic to soften but not color, then put in the mushrooms. Proceed as the recipe directs.

1⅓ pounds chanterelles	salt and freshly milled black pepper
9 tablespoons unsalted butter (1 stick plus 1 tablespoon), plus more, if needed	8 sole fillets (about 6 ounces each)
	juice of ¼–½ lemon
1 tablespoon garlic-infused oil (see page 459 and headnote)	½ cup vermouth or white wine
	2–3 tablespoons chopped parsley

Cook the mushrooms, wiped with a paper towel first if they need it, in 8 tablespoons of the butter and garlic oil in a large, high-sided if possible, frying pan, adding salt and pepper to taste, then remove to a plate or bowl while you get on with the fish. You shouldn't have to add any more butter, but do, if you feel you need to. Add the sole in a couple or so batches and cook 2 minutes on the first side, then another on the second, or until just cooked through. This should be all the cooking they need, but poke a knife in to check. Remove them as you go to a large, warmed plate big enough to hold all 8 fillets, sprinkle with salt, then get on with the rest. When all the fish is on the plate, put the mushrooms back in the pan and heat them up, adding the lemon juice to taste and the vermouth. Let the mushrooms bubble up and stir in the remaining tablespoon of butter. Pour over the sole and sprinkle with the parsley.

I don't think you need to serve anything more than a bowl of green vegetables with this—given that the dessert is not a lean one—and I'd probably choose some frozen young peas with a couple of handfuls of sugar snaps thrown in for the last 60 seconds or so of cooking time.

MASCARPONE, RUM, AND LIME CREAM

3 eggs, separated

6 tablespoons superfine sugar

3⅓ cups mascarpone

3 tablespoons dark rum

juice of 1 lime plus more, if needed

Whisk the egg yolks and sugar together till light and moussily creamy. In another bowl, stir the mascarpone together with the rum and lime juice. Stir the egg mixture in gently but firmly, with a folding movement, and taste; you may want to add a little more lime juice. Don't worry about sharpness unduly; you need that to hold the egg-enriched mascarpone in check. What you want to end up with is the creamy tartness, the taste of cheesecake, but with the whipped lightness of mousse.

Wipe the inside of the bowl you're going to whisk the egg whites in with the cut side of the lime. Then whisk the whites till stiff and fold them into the mascarpone mixture. Decant into glasses and keep somewhere cool till needed. I leave this blank and unadorned, but you could always pare a strip of lime zest, or even cut a twist of lime, holiday-cocktail style, for the top of each glass. But plain or prinked, you must get hold of some cookies to eat with.

LAMB WITH GARLICKY TAHINI
PASSION FRUIT FOOL

Again, you can more or less prepare the dessert when you get in—just leave the combining of the seed-studded pulp and sweetened cream till last minute—and you can put the lamb in its scant marinade and get on with the tahini garlic sauce at the same time. That leaves you with the lamb to cook—15 minutes at most.

LAMB WITH GARLICKY TAHINI
with thanks to Steve Afif

I figure on allowing each person a couple of lamb noisettes, meat nuggets taken from the boned lamb loin, and further provide enough for half those present to have another one each.

1 onion, chopped roughly	10 lamb noisettes, about 1¼ inches
1¼ cups extra-virgin olive oil	thick
zest of 1 lemon and juice of 2	8 tablespoons tahini
¼ teaspoon ground cumin, plus more,	4 garlic cloves, minced or pressed
for garnishing	½ teaspoon coarse salt

Put the onion into one large shallow dish in which the noisettes will fit in one layer, or divide the onion into two medium-to-large freezer bags. Add the oil, lemon zest, and cumin (dividing equally, obviously, if you're using bags). Give a good stir and then add the lamb. Cover the dish or tie up the bags and leave, turning or squishing respectively at half time, as long as you've got; frankly, though, it should be for at least 10 minutes and preferably not in the fridge. Preheat the oven to 425°F. Put a nonstick or cast-iron pan on the stove. Remove the noisettes from the marinade; you don't need to wipe them dry, just brush off the bits of onion. Sear each side for a minute or two, then transfer to a baking pan and then to the preheated oven. Ten minutes should be right for pink, but not bloody, lamb; you may need a bit longer if the meat started off very cold. You will need to check for yourself, obviously, and when cooked as you want, remove to warmed plate.

For the sauce, put the tahini in a bowl and add the garlic and salt. Stir with a wooden spoon, adding the lemon juice as you do; it will seize up here, but don't worry because it will loosen later. Slowly add some water (I find I can use about ½ cup), pouring from a measuring cup so that only a little goes in at a time, and keep stirring. When you have a smooth mixture the consistency of heavy cream, stop adding water. Put into a bowl with a spoon and sprinkle with the additional ground cumin.

I like a plateful of lemony spinach with this—if you're buying it frozen, which I do, make sure it's leaf, not chopped, spinach—and a tomato salad. If you want a carbohydrate, then bulghur wheat (see page 102) would be just right.

PASSION FRUIT FOOL

The fragrant astringency of passion fruit is just right after the palate-thickening stickiness of the tahini. This recipe comes from British TV cook Stephen Saunders' *Short Cuts* and is so good that I haven't even downsized it from his specifications, which are for six; just use this to fill 4 glasses instead, and your guests will thank you.

12 passion fruit

1 cup heavy cream

1 cup confectioners' sugar

juice of 1 lemon

2 teaspoons Cointreau

Cut the passion fruit in half, scoop out the pulp with a spoon, and leave it in a bowl. Semi-whisk the cream in a large bowl and leave it in the fridge. Put 4 glasses in the fridge too, though it won't hurt if they're not chilled. Sift the sugar and set aside.

Then, when you want to eat dessert, whisk the sugar into the cream with the lemon juice and Cointreau. Fold in the passion fruit and pour the fool into the glasses. Serve with whatever cookies you like.

ROAST COD WITH PEA PURÉE

QUICKLY SCALED MONT BLANC

The peas are actually a speeded-up, simplified version of the garlic-breathy puréed pea crostini on page 301. If the quantities given seem to specify a lot, it's because people eat a lot of it. Though be grateful if you've got some left over; it makes lovely pea soup.

If you're getting the cod from your fish seller, ask for it to be cut from the top end.

ROAST COD WITH
PEA PURÉE

cloves from 1 head garlic, unpeeled

5½ cups frozen young peas

8 tablespoons (1 stick) unsalted butter

4 tablespoons crème fraîche or
    heavy cream

1–2 tablespoons olive oil

1 tablespoon flour

salt and freshly milled pepper

4 cod fillets (about 8 ounces each)

Put the garlic in a large saucepan of cold water, bring to boil, salt, and then boil for 10 minutes. Fish out the cloves with a slotted spoon, push them out of their skins back into the water, and bring back to the boil. Add the peas and cook for slightly longer than you would if you were eating them normally. Drain, then tip into a food processor, add the butter, and process. Add the cream and process again. If you've done all this when you get in, scrape back into the saucepan so you can reheat as and when you want it.

Now for the cod. Preheat the oven to 400°F. Get hold of a frying pan that will go in the oven later; otherwise, use whatever frying pan you have and transfer the fish you cook in it later to a baking sheet. Whichever, pour the oil into the pan, put it on the stove, and, while it's heating up, put the flour on a plate, add salt and pepper, and dredge the cod fillets in it. Sear the cod fillets on each side, then transfer to the oven and bake until just cooked through, 7–10 minutes, depending on how thick they are and how cold they were before you started. Serve the juicy white fish alongside the vivid green nubbly purée.

QUICKLY SCALED MONT BLANC

My mother often made this most basic version of the traditional Italian chestnut dessert called Mont Blanc. It's just sweetened chestnut purée (from a can) scraped into a bowl and some whipped heavy cream piled on top; you can add crumbled bought meringues, grated chocolate as you like, and whisk a tablespoon each of rum and confectioners' sugar into the cream. If you can add some actual marrons glacés, too, so much the better. This is so gloopy it's easier to do it in individual glasses, even if it's not my usual style.

NEW POTATOES

It's hard to cook potatoes in under half an hour, but if you get those teeny-weeny miniature new potatoes you should keep within schedule. Or take more time but no more effort by putting 6 baking potatoes in the oven for 1–1½ hours (it all depends, of course, on your having that much time to play with), then scraping out the fleshy interior into a bowl. Warm up some milk and a huge amount of butter (I put both in a measuring cup in the microwave) and fork into the potatoes with salt, pepper, and freshly grated nutmeg.

SAUSAGE AND MASHED POTATOES

You can do very easy "sausages and mash," that simple and hearty British comfort dish, by putting some sausages in an oiled pan during the last 50 minutes of the potatoes baking. Both worth remembering for those evenings you do get back a couple of hours before you want to eat, but without the energy to do anything in those two hours.

The pea purée, while we're dealing with variations on a theme, goes just as rhapsodically well with noisettes of lamb (see page 174, only add some rosemary needles to the marinade in place of the onion).

DUCK WITH ORANGE SALSA

NOODLES WITH SCALLIONS, SHIITAKE MUSHROOMS, AND SNOW PEAS

ICE CREAM WITH STEM GINGER OR FIGS

❖

Shrimp cocktail, coq au vin, duck à l'orange—there has been in the recent past an insistent, cool-minded movement to bring these disparaged specialities of the 1960s and 1970s back into culinary fashion. I have nothing against this in principle; if it tastes good, eat it. Fashionableness—ironic or otherwise—should not count against a food any more than its unfashionableness. The pairing of duck and orange can work (see page 166 also), and work quickly. A coriander-spiked citrussy salsa—an intensely flavored, swiftly-put-together relish—is a perfect foil for the sweet and rich flesh of the soy-sprinkled duck breasts. If available, blood oranges look spectacular in this, but they tend to be hard to peel and chop. If you're in a hurry, choose a seedless, neatly peeling navel orange or substitute a papaya, though in which case don't bother about using the mint but do give a squeeze of orange along with the lime. Noodles are just right with this and, as usual, you can boil them when you get in and finish them off later.

DUCK WITH ORANGE SALSA

You may find it easier to use a grapefruit knife, if you own one, to dismantle the oranges for this; in which case, halve each unpeeled orange and use the knife to cut around the rim and through each segment, as you would if preparing a grapefruit. Cut each chiselled-out segment into two or three pieces and then, after you've done all of them, squeeze the juice from the hollowed-out orange halves over the diced flesh. (Another option follows in the recipe.) Also, I think it is better to use rubber gloves when working with the chili here, however unhygienic they may be. Otherwise your hands will infuse everything with burning heat for the rest of the evening.

4 boneless duck breast halves with skin (about 8 ounces each)

soy sauce

2 oranges, preferably seedless, peeled and pith removed (or see headnote)

½ medium red onion, minced

1 red chili, halved lengthwise, seeded and minced

3–4 tablespoons finely chopped coriander

1–2 tablespoons finely chopped mint

salt

½ lime

Preheat the oven to 450°F.

Slash the skin of the breasts diagonally, about 4 times on each, then sprinkle with soy sauce and rub this over the skin with your hand. Arrange on a rack in a baking dish, skin side up. Cook for about 20 minutes, though do look after 15 minutes; the skin should be crisp, the flesh pinkly tender.

Meanwhile, if not using a grapefruit knife to dismantle them, slice the peeled, pithless oranges crossways and then chop each slice into small chunks. In an ideal world, you might want to remove the membranes between each segment, but I don't. Stir the chili into the oranges, along with the coriander and mint. Sprinkle with salt and squeeze over the lime gradually and tasting as you do; you want the salsa to be sharp but not painfully so. Stir gently together and put aside until needed. Standing around for 15 minutes or so will do it no harm—indeed, on the contrary. To serve, either plonk the breasts, skin side up, on a plate, or cut each breast into diagonal slices about ¼ inch thick and lay them on said plate. Put the salsa in a bowl and serve alongside the duck for people to to help themselves.

NOODLES WITH SCALLIONS, SHIITAKE MUSHROOMS, AND SNOW PEAS

Just as you can boil the noodles in good time—in other words, when you can still enjoy the privacy of your own kitchen—so you can chop all the bits to go in them. I know stir-frying can tax a girl's nerves, but this is serenely manageable.

8 ounces egg noodles	8 ounces shiitake mushrooms, stemmed and chopped
2 tablespoons vegetable oil	
1 teaspoon sesame oil	4 ounces snow peas, halved or cut in thirds
4 red chilis, seeded and chopped	
6 scallions (white and green parts), sliced into ½-inch lengths	2 tablespoons soy sauce
	3–4 tablespoons chopped coriander

Boil the noodles in salted water according to the instructions on the package, then drain, rinse in cold water, and drain again. Heat the oils in a hot wok or large frying pan and stir-fry the chilis and scallions for 1 minute; add the mushrooms and stir-fry for another 2 minutes. Then add, stirring furiously, the snow peas. Give them a minute, then add the noodles, lifting them up in the pan and stirring well so all is mixed in together, pouring in the soy as you do so. Toss well and quickly, then empty onto a big round plate. Sprinkle with the coriander.

ICE CREAM WITH STEM GINGER OR FIGS

All you need to do for dessert—following one of the suggestions in the hasty-improvisations section earlier—is put a container of good vanilla ice cream and a jar of stem ginger in syrup on the table. Canned figs—the stuff of sweet trolleys in provincial British hotels, maybe—would also be just, delightfully, right after the zingily salsa'd duck.

Obviously, you can simply grill your mackerel—all you need then is a squeeze of lemon or orange juice over (a Seville orange if in season), and nothing could be better. Fish, especially oily fish, is always good when plain grilled. When I want to eat properly but in a hurry, I lunch on grilled trout, herring, or mackerel fillets with pickled ginger and soy sauce. The reason I might want to cook fish in a way that might seem a little more elaborate is that cooking in the oven I find easy when I have people over.

Mackerel poached or steamed in cider, or sometimes cider vinegar, with a sauce that may or may not contain mustard, is a fairly common way of eating in Normandy and Brittany; this version happens to be reassuringly pared down. It helps, too, that mackerel (like trout) is easily bought. Obviously, the cider intended is the French hard cider, made in the area. But don't lose sleep over finding some. Use any hard cider you can get your hands on or a mixture of half apple juice and half lager beer. Have potatoes or cabbage with caraway with this, and apples for dessert, too. The cider with the fish, and the apples after, do not cloy or bore; somehow the flavors seem to deepen rather than tire with the repetition.

MACKEREL IN CIDER

I know that the idea of cream, and quite so much of it, added to sauce that is to swathe such oily fish might sound alarming. But when you're cooking quickly, something's got to give, and I find most often that something is the contemporary concern about cream and butter. Adding either or both of these is a way of adding instant depth, texture, and accomplished finish to a dish. But if you want to add less, then I'm not stopping you.

6 skinless mackerel fillets (about
    8 ounces each)
3 shallots or I small onion, minced
I cup hard cider, or ½ cup each apple
    juice and lager beer

salt and freshly milled black pepper
½ cup crème fraîche or heavy cream
lemon juice (optional)
1–2 tablespoons chopped parsley

Preheat the oven to 400°F.

Put the fillets in a lightly buttered, shallow baking dish. Sprinkle with the shallots and pour over the cider. Season with salt and pepper and cover tightly with foil. Bake for 20–25 minutes, until the fish is cooked through. Transfer the mackerel to a warm serving plate and cover to keep warm.

Pour the cooking liquid into a small saucepan and boil, reducing by about half. Add the crème fraîche and simmer with the heat low for a couple of minutes. Season to taste, adding lemon juice if you want.

Strain the sauce, pressing with the back of a spoon to extract all the liquid. Garnish the fish with parsley and serve with the cider sauce.

With this I can think of nothing better than plain boiled potatoes and spinach with a fragrant cocoa-brown dusting of freshly grated nutmeg. But frankly, you can put all your effort into the boiled potatoes (I think peeled large floury ones are more comforting here than the ready-washed and thin-skinned waxy ones, though I am prepared to accept them as an alternative) and then just make a quick salad with watercress and thinly sliced bulb fennel. This is the perfect foil to the pungent creaminess of the fish and sauce. A small amount of grainy mustard in the salad's dressing will work well. I love my mother's cabbage with caraway here, too. Shred half a large white cabbage, either by hand or in the processor (using the slicing disc). Melt 2 tablespoons or so butter and 1 tablespoon of olive oil in a large, deep frying pan or wok. Scatter in 1 tablespoonful of caraway seeds, then toss the cabbage in. Keep stirring and tossing over high heat till the cabbage has wilted and shrunk a little (a couple of minutes or so) and then throw in about 1 cup of hot stock (I use half a vegetable bouillon cube in some boiling water) and toss, then clamp on a lid. In another couple of minutes or thereabouts, remove the lid, let bubble away for another minute, and then serve. If you want to add more butter or more caraway seeds at this stage, do; anyway, sprinkle salt and grind pepper over generously.

CABBAGE WITH CARAWAY

BUTTERED APPLES

Fry 3–4 Gravensteins, peeled, cored, and cut into eighths, in about 4 tablespoons butter until brown on each side. Sprinkle thickly with superfine sugar until that too browns and then pile onto a plate and serve with ice cream or cream (or add the cream to the juices in the pan and make a sauce that way). Ben and Jerry's Rainforest Crunch ice cream is delicious with these buttery, caramelly apples.

CHAMBÉRY TROUT

SALSA VERDE

GUSSIED-UP ICE CREAM

❖

With the herby, vermouth-poached trout serve a salsa verde, which is the perfect foil for the fish and an excellent idea for the quick cook anyway, as all you need to do is to put everything in a food processor and turn it on. The salsa verde is good with poached chicken breasts, too (see page 165).

With either the fish or the chicken, I'd go for some fava beans, which are perfect with the salsa verde—being, I suppose, an Italianate version of fava beans with parsley sauce that I ate often as a child. Otherwise go for lentils, canned if need be, with bacon lardons or strips or cubes of pancetta stirred into them. But remember that the bacon is salty and the salsa verde is salty and that canned lentils tend to be salty, so go easy. That's why pancetta, if you can get it, is a better choice. For dessert—ice cream slightly gussied up.

CHAMBÉRY TROUT

This is another easy way of cooking fish without touching it while you do so. I keep a bottle of Chambéry or Noilly Prat vermouth in the kitchen at all times, primarily because I am not much of a drinker and don't necessarily want to open a bottle of wine when I need just a little for something I'm cooking. Of course, if you've got friends coming for dinner, you might want to drink white wine with the fish, so obviously use some of that rather than the Chambéry if you prefer. In which case, use 1 cup wine, dispensing with the water.

Save the fish-poaching liquid for the salsa, which follows.

4 trout (1–1¼ pounds each) cleaned, with the heads left on

salt and freshly milled black pepper

⅔ cup Chambéry or other white dry vermouth

Preheat the oven to 400°F.

Grease a baking dish—I use an old enamel one I have that measures about 8 × 12 inches—and then put the cleaned and seasoned trout in it. Pour over the Chambéry mixed with ¼ cup water, cover loosely with foil, making sure the foil doesn't touch the fish, and bake for about 20 minutes. When the fish is ready, the flesh should be beginning to be flaky and have lost its translucency. It's probably better to take the fish out before you think it is absolutely *à point,* as you can just let it stand, still covered, and to one side, for a few minutes, in which time it will continue to cook gently, which is the best way.

SALSA VERDE

I first had salsa verde when I was a chambermaid in Florence. I was there with a school friend and we used to go, most evenings, to a trattoria called Benvenuto and eat tortellini in *brodo,* their *penne al modo nostro,* which involved an intensely garlicky tomato sauce, then moussy-sweet *fegato*—calves' liver—or, my favorite, tongue with salsa verde. Now I wonder how good the restaurant was, but then, when most of the time we were living on a bottle of wine, a loaf of bread, and a kilo of tomatoes between us a day, it seemed like heaven. Anyway, after a while we came back mostly for the clientèle, made up in significant part by the local community of transsexuals and transvestites. The most beautiful of all of them, and the one generally held to be the glorious and burnished figure-head, the presiding force and icon, was a Bardot-esque blonde, only more muscular, known as La Principessa; those less appreciative of her aesthetic construction referred to her simply as La Romana. I felt I'd arrived when she huskily called out "*Ciao bella*" to me across the street one day.

Salsa verde has, since those days, become something of a menu commonplace in Britain, but the salsa verde that gets served up is often much fancier—with mint, basil, sometimes even coriander thrown in—than Benvenuto's version, which was just parsley, capers, cornichons, anchovy, oil, and vinegar, making a semi-liquid, deep-flavored, and spiky sauce the color of pool table felt. I, too, sometimes add to that basic mixture. I might throw in arugula, bought in robust great bunches from a Greek greengrocer's; it gives a wonderful pepperiness (itself a good balance for the gratifyingly searing saltiness of the anchovies). At other times, tarragon, just a little, lends an aniseedy and hay-fresh muskiness.

After the salsa verde has emulsified, to make it creamier and more liquid I spoon or dribble in a good few tablespoons of the winy liquid in which the fish has been soaking. Normally, salsa verde has lemon added at the end if it's to accompany fish, vinegar if it's to go with boiled meats, but I tend to use vinegar more often, even with fish. And although it is not at all *come si deve,* I quite like borrowing a trick from sauce gribiche and adding some finely chopped hard-boiled egg white, too—but for practical purposes, when the idea is to cook quickly, there's no call even to consider such innovations.

Now I know most people put garlic in. But I thought I remembered that, when I had the salsa verde with tongue in Florence all that time ago, there wasn't any garlic in it. I couldn't be absolutely sure, so I asked Anna del Conte, the best Italian foodwriter in English, a great authority, utterly versed in her subject and a reassuring, illuminating recipe doctor. I felt doubtful suddenly only because every salsa verde I've eaten since has had garlic in. She reassured me, said that it most certainly wouldn't have had. Salsa verde emanates from Lombardy (where the parsley is especially prized) and garlic was then anathema to the Lombardi. Bread crumbs or some boiled or mashed potato (to thicken the mixture) are also traditional. Of course you can add garlic if you want, but I suggest not too much. I don't add bread crumbs or potato simply because I use the food processor to blend it all, and the machine automatically thickens it. It is difficult to be specific about amounts, but what you should end up with is a green-flecked, almost solid liquid that looks as if a spoon would stand up in it—even if, in fact, the spoon would, put to the test, soon sink gloopily into that thick, green, parsley-dense pond.

I large bunch parsley	5 tablespoons fish poaching liquid (from
3 anchovy fillets	Chambéry Trout, above), plus more,
I tablespoon capers, preferably packed	if needed
in salt	I tablespoon wine vinegar or lemon
2 cornichons (miniature gherkins)	juice, plus more, if needed
8 tablespoons extra-virgin olive oil, plus	
more, if needed	

Tear the parsley leaves from the stalks (don't worry about being too neat) and put them in the bowl of the food processor (don't even think about doing this sauce, or at least not if you want to get it ready quickly and with a minimum of effort, if you haven't got a food processor; just mix some oil and lemon together instead). Add the anchovy fillets (if they taste rebarbatively salty, then soak them briefly in a saucer of milk), the capers (well rinsed in cold water and drained if they've been packed in salt), and the cornichons. Pulse, then scrape the bowl with a spatula and, with the machine running, gradually pour the olive oil through the feed tube. Take the lid off to check how thick the sauce is becoming and dip in a finger to taste. Scrape down any mixture from the sides. Add more oil if needed; then when the fish is ready, spoon in some of the poaching liquid, all while processing. Taste after every small addition, adding more of the liquid if needed. Then pour the salsa verde into a bowl with a spoon and stir in the vinegar or lemon, a little at a time, adding more if needed. And that's it. Keep whatever salsa's left over in the fridge, covered with plastic film. Eccentric though this might sound, I love it, sharp and cold and salty, with hot, fat, spicy, or even not spicy, sausages.

GUSSIED-UP ICE CREAM

Again, this idea has been adumbrated earlier: to ice cream you simply add some processor-pulverized chocolate. Break 4 ounces of the best, most malevolently dark chocolate you can find into small squares and put them into the bowl of the food processor. Make sure they're cold before you start. Pulse them to dusty rubble. Empty onto a plate and put this plate in the fridge until you need it. At which time, pour the pulverized chocolate into a small bowl and put on the table alongside the container of ice cream.

Any thin fillet of meat or fish will cook quickly, but salmon is particularly useful because its oiliness stops it from drying to irritating cardboardiness in the heat. But still, exercise caution; don't overcook—just dunk these fleshy, coral-colored slices into the pan.

Balsamic vinegar is one of those ingredients whose fashionability leads people to disparage it. But the sweet pungency of the balsamic vinegar here is so right with the oily meatiness of the fish that its use is justified. After this, you can expand into a good plate of perfectly *à point* brie or camembert and another of aromatic, wine-toned grapes. Both must be at room temperature.

SALMON SCALLOPS WITH WARM BALSAMIC VINAIGRETTE

I tablespoon vegetable oil , if needed

8 scallops or thin fillets of salmon

(about 4 ounces each)

small bunch chives, snipped

6 tablespoons balsamic vinegar

6 tablespoons olive oil

Heat a heavy-bottomed, well-seasoned frying pan or good nonstick pan or griddle. Add the vegetable oil if you have any doubt about the fish sticking, put in the salmon, and cook for I minute on each side, then turn again and cook for another minute on each side. The fish should be just cooked through. Put on a warmed plate and, when all are ready, sprinkle with chives. Keep warm with tented foil.

In a small saucepan, heat the balsamic vinegar and olive oil until warm (but not hot) and dribble a little over the fish. Pour the remaining vinaigrette into a small pitcher (with a teaspoon near it, for stirring) and let people pour or spoon over as they wish. The measurements I've stipulated, strictly speaking, give you more than you need, but otherwise you would be producing such a stingy-looking puddle.

Another way of doing this, and how I always do it if there's just me eating, is to pour a few drops of oil into the pan (you can't use a griddle here) and fry the salmon in it. Then, when the fish is cooked and on its plate, I pour a few drops of balsamic vinegar into the pan in which I've cooked the fish, swirl it about, and pour it over the fish. Dot with scissored chives and eat.

What works here is the gentle balance between the sweet acidity of the vinegar and the meaty oiliness of the fish. But you could elaborate on this theme with other vinegars, or the juices of lime, lemon, or Seville orange.

If you're using lemon juice, fry the salmon in a small amount of olive oil and add (off the heat, at the end) parsley, feathery green clumps of the stuff, vigorously chopped but not minced by machine (unless you're using huge great quantities, the food processor is not the answer—you just end up with a damp green mess) in place of the chives.

If you want to deglaze the pan with lime, which makes for an intense and astringent dressing, cook the salmon first in a nut of butter. The sweetness of the butter counters the more invasively acid punch of the lime. Sprinkle over musky, pungent, freshly chopped coriander, but not much of it, just before serving. Or leave the salmon itself relatively unprinked and add the coriander, in relative abundance, to a couple of cans of drained, oil-dressed cannellini beans.

Before the cheese, you may want a green salad, or put all on the table together.

CINNAMON-HOT RACK OF LAMB
WITH CHERRIED AND CHICKPEA'D COUSCOUS
BAKED FIGS

Lamb can be cooked very quickly indeed. Many people, however, stuff, prink, and generally fuss about rack of lamb, but the truth is you need do nothing providing you buy good meat. Applying a little oil and spice will not take very long. It will make the fat crisp up better, which is a consideration, but frankly it won't matter if you don't bother. The figs afterward offer sweet, plump, ripe fruitiness and appropriately exotic voluptuousness.

If you wanted, you could cook quail instead of lamb, in which case substitute 8 quail for the lamb and add some butter, also mixed with a little cinnamon, to put into the birds' cavities.

CINNAMON-HOT RACK
OF LAMB

I scant tablespoon chili oil	**2 racks lamb (7–8 ribs each)**
½ tablespoon ground cinnamon	

Preheat the oven to 450°F.

Mix the oil and cinnamon to a paste and rub over the meat. Place on a rack over a baking dish and cook for about 30 minutes. The skin should be shiny brown and the meat within pink and tender. Let stand for 5 minutes or so before serving. Turn the oven down to 350° for the figs.

CHERRIED AND CHICKPEA'D COUSCOUS

Couscous should, traditionally, be soaked and then steamed (see page 207), but you don't have to; if you're adding bits and pieces to it, you can get away with this incorrect procedure, although expect aficionados to be shocked. It is difficult to give precise details for the couscous, as different brands give slightly different instructions. I use precooked couscous; depending on the make, you may need to add a little more liquid if you think the grains are too heavy. Check package instructions.

Now, normally, I hate fruit in savory concoctions, but the sour cherries here really do work. There is an authenticity to the mixture of sweet dried fruit and waxy nut and fragrant buttery grain. But if you don't like the idea of sour cherries, just leave them out.

The couscous will taste better if it has been steeped in stock rather than water, but by making stock I don't mean anything more arduous than stirring half a stock cube into boiling water.

½ vegetable bouillon cube	½ cup pine nuts
salt	1 can (14 ounces) chickpeas
2 cups quick-cooking couscous	2 tablespoons unsalted butter
¼ cup dried sour cherries	3 scallions (white and green parts), cut
½ teaspoon ground cumin	into thin rings
½ teaspoon cinnamon	harissa (page 208), for serving

Pour boiling water into a measuring cup to get 2 cups, add the half bouillon cube, crumbled, then pour into a saucepan and bring to the boil again. Add salt to taste. Put the couscous in a bowl, mix in the cherries, cumin, and cinnamon, and then turn into the saucepan of boiling water. Wait until it starts to boil again, put the lid on, and take the pan off the heat. Meanwhile, put a heavy frying pan on the stove and, when it's hot, toast the pine nuts. When they are beginning to turn golden, remove them.

Heat the chickpeas with their liquid in a saucepan. When the couscous is tender and has absorbed the liquid, about 10 minutes, add the drained warm chickpeas, stir in the butter, then half the pine nuts, and turn out on to a large heated plate and sprinkle with the remaining pine nuts. You will probably have more couscous than you need here, but I feel that making less than this looks so miserable and unwelcoming. Anyway, it tastes good the next day. The best way of reheating it is either by steaming (a strainer suspended over a saucepan of boiling water will do it) or a quick burst in a microwave. Stir in the scallions and eat hot with the harissa to the side.

BAKED FIGS

8 black figs

4 tablespoons unsalted butter

4 heaping tablespoons honey

½ cup red wine

4 cardamom pods, lightly crushed, or

2 bay leaves, crumbled

I cup yogurt, chilled, for serving

Preheat the oven to 350°F.

Put the figs in an ovenproof dish in which they'll fit pretty snugly. Cut each one as if in quarters, only leaving the base intact. In a saucepan put the butter, honey, wine, and cardamom and heat up. When the butter's melted, the honey's dissolved, and you have a smooth, hot, sweet gravy, pour over the figs and put in the oven for about a quarter of an hour. Remove and let sit for 5 minutes or so before eating; and when you eat, make sure it's with dollops of the satiny, cold yogurt to the side.

CHICKEN WITH SCALLIONS, CHILI, AND YOGURT

SEVEN-MINUTE STEAMED CHOCOLATE PUDDING

During my time as a restaurant critic, I became obsessed with the insistent inanities of the fashionable menu. In the end, either someone can cook or they can't, either the food tastes good or it doesn't. I object, for example, to the term *pan-fried*. I mind because what are you going to fry something in, if not in a pan? But the thing about pan-fried is not so much that it is tautologous, as that it is a con-trick. Let me deconstruct: fried is greasy, heavy, fattening, old-style food that none of us eats any more; pan-fried is modern, light, clean-living, healthy. The distorted echoes of "stir-fried" help formulate that image-by-association. But food, whether fried or pan-fried, is cooked in the same way. It's a brilliant wheeze. I could call it grilled (or even griddled) chicken and that would have been OK. But I have my doubts about the efficacy of the domestic broiler, in the first place; not everyone owns a griddle, in the second. I cannot, just cannot, bring myself to call it pan-fried chicken. So, just chicken it is.

CHICKEN WITH SCALLIONS, CHILI, AND YOGURT

The accompaniment borrows from the idea of tzatziki and all those Middle Eastern yogurt salads; I have my friends Lucy Heller and Charles Elton to thank for it. I haven't put cucumber in this recipe, but sometimes I do. Coriander is, funnily enough, easier to come by than mint these days (although mint is certainly the traditional herb to use here), so you can use either of them. The point is to have a cool, pungent accompaniment to the tender, but not strongly flavored, poultry. You can fashion it as you wish. If I use cucumber, I don't bother to salt and degorge it; it may, therefore, get watery if you leave it lying around—but, as this is a quick dinner, the tradeoff is worth it. Make sure to use whole-milk yogurt; you want this sauce to be astringent but voluptuous; and low-fat natural yogurt is too thin, sour, and depressing.

For this I would use the cut known as a suprême: a boned chicken breast half that has been skinned, usually called a cutlet. If it's easier, just buy whole breast portions, but in either case preferably from a free-range bird, and leave the skin on if you wish. It will look glorious if you happen to have a ridged griddle or grill pan to cook the breast in, but a heavy-bottomed frying pan is more than fine. Don't use a nonstick pan; you want a burnt-golden exterior and the nonstick pan pointedly can't give you that.

I think it's necessary to cook extra chicken, even if you have to fry it in two batches, just because I have never known people not to want more. And how could leftovers matter? The half cucumber used in this is optional; peel it or don't peel it as you wish. I tend to use a potato peeler to shave off strips of peel so that there's a stripey dark-green, light-green effect; this was how my mother always did it.

6 chicken cutlets (about 6 ounces each)	**I green chili, seeded and minced**
juice of 2 lemons	**2 garlic cloves, minced**
6 tablespoons olive oil, plus more,	**½ cucumber, cut into small dice (see**
if needed	**headnote; optional)**
salt and freshly milled black pepper	**3–4 tablespoons chopped coriander**
6 scallions (white and green parts) cut	**1–2 tablespoons chopped mint**
into thin rings	**1¾ cups yogurt**

Marinate the chicken in the lemon juice and 3 tablespoons of the oil. Season with salt and pepper. If the cutlets look fat and plump—you want them to cook fairly speedily—put them between 2 sheets of wax paper or plastic film and bash them, using anything heavy you can lay your hands on—a can of baked beans, say—if you're not the sort to keep a meat mallet in the top drawer in your kitchen.

To make the sauce, add the scallions, chili, garlic, cucumber, coriander, and mint to the yogurt. Stir, taste, and add salt as needed.

Remove the chicken from the marinade. Add the remaining oil to a large frying pan and, when it's hot, fry the cutlets. Turn over after 5 minutes or so and cook the other side for about 5 minutes, or until just cooked through. It may be cooked, it may need more time. You may need to add a little more oil while cooking; you certainly will if you're frying in two batches. If you want, when the chicken is cooked, you can throw the lemony marinade over it in the pan at the last minute. Arrange the cutlets on a large plate and serve the yogurt relish in a bowl with a spoon.

With this, I might give the couscous on page 186, minus the cinnamon and minus the dried cherries. A tomato salad, with or without black olives, is all you need otherwise. If you can't find any tomatoes with flavor, then a crisp-leaved green salad will do.

SEVEN-MINUTE STEAMED CHOCOLATE PUDDING

I am not a particular fan of the microwave, except for defrosting baby meals and reheating cold roast potatoes (divine, though dangerously easy to eat; I wish my Aunt Fel hadn't told me of this), but I had this chocolate pudding at the home of some friends one Saturday lunchtime and thought it was amazingly good—thick and rich and chocolatey. One thing, though—don't hide the fact that you're microwaving it; they do say the proof of the pudding is in the eating. This takes 2 minutes to prepare in the food processor, 5 minutes actually to cook in the microwave, and 10 minutes' standing time after that. If you get everything ready in advance, just throw it in the microwave 15 minutes or so before you think you'll want to eat it.

This recipe comes from Barbara Kafka's *Microwave Gourmet* and I have kept to her quantities for 8 people because I am greedy. If you—unlike me—think 4 people won't eat enough for 8, then halve the quantities and cooking time and use a 3-cup pudding basin.

10 tablespoons (1 stick plus	½ cup heavy cream
2 tablespoons) unsalted butter	⅓ cup all-purpose flour, sifted
8 ounces best-quality semisweet	½ teaspoon baking powder
chocolate	3 eggs
½ cup light brown sugar	crème fraîche or heavy cream,
1 teaspoon vanilla	for serving

Butter a 9 × 4-inch ceramic bowl or 4-cup pudding basin with 2 tablespoons of the butter.

Grate the chocolate in a food processor, then add the remaining butter, cut into 1-tablespoon pieces, and the sugar. Process until thoroughly combined. Add remaining ingredients except the crème fraîche and process to a smooth mixture.

Pour into a prepared bowl. Cover tightly with microwave plastic film. Cook at 100 percent (Barbara Kafka refers to a 600–700-watt microwave as the norm; mine is 750 watt but I leave cooking time as is) for 5 minutes, until set. Pierce the film with the tip of a sharp knife, remove from the oven, and cover the top of the bowl with a heavy plate; this will keep the pudding hot. Let stand for 10 minutes. Unmold onto a serving plate.

Put some crème fraîche or cream—I prefer crème fraîche, as the sourness sets off the palate-coating sweetness better—in a bowl on the table.

STEAK MIRABEAU

RASPBERRIES AND CREAM

❖

The steak mirabeau is a recipe from one of my favorite cookbooks, Ann and Franco Taruschio's *Leaves from the Walnut Tree* (the Walnut Tree was Elizabeth David's favorite restaurant), which is written with such love and quiet authority. You can trust this book; nothing is for effect and everything works. Innocent of illustration, *Leaves from the Walnut Tree* is far from being a chef book. Often, when I'm wondering what to cook and want to find something simple that won't take too long, I turn to it. This is just such a recipe. And it shows, too, the Taruschios' confident affection for the sort of food that glossier establishments with less secure foundations tend to eschew in a panic-stricken search for something ever new.

All you need after are raspberries and cream (see below).

STEAK MIRABEAU

Buy good-quality anchovy fillets in olive oil and drain well. You could soak them for a few minutes in milk before draining well again, if you're worried that the fillets you've got are just too unbearably salty, but do remember that the particular fierce rasp of the anchovy is what's wanted here, so don't attempt to drown it out. I love anchovies with meat (see pages 100 and 344) and, if you wanted, you could just as easily use some lamb steaks here. You could leave out the olives and the criss-crossing business, too. A tablespoon or so of cream at the end will make for a mellower concoction, but still a pleasurably bracing one.

1 tablespoon olive oil	freshly milled black pepper
2 tablespoons unsalted butter	20 anchovy fillets
4 boneless strip steaks (about	18 pitted black olives, halved
8 ounces each)	1 glass red wine

Heat the oil and butter in a large frying pan or pans and, when it's foaming, add the steaks. Cook as preferred—I like mine bloody, for which do them 3 or so minutes a side—and season with the pepper. When ready, remove to a large, warmed plate. Criss-cross the steaks with 4 anchovy fillets each and place the olive halves in the squares. (This doesn't look as dinky-do as it sounds.) Mash the remaining 4 anchovy fillets in the pan juices, add the red wine, and reduce rapidly until a glaze appears on the sauce. Pour the sauce over the steaks and serve at once.

Perfect, sweet, waxy new potatoes are what you want with this; I love, too, the iron tang of some leaf spinach just buttered and nutmegged, soaking up the wine and olive brine of the steak.

I suggest raspberries and cream for dessert: a mound of the fruit, a bowl of RASPBERRIES thick yellow cream. If raspberries aren't absolutely as they should be at the AND CREAM moment, then stick to the same ingredients but treat them with less respect. Mash 2½ cups raspberries (bar a couple of tablespoons which you've removed for later), tired fresh or just thawed frozen, sprinkled with a little confectioners' sugar, in a bowl with a fork. Whisk 1 cup, or thereabouts, heavy cream with 1–2 further tablespoons of confectioners' sugar. Fold in the raspberries and spoon this rough fool into a bowl (or individual glasses, if you prefer) and scatter the unmashed ones over the top. And you can always crumble in some shop-bought meringues, too.

WEEKEND
LUNCH

Although the dinner party remains the symbol of social eating, most eating in company among my friends actually takes place at weekend lunch. After a long day at work, many of us are, frankly, too tired to go out and eat dinner, let alone cook it. And there is, as well, the baby factor. For many people of my generation, having to get food ready after the children have gone to bed explains the popularity of the takeout menu. And even those who haven't got children are affected by the baby-sitting arrangements of their friends who have. When I was younger we stayed in bed on weekends until two in the afternoon; now that most of us are awakened at six in the morning, there is a gap in the day where lunch can go. We have got into the habit of filling it.

Lunch is more forgiving than dinner; there isn't the dread engendered by perceived but not-quite-formulated expectations; there's no agenda, no aspirational model to follow, no socioculinary challenge to which to rise—in short, no pressure. Lunch is just lunch.

And if you don't want to cook it, you don't have to. A weekend lunch can be at its most relaxed and pleasurable when it is just an indoor picnic. What matters, then, is what you buy. These days shopping is nobly recast as "sourcing"—and clever you for finding the best chili-marinated olives, French sourdough bread, or air-dried beef; there's certainly no shame in not clattering about with your own pots and pans instead.

Shopping is not necessarily the easy option. It's certainly not the cheap one. But discerning extravagance (rather than mere feckless vulgarity) can be immensely pleasurable. Indeed, I can find it positively uplifting—not for nothing is shopping known as retail therapy. Shopping for food is better than any other form of shopping. There's no trying-on, for a start. Choosing the right cheese, the best and ripest tomato, the pinkest, sweetest ham can be intensely gratifying. And in shopping for food that you are then going to prepare (even if that preparation involves no more than de-bagging and unwrapping) there is also the glorious self-indulgence of knowing that you are giving pleasure to others.

Shopping is not a quick activity—you need to be prepared to proceed slowly, haltingly. Compromise can be ruinous. Of course, some of the time we all eat food that is less than perfect, less than enjoyable even, but you can't set out to buy inferior produce—what would be the point?

Good food doesn't have to be difficult to cook, and it certainly doesn't need to be difficult to buy. But you must know what you're after. The important thing is to be greedy enough to get what's good, but not so restlessly greedy that you get too much of it. Restrict your choices, so that you provide lots of a few things rather than small amounts of many. This is partly an aesthetic dictate, partly a practical one. If you buy 4-ounce pieces of six different cheeses, everyone is going to feel inhibited about cutting some off; however generous you have been, it is only the meagerness of each portion that will be apparent. Provide, instead, a semblance—indeed the reality—of voluptuous abundance. You don't need to buy more than three different cheeses, but get great big fat wedges of each. You want munificence, you want plenty, you want people to feel they can eat as much as they want and there'll still be some left over afterwards. Start by thinking along the lines of one hard cheese, one soft cheese, and maybe a blue cheese or chèvre. You needn't stick to this rigidly; sometimes it's good just to be seduced by the particular cheeses spread out in front of you on a cheese counter. Keep your head, though; without ruling out whim entirely, don't be immoderately ensnared by fanciful names or the provocatively unfamiliar. One type of cheese no one has heard of might well be interesting, but not three. Anyway, the desire to be interesting is possibly the most damaging impulse in cooking. Never worry about what your guests will think of you. Just think of the food. What will taste good?

And you don't have to go through the ridiculous pantomime of pretending everything is homespun. If you're still getting your shopping out and unwrapping your packages when everyone arrives, who cares? Your kitchen doesn't have to look like a set from a 1950s sitcom. It is curiously relaxing to be slowly creating the canvas—arranging the table, putting flowers in a vase, chopping up herbs, and putting water on for potatoes—while talking and drinking unhurriedly with friends.

The shops nearest you will probably govern what sort of food you buy for your indoor picnic. I stick to the plainest basics: meat, cheese, bread, with tomatoes, a green salad, maybe some robustly salted, herb-speckled potatoes, the waxy-fleshed, puce-skinned ones, cooked till sweet and soft then doused in oil, scarcely dribbled with vinegar or spritzed with lemon, and with a few feathery pieces of chopped zest on them, left to sit around to be eaten at room temperature.

If you're buying ham, get enough to cover a huge great plate with densely meaty pink slices. Choose baked ham and the cured Italian stuff. I like imported

HAM

prosciutto di San Daniele better than prosciutto di Parma (the glorious, requisite, honeyed saltiness is more intense), but as long as it's well cut—and obviously freshly cut—so that each white-rimmed silky slice can be removed without sticking or tearing, that's fine—more than fine.

There is internal pressure in my home to buy bresaola—dried, salted, and aged beef fillet—too, but although I like eating it well enough, I never mind if I don't. I'd rather buy a big terrine en croûte. Salami, too, is good. I don't think you need both salami and the terrine, so choose which you prefer. If you buy a whole little salami, as with the large terrine, you can introduce an all-important Do-It-Yourself element into the proceedings. Put the salami on a wooden board with a sharp knife and let people carve off for themselves thick, fat-pearled slices of spicy sausage. This way, the individual act of cutting, slicing, serving yourself, becomes almost a conversational tool. It makes people feel at home when they're around your kitchen table. Allow yourself a few saucer-sized plates of extras—

maybe some fresh, marinated anchovies, olives steeped with shards of garlic and crumbled red chilies, astringent little cornichons, those ones that look like cartoon crocodiles in embryo, a soft, moussy slab of pâté—but, again, don't go overboard. I sometimes succumb to those Italian olive-oil-soused blackened globes of chargrilled onions, sometimes available at Italian delis, sweet and smoky and wonderful with meat or cheese or a plain plate of bitter leaves.

If you prefer fish to meat, go for the old-fashioned traditional option: a huge plate of smoked salmon—mild, satiny, and softly fleshy—with cornichons, lemon, and maybe a pile of blinis (see page 152 to make them) or potato pancakes (see page 220), thinly sliced bagels with cream cheese and/or already buttered black bread. If you have a shop or fish seller near you that sells a good-enough version of the stuff, then maybe you should get a tentacled mess of Italianish seafood salad. I quite like, too, that old-fashioned pairing of tuna and

beans. My great-aunt Myra, who was a wonderful cook, always used lima beans (just out of the can, as was, of course, the olive-oil-preserved tuna) and would gently mix the two, squeeze lemon over, and cover with a fine net of wafer-thin onion rings. Yes, proper dried then soaked and cooked and drained real beans are always better, but there's something comforting and familiar for me in that quick and effort-free assembly. It tastes of my childhood.

Smoked salmon calls for black bread, but there's something reassuring about a thick wedge of white bread, heavy with cold unsalted butter and curved over a tranche of quickly grabbed ham to make a casual sandwich. But all that matters is that the bread is good: sliced chewy sourdough, a crusty peasant loaf, or

French bread—which could be a just-bought baguette or, my favorite, the slender ficelle. I sometimes think if I see another ciabatta I'll scream.

Frankly, if you can get good enough tomatoes, I'd just leave them as they are, whole, with a knife nearby (a good, sharp, serrated one, suitable for the job) so that people can eat them in juicy red wedges with their bread and cheese, or cut them thinly and sprinkle with oil and salt to make their own private pools of tomato salad.

A green salad needn't comprise anything other than lettuce. All you need for dressing is good oil, a quick squeeze of lemon, and a confident hand with the salt, tossed with your own bare hands. You can, of course, supplement the torn leaves (and let's be frank, most of us will be opening one of those cellophane packets) with some thin tongues of zucchini (the slivers stripped off with the vegetable peeler), chopped scallions, or a handful of not-even-blanched sugar snap peas or whatever you want. There's one proviso: keep it green. There is something depressingly institutional about cheerfully mixed salads. I was brought up like this. My mother was fanatical, and her aesthetic has seeped into my bloodstream; my father takes the same line. Do not even think of adding your tomatoes—keep them separate. Cucumber tends to make the salad weepy. Give it its own plate, and dress it with peppery, mint-thick, or dill-soused yogurt or an old-fashioned sweet-sour vinaigrette.

In the same way, I am fanatical about keeping fruit separate. There is, for me, something so boarding-housey about the capacious bowl filled with waxy, dusty bananas, a few oranges, some pears and the odd shrunken apple. I want a plate of oranges, another of bananas, of apples, of pears. I even put black and white grapes on separate plates.

An unfussy, sprawled-out weekend lunch definitely doesn't demand culinary highjinks. Don't worry about dessert. You just need some tubs of good ice cream—Ben and Jerry's or whichever make you like most. Or buy a tart from a good French pâtisserie.

I like just picking at food laid out in front of me, although I am alarmed at how much I can eat, and go on eating, that way. But somehow it can be good to have a full stop put on it. Sometimes, after a deli-to-table picnicky lunch, I feel I want to eat something, well, puddingy for dessert. An English treacle tart (page 266) or sponge (created in the food processor), a chocolate pudding or apple crumble, is a proper focus, reassuring after all that ambling about and fidgety grazing.

We all have our own fallback dishes—recipes we know so well that we don't even consider them recipes any more. I often cook the same thing for close friends at weekend lunch. In order of frequency these are roast chicken, cooked in butter, with a lemon up its bottom and garlic littered around the pan; the effortless chicken with green chili and herb yogurt on page 187; linguine with lemon cream sauce (page 230); and sausages and mashed potatoes (page 245).

The following ideas for weekend lunch are just that—ideas. I have suggested two courses. If you want to have bits of prosciutto or a bowlful of olives or designer crisps on the table while you're finishing off the cooking, do.

BASIC NO-EFFORT LUNCH

ROAST CHICKEN WITH GREEN SALAD
MIXED FRUITS AND CREAM OR ICE CREAM

A roast chicken is my basic Saturday lunch, Sunday lunch, any day, or even ceremonial dinner. This explains why I singled it out in Basics, Etc. (page 7). To prepare it, follow the method there. You can use ginger to spruce it up instead of lemon. Rub the skin of a chicken with fresh ginger (make sure you've got a juicy tuber) and then cut some slices off the root and stuff the inside of the cavity with them. Gingered chicken makes for a wonderful chicken salad later; bring out that can of water chestnuts from the bottom of your pantry if you dare, use lots of crunchy green leaves and some raw sugar snap peas (or failing that, snow peas), and sprinkle with some sesame seeds that have been briskly toasted in a fatless pan before generously dousing with an orientalish dressing. Use soy, use sesame oil, use rice vinegar—one in a fairly normal vinaigrette or all three in conjunction as you wish—and eat the salad in front of the TV.

Keep the green salad to go with either the ginger or the lemon chicken simple. Two small-to-medium chickens are fine for eight and won't take long to cook. If you're on a particularly tight timetable, get the butcher to butterfly the chickens for you (in which case 1 hour at 400°F should do it). And all chicken is good eaten at getting-toward-room-temperature, especially butterflied chicken.

For dessert I often provide just a plate of mixed fruits—in winter, out of a couple of packages picked up from the freezer compartment; otherwise, whatever's in season. Frozen berries are fine providing they're sufficiently thawed and you have removed every last strawberry. Sprinkle with some sugar, the finely chopped zest of ½–1 orange (I use my zester to get the rind off and then the mezzaluna to chop it finely, although I do sometimes leave the zest as is in thin little

GINGERED CHICKEN SALAD

MIXED FRUITS

stringy ribbons), and a tablespoon or so of a liqueur of some sort. I throw all that stuff over while the berries are still frozen and then, just before eating them, I sieve over some confectioners' sugar through my tea strainer so that they look beautiful. If I can't stop myself, I add a few tiny leaves of mint from the garden. Serve with good vanilla ice cream or thick heavy cream. Normally for such desserts I prefer crème fraîche, but here I wouldn't want any hint of sourness (the fruit, after all, has that) but might rather go for a bowl of cream whipped up with sugar and perhaps a drop of real vanilla extract. Work on the principle of one 10-ounce package of berries for 4 people.

THE SLIGHTLY MORE THAN BASIC LUNCH FOR 6–8

LEMON CHICKEN

PECORINO AND PEARS, OR STICKY CHOCOLATE PUDDING

This lemon chicken is a version of the Greek *kotopoulo lemonato*—that's to say chicken roasted in portions in the oven with wine and water to make an aromatic liquid to produce, along with eggs and lemon, a sharp but deeply flavored avgolemono sauce. Obviously, you can serve it with just a green salad, especially in hot weather, but otherwise I'd do a bowlful of buttery basmati rice (quite the easiest rice to cook and the fastest, see page 272) and some peas (which in my house means frozen young peas, with some sugar added to the water along with salt and some basil with butter, a nut of which I add to the drained hot peas—chop the basil at the very last moment or else use some basil-infused olive oil).

I cook the chicken in the oven just because I find it the most relaxing way to deal with it, but if you prefer to grill or sauté it, then do so.

If it's summer or an approximation of it, then for dessert provide a lemony, crumbly wedge of pecorino and a bowlful of pears. Get the pears from a good greengrocer's rather than the supermarket and buy them on the Wednesday before if possible (Thursday at the latest) to be sure they aren't tooth-breakingly hard.

The chocolate pudding wouldn't taste right in high heat, but in more customary warmth it'll still work wonderfully.

LEMON CHICKEN

I prefer to go to my butcher for a proper, free-range bird, which he will then cut up into portions. I like the bird to be cut up small.

6 tablespoons olive oil, plus more,	zest and juice of 1 large lemon or
if needed	2 small
1 large chicken (about 5 pounds) cut	1 tablespoon dried oregano
into 8 or more pieces, or 2 small	1¼ cups white wine, plus more,
chickens (about 3 pounds each) cut	if needed
into 6 pieces each	salt and freshly milled black pepper

Preheat oven to 425°F.

Put a large baking dish on the stove (one big enough to hold the chicken, which should fit more or less over two burners) and pour in the olive oil. If you can't fit the chicken pieces in one pan and are therefore cooking them in two, you may need more oil. Turn the chicken in the hot oil for a few minutes until the pieces are golden. Add the lemon zest and oregano. Pour over the wine—you may need more—season with the salt and pepper; let it bubble up a bit, then add 1¼ cups water. Put in the oven and cook for about 30 minutes, more if the chicken pieces are large. (Check individual pieces; you may want to remove the breast portions first.) Arrange the chicken pieces on a plate that can go back in the oven while you make the sauce. Turn off the oven.

AVGOLEMONO To make the sauce, first pour the chickeny juices into a measuring cup. You need about 1 cup. You can make avgolemono in a saucepan, but you may feel safer using a double boiler, the top over (but not touching) gently boiling water in the bottom.

In this pan put 3 eggs and lemon juice and start whisking. Keep whisking until the mixture's frothy. Pour in gradually, still whisking, the chicken cooking juices. It shouldn't curdle, but if you're feeling nervous (or even if you're not, for it'll stop you needing to), put a bowl or pan of cold water next to you so that you can plunge the avgolemono pan in if it begins to look as if it's thinking of over-heating and curdling. It's ready when it's turned into a thin custardy substance.

Taste for salt and pepper and add more if needed. Pour some of the sauce over the chicken portions and put the rest in a small pitcher or leave it in its bowl and just put a ladle into it. You'll have a nice big bowlful of it.

STICKY CHOCOLATE PUDDING

This is a variant on lemon surprise pudding, in which the mixture divides on cooking to produce a sponge above the thick lemony sauce that forms below. Indeed, it is known in my house as Lemon Surprise Pudding, the surprise being that it's chocolate.

Although I didn't actually eat this as a child, it is heady with reminders of childhood foods: the hazelnuts in the sponge bring back memories of Nutella, the thick, dark, fudgy sauce of chocolate spread. The proportions below are geared toward 6 but easily feed 8. It's heavenly with fridge-cold heavy cream poured over it.

It is also child's play to make. Choose good cocoa and good chocolate and stick carefully to the exact measurements. (You can, though, use 1⅔ cups flour in place of the 1¼ cups flour and ½ cup ground nuts, if you prefer, increasing the amount of baking powder needed to 1½ teaspoons.) Use one of those standard white soufflé dishes 8 inches in diameter, or a shallow square 12-inch pan. If you've got only a single oven, it makes sense to use the shallow dish; it will take less time to cook.

FOR THE PUDDING
1¼ cups all-purpose flour
1 teaspoon baking powder
pinch salt
¼ cup good unsweetened cocoa powder
½ cup ground hazelnuts
1⅔ cups confectioners' sugar
2½ ounces best semisweet chocolate, chopped roughly, or chocolate morsels

2 tablespoons unsalted butter, melted
1 egg
¾ cup milk
1 teaspoon pure vanilla extract

FOR THE SAUCE
1 cup dark muscovado sugar or dark brown sugar
1¼ cups unsweetened cocoa powder

Preheat the oven to 350°F.

Sift the flour, baking powder, salt, and cocoa into a bowl, stir in the hazelnuts and the sugar, then add the chocolate. Whisk together the melted butter, egg, milk, and vanilla and pour into the dry ingredients. Stir well, so it's all thoroughly mixed, then spoon into the buttered dish.

Now for the sauce—not that you make it yourself (the cooking does that for you), but you have to get the ingredients together. Bring 2½ cups of water to a boil. Mix the brown sugar and cocoa and sprinkle over the top of the pudding mixture in the dish. Pour the boiled water up to the 2-cup mark of a measuring cup, then pour over the pudding. Put the water-drenched pudding directly into the oven and leave it there for about 50 minutes. Don't open the door until a good 45 minutes have passed, and then press; if it feels fairly firm and springy to the touch, it's ready. If you're using the shallow dish, it'll be ready in 35–40 minutes.

Remove from the oven and serve immediately, spooning from the dish and making sure everyone gets both sauce and sponge.

AUTUMN LUNCH FOR 6

RAGOÛT OF WILD MUSHROOMS WITH OVEN-COOKED POLENTA

CHEESES WITH BITTER SALAD

STEWED APPLES WITH CINNAMON CRÈME FRAÎCHE

You want mushrooms as fresh as you can get them. If you buy them in advance they'll probably be lying, ever more limp and bruised and unappetizingly damp, in their brown paper bag in the fridge and you'll get no pleasure at all out of the prospect of cooking them. So do your shopping on the morning before lunch.

This recipe for wild mushroom ragoût is adapted from a recipe in *From Anna's Kitchen* by Anna Thomas. I was sent it one year among many other books under review and was surprised to find myself utterly seduced by it. Any description undersells it; it might be described, showily, as a gourmet vegetarian cookbook. But it has none of the worthiness or pretentiousness that might seem to suggest. It is fresh and alive and speaks directly and intimately to the reader. I could take so many recipes from it here, as I so often cook, if not exactly from it, then inspired by it (which is more telling).

STEWED
APPLES

This ragoût is a sort of woodsy stew, odoriferously autumnal. As for the cheese afterward, I'd think about a really fulsome camembert or ammoniac gorgonzola, either paired with stringently dressed Belgian endive. Deal with the apples by peeling, coring, and segmenting about 4 Gravensteins or other cooking apples. Put them in a saucepan, cover with 5–6 tablespoons sugar (or to taste), a tablespoon of butter, the juice (and perhaps the zest) of 1 orange and 2 cloves, and/or a cinnamon stick. Cook, covered, on a low heat till the fruit is soft but not pulpy beyond recognition. Eat with crème fraîche sprinkled with cinnamon or bolstered with a whipped-in slug of Calvados. I love it with plain, sharp yogurt and maybe some soft brown sugar.

MUSHROOM RAGOÛT

1 tablespoon olive oil	3 garlic cloves, chopped
4 tablespoons unsalted butter, plus additional, if needed	salt and freshly milled black pepper
	¾ cup dry red wine
1 medium onion, minced	⅓ cup Marsala
1 medium red onion, sliced thinly	1 bay leaf
2 celery stalks, sliced thinly	½ teaspoon fresh thyme leaves

1¾ **pounds fresh wild mushrooms, or a**
    combination of wild and cultivated,
    wiped, stemmed if necessary, and
    sliced or cut into generous pieces
pinch cayenne

1 **tablespoon Italian 00 or all-purpose**
    flour
2 **cups vegetable stock, heated**
3 **tablespoon chopped parsley**

Heat 1 teaspoon of the oil and 1 tablespoon of the butter in a large nonstick frying pan or similar pan and sauté the onions and celery in it, stirring often, until they begin to soften. I sometimes find I have to add more butter. Add the garlic and some salt and pepper and continue cooking until the onions and garlic begin to brown. Add half the red wine and half the Marsala, the bay leaf, and thyme. Turn down the heat and simmer gently until the wine cooks away.

Meanwhile, in another large nonstick pan, heat the remaining 2 teaspoons oil with 2 tablespoons of the butter—again adding more butter if you like, though if you're patient it shouldn't be necessary. Sauté the mushrooms with a sprinkle of salt and the cayenne until their excess liquid cooks away and they begin to color. Add the remaining wine and Marsala, lower the heat, and allow the wine to simmer down. Then add the onions to the mushrooms.

Put the remaining tablespoon of butter in the pan in which you've sautéed the onions and let it melt. Stir in the flour and keep stirring over medium heat for a few minutes as it turns golden. Whisk in the hot stock and continue whisking as it thickens. Add this sauce to the mushrooms and onions, along with the parsley.

Simmer everything together very gently for about 10 more minutes. Serve with steamed or boiled rice—and I mostly just do a buttery pile of basmati—or polenta.

OVEN-COOKED POLENTA

This is the *polenta senza bastone* (the *bastone* is the here-unneeded wooden baton traditionally used to stir the polenta while it cooks) from Anna del Conte's *Classic Food of Northern Italy*. It's much less work than traditionally cooked polenta and infinitely preferable to the quick-cook stuff.

Bring 2 quarts water or stock to simmering point. Remove the pan from the heat and add 2 teaspoons salt. If you are using bouillon cubes (you'll need 4), here's where you add them to the water, in which case you probably won't need the salt.

Gradually add 2½ cups polenta or, more properly speaking, cornmeal, letting it fall in a fine rain through your fingers while you stir rapidly with a long wooden spoon. Return the pan to the heat and bring slowly to the boil, stirring constantly in the same direction. Boil for 5 minutes, still stirring. Now transfer the polenta to a buttered oven dish. I use an old and battered oval enamel casserole, but it doesn't much matter and you'll be able to see easily which of your various dishes will be the right size just by looking at the grainy mass. Cover with buttered foil and cook in a preheated 350°F oven for 1 hour.

CHEESES
WITH BITTER
SALAD

As for cheeses, keep in mind those that will crumble or meld into the salad on the plate. You are not looking for a cheese-and-crackers kind of assortment. The salad should be made mostly of Belgian endive. Throw in one of those packages of mixed greens (or maybe just half a package) for ballast if you want and make a strong lemony, oily dressing thickened either with 2 pounded anchovy fillets or 1 teaspoon Dijon mustard mixed with a quick grating of orange zest.

And maybe put the apples and crème fraîche on the table at the same time as the cheese and salad.

I like aromatic, unstructured food: stews, braises, soupy mixtures of vegetables to be eaten with warm mounds of rice, couscous, pasta, or just thick wedges of bread.

A thick, squashy root vegetable stew with couscous, an earthy, grainy, aromatic braise of carrots, turnips, parsnips, and squash, is the ideal soothing weekend lunch. Abroad (in Paris, mostly) I've eaten this with lamb, but I don't like the greasiness when I make it myself, unless I boil up the lamb (2–3 pounds neck pieces, generously covered with salted water) the day before and skim the fat off when cool (and see recipe for Cawl on page 94). That way you get all the glorious sweetness of the meat and the well-cooked stringiness (well, let's be frank here) that is so characteristic of this kind of stew. (See below, too, for a chicken couscous recipe.)

BOLSTERING WEEKEND LUNCH FOR 6

GOLDEN ROOT-VEGETABLE COUSCOUS OR CHICKEN STEW WITH COUSCOUS
COCONUT CRÈME CARAMEL

I think of this as particularly good for weekend lunch if you've been feeling rather fragile; the food is soothing and so, too, are the rhythms of its preparation.

You do need to do a couple of things for this in advance—put the chickpeas in to soak (see page 78) and make the crème caramel. Neither of these activities should be too demanding even on a Friday for a Saturday lunch (morning for the chickpeas, evening for the crème caramel) after a long week at work. If you hate coconut (although the taste of it is subtle rather than pronounced here), then substitute for the coconut milk the same quantity of regular milk. But after the warm spiciness of the stew, the lightly aromatic coconut custard is just right; it offers a gentle but resolute ending to the meal.

Each time I do this I use different vegetables in differing quantities, but if that sort of permissiveness makes you feel unsafe, then follow this recipe word for word the first time and then gradually, as you do it and redo it, you will find you loosen up. Don't think less of yourself for following orders to the letter. It takes time to learn when you can make free with a recipe and when it's best to rein in the improvisatory spirit. Most of my mistakes have been as a result of fiddling about with a recipe the first time I've cooked it, rather than doing it as written, and then next time seeing where I could improve or change or develop it.

I've specified already ground spices here; it is certainly better if you dry-fry and then grind your own, but actually I resort mostly to the dried ones when I make this, and I wanted to be honest rather than high-minded here. I do buy good fresh spices, though.

Use vegetable stock if you want this to be vegetarian; otherwise use any stock—chicken, beef, lamb—that you want. And the stock doesn't need to be strong; if you're using bouillon cubes or cartons of stock, then use extra water to dilute them.

This recipe requires a lot of preparation, albeit of a basic and undemanding sort. I like a drink beside me and someone to talk to (or the radio to listen to). I peel, chop, assemble solidly—and then that's it.

I use my couscoussier, but a big, deep pot will do. Obviously, you will need more or less liquid depending on the proportions of the cooking vessel, so be prepared to be flexible. Do remember that you can use extra water; there's no need to have more stock on hand. Use a couple of saucepans if you don't have anything very capacious.

Chief among the virtues of couscous is the speed with which it is cooked. I love it for its sweet, soft graininess, which needs nothing more than a nut or two of butter by way of dressing. Try to resist the modern tendency to use oil instead. When I make couscous just for myself or for the children, I often cook it just by immersing it in an equal volume of hot stock, but here I would soak, then steam it.

For serving, keep all the parts separate: the stew in one bowl, with plenty of juice; the grain in another; some harissa, that garlic-pounded paste of chilies, to the side. The culinary idea behind this is the contrast between spicy stew, spicier relish, and the plain, comforting blanket of grain. You can moosh them all up on your plate, but if they were all mixed up on the serving dish, it would be both too sloppy in texture and too monotone in taste.

Though it's not strictly necessary, if you want some meat with this, get hold of some chorizo. But make sure you buy the spicy, paprika-tinted sausages rather than salami. If you happen to live near a shop that sells merguez (which are actually more traditional for this), then just grill them and serve them instead of the chorizo. Otherwise, use a cast-iron frying pan and cover the bottom with a film of olive oil. Prick the chorizo sausages, place them in the pan, and turn them so that they are sealed on all sides. Throw in a glass of red wine, lower the heat, and cook for about 10 minutes. Remove and slice each sausage diagonally into 3 squat logs.

GOLDEN ROOT-VEGETABLE COUSCOUS

FOR THE STEW

3 tablespoons olive oil

2 medium onions, quartered and sliced
    thickly

2 garlic cloves, minced

1 teaspoon each ground cinnamon,
    cumin, and coriander

½ teaspoon paprika

generous pinch of saffron strands

3 medium carrots, peeled and cut into
    1-inch dice

2 medium parsnips, peeled and cut into
    1-inch dice

2 medium turnips, peeled and cut into
    1-inch dice

1 small kabocha or butternut squash,
    peeled and cut into 1-inch dice

½ medium rutabaga, peeled and cut
    into 1-inch dice

3 zucchini, peeled partially to make
    alternating ¼-inch strips of peel and
    flesh, then sliced ½-inch thick

4¼ cups chicken, beef, or vegetable
    stock

½ can (14.5 ounces) plum tomatoes,
    drained and roughly chopped, their
    liquid reserved

grated zest ½ large orange, plus juice
    from the whole orange (optional)

⅔ cup sultanas

1½ cans (14 ounces each) chickpeas or
    8 ounces dried, soaked, and partly
    cooked chickpeas (see page 78)

salt

few drops chili oil or 1 teaspoon harissa
    (optional; page 208)

FOR THE COUSCOUS

½ cup pine nuts

4 cups quick-cooking couscous

2 tablespoons (¼ stick) unsalted butter,
    plus more, if desired

4–5 tablespoons snipped fresh coriander
    or parsley

Heat the olive oil in a big, deep pot or the bottom of a couscoussier and turn the onions in it for a few minutes. Add the garlic, the ground cinnamon, ground cumin, ground coriander, paprika, and saffron, and stir over a low to medium heat for 5 minutes. Add the carrots, parsnips, turnips, kabocha, rutabaga, and zucchini and turn briskly, but don't worry if you can't do this very efficiently—there are a lot of vegetables. After about 5 minutes add the stock, the tomatoes, the orange zest, the sultanas (I love sultanas and hate raisins; if you feel differently, then do act differently), and the chickpeas. Turn again so that, if possible, all gets at least partially covered by the stock. Add the reserved tomato juice from the can and some water if the liquid level is looking too low. Season with the salt, taste, and, if you want to, add the orange juice. The stew benefits from an aromatic hint of orange, but don't be too heavy-handed.

Cook this fragrant, golden stew for 20–30 minutes, until the vegetables are tender but not mushy (at least not all of them—some will be beginning to fray around the edges, and that's good) and the liquid has formed a thin but not watery sauce. Taste and add chili oil or the harissa if you want it to have a bit more punch.

Meanwhile, prepare the couscous. Put the pine nuts in a hot, dry frying pan and toast until they are golden and giving off a sweet resiny aroma. Set aside. Thirty minutes or so before the stew is cooked, put the couscous in a bowl, cover it with cold water by about 1½ inches, and soak it for 10 minutes. Drain and put the couscous in either a steamer basket or the top part of the couscoussier; you may have to do this in 2 batches. Place the butter on top of the grain and put the couscous on top of the pot with the stew in it. Cover and allow to steam-heat for 5–10 minutes; the butter should have started melting by the time it's ready. Transfer to a warmed dish or flat round plate, adding more butter if you like. Fluff up with a fork and scatter with pine nuts.

To serve, pour the stew gently into a big round shallow bowl (and this should be warmed), strew with the parsley or coriander, and bring to table with the couscous.

CHICKEN STEW WITH COUSCOUS

In the Middle East or North Africa, chicken would be used primarily to flavor the broth, not to yield much meat to eat. But I figure that, if people are expecting to eat the meat, you must have 2 small chicken parts per person. Chicken is better if it is freshly jointed, so I get the butcher to cut one large chicken (about 5 pounds) into 10–12 parts. You can, however, use thighs from the supermarket.

Don't worry if the stock isn't very strong for this—the broth should be light. The point of couscous is, I stress, to have the bland grains as a base for the vegetables and chicken, moistened by the gentle broth and given heat and intensity by the harissa.

You will need to start on this a good day in advance in order to soak the chickpeas. If you prefer to use canned chickpeas, you can, but I think it's worth the effort (not in itself exactly arduous) of soaking and cooking the dried ones.

8 ounces chickpeas, soaked (see page 78), or 1½ cans (14 ounces each)

3 medium onions, 1 halved, 2 sliced thinly

1 bouquet garni (see page xx)

4 garlic cloves, unpeeled

2 drops olive oil

2 tablespoons vegetable oil

1 teaspoon ground cinnamon

½ teaspoon ground cumin

¼ teaspoon cayenne pepper

pinch salt

10–12 chicken parts (see headnote)

1 pound carrots, peeled, halved lengthways, and cut into chunks

4 celery stalks, 1 left whole, 3 sliced thinly

1 heaping teaspoon harissa (page 208), plus more, for serving

Put soaked chickpeas in a saucepan with the halved onion, bouquet garni, and the garlic, cover by about 4 inches with cold water, and add the olive oil. Cover the pan, bring to the boil, and then cook at a gentle boil for an hour. Leave in the pan.

Now for the chicken and vegetables. Pour the vegetable oil into a big pot, add the cinnamon, cumin, cayenne pepper, and the remaining onions. Sprinkle with the salt and cook for a few minutes, until soft. Then add the chicken parts. (If you want them golden, fry them in a pan first, remembering to scoop up all chickeny juices by deglazing with some water.) Cover with cold water and bring to the boil. Skim off any scum that may rise to the surface. Drain the reserved chickpeas and add them with the carrots and celery, stir in the harissa, and cook fairly gently for 1½ hours, maybe slightly less, until the chicken is just cooked through. If using canned chickpeas, drain and add them 5 minutes before the chicken is cooked, and allow to heat through. If, finally, you really feel the broth needs more flavor, don't panic; just add a bouillon cube.

Meanwhile, following the recipe on page 207, cook the couscous, starting about 30 minutes before the chicken and vegetables are cooked. Serve as for the vegetable couscous.

HARISSA

As you can buy very good harissa (but do check labels to avoid brands with fillers), I make no apology for the fact that this homemade version is fairly labor-intensive. If, however, the idea of pounding the whole spices appalls and yet you still want to make your own, then use ground spices (the caraway doesn't come ground, but can be dealt with in the processor later), reducing quantities slightly, and frying them first not in a dry pan, but in one with a tablespoon or so of oil in it. The chilies I tend to get for harissa have a definite heat, but no killer burn.

You can keep this, with a film of oil poured over the top, for ages in the fridge. And it's addictive stuff; once you start eating it, you'll want it with practically everything.

2 ounces dried red chilies	**6 garlic cloves**
3 tablespoons coriander seeds	**2 tablespoons coarse sea salt**
1 teaspoon caraway seeds	**1 tablespoon sherry vinegar**
1 teaspoon cumin seeds	**3 tablespoons olive oil**

Bring about 2 cups of water to a boil. With rubber gloves on, especially if you wear contact lenses, break open the chilies and remove the seeds. Cut the chilies into thinnish slices—I use scissors for this—and put into a small bowl. Cover with the boiling water and leave to soak for 1 hour.

Toast the coriander, caraway, and cumin in a hot dry heavy-bottomed frying pan, shaking and turning till the spices are lightly browned and beginning to give off a heady fragrance, 3 or 4 minutes. Remove them from the pan and bash to a powder with a pestle and mortar, or use a spice grinder.

I do the next step using a processor, but if you want to be truly authentic I dare say you should keep pounding. Anyway, spoon the just pounded spice powder into the bowl of the food processor. Pound the garlic and salt together with the pestle and mortar and then transfer that, too, to the processor. Add vinegar and the drained chilies, reserving the soaking water, and blitz to a fiery-red purée. Then, turn the machine on again and, with the motor running, pour the oil down the funnel. Stop, scrape up—or rather down—any mixture on the sides of the bowl, then switch on again, pouring in some of the chili-soaking liquid; you want the texture thick but not stiff. Taste to see whether you want more salt or more vinegar, or indeed more chili.

COCONUT CRÈME CARAMEL

Crème caramel is a soothing dessert to end with, and one that is not, contrary to appearances, very hard to make. It's easier to make the caramel alone in the kitchen, though. If there's anyone else there, they're almost bound to plead with you to take the darkly spluttering sugar off the heat before it's brown enough.

This version is not intensely coconutty, but after the third or fourth mouthful, a light, fluttery note of coconut begins to make itself heard. Think, too, of substituting ordinary milk, infused for 20 minutes with the zest of an orange, then strained. In which case, use orange juice, not water, to make the caramel.

I use an oval dish that has a capacity of 3½ cups. This makes a modest, though not too mean, amount for 6: boost quantities for exuberantly greedy people.

The canned coconut milk I use (because I had it in the larder the first time I made this) is called Thai Coconut Milk; it's available widely in the United States. It needs a good shake before opening and pouring over the eggs and sugar. Get the best eggs you can—not mass-produced. Use a round baking dish for this with an 8-cup capacity.

I cup superfine sugar	4 egg yolks
4 eggs	2½ cups coconut milk

Preheat the oven to 325°F and put in the dish in which you are going to cook the crème caramel.

Put ¾ cup of sugar and 5 tablespoons of water in a heavy-bottomed saucepan to make the caramel, stir to help dissolve, then put on a high heat. Meanwhile, fill a kettle with water and heat to the boiling point. Bring the sugar and water to the boil, without stirring—though I can never resist shaking a bit—and boil until it is dark golden and syrupy. Get the warm dish from the oven, pour in the caramel, and swirl it around so it coats the sides as well as the bottom. You need to use an oven mitt to hold the pan because the caramel is extremely hot. You will have to work quickly but not hysterically so. Put the dish aside somewhere cool and let the caramel harden.

Then, in a bowl, whisk the eggs, egg yolks, and remaining sugar with a fork. Heat the coconut milk and, still beating with a fork, pour it over the egg and sugar mixture. Strain into the caramel-lined dish.

Get out a roasting pan and set the dish in it. Pour the hot water from the kettle into the roasting pan to come about halfway up the sides of the dish, then convey all of this to the oven.

Start testing with your fingertips, pressing the top, after 45 minutes, but figure on about I hour before it is cooked enough. You want it set, but with a hint of wobble underneath. Remember, it will carry on cooking a little after you take it out.

Remove the dish when you judge the time to be right and let it cool. Then stick it in the fridge overnight. A bit before you want to eat it, take it out of the fridge, press with your fingers all around the edge to release the custard from the sides of the dish, then get a sharp, thin knife and trace along the sides, cutting down to the bottom of the dish. Keep calm; there is no reason why this shouldn't work. Place a flat plate over the top of the caramel dish and invert. Shake a bit, and remove the dish. In front of you should be a beautiful, gleamingly tanned mirror-topped custard, dripping with brown caramel down the sides and into a puddle around it. The crème caramel is always shallower on the plate than it looked as if it would be, but that's just what happens—or it does to me.

Put two spoons on the table and let people help themselves.

If you want to make something that takes altogether less thinking about, then I suggest a glass-filling mixture of yogurt, honey, passion fruit, and thick, rich, yellow clotted or Devonshire cream, now widely available. Passion fruit, like coconut, seems to go well after the sweet aromatic spices that waft from the stew.

YOGURT

HONEY

PASSION
FRUIT

CLOTTED
CREAM

It may seem to go against my usual ordinances to suggest making a dessert that is to be served already meted out in individual portions, but the mixture quickly becomes too gloopy to survive being served from a larger bowl. For each person, put into your chosen glass a big dollop of yogurt. On top of this pour in 1 tablespoon dark, clear, strong Greek honey or any well-flavored runny honey; stir it in a bit, not so that it is completely mixed but so that it isn't just sitting in a fat puddle on top. Now take a passion fruit, cut it in half, and scoop the seeds and pulp out on top of the honey and yogurt. Stir this in gently, but leaving most of it on top. Then on goes a generous tablespoon of the cream. Now, drizzle a bit of honey over that, but only a tiny bit—the amount that comes off the sticky tablespoon you used last time. If your kitchen lunch is completely informal, and as this dessert is best done at the last minute, assemble it at the time. And if you wanted something even simpler you could use Jane Grigson's trick—which is to have a bowlful of passion fruits and another of good cream. Eaters lop off the top of the fruit, rather as if taking the top off a boiled egg, add a spoon of cream to the pulpy cavity—and then, pleasurably, eat.

EASY WINTER LUNCH FOR 6

HAM COOKED IN CIDER WITH LEEKS, CARROTS, AND POTATOES

BAKED WINE-SPICED PLUMS WITH BARBADOS CREAM

The poet Paul Muldoon wrote wonderfully, in *Profumo,* of his mother going "from ham to snobbish ham." The plastic-wrapped, sliver-thin, and pinkly shiny kind he alluded to has its place. But the real thing is such a treat—such an ordinary treat, nothing fancy, but enormously uplifting. And it's just right for winter lunch: nothing to do except throw everything in a pan and then the whole house becomes imbued with savory, clove-scented fog. Buy more ham than you want and then eat it cold for supper with poached eggs, or in a sandwich, or chopped in a pea soup cooked with the cidery stock the ham itself was cooking in. I love nothing more, on a Saturday night in, than a bowl of thick and grainy pea soup eaten with a spoon in my right hand while my left holds (for alternating mouthfuls), a ham sandwich, good and mustardy, made with unsalted butter and white bread, real or plastic (both have their merits). The leftover stock also makes the basis for excellent risotti (see Pea Risotto, page 140, and Orzotto, page 317) and can be used to add depth and pungency to an ordinary chicken casserole.

After the ham you want something not too filling, but a moussy little number would be striking the wrong note. The plums baked in spice-deepened wine are just right, warming and comforting but not bloating, and the Barbados cream is an optional accompaniment worth serious consideration. If you think it would make life easier, then just put some crème fraîche on the table instead. And, now I come to think of it, there's a very good case for custard. Still, I like the sugar-topped yogurty cream. Do it a day before your lunch—a good 24 hours will give everything time to meld fabulously. I'd do the plums in advance, too, although if you prefer you can cook them when you want to eat them. I know it might sound odd to specify a plum recipe for winter when these aren't winter fruits, but you can get plums (from Chile, among other places) in winter and they benefit especially from being cooked like this. Only the soft, juicy ones straight from the tree in August can be eaten as they are.

HAM COOKED IN CIDER

I resist specifying the size of the ham you need; it depends how much you want left over. But I wouldn't consider getting one weighing under 5 pounds. What you're after is a mild-cure ham. I prefer to get my ham from the butcher, but I have made more than respectable boiled ham from the vacuum-packed variety bought at the supermarket.

To calculate how much time the ham needs, work along the lines of about 12 minutes per pound for a fully cooked ham, and about 18 minutes per pound for one that's partially cooked, plus 30 minutes. If it's come straight out of the fridge, you could need to add a further 20–30 minutes.

I am basing this recipe on a 5-pound ham, but armed with the information above, you can change the cooking time as you wish. Anyway, if the ham stays in the liquid longer, it'll be fine. And when you have finished lunch, put the ham back in the liquid until cool; this keeps it from going dry and stringy.

I never mind which cider I use and I have probably used apple juice, too.

1 5-pound half bone-in ham, partially or fully cooked

10 medium carrots, peeled and quartered

2 medium onions, halved, each half studded with a clove

8 leeks, white and green parts separated, the white cut into 2½-inch lengths

10 peppercorns

2 celery stalks, or the bottom sliced from a whole bunch

small bunch parsley, tied with a freezer-bag wire

1 bouquet garni (see page xx)

4½ cups hard or sweet cider, or apple juice

2 tablespoons light brown or demerara sugar (see page 460)

6 medium floury potatoes, peeled and roughly quartered

Put the ham in a large pot; add 2 of the quartered carrots, the onions, the green parts of the leeks, the peppercorns, celery, parsley (tied with a freezer-bag wire, the parsley is easier to remove later), and bouquet garni. Pour in the cider, then add cold water to cover and bring to boiling point.

Add the sugar, lower the heat, and simmer briskly (or boil gently, depending on how you want to look at it) for about 70 minutes for a partially cooked ham, 40 minutes if the ham is fully cooked. (And at about this stage you should start thinking about the potatoes; see below.) Remove the carrots, green parts of leek, and parsley and put in the remaining carrots and leeks and cook for about another 20 minutes. The ham is done at an internal temperature of 160°F for a partially cooked ham, 140°F for one that is fully cooked. When it's all cooked, remove the ham to carve it, take the vegetables out with a slotted spoon, and then put the ham on a huge plate surrounded by the leeks and carrots. Or carve it to order at the table and put the vegetables on a plate on the table by themselves.

Now the potatoes. You can do either of two things: you can boil the potatoes in a saucepan of water while the ham is cooking, or you can cook them in the ham water itself. The advantage of cooking them separately is that they offer a distinct, appropriately plain, taste. And potatoes are really at their best when they are the bland but sweet bass note to sop up and support other, stronger, tastes. Added to which, you are left with a clear stock at the end; if you cook the potatoes in with the ham, all you can do with the stock, really, is make thick soup. And unless you have a very big pot, the ham, vegetables, and potatoes, all in together, will be a very tight squeeze.

Having said that, there is something wonderful about the sweet, grainy potatoes absorbing all that appley and salty stock. You decide. (I reckon on 1 potato, quartered, per person; I might even do 1½ per person.)

In the ham pot, or separately, simmer the potatoes until just tender, 35–40 minutes. The recipes for both the plums and Barbados cream are in Cooking in Advance; see pages 116 and 117.

GOOD, THICK WINTER PEA SOUP As for dishes using ham leftovers, there are pea-based soups, risotti, and the like mentioned throughout (check the Index, too), but for a good, thick winter pea soup, all you need to do is throw into the cold ham stock a couple of handfuls of split green peas and boil away until you have a sludgy purée. A bright green fresh-pea soup is obviously not a winter meal, but if you cheat and use frozen peas (I always do), then it can be. But the grainy potage produced by the split peas is wonderfully satisfying—and you can just as well use the yellow split peas. In fact, you can use just about any legume you want; it's just that split peas need no soaking. But if you don't feel like eating a ham-based pea soup immediately after lunch, then pour the stock (in labeled quantities) into containers or plastic bags and put them in the freezer. Don't stick it in the fridge with the intention of doing something or other with it over the next few days. You won't and you'll end up throwing it away, which would be too much of a waste for me to bear even on your behalf.

You could thaw some of the stock to make my next suggestion for a kitchen-bound weekend lunch: minestrone. I haven't actually ever used ham-cooking liquid for it, but I've used chicken, beef, and vegetable stocks and all have tasted wonderful. Strangely, the best minestrone I ever made was with a stock cube (a Knorr one made for the Italian market—gusto classico, which indicates a beef and chicken broth). I think a soup like this makes one of the best sorts of weekend lunch. I love it not hot hot but a flavor-deepening lukewarm. Yes, you could serve cheese after it if you're worried that it isn't enough as it is for a main course, but you'd be wrong. This is perfect for lunch; it's so nice, apart from anything else, to be able to have bowlfuls and bowlfuls of it rather than only a politely small amount in order to make room for a main course you're almost bound to like less. For dinner, fine—have something after the soup; but for lunch—and supper, indeed—you don't need to make a multicoursed assault on people. To be frank, I'd be happy with just an orange afterwards, but I will suggest a more proper dessert in the knowledge that you don't need a recipe for peeling an orange.

If you want to do something even simpler than the recipe that follows for Baked Sauternes Custard, you could think of doing my great-aunt Myra's Moroccan orange and date salad. Oranges are peeled, their pith removed, and then cut into thin discs; dates are halved, stoned, and laid alongside. All you do is make an orangy syrup by boiling up some water, sugar, zest of the orange, and some juice, plus orange-redolent alcohol if you like, though it wouldn't be very Moroccan. Still, I don't know if there is anything really Moroccan about this salad anyway. Sprinkle a small amount of syrup over the salad and then scatter with slivered almonds. And I rather like it without the syrup, but just with orange juice and a bit of orange liqueur sprinkled over, as well as the blanched (toasted or not) and slivered nuts and maybe some ground cinnamon. I have to say, though, that I find the custard (which involves just gentle whisking and stirring) rather easier to make than the orange salad, with all that fiddly pithy business. No cooking should ever be undertaken with the single and vulgar aim of impressing anyone, but it's worth remembering as you make your choice that most people will presume that slicing a few oranges is as close to doing nothing as you can get, whereas baking a fragrantly grapey and wine-resonant custard counts as making an effort.

I think of this following menu as being particularly suitable for a weekend away; chopping and preparing vegetables is ideal work to do with either a lot of people doing bits of it each or a lot of people sitting around to talk to while you do it. Don't be put off by the formality of the term Country House Lunch. I mean no more by it than to evoke a lazy, long weekend with friends.

COUNTRY HOUSE
LUNCH FOR 6

MINESTRONE

BAKED SAUTERNES CUSTARD

MINESTRONE

There was something of a fashion in Britain recently for season-specific minestrone—a spring one majoring in peas, an autumn one containing porcini, and so on—and while all these can be fabulous, the recipe here is for a plain, basic one (if such exists) that shouldn't be too hard to throw together all the year round. I doubt, however, if you'd really want to cook this in high summer; it tends to be on the menu, as far as I'm concerned, any time between September and May. As ever, the list of ingredients is not meant to be interpreted too strictly; any vegetable, more or less, can argue its case here. I am, however, unpersuaded by tomatoes. Yes, it is normal to include them, but I resolutely (along with the

Milanesi) prefer not to. The only drawback is that the soup, after all that cooking, turns out an undeniable khaki. But it tastes so good, with an almost honeyed savoriness, that it really doesn't matter.

I have listed canned beans below, but if you want to use dried ones, then soak and cook them first. The added work is not burdensome in itself, but I do understand that activities-to-be-undertaken can take up psychological space, so to speak.

As for the work of chopping and preparing the vegetables, I like to chop the first one needed, then proceed to the next while the first is cooking, and so on. But most people want to be brisk and efficient, chop everything up in advance so that they've got an army of ingredients ready and facing them before they start, and I've followed this approach in setting the directions down.

I always freeze the rinds of old used-up chunks of Parmesan and throw one, or two if they're only little, into the minestrone while it's cooking; this brings a flavorsome unctuousness to the carroty-oniony liquor. (I sometimes toss a rind into pea soup, as well.) You should discard the cheese rind before serving the soup; I dredge it out and then chew on it as soon as it's bearable—I love its elastic stickiness. Last, the oil. I use Ligurian oil, which is sweeter and milder than the peppery Tuscan variety.

8 tablespoons olive oil, preferably Ligurian

2 tablespoons (¼ stick) unsalted butter

3 large onions, sliced thinly

5 medium carrots, peeled and diced

2 celery stalks, chopped fairly small

10 ounces potatoes, peeled and diced

3 zucchini, diced

4 ounces young green beans, cut into ½-inch lengths

8 ounces Savoy cabbage, shredded

6⅓ cups beef, chicken, or vegetable stock

rind of a finished piece of Parmesan cheese (optional)

salt, if needed

4 ounces dried white beans, soaked and cooked, or 1 can (15 ounces) cannellini beans

6 ounces small tubular pasta, such as ditalini

½ cup grated Parmesan, plus more, for serving

Get a big pot and put in the oil and butter and onions and cook until the onions are softened but not browned. Add the carrots and cook for about 3 minutes, stirring a couple of times. Do the same with the celery, potatoes, zucchini, and green beans, cooking each one for a few minutes, stirring a few times. Then add the cabbage and cook for 6–8 minutes, stirring now and then.

Add the stock. Put in the rind if you're using it, give a good stir, and season with salt if needed. (The rind will give a small saline kick of its own, and remember, if you're using bouillon cubes, that they can be very salty.) Cover the pan and cook at a gentle boil for 2–2½ hours. The soup should be thick, so you have to cook it for long enough to lose any wateriness, but it has to have enough liquid in it at this stage for the pasta to absorb while it's cooking. If the soup is too thick when you've finished cooking it but before you put in the pasta, then add some water.

Now add the white beans and cook for 5 minutes, then turn up the heat slightly and put the pasta in. It should cook in about 15 minutes. When it's ready, take out the rind, add the fresh Parmesan, and give the soup a good stir. Serve with more cheese.

First time around I love to eat this with a slug of soft, light Ligurian oil poured into it, but afterwards, when it's been left to get thicker and sludgier in the fridge, I like it heated up so that it's warm (just) but not hot and with some tube-clearing chili oil— known to the Italians as *olio santo*—to punctuate its satiny depths.

I don't want to sound too fussy, but when you serve it, if you can, give people proper soup bowls (in other words, wide and shallow rather than deep and cupped); I don't know why it should make a difference, but it does.

BAKED SAUTERNES CUSTARD

I first ate this custard at Sir Terence Conran's restaurant Quaglino's in London; it's one of the best things I've ever eaten in a restaurant, and I say that after about twelve years as a restaurant critic. There, it's cooked in caramel-bottomed individual dariole molds and turned out, a golden-topped shivering tower of the stuff on the plate, and served with Armagnac-soaked prunes. My version, based on then-chef Martin Webb's recipe, is somewhat simpler. I don't know why I still call it Sauternes custard, except that it sounds so luxuriously evocative, as it is only if you're feeling extravagant or generous (depending on how you look at it) that you will actually use Sauternes. Restaurants don't have to worry about opening a bottle just for the odd cup of it. You can get a cheapish ordinary Sauternes, but then you will find it lacks distinction in general and in particular that musky, scented note of botrytis, which was the point of using Sauternes in the first place. If you've got guests who you can count on appreciating a bottle to go with the dessert, then it is worth it. You need a little for the custard, but the rest will get pleasurably and more or less immediately used.

I like this warm, spooned straight from the dish it's cooked in (eaten about 45 minutes to 1 hour after it comes out of the oven), but it is also wonderful cold, as long as you remember to take it out of the fridge a good hour before eating it. The cold option has two things going for it: first, it makes more of a contrast with the warm soup; and second, you can do it all the day before. Of course, it would look better unmolded, but that's something I can't manage and wouldn't advise trying. Yes, I know that the gleaming construct of an unblemished, unmolded mound of smooth custard is a wonderful thing, and a gloopy scoop of it from a large oval dish is at best homely. But this is partly because we have all been too much influenced by restaurant preparation. If a dish looks homely, well then, that's how it should be when eaten at home. The taste is so wonderful, so subtle but resonant, that any amount of visual inelegance is irrelevant.

POACHED APRICOTS

Cold, especially, it would be wonderful with poached apricots. The apricots that are sold are generally in no fit condition to be eaten, but poaching will help. Otherwise, just soak and cook some good dried apricots. Then transfer fruits and soaking liquid to a pan, add water to cover (if necessary), bring to the boil, and then simmer until soft. Remove the apricots to a bowl and then boil down the liquid in the pan to a syrup. Pour over the syrup and leave till room temperature or cold (but not fridge-cold). Or you can prepare ordinary dried apricots along the lines of the eastern Mediterranean recipe for them on page 320, or indeed the poached peaches I suggest as an accompaniment to the Sauternes custard ice cream on page 340. If all this is sounding a little complicated, then fresh raspberries or strawberries doused in some of the wine you're using for the custard would do as well. But don't start thinking that you absolutely have to be doing anything; this custard is good enough alone. No, more than good enough—sublime. In some moods, any accompaniment is a distraction.

2 whole eggs	1½ cups heavy whipping cream
4 egg yolks	1 vanilla bean, if not using vanilla sugar
½ cup vanilla sugar (page 72) or superfine sugar	¾ cup Sauternes or other dessert wine

Preheat the oven to 300°F. Fill up the kettle and bring the water just to the boil. Whisk the eggs, egg yolks, and sugar in a large bowl. Put the cream and vanilla bean, if using, in a saucepan; put the wine in another. Bring the cream to just below boiling point and then remove from heat; if using the vanilla bean, cover and let infuse for 20 minutes or so. Meanwhile, bring the wine to just below boiling point. If you are using a vanilla bean, remove it after steeping.

Start beating the egg and sugar mixture again. Pour the wine over it and continue beating while you then pour in the cream. Don't go mad with the whisking. If you beat too much air in, it'll go frothy and you will have a layer of bubbles on top, which you don't want. Strain the mixture and pour into a 4-cup dish (this will help remove some froth). Put the dish into a roasting pan and pour the water into the pan to come about halfway up the sides of the dish. Cover loosely with parchment or waxed paper.

Bake for about 1 hour. The custard should be firm but not immobile; when you press it with your fingers it should feel set but with a little wobble still within. When you eat it it should be just warm, soft, and voluptuous, like an eighteenth-century courtesan's inner thigh; you don't want something bouncy and jellied. A bit of dribble doesn't matter: it might not look defined on the plate, but it will taste resolutely good on the palate.

On my last birthday, I went to the local pub for lunch. I should amplify; the pub in question is the Anglesea Arms, whose kitchen is presided over by Dan Evans, a one-time protégé of British super-chef Alastair Little. Evans's food is fresh, strong, modern, but not caricaturedly so, and eclectic but not vertiginously so. I suppose because it's a pub rather than a restaurant—although there is a properly designated restaurant space—the food is bound to be more informal, nearer to the food you would like to eat at home.

I had six oysters, then potato pancakes with quickly marinated smoked haddock, which lay on top of each pancake with a dollop of crème fraîche beneath and a flurry of snipped chives on top. This was heavenly. And, I have since found out, not hard to make. You can replace the haddock with smoked salmon, but somehow that seems to signify "no effort." Although the smoked haddock is easily prepared once you get home, you do need to go to a fish seller to get the fish cut into the requisite thin slices. If this is too much trouble, you can wander off toward other things; these pancakes are good topped with chicken livers sautéed in butter and the pan deglazed with Marsala, sherry, or muscat wine. Or you might consider a tranche of just-seared salmon (or a silky layer of the smoked stuff) with a poached egg on top.

These pancakes—crêpes Parmentier—are named in honor of the man who forced the potato into the affections of the French and who persuaded, to that end, Marie Antoinette to weave potato flowers into her hair. They aren't difficult, but you need a blini pan about 4½ inches in diameter.

THE SMALL BUT PERFECTLY
FORMED LUNCH FOR 4

CRÊPES PARMENTIER WITH MARINATED SMOKED HADDOCK

POIRES BELLE HÉLÈNE

CRÊPES PARMENTIER WITH MARINATED
SMOKED HADDOCK

When you buy the haddock (you may have to order it in advance), ask the fish seller to cut it into very thin slices, rather like smoked salmon. It won't be quite so thin, but you want him to be thinking in that direction.

I get nine pancakes out of the quantities stated, so you've got room to lose one and still give people 2 each. If you think 2 each isn't going to be enough, then just boost quantities.

FOR THE POTATO PANCAKES

1 pound floury potatoes, peeled and cut into ½-inch dice

4 teaspoons all-purpose flour

3 eggs

4 egg whites

¼ cup crème fraîche or heavy cream

¼ cup milk

salt and freshly milled black pepper

vegetable oil, for frying

FOR THE HADDOCK

3 tablespoons extra-virgin olive oil

juice of 3 lemons

sea salt and freshly milled black pepper

1 pound smoked haddock (finnan haddie), sliced very thinly (see headnote)

_____

1 cup crème fraîche

small bunch chives, snipped

3–4 tablespoons chopped coriander

Put the potatoes in a steamer basket or perforated container (a metal colander would do) over gently boiling salted water and steam until tender. Try them after 20–30 minutes, and then keep trying. At about the time they're ready, preheat the oven to 350°F and put in it a plate big enough to hold about 9 of the pancakes.

Now, put the potatoes into a bowl and add the flour, mixing well. I tend to use a hand-held electric mixer for the entire operation. Then add the eggs, egg whites, crème fraîche, and milk; mix well so that you've got a smooth, thick batter, and add salt and pepper.

Pour a film of oil into a blini pan and put it on to the heat. When it's very hot add some batter, about a half ladleful or so. The pan should be slightly more than half filled. Keep it on the heat and watch; when the pancake is ready to turn, you'll notice the top beginning to bubble and the bottom will be brown. You can judge this by slipping a spatula underneath the pancake and upturning it slightly. Having flipped it over, cook it for slightly less time than the first side. These pancakes are easy to turn anyway, so don't worry about it. And if you make a mess of the first one, just jettison it and proceed. As each pancake is cooked, put it on the plate in the oven to keep warm.

While you're cooking the pancakes, prepare the haddock. In a shallow dish big enough to take all the fish, pour in the oil and lemon juice and sprinkle on some of the salt (I know you think the fish is salty enough anyway, but it will need salt, I promise), grind over some pepper, and place the thinly sliced fish in this basic marinade for 4–5 minutes only. This means you can really wait to do this until you've more or less finished dealing with the pancakes. By this time you'll be taking the pancakes in your stride so won't worry about having to fiddle with something else at the same time.

I like serving the component parts separately, for people to assemble themselves. On one plate place the lemony fish, on another the pancakes, in a bowl the crème fraîche, and in a couple of others the snipped chives and chopped coriander. Diners should put a pancake on their plates, lay on it a piece of fish, dollop over the crème fraîche, and douse all generously with the chives and/or coriander.

ST. JOHN'S SALAD

As for salads or something to eat with or after, I would offer a salad from London's St. John's restaurant of fresh, fresh flat-leaf parsley with red onion rings and soaked, drained, and dried salt-preserved capers (or use those put up in brine). A drizzle of oil with the quickest squeeze of lemon is all you need; it is important after the intense flavors of the haddock that the salad dressing should be light.

POIRES BELLE HÉLÈNE

Now for the pears. Old-fashioned they certainly are, and my grandmother used to make them for me when I was a child. But they're not nursery food and it isn't just nostalgia that makes me dredge them up. Pears are so rarely edible when raw. When they're good, they're wonderful, but I am beginning to think Ralph Waldo Emerson was being optimistic when he wrote, "There are only ten minutes in the life of a pear when it is perfect to eat." Most pears go from hard to woolly without ever passing through the luscious ripe stage. Poaching pears is one way of dealing with all those hard, unyielding fruits in the shops; somehow, however wooden they felt raw, poached they become infused with a juice-bursting plumpness. In fact, it is a positive advantage to use what would in other circumstances seem annoyingly firm fruit. (Actually, I have rather a soft spot for canned pears; the dense graininess of the liquid-soused fruit is remarkably seductive.)

Traditionally, this dessert consists of ice cream topped with a poached pear, chocolate sauce, and, finally, candied violets. I'd rather put on the table a tub of ice cream, a plate of poached pears, a pitcher of chocolate sauce, and, if possible, a saucerful of the violets.

FOR THE PEARS	FOR THE CHOCOLATE SAUCE
4–6 firm Bartlett pears or other dessert variety	8 ounces bittersweet chocolate
juice of 1 lemon	½ cup strong black coffee, or 1 teaspoon instant coffee in ½ cup boiling water
½ cup superfine sugar or vanilla sugar (page 72)	½ cup superfine sugar
1 vanilla bean, or 1 teaspoon pure vanilla extract if not using vanilla sugar	½ cup heavy cream

1 quart best-quality vanilla ice cream
crystallized violets (optional)

Peel, halve, and core the pears and sprinkle over them the lemon juice to stop them from discoloring. In a wide shallow pan (in which the pears will fit in one layer—otherwise cook them in batches) put 1¼ cups water, the sugar, and the vanilla bean, if using. Bring to the boil, stirring every now and again to make sure the sugar dissolves, then lower the heat slightly and simmer for 5 minutes. Add the vanilla extract, if using. Put the pears into the liquid, cut side down, and raise the heat again so that the syrup boils up and the pears are covered by it. You may need to spoon the syrup over. After half a minute or so, lower the heat, then cover the pan and simmer for 10 minutes; turn the pears, cover the pan again, and simmer for another 10 minutes. Continue poaching until the pears are cooked and translucent; they should feel tender (but not soggy) when pierced. They may need more or less cooking time—it depends on the pears. Take off the heat, keep covered, and leave to cool.

Now the chocolate sauce: place the chocolate, broken up into small pieces, in a thick-bottomed pan with the coffee and sugar and melt over a low heat, stirring occasionally. Then pour in the cream, still stirring, and when it is very hot pour into a warmed sauceboat or a bowl with a ladle.

To serve, arrange pears cut-side down on a big flat plate and pour some syrup over. (Any remaining syrup will keep in the fridge or freezer and can be used to pour over apples or other fruit when making pies or crumbles. You can wash the vanilla pod, wipe it and put it in a canister of sugar.) Offer with the ice cream, sauce, and violets, if using, served separately; allow diners to help themselves.

People are wrong to be daunted by pastry, but there's no point in pretending they aren't. There is something unhelpful about suggesting you come to grips with it at the end of a long day's work, but on the weekend you can work calmly. And the weekend is just the time to eat simple, comforting food such as traditional English steak and kidney pie or rhubarb meringue pies or a soft and swollen, creamy crab tart.

The following four menus all include a pastry factor.

A SCHOOL-DINNER LUNCH FOR 4–6

STEAK AND KIDNEY PIE

BANANA CUSTARD

If you can't stomach the idea of banana custard, substitute the trifle on page 109 or provide good ripe bananas and good thick cream and put them on the table with a bowl of soft brown sugar and let everyone mash their own.

STEAK AND KIDNEY PIE

Cook the meat in its licorice-dark gravy first and then assemble the pie later with the made, cooled filing. The advantage of the two-pronged attack is that the meat is at its best when cooked, on low heat, for a good long time and the pastry needs a shorter time at a higher heat to keep it crisp but yieldingly rich. Another advantage is that you can cook the meat in advance. I make a suet dough here rather than a regular one for two reasons. The first is the most compelling—it goes so well, it fits, tastes as it should; it somehow manages to give me a nostalgic glow of satisfaction about food I was never actually given to eat as a child. The second is simply that this is the easiest of all pastries to make and roll out; just stir all the ingredients together in the bowl, roll out, and stretch any old how over the pie. Suet crust (unlike ordinary pastry, which benefits from hanging around) has to be baked the minute it's made, and it makes for a bumpy, ramshackle-looking pie.

If you don't like kidneys (and unless you've got a good butcher they can be bitter and somehow sawdusty and rubbery at the same time), then just boost the quantities of steak and add more mushrooms. These should be cremini mushrooms, if possible; regular button mushrooms can sometimes be just pretty polystyrene. I use stout rather than wine because I love it, and also because I make the pie filling in advance and don't drink enough to have an open bottle of red wine on the go. Use the best beef stock you can, but if you can't do better than a good cube, then don't lose sleep over it.

If you cannot get suet (beef fat from around the kidneys; see page 459), then use any plain pastry dough (see page 37) made with lard or half lard and vegetable shortening and butter.

This is, of course, a standard British dish, but I start it off as the Italians do their stews, with a soffritto of carrot, onion, celery, and, less orthodox, sage. If the lovage is out in the garden, then I use that instead of celery, but to be frank, it isn't for long that the desire to eat steak and kidney pie and the seasonal availability of lovage overlap. You could, I suppose, add garlic too, as the Italians would, but I don't. Not because I think it would be disastrous, but because I just instinctively don't.

4 tablespoons vegetable oil

2 medium onions, minced

I medium carrot, minced

½ celery stalk or small handful lovage
   leaves, minced

3 sage leaves, minced

2 tablespoons unsweetened butter

7 ounces cremini or regular button
   mushrooms, quartered

I heaping tablespoon chopped parsley

4 tablespoons all-purpose flour

whole nutmeg

freshly milled black pepper

I pound beef stew meat, cut into I-inch
   chunks

½ pound kidneys, cut into I-inch chunks

I cup beef stock

I cup stout or red wine

salt

FOR THE CRUST

I ½ cups all-purpose flour

½ teaspoon salt

2 teaspoons baking powder

whole nutmeg

½ cup beef suet

Preheat the oven to 300°F. Put 2 tablespoons oil in a heavy-bottomed saucepan and heat, adding the vegetables and sage. Stir around over medium heat for about 5 minutes or until softish. Remove to a heavy casserole with a lid.

Add the butter to the saucepan and sauté the mushrooms for a few minutes; add the parsley, turn well, and then transfer to the vegetables in the casserole. Sprinkle the flour onto a large plate and add an exuberant grating of fresh nutmeg and some pepper. Turn the beef and kidneys in the flour and, when all the pieces are done, heat the remaining 2 tablespoons oil in the pan and brown the meat. Don't cram the pan or the meat'll be steamed rather than seared; just do 4–5 chunks at a time, removing them to the casserole as you go. If there's any flour left on the dredging plate, add it to the frying pan, stirring as you do so. I use a flat wooden spoon-cum-spatula for this. Add the stock and stout and stir well, scraping any bits from the base of the pan, and pour over the meat and vegetables in the casserole. Season with the salt and pepper, cover, and cook for about 2 hours. You want the meat to be tender but not falling apart. But you shouldn't have a problem at this low heat anyway.

When it's ready, leave to cool. If you can't cook the pie filling in advance, then you need to decant it to make it cool more quickly. I would just pour it into a roasting pan (or anything that will take it in as thin a layer as possible) and put somewhere cold. Later, transfer to an 8-inch pie plate. Put a pie funnel (or upended eggcup) in the middle.

The pastry will need 30–40 minutes to cook, so bear that in mind when you decide when to get started on the pastry. And how easy is that? Preheat the oven to 425°F. Put the flour, salt, baking powder, and another extravagant grating of nutmeg in a bowl. Stir in the suet and then, still stirring, add water, ½ cup of it at first. You need a soft paste; add more water (or flour, if you've been too heavy-handed with the water) as you think necessary. This is a forgiving kind of pastry, so don't worry about exact calibrations.

Sprinkle some flour onto a surface, some onto the rolling pin, and some more onto the surface of the dough, and start rolling. You need a fat disc, about ¼ inch or so thick, slightly bigger than the diameter of the pie dish. You'll have rather more than this, so from the overmatter cut some strips and cover the rims of the dish with them. It helps to dampen the rims with a little cold water first. Now, lift up your circle of nubbly soft pastry and drape over the pie dish. Cobble it together somehow if holes appear and press down over the pastry rims. Put the pie in the oven and cook for about 10 minutes, then turn the oven down to 375°F and cook for another 25 minutes. Peep after 15; if the pastry looks as if it might stop browning and start burning, then cover loosely with foil. Whip the foil off, though, for the last couple of minutes. Allow to cool for 10 minutes and serve.

I think you have to have peas with this; and as it obviously isn't summer food, I mean by this frozen young peas. Potatoes aren't strictly necessary, I suppose, given the pastry, but even so, potatoes mashed with an equal volume of parsnips (or rutabaga) and more butter than anyone would like to own up to would be just right.

BANANA CUSTARD

The first time I made a banana custard, it looked so pallid; terrifying schoolgirl memories had taught me to expect the bouncy canary-yellow of Bird's custard mix, a British kitchen standby. The next time I added saffron to the custard (as long as you don't add too much, the note it strikes is intriguing rather than intrusive), which turns it from palest primrose to a yellow that would do honor to the most dazzling *tartrazine*. It is more than just a culinary joke, though, enjoyable as that is in itself. And for once, powdered saffron may be a better choice than strands. Saffron strands leave little red strings, which are beautiful enough, to be sure, but what we are after is an uninterrupted blanket of unarguable yellow.

If you hate the idea of the saffron, then leave the custard pale and uninteresting; there's no mileage in adding food coloring and no point in using a mix.

Use a dish with a 6-cup capacity and enough surface area to allow the banana slices to be spread in a single layer. The custard could also be baked (see page 339).

2½ cups milk	⅓ cup superfine sugar
good pinch ground saffron	4 bananas, firm but ripe
8 egg yolks	

Fill the sink with cold water—you may need to plunge the custard pot into this later to stop it cooking quickly.

Put the milk in a saucepan, sprinkle in the saffron, and bring to boiling point. Meanwhile whisk together the egg yolks and sugar with a fork, and just as the milk is about to come to the boil, pour it over the eggs and keep on whisking. Pour into a wide, heavy-bottomed saucepan (I use the largest one I've got) and cook on a low heat, stirring constantly with a wooden spoon. In about 10 minutes the custard should have thickened lightly. Remove from the heat and plunge the pan into the cold water in the sink and stir until cooled. If, indeed, at any stage you think the custard is about to boil or curdle, then immerse the custard pan in the cold water and beat vigorously.

Slice the bananas into a dish. I do them in coins of lengthening diagonals. When the bananas are arranged as you like them, strain the custard over and leave to cool and form a skin. This is imperative. I don't like skin on custard usually, but I recognize that banana custards must have a skin. You can make the custard in advance, sprinkling confectioners' sugar on top to prevent it forming a skin, but in that case the bananas cannot be cut and the whole assembled till the last minute.

LUNCH, TENTATIVELY OUTSIDE, FOR 8

CRAB AND SAFFRON TART

PARSLEY SALAD

BAKED CARAMEL APPLE

❖

In the heat of the summer you don't want, I think, a rich and odoriferous crab tart. But in those first early days, when it is more hope than convenience that takes you outside, or when the sun is growing weaker but still invites, toward the end of September, this is the perfect lunch—not too filling and not a parody of a picnic to be eaten under those cloudless pre–First World War skies of nostalgic collective memory.

If you think you can't manage the pastry, buy it, but making the rich crust below is not a big deal, I promise you. I tend to make the pastry the night before and leave it in a disc, wrapped in plastic film, in the fridge to be rolled out the next morning. If I've got time to start it slightly earlier in the evening, I make the pastry, let it rest, then bring it out and roll it, line the tart pan with it, and put it back in the fridge, covered with film again. Then, the next day, all I've got to do is bake it blind (see below and page 39) and then get the filling together, which is not a strenuous exercise.

CRAB AND SAFFRON TART

This recipe is adapted from food writer Simon Hopkinson's *Roast Chicken and Other Stories*. Normally I don't like tomatoes with fish, but here everything melds so harmoniously, seductively together that I forget my usual gripes. With it I'd serve the salad of parsley—flat-leaved, unchopped—capers and red onion that is copied from the salad served with bone marrow at St. John's and mentioned on page 221. The rich and fragrant creaminess of the tart is offset particularly well by it.

PARSLEY
SALAD

FOR THE PASTRY

1¼ cups Italian 00 or all-purpose flour

6 tablespoons (¾ stick) unsalted butter, chilled and cut into small dice

1 egg yolk

¼ teaspoon salt

1 teaspoon lemon juice

FOR THE FILLING

1 can (14.5 ounces) plum tomatoes, drained and chopped

2 fat garlic cloves

1 bay leaf

1 sprig thyme

¼ teaspoon salt, plus more

freshly milled black pepper

1¼ cups heavy cream

½ teaspoon saffron threads

4 egg yolks

½ pound lump crab meat

First make the pastry following instructions on page 38. Go slowly when adding the water, incorporating 1 tablespoon at a time. About 4 tablespoons should do it, but you may need more. The weather, the flour, the egg will all make a difference. When the dough coheres into an unsticky ball, press it into a fat disc and cover with plastic film and put into the fridge for about 20 minutes, more if it's a hot day, or leave overnight.

Preheat the oven to 400°F. Then roll out the pastry to fit a 9½-inch tart or quiche pan that's 2 inches deep. Bake blind (see page 39).

Remove from the oven, turn the heat down to 350°F, and get on with the filling (or if you prefer, do the filling while the pastry cooks). Put the tomatoes, garlic, herbs, the ¼ teaspoon of salt, and a few grindings of the pepper in a saucepan and reduce to a thickish sauce. Cool, remove the herbs, and spread the sauce in the bottom of the pastry shell. Warm together 3 tablespoons of the cream with the saffron and allow to steep for a few minutes. Beat together the egg yolks and the rest of the cream and add the saffron cream. Correct the seasoning. Loosely fold the crab meat into the custard and carefully pour into the tart shell. I think it's easier to pour it in while the pastry shell is sitting on its (slightly pulled out) oven rack.

Bake 30–40 minutes or until set and pale golden brown on top, but with a hint of runny wobble within. Serve neither hot nor cold but warm; this is at its paradisal, slightly *baveuse* best about 50 minutes to an hour after it comes out of the oven. And I have found that you can bring any fridge-cold leftover wedges back to optimum, faintly runny room temperature in a low microwave. Strange but true. And if you do have any left over, it is worth cutting into individual fat slices and freezing like that, only to resuscitate them for a perfect, gloriously luxurious dinner for yourself in evenings ahead.

BAKED CARAMEL APPLES

As with the crab tart, these apples are best eaten not hot but warm. If you put them in the oven just as you take out the tart, then they in turn will be ready to be taken out just as you sit down for lunch. Transfer the apples to a large plate or couple of plates and pour the juices into a saucepan. Then all you need to do at the last minute is come back to the stove to reduce and add cream to the buttery sour-sweet liquor in the saucepan before pouring it thickly over the softly cooling, glossy, and bulging apples on the plates. These are my favorite baked apples of all time and I wouldn't change a thing. If, however, you want the sauce clear and caramelish rather than dense and fudgelike, then omit the cream.

8 cooking apples	1 cup Calvados or applejack
10 tablespoons (1 stick plus	juice of 1 lemon
2 tablespoons) unsalted butter	½ cup light cream
⅔ cup light muscovado sugar or light	
brown sugar	

Preheat the oven to 350°F. Core the apples and, with a sharp knife, cut a line round each as if circling the equator. Put them in a roasting pan. Press in the butter and sugar, alternately, in the holes and press any excess on top. Pour the Calvados and lemon juice into the pan. Put them into the oven and cook for about 50 minutes or until soft.

Remove the apples to a plate or dish and pour the cooking juices and liquid into a saucepan. (I've left them to cool for about an hour and a half and they've still tasted perfect.) When you want to eat dessert, nip back inside and put the saucepan on a high heat. Let bubble till the liquid is reduced and thickened; it should be like a gooey sticky syrup. Stir in the cream and let bubble again for a few minutes and pour this fudgy sauce over the apples. Serve right away, as they are—you don't need to eat anything else alongside or dolloped on top.

SPRING LUNCH TO LIFT THE SPIRITS, FOR 6

LEMON LINGUINE

GREEN SALAD

IRISH TARTE TATIN

❖

According to my paternal grandmother, spring no longer exists, though her lament was as much sartorial as environmental: no more spring coats, you see, because no more spring weather. Actually, I suspect the change is in us rather than in the climate; our failure to recognize, let alone celebrate, the advent of spring owes rather more to the fact that we now live in centrally heated homes. The meager upturn in the weather cannot have quite the impact it must once have had. But I do think there is an idea of spring, culinarily speaking. Of course, seasonal produce has something to do with it, but not everything. For me, that idea is instantly conveyed by this lemony, creamy tangle of linguine that actually you could cook at any time of the year. It is the easiest thing you could imagine—the sauce requires no cooking, just stirring (and limply at that) and it produces food that is both comforting and uplifting. There must be something about the smell of lemons, so fresh, so hopeful, which makes this instant good-mood food. But it isn't so jaunty and astringent that you need to brace yourself to dive in.

I made this sauce once with a very fine pasta, some sort of egg tagliarini, and regretted it. You need the sturdier, but still satiny, resistance offered up by the linguine, which is why I stipulated this very pasta. Good spaghetti or tagliatelle would do if linguine are not to be found. As the sauce is the sort of thing you can throw together after a quick rummage through the shelves of the corner shop, it would be unhelpful to be too sternly dictatorial about a pasta shape that is not universally carried.

As for the Irish tarte Tatin, this is Roscommon Rhubarb Pie as chronicled by Darina Allen in *Irish Traditional Cooking*. The rhubarb and sugar are piled on the bottom of the pie dish, a scone mixture on top, and the whole turned out later in the manner of a tarte tatin. The upended pie with its bronzy pink crown of rhubarb looks beautiful and it is fabulously easy. For this, you're just mixing stuff around in a bowl, idly and imprecisely rolling it out, and then tucking the large disc of scone like a blanket over the simply chopped and sugar-sprinkled fruit.

Perhaps pastry after pasta sounds stodgy, but it won't taste like that, I promise. And the scent of lemons followed by the sharp-sweet breath of red and early rhubarb conveys the brisk but tender air of early, still faintly wintry, spring.

LEMON LINGUINE

2 pounds linguine	pinch salt
2 egg yolks	freshly milled black pepper
⅔ cup heavy cream	4 tablespoons (½ stick) unsalted butter
½ cup freshly grated Parmesan	2–3 tablespoons chopped parsley
zest of 1 lemon and juice of ½,	
plus more juice, if needed	

Fill just about the biggest pot you have with water and bring to the boil. When friends are coming for lunch, get the water heated to boiling point before they arrive, otherwise you end up nervously hanging around waiting for a watched pot to boil while your supposedly quick lunch gets later and later. Bring the water to the boil, cover, and turn off the burner.

I tend to leave the addition of salt until the water's come to the boil a second time. But whichever way you do it, add quite a bit of salt. When the bubbling's encouragingly fierce, put in the pasta. I often put the lid on for a moment or so just to let the pasta get back to the boil, but don't turn your back on it, and give it a good stir with a pasta fork or whatever to avoid even the suspicion of stickiness, once you've removed the lid.

Then get on with the sauce, making sure you've set your timer for about a minute or so less than the time specified on the package of pasta.

In a bowl put the yolks, cream, Parmesan, zest of the whole lemon and juice of half of it, the salt and good grind of pepper, and beat with a fork. You don't want it fluffy, just combined. Taste. If you want it more lemony, then of course add more juice.

When the timer goes off, taste to judge how near the pasta is to being ready. I recommend that you hover by the stove so you don't miss that point. Don't be too hasty, though. Everyone is so keen to cook their pasta properly al dente that sometimes the pasta is actually not cooked enough. You want absolutely no chalkiness here. And linguine (or at least I find it so) tend not to run over into soggy overcookedness quite as quickly as other long pasta. This makes sense, of course, as the strands of "little tongues" are denser than the flat ribbon shapes.

Anyway, as soon as the pasta looks ready, remove a cup of the cooking liquid, drain the pasta, and then, off the heat, toss it back in the pot or put it in an efficiently preheated bowl, throw in the butter, and stir and swirl about to make sure the butter's melted and the pasta covered by it all over. Each strand will be only mutely gleaming, as there's not much butter and quite a bit of pasta. If you want to add more, then do; good butter is the best flavoring, best texture, best mood enhancer there is.

When you're satisfied the pasta's covered with its soft slip of butter, then stir in the egg mixture and turn the pasta well in it, adding some of the cooking liquid if it looks a bit dry (only 2 tablespoons or so—you don't want a wet mess—and only after you think the sauce is incorporated). Sprinkle over the parsley and serve now, now, now.

As for the green salad: buy a package of the ready washed and chopped stuff or assemble your own as you wish. But keep it green; by all means add raw sugar snap peas if you like (a good idea, indeed) and some whole, tender basil leaves (equally so), but remember the idea is to provide something clear and refreshing between the pasta and the pie. A soft, round, pale green lettuce like Bibb is just right for this—nothing else, just that, in a plain vinaigrette, no interesting oils.

IRISH TARTE TATIN

Bright-hued, early spring rhubarb is indicated here, but I've used the later stuff with good results. But be stern when inspecting it before buying; there's no point in making this dessert if the fruit's woody and acrid. If it looks as if it's rusting and wilting, then don't bother.

Darina Allen specifies a 9 × 2-inch round pie pan and remarks that she also uses a heavy stainless-steel sauté pan. I use my regular stainless-steel pie dish. It's about 8 inches in diameter, 2 inches in depth, and has sloping sides. Because of the sloping sides, the pie, when turned out, looks rather celebratory, as if it were holding up the rhubarb as an offering.

2 pounds rhubarb, trimmed and cut into 1-inch pieces

1¼ cup sugar, plus additional, if needed

FOR THE SCONE DOUGH

2½ cups all-purpose flour

2 tablespoons superfine sugar

1 heaping teaspoon baking powder

pinch salt

4 tablespoons (½ stick) unsweetened butter, cut into medium dice

1 egg

¾ cup milk, plus more, if needed

1 egg, beaten, for the wash

sugar, for sprinkling

Preheat the oven to 450°F. Put the rhubarb into a pie dish or a sauté pan (see headnote) and sprinkle it with the sugar. Taste the rhubarb and add more sugar if needed.

Into a bowl sift all the dry ingredients for the scone dough. Rub the butter into the flour until the mixture resembles coarse bread crumbs. (Not hard to do by hand, but I tend to use my free-standing mixer.) Whisk the egg with the milk. Make a well in the center of the dry ingredients, pour in the liquid all at once, and mix to a soft dough. Turn out onto a floured board and roll into a 9-inch round (or the size of the dish you're using) about 1 inch thick. Place this fat disc on top of the rhubarb and tuck in the edges neatly. Brush with a little of the beaten egg and sprinkle generously with sugar.

Bake in the preheated oven for 15 minutes, then reduce the temperature to 350°F for about 30 minutes more, or until the top is crusty and golden and the rhubarb soft and juicy.

Remove the pan from the oven and allow to sit for a few minutes. Put a warm plate over the top of the pan and turn it upside-down so that the pie comes out on the plate. It is almost impossible (or I, naturally impatient and clumsy, find it so) not to burn yourself with some of the escaping hot liquid. The trick is to find a dish that is flat at the bottom with slightly upturned edges. I'm working on it.

Serve warm with, Darina Allen recommends, light brown sugar and cream. I can think of nothing nicer. For those who cannot contemplate rhubarb without custard, a good cold dollop of the stuff would be an obvious, but rewarding, choice.

ANOTHER SPRING LUNCH
FOR 6–8

PROSCIUTTO, FRESH RICOTTA OR MOZZARELLA, AND BASIL
GRILLED ZUCCHINI OR ROAST ASPARAGUS
SALAD AND BREAD
RHUBARB MERINGUE PIE

I love rhubarb; a quick glance at the entry for it in the Index will suggest how much. But my real passion goes deeper; at home I use it whenever I can get away with it. Maybe it's the relatively short season (although I find I can go from the hothouse stuff to the hardy outdoors-reared stalks with hardly a hiccup) that makes it so attractive, but if it's in the shops, I want to cook with it. I make rhubarb fool (divine used to wedge together the two vanilla-scented halves of a Victoria sponge), rhubarb and raspberry crumble (the rhubarb fresh, the raspberries always used to be from the freezer case, but more recently they're fresh too, flown in at great expense from distant points), plain stewed rhubarb, rhubarb custard pie—the pie, indeed, above—all the other rhubarb-rich recipes in this book;

and my absolute tear-inducingly comforting favorite, rhubarb meringue pie.

It isn't nostalgia that drives me—such desserts, such ingredients, were not a part of my childhood—or a kitsch longing for the retroculinary repertoire. It's the taste, the smell, the soft, fragrant, bulky stickiness of this that seduces. I cannot pretend any form of meringue pie is easy and because it takes a bit of effort, I have suggested a picnic before it.

For eight people, I get 1 pound of prosciutto (San Daniele or Parma), sliced thin, thin, thin and draped over a big plate like rumpled silk lining. Add a mound of fresh ricotta or provide fresh mozzarella di bufalo drizzled with basil oil (see recipe below) or just milkily plain and barely sprinkled with salt and pepper and olive oil. Make a salad of lamb's lettuce and romaine hearts with a light but astringent dressing; if it's in season, lay on some asparagus just rolled in oil and coarse sea salt and spread out on a baking sheet in the hottest oven you can muster, for 5–10 minutes a side, and then left to cool to room temperature or just above, and put on a plate with either some lemon wedges bundled alongside or just a sprinkling of good balsamic vinegar over. If asparagus isn't around, then get some zucchini (about 5 should do for 8 people), slice them thinly lengthways, brush them lightly with oil, and cook on a hot griddle till blistered brown. As they cook, remove them to a large plate and pour over glass-green oil, a good squirt of lemon juice, and a carpeting of just-chopped herbs—parsley, mint, marjoram, basil, some or all. Make sure there's lots of bread and you might, as well, leave some tomatoes whole in a bowl on the table, so that people can take them as they like.

PROSCIUTTO

FRESH
RICOTTA

MOZZARELLA
DI BUFALO

ASPARAGUS

ZUCCHINI

BASIL OIL

The book from which this recipe comes, *Recipes 1-2-3* by Rozanne Gold, is a clever idea. All its recipes contain just three ingredients, though further ones in the form of suggested "add-ons" are posited.

Leaves from 1 very large bunch basil   **6–10 tablespoons extra-virgin olive oil**

Blanch the basil leaves in boiling water for 30 seconds and then refresh by plunging immediately into ice water. Squeeze out as much moisture as you can and then put in a blender or processor with a small bowl and whizz with the oil until you have a thickish green purée, like liquid pool-table felt. That's it.

This makes enough for 3 balls of mozzarella.

Slice the mozzarella thickly and dribble the basil oil over it. You could equally use the basil oil over sliced tomatoes, pasta, soup, anything.

RHUBARB MERINGUE PIE
for Horatia

I don't go in for flavored mashed potatoes, flavored pasta, or flavored pastry. I think that mashed potatoes, pasta, and pastry are meant to be the base line, the comforting neutral blanket against which other more sprightly tastes can be set. But orange, in pastry, does work, and subtly. Orange, famously, sets off rhubarb—and it is used also to bind the fruits beneath the meringue topping.

Because I quite often make rhubarb jelly, I tend to have pulpy bags of frozen, poached, sweetened fruit in the freezer. For a 8-inch tart pan, about 2 cups of cooked fruit should be fine. And if the purée is already sweetened, you'll need only 1–2 tablespoons of extra sugar rather than the ¾ cup specified.

If you're using raw fruit, proceed as below.

FOR THE PASTRY

1 cup Italian 00 or all-purpose flour

6 tablespoons unsalted butter, cold, cut
    in small cubes, or 3 tablespoons lard
    and 3 tablespoons butter

juice of 1 orange

pinch salt

Make the pastry by following the instructions on page 37, freezing the flour and butter for 10 minutes and chilling half the orange juice with the salt, which you will use later to make the floury, buttery, breadcrumby mixture cohere. You will be using the remaining juice for the filling, so keep it. Go slowly, adding ice water if needed. When the dough can be formed into a ball, stop, roll it into a ball in your hands, and then press it into a disc, wrap with plastic film, and put in the fridge for 20–30 minutes. Roll it out and line a deep tart/quiche pan of 8 inches in diameter. Put back in the fridge, if possible, for about another 20 minutes and preheat the oven to 400°F.

Bake blind (see page 39) until the pastry looks cooked but not brown. Remove from the oven; you don't want the pastry hot when you put all the other ingredients in it.

FOR THE RHUBARB

1¼ pounds rhubarb, trimmed, halved
    lengthwise if wide, and cut ½-inch
    thick

remaining juice from making the pastry,
    plus more, if needed

2 eggs, separated

1¼ cups superfine sugar, plus 1 teaspoon

2 tablespoons all-purpose flour

2 tablespoons (¼ stick) unsalted butter,
    melted

¼ teaspoon cream of tartar

Put the rhubarb in a saucepan with the orange juice and heat briefly, just until the rawness is taken off them. Remove and drain, keeping the liquid.

Put the egg whites aside for the meringue and beat the yolks in a bowl. In another bowl, mix ¾ cup of the sugar with the flour and the melted butter. Then add the yolks, and enough of the orangey-rhubarb liquid to make a smooth and runny paste. Squeeze in more orange if you need more. Put the rhubarb in the blind-baked pastry shell and pour the sugary, eggy mixture over it. Put in the oven and bake until just set, 20–30 minutes.

Meanwhile, beat the egg whites until they form soft peaks, add ¼ cup of the remaining sugar, and continue to beat until glossy. I use my mixer until this point. I then change to a metal spoon and fold in the remaining ¼ cup sugar and the cream of tartar. Spoon this over the hot cooked rhubarb, making sure it is completely covered and there is no place, no gap where some rhubarb can bubble up through and over the meringue. Use the spoon to bring some of the meringue into little pointy peaks if you like (I do), but this is an aesthetic *diktat*, not a practical-culinary one. Sprinkle with the 1 teaspoon sugar and put back in the oven for about 15 minutes until the peaks are bronzy and brown-topped.

I like this cold. But for most tastes, eat it 10–12 minutes after it's been taken out of the oven.

HIGH SUMMER AL FRESCO LUNCH FOR 8

To eat outside, you don't necessarily have to cook a lot, but you've got a lot to think about. I'm talking here about a table-borne lunch outside in the garden. Choose nothing fussy, nothing that will grow waxy or dry in the heat, and nothing that will sit too heavily on the digestion. Lots of meat, quivering pots of mayonnaise in the sun's glare, bread already cut—much traditional picnic fare is ruled out. Certainly a hunk of bread, a wedge of cheese, and a peppery salami will do on cooler days, but in even moderate heat, bread gets stale in a matter of minutes. Cheese and meat quickly grow a patina of rancid sweatiness.

Pita is better—unsurprisingly—at withstanding heat; it does harden to cardboardy unpliableness if left out too brazenly, but covered with a napkin or toasted to order on a nearby barbecue, it will hold up better than ciabatta or baguette. Don't bother cooking a dessert. You could go for the Yogurt with Honey and Passion Fruit on page 211; otherwise serve grapes and plums all'Italiana—bobbing about in water- and ice-cube-filled bowls—or any amount of fruit cut up with as much dexterity as you can muster (in my case, not much), Japanese style. Tropical fruits obviously do well in the heat. Cut papayas in half, remove the black stony pips, and squirt with lime, or fill the cavities, avocado-style, with strawberries that have been chopped and macerated with a sprinkling of balsamic vinegar or with plain, unadorned raspberries.

Food that suits hot weather is—it stands to reason—food that's customarily

GRAPES AND
PLUMS

PAPAYAS

eaten in hot countries. I tend to go for the food of the eastern Mediterranean. I am not pretending to set up a taverna in my backyard; but when it's hot I want tabbouleh, hummus, garlic chicken, mint-sprinkled slices of eggplant, and the balm of juicy, cold, jade-colored wedges of cucumber.

TABBOULEH

I love this salad of cracked wheat, mint, and parsley to be very green and very sharp, but if you want it to be grainier and oilier, then adapt it as you wish. In many recipes you will find cucumber stipulated as well; by all means add this if you want, but I tend not to as after a while it makes the salad go wet and watery. I keep leftovers in the fridge to be squished into pita or a baked potato for the next day's lunch and, indeed, eaten whenever the desire overcomes me. Tomatoes seem to hold up pretty well in the dish, although I always add them just before serving the tabbouleh the first time. Perhaps it's just that I don't mind the pinkly-stained sogginess so much on my own account when it's brought out for the second. Red onions, if they're not mild, can make this very intensely oniony, so taste a bit of the onion (and the scallions—they too can vary) before you judge how much to add. Tabbouleh, surprisingly, works very well too with cold—poached or baked—salmon for a different take on a traditional summer food. Warm, pink, sweet lamb—noisettes seared on a griddle until medium-rare, let to stand for 5–10 minutes, then sliced thinly on the diagonal, heaped on a nearby plate, and sprinkled with some salt, chopped mint, and marjoram—is terrific with tabbouleh, too. Like a lot of foods with bite, once you eat this you hanker after it again.

Be very wary of using a food processor for chopping the parsley and mint for this, which must be done at the last minute to preserve their flavor. It does have a tendency not so much to chop herbs as to reduce them to a wet mush. But when you are chopping a reasonably large quantity the danger can be avoided more easily; just pulse on and off quickly and (after checking) repeatedly so that the herbs don't get pulverized before you've had a chance to intervene. Leave the leaves relatively large, too; after all, the parsley and mint are the major part of the salad itself, not flavoring in it.

1 cup medium bulghur	½ cup mint leaves
juice of 2 lemons, plus more, if needed	12 scallions (white and green parts),
⅔ cup olive oil, plus more, if needed	sliced into thin rings, or 1 large or
salt and freshly milled black pepper	2 small red onions, minced
½ cup parsley leaves	6 flavorful tomatoes

Put the bulghur in a bowl, cover it with boiling water, and leave to soak for 30 minutes. Drain the bulghur in a strainer, getting rid of as much water as possible.

Put the bulghur in a serving dish and pour over the lemon juice, olive oil, and a good sprinkling of salt and pepper. Meanwhile, finely chop the parsley and the mint.

Throw the chopped parsley and mint into the dressed bulghur and stir in the scallions. Put the tomatoes in a bowl and pour over boiling water from the kettle to cover. Leave them for a few minutes, then remove, peel, cut in half, and take out seeds. Dice the tomatoes and stir into the herbs and cracked wheat. Taste and add more salt, lemon juice, and oil if it needs it.

HUMMUS WITH SEARED LAMB AND TOASTED PINE NUTS

This isn't an obvious pairing, but I think it's an authentic one. That's to say, although I've never seen mention of it in cookbooks, I've eaten it—in both Turkish and Lebanese restaurants. And I love this combination of cold, thickly nutty, buff-colored paste and hot, lemony-sweet shards of meat, and the waxy, resiny nuts—it instantly elevates the hummus from its familiar deli-counter incarnation. You could use good bought hummus—but just dribble a little good olive oil on top, and round the edges, before topping with the nuts and lamb.

And as far as authenticity goes, I don't make any claims for my hummus recipe, for I add yogurt. Nor do I apologize for my innovation. Homemade hummus can be stodgy and sticky, and I love the tender whippedness that you get in restaurant versions (which, come to think of it, are probably brought in). If you leave out the yogurt, you may have to add a little more of the chickpea cooking liquid. Don't be afraid of making this too liquid; it'll most likely stiffen on keeping anyway. With the yogurt, I find I can still use up to 1 cup cooking liquid when puréeing the chickpeas.

I use noisettes of lamb for this because I know that they'll be lean but still satiny within. Cut the noisettes into lardons, small fingerlike strips of meat, then cut these in half horizontally. That's the size of meat you're aiming for.

I also use garlic-infused oil to sear the lamb because I like it when the lamb has a garlicky taste, but I don't want burnt shards of garlic mixed up with it. Marinating the lamb with a few cloves of crushed garlic can work, but then it doesn't sear as well. But ordinary olive oil works well too, and because the hummus itself is garlicky, you hardly risk blandness by omitting the garlic with the lamb.

The quantities in this are based on the use of a shallow wide or long dish to hold it; if you're using a deeper, smaller dish, cut back on the lamb and pine nuts.

1½ cups dried chickpeas

1 medium onion

2 bay leaves

7 garlic cloves, 3 unpeeled, 4 peeled and
chopped roughly

1 teaspoon salt, plus more

3 tablespoons olive oil

9 tablespoons tahini

juice of 1½ lemons, plus more, if needed

fat pinch cumin

freshly milled black pepper

3 heaping tablespoons yogurt,
preferably full fat, plus more,
if needed

½ cup pine nuts

3 tablespoons garlic-infused olive oil
(see page 459) or plain olive oil

¾ pound lean, tender lamb, cut in small
thin strips (see headnote)

salt

2–3 tablespoons chopped parsley

warmed pita, for serving

For the hummus, soak and cook the chickpeas following the instructions on page 78, throwing the onion, bay leaves, and the 3 unpeeled garlic cloves into the pot, too. It is imperative that you taste the chickpeas to see if they are truly cooked enough before draining them; undercooked chickpeas make for an unsatisfactorily grainy texture, and you want a voluptuous velvetiness here, no hard surfaces. When you're satisfied the chickpeas are buttery and tender, dunk a large measuring cup in to catch a good 1½ cups of the cooking liquid, and then you can drain the chickpeas with a clear conscience.

In the food processor add the chopped garlic, the salt, ½ cup of the cooking liquid, olive oil, tahini, the juice of 1 lemon, and cumin. Blitz till well and truly puréed. Taste, adding more liquid as you feel you need to loosen and soften the mixture. Process again, then grind in some pepper, add the yogurt, and give another whizz. Taste to see whether you want to add any more lemon juice (and you could want double) or yogurt, or indeed oil or seasoning. When you have a smooth yet dense purée with the intensity you like, scrape out into a bowl, cover, and keep in the fridge until about an hour before you want to eat it.

You can toast the pine nuts before then, but the lamb must be done at the last minute. To be frank, then, you may as well do them both together. Decant the hummus into a shallow round or oval bowl and put to one side for a moment.

Put a heavy-bottomed frying pan on the stove over medium heat, add the pine nuts, and shake every so often until they begin to take on a deep golden color and their resiny fragrance rises from the pan. Pour onto a plate or into a bowl and then add the garlic-infused oil to the pan.

When the oil is hot, toss in the lamb and stir furiously until it begins to crisp and brown at the edges. Add the juice of the half lemon, push the meat about once more, and empty the contents of the pan evenly over the hummus, lemony oil juices and all.

Sprinkle with salt, season with pepper, and scatter with the toasted pine nuts. Add the parsley, then serve immediately and with the pita.

TARAMASALATA

I wouldn't eat taramasalata with the lamb-heavy version of hummus here, but it's a bit like giving a present to one child: you just can't give the one recipe and leave out the other. So I add the taramasalata here. But maybe not just for that reason—in order to complete, too, the childhood picture I have of my mother stuffing bread, ritually uncased cod's roe, oil, lemon, briskly into her blender—and a really vile one at that, with an olive-green plastic top and a goblet made of dull bronze plastic, like a fourth-rate gangster's shades.

To make taramasalata, put about ½ cup smoked cod roe (or mullet roe, if you can find it) into a food processor. Add 2 slices of firm white bread, left to get slightly dry, then soaked in water and squeezed out, 2 garlic cloves, and the juice of 1 lemon. Purée to a thick, smooth paste. Then process again, while pouring about 10 tablespoons olive oil down the feed tube. Remove the lid and taste; you may need some more lemon juice and oil. I sometimes add a dollop of yogurt, as with the hummus. When it's as you like it, remove to a shallow bowl and dot with a few halved, stoned black olives, should the mood take you.

If I'm eating this with pita, I like some scallions to accompany it, too; but I have a rather deep and inexplicable love for this just spread on hot toast made from plastic white bread.

GARLIC CHICKEN WINGS

There are countless ways you could let garlic breathe its sweet, smoky breath over these bony joints; this method requires very little effort (though a little early planning) for great effect. It avoids absolutely the burning and bitterness you can get with chopped raw garlic and adds the velvet mellowness of baked garlic without the extra hour's cooking that would take. I make and eat these compulsively. I should add that children adore this, so if you've got a lot of them coming for lunch, do boost quantities.

cloves from 2 heads garlic, unpeeled	16 chicken wings
1⅔ cups olive oil	coarse salt
juice of 2 lemons	

Put the garlic in cold water to cover generously, bring to boil, and boil for 10 minutes. Then drain, push the cloves out of their skins into the processor, and blitz. Then, with the motor running, pour the oil down the feed tube till you have a milky white gloop. Add the lemon juice, pour over the chicken wings, and leave covered in fridge, fleshy side down, for 36 hours.

Take them out of the fridge a good hour before you put them in the oven and empty out into roasting pan. Preheat the oven to 425°F. Then bake, basting occasionally, for 45 minutes to an hour, until they are very well done, crisp and burnished brown. Remove from the oven, arrange on a large plate, and sprinkle generously with the salt.

EGGPLANT SLICES WITH POMEGRANATE JUICE AND MINT

I suppose pomegranates—that carpaccio-red juice, those glassy beads—always seem exotic to us, and that's partly why I like them. There is something both biblical and almost *belle époque* about them, something both ancient and vulgar. And curiously, I feel rather nostalgically inclined toward them, too. I remember digging them out of Christmas stockings, then sitting for hours with a yellow-mazed half in front of me, winkling the bitter-cased seeds out with a pin.

But they fit best in the time-stamped, opulent Middle Eastern tradition, as here, with the juice steeping pinkly a plate of eggplant slices fried in olive oil, the seeds like jewels glinting out from behind the aromatic leafiness of thickly sprinkled mint. You can fry the eggplant in advance, but don't do anything with the pomegranate and mint until about half an hour before you eat. After 20 minutes' steeping, the eggplant is at its heady best.

I don't, as I've mentioned elsewhere, salt and soak eggplant before preparing it; if you buy ones that are taut and glossy and feel light for their size, you shouldn't find them bitter. If you like, you can substitute charred, skinned red peppers for the eggplant, and pomegranate molasses (see page 459) for the fresh pomegranates. If using the molasses, make a dressing for the eggplant with 2 tablespoons each of the molasses, extra-virgin olive oil, and water. Drizzle this over the eggplant before sprinkling with salt and the mint.

On the table with this I'd put a plate of cucumbers, cut into 2-inch lengths and then each chunk cut into quarters lengthways. Add a plate of tomatoes and another of raw, scrubbed, and peeled carrots, in chunks like the cucumber, and consider decanting a jar of pickled peppers.

2 medium eggplants	**handful fresh mint**
olive oil, for frying	**salt**
2 pomegranates	

Slice the eggplant into discs about ¼-inch thick or cut lengthways to form swelling, pear-shaped slices; the bulging lengths look more beautiful, the discs are easier to eat.

Once sliced, start frying. If you've got a ridged cast-iron griddle, use that, only brush the eggplant as well as the griddle with olive oil before you start. Or use a frying pan, pouring in the oil to a depth of about ¼ inch (and be prepared to add more as you put fresh eggplant batches in to fry) and leaving the slices as they are. Whichever way, cook the eggplant briskly until the surface crisps and the interior is soft, then remove to plates lined thickly with paper towels and drape some more paper over the resting slices so that the paper absorbs as much oil as possible and the eggplant is as dry as possible. You can eat them warm or, if it makes life easier, just leave them to get cold.

Meanwhile, cut one of the pomegranates in half and remove the seeds; you'll need just enough to sprinkle over the slices. The easiest way to do this is to hold a half with one hand, cut side down, over a bowl; with the other hand take a wooden spoon and thwack the held half. After the third thwack you will have rubies raining down. Put those aside and squeeze the juice out of the second fruit. I find an electric citrus juicer the easiest way to do this, but an ordinary, old-fashioned manual one will do. (You might, though, need to get more of the fruit if juicing by hand.) Finely chop the mint. Arrange the eggplant slices on a large plate, sprinkle over a little salt, then pour on the pomegranate juice. Now sprinkle over the mint and then scatter over the pomegranate seeds, but go steady; you may find that you don't need them all. This is one of those times when less is probably more.

A COMFORTING LUNCH
FOR 4

FISH AND PORCINI PIE

ICE CREAM, CHERRIES, FLAKED ALMONDS, AND CHOCOLATE SAUCE

Fish pie is not particularly labor-intensive to cook, but it's hard to get right; if the flour/butter/milk balance is off, the sauce bubbling beneath the blanket of nutmeggy mashed potato can be too runny or too solid. Don't let nervousness make you scrimp on the milk; it's better runny than stodgy, and even an imperfect fish pie is a delicious one. What's important is not to make the sauce taste too floury (using Italian 00 flour sees to that) and not to let your desire for something comforting blunt your appetite for seasoning. I added porcini because I'd been given some by my Austrian aunt Frieda, who was coming for lunch. Perhaps it would be more correct to say great-aunt; the title is honorific but she's the generation, was the companion, of my grandmother. She was the matron at my mother and aunts' boarding school and my grandmother, not I think extraordinarily maternal, was so dreading the summer holidays that she asked Matron to stay at home with the children during them. Over forty years later, she's still here, an important figure in all our lives. I wanted to use the mushrooms because she'd given them to me. But I also thought they'd add a creaturely muskiness, a depth of tone, to the milkily-sweet fish-scented sauce. They did.

This is how I made it. You can change the fish selection as you want and boil and mash the potatoes ahead of time.

FISH AND PORCINI PIE

2 tablespoons dried porcini	4 tablespoons (½ stick) unsalted butter,
½-pound piece of cod	plus more, for dotting the pie
½-pound piece of smoked haddock	½ cup Italian 00 or all-purpose flour
(finnan haddie)	2½ pounds floury potatoes
½-pound piece of salmon	½ cup heavy cream
1 cup milk	freshly grated nutmeg
1¼ cups fish stock	salt and freshly milled black pepper
3 bay leaves	

Cover the dried porcini with very hot water and leave for 20 minutes or so. Then drain the mushrooms and strain the soaking liquid into the stock. Make sure the mushrooms are grit-free; rinse them, if necessary, and chop them finely.

Choose the dish in which you will cook (and serve) the fish pie and butter it. I use an old, very battered oval enamel cast-iron dish of my mother's, which has a capacity of about 2 quarts. Put the fish in a wide, heavy-bottomed pan—I use a frying pan, but anything that'll take them in one layer would do—and cover with the milk, the stock with its mushroom liquid, and the bay leaves. Bring to a simmer and poach for about 3 minutes. Remove the fish to the buttered dish and fork into chunks. Strain the cooking liquid into a large measuring cup, reserving bay leaves.

Melt the butter in a saucepan and add the mushrooms. Fry gently for 2 minutes, stir in the flour, and fry gently for another 2 minutes. Off the heat, very slowly add the liquid from the cup, stirring with a wooden spoon or beating with a whisk (whichever suits) as you go. When all is incorporated, put back on the heat. Add the bay leaves and stir gently until thickened. If you're going to eat it straightaway, pour over the fish in the casserole. Otherwise, remove from heat and cover with waxed paper or a film of melted butter.

Boil and mash the potatoes with the cream and season with the nutmeg and lots of salt and pepper. When you're ready to roll, preheat the oven to 350°F. Put the fish and mushroomy white sauce in the casserole, if you haven't already done so, the potato on top, with more nutmeg, pepper and butter (little dots of it here and there) added just before it goes into the oven. Depending on how hot it all is before it goes in the oven, the fish pie should need 20–40 minutes, or until lightly golden in parts on top. Test as you go. This isn't an untouchable work of art you're creating; dig a hole, taste, and then patch up with potato.

For dessert, buy the best ice cream, vanilla if you can, or make your own (see page 33). Buy a ruby-glinting jar of bottled, sourish cherries and some flaked or slivered almonds to go with it and make a glossily dark chocolate sauce (page 222).

ICE CREAM

SERIOUS LUNCH FOR 8— NO HOSTAGES

CHOUCROUTE GARNIE
QUINCE SYLLABUB

❖

In our enthusiasm for all things Mediterranean, some more northerly specialties have got lost. I love Scandinavian food, perhaps because I spent a lot of time in Norway as a child (taken by an adored au pair, Sissel), but I love too those robust, spicily sour Germanic constructs: *pflaumenpfannekuchen,* great solid pancakes bolstered with plums and weighed down with a thick layer of granulated sugar; plum tart made with shiny dark quetschen, sliced, and cooked till a reddy, coppery cinnamon on thick banks of *hefeteig,* a yeast dough; a long-steeped sauerbraten; stuffed cabbage; wurst *mit senf* (with mustard); and—we're getting there—an astringent, tangled heap of sauerkraut with boiled potatoes, juniper berries, frankfurters, the works. The choucroute garnie of the title makes this sound Alsatian rather than uncompromisingly German. But, whatever, we're talking about the same hangover-salving thing.

You can leave all the sausages in this whole, or halve or cut them into chunks as you like. If you are going to cut them, you can reduce the amount you get; you just need everyone to be able to take some of each.

CHOUCROUTE GARNIE

¼ cup goose fat

2 medium onions, finely sliced

3 smoked ham knuckles

3 medium carrots, peeled and halved

I bouquet garni made of I bay leaf,
   8 juniper berries, 2 cloves, 3 sprigs
   thyme (see page xx)

¾ pound sauerkraut

freshly milled black pepper

3 cups dry Riesling

8 Toulouse sausages or bratwurst

8 frankfurters

Melt or heat ½ cup of the goose fat in a heavy casserole—I use a large cast-iron rectangular one that fits over a couple of burners—and cook the onion in it over medium heat, uncovered, for about 10 minutes or until soft. Add the knuckles, the carrots, and bouquet garni and stir. Then add the sauerkraut and a good grinding of pepper, and mix well so that all is combined and the knuckles are blanketed by the sauerkraut.

Pour over the Riesling and bring to the boil. Add the remaining goose fat in teaspoon-sized dollops over the top of the sauerkraut. Put the lid on, turn the heat down to very low, and simmer for 2½ hours.

Grill the Toulouse sausages or bratwurst and set aside till needed. When the knuckles are cooked, remove, let cool a little, then carve and slice into chunks (neither delicacy nor finesse are exactly required), getting rid of the bones (or keeping them to flavor soup), and return to the casserole along with the sausages or bratwurst and the frankfurters, halved or cut up, if you like. Put the casserole back on the heat, covered, and let simmer for 20 minutes till all's heated through.

You can serve straight from the casserole or decant everything to a vast oval plate. With this, I like plain, that's to say unbuttered, boiled floury potatoes with some juniper berries bashed and sprinkled over on serving.

If I have leftovers, I put everything back in the casserole, stash it in the fridge, and reheat it up to 3 days later—a little something for the week.

QUINCE SYLLABUB

You cannot want much of a dessert after this, but the syllabub will seep comfortably into whatever small space is left. Turn to page 113 for the recipe, adjusting quantities as necessary.

If this sounds like too much hard work, then bring out a vast tub of yogurt, a jar of, preferably, Greek honey, and some flaked almonds you've toasted in a fatless pan over medium heat.

FINALLY, THE BASIC ALWAYS-
WELCOME LUNCH FOR 8

SAUSAGES AND MASH WITH RED WINE, CUMIN, AND ONION GRAVY

SEVILLE ORANGE CURD TART, OR LEMON CREAM WITH SHORTBREAD

❖

Sausages and mash—sausages with mashed potatoes—have to be the most grate-fully received lunch ever. For the mash, work on 8 ounces of potatoes per person, adding lots of butter, lots of cream, lots of pepper; as for the sausages, I exhort you not to be seduced by interesting-sounding combinations. I always regret falling for the wild boar and ginger, the venison and mint sausages; sausages should be just sausages. I do, though, buy my butcher's Cumberland sausages, porky, herby links, now that he makes individual ones, not just the traditional yard-long spiralled kind. A reliable choice is any honest pork sausage that is without distracting flavors.

I always cook my sausages in the oven, set at 400°F. Use a roasting pan with a little bit of vegetable oil in it and prick the sausages before cheerfully shunting them into the oven and forgetting about them. Turn them over after 10 minutes. They should be done after 20–30.

With the sausages and mash, though, an onion gravy makes all the difference; I make mine spicy and wine-dark for this, rather than the more traditional one that accompanies my roast beef (page 252). If you've got some meat stock on hand, do use it, but I have no qualms about using one best-quality beef bouillon cube to make the stock.

For dessert I give the recipe for lemon cream as well as the Seville orange tart in part to make this doable whatever the season, but also because it's incredibly easy and incredibly delicious.

RED WINE, CUMIN, AND
ONION GRAVY

You can make this in advance and reheat it later; you might need to add some water when you do.

2 tablespoons beef drippings or
  vegetable oil

8 ounces onions, sliced very thinly

1 teaspoon ground cumin

scant tablespoon sugar

2 scant tablespoons all-purpose flour

2 cups beef or veal stock (see headnote)

½ cup red wine

Heat the drippings in a heavy-bottomed, fairly wide saucepan and add the onions. Turn down the heat to low and cook the onions for about 10 minutes until soft, stirring occasionally to push them around the pot and make sure they're not burning. Stir in the cumin and cook for another 5 or so minutes. Turn the heat up and add the sugar; let the onions caramelize slightly by stirring over a medium-high flame for 3 minutes and then, still stirring, add the flour. Stir over the heat for 2 more minutes and then add the stock and wine and keep stirring—or stir now and again but with some concentration—while the gravy comes to the boil. When it does so, turn down and simmer very gently for 30 minutes, stirring occasionally.

SEVILLE ORANGE CURD TART

I ate this at influential chef Alastair Little's Lancaster Road restaurant, just after it opened, one February when the Seville oranges were in the shops, and couldn't believe how transcendentally good it was. I have introduced some muscovado sugar, which gives off a pleasurable hint of toffee-ish marmalade. I sometimes make a sweet pastry, sometimes a plain one for this. The sweet pastry is more delicate somehow, but there really is something to be said for using a plain, unfancy, nonsweet pastry, the better to set off the deeply toned curd.

3 whole eggs

2 egg yolks

½ cup superfine sugar

⅓ cup light muscovado sugar or light
 brown sugar

juice and zest of 4 Seville oranges

10 tablespoons (1 stick plus
 2 tablespoons) unsalted butter, cut
 into ½-inch cubes

1 plain or sweet pastry shell (pages 37
 and 39), baked blind and cooked
 through in a shallow 9-inch or deep
 8-inch tart pan, cooled

Make the pastry shell. In a heavy-bottomed saucepan whisk together the whole eggs, yolks, and sugars until amalgamated. Make sure to stir in and scrape up any sugar at the edges or it will burn when it's on the stove. Add the orange juice and zest and the butter. Put the saucepan over medium heat and cook, stirring constantly, until thickened; do not allow to boil. Again, take care to stir the edges as well as middle, otherwise the curd may burn. Remove the curd from the heat and pour directly into the tart shell. Eat warm, or cool before serving.

If you're not making a tart but serving the curd to be eaten with shortbread, then pour into individual glasses when it is cool enough not to splinter the glass. Or accompany with really good plain dark chocolate cookies of a delicate nature.

LEMON CREAM

I made this by accident when I had some mixture left over from a tarte au citron; I poured it into ramekins and baked it (in a bain-marie) along with the tart. I loved the lemon cream, and it's easier than pastry and less commonplace than tarte au citron.

It really does make a difference to the intense, satiny lemoniness if you leave it to steep in the fridge for 2 or 3 days before baking it. You could always use Seville oranges, too, in place of the lemons.

zest and juice of 3 juicy lemons

1½ cups superfine sugar

6 eggs

1¼ cups heavy cream

In a bowl combine the lemon zest and juice, sugar, and eggs and whisk until well incorporated. Then combine the cream with the lemon mixture and pour into a measuring cup. Cover with plastic film and refrigerate it until required, but preferably for at least 2 days.

When ready to bake, preheat the oven to 300°F. Bring a kettle of water almost to a boil. Put 8 ½-cup ramekins into a roasting pan and pour the lemon cream mixture into them. Pour hot, not boiling, water into the roasting dish to come about halfway up the ramekins, and bake 20–30 minutes. The cream should be just set but still with some wobble; it will set more as it cools, but there should always be a slight and desirable runniness about it. Remove and cool. If you're eating this soon, don't put the cream in the fridge, and if you're making it in advance and therefore need to refrigerate it, make sure you take it out to get it to room temperature for a good hour before eating.

SHORTBREAD

You do need cookies with the lemon cream; make these. There is no one way of going about shortbread, ask any Scot—this version is buttery and short (or rich), but with a certain gritty density. I find the way of shaping then baking the shortbread as specified below the easiest way to go about it, but you can press the dough into a traditional mold or push it into a jelly-roll pan and segment the shortbread when fresh out of the oven, if you prefer a more orthodox approach. Obviously, too, you can make these by hand if you don't like or don't have the machine. This will yield about 44 cookies.

8 tablespoons (1 stick) unsweetened
    butter, very soft

½ cup confectioners' sugar, plus more,
    if desired

¾ cup Italian 00 or all-purpose flour

½ cup cornstarch

pinch salt

Cream the butter and sugar in the food processor; you may need to stop and push down the buttery bits if the mixture's not combining properly. Add the flour and cornstarch and salt, and process to combine again; again, you may need to push the mixture down if it goes up the sides of the bowl.

Remove and knead into a cylinder shape. Cover with plastic film and chill in the fridge. At the same time, preheat the oven to 325°F. After about 20 minutes, when this buttery cylinder feels hard to the touch, slice into ¼-inch-thick disks—or thinner if you want and can—put onto a greased or lined baking pan, dredge with confectioners' sugar if you want a sweet, crunchy edge, and bake for 20–30 minutes, or until the tops are dry and the base is no longer doughy at all. Remember, like all cookies, they'll crisp up when they're cold.

Remove with a spatula and cool on a wire rack.

A TRADITIONAL BRITISH SUNDAY LUNCH

Proper British Sunday lunch is everything contemporary cooking is not. Meat-heavy, hostile to innovation, resolutely formalized, it is as much ritual as meal, and an almost extinct ritual at that. Contemporary trends, it is true, have hastened a reappraisal of traditional cooking. But neither nostalgia for nursery foods nor an interest in ponderous culinary Victoriana is what Sunday lunch—Sunday dinner—is all about. It doesn't change, is impervious to considerations of health or fashion; it is about solidity, the family, the home.

One of the silent, inner promises I made myself on having children was to provide a home that made a reassuring, all-comers-welcome tradition of Sunday lunch. It hasn't materialized quite yet, but few of my generation lead meat-and-two-veg lives any more. We are generally more mobile; the weekend is no longer homebound. Nor do we want to be kitchen-bound (and those with small children hardly have the time on their hands for involved cooking). The fact is that a traditional Sunday lunch is impossible to pull off without putting in at least a couple of hours by the sink and the stove. And it is far from being the sort of cooking anyway that finds favor now; the relaxed, "let's throw this with that and come up with something simple and picturesquely rustic" approach will not put a "joint"—the roast—Yorkshire pudding, and roast potatoes on the table. To cook a decent Sunday lunch needs discipline and strict timekeeping.

But with modest organization, there can be something strangely reassuring about cooking a traditional meal. It is about choreography, about timetabling, and has its own pleasures. We are so accustomed to being invited to consider cooking an art that we forget just how rewarding and satisfying it is as pure craft. My Latin teacher, Miss Plummer, who had the misfortune to teach at one of the less academic schools I frequented, used to remark, with a sort of elegiac condescension, that none of us could know the simple yet substantial pleasures of the carpenter in making a chair. But cooking does give that pleasure, and there are particular satisfactions peculiar to the making of this Sunday lunch. For Americans, such a lunch would also make a wonderful evening or holiday meal, perfect when family and friends are gathered and one wants something intimately festive.

Whenever I cook for people, I find it easier to have scribbled down in front of me the times at which I'm meant to do any key thing—put things in the oven, take them out—just because once I start talking or drinking I tend to lose track. I haven't suggested this alongside the dinner-party menus or elsewhere because I can't know what time you'll be eating and anyway have tried not to be too bossy. With full-on Sunday lunch, I have no such compunction. It has to be planned as efficiently as a military campaign.

Traditional British Sunday lunch does, of course, mean roast beef. It is essential to get good beef from a butcher you trust. You can also explain what you want, or ask what you think you should want, for how many people, how you want to carve it, and so on. A rib roast gives the best flavor, but it is very difficult to carve. But I am, anyway, a hopeless carver and believe that in cooking especially, though in everything really, it is better to play to your strengths than your weaknesses. Besides, if you can't do much more than hack at it, it's a waste. I am resigned to buying a boned roast. I have recently become very extravagant and gone for top loin; a boned sirloin would be good, too, though.

I have always found gravy problematic, but for beef I don't think you can casually deglaze the roasting dish with some red wine and hope it'll be all right. Nor does that mean the opposite extreme, the thick, floury, school gloop. Banish instant gravy powders and granules from your thoughts and your cupboards. Instead, start caramelizing your onions early and cook them slowly. This may be difficult when you're trying to orchestrate everything else for lunch, but you can easily do the gravy the day before and then just reheat and add meat juices at the last minute.

Roast potatoes are another fraught area. I have, in the past, got frantic with despair as the time for the meat to be ready drew closer and the potatoes were still blond and untroubled in their roasting pan. The key here is to get the fat hotter than you would believe necessary before you start and to continue to cook the potatoes at a higher heat and for longer than you might believe possible. And you must roughen them up after parboiling.

The heat of the fat is again the crucial element in making a Yorkshire pudding rise. There's no doubt this is easier if you have two ovens (one for the beef, one for the Yorkshire pudding), but the beef can either be cooked at a very high temperature for a quick blast and then at a moderate one for a while, or at a high-ish one all the time. You can always blast the Yorkshire pudding on a high heat while the beef is resting on its carving board.

Roast root vegetables are traditional, but I tend not to bother. With the roast potatoes and Yorkshire pudding, you hardly need more starch, though if I'm cooking roast pork, or roast beef without the Yorkshire pudding, or the usual roast chicken, I might do parsnips, either roasted alongside the potatoes or in another pan anointed with honey and put in the oven to grow sweet and burnished.

As for other vegetables, I think you need two sorts. This can make life difficult, but not insurmountably so. It's just a matter, again, of time management—the important thing is not suddenly to need about six pans on a four-burner stove. And there doesn't need to be too much chopping. Choose, for example, frozen peas and something to provide fresh, green crunch: beans, Savoy cabbage, bok choi. I love broccoli, but it is very sweet, and with the peas you don't really need any more sweetness. It's unconventional, but I do rather like a tomato salad somewhere too, especially if it's still warm outside.

I don't often make my own horseradish sauce (though see page 265 for a recipe)—I buy a good bottled one and add a bit of crème fraîche, ordinary cream, or yogurt—but mustard must, for me, be English and made up at the last minute. I don't mind having other mustards on the table, but for me the whole meal is ruined without proper English mustard.

Traditionalists will insist on a sturdy pie or crumble for dessert, but really, after all that carbohydrate, have you got room? I am immensely greedy, but I don't like that invasive and uncomfortable feeling of bloatedness that can make you regret eating much more than a hangover can ever make you regret drinking.

Now that we seem to be able to get blueberries all the year round, I often serve them with a large, shallow bowl of Barbados cream. This—yogurt and heavy cream stirred together, fudgy brown sugar sprinkled on top—has the advantage of having to be done the day before (see page 117). I love lemon ice cream after this (and it's good with blueberries, or indeed any berries, too) and I sometimes make one that doesn't need fiddling about with while freezing—you just stash it in the freezer (see page 254). Nothing is quite as good as proper ice cream, made with a custard base and then churned until solid, but home cooking is based on compromises, and a simple dessert is a compromise I am often grateful to make. You could consider a crumble (see page 41 for a recipe and adjust quantities as necessary) if only because the crumble mixture can be made up earlier and just sprinkled on the fruit as you sit down, and cooked while you eat the beef. Remember, you are not trying to produce the definitive Sunday lunch to end all Sunday lunches. Nor are you a performance artist. The idea is to make a lunch that you want to eat and can imagine sitting down to do so without bursting into tears.

I'm sorry to sound bossy, but Sunday lunch, as I've said, has to be run like a military campaign. I find it easier to decide when I want to eat and then work backwards, writing every move down on a pad that I keep in a fixed place in the kitchen. This timetable is engineered toward having lunch ready to eat at 2 P.M. exactly. I take it for granted that dessert's been made already.

All quantities and timings have in mind a lunch for about 6 adults and perhaps some children and are based on having a 5-pound roast of any of the kinds mentioned above to cook.

11:20	Start gravy
11:30	Take beef out of fridge
11:50	Peel potatoes
12:05	Put the potatoes in their water in the pan, bring to the boil, and parboil. Preheat oven to 425°F.
12:15	Put roasting pan in oven with a knob of dripping or vegetable oil for beef
12:20	Put beef in oven
12:35	Prepare any vegetables that need chopping or cleaning, etc.
12:40	Put pan with dripping for potatoes in oven
12:50	Make Yorkshire pudding
1:00	Put potatoes in oven
1:25	Put vegetable water on to heat
1:35	Put pan with drippings for Yorkshire pudding in oven
1:40	Take out beef and put in Yorkshire pudding, turning oven up to 450°F as you do so. Let beef stand.
1:45	Cook vegetables
2:00	Take out Yorkshire pudding and potatoes

THE ROAST BEEF

I think many people underplay how much meat you need. For 6 people, I wouldn't consider getting under 5 pounds—which, in other words, is about a pound per person. A roast is a sad prospect without the possibility of leftovers. For a rib you should add on about 2 pounds extra here.

For rare meat you can either cook the beef at 475°F for 15 minutes and then turn it down to 350°F and cook for about 15 minutes per pound, or cook at 425°F throughout for about 15 minutes per pound, which approach is what the timetable reflects. I usually do 15 minutes per pound and then add on an extra 5 minutes so that those who don't like rare meat have a bit of slightly more cooked beef from the ends. Those who don't like blood don't have to get it; the rest of us gratifyingly do. Use a meat thermometer to determine doneness exactly. The internal temperature for rare beef is 120°F; for medium-rare, 125°–130°F; and for medium, 140°F.

All I do to the beef is massage it with dry mustard powder after I've taken it out of the fridge. I use a knob of dripping for the pan, but you could use whatever fat or oil you have at hand.

THE GRAVY

Gravy is one of my weaknesses, which is to say I find it hard to make a convincing light and thin juice. To overcome my deficiencies, I took to following Jane Grigson's recipe for onion gravy (indeed, most of my Sunday is Grigson-based), adding a drop of Marsala to it. You don't need to—you could use some Madeira or even some sweet sherry or just add a little bit more sugar—but the Marsala brings a wonderful aromatic muskiness to the gravy. If you don't have any real beef stock, use bouillon cubes or the best beef stock you can buy. If you use a cube, dilute it well and taste before putting in salt.

You can start the gravy the day before if you want, just reheating and adding meat juices at the last minute.

I tablespoon dripping or butter, plus a
    dribble of oil
I medium onion, sliced very thinly
pinch brown sugar

2 tablespoons Marsala
I teaspoon all-purpose flour
I¼ cup beef stock

Heat the dripping or melt the butter (with the oil to stop its burning) in a saucepan and cook the onion in it at a very low temperature, stirring often. When the onion is soft, add the sugar and Marsala and let it caramelize. Cover with foil, putting the foil as near to the bottom of the pan as possible, and continue to cook, still on a very low flame, for about 10 minutes. Then stir in the flour and cook, stirring, for about 2 minutes. Stir in the stock, bring to the boil (you can turn the heat up here), then reduce the heat to very low again and simmer gently for about 20 minutes. Purée in the food processor (or you can strain it, pushing the soft onion through the strainer). Pour back into the saucepan. At the last minute, reheat and add meat juices from roasting pan. This gravy is wonderfully stress-free, as you don't have to be doing furious deglazing at the last minute.

THE ROAST POTATOES

I like roast potatoes fairly small, so I cut a medium-to-large one into about three pieces. For 6 people, I suppose, that's about 4 pounds. Well, that may be over-generous, but nothing is worse than too few.

Peel the potatoes and cut them into large chunks. Put them in cold salted water, bring to the boil, and parboil for 4–5 minutes. Drain, put back in the saucepan, put on the lid, and bang the whole thing about a bit so that the edges of the potatoes get blurred; the rough edges help them catch in the fat and so get crisp. Add 1 tablespoon or so of semolina and give the pan, with its lid on, another good shake. The semolina gives the potatoes a divinely sweet edge—not at all cloying or inappropriate, just an intensified caughtness, as it were. When my mother and aunts were young, they had an Italian au pair, Antonia, who, when required to make a British Sunday lunch (having never cooked anything other than Italian food), adopted, or rather invented, this practice. If you're unconvinced, or don't have any semolina at hand, just use flour and shake the warm potatoes around in it. The flour doesn't give the same honey-toned depth as semolina, but it helps the potatoes catch and brown wonderfully.

Put 5–6 tablespoons fat or oil in a roasting pan that will hold the potatoes comfortably and transfer it to the oven to heat. I use tablespoon-sized lumps of goose fat or some truly superb beef dripping. If you can lay your hands on neither, of course you can use oil or even vegetable fat. The fat must be hot before the potatoes go in the pan, and they must not be taken out of the oven until you are absolutely ready to eat them. They will take approximately 1 hour to cook.

THE YORKSHIRE PUDDING

I always use Jane Grigson's *English Food* for the Chinese Yorkshire pudding recipe, which is not as odd as it sounds. The story is that when a big competition was held in Leeds for the best Yorkshire pudding, the winner was a Chinese cook called Tin Sung Yang. For years it was held to have a mystery ingredient—tai luk sauce—until, Jane Grigson reports, a niece of hers found that this was a Chinese joke. Nevertheless, the recipe is different from normal—it works backwards. That's to say, you mix the eggs and milk and then stir in the flour, rather than making a well in the flour and adding the eggs and milk, and it works triumphantly; it billows up into a gloriously copper crown of a cushion. I am able to cook this for the most die-hard, pudding-proud British northerners without inhibition or anxiety. I prefer Yorkshire pudding to be in one dish rather than in those depressing, cafeteria-style individual portions, so for this amount, I use an enamel dish about 12 by 7½ inches and 3 inches deep. Cook it on the top rack of the oven but make sure the rack isn't too high up, as the Yorkshire pudding really does rise. I have had to prise it off the ceiling of the oven, which slightly dented its magnificence and my glory.

1¼ cups milk	1½ cups all-purpose flour, sifted
4 eggs	1 tablespoon beef dripping or vegetable
scant ½ teaspoon salt	oil to taste
freshly milled black pepper	

The oven should be heated to 450°F. Mix the milk, eggs, and salt, and add pepper, beating all well together. I use my freestanding mixer, the fabulous KitchenAid, but anything—hand-held electric mixer, rotary, or balloon whisk—would do. Let these ingredients stand for 15 minutes and then whisk in the flour. Meanwhile, add the dripping to the pan and put it in the oven to heat for about 10 minutes. Into this intensely hot pan you should pour the batter and cook for 20 minutes, or until well puffed and golden. Bring it, triumphant, to the table.

THE
DESSERT

The recipe for Barbados cream is on page 117. Recipes for crumbles are on pages 41 and 156; custard to go with is on page 32.

LEMON ICE CREAM

Years ago, when I bought my enormously expensive ice-cream maker, a friend of mine brought round her copy of Shona Crawford Poole's *Iced Delights* for me to play with. Naturally, the recipe I fell upon was one that didn't need an ice-cream maker. I include it here out of fondness—my sister Thomasina loved it and often made it herself.

It's very quick and easy to make. Even though I have doubts about non-custard-based ices (they freeze very hard and then melt back into a runny creaminess, so you have to be very careful about ripening them in the fridge for a good 40 minutes before eating them, rather than letting them thaw in the kitchen and thus start dripping), it's worth having this one under your belt, as it is good by itself and wonderful as an accompaniment to a tarte au citron (bought or made, but especially useful to zhuzz up a bought one), rhubarb pie, a plate of stewed rhubarb, wine-candied quinces (page 329), or any assortment of berries.

juice of 3 lemons, the zest of 2   1¾ cups heavy cream

1½ cups confectioners' sugar

Pour the lemon juice into a bowl with the zest and sugar, stir to combine, and leave for 30 minutes, if you can, to let the flavor deepen.

Whip the cream with 3 tablespoons iced water until it holds soft peaks, then whisk in the sweetened lemon juice. Turn into a shallow container, cover, and freeze—no stirring, crystal-breaking-up, mixing, or anything needed—until firm, about 2 hours. Bear in mind my comments about thawing and melting, above, when you want to eat it.

LEMON MERINGUE ICE CREAM

This is an ice cream along much the same lines. I saw this recipe of Jane and Elizabeth Pelly's in *The Women Chefs of Great Britain,* though I've changed it slightly here. The original version specified homemade meringues and homemade lemon curd, but I brazened it out with the bought stuff and suggest, for ease, that you do too. If you are using shop meringues and curd, you may have to add more lemon juice and zest or it will be too sweet. Taste to see; it needs an edge to it.

1¾ cups heavy cream   juice and zest of 2 lemons

1 cup full-fat yogurt   6 meringue nests (see headnote)

1¼ cups lemon curd

Whip the cream until fairly stiff and fold in the yogurt. Add the lemon curd, lemon juice and zest (you will find it easier to stir in the curd if you add the lemon juice to it first), and the meringues, broken up into small pieces, but not so small that they'll dissolve into dust.

Put into a container—it should really be a shallow rather than tall one—and freeze. And that's all there is to it. Ripen it in the fridge for 40 minutes before you want to eat it. You could dribble over it either some clear honey or some more lemon curd diluted to runniness with lemon juice.

Apropos of this, one year I made a summer version of lemon meringue pie, or maybe it would be better to describe it as a cross between lemon meringue pie and pavlova: make a pavlova base—see page 336—smear it with some thickly whipped double cream, as if one were spreading some butter on bread, then thickly cover that with lemon curd, then even more thickly with more whipped double cream, and then dot with some raspberries.

LATE-SUMMER SUNDAY ROAST BEEF AND YORKSHIRE PUDDING FOR 8

COLD ROAST FILLET OF BEEF

ROSEMARY AND ANCHOVY MAYONNAISE

WARM CANNELLINI OR CRANBERRY BEANS
WITH GARLIC AND SAGE

TOMATO SALAD

YORKSHIRE PUDDING WITH SYRUP AND CREAM

This, I think, is one of my favorite Sunday lunches, but you can get away with it at any time the sun is warm enough to make a cold roast fillet of beef seem a treat. It's certainly too expensive to produce if you believe people will think cold food a disappointment or an easy option.

Most of this lunch can be made in advance—you can cook the beef the day before and boil some beans in readiness for a quick sousing in sage and olive oil just before you eat. Make the mayonnaise on the morning of the day you're serving lunch and all that will need doing around lunchtime is a tomato salad or green salad to go with it. I don't think you need potatoes. You do, you see, have Yorkshire pudding coming too, not with the beef but after, as dessert, served searingly hot with golden syrup (see page 460) or honey poured over and thick whipped or, even better, clotted cream (page 457). This may sound odd, but remember that Yorkshire pudding is just a kind of popover, which specialty can be served with syrup for breakfast. This heavenly dessert version is not alone in its recasting of the traditional savory pudding. When I was young there was, tucked behind Fulham Road in London, a restaurant called the Hungry Horse where it was considered frightfully fashionable to go for Sunday lunch. One of the high points of its menu was Yorkshire pudding for every course.

COLD ROAST FILLET OF BEEF

I think people tend not to eat as much fillet as other cuts of beef, but I would still make a more generous allocation than the normal reckoning of 8 ounces per person, so instead of getting a 4-pound fillet I'd get one large fillet of 5 pounds. In fact, I'd probably take fright at the idea of skimpy portions once I was in the butcher's and then nervously settle on the heavier weight. Anyway, who's going to complain about leftover fillet sliced into cool thick slabs, smeared with mustard, and eaten with warm pebbly new potatoes and alligator-skinned cornichons or an astringent salsa verde (see page 181) or with thickly sliced floury boiled potatoes fried till crisp and blistered without, steamed creamily sweet within?

I would give the fillet about 8 minutes per pound, in a pretty hot but not searing oven (425°F). Remember that the beef will carry on cooking as it cools, and you do want it rare (or I do; adapt to please yourself). For exact doneness, roast the fillet to an internal temperature of 120°F for rare, 125°–130°F for medium-rare, or 140°F for medium. You really don't need to do much to the beef after cooking. Just anoint it with some oil. I have some olive oil that has been infused with bay and rosemary, and this is what I'd use here. Normal olive oil, with no other seasoning, will be fine enough though, or you could make your own rosemary oil, see below. I sometimes add some mashed anchovies to the herbed or herbless oil, which I then apply as the meat-massaging unguent. The meat tastes good, too, simply wiped down with mustard to which you've added 2 teaspoons of oil.

So, you anoint the fillet, roast it, let it cool, wrap it in foil, and put it in the fridge. What you absolutely must remember to do is take it out of the fridge a good 2 hours before lunch. Yes, it should be cold, but it should not have the merest smack of the refrigerator's chill about it. Alternatively, you could cook the fillet early on Sunday morning and let it cool in the kitchen to room temperature, even slightly above, so that you eat it not cold but not hot either. Always a pleasurable possibility.

If you think the fillet looks too spooky or too brown as it sits ready to be sliced, then do sprinkle with freshly chopped parsley or chives—not too many, just enough to lift it—or just carve it in readiness. You should, too, sprinkle with salt, unless of course you've mashed anchovies into it before roasting.

ROSEMARY AND ANCHOVY MAYONNAISE

Anchovy really does give something to meat (though this mayonnaise is also wonderful with crab cakes or indeed, any fish cakes).

You can use bought rosemary-infused oil, or make your own, or leave the rosemary out and let the anchovies speak eloquently for themselves.

9 anchovy fillets in olive oil, drained and minced

½ garlic clove, peeled and minced

3 egg yolks, at room temperature

1½ cups peanut or sunflower oil

squeezes lemon juice

8 scant tablespoons rosemary oil or olive oil infused with rosemary (see recipe below)

freshly milled black pepper

salt, if needed

Mash the anchovies and garlic to form a paste and then whisk together with the egg yolks in a large bowl. The egg yolks should be at room temperature. You can use an electric hand-held mixer (or, indeed, a free-standing one) but what you can't use, and I'm sorry to be a bore about this, is the food processor. Drip by slow drop, pour in the sunflower or peanut oil, whisking all the while. The mayonnaise should slowly emulsify. Squeeze in some lemon, going carefully. Don't worry if it still doesn't taste lemony enough now. Keep whisking and now add the rosemary oil, still pouring slowly. Taste and add the pepper, some salt—if, after the anchovies, you need it—and more lemon juice as wished. Cover with plastic film.

It's best not to keep mayonnaise in the fridge but rather in a cool place. If the mayonnaise develops a greasy, glassy top (this tends to happen when it's refrigerated), just skim this off with a spoon before serving.

ROSEMARY-INFUSED OIL

Put about 12 tablespoons of olive oil in a saucepan and add 3 tablespoons of rosemary leaves. Put on the heat and shake while warm and then let sizzle for a very short while, about 10 seconds. Pour through the finest mesh strainer. Don't use the rosemary-infused oil in the mayonnaise until it has cooled, though it's fine to massage a few warm tablespoons of it into the meat before roasting. This should give you enough for both.

WARM CANNELLINI OR CRANBERRY BEANS WITH GARLIC AND SAGE

It really doesn't matter whether you use cannellini or cranberry beans here. I tend, more often, to use cannellini, just out of habit, I think, but adore the soft pink specklediness of cranberry beans, too. I suppose it's just that I associate them more with soups. No matter; choose which you prefer.

1 pound dried cannellini or cranberry
   beans

1 large onion, halved

1 medium carrot, peeled and halved

7 sage leaves, 3 whole, 4 minced

7 tablespoons olive oil, plus more,
   for serving

salt

4 garlic cloves, minced

2–3 tablespoons chopped parsley
   (optional)

Soak the beans overnight in cold water. Drain them, and put them in a heavy-bottomed large saucepan along with the onion, carrot, and the whole sage leaves. Cover by about 6 inches with cold water, bring to the boil, and simmer for 1–1½ hours or until done. How long it actually takes depends on the age of the beans, but start tasting after 50 minutes and keep a beady eye on them, as you don't want them to melt into fudgy rubble. When they are tender, drain them, reserving some cooking liquid for later. Stir in 3 tablespoons of the olive oil and some salt. When they are cool, remove the onion, carrot, and sage. Cover the beans and leave in a cool place or refrigerate.

When you want to eat them, get a heavy-bottomed or, even better, terracotta dish and pour in the rest of the olive oil. Add the garlic and the minced sage leaves, then sprinkle over some salt and cook on the stove, sizzling gently and stirring all the while to prevent the garlic from coloring. You don't want it to brown, just soften. Stir in the beans, add some of the reserved cooking liquid, and warm through. Pour some more olive oil over and serve, sprinkling with the chopped parsley if you like (I always do).

TOMATO SALAD

There is no recipe to follow here—no one needs to be told how to slice tomatoes. But there is an injunction: leave them plain. You can peel them if you are up to it, but it doesn't matter if you don't. Get the best tomatoes you can and make sure they aren't cold before you start (they should never be kept in the fridge, anyway). Slice thinly, arrange on a plate, sprinkle with salt, pepper, sugar if you think they really need it (but even so, just a pinch), some finely chopped scallions, a drop or two of balsamic or else good red wine vinegar, and a drizzle of glass-green olive oil. Small cherry tomatoes should be halved or quartered and tossed with the other ingredients in a shallow bowl.

YORKSHIRE PUDDING WITH SYRUP AND CREAM

Follow precisely the instructions for Yorkshire pudding (page 253), only instead of using dripping, use vegetable oil or shortening.

While the Yorkshire pudding is cooking, pour some golden syrup or runny honey (or honey warmed to thin it) into one pitcher and some heavy cream in another, or, if you're using clotted cream, just put it in a bowl. The best vanilla ice cream you can find would also be heavenly with the blisteringly hot pudding and gooey golden syrup.

Fillet of beef is also useful when you want to make a special lunch for just a few people. Instead of fillet, you could also buy top rump roast.

A PERFECT PLAIN SUNDAY LUNCH FOR 3

TOP RUMP ROAST OF BEEF

NEW POTATOES WITH TRUFFLE OIL

YOUNG PEAS AND SNOW PEAS, OR DARK-LEAF SALAD

RICE PUDDING

For three, I would buy a roast weighing about 3 pounds or even 4 pounds. I love it cold the next day, cut into thick chips and put into a salad, with lettuce, cucumber, sliced gherkin, and scallions, with a mustardy dressing and topped with crumbled, finely chopped hard-boiled egg. And any leftover potatoes can be halved or thickly sliced and profitably thrown in, too.

Preheat the oven to 425°F. While it's heating up, put in the dish in which you're going to roast the beef; then, 5 or so minutes before you want to put the beef in, add a small dollop of dripping or vegetable oil. Work out the roasting time for the meat, based on 15–17 minutes per pound—that's if you like it bloody (see also page xviii), or cook to an internal temperature of 120°F or higher for less rare meat (see page 257). Put the meat in the dish and in the oven along with a tomato, cut in half, an onion, ditto, and 2 unpeeled garlic cloves.

When the beef is ready, remove it to a carving board or plate and let sit for 10 minutes. Meanwhile, make a thin gravy by putting the roasting pan on the stove, removing the tomato, onion, and garlic if you can't be bothered to sieve later. Add about ½ cup beef stock and the same amount of red wine and let bubble away, adding salt and pepper and maybe a pinch of sugar. Strain into a warmed jug.

NEW
POTATOES
WITH
TRUFFLE OIL

The potatoes I choose are those small, buttery, waxy-fleshed, thin-skinned ones, which can be available even in darkest winter. New potatoes, unlike baking ones, should be put into a saucepan of boiling water, salted, and cooked for the 30 minutes or so they need. Drain them and return them to the pan with a fat dollop of unsalted butter. Shake the pan gently so the potatoes are all glossily covered. Grind over some white pepper (though, of course, black pepper wouldn't be a catastrophe) and add a few drops of truffle oil, tiny bottles of which can be bought at specialty food stores. You don't need much; if you have too heavy a hand, you will begin to notice a positively barnyard fragrance wafting from the pan. I like these potatoes warm rather than hot, so leave them with the heat turned off but the lid on before decanting them into a warmed bowl.

In winter, I'd make a buttery mixture of peas—good frozen young peas—and just-cooked snow peas. In summer, I love a peppery salad with the soft, pink, sweet meat. Any strong dark leaves in more or less any combination would work: tender spinach, watercress, arugula, mizuna, or unchopped, robust flat-leaf parsley. Use oil—stick to olive if you've made the truffle-scented potatoes, or else a nut oil—and lemon juice for the dressing; nothing fancy, but remember to add salt while tossing. I think a salad like this is better on a large flat plate rather than in a normal salad bowl.

RICE PUDDING

Everyone is convinced of the importance of getting a rice pudding absolutely right, but unfortunately no one agrees what that means. Definitely it shouldn't be gummy, though neither should it be watery; the rice shouldn't be too firm, but it shouldn't be mush either. And between those two extremes, there is room for intense disagreement. For me there is indeed such a thing as a too-creamy rice pudding; I like it milk-white, sugary but pure tasting. I live with someone who regards an almost butter-yellow, fat-thickened, rice-beaded soup as so much perfection attained. I loathe and detest skin on rice pudding (but rather less than I hate and fear skin on custard)—just writing the words makes me shiver. I concede, though, that for most people, in Britain at least, the skin is almost the best part.

The rice pudding below cannot quite straddle all these oppositions—but, bearing in mind these proportions, you can alter the ingredients, adding cream, light or heavy, or melted butter, to make it as rich and softly fatty as you like. And if you want to add raisins, do; just don't tell me about it.

3 tablespoons unsweetened butter, melted	2 cups milk
4 tablespoons medium- or long-grained rice	½ teaspoon pure vanilla extract, if not using the vanilla sugar
2 tablespoons vanilla sugar (page 72) or superfine sugar	whole nutmeg

Preheat the oven to 300°F. Use some of the melted butter, about half, to grease an ovenproof dish with a capacity slightly over 4 cups. I like to use an oval cream stoneware dish for this. In this dish put the rice, then the sugar, and then pour over the milk and vanilla, if using. Pour the rest of the melted butter on top of this (if you're going to have a skin, the butter will ensure it) and then grate over some nutmeg. Put in the oven and bake for 2½ hours, giving a good stir after the first half hour and first hour. If you angle a wooden spoon in slightly aslant, you won't disperse too much of the nutmeg on the top.

It's British-traditional to eat this with jam, but I prefer the also-British golden syrup—with or without heavy cream.

The idea of a luncheon party is somehow vulnerably old-fashioned, but occasionally you want to invite people to a lunch with a more celebratory feel about it.

LUNCH-PARTY LUNCH FOR 8

SPINACH, BACON, AND RAW
MUSHROOM SALAD

BAKED SEA BASS WITH ROSEMARY

BAKEWELL TART WITH FRESH RASPBERRIES

SPINACH, BACON, AND RAW
MUSHROOM SALAD

Lazy as I am, I wouldn't consider making this salad if I had to wash, drain, and stem everything. Instead, I buy spinach in packages. I think I'd get 3 10-ounce packages for this, although a wiser woman might stop at 2, and then 8 ounces or so of those firm but otherwise unexceptional button mushrooms. Wipe them if you must, but otherwise just slice them finely-finely, so that you have masses of wafer-thin mushroom-shaped slices. Get some bacon—about 8 thin slices of the best (unwatery) kind available—and fry or grill it till ochre-tipped and crisp, and then crumble it into the mixture of mushrooms and young spinach leaves. I like a garlicky dressing: peel 2 garlic cloves and fry them gently in about 4 tablespoons good olive oil. Don't let the oil hiss and sizzle and don't let the cloves burn. Take the pan off the heat and leave the oil to cool. Remove the cloves, squeeze some lemon juice into the pan, sprinkle in some salt, and grind in some pepper—and that's your dressing.

I sometimes do a version of this salad with whole fried, peeled garlic cloves and/or croutons, too.

BAKED SEA BASS WITH ROSEMARY

Sea bass is such a wonderful fish and, cooked whole, has inevitably something festive, something important, about it. A sea bass, boned, with fistfuls of rosemary stuffed inside and baked, is easy to cook, looks beautiful, and has that perfect simplicity of taste that throws any amount of chi-chi food into a cocked hat. I take it for granted, while talking blithely of how easy it is to do, that you won't be boning it yourself. But, as there's no point buying fish like this unless you can be positive it's the best and freshest possible, you will, anyway, be roping in a fish seller for this.

The advantage of stuffing a boned, whole fish with herbs (and if you haven't got any rosemary growing in the garden, indeed haven't got a garden, buy a small plant rather than masses of supermarket packets of the stuff) is that although it sounds like more work than just baking fillets, it isn't, because the timing, although still crucial, isn't quite as cut-throat. Also, you can keep the fish waiting in its foil package while you have the first course, whereas single pieces of fish really would be tricky to leave hanging around. And although you can't make this really in advance, you can stuff the fish and wrap it in foil a good 1–2 hours before putting it in the oven.

I find it easier to serve 2 smaller rather than 1 larger fish, simply because it can be a tight squeeze fitting a fish over 4 pounds in my oven. But if you can, do—one enormous bass does look splendid. And if you prefer, you can buy small sea bream, using one per person. Ask your fish seller to bone the fish entirely for you. Explain that you want to serve the fish whole, stuffed, then cut into slices.

2 tablespoons extra-virgin olive oil,
　preferably Ligurian, plus more,
　for oiling baking foil
2 3-pound whole sea bass, boned

about 20 4-inch sprigs fresh rosemary
coarse salt and freshly milled black
　pepper

Preheat the oven to 375°F.

Oil two pieces of foil big enough to wrap each fish in and lay the fish on top. Stuff the cavities with the rosemary sprigs, plonk the fish on the foil, dribble the 2 tablespoons of oil over, sprinkle with the salt, and grind over pepper. Make packages with the foil, twisting the ends very tightly but keeping the packages themselves baggy. You can leave in a cool place, or fridge if it's a hot day, for an hour or so, then put in the oven for 20–25 minutes. Keep in unwrapped foil packages until you've eaten your first course, then remove to two oval plates (or one, if you can fit both fish on it) and serve by slicing after removing the rosemary to one side. Spoon over the oily, rosemary-scented juices.

New potatoes, either boiled or roasted, are wonderful with this, as are puy lentils, cooked, then tossed in an oil-softened dice of garlic, onion, celery, and carrot and sprinkled with parsley.

BAKEWELL TART WITH FRESH RASPBERRIES

Bakewell tart, or Bakewell pudding, is a traditional British almond-rich "pie," usually made with jam. We had it at school: sweet, stodgy, dense and heavy, a rigid disc of pastry smeared with red jam and topped with a sandy paste that itself bore the weight of a hardened pool of graying white icing. It had its charms, but I don't intend to emulate them here. This version is bold with almonds; the traditional frangipane topping is rich with them, of course, but here the pastry also has a good couple of tablespoons of them, which both lightens the texture and stops it from going soggy. This is important, as this version includes fresh raspberries, which create an altogether less stodgy, more elegant pie, but more seepage. If you can get really wonderful, sweet, and raspberry-tasting raspberries, then you can probably do without using jam. But I find that the raspberries that are in most shops tend to perform better with about 3 tablespoons of best-quality (even sugar-free—that is, additional-sugar-free) jam.

This is fabulous, the sort of dessert people who say "I don't eat desserts" have second helpings of. Serve with more fresh raspberries and a pitcher of heavy cream or crème fraîche on the table alongside.

FOR THE PASTRY	FOR THE FILLING
1½ cups Italian 00 or all-purpose flour	8 tablespoons (1 stick) unsalted butter, very soft
pinch salt	
¼ cup ground almonds	1 cup superfine sugar
½ cup confectioners' sugar	3 eggs
8 tablespoons (1 stick) unsalted butter, diced	1 cup ground almonds
1 egg yolk	3 tablespoons raspberry jam (optional)
	12 ounces (2 pint boxes) raspberries
	2 tablespoons flaked almonds

Preheat the oven to 400°F. Make the pastry by hand, in the processor, or in a freestanding electric mixer as you like. If you're making it by hand, sift the flour, salt, the ground almonds, and sugar into a mixing bowl. Add the diced butter and cut in the flour mixture using a round-bladed knife or pastry blender or as you do normally. When the butter has been reduced to flakes, use your fingertips to rub it into the flour. And then, when it looks like fine crumbs, stir in the egg yolk to make a soft but not sticky dough.

You may need to add a few drops of ice water if some crumbs of pastry remain at the bottom of the bowl. Wrap the disc of dough—as usual—in plastic film or foil and let it rest in the fridge for 15–20 minutes.

Roll out the pastry and use it to line a deep 10-inch tart or quiche pan, prick the dough, and then put the pan in the fridge while you make the filling.

Melt the butter, then put it to one side for a moment. Beat the sugar and eggs together and then, still stirring, pour in the melted butter. When all's mixed, stir in the ground almonds. That's all there is to it.

Spread the jam, if using, on the base of the tart shell, then cover with the raspberries. Pour the egg mixture over that and then scatter with the flaked almonds.

Bake for 35–45 minutes until the tart looks golden and swollen. Remove and let stand until warm.

BEEF ONCE MORE STEWED, FOR 6

STEWED BEEF WITH THYME AND ANCHOVIES

FRESH HORSERADISH SAUCE WITH CHIVES

BAKED OR MASHED POTATOES AND CORNICHONS

TREACLE TART WITH VANILLA ICE CREAM

Sometimes a stew is just what you want for lunch. This is a particularly special one, elegant yet bolstering; turn to Cooking in Advance, page 75, for the recipe. As suggested there, I like this with baked potatoes and some cornichons, their vinegariness contrasting beautifully with the salty mellowness of the stew.

It may seem odd to suggest giving horseradish sauce with stew, but think of this as a raita, rather. Again, this is about contrasts—the rasp of the horseradish, the cold, sour creaminess of the sauce, provide both foil and balm. And it's heavenly dolloped into the potatoes, too. The recipe for this comes from British food writer Arabella Boxer's *Herb Book,* though I have to say when I couldn't get any fromage frais for this once, I made this with crème fraîche and nonfat yogurt (well, that's what I had in the fridge), half and half, as I suggest you do here, and it was wonderful, too. If you haven't got oven space for the potatoes, though the treacle tart should leave room, consider mashed instead.

FRESH HORSERADISH SAUCE WITH CHIVES

I don't normally make real horseradish sauce, as I've already confessed, but I give you an adaptation of Arabella Boxer's recipe, which is staggeringly good.

Some greengrocers have fresh horseradish root (and you can stash some in the freezer) but, if you can't find any, use instead bottled prepared horseradish.

¾ cup crème fraîche	I teaspoon Dijon mustard
¾ cup yogurt	2 teaspoons white wine vinegar
¼ cup grated fresh horseradish or	salt
bottled prepared horseradish	½ cup chopped chives

Beat the crème fraîche and yogurt together till smooth, then stir in the horseradish, mustard, vinegar (1 teaspoon only if using the bottled kind), and a good pinch of salt. Stir in the chopped chives. Turn into a clean bowl and serve.

TREACLE TART

Treacle tart, that traditional British pie of lemony, bready, caramel-dense syrup, should be thin and chewily crisp rather than deep and fat-bellied. It should be warm, too.

Some people will try to persuade you of the superiority for treacle tart of a buttery sweet pastry, the sort the French use for fruit flans and lemon tarts. I am not convinced. I think the intense sweetness of the filling is better served by a plainer crust and that the important thing is to get the pastry as thin as possible. Ordinary pastry dough (see page 37) is really a snap to make; even I, so undeft as to be embarrassing, can roll it out thinly and drape it silkily over a waiting 8-inch tart pan. You can use the crust recipe below or the one for jam tarts on page 449. Traditionally, a treacle tart is covered by a latticework of pastry. I like it plain, but if you want to you can cut out strips from the leftover pastry you'll have and make a criss-cross design to cover before putting it in the oven. It isn't traditional, but the cream gives a soft roundedness to the sweet filling and stops it from drying out.

If you don't want to go in for baking, buy a pot of ice cream and make the butterscotch sauce on page 275.

FOR THE PASTRY	FOR THE FILLING
¾ cup Italian 00 or all-purpose flour	⅔ cup golden syrup
2 tablespoons (¼ stick) cold unsalted	½ cup fresh bread crumbs (see
butter, diced	page 22)
2 tablespoons vegetable shortening,	juice of I lemon plus the zest of half
diced	3 generous tablespoons heavy cream
I tablespoon lemon juice	

Make the pastry according to the instructions on page 37, using a few tablespoons ice water and the lemon juice to bind, and let rest in the fridge. Roll out to line an 8-inch tart pan and then put back in the fridge for about 30 minutes. You can do this a day or so ahead.

Preheat the oven to 400°F and put a baking sheet in to warm up, too.

For the filling, put the syrup in a saucepan on the stove and, when warm and runny, add the bread crumbs, lemon juice, and zest and heat until warm and runny-ish. Leave for 5 minutes, then stir in the cream. Pour or spoon this mixture into the prepared pastry, place on the baking sheet, and bake for about 15 minutes, then turn the oven down to 350°F and bake for another 15–20 minutes or until the pastry is golden and the filling is slightly firmed on top.

I like this best hot, with cold, cold vanilla ice cream.

ELEGANTLY SUBSTANTIAL TRADITIONAL ENGLISH LUNCH FOR 8

ENGLISH ROAST CHICKEN WITH ALL
THE TRIMMINGS PLUS SOME

TRIFLE

When you speak to English ladies of a certain generation, you will notice that they use "meat" to mean "beef." Thus "We ate meat only once a week" doesn't preclude the consumption of vast and daily, or twice daily, platefuls of ham, pork, chicken, and lamb. A fine English Sunday lunch was roast chicken as it always used to be done, with parsley and thyme stuffing, bread or onion sauce, roast potatoes and sausages, and honey-roast parsnips, rather than the modern take (lemon, garlic, onions, olive oil—see page 7), much as I love it.

A traditional English "pudding," meaning dessert, is what you want after; of course, any pie or crumble or indeed steamed sponge pudding would be just fine, but a trifle would be perfect.

ENGLISH ROAST CHICKEN WITH ALL THE TRIMMINGS

If you want the stuffing to be a stiff rather than dense and crumbly mass, add a beaten egg to combine before stuffing the birds.

4 tablespoons (½ stick) unsalted butter	2 cups fresh bread crumbs
drop oil	leaves from about 8 sprigs fresh thyme
1 medium onion, minced	or 3 teaspoons dried
6 slices bacon, minced	6 tablespoons chopped parsley
1 pound button mushrooms, minced	zest of 1 lemon
salt and freshly milled black pepper	2 chickens, about 3½ pounds each

Preheat the oven to 400°F. Put 2 tablespoons of the butter with oil in a heavy-bottomed saucepan and, when melted, add the onion and bacon. Fry together, over medium heat, for about 10 minutes or until onions are soft. Remove the bacon mixture and, in the same pan, melt the remaining butter and cook the mushrooms, covered, with some salt and pepper, for about 5 minutes. Remove to a plate to cool. Put the bread crumbs in a large bowl and mix in the thyme, parsley, and lemon zest, seasoning with salt and pepper to taste. Stuff the birds and roast 15 minutes per pound, adding 10 minutes to the chickens' cooking time, or until the juices run clear when the chickens are pierced between a thigh and the body.

SAUSAGES   As for the sausages, what I do is get 3–4 little sausages, pork and as plain as possible, per head, then I cook them slightly in advance for 30–40 minutes in a 400°F oven. Then, just about 15 minutes or so before eating, I put them back in the oven the chickens have just been taken out of to heat up.

POTATOES   The potatoes really need a hotter oven—turn to page 253 for the method for making them—but if you haven't got a double oven, you will just have to let the chickens stand for a while and turn up the oven to 425°F. Roast about 3 pounds of potatoes for 20 minutes or so (in which case cover the reheating sausages with foil). If you like living dangerously, you can brown the potatoes by putting them, hot fat, baking pan, and all, on the stove. But don't say I didn't warn you.

The recipe for bread sauce can be found on page 58. The following onion sauce, however, was what my mother more often cooked to go with roast chicken, whether it was stuffed as above, or just with a squeezed-out lemon half.

ONION SAUCE

Many people like a Frenchified onion sauce, with the onions almost minced and disappearing into a velvety mush. I love this sauce as we ate it at home, the onions boiled, drained, and some of the water added to the milk to make the white sauce. Three things: I don't bother to fish out the cloves and bay from the milk. If you don't want to add cream, and I often don't, just make the initial milk up to 3 cups instead. And you may substitute 6 leeks, each cut into 3 pieces, for the onions. We nearly always ate leeks cooked like this in white sauce, at home, and they are particularly good, too, with roast pork or ham.

2½ cups milk	6 tablespoons (¾ stick) unsalted butter
2 cloves	¾ cup Italian 00 or all-purpose flour
I bay leaf	½ cup heavy cream
6 small or medium onions, halved	freshly milled white or black pepper
salt	whole nutmeg

Pour the milk into a saucepan, add the cloves and bay leaf, and bring to boiling point. Just before it boils, remove from heat, cover, and let steep for 20 minutes or so while you cook the onions.

Put the onions into a saucepan and cover with cold water. Bring to the boil, add salt, and cook, covered, at a gentle but insistent simmer until the onions are soft—20 minutes should do it. Onions retain heat ferociously (which is why an onion, boiled and wrapped in a tea towel, was always used as a remedy for earache, staying warm for hours as it was pressed against a throbbing head). Pour the onions into a colander suspended over a wide-necked measuring cup or other saucepan. Let them drip in for a good 5 minutes. Then add 2 cups of the oniony water to the milk. If you haven't got that much, just make up the extra with more milk.

Now make the sauce: put the butter in a saucepan over a low to moderate heat and, when it's melted, stir in the flour and cook, stirring, while the roux turns nutty, for 2 minutes. Make sure it doesn't brown, though.

Off the heat, slowly pour in the milk and onion water, stirring all the time. I use a plastic whisk for this. Do it gradually, so the liquid is smoothly incorporated into the roux. Put back on a low heat for about 15 minutes until the sauce is cooked; it should be smooth, very thick (the onions and cream will thin it in a minute), and velvety.

Stir in the onions and leave covered with a piece of buttered or wax paper until you want to eat it, at which time reheat and then stir in the cream. Season with salt and pepper and add a grating of nutmeg.

Serve not in a gravy boat (it's too thick) but in a bowl with a spoon.

I like peas with this as well as the parsnips. Normally I'd allocate a medium-sized parsnip per person but—with so many sausages—it's probably more sensible to work along the lines of 3 parsnips per 2 people. Peel them, cut them into 4— that's to say, cut them in half crossways and then cut each half lengthways—and parboil them in boiling, salted water for 3–5 minutes. In a baking dish in which they will fit in one layer, melt some fat—good dripping or lard is best; however, if you blanch at the very idea, do use oil. Put in the parsnips, toss well so that they're coated, and drizzle about 3 tablespoons runny honey over them. Roast them in the oven for about 30 minutes at 425°F or 40 at 400°F. And give them a blast, the oven turned to very high, at the end of cooking while the chicken is resting. When they're ready they should be tender at the prod of a fork within but brown and shiny and crisp without. If you can't find room to roast the potatoes and the parsnips separately, then throw them all in together, but you will then have to forget the honey over the parsnips. It's not ideal for the parsnips to be cooked at the high heat the potatoes require (you will end up with perhaps more burnt and crusty exterior than you'd like and rather less sweet and creamy interior), but it's not the end of the world.

GREENS

I think as a third vegetable, if you're willing to go the extra mile, you need something grassy and unsweet, and for that reason I'd choose kale or greens of some sort rather than white cabbage. Spinach is not at all a bad idea either—I am quite equable about the idea of frozen whole leaf spinach. If you do fresh spinach for 8 people, you will have to be carting pounds of the stuff back from the store.

TRIFLE

For the proper English trifle, see page 109. The rhubarb, muscat, and mascarpone one (page 107) has an awful lot going for it here too.

SPRING-SCENTED LUNCH FOR 8

TARRAGON FRENCH ROAST CHICKEN

GERMAN LEEKS AND WINE, RICE, PEAS, AND SNOW PEAS

LEMON PIE

GERMAN
LEEKS AND
WINE

With tarragon chicken, I like rice or mashed potatoes, to mop up the chickeny juices. And I'd adapt Jane Grigson's recipe for German leeks and wine. You cut clean leeks into pieces 2½–3½ inches long, depending on the overall size of leek. (And work on the principle of 3 logs, that's to say probably 1 leek, per person.) Stew these logs slowly in butter in a covered pan for about 5 minutes, turning them occasionally—they should all be buttery. Then, pour in ¾–1 cup dry white wine (more if the arrangement of the pan seems to demand it) and keep cooking over a low heat, lid on. After about 10 minutes, when the leeks are ready (tender but not squishy), remove them to a dish and, if there's too much liquid left, boil down the juices. Whisk in a knob of butter and pour over the leeks. Use white pepper, not black, or it'll just look as if you haven't cleaned them properly.

TARRAGON FRENCH ROAST CHICKEN

Don't go mad with the tarragon for this; it's wonderful used with a light hand but suddenly whiffy when thrown in with too much exuberance. A straggly bunch comprising about 10 sprigs should be more than enough, which is about as much as is contained in those irritating see-through plastic envelopes you find at the supermarket.

This should also give you wonderful leftovers for salad or sandwiches.

6 tablespoons (¾ stick) unsalted butter

small bunch tarragon, leaves chopped, stalks reserved

I scant teaspoon sherry

freshly milled white pepper

2 large chickens, 4–5 pounds each

2 cups chicken stock, homemade or from a well-diluted cube

salt

Mix the butter well with the tarragon leaves. Add the sherry and a good grinding of white pepper. Push your fingers underneath the skin of the chicken so that you've got a pocket between breast and skin. Be careful not to break the skin, so proceed slowly. Smear most of the tarragony butter onto the breast, pat the skin back over, and dot the rest in the space between leg and body.

Preheat the oven to 400°F. Heat up the chicken stock and pour it into the bottom half of a roasting pan fitted with a rack. Add to the hot stock the stalks of the freshly chopped tarragon. Sit the chickens on the rack. If you're not sure about the quality of your chickens, make a domed lid with foil to retain moisture; it should be baggy over the chickens, fastened around the pan's edges. Keep the foil on for just 1 hour, though. Otherwise, just let the chicken sit on its rack over the hot stock, untended.

Roast the chicken for 15 minutes per pound plus 10 minutes. (If you're cooking a lemon pie at the same time—and the sour-sweet intensity of the lemons and the old-fashioned comfort of the pie are just right after the herbal hit of the buttery tarragon—you can have the oven on at 375°F and just make sure the chicken has 15 minutes or so longer in the slightly cooler oven, or cook the lemon pie in advance.)

When the chickens are ready—golden, and the juices run clear when pierced between a thigh and the body—take them out of the oven and switch it off. Pour off the pan juices and either put the chickens in their pan back in the oven to keep them warm or let them wait on their carving board. I don't mind what temperature chicken is when I eat it, and actually, there's a lot to be said for that puffed-breath warmth.

Pour the chicken-tarragon juices into a measuring cup. Pour some off into a small saucepan to boil down into a gravy-ish sauce. Obviously, taste for salt and pepper, too.

FOOLPROOF RICE

For 8 people, you need 4 cups of basmati rice and 4 cups of water. Pour the rice into a large strainer and hold it under the cold running water for a while to soak and rinse the rice. Shake well to drain. Melt 3 tablespoons of butter in a heavy-bottomed saucepan (which has a lid that fits) and stir in the rice till it's all coated. Then add the water, bring to the boil, add a good pinch of salt, then cover and turn down the heat to absolute minimum. For preference, use a heat-diffuser. Cook for 30–40 minutes or until all the water is absorbed and the rice is cooked. You can leave it with the lid on but the pan off the heat for 10 minutes or so without harm. You might consider, too, siphoning off some of the chicken stock from the chicken's roasting pan to add to the water and lend flavor to the rice while it's cooking.

All I want else with this are some snow peas, possibly with some buttery young peas stirred in.

LEMON PIE

I first came across a recipe for lemon pie (as distinct, very, from lemon meringue pie and lemon tart) in Norma MacMillan's In a Shaker Kitchen, a book I curl up with and read in a metaphorical fog of home baking after another stressed-out urban day. Reading recipes for chicken pot pie and maple wheat loaves is a wonderful antidote to modern life. The Shaker version of lemon pie takes lemons, slices them, macerates them in sugar, and then adds beaten egg yolks to this viscous sherbety mix and cooks it in an old-fashioned double crust. For me, it has the edge on both lemon meringue pie (the least impressive example of the type—and, if you want a meringue-topped pie, please just turn to the rhubarb-filled, meringue-topped, orange-fragrant pastry based version on page 234) and tarte au citron. I noticed that when I made it with sliced lemons, most people left pithy piles of politely regurgitated rubble on their plates. So I now cut off the pith after zesting and before slicing them. The easiest way to do this, I find, is by standing a lemon on a chopping board and then cutting thin slices off downwards. Don't worry that you're carving the lemons into interesting geometric forms; you can afford to lose some of the flesh along with the pith anyway, and besides, it doesn't matter what they look like. And don't worry, either, about this being a bit of a sweat—it doesn't take longer than a few clumsy swipes of a knife.

In effect, what you are making is a nubbly lemon curd, but even when you get rid of the skins, the fruit will hold up enough to create a proper pie filling rather than just goo. But although it's solid enough, it isn't stiff, and you'll need a spoon rather than a cake slice to serve it out.

4 lemons, zest removed and reserved, pith removed and flesh sliced ¼-inch thick (reserve any juice from the cutting)

2 cups sugar, plus more, if needed, and for sprinkling

FOR THE PASTRY

2¼ cups all-purpose flour

1 teaspoon baking powder

pinch salt

6 tablespoons (¾ stick) cold unsalted butter, cut in small dice

6 tablespoons cold vegetable shortening, cut in small dice

1 egg yolk

4 eggs

2 tablespoons unsalted butter, softened

Seed the lemon slices and put them in the bowl with the zest, adding the reserved juice. Pour over the 2 cups sugar and turn well (but gently; as much as possible, you want the lemon slices to hold their shape) so that all the lemons are coated with sugar. (And don't use anything metal; a wooden spoon or plastic spatula will do fine.) Cover and put the bowl in a cool place (or the fridge) for at least 12 hours or preferably 24.

Make the pastry following the instructions on page 38, adding a few tablespoons of ice water to the egg to bind the dough.

Divide the dough into 2 portions, one marginally bigger than the other, and then press each into a flattened ball, cover both discs with plastic film, and put in the fridge. The pastry will need to rest in the fridge for at least 20 minutes, but you can leave it in for days as long as you remember to take it out so that it isn't icy cold when you start rolling.

When you're ready to cook the pie, preheat the oven to 375°F. Roll out the slightly larger disc of pastry and use it to line a pie dish 9 inches in diameter and 2 inches deep. I have a stainless-steel dish of these dimensions that I am very fond of, not least because the pastry never seems to stick to the metal; I am not keen on ceramic pie pans.

Beat the eggs and stir them, with a wooden spoon or spatula, into the lemon mixture until well combined. Spread the softened butter on the base of the pastry (much as you would butter a slice of bread), then (tasting it first) pour in the lemons and their eggy-sugary juices. Sprinkle with more sugar if you feel they need it. Wet the rim of the bottom crust with water, roll out the other disc of pastry, and place on top. Crimp the edges to seal and cut some slits in the center to let steam escape.

Cut a strip of foil, enough to cover, loosely, the perimeter of the pie dish, so that the thinner, crimped edges don't burn. I find the pie needs about 1 hour in full, but you should start checking after about 45 minutes; it's done when the filling is firm to the touch and the crust golden. I keep the foil on for about 30 minutes. You can always do it the other way round, if you like—that's to say, leave the pie uncovered for 30 minutes and then put the foil on to stop it burning.

Remove from the oven and put the dish on a rack. Sprinkle with sugar and serve from the pie pan, hot, warm, or cold.

Even I cannot live by roast chicken alone, so I move on. I love duck for weekend lunch, if only because it is made to pick at as you sit around the not-cleared table, lazily finishing up whatever remains. There are drawbacks: it is not easy to carve and it doesn't go very far. Keep it, then, for when there are just four of you, along with a child or two, as well. The recipe I use makes the carving point less pertinent; you can almost treat it like crispy Peking duck. What you can carve, carve, and as for the rest, pull it into soft strips and gloriously crispy shreds.

With duck, how can you not have peas? Some will want also plain potatoes, to offer a foil to the rich and unctuous meat.

Don't go berserk over dessert. Yes, a sharp and fragrant fruit tart would be lovely (and my Seville orange curd tart—see page 246—is an obvious contender here, evoking as it does another traditional culinary conjunction with the duck), but just as good, certainly easier, perhaps even more judicious dessert, would be a heaped mound of tropical fruit salad. Get papaya, get mango, some headily perfumed melon, and, just for the look (there's certainly no taste), slice some star fruit into the bowl, too. The juice of the fruit (cut them over the bowl so you don't lose any) should provide some liquid, which you can supplement with squirts of lime juice and the pulp of a couple of passion fruits. And although it might sound excessive—well, it is excessive—I serve with it a pitcher of warm, even hot, butterscotch sauce. You may not believe me before tasting it, but this is an ecstatically successful culinary combination.

RELATIVELY EASY LUNCH FOR 4

SOFT AND CRISP ROAST DUCK

PETITS POIS À LA FRANÇAISE AND POTATOES

TROPICAL FRUIT SALAD WITH BUTTERSCOTCH SAUCE

The reason why this is relatively easy, if not just plain simple, is that quite a bit of it can be done in advance. The ducks can be poached in advance, and then all you need to do is roast them. The peas can certainly be done slightly in advance. The fruit must definitely be bought quite a bit in advance. Nearly all fruit is sold before it is anywhere near ripe these days, so unless you're very confident, I wouldn't consider buying fruit to eat on the weekend any later than Wednesday. And you probably don't need me to say this, but don't keep the fruit in the fridge.

The recipe for the duck is on page 89; for 4 adults, you will need 2 ducks (and that'll provide enough for a few smallish children, too, who love this) and the recipe for the peas is on page 105. For just four, you need to think of using about 2 pounds of unshelled peas or about 2 cups of frozen young peas.

QUICK
STOVETOP
BUTTERSCOTCH
SAUCE

To make a quick stovetop butterscotch-toffee-ish sauce for the tropical fruit, melt 3 tablespoons light muscovado or light brown sugar, 2 tablespoons superfine or granulated sugar, 4 tablespoons (½ stick) unsalted butter, and ½ cup golden syrup or light corn syrup together in a heavy-bottomed pan. When smooth and melted, let it bubble away, gently but insistently, for 5 minutes or so. Then, off the heat, beat in ½ cup light cream and ¼–½ teaspoon best-quality vanilla extract. (Or maybe add instead a slug of rum.) You can pour the sauce into a pitcher or bowl with a ladle and serve hot, or you can do it in advance and reheat.

MINT,
ORANGE, AND
RED CURRANT
JELLY

Respectful though I am in general of tradition, I don't like English-style roast lamb. Nostalgia makes me forgiving of red currant jelly or mint sauce, but neither is my first choice. You could consider an amalgam of mint and red currant, which works better than either sauce on its own. Decant your jar of bought good red currant jelly, grate over the zest of ½–1 orange, and add 1 heaping tablespoon (or more, if when you taste it you feel it could do with it) chopped mint. I use my mother's rusted-up old Moulinex herb mill; I hold it over the bowl of jelly and just turn the handle till I think I've got enough. Hold one of the orange halves over the bowl and give it a squeeze. Stir everything together and, if you made a mess, decant the jelly into a clean bowl for serving.

Lamb is best, I think, when the sweetness of the meat itself is in relief, rather than rudely overtaken by a less subtle sugariness. This means serving it warm rather than hot and, if eating it cold, at room rather than at fridge temperature. The smoky sweetness of peppers is perfect here; they complement rather than compete with the lamb's almost musky meatiness. Most people give you leg of lamb, but you should try shoulder—the flavor is deeper, more rounded, and the texture is fat-irrigated and plumply velvety. I am an awful carver and end up hacking an unboned shoulder into oblivion; a boned shoulder solves the problem.

LATE-SUMMER LUNCH FOR 6

ROAST SHOULDER OF LAMB WITH RATATOUILLE

GREEN SALAD WITH GREEN BEANS

TRANSLUCENT APPLE TART

I've called this a late-summer lunch because this is when it is eaten at its best—the air still warm, the wind beginning to bluster limply; it may be a late, weak August, it may be early September. But, hell, you could eat it anytime, even in the depths of winter. Mostly, I hate too much Mediterranean sprightliness when the weather is shoulder-stoopingly brutal, but the soft stewiness of ratatouille (or at least, that's the way I like it) accommodates itself elegantly enough to an alien climate.

The recipe for ratatouille is on page 102.

ROAST SHOULDER OF LAMB

3 garlic cloves, peeled and minced

leaves from 1 sprig rosemary, minced

1 tablespoon olive oil

1 4-pound boned shoulder of lamb

coarse sea salt

Preheat the oven to 425°F.

Put the garlic and rosemary in a bowl with the olive oil and stir and mash together. Get a sharp knife and stab the lamb in several places. Using your fingers, push small amounts of the garlic mixture into the cavities and, if there is any left in the bowl, thin it out with a little more olive oil and coat the top of the lamb with it. Sprinkle with the salt and roast for 30 minutes per pound plus 20 minutes, or to an internal temperature of 130°F, for pink meat. Then let stand for a good 10 minutes before carving.

If you're in a hurry, you can stud the lamb just with garlic, in which case cut the garlic lengthways into thin slivers and push them into the cavities. And you could, if you wanted, smear the top with a spoonful of good pesto. I'm not mad about the cheese element, but I have been reduced to this, and it works, which is why I pass it on.

If you want a gravy, just remove as much of the fat as you can, put the pan on the stove, and add a glass of red wine. Taste to see whether salt or water is needed. You don't need to make much gravy, just enough to drizzle over the carved slices of meat, not so much as to provide a puddle on the plate.

GREEN SALAD WITH GREEN BEANS

You've already got the sweet soft mush of the ratatouille; what you want here is something crisp and fresh and plain. I'd stick to the paler lettuces—one soft Bibb or Boston lettuce and a romaine heart or two, the leaves just separated, not torn into chunks. Get about 4 ounces green beans, trim the ends, and halve them so you have a pile of short lengths and cook them in salted boiling water until they're tender-crisp, about 5 minutes. You want them to have bite, but not too much; green beans are horrible undercooked. While they're cooking, fill the sink with cold water and chuck in a few ice cubes. As soon as the beans are tender-crisp (start tasting after 5 minutes), drain them and then plunge them into the sink of icy water. Drain again and dry, either on a paper towel or in a salad spinner, toss with the lettuces, adding some tender little basil leaves, whole, or some chopped fresh parsley or the tiniest grating of lemon zest. Make the simplest dressing of olive oil, salt, and lemon juice or vinegar (using hardly any lemon or vinegar and even less if you've grated in some zest) and maybe a dot of mustard, if you like.

TRANSLUCENT APPLE TART

I came across this tart one Sunday lunch at the house of friends. When I arrived the pastry was being made; in the brief pause between first and second helpings of the main course the apple was grated relaxedly into the butter mixture, and then, at the end, we ate it. And it reminded me how nice it is to see food being prepared rather than just being presented with the finished product. The lack of anxiety in the cooking inevitably transferred itself, and that's a salutary lesson. The recipe is adapted from Jane Grigson's comforting and instructive *Fruit Book*. She, in fact, calls it Apple Cheese Cake or Apple Curd Tart, but she makes the comparison between this and the old-fashioned southern American specialty called transparent pie, in which the custardy filling made with melted butter in place of cream or milk becomes translucent as it cooks. The word *translucent* evokes the light and melting delicacy of this tart, and I can't help finding the idea of cheese and curd a distraction. The only drawback for me is that it needs only one apple, thereby hardly relieving me of the reproachful mound of cooking apples in my garden in August and September.

I find it easier to get the pastry made, rested, and rolled out, and the tart shell lined, the evening before. Pâte sucrée, Jane Grigson stipulates, but I use my foolproof sweet pastry dough (page 39) instead. I have made this with bought puff pastry and it's still good; I should think bought pie crust would do as well. But you must believe me when I tell you how easy my pastry is. You are not baking this blind, so once the pastry is in its pan, you can proceed to fill and bake it.

I recipe plain pastry dough (page 37)	I egg
4 tablespoons (½ stick) unsalted	few drops pure vanilla extract, if not
butter	using vanilla sugar
⅓ cup vanilla sugar or superfine sugar	I cooking apple

Preheat the oven to 425°F.

Prepare the pastry and line a 9-inch tart pan with it. Melt the butter and sugar together over such a low heat that they become no more than tepid. Remove from the stove and beat in the egg and vanilla extract, if using. Quickly peel, core, and grate the apple coarsely, and stir thoroughly into the butter mixture.

Pour and spread over the pastry-lined pan and bake for about 15 minutes, until golden brown. Lower the heat to 350°F and cook for a further 15–20 minutes, until nicely colored.

As with most desserts, it is best to time this to come out of the oven not long before you're sitting down; it will be warm but will have had time to settle. But this, as Jane Grigson says, is wonderful whether hot, warm, or cold.

FRANCO-AMERICAN LUNCH
FOR 6

GIGOT BOULANGÈRE

SLICED GREEN BEANS OR GREEN SALAD

SUMMER SLUMP

I've mentioned that I like lamb as cooked by the French, and a gigot boulangère is particularly glorious, both dignified and comforting.

After the garlicky lamb, do something simple. If you want it to be a "made" dessert rather than plain fruit or ice cream, then I'd go for a slump, which is a fabulous, homey dessert (as is grunt, which has a synonymous application) of fruit baked with little dumplings on top. This is easy and suits late summer, when fruit's around, though you can use frozen.

GIGOT BOULANGÈRE

Shoulder, not leg, of lamb baked over potatoes is probably the origin of this dish; the shoulder would have been boned and so, really, should the leg. But don't worry about it, nor about making this historically authentic. We no longer take the roasting pan or casserole over to the baker's to cook in his oven (hence the name), so we can liberate ourselves from the other connotations of the dish without going into a frenzy of culinary self-doubt. Elizabeth David specifies new potatoes to go underneath the roast, and feel free to do likewise. The French certainly eat waxier potatoes than we do. I specify floury potatoes simply because that's the way I have always eaten this.

1 whole bone-in leg of lamb, about 7 pounds, hip bone removed (have your butcher do this)	3 bay leaves
	2–3 shallots, halved, or 1 large onion, quartered
3 garlic cloves, peeled, slivered lengthwise, and the slivers halved	6 or 7 sprigs fresh thyme or 1 teaspoon dried
8 tablespoons (1 stick) unsalted butter, plus more for greasing the pan, softened	3½ pounds floury potatoes
	salt and freshly milled black pepper
	1 cup lamb stock or water

Preheat the oven to 400°F.

Stab the lamb in several places with the point of a sharp knife and insert the garlic slivers. Cut a quarter of the butter off and put it to one side.

Crumble the bay leaves and put them and the shallots in a food processor. Reserving a couple of sprigs, hold the rest of the thyme over the bowl and, squeezing each stem by turn, pull downwards so that the leaves fall into the bowl. Pulse until everything is chopped finely. Naturally, you can do this by hand if you prefer.

Butter a deep roasting pan large enough to take all the potatoes and the lamb; an ordinary high-sided one will do, and indeed is what I use. Peel the potatoes and slice them thinly but not transparently so, blanch them for 2–3 minutes in boiling salted water; drain, dry, and layer them on the bottom of the dish, dotting with the larger quantity of butter and seasoning with the salt, pepper, and the onion mixture as you go.

Pour the stock over the potatoes, put in the oven, and bake for 30 minutes before adding the lamb.

Rub the top of the lamb with the rest of the butter and the leaves from the remaining sprigs of thyme. Sit the lamb on top of the potatoes and roast for 1 hour, then raise the heat to 450°F and cook for another 30 minutes or to an internal temperature of 130°F. This should give you pink but not underdone meat, but test after about 1¼ hours to see if it's how you like it.

Let the meat rest in the turned-off oven with the door open for about 15 minutes before serving. Even though it doesn't look as lovely, remove the lamb to a board to carve it. You can always put the slices back on top of the potatoes in the pan before you serve it.

SUMMER SLUMP

Note that the fruit layer in this is quite liquid—most like a fruit soup. If you haven't got fresh fruit to make it, use frozen red berries (not strawberries) and avoid framboise or a fraise liqueur. Make the dough for the dumplings ahead, if you like, and hold it in the fridge.

To make enough slump for 6, then (though it would stretch to 8—it's just that I hate stretching), you need:

FOR THE FRUIT

2¼ pounds fruits, such as raspberries, blackberries, cherries (stoned), or blueberries, any combination, fresh or frozen

½ cup sugar, plus more, if needed

4–5 tablespoons water or suitable liqueur, such as crème de cassis or an orange liqueur

FOR THE DUMPLINGS

1 cup all-purpose flour

1 teaspoon baking powder

pinch salt

2 tablespoons superfine sugar

2 tablespoons ground almonds

6 tablespoons (¾ stick) unsalted butter, chilled and cut into small dice

milk to bind

Preheat the oven to 375°F. Put the fruit in a baking dish—I use one of those oval old-fashioned cream stoneware bowls, but any pie or baking dish that has a capacity of about 10 cups should do. Sprinkle the fruit with the sugar; taste and add more if you think it's needed. Add the water or suitable liqueur and put, covered (with lid or foil), in the oven.

Meanwhile, get on with the dumplings. Sift the flour and baking powder into a bowl, add the salt, the sugar, and the almonds (almond dumplings are not usual, but I prefer them here). Stir them together and then throw in the butter and rub into the dry ingredients until the mixture is crumbly. You could do this in a free-standing electric mixer, but I wouldn't try a processor.

Pour in enough milk—about 2 tablespoons—to bind the dough; it should be soft but not too sticky to form into balls the size of small walnuts (remember, they will swell while cooking and then they should grow up into the size of proper walnuts). This quantity of dough should make about 24 little dumplings. Take the fruit out of the oven when it's simmering—15–35 minutes, depending on whether the fruit is fresh or frozen. Take off the lid, stir the fruit, and taste for sweetness, adding more sugar if necessary. Put the dumplings in the dish, cover again, and bake for another 15–20 minutes, by which time the dumplings should be cooked, beautifully swollen and no longer doughy. I like this with ice cream, but cream, old-fashioned runny cream rather than those stiff restaurant mounds, can be just right, too.

If you want something plainer, or rather even less trouble, just get masses of blackberries, cover a vast plate with them, and do nothing save sprinkle them with superfine sugar. Pour a great deal of heavy cream into a pitcher and put it on the table alongside.

This was never going to be a comprehensive list of suggestions, but I am loath to move on without mentioning one more traditional—and this time British traditional—way with lamb, and that's with caper sauce.

Caper sauce in fact goes, or always went, with boiled leg of mutton. But no one eats mutton any more. It's extravagant to boil lamb. It would be awful, though, if caper sauce disappeared, so just make it to go with plain roast lamb instead.

The best way to get some lamb stock to flavor the caper sauce is to roast lamb for 15 minutes in a very high oven, turn it down to 400°F, and add about 2 cups of water and an onion, halved, to the dish. I've got one of those roasters that is made of a punctured dish over a deeper pan and I put the lamb on the rack and the water and onion in the pan below. Don't cover the lamb; you want the top to crisp. (For cooking times, check table on page xviii.) Otherwise just buy a tub of chicken stock for the sauce.

For a richer sauce, stir in, at the end, an egg yolk beaten gently with about 5 tablespoons heavy cream.

CAPER SAUCE FOR
ROAST LAMB

Make this sauce while the lamb is resting prior to carving. If you've braise-roasted the lamb as mooted above, try to remove as much fat as you can from the roasting pan. I am hopeless at it, so what I suggest is that you pour the juices into a measuring cup and mop the top, where the fat is, with some paper towels. If you find those gravy dividers effective, use one of them, but I find that they're made so big that the top of the liquid—let alone the unfatty part below—never even reaches the spout. Pour about 1 cup of the juices into the milk required and warm.

4 tablespoons (½ stick) unsalted butter

½ cup all-purpose flour

1⅔ cups milk

1 cup lamb or chicken stock

3 tablespoons capers plus 1 teaspoon
    vinegar, or more, from the jar

1 tablespoon chopped parsley (optional)

salt, if needed

freshly milled black pepper

Using the butter and flour, make the roux for the sauce (following the recipe for béchamel on page 19), pour in the milk and lamb stock as normal, and cook until thick. Stir in the capers (adding more if you want it more capery) and the 1 teaspoon of vinegar from the caper bottle. Taste and add more vinegar if you think it's needed. I like this fairly sharp and might well add another teaspoon of caper juice, but proceed cautiously. If using, add the parsley. Season, if needed, with salt and do not be reticent with the pepper.

To be frank, although it's hardly traditional, I love caper sauce with roast pork, too. Its sour-noted velvetiness goes wonderfully with the densely woven sweetness of the meat. More often, though, I go for onion (or leek) sauce, but habit plays a large part in the lunch repertoire, I do see.

For regular, ordinary weekend roast pork I get a fresh ham; ask the butcher for boneless knuckle-half, a 6–8-pound cut. Roast it at 425°F for 1 hour and then turn it down to 325°F. To work out the total cooking time, think along the lines of 22–25 minutes per pound plus 25 minutes, or cook to an internal temperature of 160°F.

If you're going to do just plain fresh ham, then follow the instructions for roast potatoes given with the roast beef (page 253) and work a timetable out for yourself. At least you're not bothering with the Yorkshire pudding, so there are fewer major factors to take into consideration. With this I love sliced green beans and cabbage—huge bowlfuls with butter and black pepper or, as my mother often made it, with caraway seeds. The only time I like red cabbage is with pork, too, so I'll give a recipe for that while I'm about it.

SWEETLY NOSTALGIC LUNCH
FOR 6

ROAST FRESH HAM

ROAST POTATOES

RED CABBAGE COOKED IN THE VIENNESE FASHION

STEM-GINGER GINGERBREAD WITH SHARP CHEESE,
OR APPLE BUTTERSCOTCH TART

ROAST FRESH HAM

If at all possible, get your ham with its skin, and roast according to the method above. And, to make sure the skin becomes a true crackling and not damp, chewy rind, make sure you don't cover the ham while it's in the fridge (plastic film will give it a very sloppy kiss of death). Score it with a sharp knife before roasting. I do it the easy way: I ask the butcher to score it; his knives are better than mine, for a start. Besides, the purpose of going to a good butcher is to make sure the meat is beautifully handled, cut, and prepared as well as fresh and well chosen.

If you're stuck with scoring the skin yourself, then take a sharp knife and cut lines on the diagonal at about 1-inch intervals. If you want, you can then do the same the other way, so you have a diamond pattern etched into the rind. But that's not necessary, and it is easier not to.

I like to rub English mustard powder onto the scored, wiped skin, or the surface fat if the ham is rindless (give it a quick go-over with some paper towel just to make sure it's really dry). Or you can sprinkle on salt. Some people dribble vinegar on, but I am not convinced.

A tip from my butcher, David Lidgate: to make sure the crackling is properly crunchy all over, when you take the ham out of the oven, quickly peel off the crackling, cut it into 2 or 3 pieces, and put it in a hot tray and back into the oven, turning it back up to 425°F as you do so. Start carving and when you're done, take out the crackling, break it into more pieces, and put it on a plate in the middle of the table for people to take as they like. The pieces of crackling that come from the nether parts of the leg will obviously be damper and take longer to crisp than those from the top part, so don't take all the crackling out of the oven at the same time.

My mother loved red cabbage, so I am fond of this dish. On the whole, I don't like savory food that's fruity and jammy, but in the right weather and in the right mood, it can be fabulous, aromatic, and warming, and with just enough edge to stop it from cloying. I prefer it with roast pork rather than the more usual goose or duck. I think it actually benefits from being eaten with a meat that offers light to its shade. I love it with sausages, too. And it works beautifully with just-fried, still-moussy calf's liver.

The advantage of fruity stewed red cabbage is that it can be made in advance and moreover is the better for it. This recipe comes from a lovely book, Arabella Boxer's *Garden Cookbook*, which I picked up at a dusty second-hand bookshop. This book came out in the mid-1970s, so it is exactly contemporaneous with my memories of the red cabbage my mother used to cook. I seem to remember, though, my mother always used brown sugar, and a rich molasses-y one at that. And I had no idea that the culinary style this invoked was Viennese, but I rather love the idea—it certainly adds charm.

RED CABBAGE COOKED IN THE VIENNESE FASHION

I large red cabbage, quartered, cored, outer leaves removed and discarded

½ cup beef dripping or other fat, such as vegetable oil, butter (with a drop of oil added to prevent burning), or rendered chicken fat

I Spanish onion, chopped

2 tablespoons light brown sugar, plus more, if needed

I large cooking apple, unpeeled and cored

3 tablespoons red wine or cider vinegar, plus more, if needed

salt and freshly milled black pepper

1¼ cups beef stock

I tablespoon all-purpose flour

¼ cup tablespoons cream, sour cream, or crème fraîche

Shred the cabbage finely. Even by hand this doesn't take long. And as this recipe predates the food processor, I tend, nostalgically, to eschew machine cutters here. Illogical of course—I use an electric mixer for pastry happily enough. But then I never saw my mother make pastry.

Melt or heat the fat in a deep, heavy casserole. Add the onion and cook until it starts to soften and color. Add the sugar and stir around until all is golden. Put in the cabbage and mix well. Chop the apple and add it to the cabbage. Add the vinegar and season with the salt and black pepper. Stir well, cover, and cook for 15 minutes over a low heat.

Heat the stock and pour into the casserole. Cook for 2 hours on top of the stove or in a 325°F oven. When the time is up, mix the flour and cream to a paste in a cup and add it to the cabbage by degrees, stirring all the time, on top of the stove.

Cook over a low heat for 4 or 5 minutes to cook the flour and thicken the sauce. Taste and add more sugar or vinegar if necessary—the sweet and sour elements should be nicely balanced, not like the culinary outpourings of a provincial Chinese takeout, so go steady—or add more salt and black pepper.

If you are making this in advance—which is always a good idea—reheat it, covered, in its casserole for an hour at 350°F, or on the stove for markedly less time. Serves 6–8.

If you're not making the cabbage, turn to page 327 for a recipe for applesauce, only I wouldn't strain it here. My grandmother always ate horseradish with her pork; you could think of doing likewise. Similarly, if I weren't bothering with the red cabbage, I'd cook an apple dessert like baked apples, apple crumble, apple pie, or—especially good after the pork—this sour-sweet apple butterscotch tart. Otherwise, dense, wet and aromatic gingerbread (page 114) and some sharp and crumbly cheese such as Lancashire or Wensleydale would be perfect.

APPLE BUTTERSCOTCH TART

I recipe Plain Pastry Dough (page 37) made with I cup Italian 00 or all-purpose flour

I pound cooking apples (or substitute rhubarb or blackberries), peeled, cored, and sliced fairly thinly

⅔ cup light muscovado sugar or light brown sugar

¼ cup all-purpose flour

pinch salt

2 eggs

¼ cup heavy cream

Make the pastry and line an 8-inch tart pan with it. Fill the shell with the apples and spread over the top a walnut-colored butterscotch paste made by mixing the sugar with the flour, salt, and the eggs beaten with the cream. Bake at 425°F for 10 minutes, and then lower the heat to 350°F and cook for another 20 minutes or so or until the pastry is golden and the filling is set.

If you want a dessert that is altogether lighter (and can be cooked in advance), then try the rhubarb and muscat jelly (page 312), substituting freshly squeezed orange juice for the muscat if you want something suitably alcohol-free for children (although I wouldn't presume they'd dislike the unctuous grapiness of the wine). There is an established culinary connection, anyway, between rhubarb and pork; the Swedes eat rhubarb purée with pork much as we do applesauce. I suggest some variation on this theme—just get a stick or two of rhubarb, cook until it turns into a pinky-khaki mush, and, when it's cool, stir it into a cup of bought horseradish sauce.

CALMING WINTER LUNCH FOR 6

ROAST PORK LOIN WITH ROAST LEEKS

CLAPSHOT, A VEGETABLE PURÉE, WITH BURNT ONIONS

CUSTARD TART

Much as I love roast fresh ham, I don't cook it that much; roast boned and rolled loin, without the rind, is my more regular pig-out. I feel at ease with it, even though the flesh can tend to dry stringiness. Ask the butcher for rib-end of loin (hard to carve, but wonderful tasting). And put a little liquid in the roasting pan so the meat grows tender in its own small pool of odoriferous steam. Anything will do—a glass of wine or cider, some stock, water mixed with apple juice, the leftover liquid you've cooked carrots in.

Cooking boned and rolled pork loin bears almost any interpretation or elaboration. By elaboration, I mean not to imply complexity of culinary arrangement

WITH GARLIC
AND FRESH
GINGER

WITH DRIED
BAY LEAVES

GROUND
CLOVES,
CINNAMON,
AND
CARDAMOM

but wide-rangingness. If you want, at other times, to add a modern, fusiony note, make a paste of garlic and fresh ginger and smear that over the roast. If you want something altogether less vibrant, then pulverize some dried bay leaves, and press these against the fat. Or rub in ground cloves, cinnamon, and cardamom to produce an almost Middle Eastern waft.

Get the butcher to remove the bones and give them to you so you can cook them around the joint, which will make the gravy. And while you're about it, ask him to chop them up small. The loin should be left elegantly wrapped in its pearly coating of fat. If there's not enough fat on the joint, it will end up too dry.

ROAST LOIN OF PORK

You will need a boned loin of about 4 pounds. If you're a good carver, don't bother with boning, but have the butcher cut through the chine bone to ease carving.

Preheat the oven to 425°F. Work out how long the loin needs—and at roughly 20 minutes per pound, for a 4-pound roast that's about 80 minutes, or cook to an internal temperature of 150°–155°F. About halfway through the pork's cooking time, throw a glass of wine (or whatever you're using; cider would be very good here) into the pan.

I am not one of nature's gravy makers, and therefore I do everything to make life easier for myself—and frankly suggest you do too. As for this gravy, all you need to do is pour the winy juices from the meat dish into a sauceboat or bowl, removing fat if you can and if you need to. Taste it; you may need to add a little bit of water, you may just want to use it as is. I am not, on the whole, a thick-gravy person; you may be. For a recipe for applesauce to go with, see page 328, only again I wouldn't strain it here.

ROAST LEEKS

For 6 people, get about 8 not-too-fat leeks (although one each would probably be enough, I'd always rather have over). Once you've made sure they're clean, cut them on the diagonal into logs about 3 inches long. Pour some olive oil in a roasting pan and turn the leeks in it so they're glossy all over. Sprinkle over some coarse sea salt and roast for about 30 minutes at 425°F. I usually roast them at a higher temperature and for slightly less time, but it would be absurd to complicate matters, as you're going to have the oven at this temperature anyway.

I love these leeks blistered sweet on the outside, suggestively oniony within their slithery center. I know that there are going to be onions themselves with the clapshot, but the pork can take the double helping of allium. If you feel otherwise, make a large, iron-dark bowl of butter-drenched kale. Kale, indeed, is a feature of traditional clapshot; this recipe makes do without and it is tempting to make up the shortfall. If you wanted to add a slightly more modern touch, then simply get some bok choi or choi sum and steam or stir-fry it with or without lacily grated ginger.

CLAPSHOT WITH BURNT ONIONS

I got the idea for this traditional British dish from a supermarket recipe collection. It is a modern take on old-fashioned clapshot, which is a delicious hodge-podge of various vegetables cooked and mushed together. This is something not so stylish as to be self-conscious but not so hearty as to be indigestible.

2 pounds rutabagas, peeled and diced

2 pounds floury potatoes, peeled and quartered

8 tablespoons (1 stick) unsalted butter

salt and freshly milled black pepper

whole nutmeg

4 tablespoons olive oil

2 large onions, very thinly sliced

2 tablespoons superfine sugar

Put the rutabagas in a saucepan of boiling, salted water and simmer for about 5 minutes. Add the potatoes and simmer for 25–30 more minutes until both are just cooked. Don't overcook or they will disintegrate into potato soup. Drain thoroughly.

Dry the rutabagas and potatoes slightly by putting them back in the saucepan (which you've wiped dry) and placing it over a low heat. Then mash—with a potato ricer or mouli—with the butter. Season with the salt and pepper to taste, adding a good grating of fresh nutmeg.

While the potatoes and rutabagas are cooking, get started with the onion-burning. Heat the oil in a heavy-bottomed frying pan over low heat. Add the onions to the oil and cook slowly for about 30 minutes until crisp and golden brown, stirring and scraping from time to time. Turn heat to high and sprinkle with sugar and stir continuously for a further 3 minutes or so until the sugar caramelizes and the onion darkens.

Put the clapshot in a serving bowl and top with the burnt onions.

CUSTARD TART

I adore custard tart—I love its barely vanilla-scented, nutmeggy softness, the silky texture of that buttermilk-colored eggy cream, solidified just enough to be carved into trembling wedges on the plate. It isn't hard to make, but I botch it often out of sheer clumsiness. But now I have learnt my lessons, and pass them on to you.

One—pour the custard into the pastry shell while the pastry is in the oven, so that you don't end up leaving a trail from kitchen counter to stove, soaking the pastry shell in the process. And two—don't be so keen to use up every last scrap of that custard, filling the shell right to the very brim so that it's bound—as you knew it was—to spill, making it soggy and ruining the contrast between crisp crust and tender filling. If you can manage to do both those things, then you can make a perfect custard pie. I won't promise it's an easy exercise, though.

If you want to eat it cold, this makes life easier, as you can arrange to have free play with the oven the day before. But, at its best, the custard should still have a memory of heat about it. Make it before you put the pork in the oven and let it sit for 1½ hours or thereabouts, gently subsiding into muted warmth in the kitchen.

If you can't be bothered to make the pastry yourself, you have a choice: either you can use a bought crust, or don't bother with a crust at all and make a baked custard. For a baked custard, make double quantities of custard, then pour it into a pie dish (with a capacity of just over 4 cups), stand the pie dish in a roasting pan filled with hot water, and bake in a 300°F oven for about 1 hour.

If you don't keep vanilla sugar—although I do recommend it; see page 72—then just add vanilla extract to the mixture. Of course you can always add an actual vanilla bean to the milk and cream when you warm them, but actually I don't like baked custard with too much vanilla; I like the merest musky suggestion of it.

I recipe Rich Pastry Dough (page 38)	¼ teaspoon pure vanilla extract, if not
I egg, separated (reserve the yolk for	using vanilla sugar
the custard)	I ¼ cups light cream
FOR THE CUSTARD	⅔ cup milk
3 eggs plus the reserved yolk	pinch ground mace
2 tablespoons vanilla sugar or	whole nutmeg
superfine sugar	

Preheat the oven to 400°F. Make the pastry, line an 8-inch tart pan with it, and bake blind for about 20 minutes, following the instructions on page 39. Take out of the oven and remove the beans and paper or foil. Beat the egg white lightly, brush the bottom and sides of the cooked pastry shell with it (the idea being to seal the pastry so the custard won't make it soggy later on), and put back in the oven for 5 minutes. Turn down the oven to 325°F.

For the custard, put the eggs, yolk, and sugar and vanilla, if using, in a bowl and whisk together. Warm the cream and milk in a saucepan with the mace and pour into the egg mixture. Stir to mix and then strain into the pastry shell as it sits on the pulled-out rack in the oven. Grate over some nutmeg. Push the shelf back in carefully but confidently (tense hesitation can be disastrous, far too jerky), shut the door, and leave the custard pie in the oven to bake for about 45 minutes. Take a look though, after about 35 minutes. The custard, when it's ready, should look more or less solid but still with a tremble at its center.

Take out of the oven, grate some more nutmeg over it, and leave until it reaches tepid heaven.

If pork is not cooked often enough, salmon is overexposed. It can, though, be just right.

SPRING LUNCH FOR 8

SALMON BAKED IN FOIL

TABBOULEH AND FENNEL SALAD, OR PEAS, AVOCADO, AND MINT

ALMOND SPONGE WITH ORANGE SYRUP

This is the perfect menu for a sprightly April; the salmon makes you feel summer's on the way, and the fragrant and tender sponge offers comfort because it isn't.

SALMON BAKED IN FOIL

My grandmother swears that the way to cook a whole salmon is to cover it with cold water, bring it to the boil, let it simmer for 10 minutes, then turn it off. When it's cold, she says, it will, whatever its weight, be perfectly *à point*.

If you don't own a fish poacher (as I don't), then baking salmon in the oven, wrapped in foil, is the best and simplest way to cook it. Everyone has their own way, and I notice that cooking at high temperatures is gaining fashionable ground, but this is the basic method. Heat the oven to 300°F. Get a piece of foil large enough to wrap the fish loosely—for 8 you should have a salmon of 5½ pounds or so, which is probably as big as you'll be able to get in your oven. Butter the fish if you are going to eat it hot; oil it if you're going to eat it cold. Lay the fish on top of the greased foil, season with salt and pepper, squeeze over the juice of ½ lemon, then twist the edges of the foil together lightly. The foil envelope should be well sealed but baggy.

Put the parcel into the oven; I always put the foil parcel directly on the rack, not having a pan big enough. I rely on my aunt Fel's way, which is to cook the fish at this fairly low heat for 12 minutes per pound. If you like your salmon fashionably orange in the middle, rather than flaky peachy pink, cut the overall cooking time by about 15 minutes. I also pass on a tip from fish seller Steve Hatt, who reminds me to make the join of the foil on the back of the fish so that you can quickly unwrap a bit and poke a knife in to see if the fish is coming away from the bone and is therefore ready.

When the salmon's had its time, remove from oven, unwrap the foil, and leave it to cool in the opened parcel if it's to be eaten cold. If you're going to eat it hot, let it stand like that for 15 minutes, then finish unwrapping and put it on its plate. Either way, surround the salmon with lemon quarters together with watercress if you're going in for a traditional look; otherwise, you could supplement the lemon wedges (which are necessary, though of course don't need to be on the same plate as the fish) with arugula, mizuna, or flat-leaf parsley. I am not much of a garnish queen, but there is something about an unadorned fish on its platter that makes it look beached.

TABBOULEH

If the salmon is to be eaten cold, which I do prefer, I might have it with tabbouleh (see page 236)—not just to work against culinary expectations but because they are wonderful together. But old pairings do work and I think of peas as going with salmon as much as I think of them partnering ham. My great-aunt Myra, who was a wonderful cook, used to make a summer salad of peas, avocado, and mint (very British seventies); turn to page 343 if you're interested.

PEAS,
AVOCADO,
MINT,
FENNEL, OIL,
LEMON

To go with the tabbouleh, though, just slice some fennel bulbs very, very thinly, drizzle over oil, and squeeze over lemon. Add salt, pepper, and the finely chopped aniseedy fronds that you removed before slicing. I love this almost medicinally pure taste against the oily denseness of the fish.

I normally avoid too much same-color food. However much I resist emphasis on the look, rather than the taste, of what you're eating, appearances do count for something. But all rules, all generalizations, culinary or otherwise, are to be challenged. Here I evince the culinary proof: the dessert I suggest, the almond sponge drenched in orange syrup, is exactly what you want, despite being a tonal echo of the course before; the recipe for it is on page 115.

I know how to observe the proprieties, mutter damply about the cold, exclaim with joy at the prospect of warmth and sun and dusty summer heat, but the truth is I love winter food, winter cooking, best. I welcome it, and in January particularly, when I make first sightings of early hothouse rhubarb, almost bubblegum pink.

WELCOMING JANUARY LUNCH FOR 6

BRAISED PHEASANT WITH MUSHROOM AND BACON

PIG'S BUM

This is such a wonderful winter lunch; in January, the memory of all those slabs and plates of meat from Christmas is near enough to make one weepily grateful for a sweetly steamy bowl of stew. The dessert afterwards—as glorious as its name—is the result of a conversation I once had with British chef and restaurateur Antony Worrall Thompson. I'd been, I think, recounting the gastronomic glories of rhubarb; he'd countered by telling me of a steamed pudding he'd had at prep school they always called pig's bum, because of the peculiar form and coloration of this stodgy rhubarb steamed sponge. I, understandably, was entranced. I have no idea how my version of this pudding measures up to his remembered original, my inspiration, but I have grown as fond of it as I could never become of any of the puddings I remember from the school lunches of my past. Note that if the pudding is prepared with later-season rhubarb, it won't be as piggy-pink.

The recipe for the pheasant stew is on page 101, and with it I'd have the bulghur mentioned there, too; but as the steamed pudding that follows is actually rather light, you could wallow in a pile of buttery mashed potatoes first if you—quite understandably—wanted.

The pudding needs 2½ hours to cook, but you need do nothing to it while it's cooking, except to make sure there's enough water in your steamer to keep the pudding cooking at full heat, so don't regard the time as a major problem. Besides, the pheasant stew can be made in advance, so you're hardly giving yourself a terrible morning in the kitchen.

PIG'S BUM

¼ pound rhubarb, trimmed and chopped into 1½-inch pieces

½ cup plus 1 tablespoon sugar

1 cup all-purpose flour

1½ teaspoons baking powder

pinch salt

8 tablespoons (1 stick) unsalted butter, very soft

2 eggs

1½ teaspoons baking powder

1 teaspoon pure vanilla extract

1–2 tablespoons milk, if needed

Butter a 4-cup pudding basin (preferably one with a lid) or deep bowl, remembering to butter the inside of the lid too; if it hasn't got a lid, you will just have to wrap it in foil later.

Put the rhubarb in a saucepan with the tablespoon of sugar and ½ cup of water; bring to the boil, reduce the heat, and simmer, covered, over medium heat till it's cooked to a pulp, about 5 minutes. Drain and let cool. Put a full kettle on to heat up the water for steaming later.

Put all the remaining ingredients except the milk into the food processor and mix till smoothly combined; you must see no lumps of butter, or indeed of anything. Then add the rhubarb purée—you should have 4–5 tablespoons—and pulse quickly so that that, too, is combined in the sponge batter, though it doesn't matter if what you have is a pale yellow mixture shot through with strings of pink. If it's still a little stiff, add the milk, a tablespoonful at a time, until smooth and soft. Now dip a spoon in and lick—not because I think you need to add anything, but because the taste of this is better than almost anything; it reminds me of the boiled sweets I used to buy as a child, two-tone affairs called rhubarb and custard, that left the inside of my cheek rough with sugar-shock.

Anyway, pour the boiling water from the kettle into the bottom half of a steamer or just any big pot (in which case you need the water to come about halfway up the pudding basin), put it on the heat, and pour the mixture into the prepared basin. Put the lid on or cover with foil, then wrap all over with foil again—and really wrap, so no water can come in. When the water's boiling, lower the basin in or set it above on the steamer. Cook for 2½ hours, making sure the water never runs dry or stops bubbling. Remove the foil and unmold the pudding onto a plate.

You do really need custard with this. How could you think otherwise? I normally like hot custard, but cold is right here. This makes life easier, as you don't even have to think of fiddling about with it at the last minute. Turn to pages 31–33 for recipes.

From pig's bum to ham: it's an obvious step. I love ham poached in water or cider and then its rind stripped off, the glutinous fatty wrapping underneath pressed with mustard and sugar, scored with a sharp knife and studded with cloves, and then glazed in a hot oven. That was my mother's way. To poach the ham, see the recipe on page 212. When the ham's cooked, either way, strip it, score it (and I have only just worked out how to do this without burning my fingers—leave it to cool, the obvious and right thing to do), and then smear it with glaze before poking in cloves at the interstices of the criss-crossing diagonal slashes. My mother's glaze was simply a stiff paste made of English mustard powder, muscovado sugar, and a drop or two of orange juice. Marguerite Patten, the venerable British cookbook writer, suggests (in *Classic British Dishes*) a wonderfully malevolent-sounding glaze of black treacle—use molasses—blended with a little crushed pineapple (from a can, presumably) and sugar, which should keep the Hawaiian pizza brigade—and those who sneer at it—happy.

I am much taken with the American way of cooking a ham in Coca-Cola. In an age that solemnly tells you that cooking can produce food only as good as the ingredients that are provided (that's the whole history of French cuisine dispatched then), there is something robustly cheering about this dish. I'd be tempted to stick to the same idiom with dessert, too. By that I don't necessarily mean some sugary example of kitchen kitsch, but one of those unpretentious pies that Americans do so well.

WHITE-TRASH LUNCH FOR 6

HAM IN COCA-COLA

PARSLEY POTATOES, SNOW PEAS, AND YOUNG PEAS

CHERRY PIE

HAM IN COCA-COLA

I cannot urge you to try this strongly enough. The first time I tried it, it was out of amused interest. I'd heard, and read, about this culinary tradition from the Deep South, but wasn't expecting it, in all honesty, to be good. It is—I'm converted. I have to make myself cook ham otherwise now, though often I don't bother with the glaze but just leave it for longer in the bubbling Coke instead. But, if you think about it, it's not surprising it should work. The sweet, spiky drink just infuses the ham with spirit of barbecue. Don't even think of using Diet Coke.

2 liters Coca-Cola	2 cups dark muscovado sugar or dark
I 5-pound half bone-in ham, partially	brown sugar
or fully cooked	I tablespoon mustard powder
I medium onion, halved	2 tablespoons Dijon mustard
I cup freshly made bread crumbs	

Remove and reserve 2 tablespoons of the Coke.

Put the ham in a large pot or Dutch oven, add the onion, then pour over the larger quantity of the Coke. Bring to the boil, reduce to a good simmer, put a lid on, though not tightly, and cook for about 1½ hours for a partially cooked ham, 1 hour if the ham is fully cooked. The ham is done at an internal temperature of 160°F for a partially cooked ham, 140°F for one that is fully cooked. Do take into account that if the ham's been in the fridge right up to the moment you cook it, you will have to give a good 15 or so minutes' extra cooking time so that the interior is properly cooked.

Meanwhile, preheat the oven to 425°F.

When the ham's had its time, take it out of the pot (do not throw away the cooking liquid) and let it cool a little for ease of handling. (Indeed, you can let it cool completely, then finish off the cooking at some later stage if you want.) Remove any skin, leaving a thin layer of fat. Mix the bread crumbs, sugar, and the mustards to a thick, stiff paste with the reserved 2 tablespoons of Coke. Add a drop at a time because the one thing you don't want is a runny mixture. Slap the mustardy crust on the ham and put it, crust-side up, on a rack in a roasting pan and cook in the hot oven for 10–15 minutes, until the crust is just set.

Or if you want to do the braising stage in advance and then let the ham cool, give it 30–40 minutes, from room temperature, in a 350°F oven.

With this I serve a large bowl of floury, large-chunked boiled potatoes, leafily covered with fresh chopped parsley—and I mean covered, not sprinkled. But mashed potatoes are wonderful with this, too, truly. For the peas, cook about 2½ cups frozen young peas in copious boiling water until almost tender, about 3 minutes. Add several handfuls of snow peas, any strings removed, and allow them to blanch and the young peas to finish cooking, about 1 minute. Drain the lot, stir in some butter, and season with salt and pepper.

This ham, not surprisingly, is sensational cold, in sandwiches, and the cooking liquid makes a quick, no less fabulous, version of the South Beach black bean soup. I throw a pound of dried black beans in the liquid, adding about a cup of water and the juice and zest of a lime. When cooked and puréed as usual, I eat it with some more lime squeezed in, or some drops of balsamic vinegar stirred in, a dollop of sour cream or somesuch, and a handful of earthily pungent, eye-searingly green, just-chopped coriander.

CHERRY PIE

My generation is, effectively, American-reared, so I suppose it's not surprising if we British have a certain kitchen nostalgia for these foods we've never eaten, only seen in films or read in those exotically demotic stories and novels. And you don't get much more evocatively down-home than a cherry pie. If you were serious about such matters you'd be stoning the fresh cherries yourself, but apart from a brief burst of enthusiasm when I got a friend to bring over a cherry stoner with her when she came to visit, I stick to good bottled ones. Morello cherries in glass jars are just dandy.

Serve à la mode or dollop on some far more grown-up crème fraîche instead.

FOR THE PASTRY

2 cups all-purpose flour

1½ teaspoons baking powder

pinch salt

8 tablespoons (1 stick) unsalted butter, diced

2 egg yolks beaten with ¼ teaspoon pure vanilla extract, pinch of salt, and 2 tablespoons of ice water

FOR THE FILLING

1 tablespoon unsweetened butter, melted

½ cup plus 1–2 tablespoons sugar

1 tablespoon Italian 00 or all-purpose flour

1 24-ounce jar morello cherries in syrup, syrup drained and 2 tablespoons reserved

1–2 tablespoons superfine sugar

Preheat the oven to 400°F. Put in a baking sheet to heat up.

Using the pastry ingredients, make the pastry according to instructions on page 38 and then divide it into two discs. Roll out one disc and use it to line an 8-inch shallowish pie plate. For the filling, make a paste with the melted butter, the sugar, flour, and the reserved cherry syrup. It will be stiff, not runny; the cherries will leak out more as they bake and you don't want soggy pastry.

Roll out the other disc, and then add the cherries and the paste to the pie dish. Moisten the edges of the pastry and top with the remaining pastry. Cut off the overhang, crimp the edges, and, if you're up to it, cut out some little cherries to decorate. Make a few slashes in the top with a sharp knife for the steam to escape and then put on the hot baking sheet in the preheated oven.

After 15 minutes, cover loosely with foil, turn down the oven to 350°F, and bake for another 18 minutes, or until the crust is golden and thick juices bubble through the slashes.

Remove, sprinkle with the superfine sugar, and let cool for about 40 minutes before eating.

I am aware that the culinary spirit of the age is not ferociously carnivorous and that my blood-oozing joints of well-hung beef and fat-girdled pork risk offending modern quasi-vegetarian sensibilities. But I have wanted to concentrate on this sort of meat cookery simply because it seems to hold such unnecessary terrors for people now. There's enough written on pan-Asian stir-fries and Italo-Thai noodle dishes and you're unlikely to need any more, at least for the time being.

Of course I don't expect anyone to eat this sort of food every weekend without fail—no one's telling you you can't have pasta, for God's sake—but the particular focus it offers is worth exploiting. For food like this, more than any other sort, is what cooking at home rather than eating in a restaurant is all about.

DINNER

I'm not sure I like the connotations of the term *dinner party*, but I think we're stuck with it. Kitchen suppers—which is perhaps what this chapter should be called—sounds altogether too quaint, even if it evokes more accurately the culinary environment most of us now inhabit. So let's just call it dinner, which is what it is. The modern dinner party was, in Great Britain, the invention of the post-war, post–Elizabeth David brigade of socially aware operators, and in the United States was ushered in by the great Julia Child. In both cases, this dining was about Entertaining-with-a-capital-E. Not only was the food distinctly not home food, it wasn't even restaurant food; what was evoked was the great ambassadorial dinner. But *autres temps, autres moeurs;* most of us don't even have dining rooms any more. Yet people often still think they should be following the old culinary agenda; they feel it is incumbent on them not so much to cook as to slave, to strive, to sweat, to perform. Life doesn't have to be like that. As far as I'm concerned, moreover, it shouldn't be like that. I find formality constraining. I don't like fancy, arranged napkins and I don't like fancy, arranged foods.

That's not to say that I feel everything should be artfully casual; the this-is-just-something-I've-thrown-together school of cookery can be just as pretentious. What I feel passionately is that home food is home food, even when you invite other people to eat it with you. It shouldn't be laboriously executed, daintily arranged, individually portioned. It's relaxed, expansive, authentic—it should reflect your personality, not your aspirations. Professional chefs have to innovate, to elaborate, to impress the paying customer. But the home cook is under no such constraints. (Indeed, you don't have to cook much at all if you are prepared to shop well.) I once went to a dinner party a good friend of mine gave, and she was so anxious, she'd been up till three in the morning the night before making stocks. She said scarcely a word to any of us after opening the door, as she was in the middle of the first of about five courses. The food was spectacular, but she spent most of the evening ever more hysterical in the kitchen. At one point we could, as we stiltedly made conversation between ourselves, hear her crying. The fault wasn't her competence, but her conception: she felt that her dinner party must be a showcase for her culinary talents and that we must all be judging her. Some cooks, indeed, seem to resent their guests for interrupting the cooking, rather as doctors and nurses resent patients for interrupting the nice, efficient running of their hospitals.

Restaurants need to be able to produce food in short order. But unless you want to stand in your kitchen handing hot plates out to your friends at the table, you need not and should not. Avoid small portions of tender-fleshed fish that have to be conjured up at the last minute and *à point,* and anything that will wilt, grow soggy, or lose character or hope as it sits, sideboard-bound and dished up. Don't make life harder on yourself. I am working on banishing the starter from my dinner-partying life. (Truth to tell, I don't have much of a dinner-partying life, but, in theory, I do invite friends for dinner.) This is not so much because cooking the starter is difficult—in fact it is the easiest course of any of them—but because clearing the table, timetabling the whole meal, keeping the main course warm, can all add to the general tension of the evening.

Besides, our lives are so different now. Because working hours are longer, we eat dinner later. And if dinner doesn't start till nine or nine-thirty, then it is going to be a very late evening if you sit down to three courses. And you don't want to miss out on the general hanging around with a drink beforehand. I am more of an eater than a drinker and tend to get unbearably anxious if the drinking goes on for hours with no sign of the eating to come, so I try to amalgamate the two. I am, in effect, not really banishing the starter, but relocating it, refashioning it. Now, I can't pretend that serving bits with drinks is an original idea, but I suggest that you think of them as the starter. There is no dinner party I would give where I couldn't just make a plate of crostini to eat as a first course.

Normally, I make a couple of different sorts. I don't assemble the crostini in advance, but I often make the mixture with which they're going to be spread days ahead and keep slices for toast, ready-carved from baguette or ficelle, bagged up in the freezer.

CROSTINI

I figure on getting about 40 usable slices from a ficelle and maybe 50 from a baguette, which seems to be longer as well as thicker. A baguette is commonly used for crostini, but I prefer the ficelle. I like its relative spindliness; the smaller rounds it makes mean you can eat crostini in one bite; and the string loaf seems to have a less tooth-resistant crust. But whichever loaf you're using, cut in straight-knifed rounds rather than diagonally, as usually advised, because it's easier to keep the slices compact and easy to eat that way.

To make the crusts for the crostini, cut the loaves into slices ¼–½ inch in width. Let your instinct guide you; you probably know yourself just how thick or thin you want them to be. The crostini are no more than slices of bread dabbed with oil and toasted in a hottish oven. Preheat the oven to 400°F and, using a pastry brush or just your fingers, dip in oil and lightly cover each side of each slice of bread. I find 40 slices use up about 8 tablespoons of oil. And, unless specified below, always assume that olive oil (extra virgin, the usual specifications) is indicated. Put the oil-brushed slices on a rack in the oven for 5–10 minutes. The length of time the bread takes to brown depends in part on how stale it was to start with (and stale is good here). Turn the bread over as it turns pale gold. Remove when cooked and leave the uncrowned crostini some-where to get cool. You should toast them no more than 2 hours before you eat them. Don't spread anything on them until wholly cold. And then you can put just about anything on top.

All the quantities below make enough for 20 crostini. I would make at least 5 per person, and probably two different kinds.

CHICKEN-LIVER CROSTINI

This is your basic crostini, really, the Tuscan version of chopped liver. (Speaking of which, if you want to be rakishly cross-cultural, I suppose you could, as the malapropism of a friend's Yiddish-speaking uncle has it, throw kasha to the winds and smear this stuff on toasted bagels instead.)

Use whatever grapey alcohol you want: vin santo, Marsala, muscat, white wine, vermouth, or sherry. I've specified Marsala because it's what I keep near-est to me by the stove; I suspect a Tuscan would stipulate vin santo. You could use some of this in the crostini and keep the rest for dinner; pour it into glasses and give people those almond-studded biscotti known as cantuccini to dunk.

½ pound chicken livers

milk, for covering the livers

⅓ celery stalk

I garlic clove, peeled

I shallot or I scallion (white and green parts), chopped coarsely

I heaping tablespoon chopped parsley, plus more, for garnish

2 tablespoons olive oil

½ tablespoon tomato purée

4 tablespoons Marsala or other wine (see headnote)

salt and freshly milled black pepper

I heaping teaspoon capers, rinsed, drained, and chopped

2 anchovy fillets, wiped and chopped

I tablespoon unsalted butter

Remove any bits of green or gristle you can see in the chicken livers, then put them in a dish and pour milk over to cover. Leave for about 10 minutes. Put the celery, garlic, shallot, and the tablespoon of parsley in the processor and chop finely. Heat the oil in a heavy-bottomed frying pan and add the vegetable mix. Cook at low to moderate heat, stirring regularly, for about 5 minutes, perhaps slightly longer, until soft but not colored. Drain the chicken livers, wipe them dry with a paper towel, and chop them using a knife or mezzaluna. Add them to the pan and cook, prodding, pushing, and stirring with your wooden spoon or spatula until that characteristic claret-stained rawness has disappeared; they should still, however, be pink and moussey within. Stir in the tomato purée and cook, stirring, for a minute or so, then add the Marsala. Let this bubble mostly away, then taste and add salt and a good few grindings of pepper as needed. Turn down the heat and let cook gently for another 10 minutes or so.

Then decant the contents of the pan into a food processor, add the capers and anchovies, and give the merest pulse; you want this chopped but not puréed. (You could always use a knife.) Pour back into the pan with the butter and cook for a few final minutes at gentle heat while you stir. Remove from the heat and let cool before spreading. Sprinkle some more parsley over, once spread.

If you want to use duck livers, forgo the capers and anchovies, but add instead, at the beginning with the celery mixture, the very finely chopped zest of ½–1 orange. And I use Grand Marnier, either in place of the Marsala, or half-and-half, with a spritz of the orange's juice. DUCK LIVERS

PEA AND GARLIC CROSTINI

I warm to the Day-Glo vibrancy of this concoction; just like the future, so bright you gotta wear shades. But it is seriously good: the sweet pungency of the roasted garlic gives resonance and depth; the Parmesan supplies edge and the butter unctuousness. And it's a doddle to make. This amount will give enough for a few extra crostini.

1 head garlic	2 tablespoons freshly grated Parmesan
1 teaspoon olive oil	salt and freshly milled black pepper
8 ounces frozen young peas	1 tablespoon chopped mint
1 tablespoon unsalted butter	

Preheat the oven to 400°F. Lop the top off the head of garlic; you want to see the tops of the cloves just revealed in cross section. Cut a square of foil, large enough to make a baggy parcel around the garlic, sit the garlic in the middle of it, drizzle over the oil, and then make said parcel, twisting the ends slightly. Put in the oven for 50 minutes to an hour, until the garlic is soft.

Cook the peas in boiling salted water as you would normally, only for a fraction longer. Drain and tip into a food processor. Squeeze out the soft, cooked cloves of garlic and add them, then the butter and Parmesan. Process to a nubbly but creamy purée. Season with the salt and pepper and cool before spreading. Sprinkle each crostini with a pinch of the mint.

ROAST PEPPER WITH GREEN OLIVE PASTE CROSTINI

If you find the charring and skinning of the peppers too labor-intensive for the effort-sparing strategy of the drinks-accompanying starter, buy them from a good Italian deli. I spread green olive paste on the toast first and top it with a soft tangle of peppers cut into strips, their skins already burnt off by someone else. If you do want to do your own, you'll need 2 red and 2 yellow peppers; see page 86 for the method. In either case, sprinkle with chopped parsley.

GORGONZOLA WITH MASCARPONE AND MARSALA CROSTINI

Marsala with gorgonzola is a translation of the British tradition of mixing port with Stilton. The nutmeg and mascarpone sweeten and blunt the pungency of the gorgonzola; even those who think they don't like blue cheese find this gratifyingly edible. If you're fed up with Marsala, use white port—my mother always kept a decanter of this in the dining room, and so I have a peculiar nostalgia for it.

This is the easiest crostini topping I can think of. When I make the little toasts, I sometimes anoint them with walnut rather than olive oil.

4 ounces gorgonzola, crumbled	whole nutmeg
⅓ cup mascarpone	1 tablespoon chopped parsley
2 tablespoons Marsala	

Put the gorgonzola in a bowl with the mascarpone and the Marsala and mash together using a fork. Add a good grating or two of fresh nutmeg and stir again. Cover the bowl with plastic film and put in the fridge until you need it, but remember to take it out a good 30 minutes before you do, to make it easier to spread.

Sprinkle each crostini with a pinch of the parsley before serving.

LENTIL AND BLACK OLIVE CROSTINI

This looks good on a plate with the paler gorgonzola crostini, above. The idea is adapted from the glorious recipe for black hummus in *Recipes 1-2-3* by Rozanne Gold and is, in effect, just a purée of cooked puy lentils and bought tapenade with a spoonful of Cognac added. Remember that although it looks suitable for vegetarians, it isn't—the tapenade contains anchovies.

⅓ cup puy lentils

large pinch sea salt, plus more,
    if needed

6 black peppercorns

3 tablespoons tapenade (black olive
    paste)

1 teaspoon Cognac

5 cherry tomatoes, blanched, peeled,
    and diced

1 tablespoon chopped parsley or
    snipped chives

To make the purée, put the lentils in a saucepan with the salt and the peppercorns. Pour over about 2 cups cold water and bring to the boil. When boiling, turn down the heat, cover, and simmer for 35 minutes, or until the lentils are soft. Drain the lentils, reserving ⅓ cup of the cooking liquid. Let cool for 15 minutes.

Then all you do is put the lentils in a food processor with the tapenade and process until fairly smooth, adding 2 tablespoons to ⅓ cup of the reserved cooking liquid, as needed, to make a spreadable (but still nubbly) paste. Remove to a bowl, stir in the Cognac, and leave to cool. Cover and stick in the fridge—for days on end, if you like. You might need to add salt, or it might taste very salty, but don't be alarmed; on the toasts it will all mellow and come together. Spread on the crostini, sprinkle with the tomatoes and parsley or chives, and serve.

MUSHROOMS CROSTINI

Get a mixture of wild and cultivated mushrooms from your local greengrocer or buy a packaged blend from the supermarket. If you want to save time, instead of chopping the garlic you can fry the mushrooms in garlic-infused oil.

2 tablespoons olive oil

1 fat garlic clove, minced

leaves from 2 thyme sprigs, minced, or
    a pinch dried

8 ounces mixed mushrooms, wild and
    cultivated, wiped and minced

scant tablespoon freshly grated
    Parmesan

salt and freshly milled black pepper

1 teaspoon chopped parsley

Pour the olive oil into a pan and, when still cold, add the garlic and thyme. On the heat, cook for about 1 minute, then add the mushrooms, stir and cook until soft and fragrant, and then stir in the Parmesan. Salt and pepper robustly to taste. Put the mixture in a processor to make a coarsely chopped mixture (easier to spread), if you like, but make sure you don't make a purée. Spread while still just warm and sprinkle the crostini with the parsley.

SHRIMP AND EGGPLANT CROSTINI

This is not as fiddly as it might sound, as all you do to the eggplant is bake it (if you're making the garlic and pea crostini, you can roast the garlic for that at the same time), and there aren't enough shrimp to make peeling them a nightmare. The eggplant tempers the heat of the pepper-spiked shrimp and makes them more spreadable. I get the shrimp from the fish seller at my local supermarket.

1 medium eggplant	6 ounces unpeeled shrimp
1 tablespoon olive oil	1 teaspoon chopped coriander or
1 fat garlic clove, minced or sliced finely	Thai basil
1 dried red chili pepper	

Preheat the oven to 400°F.

Put the eggplant into the oven straight on the rack and bake for 1 hour, by which time it should be soft-fleshed and cooked. Remove and leave till cool enough to handle, which won't be long. Put a strainer over a bowl and scrape the flesh of the eggplant into the strainer so that it drains. Let it stand there until it's cool, by which time it should be dry and all the excess liquid should be in the bowl.

Put the oil into a heavy-bottomed frying pan, add the garlic, and crumble in the chili. Sauté for 2 minutes, then throw in the shrimp and stir around the hot pan until the livid gray carapace turns holiday coral—2 minutes and they should be cooked but still tender. Remove from the heat and, as soon as you possibly can, peel the shrimp. Put everything—except the shells—into a processor and pulse to chop; you really need a mini one for such a small amount. Add the eggplant pulp and give another pulse. You need something spreadable but not smooth. Spread the shrimp mixture onto the crostini when you want to eat, and sprinkle with the coriander.

BEANS WRAPPED IN PROSCIUTTO

One doesn't want to wade too deep into canapé land, but I would feel I was doing less than my duty if I didn't faithfully report my other most-relied-upon starter-stand-in: beans wrapped in prosciutto. I saw these little bundles of green beans tied around the middle with Parma ham in an Italian delicatessen and went straight back home and made my own. Top and tail some green beans and cook them in boiling salted water. Remember that the beans need decent cooking, not mere dunking in hot water. Drain them, wait for them to cool, dip them in balsamic vinegar, then cut raggedy thin slices of Parma ham in strips and tie them round the bean-bundles.

You may take it for granted that whatever starter I suggest, you can always whip it away and provide the crostini or the fascist beans—I refer to their bundling only, there's no darker connotation here—in their place. I won't say that again. The following menus and recipes are merely suggestions, ideas for you to work on, ignore, play around with as you like. There's no right answer, nor one way only to organize a dinner, compose the food. But at least being shown one path gives you the freedom to study the terrain and choose another. That choice might often mean not cooking at all, or very little. No one, for example, ever has to make a dessert. I am more than happy to get some perfect creation from the pâtissier, to buy ice cream and good cookies. But the relatively low effort needed to make any sweet thing will be repaid in gratifying disproportion by the pleasure of your guests. I propose only—you dispose or not, as you wish.

My menus, or sketches for menus, often give alternatives, an easier route, or different seasonal choice. The reasons are simple, but important. Sometimes we've got hours in which to cook, sometimes we haven't; it's as simple as that, and I wanted to show how speediness can be accommodated into a menu without ditching the whole thing. I wanted to show, too, why I thought one starter went with the particular main course, and how those principles or sensory judgments remain true even if their application is somewhat different. Thinking aloud seems to me the best way to offer direction, a sort of enthusiastic culinary companionship—without, I hope, being insufferably bossy. If I were in the kitchen with you, or you with me, these are the things we'd be talking about.

I make a distinction between dinners and kitchen suppers, but it is a slim one. At no time will you find me fiddling about with table decorations or doing clever things with the lighting. But there is a difference between a structured plan to bring people together over food and just having the usual suspects round after work. I don't get up at five in the morning to buy bucketloads of flowers from the market (and people do, you know), but I do want things to look beautiful. Cheaper than flowers, and more useful because it doesn't interfere with people's line of vision as they're sitting at table trying to talk to each other, is to use food rather in the manner of a still life. A bowl heaped with lemons or limes will always look beautiful. Eggplants, either those skin-stretched vast glossy ones or the compact, purplish babies, look fabulous. As I've said, I don't like bowls of mixed things, but sometimes I have on the table a plate or low bowl of pomegranates mixed with pale, bark-colored dried figs, their once-red interiors just showing through the split skin, like spiky-toothed gums Crayola-colored an orange-scarlet.

As I am not a vegetarian, I don't ever purposefully arrange a totally meatless and fish-free three-course dinner. And no vegetarian needs tips on meat-free cooking from a committed carnivore like me. But if you want to cater for vegetarians and suchlike, you need to make sure there is food they can eat without designing the dinner around them. I deal with it by having a vegetable starter (which I do often enough, anyway), soup or salad, say, and then I provide the vegetarian with a plate of wild mushrooms cooked with butter (olive oil for vegans) and garlic and thyme while everyone else eats their main course. The advantage is that a thick, dark stew of mushrooms is easy to do while you're getting on with the starter, or before, and can sit in the pan to be reheated when it's needed. And it goes well, without adaptation, with the potatoes and vegetables you'll no doubt be doing anyway. The difficulty with doing vegetarian pasta of some sort is that it sets the eater entirely apart, but with the mushrooms she, or he, has just one different component.

There's no need to make a big song and dance about what you drink with what, but I wanted to offer something good in the way of guidance. Following each menu, then, are brief notes by that distinguished but relaxed Notting Hill wine merchant, John Armit. He begins:

JOHN ARMIT'S WINE RECOMMENDATIONS *In general I have chosen one wine, although you could always choose to have two, say a white with the starter and a red with the main course. Many people would also choose a dessert wine: a muscat or a Sauternes from France, or a sweet German wine.*

WINTER DINNER, WITH SUMMER POSSIBILITIES, FOR 6

CAESAR SALAD

LOIN OF PORK WITH BAY LEAVES AND LENTILS OR CANNELLINI BEANS

RHUBARB IN ICE CREAM, CUSTARD, JELLY, OR TRIFLE

❖

This is perfect in January, when the rhubarb is new, trim-limbed, and Barbie pink; how you cook it, eat it, is up to you. I have tried to limit my suggestions, but not that hard—I want still to urge you rhubarbward. This menu works too in summer, when the rhubarb may be nearer khaki-colored and have slightly more spreading thighs, but will still have that peculiar mixture between delicacy and resonance. In summer I'd cook the pork maybe slightly in advance and leave it to cool for an hour before slicing it thickly and arranging it on a large, oval plate.

CAESAR SALAD

In my years as a restaurant critic I railed against the messed-about Caesar salad. So many chefs want to do their bit—to shave the cheese rather than grate it, so you lose that fabulous leaf-thickening coating, to throw in whole fresh anchovies, to substitute designer lettuce—and every addition is a loss. Perfection cannot be improved upon. And so what am I doing here, replacing the classic garlic croutons with small cubes of garlicky roast potatoes? Well, I do this because this is how it happened. Let me explain.

The first time I made the ceviche (see page 314) for dinner one summer, I thought it might be wonderful with some hot and salty crouton-sized, roast, diced potatoes. Reader: I was not wrong. After that, and because anything that's in the oven gives me less grief than anything ever does on the stove, I took to roasting a small dice of potatoes and using them in place of croutons in salads all the time. I get a freezer bag, put in the potatoes unpeeled but diced, about ½-inch square, maybe slightly smaller sometimes, throw chopped garlic after them and then add 2 tablespoons olive oil. (When I'm in a hurry, I forget the garlic and use garlic-infused oil instead.) I shake the bag about so that the oil disperses and covers all the cubes of potato, empty them onto a baking pan, and then roast them for 45 minutes to 1 hour in a 400°F oven. When they're glistening brown, I lay them on some paper towels and sprinkle with coarse sea salt. Then I chuck them into some dressed, tossed leaves—and, let me tell you, that's all you need.

As I said, a Caesar salad is perfect in its original incarnation, but if you add potatoes in place of the croutons for a first-course Caesar salad, you won't need to bother with potatoes for the main course. So that's one less thing to worry about or find burner or oven space for; lentils or cannellini are both vegetable and filler.

This then is what I call, in my notes, *Caesar, mia*.

If you want to add anchovies—which aren't actually a feature of Caesar Cardini's original version but are so often used they almost count as authentic, and are certainly good in it—just mash one or two up with the olive oil before anointing and tossing the salad.

8 ounces floury or boiling potatoes,
  peeled and diced

2–3 large garlic cloves, to taste, minced

about 6 tablespoons extra-virgin
  olive oil

2 eggs

leaves from 4–6 heads baby romaine
  lettuce or 2–3 heads regular romaine

pinch salt, plus more, if needed

freshly milled black pepper

drops Worcestershire sauce

juice of 1 lemon

⅓ cup freshly grated Parmesan

Make the "croutons" using the potatoes, garlic, and 2 tablespoons of the oil as directed in the headnote. You don't want them to go on the salad when searingly hot, so cool on some paper towels for about 10 minutes.

Put some water on for the eggs, put a matchstick into the pan (this stops the white flowing out if the shell cracks), and then, when boiling, lower in the eggs and boil for exactly 1 minute. Remove and set aside.

Tear the romaine leaves into eatable sizes and toss with the remaining 3–4 tablespoons olive oil to coat well but lightly. Sprinkle over the salt and several grinds of pepper and toss again. Shake over about 6 drops of the Worcestershire sauce, drizzle over the lemon juice, break in the eggs, and toss to blend. Correct the seasoning. Toss with the cheese and then with the potato croutons at the very last minute, as you bring it to the table—no sooner, or the salad will wilt.

LOIN OF PORK WITH BAY LEAVES

If you've got time, leave the pork in its marinade-rub for 12 or even 24 hours. But otherwise, just do the necessary when you get home in the evening. By roasting the pork at 400°F you can accommodate both croutons and meat. You want the loin boned with a very thin layer of fat still on and tied at regular intervals. That's why I go to the butcher. And ask him to chop the bones and give them to you to take home while he's about it.

6 tablespoons extra-virgin olive oil

4 garlic cloves, bruised and crushed with
  the flat side of a knife

1 teaspoon salt

6 peppercorns, bruised

16 bay leaves, 6 crumbled, plus more
  whole leaves, for garnish

1 medium onion, sliced finely

1 4-pound boneless pork loin (see
  headnote)

½ cup white wine

In a small bowl mix the olive oil, garlic, salt, peppercorns, and crumbled bay leaves and rub the mixture all over the meat. Put the pork on a large dish or in a large plastic bag and cover the dish or tie up the bag and leave in the fridge if you've got steeping time; otherwise—if you're about to start cooking it—just leave it out.

Preheat the oven to 400°F. Line a roasting pan with the onion. Strew over the onion 10 whole bay leaves. Place the pork, including its marinade, on top and the bones all around, if they fit and if you've got them. Roast in the oven for about 1¾ hours or to an internal temperature of 150°–155°F, basting regularly.

Remove the pork, scraping burnt bits off, to a plate or carving board and let it sit. On the stove at moderate heat, pour the wine and ½ cup boiling water over the bones, bay, garlic, and onion. Let it bubble up and reduce by about a third, and then remove the bones gingerly and strain the liquid contents into a saucepan. Heat, correct the seasoning, and add liquid as you like to make a good, thin, not-quite gravy.

Carve, put the slices on a big warmed plate, sprinkle with salt, and pour over a little of the juice-gravy, then tent with foil and leave in the turned-off oven while you eat the starter. It is a bit prinky, I know, but it will look fabulous if, when you take it out, you arrange, Napoleonically, some more bay leaves around the edges of the dish with the bay-scented pork.

PUY LENTILS OR CANNELLINI BEANS

Puy lentils or cannellini beans, or indeed any legumes, would do with this. The lentils have the advantage of not needing to be soaked. And I would leave them pretty plain—for 6 people, if it's the only vegetable, just use 1 pound. Cover with abundant water, then bring to the boil, add salt, and simmer for 30–45 minutes. Drain, put the pan back on the heat with some oil (not too much, though; you'll have the meat-juice gravy to pour over later) together with 2 garlic cloves, minced or sliced, and the finely chopped zest of ½ lemon. Turn in the warm oil for a minute or so, then put the lentils back in and toss well, tasting for salt and pepper as usual. Treat soaked beans similarly, only they'll need longer cooking (you won't get arrested for using canned, but I can't pretend they're as good), and I'd omit the lemon zest and add a little more garlic. Sprinkle over some chopped parsley when they're in their serving dish.

Now for the rhubarb. Even in winter, I love this rhubarb ice cream. It's not just the taste—which is delicate-scented perfection—but its very extraordinariness, its almost exotic rarity, which is all the more distinctive for the markedly unexotic nature of its chief ingredient. Now that you can buy so much good ice cream in the shops, it often seems hardly worth making your own, but this one you couldn't buy. If you haven't got an ice-cream maker (not that ice cream is impossible without; see page 254), then make the rhubarb custard. To call this custard an invention would be pushing it, but it is one of my favorite culinary accidents. It came about simply because I was stewing some rhubarb and forgot felt I really had to do something with the ensuing, practically formless pulp, so I stirred it into some eggs, sugar, and milk, poured it into a dish, put that dish in a pan of water, and baked it. The result was ambrosial. And typically, because I'd done this as a last-minute damage-limitation exercise, I hadn't any precise idea of the ratio of rhubarb to the other custard ingredients. I had to do it three more times before I got it to taste as good as it had the first accidental time. Take it out of the oven about 1 hour before you want to eat it. This really does mean you could do with a double oven if you're eating the pork hot. But you could always bake the custard first—it won't really be warm, but it shouldn't be cool, either.

My rhubarb and muscat jelly is, in a different way, a kitchen accident as well. I'd been making some rhubarb fool and ended up with half a measuring cup of excess pink syrup. I decided to make a jelly out of it, and muscat seemed like a good idea (and see below). This, in turn, led to the rhubarb, muscat, and mascarpone trifle (and refer, you must, to page 107). The last of my suggestions here is the rhubarb meringue pie on page 234; but look up rhubarb in the Index if you're up for more.

RHUBARB ICE CREAM

I can't pretend this is the easy option. If you want to make something simple, cook the rhubarb as below, but just stir it into some whipped heavy cream and make fool instead.

If you've got vanilla sugar, then use that; otherwise, you can add a vanilla bean, halved lengthways, to the rhubarb as you cook it, or just stir in best vanilla extract before you freeze the custard mix. And if you're using summer rhubarb, which won't make the perfect blush-pink cream of the early growth, nothing's to stop you adding the merest pin-drop of pink food coloring.

2 pounds rhubarb, trimmed	3 egg yolks
1½ cups vanilla or superfine sugar, plus	1¼ cups heavy cream
¼ cup superfine sugar or more,	1½ teaspoons pure vanilla extract, if not
if needed	using vanilla sugar
1¼ cups light cream	

Preheat the oven to 375°F. Put the rhubarb in a baking dish with the 1½ cups sugar. Cover with foil and bake in the oven for 45 minutes to an hour until utterly soft and cooked. You can cook it on the stove, but the color won't stay as bright. Drain, reserving the juice, and put the pulp in a bowl to cool. Beat well with a fork so it's smooth.

Put the light cream on to boil, but take off the heat just before it does. Pour it over the yolks beaten with the ¼ cup sugar. Half-fill the sink with cold water (this is because you need to stop the custard cooking as soon as it's thickened) and then get on with the custard by putting the cream mixture into a clean saucepan on lowish heat. Stir with a wooden spoon constantly. In about 10 minutes the custard should have thickened (see page 32 if you need more information here). Plunge the pan into the cold water in the sink and carry on stirring energetically for a minute or so. When it's cool, stir in the rhubarb pulp. Then whip the heavy cream and add to the fruit custard. Taste, as you may well need more sugar; add it 1 tablespoon at a time, but remember, when the mixture's frozen, the sweetness will seem reduced. Add the vanilla extract here, too, if you haven't used vanilla sugar.

Freeze in an ice-cream maker, or see page 331.

For some reason this is fabulous with really good dark chocolate cookies, or else those plain discs of dark thin chocolate. As for the reserved rhubarb cooking liquid, add a slug or two of muscat wine (or sugar and water) and boil down till you've got a thick syrup, pour into a small pitcher, and let people dribble it over their ice cream, or freeze it, unreduced, and make jelly with it later. The ice cream is best enjoyed as soon after churning as possible.

RHUBARB CUSTARD

2¼ pounds rhubarb, trimmed and cut
    into 1¼-inch lengths
½ cup sugar
4 eggs
4 egg yolks
½ cup vanilla or superfine sugar plus
    more, if needed

1 vanilla bean or 1 teaspoon pure
    vanilla extract, if not using vanilla
    sugar
2½ cups milk

Put the rhubarb into a large saucepan with ½ cup water and the ½ cup sugar. Put the lid on and bring to the boil. In about 5 minutes you should have pulp. Pour it into a strainer over a bowl or large measuring cup to catch juice, but don't push it through the strainer.

Preheat the oven to 325°F. Put the kettle on. Set an ovenproof dish with a capacity of 7–8 cups (I use one of those oval cream stoneware dishes, the sort that rhubarb custard was just meant to be in) on a baking sheet. In another bowl, beat together with a fork the eggs, egg yolks, and vanilla sugar, if using, or superfine sugar. Taste for sweetness and add more sugar, if needed.

If using the vanilla bean, add it to the milk. Bring the milk to a boil and, beating with a fork, add the milk to the egg mixture. When combined, stir in the vanilla extract, if using, and the well-drained rhubarb. Do this gently; you don't want an homogenous all-rose affair but a pale, yellowing-parchment cream shot through with that gloweringly intense taffeta pink. Pour into the baking dish and pour the hot water around the dish, to come around halfway up.

Bake for 45 minutes to 1 hour or until, when the top is touched, the custard quivers but is not liquid. Remove from the pan of water; the custard will continue to set as it stands in the kitchen waiting to be eaten.

RHUBARB AND MUSCAT JELLY

This is spectacular—it's beautiful when the poached rhubarb, fresh out of the oven, sits in its orange-flecked juices, and just so pretty, when it's set and shining and the sweetest pale fuscia. But because of that color, don't set it in a ring mold—it makes it look slightly gynecological. I use an old-fashioned, bulbously curving castle mould. You can get them now made in plastic, which is easier to unmold than the old copper ones.

When the new season's rhubarb comes in, clementines are available, so I often, in place of the orange called for, just halve a clementine, squeeze in the juice by hand, and then throw in the consequently crushed and pulpy peel. Blood oranges are, however, best. They intensify the already vivid tints.

As for the wine, of course use whichever muscat you like.

2 pounds rhubarb, trimmed and cut into
  ½–1-inch lengths

1⅔ cups superfine sugar, plus more, if
  needed

juice and zest of 1 orange, plus more
  juice, if needed

8 leaves gelatin or 2 envelopes
  granulated gelatin

About ¾ cup muscat wine

Preheat the oven to 375°F.

Put the rhubarb into a large ovenproof dish. I find a rectangular one measuring 12 × 8 × 2 inches perfect for the job. Sprinkle over the sugar, add the orange juice and zest, and 2 cups of water, and cover, either with a lid or with foil. Bake for 1 hour. Take out of the oven, remove lid, and let cool.

Strain carefully into a large measuring cup. I find this gives about 3 cups. Put the pulp aside (you can freeze it for use in the custard or trifle). If using granulated gelatin, soften it in ¼ cup of the muscat, about 5 minutes. Heat the mixture in the top of a double boiler over simmering water until the gelatin has dissolved, about 1 minute, and add to the rhubarb juice. Pour the remaining muscat into the juice to bring it up to 3¾ cups; if not using granulated gelatin, add the muscat as is to the juice to the required measurement. Taste; you may want some more sugar or a squeeze more orange or, indeed, more muscat.

Lightly oil a 4-cup jelly mold by dabbing a paper towel in some suitably flavorless oil and then rubbing it over the interior of the mold. Soak gelatin leaves in a dish of cold water until softened. Put 2 ladlefuls of rhubarb and muscat syrup in a saucepan and bring to a boil. Squeeze out the gelatin leaves and whisk into the syrup. When they've dissolved, pour the contents of the pan back into the measuring cup. If you want to make sure everything's well enough blended, you can pour from the cup to the pan and back into the cup again. Pour into the jelly mold and place in the fridge to chill and set, about 6 hours or overnight.

An Italian red, preferably a 1997 or 1998 Dolcetto d'Alba from Giacomo Conterno or Bruno Giacosa, would be perfect here.

EXTRAVAGANT BUT STILL ELEGANT DINNER FOR 8

HOT SAUSAGES WITH ICE-COLD OYSTERS, OR CEVICHE WITH HOT GARLIC POTATOES

THE TENDEREST CHICKEN, WITH GREEN SALAD AND GARLIC POTATOES

CHOCOLATE RASPBERRY PUDDING CAKE WITH RASPBERRIES AND YOGURT

❖

This is the sort of dinner I dream of, the perfect birthday dinner party for someone who likes oysters and whose birthday (like mine) falls on a suitable date. You can get oysters all the year round now (or some types), but they're still best in winter. Buy an oyster knife at the same time as your oysters, 6 per person. Ask the fish seller for proper instructions as to cleaning (if necessary) and opening. And you'll need either coarse salt or crushed ice to set them on. I used to eat oysters and sausages at chef Alastair Little's first, eponymous restaurant in Frith Street in London. He served the most inspired starter in town—cold, cold oysters with hot, spicy Chinesey sausages.

My way is to get cocktail sausages from my butcher and then roll them in a roasting pan in chili oil to spice. (You can also "make" cocktail sausages by twisting thin-diameter regular sausages to divide them into smaller links.) If the chili oil isn't ferociously hot, add some drops of Tabasco. Cook them for about 35 minutes in a 350°F oven. Fabulous. But don't forget finger bowls. Cooking them in the oven is the easiest way, but if that creates problems with the chicken, cook the sausages in a frying pan on the stove.

If you balk at oysters, replace this course with something that strikes some of the same notes, such as ceviche, in which the cold, soft flesh of the fish is offset by some searingly hot and salty crouton-sized cubes of garlicky roast potatoes. If you're making this potato-spiked ceviche, you will have to miss out the potatoes with the chicken.

CEVICHE WITH HOT GARLIC POTATOES

Ceviche—fish that is "cooked" by the acids of a citrus marinade—is about as effortless as you can get. Often, the fish is served with avocado, but I feel that the texture somehow is both too samey and too squashy. I prefer it like this.

The recipe lists turbot, scallops, and salmon, but you could use a cheaper combination of fish if you wanted, substituting brill, sole, or flounder for the turbot if, in any case, the latter is unavailable. You must, anyway, get the fish from a fish seller rather than a supermarket, and explain that you will be eating it raw. The fish seller will tell you which fish are fresh enough and suitable. And don't be put off by the idea of raw fish; it does actually taste—and look—cooked by the marinade.

¼ **pound very fresh salmon, cut into**
   ½ × 1½-inch strips
½ **pound very fresh turbot, brill, sole, or**
   flounder, cut into ½ × 1½-inch strips
4 **sea scallops, each cut into 3 discs**
juice of 3 limes
juice of 2½ lemons
juice of 1 orange
1 **tablespoon plus 1 teaspoon balsamic**
   vinegar
¾ **pound new potatoes, cut into**
   large dice

3 **tablespoons olive oil or 1 tablespoon**
   olive oil and 2 tablespoons garlic-
   infused oil
3 **garlic cloves, if not using the garlic-**
   infused oil, peeled and smashed
   or minced
1 **bunch watercress**
salt
3–4 **tablespoons chopped coriander,**
   for garnish

Put the fish and scallops in a large dish, cover with the citrus juices and balsamic vinegar, and leave in the fridge for 6 hours. Preheat the oven to 400°F. Put the potatoes in a plastic bag with 2 tablespoons of the olive oil and the garlic, or the garlic-infused oil only. Transfer to a roasting pan and bake for about 40 minutes, or until the potatoes are brown and crisp.

While the potatoes are cooking, put the watercress on a large plate, and take the seafood out of its marinade and arrange it on top. Take out 3 tablespoons of the marinade, put in a cup, and stir in the 1 tablespoon olive oil and make a dressing (add more oil if you like) to pour over the creviche and watercress. At the last minute, sprinkle some salt on the potatoes and toss them over the watercress and among the seafood. Sprinkle the coriander on top.

THE TENDEREST CHICKEN

The title tells no lie. The buttermilk marinade stops the flesh from drying and turning stringy, even after it has been blitzed in a hot oven. Although I would advise getting a proper free-range chicken, this method will work miracles on inferior supermarket birds. Incidentally, despite its name, buttermilk is very low in fat, which makes it useful if you want to keep a skinless portion (for virtuous reasons) as moist as possible.

I quart buttermilk

10 garlic cloves, minced

2 tablespoons Dijon mustard

1 tablespoon soy sauce

2 large chickens, about 4 pounds each,
    each cut into 8 pieces

3 tablespoons unsalted butter, melted

3 tablespoons olive oil

salt and freshly milled black pepper

Pour the buttermilk into a large bowl and stir in the garlic, mustard, and soy sauce. (You may find this easier to do in 2 batches in separate dishes.) Add the chicken pieces, turning to cover, and then pour the entire contents into 2 plastic bags and tie with elastic bands. Leave in the fridge for at least 8 hours.

Remove the chicken from the marinade and wipe totally dry with paper towels. Preheat the oven to 425°F. Combine the butter and olive oil; season with salt and pepper. Arrange the chicken, skin side up, in 2 oiled baking dishes, brush over with the butter mixture, and bake. It's difficult to say exactly how long it will take; evidently it depends on the size of the chicken. Poke and test. I tend to give the dark meat portions 30–40 minutes, breasts 20–25. Either take the breasts out first and keep them warm, or put the thighs and legs in 10 or so minutes before the breasts.

GARLIC
POTATOES

The chicken can be kept warm, but the potatoes most definitely cannot wait; they must stay in the oven till the very last minute, so put them in the oven 35 minutes before you plan to eat the starter. For 8 people, I'd get 8 decent-sized (about 8-ounce) baking potatoes, and leave them unpeeled but cut into square chunks of about 1 inch. Get 2 heads garlic and throw the cloves, separated but unpeeled (or use garlic-infused oil), with the potatoes into a roasting pan. Slick the potatoes and garlic with oil and cook at 425°F for about 45 minutes. When you take them out of the oven, sprinkle with coarse sea salt and fresh chopped parsley.

As for the green salad, go for one with plenty of crunch and absolutely no GREEN SALAD garlic in the dressing. And I'm presuming you've had bread on the table since the first course, so we needn't even mention it now.

Now, for dessert. First, the logistics. You want this warm, not hot, so you can cook it before putting the chicken in, taking it out in time to allow the oven to get hotter for the poultry. The sausages can go into the oven with the dessert at 350°F, but for 10–15 minutes longer than if they're cooked at 400°F. Reheat them on the stove and they'll brown up in the pan then.

CHOCOLATE RASPBERRY PUDDING CAKE

I call this a pudding cake because its texture is simply a mixture between pudding and cake, though lighter by far than that could ever imply. Think, rather, of a mousse without fluffiness; this is dense but delicate. And it's heavenly tepid, when the cakiness of the chocolate sits warmly around the sour-sweet juicy raspberries embedded within, like glinting, mud-covered garnets. This should be eaten an hour or so after it comes out of the oven. It gets more solid when cold, and loses some of that spectacular texture. If you have any left, wrap it in foil and heat it up in the oven, or warm it up a slice at a time in the microwave before eating it.

Use fresh raspberries or well-thawed frozen ones, adding more if frozen. But the cake works unfruited, too. Just replace the raspberry liqueur with a tablespoon or so of dark rum and serve with coffee ice cream.

This is so easy to make (a little light stirring, that's all) that it's almost more work to type out the instructions than to make the cake itself. Serve it with lots more fresh raspberries, and yogurt, whipped heavy cream, or crème fraîche.

1½ cups all-purpose flour
1½ teaspoon baking powder
pinch salt
⅓ cup best-quality unsweetened cocoa
   powder
8 tablespoons (1 stick) unsalted butter
1 tablespoon framboise
½ cup superfine sugar
½ cup light muscovado sugar or light
   brown sugar

8 ounces best-quality bittersweet
   chocolate
¾ cup black coffee and ¾ cup water, or
   instant coffee made up with
   2 teaspoons instant coffee and
   1½ cups boiling water
2 eggs, beaten slightly
8 ounces raspberries plus more,
   for serving
confectioners' sugar, for dusting

Preheat oven to 350°F.

Butter an 8-inch springform pan and line the base with baking parchment. Sift the flour, baking powder, salt, and cocoa powder together in a bowl and set aside. Put the butter, framboise, sugars, chocolate, and coffee with water in a heavy-bottomed saucepan and stir over low heat until everything melts and is thickly, glossily smooth.

Stir this mixture into the sifted flour and cocoa. Beat well until all is smooth and glossy again, then beat in the eggs. This will be runny—don't panic, and don't add more flour; the chocolate itself sets as it cooks and then cools.

Pour into the prepared pan until you have covered the base with about an inch of the mixture, and then cover with raspberries and pour the rest of the mixture on top. You may have to push some of the raspberries back under the cake batter by hand. Bake for 45–50 minutes, until the top is firm and probably slightly cracked; don't try to test by poking in a skewer as you don't want it to come out clean—the gunge is what the cake is about. When it's ready, take the cake out of the oven and put on a rack. Leave in the pan for 15 minutes and then turn out.

When you're just about to eat, dust the cake with the confectioners' sugar tapped through a strainer. Serve with the additional berries, piled in a bowl.

Sancerre, the perfect wine with oysters, will not be overawed by the spicy sausages; a good Bordeaux has the harmony and complexity to suit the garlic and buttermilk-marinated chicken.

TARTED-UP HOMEY DINNER FOR 6

ENDIVE AND MUSTARD SALAD

HAM WITH PEA ORZOTTO AND ROAST LEEKS

POACHED PISTACHIO-SPRINKLED APRICOTS STUFFED
WITH CRÈME FRAÎCHE

One of the reasons I love this menu is for its central side dish, if this is not a contradiction in terms. The pea orzotto is a kind of barley risotto or stew, only this is better, sharper, smarter. Because pearl barley has less gluten than rice, it doesn't get sticky if it stands around after it's been cooked. It's true that the actual stirring and whole process of the absorption of the stock to make a risotto takes longer with pearl barley than with rice, but an extra fifteen minutes' effort in advance is nothing compared to the hell of having to get everything ready from scratch at the last minute.

But another reason I'm keen on this menu is that it shows how by changing the details you can change the whole; with boiled potatoes and carrots, the ham in cider is a not particularly partyish weekend lunch (which, indeed, is where you'll see the recipe; turn to page 212, only lose some of the veg); with the orzotto and oven-charred leeks, the endive salad and the pistachio-sprinkled apricots, it is dinner-party food that knows not from trinked up and tweaked. The ham takes some time to cook, so you've either got to get home from work early or do it on the weekend.

The endive salad is just the right starter; the salt-sweetness of the ham, peas, and barley needs the near-wincing astringency of those sword-sharp leaves; the soft-bellied tenderness of the poached dried fruit and its Arabian Nights aromatic muskiness complement and elevate what's gone before.

ENDIVE AND MUSTARD SALAD

I tablespoon sherry or cider vinegar	6 tablespoons extra-virgin olive oil
I scant tablespoon Dijon mustard	leaves from 6 small or 4 large heads
large pinch salt	Belgian endive
2 tablespoons crème fraîche	

To make the dressing, use a fork to whisk the vinegar, mustard, salt, and crème fraîche together in a little bowl and, whisking still, very slowly pour in the olive oil so that you have a smooth, thick, emulsified dressing. I like this with punch. You may prefer a different balance. Divide the leaves among 6 plates and pour over the dressing.

PEA ORZOTTO

You can very well use crème fraîche for this instead of the heavy cream specified, as you need crème fraîche anyway for the dessert, below, and the salad dressing, above. Though in which case, use a little bit more cheese. If you have no home-made stock, use best-quality commercial stock or bouillon cubes.

about 2 quarts chicken or vegetable stock	I 10-ounce package frozen young peas, thawed
6 tablespoons (¾ stick) unsalted butter	salt
drop oil	¼–½ cup heavy cream or crème fraîche, plus more, if desired
I medium onion, minced	2 tablespoons freshly grated Parmesan
I¼ cups pearl barley	
½ cup white wine or vermouth	

Heat the stock in a saucepan and keep it just simmering.

Melt 2 tablespoons of the butter, with the drop of oil to stop it burning, in a large, heavy pan. Put in the onion and fry for 5–7 minutes or until it is soft but not brown. Then add the pearl barley and stir well, for about I minute, until the grains are coated and glossy with fat. Pour in the wine and let it bubble and reduce, and become absorbed into the onion and barley mixture.

Add a ladleful of the hot stock and, stirring, wait for it to be absorbed. Then add another ladleful, and so on until the stock is all absorbed and the barley cooked al dente. After the first 10 minutes or so you can add a couple of ladlefuls at a time and you needn't be quite as diligent as earlier about stirring, but don't walk away from the pan. This process will take 35–45 minutes. You can leave it now and come back and finish the dish off *à la minute.* If you are leaving the orzotto for only an hour or so, then leave it in its pan, adding just a film of stock or hot water so that it doesn't dry out. If you are leaving it for longer (and I have successfully made it a couple of days in advance), you must decant it into a wide dish so that it will cool quickly and not carry on cooking. Cover and put to one side.

Now for the final touch; sauté 1 cup of the peas in 2 tablespoons of the butter for 2 minutes or until just cooked but still sweet, firm, and pea-like. Put aside and sprinkle with a little salt. Sauté the remaining peas in the remaining butter, this time for 4–5 minutes. Add a ladleful of stock, let it reduce, and then purée the peas in a blender. Just before serving, heat up the orzotto and stir in the whole peas, the puréed peas, the cream to taste, and the Parmesan. (If you were eating this without the ham, you should probably triple the amount of cheese.) Let stand, loosely covered, for 5–10 minutes (you could eat the starter while it's resting), as this somehow lets the textures and flavors more exuberantly and exquisitely cohere.

If you want to create your own orzotti, use this recipe as a guide or follow any risotto recipe, remembering that barley takes longer to cook, requires more stock, and has to have cream for the final stirring or *mantecatura.* (I particularly recommend making a saffron orzotto in place of the usual risotto Milanese to accompany osso buco.)

ROAST LEEKS

As for the leeks: preheat the oven to 450°F and pour some good olive oil into a couple of roasting pans. I figure on 1 medium, fairly trim leek, well cleaned and dried, per person, based on the supposition that each one gives you 3–4 segments. Roll the leeks in the oil, sprinkle with coarse salt, and bake them about 25 minutes all told, turning them once. Obviously, if they're those huge fat ones, add about 10 minutes. When done, they should be bronze and glistening, and burnt in places. Remove to a plate and sprinkle with a little more coarse salt. They'll keep the heat well, so if it makes it easier to take them out of the oven when you eat the salad, do so.

POACHED PISTACHIO-
SPRINKLED APRICOTS STUFFED WITH
CRÈME FRAÎCHE

This recipe comes via *The Cooking of the Eastern Mediterranean* by Paula Wolfert (she of the food of southwest France and Morocco). This is another dish you need to start preparing in advance, but as the very fact of a dinner party suggests planning (unless you're calling friends at the last minute, in which case we're talking about a slightly different thing), this is an advantage, surely.

Paula Wolfert suggests a mix of mascarpone and heavy cream as the best imitation of kaymak, the thick Turkish buffalo-milk cream properly used to stuff the apricots, but I prefer crème fraîche, which is lighter and less cloying. You could also use full-fat yogurt.

10 ounces good dried apricots,
    preferably Turkish

⅓ cup sugar

seeds from 6 crushed cardamom pods

2 scant teaspoons lemon juice

1 cup crème fraîche

4 ounces shelled pistachios, chopped
    very finely or ground using a pestle
    and mortar

Soak the apricots in 2½ cups of water overnight.

Next day, preheat the oven to 300°F and put in it a nonreactive ovenproof baking dish large enough to hold the apricots later. Pour the apricot-soaking liquid into a saucepan and add the sugar, cardamom seeds, and lemon juice and bring to the boil. Add the apricots and then pour them and their liquid into the heated baking dish. Cover with foil and cook for 1½ hours. Remove from the oven and let the apricots cool in the syrup. Chill well.

Before you want to serve them (and I have done this a good half-day before to no deleterious effect), lift out the apricots to drain. Carefully open each one and stuff with 1 teaspoon crème fraîche. Place on a flat plate or serving dish, spoon over some syrup, and dust with the pistachios. It is this final touch that makes all the difference, so don't be tempted to leave it out. And don't, either, serve this straight from the fridge; too-cold food kills the taste and the whole pleasure of it.

This is one of those desserts that is so simple that it almost cannot help but become an instantly reassuring part of your kitchen repertoire.

A Barbera from a great Italian grower, such as Angelo Gaja, will be ideal with the mustard, the ham, and the peas.

EARLY AUTUMN DINNER FOR 6

GUACAMOLE WITH PAPRIKA-TOASTED POTATO SKINS

COD WRAPPED IN HAM, WITH MASHED POTATOES AND
SAGE AND ONION LENTILS

HAZELNUT CAKE, WITH RED CURRANT AND PEACH SALAD

This is the sort of food I want to eat when I'm holding onto summer, despite the sad, gray-skied truth of the actual weather on the streets. These are the strong flavors of hotter climates—lime, chilies, coriander, the honeyed saltiness of cured ham—banked down, with mashed potatoes, cod, buttery sage, for northern palates. After this starter, the culinary equivalent of a mariachi band, you need to strike some calmer notes, and the unexotic fish, potatoes, and sage-and-onion-spiked lentils do exactly that.

Dessert is another version of cake with berries; here the hazelnut, almost meringuey, sponge and the sharpness of the red currants and peaches provide a foil to the dominant tastes beforehand. When red currants aren't around or available, or the only peaches you can get are stone-hard and green-tasting, substitute whichever fruits you want, but think of something, even if it's just a thawed package of frozen mixed fruits; the cake wouldn't work, here, just on its own.

In most instances I provide a couple of portions extra—6 pieces of chicken, say, for 4 people—so there's never an emptied serving plate after the food's been doled out. Here, I don't—the guacamole before is more filling than most starters, and there are two carbohydrates to go with. Speaking of one of them, I love the potato skins with the guacamole, and they can scarcely be thought of as difficult to make in what is anyway a very uncomplicated culinary exercise. To make the skins, you bake the whole potatoes first, remove and reserve the pulp, season, and return the skins to the oven to heat and crisp slightly. This makes life easier for the second course—you already have your potato pulp ready-cooked and more or less mashed, and you've had no peeling to do earlier. You could, however, dispense with the potatoes and provide tortilla chips instead, in which case just do more lentils and add a lower-effect second vegetable.

But read through all the recipes that make up this menu and you will see that this is actually a very low-effort enterprise. As long as you've got some gadget that whisks the egg whites for the cake, you can handle this dinner after getting home, late and tired, from the office. Just remember, of course, to get started on the cake and put the red currants to steep as soon as you get in.

GUACAMOLE

This guacamole doesn't include the tomatoes you sometimes find in it. It makes such a difference—it's fresh and sharp, but instead of the usual mush, you end up with a perfect buttery-yellow and jade clay.

The quantities I give are restrained. That's not to say that the portions are stingy, but that people will eat as much as you make, and you must leave room for later.

Although it's eaten first, and you can do some chopping in advance, the actual avocado mixture must be made at the last minute.

3 ripe avocados	½–1 fresh green chili, or to taste,
scant teaspoon salt	minced
juice of 3–4 limes, to taste	4 scallions (white and green parts),
4 tablespoons fresh coriander, chopped	sliced finely

Get everything, bar the avocados, prepped when you get home.

Just before you want to eat, peel and stone the avocados and put the flesh in a bowl. Don't worry about how you do it and how pulpy you make the avocado, as it will be mashed. Dissolve the salt in the lime juice and pour it over. Then add the other ingredients and mash with a fork until you have a rough lumpy mixture. At all costs avoid turning it into a smooth purée; by its nature the avocado will be smooth anyway, but you want as many soft but form-holding clumps as possible.

PAPRIKA-TOASTED POTATO SKINS
AND THEIR MASHED PULP

9 medium baking potatoes	freshly milled black pepper
1¼ cups milk, warmed	whole nutmeg
4 tablespoons (½ stick) unsalted butter	1 heaping teaspoon paprika
or more, if desired	4 teaspoons olive oil, plus more,
1 heaping teaspoon fine sea salt, plus	if needed
more	

Bake the potatoes for 1–1¼ hours in a 400°F oven or until the skins are crisp and the flesh soft. Take them out of the oven, but leave the oven on.

Halve the potatoes lengthways and, with a spoon, scoop out the innards into a bowl, leaving a thin layer lining the skins. When all the potatoes have been emptied into the bowl, mash with the milk, the butter (add more, if you like, or less, for that matter), salt, pepper, and freshly ground nutmeg to taste. Put aside to reheat later (don't put the potatoes in the fridge; just leave the bowl, covered, in a cool place) and get on with the skins.

Halve the skins again perpendicularly to your work surface, so you have 4 long "boats" per potato. Mix the paprika with the heaping teaspoon of salt. Pour the olive oil into a bowl. With a pastry brush, dab the skins on both sides lightly with oil (use more if needed) and then sprinkle the salt mixture over the interior of the skins. Put in the oven and bake for another 12–15 minutes. Remove to a wire rack and, when cool, arrange on a couple of plates. These taste just right with the coriander-heady, mouth-filling creaminess of the guacamole. Serve the mashed potatoes, reheated in a double boiler, with the cod.

COD WRAPPED IN HAM

Get a few extra slices of prosciutto for patching up, if necessary, the ham-wrapped packages. You can get all your parceling-up done and then leave the wrapped cod in the fridge. But you don't want the fish sitting around once it is cooked, so I'd put it in the oven as you sit down to eat the first course.

6 cod fillets, about 8 ounces each

6 tablespoons (¾ stick) unsalted butter, melted

8 slices prosciutto, preferably prosciutto di Parma, or other cured ham, sliced thinly

Preheat the oven to 400°F. Get out a couple of baking sheets, preferably nonstick. Brush the pieces of cod with the melted butter, wrap with ham, and then brush with butter again. (If you're doing this part in advance, leave the final buttering till just before you bake the fish.) Put in the oven and bake for 15 minutes or until, if you peek beneath the cod's ham jacket, the fish appears opaque. Remove and place on top of the lentils.

SAGE AND ONION LENTILS

1 pound puy lentils

5 garlic cloves, peeled, 2 minced

2 medium onions, plus 1 large onion, minced

12 sage leaves, 6 whole, 6 cut into thin strips, plus more strips, if desired

1 celery stalk, halved, or 2 sprigs lovage

1 heaping teaspoon salt, plus more, if desired

6 tablespoons extra-virgin olive oil, plus more, if desired

scant ½ teaspoon prepared English mustard

freshly milled black pepper, if desired

lemon juice, if desired

Put the lentils in a large saucepan; add the whole garlic cloves, the 2 medium onions, the 6 whole sage leaves, and the celery or lovage. Cover generously with cold water and bring to the boil. When it starts boiling, add the salt and then lower the heat to a firm simmer and let cook for 35–40 minutes, or until the lentils are just cooked. You want some texture to remain, so don't overcook. Drain, and taste the lentils while they're in the colander. If you think they need it, add more salt then and there, but remember that the ham is salty.

Put the pan back on the heat, add the olive oil, and, when hot, throw in the minced onion and the remaining sage leaves. Cook for 5–10 minutes (it will depend, among other things, on the diameter of your pan) until the onion has lost its rawness and then some. Stir in the minced garlic and cook for another minute or so. Add the mustard, then put the cooked lentils back. Turn the lentils well in the sage and onion mixture. Taste to see if you want to add anything else—more salt, more sage, more oil, or some pepper or lemon juice. Leave in the pan until you're ready to eat them, and then turn the lentils onto a large, warmed plate and place the cooked cod on top. This looks wonderful—the pebbly, oil-wet khaki-blackness of the lentils like a cobbled street underneath the cat's-tongue-pink slabs of ham-wrapped fish.

HAZELNUT CAKE

This cake happens to be a brilliant way to use up freezer-stored egg whites. It looks wonderful—a toasty, speckled brown, bulging-sided disc. And it tastes extraordinary: a nutty, tender sponge, with the almost-stickiness of meringue and the aromatic dampness of marzipan. The amount below will probably give you leftovers, but the cake stays all-too-eatable.

2 cups hazelnuts, toasted and skins removed	½ teaspoon salt
	grated zest 1 lemon or ½ orange
1½ cups superfine sugar	⅔ cup Italian 00 or all-purpose flour
8 large egg whites	

Preheat the oven to 350°F. Butter a 9-inch springform pan, and line the bottom with a disc of parchment.

Grind the nuts and sugar together in a food processor. Whisk the egg whites with the salt until you have stiff peaks; if you have a mixer to do this, so much the better. Fold in the sugar-nut mixture, to which you've added the lemon or orange zest, gradually and gently. Don't get too nervous about this, though—I once tipped about half the bowl in at once and then folded it in far too vigorously, and although the cake was a mite flatter than it might have been, it was still fabulous. Anyone eating who hadn't seen my characteristic act of clumsiness wouldn't have known anything was other than it should be.

When the sugar, nuts, and zest are incorporated into the cloudy mountain of egg whites, sift over the flour. What I do is put the flour into a strainer that I hold over the bowl, giving the strainer a tap every now and again, folding in as I do so.

Pour this mixture into the prepared pan and put it in the preheated oven for 1 hour or until a fine skewer comes out clean. Take the cake out of the oven and let cool in the pan for about 10 minutes, then release the springlock and remove to a wire rack to cool.

RED CURRANT AND PEACH SALAD

I had the idea of making a red currant salad, if that's what we're calling it, to go with the hazelnut cake, out of some vague not-quite-memory of ribiselkuchen, that Austrian pudding cake made of hazelnut-meringue sponge and red currants; there seems to be some special affinity between these nuts, this fruit. The peaches or nectarines used here lend a fleshy mellowness to balance and sweeten, which is needed, as the currants are, even with the sugar, undeniably sharp. Even though you're going to be pouring mountains of sugar over the red currants, you don't actually eat all the syrup it makes. Or not at this sitting. For I can't bring myself to throw this away, but boil it down after and use it to glaze other fruits in open tarts, or to flavor apples in an otherwise plain two-crust pie or—much easier this—to pour over some vanilla ice cream sprinkled with a fresh lot of hazelnuts, this time roughly chopped.

It's easy to be strict about quantities for baking, but I cannot quite bring myself to sound anything but vague when it comes to what you do to make a fruit salad, especially such a simple, two-fruit arrangement. But let me just say that for 6 people, I'd think along the lines of 3 pint baskets red currants and 3 peaches or nectarines. Remember, this is to be eaten with cake. Put the stemmed currants into a dish and pour ½ cup superfine sugar and the juice of an orange over them; in another hour do the same, and an hour later the same again, so that in total you've used 1½ cups sugar and 3 oranges, though taste as you go along to make sure you need the extra sugar. Turn the currants in the sugary juices every now and again—whenever you think about it. I think these are at their best—sticky, shiny, scarlet jewels, still sharp enough once you bite, but not so sharp that you wince—after 3½–4 hours' sitting time, but we're not talking precision timing here. It's fine if you start when you get in; just turn the currants in their syrup more often.

Before you sit down to dinner, put a kettle on to boil and the peaches or nectarines in a bowl, then pour the boiling water over them. Leave for a few minutes, then drain and peel. Or leave them with their skins on. Cut each fruit into about 8 fine slices. Drain the currants and put on a big plate and add the peaches as pleases you. Dribble over the now coral-red sugary orange juices, tasting first to make sure they're as you like them. Leave until the end of dinner, when the fruit can join forces on the table with the cake. I serve no cream of whatever sort; it would taste all wrong with this particular cake. Besides, we're looking for a little uplift here.

A Rhone red, such as a Gigondas or Chateauneuf du Pape—something powerful, ripe, and opulent—will suit the ham and lentils, or a Pinot Noir from Oregon, such as Ponzi.

DEEPLY AUTUMNAL DINNER FOR 8

CHESTNUT AND PANCETTA SALAD

ROAST VENISON FILLET WITH APPLE PURÉE AND ROSEMARY SAUCE

PEAS AND CELERIAC MASH

QUINCES POACHED IN MUSCAT WITH LEMON ICE CREAM

MARSALA MUSCOVADO CUSTARD WITH OR WITHOUT MUSKILY SPICED PRUNES

❖

I don't think one needs to be putting on a theme park of the seasons quite, but autumn is a hard one to resist. One can get a little too taken with all those mists and mellow fruitfulness, become a little too parodically bosky and lost in shades of prune and plum, but this menu seems to me to stop just this side of all that. The chestnuts are coming into season (even if I do recommend the canned or bottled peeled ones) and, although venison is available all the year around now, it still feels autumnal, especially when paired with another seasonal—apples. And we have such a short time to take a stab at quinces, we may as well exploit it as we can. For those who don't feel up to tackling this once commonly eaten, now almost exotically unfamiliar fruit, I suggest an eggy and creamy baked custard, buff-colored with Marsala and fudgy muscovado sugar. And if that's too much to ask, then all you need to do is provide cheese (gorgonzola, Roquefort, or Stilton and maybe something blander for those who don't know a good thing when they taste one) and a gorgeous plate of grapes, preferably those ambrosial fat and sepia-tinged muscat grapes, if you can get them.

CHESTNUT AND PANCETTA SALAD

I got the idea for this from two independently wonderful chestnut and pancetta soups I had, within a few weeks of one another, at the restaurant Moro and the River Café in London; these two ingredients seem to do something to one another when put together; they become more themselves—one salty, the other sweet—at the same time as fusing into something greater, transformed. This salad lets them do whatever it is they do even more baldly; there's not just the contrast between salt and sweet, but between crisp and almost fudgily dense. But despite these rich textures and strong flavors, this manages to be a light, unclogging starter. I think the trick is to resist the temptation to boost the quantities of its main ingredients.

Use a slightly bitter leaf, such as escarole, though if that's not to be found, frisée will be fine, and make sure you get good, proper Spanish sherry vinegar; otherwise you just get acidity, not intensity.

I'm not stopping you from buying, peeling, and preparing your own chestnuts (in which case double the quantities here), but I use those canned peeled and cooked whole chestnuts, which are available at many supermarkets.

1½ heads escarole	2 cups canned whole chestnuts
¼ cup plus 2 teaspoons extra-virgin olive oil	1 teaspoon Dijon mustard
	1 teaspoon sherry vinegar
8 ounce pancetta, cut into fine dice or thin strips	

Tear the escarole into manageable pieces and cover 2 large plates—mine are about 12 inches in diameter—with them. Put the 2 teaspoons oil in a frying pan and place on the heat. Toss the pancetta into the pan; in about 4 minutes it should have given off a lot of its fat and become crisp and dark golden in bits. Add the chestnuts and toss them in the hot fat with the pancetta. Don't worry about these breaking, as inevitably they will. I actually prefer it if the chestnuts are slightly rubbly. When they are warmed through, a matter of a minute or so, remove them and the pancetta with a spatula or slotted spoon to the escarole-lined plates. Stir the mustard into the remaining olive oil and, off the heat, stir this into the bacony fat. Mix well and keep stirring and scraping as you add the sherry vinegar. Pour this over the salad, toss deftly, and serve.

ROAST VENISON FILLET

This venison dish has a mixed provenance, as most things do in the kitchen, but its chief inspiration is the recipe for saddle of roedeer, a small, agile Old World deer, from Inverlochy Castle in Fort William, Scotland, to be found in *The Gourmet Tour of Great Britain and Ireland* by Sir Clement Freud.

I know it might look fussy, but you can make the rosemary sauce part-way in advance, and the applesauce wholly in advance, so all you need to do on the night is cook the venison and reheat the sauces, adding juices from the marinade and the roasting pan to the rosemary sauce.

1 bottle full-bodied red wine

1 celery stalk, diced

1 medium carrot, peeled and roughly
chopped

1 medium onion, peeled and roughly
chopped

3 juniper berries, crushed

12 black peppercorns

2 sprigs thyme, or ½ teaspoon dried

2 bay leaves

---

2 trimmed venison fillets (about
1 pound each), from the tenderloin

FOR THE SAUCE

3 cups beef stock

1 medium carrot, peeled and coarsely
chopped

1 leek (white part only), coarsely
chopped

2 shallots, coarsely chopped

1 celery stalk, coarsely chopped

2 cups red wine

8 rosemary sprigs

salt and freshly milled black pepper,
if needed

3 tablespoons unsalted butter, cold and
cut into cubes

FOR THE APPLESAUCE

3 tablespoons unsalted butter

3 cooking apples, peeled, cored, and
chunked or sliced

½ cup sugar, plus more, if needed

pinch salt

3 cloves

juice of ½ lemon, plus more,
if needed

---

1 tablespoon unsalted butter

1 teaspoon olive oil

Heat the ingredients for the marinade in a saucepan. When it comes to the boil, remove from the heat and let cool. Marinate the venison fillets in this for 24 hours, preferably in a cool place, or else in the fridge.

To make the rosemary sauce, put the stock in a saucepan with the chopped vegetables, bring to the boil, and then cook furiously until reduced by half. Add the wine and rosemary and reduce to about 1 cup. If you're doing this in advance, you can cook it till this point, reheating and resuming from here on the night. Add 8 tablespoons of the marinade and reduce, again, to 1 cup. Strain into a clean saucepan and, when about to serve, put back on the stove, taste, and season with the salt and pepper, if needed. Beat in the butter, 1 cube at a time, to make the sauce smooth and glossy.

To make the applesauce, put all the ingredients in a heavy-bottomed saucepan. Cover and cook over medium heat for 10–15 minutes or until the apples are a soft, collapsed heap. Lift the lid every now and again to prod and stop from sticking. Pass the apple mixture through a fine strainer, tasting to see whether you need more sugar or lemon juice, and reserve till needed. If it's too runny, boil down; if too stiff, add butter and liquid.

To cook the meat, preheat the oven to 450°F. On the stove, in a heavy frying pan that will go in the oven, melt the butter and oil and sear the fillets on all sides. Transfer to the hot oven and roast for 20–30 minutes. The venison should be browny-puce within (the game equivalent of *à point* pink), but not imperial purple.

Remove the venison to a warmed plate or carving board and wrap or tent it loosely with foil to keep warm. If you want, add the juices from the pan to the rosemary sauce. Before you carve the fillets, pour into the gravy, as well, the juices that have run out of them onto the board as they wait.

I would carve the fillets into slices and arrange on 1 or 2 oval plates, so people can take what they like, and hand the sauce round separately, having ladled a little over the soft, sliced meat first. Depending on its provenance, the meat can be intense; taste and, if this is so, offer 2 to 3 slices, even if they're small ones, initially (you know how I am about portion sizes generally, so you know you can trust me here). The same goes for the sauce—only a little is needed; too much would ruin the balance as well as finish the sauce up too soon.

Despite the sweetness of the meat, it seems that it's sweetness, again, you look for in the vegetables. Frozen young peas come into this category and they rupture the mood of autumnal color coordination, which can't be a bad thing.

And with the peas, I want potatoes, mashed with their own weight of celeriac, lots of butter, plenty of nutmeg. For 8 people who eat rather than pick at food, you should think along the lines of 2 pounds of both potatoes and celeriac. Celeriac is no fun to peel, but plenty of fun to eat; suffer in smug silence—your reward comes later.

PEAS AND
CELERIAC
MASH

QUINCES POACHED IN MUSCAT

I'll poach anything in muscat wine, given the chance, but this mixture of honey-sweet wine and fruit from, and perhaps not just metaphorically, the garden of Eden is more than mere culinary opportunism. It is gloriously, impeccably right.

I poach the quinces in the oven rather than on the stove, because it is easier to control the heat this way, and thus to keep the fruit poaching so gently that they keep their form and the liquid its almost ruby clarity. For, as the quinces cook, they become a grainy, glorious burnished terra-cotta and the wine in which they steep also grows rosier. If you can get hold of some of that Greek red dessert wine, then do; the fruits and their syrup will glow.

The only hard bit is the preparation of the quinces, and when I say hard, I mean strenuous rather than labor-intensive. These fruits are rock-hard, and coring and quartering takes strength. But you do nothing to them as they cook, so the tradeoff's worth it. They can be done in advance and eaten cold. Four quinces may not seem many for 8 people, but they are so temple-achingly sweet that you don't want to eat enormous amounts. A mouthful or two is ambrosial.

I suggest lemon ice cream with this because, in the first instance, I love that particular combination and, in the second, because there's a no-churn recipe (see page 254) that you can make relatively effortlessly. And I love the ice cream just with the syrup, too. But no one's going to argue if you just put out a bowl of crème fraîche, or indeed yogurt, to go with the quinces instead. It's the combination of the grainy, sweet, and perfumed fruit and cold near-sour creaminess you're after. It's up to you how you do it.

4 quinces	1 cinnamon stick
3 cups muscat wine	3 cloves
2½ cups sugar	3 cardamom pods
2 bay leaves	6 peppercorns

Preheat the oven to 325°F.

Fill a bowl with cold water and add a squirt of lemon juice to it; this is to put the quinces in to stop them browning. Peel the quinces, quarter them, and core them. You might need to do a bit of chiseling with the point of a knife, but don't worry if you can't get every last bit of core out. As you work, submerge the quinces in the acidulated water. Keep the peel and trimmings; they will help the syrup to thicken.

To make the syrup, put the wine, 1¼ cups of water, sugar, bay leaves, and spices in a saucepan and bring to the boil. Put the quince peel and cores in the bottom of an oven-proof dish and then put the quartered quinces on top, pour over the wine mixture, cover—either with a lid or, securely, with foil—and put in the oven for 2½ hours, or until when you take them out, the quinces are the fleshy-brown color of old-fashioned Band-Aids. Let them cool in the dish, with the lid on, and when you look at them next, they'll have deepened and darkened further.

When the quinces are cold, remove with a slotted spoon and put in a glass bowl. Strain the syrup into a saucepan and reduce; taste every now and again (without burning your tongue) to see how far you need to go. Let cool slightly and pour over the quinces waiting in their bowl. A warning, however: the syrup will thicken as it cools anyway; I too often overreduce it and end up with quince toffee. Any superfluous syrup can be kept, or reduced and kept, to use in place of sugar in apple pies or crumbles. Quinces are traditionally used in these dishes and the syrup gives you that extraordinary mixture between super-homeliness and the exotic without any further peeling.

MARSALA MUSCOVADO CUSTARD WITH MUSKILY SPICED PRUNES

This recipe is really just a variant of the Sauternes custard on page 217: it occurred to me that the particular combination of ingredients in zabaglione (see page 154) worked so well, it might taste equally good translated to the dense fabulousness of a baked custard. (I add muscovado sugar to boost innate tendencies.) It does. I'd consider serving it with some spiced prunes, only bear in mind that prunes can never win unanimous support. To cook the prunes, make some tea up with 2 cups boiling water and an Earl Grey tea bag (which you discard when the tea's strongish). Pour into a wide, heavy saucepan, adding a cinnamon stick broken in two, a star anise, a clove, the peel of about ⅓ orange pared from the fruit with a vegetable peeler, ½ cup Marsala, and ½ cup light muscovado sugar or light brown sugar. Bring to the boil, reduce to a simmer, and put 8 ounces (this gives you about 32) pitted prunes into the spicy tea syrup, then poach gently for 20 minutes.

Leave for at least 24 hours, 36 if possible; these just get better and better. The worse quality they are to start with, the longer you should let them steep. Obviously, this dessert is best with those wonderful, tender-bellied Agen prunes, which are available in packages, but I've used tight, wrinkled, hard-skinned ones that look like cheap teddy bears' noses, and they've ended up pretty damn fabulous.

If you want this viscous, shiny syrup even stickier and thicker, strain the poaching liquid (putting the prunes and the beautiful spices into the serving bowl) into a smaller pan, then reduce till you have a tight puddle of almost-liquid molasses. When it's a little cooler, spoon the quantity you need back over the prunes. And you can eat the rest of the syrup stirred into yogurt for your breakfast. For the custard, then:

2 cups heavy cream

½ cup Marsala

4 egg yolks

2 eggs

¼ cup light muscovado sugar or light
   brown sugar

2 tablespoons superfine sugar

whole nutmeg

Preheat the oven to 300°F and put the kettle on. In 2 saucepans, bring the cream and Marsala separately to a boil, but take off the heat before they actually do. Beat the egg yolks and whole eggs in a bowl with the sugars. Pour first the hot Marsala and then the heated cream onto the egg mixture, beating as you do so. Go steady, though—you just want to combine them all, not whip air into them. Put an ovenproof dish—one of those oval bowls with about 4-cup capacity—in a roasting pan and pour into the pan from the kettle some just-off-the-boil water to come halfway up the dish. Now pour the custard, through a strainer, into the dish, grate over some nutmeg, cover loosely with some foil, and bake for about 1 hour, but start checking after 45 minutes. You want the custard just set; it will carry on cooking as it cools. I like this best 1–1½ hours after it's come out of the oven.

 Try a relatively young red Burgundy, which has a bit of acidity, but a soft, round, voluptuous, velvety flavor.

CAMP, BUT ONLY SLIGHTLY, DINNER FOR 6

LITTLE GEMS WITH GREEN GODDESS DRESSING

PHEASANT WITH GIN AND IT

MASHED POTATOES AND SWEET-AND-SOUR CABBAGE

PAVLOVA WITH PASSION FRUIT

❖

All of these courses may sound like comic turns, a culinary joke made by someone with an overdeveloped sense of kitsch. I admit I am that person, but you don't have to apologize for this menu, or to explain it, or do anything to it other than cook it.

Little gems are small tight-budded English lettuces, for which romaine hearts make a fine substitute; I couldn't resist keeping little gems in the menu, if in name only.

The pheasant is the better for being cooked in advance, and the pavlova can be made the day before. You can store the meringue in a tin before using it but, to be frank, I just don't take it out of the oven. I cook it and leave it till I want to anoint it with cream and passion fruit. It is the astringency of the passion fruit that makes this work so well after the sweet herbalness of the gin-and-vermouth-cooked game. (The "It" in Gin and It is short for Italian, which refers to the red vermouth used.) You want the soft, sweet creaminess of the meringue, but you need the sharpness, too.

This is where the starter—a spirit-lifting winter salad—comes in, too. You can get fresh herbs all year round now, so you don't need to turn to the dusty dried stuff, even if the original did.

LITTLE GEMS WITH GREEN GODDESS DRESSING

The original green goddess dressing (created by the Palace Hotel in San Francisco in honor of George Arliss's performance in the play of the same name in the early twenties) was a mayonnaise-heavy affair; I've lightened it slightly, chiefly by using crème fraîche in place of the mayo. But it's much the same otherwise: thick with anchovy, chopped herbs, and scallions, and sharp with tarragon vinegar. To the lettuce, I've suggested adding some waxy sliced potatoes (despite the mash that's to come) and cornichons. If you want to keep this sprightlier, lose the potatoes by all means. I love, uncharacteristically, the vinegariness of the cornichons, but if you don't, then substitute a handful of raw sugar-snap peas.

½ pound boiling potatoes

4 anchovy fillets, drained and minced

2 tablespoons milk

2 tablespoons tarragon vinegar

6 tablespoons crème fraîche

8–10 tablespoons extra-virgin olive oil

1 scallion (white and green parts), sliced finely

3 tablespoons chopped tarragon

4 tablespoons chopped parsley

salt, if needed, and freshly milled black pepper

4–6 romaine hearts

18 small cornichons, or fewer gherkins, sliced

Boil or steam the potatoes, and when cool, slice into thick coins. I'm happy to leave the skins on, but it's up to you.

To make the dressing, pound the anchovies, preferably using a pestle and mortar, but a fork should do. In a bowl, and definitely using a fork, whisk together the anchovies, milk, vinegar, and crème fraîche till smooth. Slowly add the olive oil, as needed, still whisking with your fork. Stir in the scallion, tarragon, and 2 tablespoons of the parsley. Check for seasoning, adding salt, if needed, and pepper to taste. Separate the lettuce leaves and put in a large bowl; add a few tablespoons of the dressing and mix well with your hands to combine, adding the potatoes and more dressing as you need to coat well but not heavily. And this is a thick dressing, so you will have to turn the lettuce leaves in it slowly but for quite a time to make sure it's mixed in smoothly.

Arrange on a large flat plate or a couple, and toss over your cornichons and sprinkle with the remaining parsley.

PHEASANT WITH GIN AND IT

The method for this stew is based on Anne Willan's recipe on page 101, but the idea is quite other. It came to me one day when I was, as usual, adding white vermouth to something in place of white wine. I wondered when and if ever red vermouth could be used. From there my mind turned to the red vermouth my maternal grandmother used to drink in her gin and its, and this thought, in its turn, led to this dish.

Juniper berries are conventionally added to game, and gin is really just alcoholic juniper. The sweet vermouth adds a quite beautifully rounded herbalness.

You end up with a velvety, dark-flavored gravy. You don't absolutely have to have mashed potatoes to soak it up, but I'd miss them. For 6 people, I'd think 3 pounds of potatoes would do, but add plenty of butter, plenty of milk or cream, and a good grating of fresh nutmeg as you mash.

Get hen pheasants if you can, as they're plumper and more tender. If you can't get hold of any game stock, then use chicken stock. All you need to do to crush the juniper berries is lean on them a little with a pestle in a mortar, or put them in a bag and pummel once with a heavy weight—a can of baked beans or something like that. You'll need also to peel 30 pearl onions—sorry!

FOR THE MARINADE

6 tablespoons gin

2 cups sweet vermouth

1 large orange, unpeeled and cut into
   thick slices

9 peppercorns

9 juniper berries, crushed slightly

1 large onion, peeled and
   chopped

6 bay leaves

1 cup olive oil

¼ teaspoon salt

_____

3 plump pheasants, preferably hen, cut
   into 4 pieces each

4 tablespoons (½ stick) unsalted butter,
   plus more, if needed

3 tablespoons olive oil, plus more,
   if needed

1 pound portobello or cremini
   mushrooms, whole, halved, or
   quartered, depending on size

30 pearl onions, peeled

10 ounces pancetta, cut in lardons
   or diced

¼ cup Italian 00 or all-purpose flour

3 tablespoons sweet vermouth

5 cups game or chicken stock

9 juniper berries, crushed slightly

3 garlic cloves, chopped

freshly milled black pepper

few drops soy sauce

3–4 tablespoons chopped parsley

Mix the marinade ingredients together, submerge the pheasant pieces in the mixture, and leave for 24 hours. If you can't do it before the morning of the same day, that should just about be OK, but don't cut it any finer. I find it easiest to divide the pheasant and marinade between a couple of plastic bags, well tied.

When you're ready to cook, remove the pheasant pieces and pat them dry with some paper towels. Put the butter and oil in a frying pan that will take the pheasant later and put it over medium-high heat. When hot, brown the pheasant pieces in it; you may need to do this in batches. Remove to a plate and add the mushrooms to the pan. Soften these and then remove them, too. Next you're going to brown the onions, and you might need to add more butter and oil, as the mushrooms may greedily have eaten it all up. The onions should be well browned; devote about 15 minutes to this. Now remove the onions and add the pancetta and brown in the hot fat. To the crisped pancetta, add the flour and cook, stirring, on a low heat for about 5 minutes. Then throw in the vermouth and give a good prod and stir, to scrape up bits and combine. Gradually add the stock and then strain in the marinade. Return the pheasant, onions, and mushrooms to the casserole and add the juniper berries, the garlic, a good grinding of pepper, and generous shake of soy sauce. Cover and simmer gently for 1½ hours or in a preheated 325°F oven for 2 hours.

But keep an eye on it. You will probably have to take out the little tender legs after an hour and let the big, tougher breast pieces (yes, it is that way around) cook longer. When everything's tender, remove all the pheasant pieces and strain the liquid into another pan, reserving the mushrooms, pancetta, and onions. If you've got time to let the liquid settle so you can skim off excess fat, so much the better. Reduce the sauce so that it concentrates and thickens; it should be loose and thin, but not watery. Boil it down until it tastes right to you and then put the sauce, pheasant pieces, reserved mushrooms, onions, and pancetta back in the original pan and reheat gently. And if you want, you can keep it in the fridge for up to 3 days until you want to reheat it. Serve sprinkled with the parsley.

If you've got any leftovers, bone and chop the meat and reheat with the gravy to make a wonderful sauce for yourself to go with tagliatelle or pappardelle.

SWEET-AND-SOUR CABBAGE

This has to be cooked at the last minute, but it doesn't take long. You could cook it while someone else is clearing the table after the first course, or as people are helping themselves to the pheasant and mash. If I can bear to get up in the middle of the meal and do this, anyone can. You could use a processor to chop the cabbage, if you like the string-thin shreds it makes; the important thing is that it's sliced, not chopped.

1½ tablespoons sugar	1 large cabbage, green or white, sliced
3 tablespoons white wine vinegar	finely, tough stalk discarded
1½ tablespoons salt	few drops soy sauce
3 tablespoons light vegetable oil	

Mix the sugar, vinegar, and salt. Heat the oil in the largest frying pan or similar that you have; if you've got a large wok, then that would do.

Toss the cabbage with a couple of wooden forks or spatulas in the hot oil for 2 minutes until it is all covered in oil and just beginning to wilt. Add the soy and then pour on the vinegar mixture. Toss again in the heat and let it cook for 1 minute or so more, and then serve at once, while it's hot and crisp and juicy.

PAVLOVA WITH PASSION FRUIT

This pavlova version comes, appropriately enough, from an Australian book, Stephanie Alexander's compendious, addictive *Cook's Companion.* I was taken by her family tip of turning the cooked meringue over before smearing it with whipped cream, so that (in her words) the marshmallow middle melds with cream and the sides and the base stay crisp.

4 egg whites at room temperature

pinch salt

1¼ cups superfine sugar

2 teaspoons cornstarch

1 teaspoon white wine vinegar

few drops vanilla extract

1¼ cups heavy cream, whipped until
 firm

pulp of 10 passion fruits with pips

Preheat oven to 350°F. Line a baking sheet with baking parchment and draw a 8–9-inch circle on the paper. I often don't, and just imagine what size the circle should be as I dollop the meringue on. This seems to work fine.

Beat the egg whites with the salt until satiny peaks form. Beat in the sugar, a third at a time, until the meringue is stiff and shiny. Sprinkle over the cornstarch, vinegar, and vanilla and fold in lightly. Mound on to the paper on the baking sheet within the circle; flatten the top and smooth the sides. Place in the oven. Immediately reduce the heat to 300°F and cook for 1 hour; the pavlova will color slightly. Turn off the oven and leave the pavlova in it to cool completely.

Invert the pavlova onto a big, flat-bottomed plate, pile on cream, and spoon over passion fruits scooped—pips and all—from their shells. Don't be tempted to add other fruit.

A super Tuscan, such as Sassicaia or Oinellaia, made from the Cabernet Sauvignon grape, or a great California Cabernet Sauvignon, has wonderful, mineral flavors and will not be overpowered by the Gin and It.

SUMMER DINNER, WITH WINTER POSSIBILITIES, FOR 6

GRILLED PEPPER SALAD

MARINATED, BUTTERFLIED LEG OF LAMB, WITH GARLIC POTATOES

WATERCRESS AND RAW MUSHROOM SALAD

POACHED PEACHES WITH SAUTERNES CUSTARD OR ICE CREAM, OR
SAUTERNES AND LEMON BALM JELLY

In summer, I cook the lamb on the outdoor grill—in winter, in a hot oven. You might want to modify the menu otherwise—only you can tell exactly what mood the weather puts you in and how you want, culinarily, to respond. In winter, of course, you won't get the peaches, or if you do they'll be expensive and, worse, probably unsalvageable by poaching. You could, then, just make a Baked Sauternes Custard (page 217) and eat it without the fruit to accompany it, or soak and then poach some dried peaches or apricots, or a mixture of each. If you find some peaches you think you could do something with, then follow the recipe for sugar-sprinkled roast peaches (page 171). I couldn't stop myself from adding the recipe for Sauternes and lemon balm jelly, too. The advantage of this—apart from the spectacular but delicate beauty of its taste—is that it is pathetically easy to make. And when it's really hot, it's not just that you don't feel like eating excessive amounts of food, but that you don't want to spend excessive amounts of time in the kitchen.

GRILLED PEPPER SALAD

I never, ever, no matter what I'm cooking, use green peppers. If you want to add those expensive Dutch orange ones to this mix of red and yellow pepper, do, but that's as permissive as I'm going to get.

If you like, you can do this the traditional way and arrange the peppers in a dish, make up a plainish oil and vinegar dressing, and arrange anchovy fillets in a lattice on top (dotting between the crosses with halved or pitted whole black olives as you wish), but I prefer to make up a salty, khaki-stained anchovy dressing, which may spoil the glazed Chinese lacquer effect of the oil-slicked peppers but does something extraordinary to blend and transport the flavors—sweet, salty, oily, sharp—so that you have a glorious, explosive fusion.

4 yellow peppers

4 red peppers

5–6 tablespoons extra-virgin olive oil

2 garlic cloves, peeled and minced

3 anchovy fillets in olive oil, drained
and minced

I teaspoon lemon juice, plus more,
if needed

2–3 tablespoons chopped parsley

Char and peel the peppers as directed on page 86. Whatever you do, don't peel them under running water; you will lose all those sweet peppery juices. Peel them, rather, over a bowl to catch all those sweet drips. Don't be neurotic about getting every last bit of skin off; most will come off easily enough, and the rest you can live with.

Cut the peppers into strips and pile into a shallow bowl. In a heavy-bottomed pan, combine the olive oil and garlic and heat, stirring once you see it's got warm. After about 30 seconds, stir in the anchovies and keep stirring on low heat until they've melted into the oil. Then pour in the juices you caught from the peppers as you peeled them. Take off the heat. Add the lemon juice, taste, and add more if you like. Pour over the peppers, turn well to coat, then cover tightly with plastic film and leave to macerate for at least 3 hours, though 24 in the fridge would be even better. Sometimes I leave this for about half a week in the fridge and it is all the more silkily fabulous for it—as long as you remember to let it come to room temperature before you even think of eating it.

Transfer to a large plate, preferably a white one, to serve, and cover with the parsley.

There are quite a lot of peppers for 6 people, but that's for two reasons: the first is that I find people want them to stay on the table, within greedy arm's reach, with the lamb; the second is that if you're going to do some peeling, you may as well try for some leftovers later.

BUTTERFLIED LEG OF LAMB WITH GARLIC POTATOES

This is one of my most regular regulars. It is the flattened, boned leg that, opened up, makes a vaguely butterfly shape. In summer I cook it on the grill in the garden. This year I started doing it in winter, as well, in a 425°F oven for about 45 minutes, and it was wonderful. Regular lamb may not be as tender as baby or spring lamb, but the taste can be deeper and better, really, and the marinade sees off any potential toughness, despite the unforgiving heat of the oven. I don't serve a sauce with this, except for the deglazed meat juices in the pan. In summer there aren't even any meat juices, as they've disappeared into the flames, but no one seems to mind.

You must go to a butcher to get the lamb butterflied, unless you feel able to do it yourself. I've never tried but I keep meaning to learn. Because it takes so little time to cook, this is a very good way of accommodating a lamb roast into an after-work dinner-party schedule. And think of it more as a steak in that the cooking time is more to do with its thickness than its weight.

1 5-pound butterflied leg of lamb	2 rosemary sprigs, minced
1¼ cups extra-virgin olive oil	6 peppercorns
zest of 1 lemon	4½ pounds potatoes, cut into ½-inch
4 garlic cloves, crushed with the flat	dice
of knife	

Put the lamb with all the rest of the ingredients in a big plastic bag, refrigerated, for up to 30 hours, if you can, turning once or twice. Take it out of the fridge when you get back from work (or midafternoon, if it's the weekend and if the weather's not too hot) to let the oil in the marinade loosen and warm.

Preheat the oven to 425°F. Take the lamb out of the bag and put in a roasting pan. Pour the marinade into 2 baking dishes; these are for the potatoes, which need to roast about 1 hour, or until golden. Turn the potatoes in the marinade in their pans, using your hands to make sure the potatoes are well slicked in the heady oil, and put them in the oven. Roast the lamb for about 45 minutes or to an internal temperature of 130°F for medium or pinkish. Because you need the lamb to rest 10–15 minutes before carving, put the potatoes in at the same time as the lamb—a squeeze in one oven, but not impossible. And you can always cook the lamb first and eat it lukewarm. Transfer the lamb to a carving board, reserving the oily juices it leaves behind; serve this as a sauce.

For the salad, buy 2–3 bunches of watercress and slice about 6 ounces of ordinary button mushrooms thinly. For the dressing, I just mix some extra-virgin olive oil with lemon juice—basic and good.

WATERCRESS, RAW MUSHROOM SALAD

POACHED PEACHES WITH SAUTERNES CUSTARD

The difficult thing about real custard is the tedium of the stirring and its necessity; the possibility of curdling is never far away. Difficult is perhaps not the right word, but certainly the prospect of making pouring (as opposed to baked) custard can feel too daunting, and I realized I went out of my way to avoid it. Then I hit upon an idea—why not make a runny custard in the oven? I thought I could do it in advance and strain it to make sure no skin got in and then reheat it in a bain-marie on the stove when I wanted it. I doubted it would work because it seemed to me that if it was such a good idea someone would have come up with it before. But it did work; evidently I am either lazier or more fearful than other food writers, or both.

SAUTERNES CUSTARD (OR ICE CREAM)

If you don't want to use Sauternes, substitute any reliably honeyed dessert wine.

2 cups light cream

1 vanilla bean or ½ teaspoon pure
   vanilla extract, if not using vanilla
   sugar

1 cup Sauternes

7 egg yolks

⅓ cup vanilla sugar or superfine sugar,
   plus more, if needed

Preheat the oven to 325°F. Bring a kettle of water to a boil. Get out a roasting pan and put a wide, shallow bowl or an oval dish with a capacity of about 5 cups in it. Put the cream in a saucepan with the vanilla bean, if using, the wine in another, and bring both to the boil, but watch out that the cream never actually does boil. Remove them both from the heat.

If using the vanilla bean, allow the bean to steep in the cream for 20 minutes, then remove it. If using vanilla extract, add it to the cream now. With a fork, beat the yolks and sugar together and pour in first the wine and then the cream, beating all the while. Remember, though, you're beating to combine the ingredients, not whisking to get air in. Taste and add more sugar if needed. Strain the custard into the dish and pour water from the kettle into the roasting pan to come up about halfway. Cover the pan with foil; the idea is to make for a steamy atmosphere that will prevent a skin from forming. Put in the oven and cook for 1–1¼ hours or until set (or cook in a saucepan on the stove as usual).

Take out of the oven and out of the pan of water and let cool for about 20 minutes. Then strain into the top of a double boiler; this is presuming you will want to eat it warm. In fact, you can do three things with this: leave it as it is and let people spoon it over the peaches cold; reheat it till it's warm, not hot, when you're about to serve dessert; or put it when cold into an ice cream maker and follow the manufacturer's instructions. All three options are ambrosial.

POACHED PEACHES

I never think of myself as someone who likes cooked fruit—it's hard to believe that anything could improve on its natural and fresh state—but these peaches are a revelation. I wouldn't poach peaches with flesh as green and hard as young almonds, but ones that are slightly resistant, slightly lacking in that fragrant juiciness that is owing to the peachy estate, take on a plump but well-toned fleshiness and an aromatic roundedness that you couldn't believe could be brought about by just a pan of water and a mound of sugar. It's true that the vanilla you flavor the sugar with, the wine you scent the water with, each do their bit—but even with the plainest syrup, a dull and reticent peach can be transformed.

White peaches are my favorite here. Leave the skins on before immersing them in the softly bubbling syrup, and peel them later; you're left with a plate of perfect, pale mounds splodged pink, like the cheeks of a painted mummer. They look like something out of a children's fairy tale. You feel you should be drinking mead out of a jewel-studded goblet and wearing a wimple with a fetching organza veil.

The procedure is simple.

½ cup Sauternes, or the same wine used
   for the custard, above

3½ cups vanilla sugar or superfine sugar

1 vanilla bean or 1 teaspoon pure
   vanilla extract, if not using vanilla
   sugar

8 peaches, preferably white, halved
   and stoned

Put 3 cups of water, the wine, sugar, and the vanilla bean, if using, in a big saucepan, give a good stir so that the sugar begins to dissolve into the water, and bring to the boil. Let boil for 5 minutes and add the vanilla extract, if using. Lower to a firm but not exuberant simmer.

Lower the peaches a few halves at a time—I fit 4 in one go—cut-side down into the simmering syrup. Poach for about 5 minutes or until the peaches feel tender but not flabby. If you know they're in prime condition, then figure on 3 minutes, but you could need to poach them, gently, for 10. I use a fork to test for doneness, prodding into the underside so the fork marks won't ruin the beauteous display later. With a slotted flat spoon, delicately remove the peaches to a nearby large plate and cook the remaining ones in the same way. Strain the syrup into a container, remove a ladleful, put it back in the saucepan (freeze the containerful for the next time you make this), and reduce. You want to end up with a syrup that will cling tightly to the peach cheeks when you pour it over them, but not so much that it sticks. Anyway, let both the syrup and the peaches cool for now, and when they're cool, remove the skins, arrange the peaches on the serving plate, and pour the scant amount of syrup over them. They'll be fine for a good few hours like this.

SAUTERNES AND LEMON BALM JELLY

Charlotte Brand, friend and cook, put me on to this recipe. I've got masses of lemon balm in my garden, but you can substitute an equal amount of lemon grass.

I use a 5-cup ring mold and pile pale fruit—golden raspberries and white currants if I can get them—dusted with confectioners' sugar to fill the hole in the unmolded jelly. Of course you don't have to choose Château Yquem, but do select wine good enough to give to friends without making wry-mouthed apologies for it. You don't need a full bottle for the jelly, but as you want some dessert wine to drink with the dessert, there's no point buying a half bottle.

Turn to the recipe for Scented Panna Cotta with Gooseberry Compote (page 45) for comments about gelatin. Make this a day ahead, if you're concerned about its having enough time to set.

8 leaves gelatin or 2 envelopes granulated gelatin	I ounce (I cup tightly packed) lemon balm leaves
juice from 1½ lemons	about 1½ cups Sauternes or other wine
1⅔ cups superfine sugar, plus more, if needed	that can accompany dessert

If using granulated gelatin, soften it in the lemon juice, about 5 minutes, then heat it in the top of a double boiler over simmering water until the gelatin has dissolved, about 1 minute. Reserve. Bring the sugar and 3 cups of water to the boil and boil for 5 minutes. Remove from the heat and pour off ½ cup. Infuse the lemon balm in the remaining syrup until cold.

Strain the syrup, measure it, and add enough Sauternes to make 3¾ cups, and set aside. Soak the gelatin leaves, if using, in cold water for about 5 minutes, until they're soft. Warm ⅓ cup additional Sauternes, squeeze out the gelatin leaves, if using, then dissolve them in the Sauternes. Combine the syrup, gelatin mix and (reserved) lemon juice, which should bring the liquid up to 5¼ cups; check the sweetness and add more sugar if needed.

Dab a paper towel with vegetable oil and smear the inside of the ring mold with it. This will make it easier to unmold later. Pour the jelly mixture in and put it in the fridge to chill for 4–6 hours or until set.

To unmold, you might need to place the mold quickly in a sink slightly filled with hot water. But make sure it is only quickly. It's better to keep putting it back in if it doesn't come out cleanly and easily rather than leave it in and have it start to melt.

 A rich white Burgundy or Californian Chardonnay are rich enough to complement the lamb, the garlic, and the mushrooms.

MIDSUMMER DINNER
FOR 8

PEA, MINT, AND AVOCADO SALAD

BEEF FILLET WITH RED WINE, ANCHOVIES, GARLIC, AND THYME, OR TAGLIATA

NEW POTATOES AND WARM SPINACH WITH LEMON

STRAWBERRIES IN DARK SYRUP WITH PROUST'S MADELEINES

❖

This, to me, is the perfect dinner: simple, impeccable, beautiful. Of course, it doesn't have to be a June dinner, or even eaten in summer—I cook the beef all through the year and I'm such a fan of the frozen pea that I've got no reason to ration the unfashionable but deeply pleasurable salad, either. But when all the food comes together like this, it works at its best. I've given two choices for the beef simply because fillet for 8 is not always going to be a practical suggestion. If you want to make this a more formal dinner, then try the wine- and anchovy-braised fillet. The tagliata variation, a fat slab of meat cut from all along the rump, marinated, cooked briefly, then carved in squat, juicy slices on the diagonal, is the best thing you can do with your outside grill, *pace,* perhaps, the butterflied lamb of the menu preceding this. But if you're kitchen-bound, a 425°F oven is absolutely fine for roasting the meat.

The tagliata needs marinating for a day, and the strawberries need macerating for 3 hours. If you wanted to strike a more voluptuously grand note, you could end instead with the white tiramisu; see page 111.

PEA, MINT, AND AVOCADO SALAD

This is one of my great-aunt Myra's recipes. Of course, you can use frozen peas, but it's a pity at midsummer, and feels odd somehow, like having a light bulb on in brightest daylight. Alternatively—and this is probably the genuine compromise position—you can shell and cook the peas in advance and leave them steeped in the dressing. Nothing beats freshly shelled, just-cooked new peas, but we must be prepared to bend a little for our sanity's sake.

9 tablespoons extra-virgin olive oil, plus more, if needed

1½ tablespoon good white wine vinegar

fat pinch superfine sugar

bunch of mint, chopped

1 pound shelled peas (about 3⅓ pounds unshelled)

1 package (10 ounces) mixed salad greens

2 heads Belgian endive, separated into leaves

3 ripe avocados, cut into bite-size chunks

First make the dressing: put the oil, vinegar, and sugar into a large bowl and then put in a decent handful of the chopped mint. Stir well so all is amalgamated. Cook the peas for 2 minutes or so in salted boiling water, just so that they're ready, but not soft. Taste after 2 minutes and then keep tasting. Drain the peas in a colander, put them straightaway into the bowl of dressing, and let steep for an hour or up to a day.

Just before serving, stir in the mixed greens, the endive, and avocado. You may need to drizzle a bit more oil in it after tossing. Serve this on a big plate. Sprinkle with some more of the chopped mint.

BEEF FILLET WITH RED WINE, ANCHOVIES, GARLIC, AND THYME

I love this particular combination; see, too, the more wintry, homey version on page 100. If you can find some wild arugula, with those tiny William Morris leaves, use it to edge the borders of the serving plate. This doesn't just serve a decorative purpose—its pepperiness perfectly offsets the salty pungency of the anchovy–red-wine sauce.

1 tablespoon extra-virgin olive oil

4 tablespoons (½ stick) unsalted butter, 2 tablespoons cold and cut into small dice

8 shallots, sliced or minced

salt

2 teaspoons fresh thyme leaves or 1 scant teaspoon dried

8 garlic cloves, peeled and crushed with the flat of knife

12 anchovy fillets, packed in olive oil, drained and minced

2 1½-pound pieces beef fillet, trimmed

2 teaspoons superfine sugar

¼ cup tablespoons brandy

1¼ cups good red wine

freshly milled black pepper

In a heavy-bottomed Dutch oven or casserole in which the fillets will fit comfortably (no scrunching at the ends and they mustn't touch each other), heat the olive oil and 2 tablespoons of the larger quantity of butter. Add the shallots, sprinkle with a little salt, and sauté on a lowish heat for about 5 minutes or until soft and transparent but in no way coloring. Add the thyme and give 2 more minutes, stirring, then add the garlic and push about the pan too. Now add the anchovies and cook until they've started fusing with the oniony, buttery, oily mess in the pan. Remove this mixture to a bowl for a minute so you can brown the meat and turn up the heat. Sear the fillets on all sides, sprinkling with the sugar as you do so, till you've got a good crusty exterior. Add the brandy, let it bubble up a bit, then pour in the wine. Return the shallot mixture to the pan. Lower the heat and turn the meat over. Give everything a good stir to make sure the shallots, garlic, and so on are not burning or sticking. Cover and cook for 10 minutes—the meat is braising, frying, and steaming all at the same time; as it cooks it breathes in flavor. Uncover, peek in, prod, or poke; if the meat is springy, it's rare; springy but with some resistance, medium-rare to medium. Turn the meat over, cover again, and leave for another 5–10 minutes, depending on your findings and taste.

When the meat is almost as you like it, remove it from the pan (it will cook a little more as it rests) and get on with the sauce. And you can do all this before you sit down for the first course. Fish out the garlic with a spoon. Then turn up the heat and let the sauce bubble up a good bit, and taste, adding salt, if needed, and pepper. You may want to add some water. Take off the heat, but warm up before serving, at which time you should first pour into it the meat juices that have run out of the fillet as it stands and whisk in the remaining diced butter. Carve the fillets, arrange on a large, warmed plate, and drizzle over some of the sauce, leaving the rest in a sauce boat or pitcher for people to pour for themselves.

TAGLIATA

If you're going for the tagliata, get 2 beef slices, each about 1¼ inches thick, cut from along the whole length of the rump (about 1 pound per piece), and put each in a large freezer bag to marinate with a clove of garlic squished with the flat of a knife, ½ cup extra-virgin olive oil, the zest of ½ lemon, a few peppercorns, and a heaping teaspoon of fresh thyme leaves or ¼ teaspoon of dried. Tie or knot the bags and put them in the fridge for 12 or so hours. Remove and let come to room temperature before cooking as above. It's hard to say how long they'll take; it so depends on how you like your meat. I like mine pretty well still quaking and trembling on the plate—20 minutes or so, depending on how my oven or outdoor grill is behaving. Test by prodding before you start poking knives in—to elaborate on the above, if it's very, very soft and bouncy, it's blue; springy, rare; springy but with resistance, medium-rare to medium, depending on that resistance; hard—well, you know the answer to that. Take the steaks out, let them stand for 10 minutes, then carve thickly or thinly as you like, crosswise and on the diagonal. If you've roasted the meat, you'll have some meat juices; deglaze with a little red wine or Marsala, strain, adding a few more chopped thyme leaves to the clear ruby juices, then dribble over the carved meat. There won't be enough for a sauce boat. Put a plate of lemon quarters on the table too, for squeezing over the meat as you eat.

NEW POTATOES

Proper new potatoes need nothing more than a brisk rubbing before cooking and the lightest anointing with butter after. As to the cooking itself—these are best steamed, but it's pretty well impossible to steam enough for 8 people, so just boil them, but make sure you don't overboil them. I'd work on rations of about 8 ounces a head; this sounds like a lot on paper, but on the plate it somehow isn't.

WARM SPINACH WITH LEMON

You've got enough going on with everything else, so I'd use packaged spinach, or even frozen (providing it's whole leaf, not chopped). Get 4–5 packages of the fresh stuff, 3 of the frozen. And you're not doing much more than wilting the former, thawing the latter. Add butter, olive oil, and a bit of lemon juice, or else a good sprinkling of sumac, that sour, citrussy, Middle Eastern ground-berry spice.

e some wedges of lemon around the edges of the dish. A little grating of
ı nutmeg does something extraordinary here, too. The spinach should be at
m temperature.

STRAWBERRIES IN DARK SYRUP

The darkness of the syrup in question comes from balsamic vinegar. Well, wait;
this is not a sprightly, modern, hardly-dressed salad, but one with a syrup of gar-
net depths and intensity. The balsamic vinegar seems to make the red of the
strawberries against it shine with the clarity of stained-glass windows. And it
tastes as it looks, deep and light at the same time.

If you have some syrup left over after dinner, you can boil it up so that it
reduces and thickens and you'll have the world's best-ever, most intensely straw-
berryish ever, sauce to pour over vanilla ice cream. There won't be enough this
way for more than just you, but do it anyway; it's a heady experience.

Steep 2 pounds of strawberries, hulled and halved, in 2 tablespoons (I find it
easier to drizzle this over in 6 teaspoons) balsamic vinegar (the best you can
afford) and 10 tablespoons superfine sugar. Cover with plastic film and give the
dish a good but gentle shake to make sure all the berries get some sugar and
some vinegar on them, and leave for 3 hours.

Please—no cream, or similar, with these. But any form of sponge or cake
would be fine. Because we are talking ecstatic culinary experience here, it seems
entirely appropriate to produce some madeleines. The recipe here comes, naturally enough, from *Dining with Proust,* so we are really talking about:

PROUST'S MADELEINES

As you need to leave the batter for 1½ hours, you may have to think of baking
them as you eat the first two courses. You can eat them—warm and fragrant—as
cake-cookies for dessert. Obviously, you need to buy the special molds for these
shell-shaped cakes, but that's not difficult now. I use ones that can take 2 tablespoons of the mixture below, but they are best when you fill them with just 1
tablespoon. You may, then, need to bake them in two batches. This makes about
two dozen.

8 tablespoons (1 stick) unsalted butter, melted and cooled

1 tablespoon clear honey

2 eggs

½ cup superfine sugar

pinch salt

¾ cup Italian 00 or all-purpose flour

confectioners' sugar for serving

Mix 6 tablespoons of the butter with the honey. Beat the eggs, sugar, and salt in a bowl for about 5 minutes with a mixer until it's as thick as mayonnaise. Sprinkle in the flour; I hold a strainer above the egg and sugar mixture, put the flour in it, and shake. Fold in the flour with a wooden spoon and then add the melted butter and the honey. Mix well, but not too vigorously. Leave to rest in the fridge for 1 hour, then take out and leave at room temperature for 30 minutes. Preheat the oven to 425°F. Brush the remaining butter over the cavities in the madeleine molds and fill them with the cake mixture. Don't worry about filling the cavities; in the heat of the oven, the mixture will spread before it rises.

Bake 5–10 minutes or until lightly golden on top and golden brown around the edges. Mine seem cooked after about 7 minutes, but not all ovens are the same, so be alert from 5 minutes. Turn out and let cool on a rack, then arrange on a plate and dust with confectioners' sugar.

 A really good Burgundy is always the perfect wine with beef.

INDIAN SUMMER DINNER FOR 6

PEA AND LETTUCE SOUP

LAMB WITH CHICKPEAS

COUSCOUS SALAD

TURKISH DELIGHT FIGS WITH PISTACHIO CRESCENTS

❖

This is the sort of food to eat when the days are unexpectedly warm but the nights are nevertheless beginning to get cooler. You're still in the mood for summer food, but you need ballast too. This food, like that in the previous menu, is as suited for eating on a table in the garden as it is for a windows-shut, curtains-closed dinner inside.

PEA AND LETTUCE SOUP

This is best prepared with fresh peas and a homemade vegetable stock. For the stock, shell the fresh peas, then combine their pods, some parsley stalks, peppercorns, onion, half a carrot, a stalk of celery, and, of course, water. Simmer for about 1 hour and strain. If I don't feel like tackling fresh peas, or they're not available, I use frozen young peas and either chicken stock or vegetable bouillon cubes. I find it easier to start the soup off with thawed peas, but if they're still frozen, it couldn't matter less. If you've got any basil-infused oil, you can use that for softening the vegetables at the beginning. I know mint is the usual herb here, but basil seems to enhance the fruity sweetness of the peas.

2 tablespoons olive oil	5 cups light stock (see headnote)
4 scallions (white and green parts), sliced finely	1 teaspoon sugar
	1 tablespoon dry sherry
zest of ½ lemon	salt and freshly milled white pepper
1 pound shelled fresh peas or frozen young peas	3–4 tablespoons heavy cream, plus more, if desired
1 Boston or Bibb lettuce, roughly chopped	large handful basil leaves

Put the oil in a saucepan and, when it's warm, add the scallions and zest, stir a bit, and then add the peas. Turn well in the oil, and then add the lettuce and cook till it wilts and then collapses into the peas. Pour over the stock, sprinkle over the sugar, and bring to the boil. Turn down to a simmer and cook gently and uncovered till the peas are soft, about 10 minutes. Purée in batches, in a blender if possible. You don't get that velvety emulsion with a processor, though you can sieve it after processing, which will do it. Or use a food mill.

Pour back into the saucepan, add the sherry, and cook for a minute or so before tasting and seasoning with the salt and pepper, bearing in mind you'll be adding some cream and eating it cold. Let it cool a little, then stir in the cream and let it cool properly before putting it in a tureen and into the fridge.

Just as you're about to eat, taste for more salt or pepper, add more cream if wanted, and then shred the basil and add a good bit to each bowlful after ladling it out from the tureen.

LAMB WITH CHICKPEAS

For this, it's up to you whether you use whole loin, which you roast and then slice, or individual noisette discs, which you grill, griddle, or fry; the former tastes better, but the latter look better. I can never carve from the entire rolled loin without it unfurling all over the place, but of course you do get the tender, uncharred sides from the middle of the roll. When you cook the individual noisettes, you're sealing each slice in the heat. But the marinade will help to ensure that this wonderfully tender cut won't coarsen in cooking. Make sure that you're using the best lamb you can afford.

I think it's easier to cook the chickpeas in advance and do the lamb on the evening itself, having put it in its marinade the night before or the morning of your dinner.

Soak 1 pound of chickpeas in abundant water and with a paste made from 3 tablespoons flour, 3 tablespoons salt, and 1 tablespoon baking soda (as directed on page 78). Leave for 24 hours. Drain, running the cold water over them in the colander as you do so, then put them in a saucepan with 5 garlic cloves, peeled and bashed, 2 bay leaves, 2 small onions, peeled but left whole (makes them easier to remove later), and the leaves from a large sprig of rosemary. The bitter, boiled shards of rosemary will get in everyone's teeth and ruin the creamy sweetness of the cooked chickpeas, so put them in tied cheesecloth or a tea infuser.

Cover again with abundant water, add 1 tablespoon olive oil, put the lid on, and bring to the boil, but do not uncover the pan; you'll have to listen closely to hear when it's starting to boil. Turn down slightly and let the chickpeas cook at a simmer for about 2 hours. You can check them after 1½ hours, but keep the lid on till then. When tender, drain, reserving a cup of the cooking liquid. Leave, even up to a couple of days, till you want to eat. It would be better to remove the skins around each butterscotch-colored pea, and I often start doing this, but have never yet completed the task.

To reheat, put 8 tablespoons olive oil and 6 garlic cloves, peeled and chopped, in a large, wide pan on moderate heat. I like to use a terra-cotta pot for this. Add to this 1–2 fresh red chilies, to taste, seeded and finely chopped, or crumble in a dried chili pepper. Add the drained chickpeas and turn well. Meanwhile, take 3 good-sized tomatoes, blanched, peeled, seeded, and roughly chopped, and add to the chickpeas. Salt very generously, stir well, and taste; you may need to add some of the cooking liquid. You don't want this mushy exactly, but you want a degree of fusion, of fuzziness around the edges. Take off the heat and cover until you've dealt with the lamb.

If you're going for the whole-loin option, think along the lines of getting 3 1-pound loin pieces (although I might well get 4) and then roasting them in a 425°F oven for 20–40 minutes, depending on your oven and the age and thickness of the meat. You do not need to marinate the rolls.

As for the individual noisettes, I work on the assumption that you have to give each person 2, and then allow for half of those present to have more. For 15 noisettes of lamb, make a marinade out of ½ cup plus 2 tablespoons olive oil, 4 garlic cloves, crushed, 1 medium red onion, chopped, and 1 small fresh red chili pepper, seeded and sliced. I find the easiest, most efficient way of doing this is by dividing the lamb and its marinade between 2 plastic bags. Leave overnight or for as long as you can.

Just before you're about to sit down for your first course, take the lamb out of its marinade. You can drain the marinade and use that in place of the olive oil for sautéing the chickpeas, above, in which case use a smaller amount of chili. Cook the lamb either by frying it in a cast-iron pan or a griddle, or by giving it a few minutes each side under a very hot broiler. Alternatively, sear the meat in a pan, then give it about 10 minutes in a 425°F oven. To keep the lamb pieces warm, leave them in a low oven on a dish covered with foil while you eat your soup.

When you serve, arrange the chickpeas on a big, flattish bowl (again, a terra-cotta one is perfect) or a couple of big plates, and place the lamb over them. Chop over some fresh, flat-leaf parsley—or coriander, if you feel infused with the mood of late-summer headiness.

COUSCOUS SALAD

Sometimes I provide just a couple of small bowls filled with well-chopped red onion for people to sprinkle over the lamb and chickpeas as they like. The alternative is the couscous salad, which, in effect, is panzanella, only using couscous in place of the bread. I often put basil in it, but this dinner has enough going on as it is without introducing another forceful character, so I suggest parsley.

I cup quick-cooking couscous	freshly milled black pepper
I teaspoon salt, plus more, if needed	6 ripe tomatoes
6 tablespoons olive oil	½–I small red onion, to taste, minced
2 tablespoons best red wine vinegar, plus more, if needed	I cucumber
	½ cup chopped parsley

Put the couscous into a bowl with the salt and pour over I cup boiling water. Cover and leave for 15 minutes. Fluff up with a fork and add the olive oil and some pepper, and put in another bowl (or leave in the same one, if you're in no hurry) to cool. Prepare the tomatoes by blanching, peeling, seeding, and dicing, only make sure you don't leave them in the hot water too long. Cut the flesh into neat small dice.

When you're about to put the main course on the table, dice the cucumber and stir, along with the tomatoes, onion, and 7 tablespoons of parsley, into the couscous with a fork. Add salt and more vinegar if you think it needs it.

Arrange on a plate and sprinkle on the remaining parsley.

TURKISH DELIGHT FIGS
with thanks to Pat Harrison and Masterchef

These figs are beautiful but not in an art-directed way—the purple-blue fruits are cut to reveal the gaping red within, so that they sit in their bowl like plump little open-mouthed birds. When they're slicked with the flower-scented syrup, they become imbued with Middle Eastern sugariness, and the aromatic liquid itself absorbs and takes on a glassy pink from the figs. Perfect symbiosis.

Two figs a head should do it—they are very sweet, very intense—but if you can find only small figs, increase this to 3 per person. They're wonderful, anyway, the next day.

2½ cups sugar	juice of I lemon
2 tablespoons rosewater	12 ripe purple figs
2 tablespoons orange-flower water	

Dissolve the sugar in 2½ cups water in a small, heavy-bottomed saucepan over a low heat. Increase the heat, bring to the boil, and boil rapidly for 5 minutes. Add the rosewater, orange-flower water, and lemon juice. Bring back to the boil and simmer for 2 minutes.

Carefully cut the figs vertically into quarters, leaving them intact at the base. Arrange on a flat, heatproof dish and spoon the hot syrup over them. Set aside to cool, basting with the syrup occasionally. Serve at room temperature, with yogurt and pistachio crescents (below).

PISTACHIO CRESCENTS

These accompanying pistachio crescents, which resemble the hazelnut-smoky Middle-European kipferln, are rich and tender—almost soft and definitely friable. Their powdery texture is compounded by the blanket of confectioners' sugar with which they are thickly, mufflingly coated; they have a one-thousand-and-one-nights feel, which is just right with the rosewater scent of the fig-basting syrup. And they're not hard to do. The amount below makes about 12 aromatically gritty crescents.

3 ounces shelled pistachios	½ cup Italian 00 or all-purpose flour,
4 tablespoons (½ stick) unsalted butter,	sifted
softened	pinch salt
2 tablespoons confectioners' sugar, plus	
more, for dusting	

Preheat the oven to 325°F. Grease 2–3 baking sheets or, better still, cover them with Cook-Eze (see page 462).

Toast the pistachios in a heavy-bottomed frying pan with no fat for a few minutes so that their rich, waxy aroma is released. Pour into a food processor and pulse until pulverized.

With a wooden spoon, beat the butter until creamy—you are getting it ready to absorb the sugar with hardly any additional beating—and then duly spoon the sugar into a tea strainer suspended over the bowl with the butter and push it through. Beat a while longer, until the butter and sugar are light and incorporated, almost liquid-soft, and then add the flour and salt. Keep stirring composedly and then add the ground pistachios, beating until just mixed. The dough will be sticky but firm enough to mold with your hands. If it feels too mushy, put it in the fridge for 10–20 minutes. To make the crescents, flour your hands lightly and then take out small lumps of the dough—about 1 scant tablespoon at a time if you were measuring it, but I don't suggest you do—and roll them between your hands into sausages about 2 inches long. Slightly flatten the sausage as you curl it round to form a little bulging snake of a crescent and put on the prepared baking sheet. Carry on until all the dough mixture is used up. And, by the way, don't be alarmed at how green these snakes look: cooked and dredged with confectioners' sugar, the intense lichen-colored glow will fade.

Bake for about 25 minutes, though start checking after 15, or until the tops are firm and beginning to go blondly brown; the crescents will be soft just below the surface. Let the cookies sit on their baking sheets out of the oven for a few minutes and then remove to a rack. Go carefully—they are, as I said earlier, intensely friable. Dredge them with confectioners' sugar very thickly indeed (again, I use a teaspoon to push the sugar through a tea strainer) and leave to cool. You can do these ahead, and just dust over a little more icing sugar as you serve them.

 A Californian Zinfandel has the aromatic spicy quality to be ideal with this meal.

MILDLY WINTRY DINNER FOR 8

ONION TART WITH BITTER LEAVES

ROAST MONKFISH, PUMPKIN PURÉE, AND MIXED MUSHROOMS

ALMOND AND ORANGE-BLOSSOM CAKE WITH RED FRUIT

❖

I think of this as a very calm menu; there's enough food to warm but not so much that everyone will go staggering about afterwards vowing to turn macrobiotic.

There aren't potatoes with the monkfish—the pumpkin purée is starchy and filling—so you can comfortably accommodate the cream and the pastry in the tart. The cake for dessert is cooked in advance.

ONION TART

If you make and roll out the pastry the day before, along with caramelizing the onions, all you'll have to do on the night itself is take it in and out of the oven a few times, and beat some eggs and cream together. In other words, it's entirely manageable. Try to arrange things so that the tart comes out of the oven about 40 minutes before you want to eat it. This means that if you're planning to sit down to dinner at 9 P.M. it should go in, fully assembled, at 7:40. You should get your blind-baking under way, then, as soon as after 7 P.M. as possible.

FOR THE PASTRY

1 cup Italian 00 or all-purpose flour

4 tablespoons (½ stick) unsalted cold
    butter or 2 tablespoons each lard
    and butter, diced

1 egg yolk beaten with a pinch of salt
    and 1 teaspoon of crème fraîche

FOR THE FILLING

2 tablespoons unsalted butter

drop oil

1 pound onions, sliced very thinly

salt

1 teaspoon sugar

4 tablespoons Marsala

freshly milled black pepper

2 eggs

1 egg yolk

1¼ cups crème fraîche

whole nutmeg

Prepare the pastry using the listed ingredients and following the foolproof recipe on page 37. For the filling, melt the butter with the drop of oil in a heavy-bottomed frying pan, add the onions and sprinkle over with the salt, and sauté over medium to low heat for 12 minutes, until soft and transparent; then stir in the sugar, reduce the heat further, cover the onions tightly with foil, and cook for another 20 minutes on the lowest heat, until tender (almost mush) and golden brown. Remove the foil, turn up the heat, add the Marsala, and let cook, on a moderate heat, stirring every now and again to make sure nothing sticks or burns, for another 8 or so minutes. By this time the onions should be a well-stewed, darkish brown tangle. Taste and season with salt and pepper, and then remove to a bowl to cool a little.

While all this is going on, roll out the pastry to line a deep, 8-inch tart pan or 9-inch shallower one, and leave in the fridge to rest for 15–20 minutes. Preheat the oven, to 400°F, making sure there's a rack in there for the tart to sit on later. Line the pastry shell with foil, fill with beans, and bake blind for 15 minutes. Remove the beans and paper, wrap foil over the edges, and give the naked shell another 12 minutes. Remove and let it cool a little. Turn the oven down to 350°F.

Combine and beat the eggs, egg yolk, crème fraîche, and ½ teaspoon of salt. Add a good grinding of black pepper and even more of nutmeg. Line the pastry with the soggy, caramelized onions and then pour over the egg mixture. Leave it rather insufficiently filled until you've staggered over to the oven and put the pan on the rack; then you can spoon or pour in as much of the remaining egg mixture as you dare without it spilling over and down the sides and ruining the pastry. Give another grating of nutmeg on top and bake in the oven for 30–40 minutes, or until set but not firm.

I make a variation on this, replacing the ordinary onions with red onions, the Marsala with red wine, and the crème fraîche with yogurt.

BITTER LEAVES

To go with the onion tart, make a bitter salad out of Belgian endive and treviso, that elongated raddicho, or, if you're lucky enough to find it, those young greens called *cicorie* by the Italians. Make the anchovy dressing the easy way by adding 1–2 drops anchovy essence to fillets, mashed into an emulsion of olive oil and lemon juice; add a pinprick of honey (very Apicius) if you think the balance needs adjusting. You can dispense with the onion tart altogether and make the salad the focal point, and sole constituent, of the starter. If so, make a dressing by mashing some anchovies to a paste with some thyme, adding a spritz of lemon juice and then as much oil as you need, gradually.

ROAST MONKFISH

Ask your fish seller for four approximately 1-pound pieces of monkfish tail; these are going to be easier to get than a couple of great, walloping ones. Have them trimmed and skinned, but with the bone in if possible, for flavor (it's such a big bone, you can just lift it out of the fillets as you serve).

You hardly do anything to them, and what you do you do at the last minute—just before you sit down to the starter.

Preheat the oven to 375°F and, on the stove, sauté the fish a couple of minutes each side in about 3 tablespoons, more if you feel you need it, of butter and a drop or so of olive oil. I use a nonstick frying pan that will go in the oven later. If you've got any pan that you can use on the stove and in the oven and will fit all the fish, then use it; otherwise, use an ordinary or nonstick pan and transfer it to a baking dish, making sure to pour the frying juices over before baking.

When you've sautéed your fish, sprinkle over some sea salt and a bit of lemon zest, transfer to the oven, and bake for 20 minutes or until just cooked through and the flesh has lost its glassiness. Arrange the monkfish on a large plate, removing each fillet's central bone as you do so. Put the pan or baking dish with its lemony, salty juices on the stove for a moment, stir in some boiling water and grate over some pepper, and then dribble a mere tablespoon or so over the pale firm fish on the plate. But taste and adjust to suit before doing anything. If you want to strew watercress or big and flat-leafed parsley around the edges of the dish, do.

PUMPKIN PURÉE

If you can, get three small (i.e., about 2 pounds each) pumpkins rather than one huge tough, more watery, less flavorsome one. For each 2 pounds of pumpkin, you need about 4 tablespoons of butter.

Preheat the oven to 400°F. Quarter each little pumpkin. Remove the seeds (though leave the skin as is) and cut out squares of foil big enough to wrap the chunks in securely. Place each piece of pumpkin in the middle of its foil and dollop on 1 tablespoon unsalted butter, then some salt (this does taste better than just using salted butter, I promise you) and pepper in each quarter's deseeded cavity. Wrap loosely in the foil, but twist the edges tightly to seal it absolutely. Place these packages on one or two baking sheets and bake for 45 minutes or until the flesh is soft.

Remove, but leave the pumpkins in their packages on their baking sheet(s) till cool enough to touch, or—if you're doing this in advance and then reheating, as I most often do—leave until completely cool. Then open the parcels into a bowl or pan (or, if you want your purée baby-food smooth, into a processor) so that all buttery juices are saved, and, using a spoon, scrape out the cooked flesh. Mash with a masher, whip with a wooden spoon, or purée in any other way you like; the pumpkin will be soft enough not to need more than pushing to turn it into purée. There is enough butter in this; you do not need to add anything, except salt to taste, later. Any leftovers make wonderful soup.

MIXED MUSHROOMS

If you can't get a variety of fresh mushrooms, use about 2 pounds of those mixed sliced mushrooms you can pick up in ready-assembled packages in the supermarket.

1 ounce dried porcini

8 tablespoons (1 stick) unsalted butter

2 tablespoons olive oil

4 shallots, minced

2 very fat garlic cloves, minced

8 ounces cremini or portobello
mushrooms, chopped into small dice

8 ounces button mushrooms, sliced
thinly

8 ounces chanterelles or other wild
mushrooms

8 ounces shiitake mushrooms, stemmed
and halved

1 ounce trompettes de mort or other
wild mushrooms

2 tablespoons dry sherry

2 tablespoons freshly grated Parmesan

2 tablespoons chopped parsley or
1 tablespoon chopped chives

Put the dried porcini in a large measuring cup and pour over hot but not boiling water from the kettle to come up to the 1¼-cups mark. Put half the butter and the olive oil into a large frying pan. Turn on the heat and then add the shallots and garlic and cook on a low to medium heat for about 15 minutes or until very soft indeed but not browned. A nonstick pan is good for this, as the shallots tend to stew in nonstick pans rather than fry, which is what you want here. After the dried mushrooms have soaked for 20 minutes, strain them, reserving the liquid, and finely chop. Add them to the softened shallot and garlic mixture and then, 2 minutes later, add the rest of the butter and all the mushrooms and cook, covered, for 7–10 minutes, stirring and turning often. You may need longer, but you'll tell at a glance when they've cooked down. Uncover, turn up the heat, add the strained mushroom-soaking liquid and the sherry, and let it all bubble away until the liquid is syrupy. At this point I turn off the heat and leave the mushrooms to cool and be reheated later.

At which point, warm them up and, when hot, add the cheese. Remove to a serving bowl and sprinkle with the parsley or chives.

The three components of this course not only go well together, but the polished-panelling Murillo tones of the mushrooms, the smooth, unsubtle bright orange-ness of the pumpkin, the plump, untroubled white of the fish, look wonderful next to one another on the table. And the tastes have the same rightness: the simplicity of the fish, the aromatic earthiness of the mushrooms, the sweetness of the purée—the perfect trio. Don't introduce a salad or anything else—except bread, preferably a baguette, to soak up the copiously delicious juices.

DESSERT

Fruit and cake are just what you need here; you don't want to interfere with the simplicity and clarity of what's gone before. The almond and orange-blossom cake needs to be made a day or so in advance (the recipe for it is on page 115); serve any fruit you want with it, but with a damp cake like this fragrant one, no cream. Raspberries are my favorite, but they may be too expensive or too flavorless, or just nonexistent. Some stores stock European brands of bottled, not-too-sweet red cherries; drained, with some of the syrup reduced and spooned over them, they'd be just right. But never disparage the frozen package of mixed fruit; grate some orange zest over before thawing and dust them with confectioners' sugar before serving.

Try a Spanish red, ideally from the Ribeiro del Duero region, which has a fleshy, flinty quality and is harmonious and generous in character.

SIX IDEAS FOR KITCHEN SUPPERS

As all my meals are eaten in the kitchen, the demarcation between the recipes to follow and those you've just read is meaningless. But, interior design apart, we all know what we mean by a kitchen supper. I take it to be a meal without a procession of courses, just food on the table, and not necessarily much notice in which to plan or cook it (although do look at Cooking in Advance, page 75, as most of the recipes there are for just this sort of laid-back thing). As far as I'm concerned, if sausages and mash (with apple rings fried in butter, please, like my grandmother used to make for me) would be appropriate fare, a tub of good, bought ice cream an acceptable dessert, and it's in the evening, it's a kitchen supper.

All recipes serve four abundantly, which is the way I like it.

BLAKEAN FISH PIE

So-called because the intense yellow of the saffron-tinted sauce reminds me of one of those beautiful Blakean sunbursts. The saffron itself adds more than just depth of color; it headily redeems the bland, cotton-woolly fish you buy in those plastic-wrapped polystyrene trays at the supermarket—useful when you can't get to a fish seller.

You can cook the potatoes first, mash, and set them aside while preparing the fish, or, if it suits you better, cook the fish and sauce first, set them aside, and do the potatoes after.

1 medium carrot, peeled, halved lengthwise, and quartered

½ cup white wine

large pinch salt

1 bouquet garni (see page xx)

2 pounds floury potatoes, cut into chunks

8 tablespoons (1 stick) unsalted butter

8 ounces cod fillets, skin removed

8 ounces haddock fillets, skin removed

8 ounces salmon fillets, skin removed

about ½ cup light cream

¼ cup Italian 00 or all-purpose flour

pinch mace

½ teaspoon powdered saffron or ground saffron threads

5 ounces cooked, peeled shrimp

whole nutmeg

Put the carrot in a deep frying pan with ½ cup water, the wine, salt, and bouquet garni. Bring to the boil, turn off the heat, let cool, and reserve. Cook the potatoes in salted water and mash with 6 tablespoons of the butter. (The best instrument for this is a potato ricer. It's cheap and you don't need to peel the potatoes; the skins stay behind as you push the potato through.) Set aside.

Put the white fish in the reserved carroty water and wine, bring to simmering point, and poach for about 3 minutes. Remove to a plate, and add the salmon and poach for about 3 minutes. Add to this the white fish. Strain the liquid (keeping the bouquet garni) into a measuring cup, and make up to 2 cups with the cream.

Melt the remaining 2 tablespoons butter in a saucepan and stir in the flour and mace. Cook, stirring, for a few minutes. Then, off the heat, stir in the cream mixture slowly, beating all the time to prevent lumps. When it's all incorporated, put back on the heat and throw in the sodden bouquet garni. Keep cooking and stirring until thickened—about 5 minutes—then add the saffron powder or threads and cook, stirring, for another 5 minutes. Set aside for 10 minutes (or, if you're doing this in advance, let it cool altogether).

Butter a 5½-cup dish and put in the cooked fish and the shrimp. Pour over the saffron sauce (take out the bouquet garni) and mix in. Cover with the mashed potato. Make sure the potato completely covers the pie dish so that no sauce can bubble up and spill over. Grate over some nutmeg and cook in an oven, preheated to 375°F, for 20–40 minutes (depending on how cold the pie was when it went in) or until the potatoes are golden here and there and the filling is hot. Eat with peas. You must.

THE IRISH CLUB'S IRISH STEW

When I was a child I remember eating a distinctly nasty Irish stew: watery, greasy, and singularly unvoluptuous. I haven't been particularly won round by eating it in Ireland, either. But I recently had a bowlful at the Irish Club in London's Eaton Square, and it was velvety in its unctuousness, the meat and its gravy both infused with that sweet, tender viscosity. I don't think I have ever been so bowled over by something I've ordered. Actually, I didn't order it, or not initially. I had played safe and asked for the Irish smoked salmon with soda bread. But then I tasted the stew and felt pierced with envy. I am happy to eat from other people's plates; indeed, I don't feel there's any point going out if I can't do that. But this was different: I wanted my own, and lots of it. The Irish Club's Irish Stew, with its inclusion of veal stock (and chicken stock, for that matter), and whole lamb chops, which diners gnaw on, may offend purists, but experiences as voluptuous and pleasurable as this are always going to offend them anyway. Don't worry about making your own veal stock—there are good commercial versions available—but it's important not to leave it out, as that's what produces, or helps produce, the requisite seductive stickiness.

¾ cup pearl barley

3 pounds rib lamb chops not less than
    1 inch thick, trimmed of any fat

5 medium onions, chopped, or
    12 boiling onions

5 medium carrots, peeled and chopped,
    or 12 baby ones, peeled

3 large parsnips, peeled and chopped

1¼ cups chicken stock

1¼ cups veal stock

salt and freshly milled black pepper

leaves from a medium rosemary sprig,
    minced

3 sage leaves, minced

1 tablespoon chopped parsley

8 medium potatoes, peeled and sliced
    about ¼ inch thick

Cook the barley 20 minutes in boiling salted water, drain it, and reserve.

Preheat the oven to 325°F. In a casserole in which you're sure everything's going to fit, brown the lamb. You shouldn't need to add any cooking fat to the pan. Remove the meat. Add the vegetables to the casserole, turn them in the fat, and cook for about 5 minutes, stirring frequently, until slightly softened. Meanwhile, combine the stocks and heat.

Remove the vegetables to a plate for a moment, then layer the casserole with the chops, the vegetables, and the parboiled barley, seasoning well with the salt and pepper and sprinkling with rosemary, sage, and parsley as you go. Pour over the warmed stock and arrange the potatoes on top overlapping like a tiled roof, and season again. Cover the casserole so that the potatoes steam inside. Put in the oven for 1½ hours, or until the potatoes are soft and the meat is thoroughly cooked. If you want the potatoes browned on top, dot with butter and blitz under the broiler or in a turned-up oven when cooked.

The whole point of this stew is that it needs no accompaniment—except for bread, and lots of it.

SPANISH STEW

This stew is both plain and yet intensely flavored—the thickly sliced, fat-pearled, paprika-bright sausages ooze oily and orange into the sherry-spiked broth; the potatoes cook placidly alongside. It takes a few minutes to assemble, and then you just stick it in the oven. The thing that does make a difference is the chorizo itself; you need the proper, semidried (sometimes called fresh) sausages rather than the naturally drier and stouter-waisted salami. What you must guard against are those tight-fleshed, too lean and unyielding, so-called Spanish-style chorizo.

1 tablespoon olive oil	1 bay leaf
1 medium onion, minced	½ cup dry sherry
3 garlic cloves, finely minced	2¼ pounds waxy potatoes, halved
8 ounces semidried chorizo sausages,	salt and freshly milled black pepper
sliced thickly	3–4 tablespoons chopped coriander

Preheat the oven to 400°F. Pour some water into a kettle and bring to a boil.

Put the oil in a wide rather than deep pan that will go in the oven later—an oblong enameled casserole or round terra-cotta dish or suchlike—and put over medium-low heat. Add the onion and cook for 5 minutes or so, until beginning to soften. Add the garlic and cook, stirring, for another couple of minutes. Add the chorizo, the bay leaf, and the sherry, stir, and add the potatoes. Stir and pour over water from the kettle to cover, but only just; don't worry about the odd potato poking above water-level. Simmer for 10 minutes and season with the salt and pepper.

Put the dish in the oven, uncovered, and cook for 35–40 minutes, or until hot and the potatoes are tender but not crumbling. Remove, ladle into bowls, and sprinkle over the coriander as you hand them round. You need lots of (unbuttered) bread with this, but not much else—perhaps a pale, crunchy, and astringent salad after.

ONE-PAN CHICKEN

This is very easy, very quick. Don't be too hung up about the quantities below; they're nothing more than a guideline.

olive oil	16 garlic cloves, unpeeled
1 3½-pound chicken, cut into 8 pieces	3 red peppers, seeded and quartered
2¼ pounds new potatoes, cut into	coarse sea salt
½-inch dice	½ cup chopped parsley
3 medium red onions, cut into segments	

Preheat the oven to 425°F.

Get 2 baking dishes and pour in some olive oil to coat. Arrange the pieces of chicken, the potatoes, onions, garlic cloves, and peppers on them. (If you want to use 3 dishes and have got the room, do; the less packed everything is, the crisper the potatoes will be.) Then drizzle some more oil over, making sure everything's glossy and well slicked (but not dripping), sprinkle with the salt, and bake for about 45 minutes.

When done (and test all component parts), strew over the parsley and—I always do this—serve straight from the baking dishes. A green salad's all you need with it, but puy lentils do go well.

INVOLTINI

Don't serve this dish of provolone-stuffed fried eggplant piping hot, but warm. The quantities of stuffing make enough for 12 rolls, so I sauté only the best 12 slices of eggplant and then stop. If you feel 3 rolls per head will just not do, scale up accordingly. I never salt eggplant; just make sure you buy ones that are bouncily firm and shiny. You can cook the eggplant in advance, if you like; also, if you prefer, strew additional provolone over the involtini rather than mozzarella before baking.

olive oil for frying

2 large eggplants cut lengthways into
   2-inch slices

FOR THE STUFFING

6 ounces provolone cheese, cut into
   very small cubes

½ cup pine nuts

⅓ cup raisins, soaked in water until
   plump, then drained

¼ cup extra-virgin olive oil

2 tablespoons fresh white bread crumbs

1 garlic clove, crushed or minced

2 tablespoons freshly grated Parmesan

1 tablespoon chopped fresh basil

salt and freshly milled pepper

1 egg, beaten

½ cup tomato purée

8 ounces mozzarella, cut into 2-inch
   slices

Preheat the oven to 375°F.

Fill a large frying pan with about 2 inches of the oil and heat. Add the eggplant slices, a few at a time, and fry until golden on both sides. As they're done, remove them to paper towels to drain. You will have to add quite a bit more oil as you go, so don't panic about it. Leave the eggplant slices to cool as you make the stuffing.

In a bowl mix together the cheese, pine nuts, raisins, olive oil, bread crumbs, garlic, Parmesan, and basil; season with the salt and pepper and bind with the egg. Lay out the cooked eggplant slices on a work surface and divide the stuffing between them (I find 1–2 tablespoons per slice about right). Roll them up tightly to secure the filling and put them, as you go, into a lightly greased gratin dish into which they'll fit snugly.

Pour over the tomato purée. Arrange the mozzarella down the center, in a line lengthways like a snowman's buttons. Drizzle with olive oil, season with salt and pepper, and bake in the oven for 25–30 minutes, or until the cheese is melted and blistered and the sauce is bubbling. Let stand for a bit before serving.

TAGLIATELLE WITH CHICKEN FROM THE VENETIAN GHETTO

This recipe comes from one of the best food books I've read, Claudia Roden's *Book of Jewish Food.* It is rather far removed from the sort of food I think of as typically Jewish in Britian, which might be comforting but lacks many of the other culinary virtues.

Of course you can use raisins; I prefer sultanas.

I 3½-pound chicken	½ cup pine nuts, lightly toasted
2 tablespoons extra-virgin olive oil	I pound tagliatelle
salt and freshly milled black pepper	2–3 tablespoons chopped parsley
leaves from 3 rosemary sprigs, minced	
⅓ cup sultanas, soaked in warm water for 30 minutes	

Preheat the oven to 350°F.

Rub the chicken with the oil and sprinkle with the salt and pepper, then place it breast down in a roasting pan and roast for about 1½ hours, or until well browned, turning it over toward the end to brown the breast. It's done when the juices run clear, not pink, when you cut into the thigh. When the chicken's nearly ready, put abundant water on for the pasta, salting it when it boils.

Take the chicken out of the oven and take the meat off the bone, leaving all that glorious burnished skin on, and cut it into small pieces. I do much of this by just pulling, without a knife, but if you haven't got asbestos hands, use a knife and fork or wait till it's cooler.

For the sauce, pour all the juices from the roasting pan into a saucepan. Add the rosemary, the drained sultanas and the pine nuts. Begin to simmer the sauce when you are ready to cook the pasta.

Cook and drain the pasta, and toss it with the sauce, chicken pieces, and parsley in a large warmed bowl. No cheese, please.

The last suggestion in this section is less a recipe than, for me, a way of life: boiled chicken with rice and egg and lemon sauce. This is the food of my childhood, a taste that roots me in my past. When my brother, Dominic, and Rosa got married, this is what he asked me and my sisters to cook for him the night before. For us, this is the most significant kitchen supper.

Exact quantities would not be in the spirit of things, but all you do is put a chicken, preferably a hen, or 2 younger chickens in a pot, throw in chunked carrots, an onion or two, some leeks, a stalk of celery, some parsley stalks, and peppercorns, cover with water, and add salt.

Bring to the boil and then simmer 2–3 hours for a hen, 1–1½ hours for younger birds, often skimming the foam that rises to the surface. About 40 minutes before the end of cooking time, remove as many of the vegetables as you can fish out with a slotted spoon and add fresh carrots and leeks (and if I'm not in the mood for rice, I might add peeled halved or quartered potatoes, too). If you've not been able to get a hen, the consequent stock will not be much stronger than water. In that case, either cook the chicken in stock instead of water to start or add a couple of stock cubes in place of the salt. Assuming you're using rice—and I like plain basmati—cook it separately in time to serve with the finished dish.

The egg and lemon sauce, my mother's sauce, is really just a loosened, saffron-streaked hollandaise, without the ceremony. In the top of a double boiler, over simmering water, put a couple of egg yolks, a pinch of saffron threads, and a grinding of pepper (my mother always used white), and start beating with a whisk. Cube by softened cube, add some butter—until it's thick and pale yellow—then, always beating, add a ladle or so of the chicken stock from the neighboring pot. Keep whisking, though more gently perhaps now, and when you have a thickened but still runny warm sauce, add a squirt or two of lemon. Transfer to a bowl with a plate beneath it and place on the table with its own little ladle. I bring the whole chicken to the table and carve it there; diners help themselves to the sauce.

As for dessert for any of the kitchen suppers, if I'm in the mood to make one, I make what I feel like eating, whether it comes from my dinner-party repertoire or is something I might otherwise think of having after a weekend lunch. By not suggesting any particular desserts here, I'm not depriving you; all the sweet thangs mentioned in any chapter of the book are listed in the Index.

LOW FAT

This is not the healthy foods chapter; it's not a healing, nurturing place where bad dietary consciences can come to self-congratulatory rest. You will not read about toxins and chai levels, about chakras and meridians. Nor am I interested in blood-sugar levels or cholesterol. Let's be frank: the issue here is vanity, not health; whether your jeans will zip, not what your oxygen uptake is. No one likes to own up to such a narcissistic preoccupation as mere appearance. Dieting claims almost a moral status when health comes into play. With what piety and smugness do the dietetically pure wave away those wicked, fat-clogged foods and show us, sinners all, the way, the truth, and the Lite.

I don't disparage the shallow concerns of the ordinarily vain, which, after all, I share. What I hate is all this new-age voodoo about eating, the notion that foods are either harmful or healing, that a good diet makes a good person and that that person is necessarily lean, limber, toned, and fit. Quite apart from anything else, I don't see the muscular morality argument. Why should a concern for your physical health be seen as a sign of virtue? Such a view seems to me in danger of fusing nazism (with its ideological cult of physical perfection) and puritanism (with its horror of the flesh and belief in salvation through denial).

So I take it for granted that anyone wanting to read here about low-fat food is doing so because they want to improve their *ligne*, not their soul. More, I assume that anyone in need of diminution likes food. It is, after all, those of us who enjoy eating who tend to put on weight in the first place. All too often, though, the sort of people who espouse what I refuse to describe as "healthy eating" care little for food—and it shows.

Good low-fat food takes time, preparation, and thought. This puts a lot of people off, but it's part of the lure for me. I love the whole business of food. One of the things that makes me miserable about diets and dieting (more so than the obvious restraints) is that all too often they reduce food not merely to fuel but to medicine. I like the ceremony of food preparation, the shopping, the chopping, the stirring, and attending.

Calorie intake is crucial. I shouldn't need to say this, it is both so obvious and has been known, and scientifically proven, for so long, but as every contemporary dietary trend is against it, you do need to be reminded and you do need to take note: if your energy intake in the form of calories exceeds your energy expenditure—what it takes to keep you going plus any exercise you want to take to boost it—then you will put on weight; if the latter exceeds the former, you will lose weight. It can't—pending findings, rather than wishful theories, to the contrary—not work. Everyone has their pet excuse, their alternative explanations—it's metabolism, what you eat with what, the intrinsic properties of certain foods, or all down to allergies and intolerances.

Despite, however, a firm belief in the ungainsayable truth of the calorie-intake theory of weight control, I wouldn't begin to suggest that's all there is to it. Put at its plainest, we know that what makes us fat is eating too much, but that says nothing about why we might eat too much, why we get fat, why we might find it difficult to lose those self-destructive, self-sabotaging habits. I'd have found it very difficult to embark on a diet and stick to it unless I'd first tackled why I'd put on weight. I don't imagine I'm very different from most women in that I turn to food when I'm unhappy or under stress. And of course, like most women, too, my eating habits and whole attitude toward food have been influenced by my mother's eating habits and her attitudes toward food. I make this point not because I have any particular impulse toward self-revelation but because I do want to make it clear that I know dieting is not as easy as just eating less. Having said that, you won't lose weight unless you do. And for all my long-held beliefs that fat was a feminist issue, that the modern tyranny of the scales was both ideologically and physically damaging, and that intolerance of the unthin was dangerous, I have to admit that I felt awful when I put on weight after the birth of my first child and better when I lost it.

If you stick to eating foods that are not high in fat most of the time, it is likely that your calorie intake will, anyway, be curtailed. I find (when I'm trying to lose rather than just not put on weight) I keep an eye on calories too, as I somehow seem to be able to consume such vast platefuls of food that I can, with relative ease, go calorifically stratospheric while virtuously applying low-fat principles. And if you want to, then I advise you to scour the bookstore shelves for a calorie guide that you can both read and fit into pocket or purse. When I draw up my own dietary accounts, my sums are not exact or scientifically correct. That's to say, I erroneously zero-rate soy sauce, Vietnamese or Thai fish sauce, all herbs, cabbage, carrots, onions, mushrooms, zucchini, snow peas and sugar-snaps, green or French beans, spinach, chard, bok choy and all that sort of leafy stuff, all lettuces, baby corn, baby asparagus, turnips, leeks, and pretty well any vegetable that isn't starchy.

But even when I just want to counteract an intensified bout of eating, either as a result of work or in the general run of a greedy life, I would never go below 1,250 calories a day. And on the whole, I don't count the calories, I just concentrate on the following type of eating.

Much as I hate the false witnesses of the various new-age health movements, I accept that, in order to make this whole thing work, you need to get in the mood, adopt something of the mindset; you need to shift into the my-body-is-a-temple mode. This way none of it feels like self-denial or deprivation; it feels like giving yourself something, doing something positive for yourself. For all the intellectual muzziness or rapt self-absorption involved, this is crucially important. As the one-time mayor of New York, Fiorello la Guardia, put it, if the ends don't justify the means, I don't know what does.

There is no one easy way to lose weight—different people find different ways; it's a case of what works for you. This is what works for me.

BEFORE YOU START

Because so much of this is about getting your head in gear, what you must do at the beginning is psych yourself up. And because you also need to make it easier for yourself, on a practical level, by having all the right foods around, you can combine the two by going on a mood- and scene-setting shopping expedition. This does two things: it helps banish any residual feelings of dismay about imminent deprivation (you are, after all, buying things for yourself and, moreover, things to eat) and it helps propel you into just that arena of obsession that is necessary to the successful outcome of any diet. Yes, yes, yes, to be too obsessed is a bad thing, and no, no, no, I am not for a minute suggesting you totter down the first steps toward anorexia and bulimia and associated eating disorders, but we all know that the less we're trying to eat, the more we think about it, so it makes sense to exploit that. Here, it means getting every little thing right to facilitate the cooking and, later, it means thinking at length about what you're going to cook and how. The planning is not only a necessary part of losing weight; it also satisfies the part of the brain that wants, in a normally greedy person—and who else would need to be concerned with all this?—to be occupied with food.

I find just drawing up a shopping list of diet-enhancing ingredients fills me with all the zeal, good vibes, and necessary I-can-do-thisness to make me feel positively impatient for it all to start. My stock list would be something like this.

best-quality vegetable bouillon cubes and a small selection of other
packaged stock, including Thai pork and tom yam
(a spicy, citrus-y broth) cubes

about 92,000 types of soy sauce (tamari soy, shoyu, light soy,
dark soy, Japanese soy, citrus-flavored soy, Indonesian kecup
manis, the lot)

teriyaki sauce and sukiyaki sauce (both these are really just soy sauce with
other ingredients, itemized below, added for you)

Thai or Vietnamese fish sauce, nam pla or nuoc mam

sake

dry sherry

vermouth

mirin

rice vinegar

miso

instant dashi (sometimes called dashi-no-moto or hon dashi)

few packs Japanese instant miso soups and ramen noodle soups

Japanese pickled ginger

balsamic vinegar

good red wine vinegar

various mustards—English, powder and made, Dijon, Meaux,
tarragon, and other flavors you like

various dry pastas and noodles (Italian short and long and Asian rice,
buckwheat, and egg noodles)

Tabasco, red and green

chili sauce

comprehensive collection of spices

dried shiitake mushrooms

basmati rice

garlic

onions

shallots

lemons

limes

dried red chili peppers

good bought low-fat tomato sauce for pasta (check nutrition tables on
bottles in the stores and try out till you find one you like)

toasted, or fragrant, sesame oil (yes, really)

garlic-infused oil (ditto)

IN THE FRIDGE

There is no way you can make sure of an adequate supply of all the ingredients
you might like to use without also having, sporadically, to throw away stuff that's
gone off. Even the exotic ingredients can mostly be found at the supermarket.

one each, at least, of each package of supermarket prepped vegetables

bok choy or similar leafy greens

salad stuff

bunch each of coriander and flat-leaf parsley

lemon grass

Thai basil

fresh rice sticks and somen noodles

shrimp paste

miso (I add it here, too, as it goes in the fridge once opened and I buy
containers from a Japanese shop, for preference, not awkward-to-use
plastic bags of it)

fresh chili peppers

fresh ginger

scallions

a ready-prepared but nonfrozen meal (see below)

fat-free fromage blanc

fat-free yogurt

very-low-fat fruit yogurts

FOR THE FREEZER

kaffir lime leaves

one or two bagged-up portions cooked rice

some ready-prepared (either by you or the supermarket) frozen meals

¼-cup portions of good Cheddar, shredded

1 steak, well wrapped

1 chicken cutlet, well wrapped

sliced bread

frozen whole-leaf spinach

frozen raspberries or mixed fruits

Bread, good bread, is one of my weaknesses, and I can eat an entire loaf without difficulty. If I'm having a poached egg on toast, as part of my dieting intake, I want to make sure I know I've eaten it. For this I need proper bread. I go to a French bakery and buy a couple of loaves of their pain du campagne (sludge-colored and grainy with a toothsome, tough hide) or other round country loaf, which I get put through their slicer and bagged up. I put these bags in the freezer. I can then toast, slice by single slice, as needed, from frozen, and it's not quite so easy to chomp through an entire loaf without thinking.

EQUIPMENT

If you're keeping food in the freezer, a microwave is a near-essential piece of equipment. I figure that most of us who need (and often repeatedly) to lose weight are those for whom instant gratification takes too long. I seek to minimize damage (it's awe-inspiring how many calories you can consume, standing up, just while the dinner's cooking) by having a supply of food I can get from frozen to cooked in a few minutes.

I am not going to suggest that you rush out and buy a great number of gadgets. Many of you will already have a food processor and a microwave. I think there is really only one other essential item and that's a good nonstick frying pan. The only other piece of equipment I'd mention isn't essential but is useful: a griddle. No one needs reminding about plain grilled fish or chicken, but I find too much of this stock-diet food immensely depressing. Most domestic broilers are just not hot enough, so that all lean cuts dry out before they are cooked—which is where the griddle comes in. By this I mean one of those heavy cast-iron slabs, ridged on one side for meat and vegetables, smooth on the other for fish. You do need to oil this to some extent, and I use here an oil and water spray I make myself (pinching the idea from the low-fat culinary evangelist Sue Kreitzman) by buying an atomizer and filling it with one part best olive oil to seven parts water. You can, of course, just buy an olive oil spray from the supermarket if it makes life easier. The griddle's good for giving that charcoal-striated edge to otherwise plain foods, and the searing heat that comes over cast iron seems to make food taste more acutely of itself, keep it juicier, and make it look better. On the down side, it is very heavy (often I feel just too limp-wristed even to contemplate dragging it out of its drawer beneath the lower oven) and can be nightmarish to wash up; the feel of scourer against cast iron is rather like nails down a blackboard.

Dieting demands exact measurements. You need scales, proper teaspoon and tablespoon measures (the whole set, indeed, comprising ¼- and ½-teaspoon measures, too), and, of course, measuring cups.

BASIC PRINCIPLES

Immerse yourself in the desirable ethos before you begin and settle into good habits once you do. Alcohol is immensely useful in bringing real depth of flavor to food cooked without fat, but if you really want to lose weight, I think you have to give up drinking. I am more of an eater than a drinker so I don't mind, but I know this is difficult for many people. It's not just the calories in the alcohol; even a small drink makes me feel positively insouciant about weight, diet, food, calories, all of it. This is a wonderful feeling while it lasts, but dismal when—several thousand calories later—it stops. Also, if I drink enough to give me even a little shadow of a hangover, I have to eat vast amounts of fatty, stodgy food the next day to absorb—or so it feels—all the excess alcohol of the previous evening.

With eating I am less rigid. For just as I find a balance between large portions of low-fat and small portions of relatively high-fat food the best way of maintaining interest in what I'm eating when trying to lose weight, so I find I can stick longer to any diet if I keep a balance between repetition and variety. For example, I find it uncomplicates matters if every day I have the same breakfast and more or less, but not exclusively, the same lunch. Dinner I like to vary, and as much and as thought-consumingly as possible. Those who can't make their own lunch (although many workplaces have rudimentary cooking equipment now) might prefer to swap lunch with dinner, though I must say I'd find it hard to stick to a diet if I ate the same dinner every night. I need to feel dinner is a proper, celebratory meal, when the food I eat is food I can concentrate on, think about, both beforehand and afterward. Breakfast is about ⅓ cup oatmeal (preferably organic, or it's just a slimy, too-smooth wallpaper paste) cooked with a scant cup water and eaten with 1 tablespoon golden syrup. If I know I will just stagger into the kitchen in the morning and get that underway, it stops me from deciding on the spur of the moment to put a couple of pieces of toast on, slather them with butter, then heap them with marmalade.

Although a low-fat diet makes things easier in terms of losing weight, for me a low-sugar one doesn't. I found that if I used hardly any sugar (or some ghastly sugar substitute), the food I ate just wasn't as filling. The same's true with hot drinks. I don't take sugar in tea, but I do in coffee. For ages I used one of those powdered ersatz sugars, the sort that fizz up spookily after you add them to the filled-up mug; then I just went back to sugar. What I found was that if I had a mug of coffee with sugar, it filled me up as if I'd eaten food (which of course I had, in the form of the calorie-bestowing sugar). Having said that, I virtually inhale all those fizzy, Nutra-sweetened drinks, the ones we are finger-waggingly told to give up in the name of cellulite-banishment, when I'm trying to lose weight.

Now, lunch: the most filling and somehow undiet-tasting lunch I found was a baked potato with cheese. Diet books and magazines advocate reduced-fat cheese; I cannot. Despite my love for the well-piled plate, I would prefer to have a small piece of some proper, good cheese than double, quadruple the amount of some low-fat, depressing variant. (Yogurt and fromage blanc, however, somehow taste low-fat even when they're not really, so you may as well go for the low-fat ones.) Food shouldn't be tampered with so that all its rightful, taste-giving properties are taken out of it. Try to find a way of cooking food that's meant to be low fat rather than eat strangulated versions of food that was born to be saturated in the stuff. That is one of the reasons why most of my diet-minded suppers (see below) are Thai and Japanese, or otherwise Asian in tone, if not directly; these cuisines quite naturally don't use a lot of fat in many of their dishes, so the food tastes right, is right, cooked like that. Fake diet food, like reduced-fat Cheddar, which tastes like bitter rubber, is a waste of your time. In your baked potato, real, strong Cheddar in a smaller quantity will have more taste, and will melt more seductively into the floury flesh, so that you won't even feel that you're getting less for your calories: 1 ounce true Cheddar comes to about the same calorie count as a similar reduced-fat cheese. So we're not even talking about much less in quantity. To be this precise (or obsessive) about calorie counts, it is easier to buy well-labeled packaged cheese. You also need electronic scales. And the grater and the freezer. Were I to have a chunk of Cheddar in the fridge, I'd eat it. So instead I keep a large supply of bagged-up grated cheese, all weighed and uniform, at 100 calories a bag. (And this principle is worth applying to any food that is permissible for your diet in individual portions but not eaten *en bloc*.) Each lunchtime, I take the little frozen bag out to thaw as I put my potato in the oven to cook. It is a routine, a ritual. If you work in an office that has a microwave, you'll have to make do with that. (I absolutely can't take a packed lunch anywhere with me or I'd eat it by eleven in the morning. I can feel it throbbing away beneath the desk or in my bag and just can't concentrate until I get rid of it.) This is the advantage of the baked potato option—it becomes routine,

BAKED
POTATOES

CHEESE

which prevents lunch being a significant, decision-provoking issue, but somehow makes it a reassuring fixed point; and it's there, but uncooked till the moment of blitzing, so you can't just wolf it down.

A potato that weighs about 7 ounces raw, which is a goodish-sized potato, plus my 100-calorie package of cheese, makes a lunch of 250 calories. Include my breakfast, of just above 150 calories, and I've still got quite a lot of calories saved for the evening. But I want to offer up one more pearl of dietetic wisdom. Don't allow yourself to get too fiercely and unforgivingly hungry. If you leave eating till you could scrape the wallpaper off and eat that, then two things will happen: the first is that you will be jumpy and depressed; the second is that you'll be so hungry you won't be able to stop eating when you're full up. The more nagging hunger you feel during a diet, the more likely you are to ditch it.

YOGURT

FROMAGE
BLANC

If you need to eat between meals, don't allow yourself to feel you've failed or that you've given in or whatever it is that makes people inflate with self-reproach and then eat double. Instead, take a low-fat yogurt or fromage blanc from the fridge. The yogurt is about 70 calories for a 6-ounce cup, the fromage blanc, 60 calories for 4 ounces, and, small as these quantities are, they fill you up quite efficiently for a while. Of course it would be better in any number of ways to have an apple or an orange, but sometimes you need the gloop too. Reconcile yourself to this now, count it in, and then move on, sister. It's all very well getting hungry when you're at home, because you can be sure to find something suitable to eat. But it's more difficult when you're out. Pretzel sticks are 120 calo-

PRETZEL
STICKS

ries per ounce and low-fat with it. And because they're so salty, they feel filling (strong tastes do that; see more on this below), plus they're portable. If you had a huge drum of pretzel sticks in front of you, you'd find it difficult to stop eating after your 120 calories' worth, so weigh and stick to a 1-ounce allotment. A bar of chocolate with about 230 calories, or a bag of chips at about 150, are not disasters, either. There are times when chocolate is what's needed and it's better to have just one bar, count it in, and adjust your eating for the rest of the day accordingly, than to brood obsessively on it, have grilled fish for dinner, and then go out, buy, and eat the entire contents of the all-night deli and live, self-flagellatingly, to regret it.

A diet that eliminated all fats would be extremely bad for you (and unpalatable). My point is to find balance, not to veer off into extremes. And to vary pace and plate, I often prefer a small portion of something high-fat bolstered by forests of green vegetables. One of my regular dinners when trying to lose weight is a supermarket-purchased package of macaroni and cheese. Now, I am not going to claim that this is a low-fat food, but there is not very much of it, and what there is is filling. When I'm too hungry or too tired to cook, I have one of those, with a whole package of ready-prepped lettuce and some other green vegetable with strong mustard on the side. Given that the macaroni is under 500 calories for a 12-ounce portion and I don't count calories in vegetables, this is a trim little dinner all told. Anyway, I can't reiterate too often the need for balance and variation. The thing to remember is to pile, next to almost anything you're eating, a huge amount of soy-dressed or lemon-squeezed leafy or crunchy vegetables.

Much, as Byron wrote in *Don Juan*, depends on dinner. If I eat well at night, and not only eat well but make something of a ritual pleasure out of the meal, I don't feel that edginess, that diet-deprivation thing, that boredom above all else, that can make it all intolerable. Dinner has to feel civilized, or life doesn't feel civilized.

First, stagger the food, so it feels as if you have a wonderful procession of things to eat, not a great mound of stuff on a plate. These quiet rituals—and the low-fat, health-store foods they involve—create a pleasantly virtuous and serene mood. A girlfriend and I refer meaningfully to such meals as temple food. And, as the Japanese know, it makes a difference. If I've decided to have a salmon steak, seared speckly brown and tangerine without, still Fanta-colored within, and some still-crunchy broccoli with soy and a few pinprick dots of sesame oil alongside, I might—to prolong my eating evening—make some grilled zucchini to eat before or drink a bowl of miso soup, and, afterward, peel and finely slice an orange and drizzle over with orange-flower water. This is to make me feel it's something special that I'm eating.

SALMON

This is a regular supper-enhancer. Get in from work, put a griddle, corrugated side up, on the stove, and then slice a few zucchini down the length of them so that you have thin, long, butter-knife-shaped strips. Spritz the griddle with your water-and-oil spray, then cook the zucchini strips briefly on each side till they're tigered brown. Remove, sprinkle with salt, chop over some herbs—parsley, mint, coriander, any one or all three—douse with lemon juice, and just eat.

ZUCCHINI

Another fatless and, in my book, calorieless picking-food is charred, peeled, and sliced peppers (see page 86 for the method) over which you've sprinkled a drop or two of good balsamic vinegar, squirted a little orange juice, and sprinkled a little salt and more than a little chopped flat-leaf parsley. And this is transcendental in January when the Seville oranges are sometimes around. Their particular biting but fragrant sourness points up the oily sweetness of the skinned and softened peppers. Pomegranate juice (use an electric squeezer) is heavenly, too. (I like to keep this soused tangle of peppers on standby; leave to steep in the fridge

PEPPERS

SEVILLE
ORANGES

and add grassy clumps of freshly chopped flat-leaf parsley whenever you eat it. This oil-free peperonata also happens to make a fabulous sandwich filling.)

LEMONS AND NUTMEG

But this flavor-intensifying principle works all year round. Just use lemons. It's not only broccoli whose sweetness is made the more vibrant with a squirt of lemon, but all greens. Nutmeg—with all of the above—works in a different but equally effective flavor-enhancing way. And any of the soys can be substituted for the lemon. Make a tomato salad, leafy with basil, dressed just with a few drops of good balsamic vinegar. Roasting vegetables also seems to make them taste more emphatically of themselves; leeks (see page 319 and reduce the oil a little), or asparagus, or, indeed, more or less any vegetable can be cooked with a very little oil (if you use none at all, you'll just have a wizened, limp mess) in a fiercely hot oven. To look at they'll be muted, but the flavors will be kickstarted into vibrant life.

TOMATOES

LEEKS AND ASPARAGUS

The trick is not to become bored and therefore to use as varied a collection of vegetables as possible. Fennel can be sliced thinly and baked in a small amount of stock in a moderate oven for about 40 minutes, or eaten as a salad with lamb's lettuce and lemon juice. Add an equal amount of white wine to salted water, bring to the boil, and add leeks cut into about 4-inch lengths and cook until tender. Cauliflower can be broken into florets, dusted with ground cumin, and baked in a very hot oven for about 20 minutes until it tastes sweet and charred and spiced; actually, I think this is the best way to eat cauliflower, diet or no diet.

FENNEL

CAULIFLOWER AND CUMIN

Chop any vegetable on hand and cook in a method that combines stir-frying with steaming; throw a small amount of stock in a wok and on a high heat add ginger, garlic, scallions, sugar-snaps, broccoli, fennel, carrots, and baby corn. But all this isn't just to ring the changes with what might otherwise be thought of as standard diet food. The more strongly food tastes, the fuller it makes you. It's the depth of the flavor that helps atone for the lack of fat. In the days when I was the hostage of a sandwich bar at lunchtimes, I'd have a low-fat cottage cheese sand-wich—no butter—but with anchovies; the saltiness, the aggressive and indelicate invasiveness of those cheap and unsoaked tin-corroded fish made me feel, after it was finished, that something actually had been eaten, whereas a plain cottage cheese sandwich, even on whole-wheat, hardly has the force of personality to make itself felt. You're not eating; you're giving the mime performance of a person lunching on a sandwich.

VEGETABLES WITH GINGER AND GARLIC

ANCHOVIES

That's where Thai, especially, and other Southeast Asian cuisines come in; they draw on intense flavors, have a vivid culinary vocabulary, and fill you with-out supplying much in the way of fat. Italian food, it's true, is also strong and direct and robustly flavored, but it uses more oil, and that oil, green, pungent, evocative, is not an optional extra. It's an essential part of the food. And I know it's supposed to be life-enhancing and healthy but it will still, all oils being equally fattening, make you put on weight. Not that all Italian food uses a lot of it, nor does olive oil have to go completely from your regime. You need only a little. If you add, at the end (rather than at the beginning) of cooking, one teaspoon, a few drops of it even, the glorious taste will come through, virtuous drabness will disappear, and flavors will be revitalized. I often, too, stir about a quarter of a teaspoon of garlic-infused oil into some lemon-squeezed spinach; sesame oil makes itself pungently felt in the most minute quantities.

My concern here is how you go about leading the low-fat life in your own kitchen, but there is one important piece of advice to be applied in the world beyond it. Never say diet. By that I don't mean you should banish such a foul four-letter word in favor of the smug-speak term, Healthy Eating Plan, but simply that you should never talk about it. Not out loud. Not in public. In the first instance, talking about dieting is a big bore and, in the second, everyone will try, if only out of politeness, to talk you out of it. The third, crucial, element is pure vanity; if you tell people you need to lose weight they will notice that yes, maybe you do need to.

The fortunate truth is that no one is really interested in anyone else. If you don't tell them you're on a diet, they won't even notice. You can eat as little as you want without drawing attention to it and therefore without inviting comment or sabotage, or allowing yourself to use the excuse of others to sabotage the diet yourself. If you want to diet, then you have to take the responsibility yourself, not draft everyone else into the diet police.

When you're invited to dinner, don't warn people of your diet or draw attention to it while you're there. It's so aggressive to do that, so self-centered, and so dispiriting. And you'll just be a party-pooper. Once people know about the diet, they'll feel that you can't really enjoy yourself until you eat and drink to Rabelaisian excess. They'll feel you're being dried up and puritanical and drained of joie de vivre. But if you don't make an issue of it, they won't think of looking at your plate.

I find it very difficult to leave food, but if you really want to and can, then be the one to jump up and clear the plates so no one else sees. You have an easy excuse for not drinking; just say you're driving. But, again, there is no need for anyone really to notice. Just let your glass be filled, but don't drink it.

There may well be nobler spirits out there, but I find the assault on one's vanity the hardest thing about dieting. It's bad enough you need to lose weight, but drawing other people's attention to it is quite intolerable. And it's not just weight gain I don't like people to notice—I can't bear references to weight loss, either. Call me paranoid, but every time someone says "You've lost weight!" I hear "You were fat!"

There is a vexing circularity about the dieting business: it's easiest to lose weight if you feel self-confident, but it is weight loss that makes you self-confident. But you can work the con trick on yourself. Just as Pascal believed that the act of going to church, of going through the motions of the faithful, led to faith, so if you act thin, you will get thin. "Eat like a thin person" is the best form of dietary advice. And behave like a thin person, too, which means don't go on about being fat.

Most of the recipes that follow are for one; some are for two. I take the line that that's how we tend to eat when trying to lose weight. Not everyone wants to get into the strict diet account-keeping needed for a calorie-counted diet, but you may follow the recipes below in the knowledge that all the food here is low-fat and programmed for diminution.

QUICK STUFF, OR SUGGESTIONS FOR ALMOST-THROWN-TOGETHER SUPPERS

STEAK

Although I subsist mostly on carbohydrates and vegetables when I'm trying to lose weight, I like red meat every now and then when I'm not eating so much; it's filling, it makes me feel better (in France doctors can still prescribe steak and red wine for patients who are run down), and it seems an efficient use of restricted calories. Fillet is one of the leanest cuts and yields the right, slight, single-portion size (I aim for about 4 ounces to make room for other components, before or after), but if I've got a friend over, or just feel like a meaty blow-out, I buy an 8-ounce, ¾-inch-thick slab of rump, put it on the griddle, and cook till crusty without, tender and bloody within. Then I take it off the griddle, sprinkle with salt, and leave it to rest on a plate for 5–10 minutes.

Meanwhile, I slice some tomatoes and sprinkle them with salt and balsamic vinegar, or I wilt some spinach. I pour off the juices that have collected on the plate with the steak into a bowl, add some soy sauce or bottled (or make your own, see below) teriyaki sauce. Then I slice the meat in thin slices diagonally across, arrange them on the plate, pour over the bloodied soy, and thickly feather it all with freshly chopped, cave-breath, pungent coriander. If you want a more

Italianate version, substitute lemon juice for the soy and arugula for the coriander. Either way, I like to eat this with hot English mustard on the side.

FISH

Salmon and tuna are the fish world's equivalent of steak. They are oilier than those pallid, white-fleshed varieties, but they are denser, heavier, too, and more robust in flavor. If you can afford the best bass or sole, then just grill and eat it. Squirt with lemon, sprinkle with salt, and, if you're not being unnecessarily, obsessively strict, dribble over the merest ¼ teaspoon of the most beautiful olive oil (the milder Ligurian for choice) to bring out the sweet, smoky depths of the fish.

POISSON AU POIVRE

Both tuna and salmon can be treated in the same way as steak, either plain broiled or grilled and dressed in soy and herb-sprinkled as above, or coated in crushed pepper and grilled or dry-fried in a nonstick pan to create a juicy piscine take on the bifteck bistro original, poisson au poivre.

TATAKI OF TUNA

At its most basic, tataki of tuna is just a small, thick, fleshy piece of tuna, about 8 ounces, cut from the tail, seared on all sides on a smooth griddle or heavy frying pan, and left rare within. It is then left to cool, dunked in ice water, dried well, and sliced very thinly (see, for interest and comparison, though not for low-fat consumption necessarily, the carpaccio on page 138). Slice some scallions into 1½-inch lengths and cut these in half lengthways, too. Arrange on a plate. Then cut the tuna into very thin slices diagonally across. You will see the outline of the brown-crusted exterior, the ruby fleshiness within. You can dress the tuna with ½ tablespoon lime juice mixed with a pinch of sugar and 1 tablespoonful soy sauce and/or serve a piercingly hot dipping sauce of wasabi powder mixed to a thin paste with soy. And if you want to intensify the contrast between the fish steak's soft, sweet interior and seared, almost bitter, crust, then dredge the tuna in some wasabi powder, too, before grilling it. Sprinkle with coriander and eat with a cucumber salad made by cutting a decent chunk of a cucumber in half, scraping out the seeds, and then cutting the two halves finely so that you have a mound of jadelike, glassy half-moons.

SUGAR-SPICED SALMON WITH CHINESE HOT MUSTARD

From a quirky American book called *Pacifica Blue Plates* by Neil Stuart, I picked up a way of cooking salmon that has contrast and impact. The title—Sugar-Spiced Salmon with Chinese Hot Mustard—takes almost longer to write than the recipe does to cook. I've adapted the original idea (leaving out the stipulated ¼ teaspoon cocoa), but the result, the almost uncooked Day-Glo interior, the crisp, dull bronze but sharp-spiced seared casing around, provides the satisfactions of the original. For an 8-ounce juicy, thick salmon fillet (cut from the top end of the fish), mix ¼ teaspoon each ground ginger, cinnamon, cumin, cayenne, sugar, salt, and (Colman's) mustard powder. Heat a griddle (smooth side up) or a nonstick pan and, when hot, thickly dredge the fish in the spice mixture and cook for 2–3 minutes per side, or until seared and bronze without, still rare and coral-fleshed within. Remove and let stand while you make the purportedly Chinese hot mustard sauce, just by mixing a teaspoon and a half each of sugar and mustard powder with 1 teaspoon of warm water. I like this with barely cooked sugar-snaps. And the hot, sweet mustard sauce will jumpstart even the dullest piece of plain grilled farmed salmon. If you can find or afford wild salmon, let nothing interfere; save some lemon or the merest ghost of some freshly chopped tarragon.

RICE

Rice and broccoli, doused in ordinary soy sauce or citrus-seasoned soy or sukiyaki sauce, is a quick bowl-to-mouth supper. Basmati rice takes about 10 minutes, though if you keep some frozen in bags, you can nuke a portion in the microwave as soon as you walk in through the door in the evening. (I'm not mad about microwaved broccoli, though.) Sometimes a little bowlful of rice eaten immediately can stop you eating everything in the fridge later. In my more temple-food moods, I go in for brown rice, but it takes ages to cook and sometimes feels like a virtuous rather than a pleasurable choice. Where brown rice really works is in a salad; let the rice get cold, keep it in the fridge, and then you can make a quick supper by adding soy (by itself or with dashi and mirin added), chopped scallions, sugar-snaps, mint, and coriander.

A LITTLE SOMETHING ON TOAST

Less exotically, you should never forget the filling and comforting properties of baked beans or poached eggs on toast. As long as you get whatever's covering the toast on top of it the minute the toast pops out of the toaster, the lack of butter won't be a lastingly significant loss.

SMALL BIRDS

A 1-pound poussin is about 400 calories, skin and all—about half that if you can eat it without the skin. I prefer to double my caloric intake by eating it burnished and crisp-skinned; it feels like so much more of a treat. I often cook a couple of these when a girlfriend comes for supper; with it you can make any salad or vegetable you like. I like the lemony, herb-dense, grated beets on page 391.

I also love grouse, partridge, and quail, admittedly not everyday items. Eating the whole of something makes you feel less deprived. Roast grouse plain, which is no hardship either in terms of cooking or eating, and almost braise partridge by cooking it in the oven in a little puddle of stock and chopped vegetables. Shred the cooked meat and stir it into some carrot, onion, and garlic-studded lentils. See also the recipe for lacquered quail, page 389.

TEMPLE FOOD

Not all the recipes that follow are time-consuming, but I feel they come more into the category of thought-about cooking than the let's-just-throw-this-into-the-pan mode of food preparation.

AROMATIC CHILI BEEF NOODLE SOUP

This satisfies just about every principle of low-fat cookery, as far as I'm concerned—it's filling, fragrant, resonant with flavor, and beautiful to look at; it feels like a treat. And there's a lot of it. Defatted real stock is best, but you can use good bouillon cubes or instant dashi. You can do almost whatever you want to this recipe: cut the steak into strips before marinating it rather than leaving it whole; use duck breast (fat removed and meat sliced before cooking) or venison (sliced after) instead of beef; use any vegetables; use any sort of noodle. See also the recipe for Sunday Night Chicken Noodle (page 145), only use ½ teaspoon of oil when you stir-fry the chicken shreds.

I often make this for my supper using thin slices of pork that have been first dunked, then roasted, in a barbecuey marinade. The recipe for these is on page 399. For this soup variation I use pork bouillon cubes bought from the Thai shop and use bok choy or choy sum or other leafy, cabbagy greens—watercress is nice, too.

2 ounces dried egg noodles

FOR THE STOCK

2 cups beef stock (see headnote)

½-inch piece fresh ginger

1 dried red chili

¼ teaspoon ground cinnamon

1 garlic clove, crushed with the flat
   of a knife

FOR THE BEEF

2 teaspoons soy sauce

¼ teaspoon ground cinnamon

½-inch piece fresh ginger, chopped or
   put through a garlic press

1 garlic clove, minced

1 teaspoon sugar

1 teaspoon chili sauce

4 ounces sirloin steak

2 ounce sugar-snap peas, cut into
   2–3 pieces each

2 ounces (small bunch) bok choy,
   chopped

2 tablespoons chopped Thai basil or
   coriander

Cook the noodles as directed on the package, drain, rinse in cold water, and drain again. Reserve.

Bring the stock with its allocated aromatics to the boil, then leave to simmer, covered, while you get on with the beef.

In a bowl combine the beef seasonings and then put the beef in. Wipe the bowl with the beef to cover one of its sides with the chili-cinnamon mixture, then turn the beef over to marinate. Leave for 30 minutes. As you put the beef aside, turn the heat off under the stock, but leave the pan with the lid on to let the flavorings infuse the liquid.

Sear the steak on both sides in a hot, nonstick pan. Cook for 2 minutes more on each side on slightly lower heat, then remove the steak to a board to rest a second while you get on with warming the aromatic soup and noodles.

You can either strain the stock into a new saucepan or leave the bits in to be fished out as you eat. Do whichever you prefer, but bring the stock back to boiling point, cook the sugar-snaps and bok choy in it for a minute or so, and put in the cold noodles to heat. After another minute, or when the noodles are hot, add the Thai basil, if using, and pour into a bowl. Slice the steak into thin slices on the diagonal and lay on top and sprinkle with the coriander, if using. Eat with a spoon and soy sauce.

Serves 1.

MUSHROOM UDON SOUP

This is very plain, very calming—the sort of supper I might make myself to get back on track if I've gone out and had duck confit with mashed potatoes for lunch.

Dashi is Japanese stock (what *brodo* is to the Italians) and, although you can make it yourself, I advise buying dashi-no-moto, which is the dashi equivalent of stock cubes. I buy mine in a liquid version, which you mix in the ratio of 1 teaspoon of dashi-no-moto to 1 cup water. If you have problems finding the instant dashi liquid, see page 462 for a source.

8 dried shiitake mushrooms, soaked in
   1¼ cups hot water for 10 minutes
   to soften
few drops soy sauce
1 teaspoon liquid instant dashi, plus
   more, if desired

2 ounces dried udon noodles
few drops sesame oil (optional)
2 tablespoons chopped parsley or
   coriander

Strain the mushroom water into a saucepan and add the soy sauce and instant dashi. Remove the stalks from the mushrooms, squeeze the caps a little to release excess water, and add the caps to the pan. Bring to a boil and add the noodles. When cooked, pour into a bowl and sprinkle over the merest drop or two of sesame oil, if using, more dashi to taste, and the parsley or coriander.

Serves 1.

The following recipe has almost the same ingredients, but is very different in character: more bolstering, stronger-flavored, and generally just more solid.

BRAISED DRIED SHIITAKE MUSHROOMS
WITH SOBA NOODLES

Like the recipe above, once you've got yourself organized, this is a good pantry standby. The braised mushrooms come via the *Japanese Vegetarian Cookbook* by Patricia Richfield; I add them to a capacious plateful of cooked and soy-tossed buckwheat soba noodles. The graininess of the buckwheat is just the right foil to the dense-flavored and salty shiitake.

8 dried shiitake mushrooms, soaked in 1¼ cups hot water for 30 minutes to soften

1 teaspoon vegetable oil

1 teaspoon sake

4 tablespoons mirin

3 tablespoons Japanese soy sauce

3 ounces soba noodles

drops sesame oil

2 tablespoons chopped coriander (optional)

Drain the mushrooms, reserving ½ cup of the soaking water and straining it. Remove the stems and discard; squeeze the caps a little to remove excess water.

Heat the oil in a small frying pan, add the mushrooms, and stir-fry for 2 minutes. Mix the sake, mirin, and 2 tablespoons of the soy sauce with the reserved mushroom-soaking water and pour over the mushrooms in the pan. Bring to the boil and simmer over a low heat, stirring occasionally, until most of the liquid has evaporated, about 15 minutes. Meanwhile, cook the noodles according to the package instructions, drain, rinse with cold water, drain again, and toss with the soy sauce, and sprinkle with a drop of sesame oil. Toss again and put on the plate. Pour the mushrooms from the pan on top of the noodles. Sprinkle another drop or two of sesame oil over the noodles; add some coriander if desired.

Serves 1.

SEAWEED AND NOODLE SALAD

This is not an authentic dish, insofar as I didn't get it from any Japanese source, just from the happy ransacking of my own larder. Don't worry about which noodles you use. I like the starchy, fresh Japanese ones, but they're not very easy to find; dried Chinese egg noodles will do fine. Neither of the two seaweeds required—wakame or arame—is very hard to get hold of and, because all you have to do is soak them briefly, they aren't hard to use. This tastes good, too, just with the fleshy green wakame or without any seaweed at all, just as a plain noodle salad. If you want to forgo the sesame oil, you can; fatless, the dressing is slightly more astringent, but that isn't necessarily a bad thing.

2 ounces dried soba noodles	½ teaspoon sugar
¼ ounce wakame	I tablespoon prepared dashi or
¼ ounce arame	I tablespoon water with a pin-drop
4 teaspoons Japanese soy sauce	of liquid instant dashi
I tablespoon sake	I teaspoon sesame oil (optional)
2 teaspoons mirin	I scallion (white and green parts),
2 teaspoons rice vinegar	minced

Cook the noodles in boiling water for as long as the package directs, then drain, refresh in cold water, and drain again. Set aside. Meanwhile, soak the seaweeds in water, again as the packages direct; about 5 minutes for the wakame and 15 for the arame should do it. Drain well.

Make the dressing by putting the soy, sake, mirin, rice vinegar, sugar, dashi, and sesame oil, if using, in a small jar and shaking, or mix together in a bowl. Combine the noodles, which should be either at room temperature or cold, and seaweeds and toss with the dressing. Put into a serving dish and sprinkle with the scallion.

Serves 1.

I like to eat this, perhaps even more in its seaweedless state, with plain mackerel fillets, blistered under a hot broiler, then sprinkled with coriander. I love the contrast between hot, crisp-skinned oily fish and cold, slippery noodles.

Salmon teriyaki is better known (and by all means substitute a salmon steak or thick chunk of fillet), but I love the preposterously underrated mackerel.

MACKEREL TERIYAKI

I like this with plain boiled rice or just a huge pile of greens, Chinese or otherwise.

2 tablespoons soy sauce	I teaspoon sugar
2 tablespoons sake	2 mackerel fillets, about 6 ounces each,
I tablespoon mirin	skinned and halved

Put all the ingredients except the mackerel in a saucepan and bring to the boil to dissolve the sugar. Set aside.

Let a nonstick pan get very hot, then put the mackerel fillets in and cook for 2 minutes. After 2 minutes, turn the mackerel over and add the teriyaki marinade to the pan. Baste the fish and turn once again before removing it with a slotted spatula. Leave the sauce to bubble up in the pan until it's dark and syrupy and thick, but keep an eye on it, as you don't want it to burn stickily dry. Pour this reduced teriyaki marinade over the fish.

Serves 2.

BLACK COD MARINATED IN DEN MISO

At Nobu in New York I had the most fabulous black cod in miso; the flesh was soft and dense, the crust charred black and sweet with grill-caramelized sake. If you can't find black cod—more properly known as sablefish—substitute any fatty fish, such as salmon. The miso permeates the fish, but not intrusively. The fact that the preparation needs to be done in advance means you need to plan ahead, but the cooking itself is undemanding.

I've specified quantities for 2. For 1, halve quantities of the marinade only if you've got a dish small enough to fit the one piece of fish snugly, or the amount of marinade won't cover it.

½ cup white miso

2 tablespoons sugar

2 tablespoons sake

2 tablespoons mirin

2 chunky pieces of black cod (sablefish) fillet, about 5 ounces each

Combine all the ingredients except the fish, put into a heavy-bottomed pan over moderate heat, and cook for about 20 minutes, stirring often. You mustn't let the sugar burn and stick at the bottom. Set aside and let this den miso cool.

Put the sablefish pieces in a shallow dish with the den miso, making sure they are thoroughly covered. Cover with plastic film and marinate for 2–3 days in the fridge.

When you want to eat, preheat the broiler. When it's hot, take the fish out of the marinade and broil on each side until brown and slightly caramelized. This is wonderful served, not entirely Japanese-style, with a bowl of broccoli suffused with lemon or just a huge wigwammed mound of snow peas. Serves 2.

CAMBODIAN HOT-AND-SOUR BEEF SALAD

I first ate this at one of Vatchcharin Bhumichitr's London restaurants, Southeast W9, and found it spectacular. It's again an example of how the best low-fat food comes from recipes that are not specially adapted to make them so. My version is a slightly anglicized take on the recipe for the beef salad called *plea saj go* as gratefully found in Vatch's wonderful *South-East Asian Cookbook*. I have reduced the number of chilies, used shallots in preference to onion, and, as Vatch himself suggests, substituted mint for the stipulated chili leaves. But sometimes, when I can't find mint in the stores and there's none in the garden, I use arugula or a handful of watercress and baby spinach instead. In short, I don't set about doing this as if I were expecting a Cambodian delegation for dinner; I just cook it as I like it.

Although this amount serves 2 if you're eating other things—a dreamy and mild noodle soup to start, a ripe mango for dessert—I often make it just for me. I don't alter quantities; I just don't eat anything else, except perhaps for a sweet, salving banana after.

lettuce leaves, for covering a
   serving dish
8 ounces sirloin steak
2 tablespoons fish sauce
2 tablespoons lime juice
I teaspoon sugar

1–2 red or green chilies (depending
   on size and heat desired), seeded
   and minced
I shallot, sliced finely
handful mint

Preheat the broiler.

Cover a serving dish with the lettuce leaves and set aside. Broil the steak; it should be rare, really, but obviously, cook it as you prefer. When it's done, remove to a board on which to carve it and pour any juices in the broiler pan into a bowl. Cut the steak into very thin slices across and put these with any more juices that run out into the bowl as well. In another bowl, mix the fish sauce, lime juice, sugar, chilies, and shallot, stirring well. Then mix the contents of the 2 bowls, adding the mint leaves; quickly turn out on the lettuce and serve while still warm.

Serves 2.

THAI-FLAVORED MUSSELS

I have called these Thai-flavored rather than Thai because they emanate directly from my kitchen, and I am not Thai and have never even been to Thailand. So this dish is authentic, but in the sense that it is authentically how I cook it. It takes about 2 minutes, and as mussels come cleaned now, there isn't even any bearding or barnacling to do over the kitchen sink. I use kaffir lime leaves, as I keep a stash of them in my freezer, but you can substitute lemon grass. And frankly, it's still worth doing even if you can get neither.

Use whatever stock you want here: vegetable, chicken, fish, dashi, from the pot, freezer, tub, or packet. Whether you use red or green chili here is immaterial in terms of flavor; the red one, I think, just looks a little better.

½ cup light stock (see headnote)

1 shallot, minced

2 garlic cloves, sliced or minced

3 kaffir lime leaves, chopped or shredded, or one 4-inch-long piece of lemon grass, minced

½-inch piece ginger, minced

20 mussels (about 12 ounces), preferably cultivated, or cleaned and bearded

1 fresh chili pepper, seeded and chopped or sliced finely

1 tablespoon lime juice

1 tablespoon mirin

1 tablespoon fish sauce

½ cup chopped coriander

Bring 2 cups of water to the boil. Put the stock, shallot, garlic, lime leaves, and ginger in a saucepan, cover, and let it bubble away at a moderate to high heat for 3–5 minutes or until you have a thickish, softish mess at the bottom of the pan. Check to make sure it isn't either burning or just getting too dry for comfort, and add a bit of boiling water if it is. Meanwhile, put the mussels in a sinkful of ice-cold water. Chuck away any that don't sink and then, as you remove them, make doubly sure by chucking away any that don't shut when you tap them sharply. I wouldn't expect you to have to throw many away, so don't worry unduly.

Add the chili to the mixture in the pan. After about 30 seconds, or just long enough to get them out of the sink, add the mussels and then throw over them ½ cup boiling water, and the lime juice, mirin, and fish sauce mixed together. Cover, give the pan a shake, and leave on a high heat for about 3 minutes, by which time the mussels should have steamed open. Add half the coriander, shake again, and pour into a noodle bowl. Sprinkle over the remaining coriander and eat. It's probably just as well this is enough for one, as you will have to spit out the shreds of kaffir lime leaves—or lemon grass if you used that—as you come upon them.

Serves 1.

THAI CLAM POT

This recipe comes by way of a book that I have to force myself not to cook my way through—*Asian Noodles* by Nina Symonds—and, I should own up, is barely scaled down, although its specifications are for six people and mine are for two. I like a lot of liquid—I want an aromatic broth with the noodles and clams submerged in it, and enough of it to drink from the bowl or slurp from a spoon once the noodles and clams have been greedily eaten. But then, I like a lot of noodles, too. And this still works wonderfully with half the amount of noodles, if you're in super-virtuous mode.

Getting the Thai basil may be a problem. If you can't find any—I go to a Thai shop near me, indeed I practically live in it—beg and plead with your supermarket to stock it; otherwise settle instead for some fresh coriander. I would make a fuss—nicely, of course, because it wasn't that long ago that coriander would have been available only in specialty markets—and Thai basil really is extraordinarily wonderful, as aromatic as licorice. For that reason, I wouldn't substitute ordinary Mediterranean basil, wonderful as it is; they may share the same name, but the celestial pungency, the almost medicinal herbalness of the Thai basil, is not at all the same as the summery and gorgeous scentedness of the Mediterranean plant. Coriander, again, is different, but the quality of pungency is there.

The shells hold up the very gratifying wolfing-down, so I remove most of them before ladling the clams into waiting bowls.

1¾ pounds small clams, well washed	1 dried red chili pepper
salt	½ cup sake or Chinese rice wine
8 ounces fresh or 4 ounces dried somen or angel hair pasta	good handful Thai basil, shredded finely
1 scant teaspoon oil	2 tablespoons fish sauce, or to taste
3 garlic cloves, crushed with the flat of a knife and sliced finely	
2 scallions (white and green parts), cut into ¼-inch lengths and crushed with the flat of a knife	

Fill the sink with cold water, add 1 teaspoon baking soda, and leave the clams to soak for an hour. Drain and chuck out any that haven't opened.

Bring a large pot of water to a boil; add salt and then the noodles. Cook as instructed on the package or by the shopkeeper (my fresh somen take 1 minute) and then drain, rinse, and set aside.

Put a large, heavy pot (big enough to take everything later) on a high flame, add the oil, and heat until hot, about 30 seconds. Add the garlic and scallions, crumble in the chili, and stir-fry for about 10 seconds or until fragrant. Add 1¼ cups water and the rice wine, cover, and bring to the boil. Add the clams, cover, and bring back to the boil. Reduce the heat to medium-low and cook, shaking the pot from time to time so that the clams steam evenly, for 2–3 minutes or just until the clams open.

Add the basil, stir gently, cover, and cook for 30 seconds, then stir in the fish sauce. Divide the noodles between a pair of capacious bowls, ladle the clams and broth over, and eat immediately. Serves 2.

VEGETABLE MISO BROTH

This is essential to my low-fat eating moments. I cook it more than I cook any-thing else and every time I do it, I make it differently. Basically, I just boil, in salted water, various vegetables, any that I feel like, putting them in the pan in the order they'll take to cook (thus turnips first, watercress last) and then drain-ing them into a bowl. Over this bowl I pour over about 2 cups of salty soup made out of some vegetable bouillon cubes and 1 tablespoon miso. Sometimes I add ginger to the broth and stir in some pickled ginger while I'm eating it. But mostly it's just plain vegetables, chunked and still crunchy, with that almost creaturely, emphatically aromatic, miso-thickened broth.

The quantities I give below are to be viewed as sketchy; ignore or add to them as you wish.

2 medium turnips, peeled and quartered	handful watercress
I medium carrot, peeled and cut into large chunks	I vegetable bouillon cube
	I heaping tablespoon miso, or more to taste
I½ cups broccoli florets	2 tablespoons chopped parsley or coriander (optional)
I medium zucchini, halved lengthways and across	
handful of sugar-snap peas, each chopped into 2–3 pieces	

Put a large pot of water on to boil, and when boiling, add salt. Then add the turnips. After about 5 minutes, add the carrot. After another 7 or so minutes, add the broccoli. Give this 2–3 minutes, then chuck in the zucchini, and after another minute the sugar-snaps, which only need to blanch to be cooked. Throw in the watercress and then empty the entire contents into a colander in the sink.

Meanwhile, make the broth. Pour 2 cups boiling water into a large measuring cup and stir in the bouillon cube. Add the miso; taste and add more, if you wish. Put the drained vegetables into a noodle bowl, then pour over the miso broth. Add the parsley or coriander, if using. Eat. Serves 1.

LACQUERED QUAIL

Food that is fiddly, or takes time—artichokes, unshelled lobster—is worth con-sidering when you're trying to eat less. It's a variation of the old trick of eating off smaller plates, but piled high, so that you're conned, somehow, into thinking you're eating more.

In this, the lacquer effect is brought about by brushing the quail with pomegranate molasses (which you can get in Middle Eastern and specialty food stores) mixed with soy sauce, much the same way as the Chinese use maltose to help along that beautiful burnished glow on their roast ducks. You can butterfly the quails yourself, following instructions on page 134, or just ask your butcher to do it for you.

2 quails, butterflied	2 teaspoons pomegranate molasses
2 teaspoons soy sauce	

Preheat the oven to 450°F.

Line a small baking dish with foil, shiny side up, and put the quail in skin-side up. Put the soy sauce and pomegranate molasses in a small saucepan and bring to the boil. Let it bubble away for 30 seconds or so until thick and sticky and pour over the quail, using a pastry brush to dab it all over.

Roast the quail for about 15 minutes or until cooked through and crisp-skinned, then remove and eat with your fingers as soon as the quail have cooled down just enough for you to bear it. Serves 1–2.

JAPANESE-FLAVORED SOUR-SWEET CABBAGE

Sometimes I make myself a bowl of Japanese-flavored sour-sweet cabbage to eat after this. Shred about 8 ounces cabbage finely, then toss it in a hot non-stick pan in which you've already put ¼ teaspoon sesame oil. Keep turning and tossing the cabbage until it wilts impressively, then throw in a mixture made from 1 tablespoon each of soy sauce, mirin, and rice vinegar. Give this—still stirring and lifting up the cabbage frantically—another minute, then remove to a bowl and sprinkle over some Japanese seven-spice mixture, if you've any at hand.

Serves 1–2.

BEET GREENS AND BUCKWHEAT NOODLES

I began this tranche of recipes with noodles and I'll end it with noodles. I love beet greens but am not mad about beets (with some exceptions, and they're listed below, so don't worry about what you're going to do with the rejected roots now). I use Japanese soba noodles for this—often sold at the supermarket—and make a vast plateful; I want nothing else after.

In place of the soy sauce, mirin, and rice vinegar, you can use an equal quantity of sukiyaki sauce.

leaves and tender stalks from 2 pounds	I tablespoon mirin
bunch beets, chopped	I teaspoon rice vinegar
2 ounces soba noodles	salt
I tablespoon Japanese soy sauce, plus	2 tablespoons chopped parsley
more, as needed	

Put a pot of water on for the noodles, adding salt when it boils. Put the beet leaves and stalks in a sink filled with cold water. Remove, drain, and cook in just the water clinging to the leaves and stalks, no more, in a heavy-bottomed or nonstick frying pan with the lid on to get the steam rising. Meanwhile, cook the noodles in the boiling water, drain them, and toss with the soy sauce, mirin, and rice vinegar.

Then, when the beet greens are all but ready, sprinkle with salt and throw in the noodles, adding more soy sauce as needed. Stir around in the pan until the buff-colored noodles take on a deep, bronzy pink. Remove to a large plate and cover with the parsley.

Serves I.

The following two recipes are both for beets, but because they're for the beets you've got left from the recipe above, I make no apology for the purplish onslaught. I had never eaten beets raw until I came across Stephanie Alexander's recipe in her *Cook's Companion* for grated beets with lemon juice and chopped herbs, arranged around a central dollop of yogurt. I cannot tell you what a revelation it is. Something spooky can happen to beets when they're cooked (and I don't mean because of the vinegar that is often added): it's as if the sweetness has a slightly putrid edge. Raw, the sugariness has a spiky sharpness about it that stops it from cloying, even in large quantities.

SHREDDED BEET SALAD WITH YOGURT

I have adapted the recipe a bit and also substituted fat-free yogurt. And as it's what I make to go with roast poussin when a friend comes for a low-key, low-fat supper, I give quantities for two naturally big eaters.

Peel the beets wearing rubber gloves if you don't want to come over all Lady Macbeth later. Try changing the herbs, too. With chopped dill and dry-toasted mustard seeds, the salad's magnificent with salmon, for example.

good handful coriander	juice of I lemon
good handful mint	⅔ cup fat-free yogurt
2 large or 4 small beets, about	
1½ pounds, peeled and cut in small	
chunks	

Put the coriander and mint leaves in the processor, chop, and remove. Using the grating disc, grate the beets by pushing them through the feed tube until you have a wonderful pile of dark crimson shreds. Toss these in a bowl with the herbs and lemon juice and then arrange them in a ring around the edge of a plate. Fill the hole in the center with the yogurt.

Serves 2 with leftovers.

BEET SOUP

It seems odd not to be convinced about beets but to be passionate about this because, in a way, this thick, velvety soup is the sweet, smooth essence of beet. It's difficult to say how many it will feed, as I make a big quantity and just keep a pitcher of it in the fridge for a few days.

2 large or 4 small beets, about 1½ pounds	1 tablespoon balsamic vinegar
1 teaspoon Dijon mustard	buttermilk or yogurt (optional)

Put the beets in a large pot, cover with cold water, bring to boil, and boil for 2 hours or until tender. Maybe 1¼ hours if they're small. Beets take much longer to cook than anyone ever tells you (rather like chickpeas).

Remove the cooked beets (retaining the cooking liquid) with a slotted spoon and gingerly pull off their skins before putting in a processor or blender together with the mustard and balsamic vinegar. Purée, adding the cooking liquid till the texture is as you like it. Keep some of the cooking liquid, as well, as the soup will thicken as it sits in the fridge and you will need to thin it out later. But if you want just to freeze individual portions, you can add water as necessary when you reheat. This soup is wonderful with a slash of buttermilk or yogurt added as you eat it.

RESTRAINED MUSHROOM RISOTTO

A low-fat risotto might sound suspect, but this one works because of its intense, mushroomy depth of flavor. This is the sort of thing I'd make when I have a girl-friend over to dinner, cooking it while we're talking. I have specified garlic-infused oil and porcini stock made from cubes (see pages 457 and 459) just because this makes it easier for a scrabbled-together after-work supper; you can, however, use chicken, veal, or vegetable stock, as you wish. Boost whatever stock you use with dried porcini and their soaking liquid, as directed.

⅓ ounce dried porcini

1 teaspoon butter

2 teaspoons garlic-infused oil

1 small onion, minced

8 ounces mixed cultivated and wild
mushrooms, chopped or sliced, as
size and shape recommend

⅔ cup arborio rice

¼ white wine or vermouth

1¼ cups stock made from porcini stock
cubes, or chicken, veal, or vegetable
stock, heated

2 tablespoons freshly grated Parmesan

3 tablespoons chopped parsley

Soak the porcini in warm water to cover until soft, about 20 minutes; drain and chop them. Reserve the mushrooms and their soaking liquid.

In a small frying pan or medium saucepan, heat the butter and oil. Sauté the onion gently until soft but not brown. Add the mixed mushrooms and cook for a few minutes. Stir in the rice and cook for 2 minutes. Pour in the wine and let it bubble away until it's absorbed. Combine the reserved porcini and its liquid with the stock and add a ladleful of the mixture to the rice. Cook, stirring, until the stock has been absorbed. Carry on adding ladlefuls and then stirring over a low to medium heat until all the stock has been absorbed and the rice is creamy and just cooked, tender but still firm to the bite. In other words, until it tastes like risotto, which should take 18–20 minutes. Stir in the Parmesan and parsley.

Serves 2.

LINGUINE WITH CRAB

This is one of the few non-Asian low-fat recipes that you could cook for a dinner party, although I always find pasta panic-inducing in large quantities. Crabmeat is so intensely flavored that fat is not required to add depth. The recipe might seem to be masquerading as an Italian dish, but that is not the intention; really the flavors are borrowed from Thai and Korean crab cakes, but they make a wonderful, resonant pasta sauce.

1 garlic clove, minced

½ fresh red chili pepper, sliced finely,
with seeds

3–4 tablespoons chopped coriander,
to taste

grated zest of 1 lime, plus a squirt of
the juice

2–3 scallions (white and green parts),
sliced finely

2 teaspoons olive oil

½ cup white wine

salt

6 ounces linguine

4 ounces lump crabmeat

2–3 tablespoons chopped parsley

Put water on for the pasta. When it's almost boiling, start on the sauce. Sweat the garlic, chili, half the coriander, half the lime zest, and the scallions in olive oil until softened.

Add the white wine and simmer for 5–10 minutes, stirring occasionally, until it reduces and thickens to an almost sludgy texture.

The pasta water should be boiling now, so add salt, put in the linguine, and cook according to package directions. Just before the pasta needs draining, stir the crabmeat with the remaining coriander and lime zest into the white wine mixture. Add the squirt of lime juice. Just before draining the pasta, lower a measuring cup into it and fill it up with the pasta cooking water. When the pasta's drained, add it to the sauce or, if you prefer, put it into a warmed bowl and stir the sauce into it. Add some drops of cooking water if the sauce needs help to coat the strands of pasta. Bear in mind, though, that this strong-tasting sauce is meant to cover elegantly and sparsely; in this sense only, perhaps, it is an Italian sauce. Sprinkle with the parsley and eat quickly; the thinner the pasta, the faster it clumps as it waits.

Serves 2.

SALAD DRESSINGS

It's one of the fallacies of trying to lose weight that the easiest thing to eat is a salad. There is no such thing as a decent low-fat salad dressing. I have tried everything. So I have come up with dressings that don't exactly duplicate vinaigrette but will coat leaves without making you wince.

MISO-MUSTARD DRESSING

½ teaspoon miso

½ teaspoon grainy mustard

¼ teaspoon strong, clear honey

juice of ½ orange

Mix everything together well and dress the salad. What else is there to say, except that you could add a splash of buttermilk as well.

DIJON MUSTARD DRESSING

Having said that low-fat dressing mustn't ape proper dressing, I can see that this one does. But somehow it pulls it off.

½ teaspoon Dijon mustard

½ teaspoon balsamic vinegar

juice of ½ orange

drops of soy sauce, to taste

Put the mustard in a bowl and slowly stir in the vinegar and orange juice. Taste and add soy as wanted.

THICK MISO DRESSING FOR BEANS

The dressings above are runny and good for the robuster leaf salads—radicchio, frisée, or something with bite. This, though, is rich and thick and wonderful stirred into warm or cold beans.

1 heaping tablespoon miso	drop or two sesame oil
1 scant teaspoon balsamic vinegar or	
rice vinegar	

In a little bowl, stir together the miso, balsamic or rice vinegar, and a tiny drop or two of sesame oil, and mix to the consistency of a thick dressing by adding a couple of tablespoons of water.

ROAST GARLIC AND LEMON DRESSING

This dressing takes rather longer to make, but you are not required to exert yourself while the garlic's in the oven, so it's still not the biggest deal.

1 head garlic	juice of ½ lemon, plus more,
1 teaspoon vermouth	if needed

Preheat the oven to 400°F.

Lop the top off the garlic, just so you see the cloves in cross section. Cut out a square of foil big enough to wrap the garlic in. Place the garlic in the center of the foil and bring up the sides, so that when you add the vermouth it doesn't all dribble out. When the vermouth's in, close the parcel by twisting the edges of the foil together and bake for 45 minutes–1 hour. Remove, let cool a bit, then squeeze the garlic into a bowl. Add the lemon juice slowly to the roast garlic purée, stirring as you do. If the dressing is as sharp as you want it to be before it's as runny (though this is meant to be a thick dressing) as you want it to be, beat in a little water. Otherwise, add more juice.

THE STATUTORY
COOK-AND-FREEZE-AHEAD SECTION

Freezing some low-fat food will get you in the right frame of mind while setting the stage with the necessary props.

VEGETABLE CURRY IN
VEGETABLE SAUCE

This is a recipe from Sue Kreitzman's *Low-fat Vegetarian Cookbook*, which is so utterly virtuous that I regard it as eating that doesn't count. I don't cook it for other people; it's what I keep for myself to balance out a week of intense going out or overeating at home. This amount makes about enough for 6 huge portions, which I freeze individually and thaw when required. Yes, it can go soggy and fuzzy around the edges, but I don't mind.

If I am being very severe, I eat this with just a raita made with fat-free yogurt, minced scallions, grated fresh ginger, and chopped mint and coriander. If following a middling path, I add some plain steamed couscous. If I feel I have nothing for which to atone, I buy hot, soft nan bread from my local Indian takeout to mop up the aromatic juices and eat nothing else that night, bar some fruit. This recipe is, I admit, time-consuming and labor-intensive, but is the low-fat culinary equivalent of a key text. You should tackle it when you're all fired up to start. Put aside one Sunday evening and don't think of doing anything else at the same time. It's a worthwhile investment.

2 large onions, each cut into 8 pieces

2 garlic cloves, crushed

1 tablespoon each ground cumin, ground coriander, and paprika

½ teaspoon each ground allspice, ground cardamom, and ground ginger

1 teaspoon cayenne pepper

2½ cups vegetable stock, plus more, if needed

3 red or yellow bell peppers, peeled, deseeded, and chopped coarsely

3 large carrots, chopped coarsely

¾ pound button mushrooms, halved or quartered

2 medium turnips, cut into ½-inch pieces

1 large cauliflower, separated into florets

1 small parsnip, cut into ½-inch pieces

1 fennel bulb, quartered and cut into ½-inch pieces

3 celery stalks, cut into ½-inch pieces

salt

juice of ½ large lemon

3 medium zucchini, cut into ½-inch pieces

8 ounces green beans, cut into ½-inch pieces

Put the onion, garlic, spices, and half the stock in a heavy-bottomed saucepan. Cover, bring to the boil, and boil for 5–7 minutes. Uncover and stir in the peppers, carrots, and mushrooms. Reduce the heat slightly and simmer, stirring frequently, until the vegetables and spices are "frying" in their own juices and the vegetables are tender. Allow to cool slightly.

Remove and purée half the mixture in a blender or food processor, then return the purée to the pan.

Add the turnips, cauliflower, parsnip, fennel, and celery. Stir together very well. Add the remaining stock or enough to almost to cover the contents of the pot, season with salt, and bring to the boil.

Reduce the heat, cover, and simmer for 15 minutes. Uncover, squeeze in the lemon juice, and add the zucchini and beans. Simmer uncovered for 10 minutes more, or until all the vegetables are tender.

Portion this to suit your appetite.

BEEF BRAISED IN BEER

This is pretty much the English version of carbonnade, the Belgian dish of beef stewed with beer. The beer used should be stout, and I use Sam Smith's Imperial Stout, which is available in America. The prunes—which are authentic, in the sense here of traditional—give a richness and depth, and so very little fat is needed or ends up in any one of its six portions. (Incidentally, prunes, puréed, can be used to replace their weight of butter in baking.) Like all stews, this is best cooked in advance and then reheated. And because the beef is cooked slowly, you can use very lean stewing beef and it will still be velvety and tender.

Accompany this with mounds of green vegetables. And you could also make a version of the horseradish-chive sauce on page 265 using fat-free yogurt.

1¼ cups stout	2 tablespoons vegetable oil, or butter
8 ounces pitted prunes	and the merest drop oil
1 teaspoon English mustard powder	2 medium onions, sliced finely
¼ cup all-purpose flour	10 ounces medium carrots, peeled and
2½ pounds stewing beef, cut into	cut into thickish sticks
thick strips	salt

Preheat the oven to 300°F.

Pour ⅔ cup water and the stout into a bowl, add the prunes, and soak until soft, about 2 hours.

Mix the mustard powder into the flour and coat the beef with it. In a frying pan, heat 1 tablespoon of the oil and cook the onions in it for about 5 minutes; stir in the carrots and cook for 5 minutes more. Place the vegetables in a casserole and stir the prunes in with their liquid, with a pinch or two of salt to taste. Add the remaining tablespoon oil to the frying pan and brown the meat, then add meat to the casserole. Cover and cook in the oven for 2½–3 hours.

When it's cool, bag up into 6 equal portions and freeze. To do this, either thaw and reheat gently in a saucepan, or microwave the still-frozen stew.

HALF-COQ AU VIN

I don't pretend this is the real thing, in the sense of the Elizabeth David adumbrated original. But it is a good chicken stew, cooked in wine, which borrows from the cuisine bourgeoise classic without running too severely into debt. Again, this is something I like to make for myself to reheat and eat alone for dinner when I want something proper and comforting and old-fashioned.

2½ cups red wine	1 medium onion, minced
1 celery stalk	2 ounces Canadian or Irish bacon, in
1 medium carrot, peeled and quartered	one piece if possible (otherwise
2 garlic cloves, peeled	3 slices), diced
1 sprig thyme	6 ounces baby button mushrooms
few sprigs parsley	6 ounces pearl onions, peeled
3 peppercorns	heaping tablespoon all-purpose flour
3 bay leaves	1¼ cups chicken stock
1 tablespoon olive oil	3 tablespoons brandy
6 skinned chicken thighs	2–3 tablespoons chopped parsley
salt and freshly milled black pepper	

Put the wine, celery, carrot, garlic, thyme, parsley, peppercorns, and the bay leaves in a saucepan on the heat. Bring to the boil, reduce the heat slightly, and let bubble away until reduced by half. Strain and reserve.

Then, in a casserole that will take everything later, heat the oil, add the chicken, and brown a little; you will have to turn often to prevent the chicken from sticking, but persevere—the chicken will color. Season with the salt and pepper, turn in the pan, season again, and remove for a while.

The chicken, although it's lean, should have left a few oily juices in the casserole. Add to these the onion and bacon and cook, over medium to medium-low heat, stirring regularly, for about 5 minutes or until soft. Add the mushrooms and pearl onions and cook, pushing and prodding, for a further 3 or so minutes. Sprinkle over the flour, stir well to coat and cook out the flouriness, and cook over low heat for another 3 or so minutes. Gradually stir in the stock and the reserved wine. Replace the chicken thighs. Cover and cook very gently for 45 minutes to an hour or until the chicken has just begun to loosen on the bones.

When the chicken is cooked, heat the brandy in a ladle over a low flame and tilt the ladle until the brandy ignites. Pour this into the casserole and stir well. The sauce-gravy should be just about right now—neither floury nor watery—but should you find it too runny, remove the chicken, raise the heat, and reduce to thicken a little more. Return the chicken to the pan, baste with the sauce, and sprinkle over the parsley. You will need, or might want, to add freshly chopped parsley if and when you freeze, defrost, and eat each individual portion.

CHAR SIU

This, to borrow from Dr. Jonathan Miller, is not quite char siu, it's just char siu-ish.

I've given a couple of different marinades for this basically Chinese-influenced barbecued pork; choose whichever you prefer, taking into account what is most convenient for you to produce. The first is adapted from *Tiger Lily: Flavours of the Orient* by Rani King and Chandra Khan; the second is just something I did with the ingredients I had lying about in the fridge.

In both instances, the pork is the same, as is the cooking method; it's just the marinade that differs.

10 ounces pork tenderloin	**MARINADE 2**
MARINADE 1	2 tablespoons soy sauce
4 tablespoons soy sauce	2 tablespoons prune juice
2 tablespoons ketchup	2 tablespoons mushroom ketchup
3 tablespoons hoisin sauce	2 tablespoons miso
2 tablespoons sweet sherry	2 tablespoons mirin
2 tablespoons honey	I tablespoon sesame oil
2 scant tablespoons dark muscovado	2 garlic cloves
sugar or dark brown sugar	2 tablespoons light muscovado sugar or
	light brown sugar

Cut the tenderloin in half across. For either marinade, mix the marinade ingredients together in a large bowl. Get 2 plastic freezer bags and put a piece of pork in each, then pour half the marinade in one and half in the other. Tie both up and squish, seeing that the pork is coated. Lay both bags in a shallow dish and put in fridge for 24 hours.

To cook the pork, preheat the oven to 450°F.

Take the pork out of the marinade, reserving the marinade, and put the meat in a foil-lined roasting pan. Roast for 15 minutes, then turn the oven down to 325°F and give it another 20–30 minutes, basting regularly. You want the meat to be tender and still faintly pink within. If you think it looks as if it might be drying up, then add a little water to some of the remaining marinade (the second version is more liquid anyway) and spoon it into the pan.

When the pork is cooked, remove it from the oven and let it cool. When cool, cut it into very thin slices and put 4–5 of them (about 2 ounces) into freezer bags, one portion per bag, and freeze (see page 38 for usage). I keep any marinade that's left over and freeze it for the next batch of pork.

DESSERT

Dessert—in its more solid, substantial, and comforting sense—is not the stuff of which low-fat meals are made. That's not to say it is completely out of the dietary question. For one thing, it's important to have something at hand at the end of an anyway abbreviated supper, something to stave off that moment of loneliness and despondency that always threatens to settle when you realize that eating is over for the day.

I have not got a particularly sweet tooth; my weakness will never be cookies or cakes or puddings—it's bread and cheese that, once I start eating, I can't stop. But somehow, when I go on a diet (even if I never even mouth the word to myself, let alone say the word out loud), I suddenly want double-chocolate pecan cake or any other revolting concoction so long as it's high-fat. It may be psychologically predictable and embarrassing, but there it is. I deal with this, in the main, by not forbidding myself such stuff; I buy a candy bar of some sort and as these are all calorie-counted, I can then figure them into my overall intake. There are times when it's preferable to eat a vast bowl of steamed greens doused with soy and then a sugar-heavy, fat-saturated dessert for supper rather than a virtuous, balanced, and more orthodox combination.

The one thing I don't recommend, though, is trying to concoct low-fat versions of intrinsically high-fat food. Tiramisu made with fat-free sour cream, cocoa powder, and aspartame is not the answer (whatever the question is, it's not the answer). It's not just that it will taste horrible but that you will still feel deprived. Occasional guilt-free indulgence (to borrow from the dieter's lexicon) is a much better route. And actually, it's surprising how little you need to eat of something high-fat to feel satisfied—in other words, the dessert in its entirety might be vertiginously calorific, but you may not be eating even a couple of bananas' worth of calories of it. Though I do take the point that those of you who truly do manage to eat only a small amount of anything are probably not those for whom this chapter is intended.

And if you can't make smaller portions for yourself, then buy them. If you were to give yourself about a quarter-cup of ice cream, you'd weep; it would hardly cover the bottom of a bowl. But if you buy those little individual ice cream cups (Häagen Dazs makes them, and their low-fat yogurt pops are good, too), you aren't scraping out a meager portion but eating the entire serving, which feels like more. Again, it's about trying to avoid feeling deprived. Also, you are less likely to speed through the rest of the freezer eating all those unopened little cups, whereas just lifting off the lid to an already opened large container and digging in, spoon by guilty spoonful, is all too easy. It's like breaking large bills; once you do it, they get spent.

There's a lot on the market now that comes in pathetically small portions; here, at least, you can work it to your advantage. But beware of distracting yourself or getting yourself in the wrong frame of mind; so much of all this is in the head, that if you get yourself out of the mood, you can just end up making it harder for, if not actually sabotaging, yourself. This, again, is where the temple food idea comes in. You want to make a fetish, almost, out of eating the food that's going to make all this easier. So as far as dessert is concerned, this really means fruit. The same principles apply: make it look beautiful and take longer eating it.

And for this you naturally don't need recipes; the list of ideas that follows is presented just to jolt your memory and help you draw up your shopping lists.

- Peel and de-pith an orange, slice it finely, and arrange serenely on a plate. Pour over a drop or two of orange-flower water and sprinkle over a pinch of ground cinnamon.

- Cut a papaya in half, get rid of the seeds, and fill the cavities (avocado-style) with raspberries or chopped strawberries.

- Or peel the papaya before scooping out the seeds, then put it cut side down on a plate, slice across thinly, and fan out, this time nouvelle-cuisine style, and squeeze the juice of a lime over the fleshy pink slices.

- With a sharp knife, make an incision, skin-deep, all around (lengthwise rather than through its equator) a mango—the best are the little Asian ones, sometimes available—and then peel off one side's skin. Hold the mango over a plate and, with the knife, do some cross-hatching, right through to the stone, to form little squares; then take the knife and slice it downwards, scraping the stone and therefore cutting off all the little squares, which will then drop into the plate. Do the same to the other half. Or just eat the mango, peeled but otherwise left as is, in the bath.

●Make yourself a kind of Japanese food plate with as much dexterity as you can muster; arrange melon, pineapple, kiwi, orange, artfully chiselled—and then, with quiet ceremony, eat them.

●Hull and halve good strawberries; sprinkle over some balsamic vinegar.

●Cut crosses in figs—as if quartering them without cutting right through them—so that they open like bird-throated flowers. Eat as is if they're perfect; otherwise, dust with vanilla sugar, a pinch of confectioners' sugar mixed with ground cinnamon, or honey diluted with rosewater, and blitz them under a searing broiler.

●Make a tropical fruit salad by chopping some or all of papaya, melon, mango, or pineapple, and pour over the seed-crunchy pulp of one or two passion fruits mixed with the juice of half an orange.

●The perfect peach should be eaten alone and unadulterated. But less good, and more prevalent, specimens need both bolstering and camouflage. Tip some blueberries into a bowl and, holding a peach over it, slice the peach into segments, then stir in. (This, too, symbiotically, is a way of salvaging inferior berries.)

●Never forget watermelon in summer; keep it well wrapped in the fridge and carve off great wedges of it to eat as you want. And make a salad by cutting chunky squares of watermelon, adding pomegranate seeds (see page 241 for advice as to the best way to release them from their pithy nest) and only a small amount of freshly chopped mint.

●The health-farm special: if you can manage to keep pumpkin seeds in the cupboard without raiding it and eating the rest of the opened packet in one go, then keep pumpkin and flax (the latter less bingeworthy) seeds in store to sprinkle, in teaspoonfuls, over some fat-free yogurt. Add a teaspoon of oatmeal and another of runny honey. Dried banana chips are wonderful, but safest to avoid, though a small fresh, sliced banana is worth considering. And try to get Greek mountain honey, as you get maximum sweetness and flavor for your teaspoonful. Just banana, yogurt as above, and a sprinkling of brown sugar eaten after a couple of minutes' steeping (enough time for the sugar to go caramelly but not enough time for the banana to go black) is wonderful and very—all things being relative—filling.

- Fill a bowl with cold water and ice cubes; to this add, simply, a small bunch of grapes.

- Ditto, but with a couple of handfuls of cherries.

- Not quite temple food, but relatively restrained all the same: fold some raspberries or blackberries into a small bowl of fat-free yogurt, add a teaspoon of confectioners' sugar, and crumble in a meringue.

FEEDING BABIES AND SMALL CHILDREN

Good eating starts in the cradle. Nutritionists and obstetricians would probably insist that it begins much earlier, but I am talking not so much of the food necessary for good health but the food necessary for a good life. Certainly, they sometimes overlap, and for a child they are inextricably linked. The moment a baby is put to the breast, he or she learns that eating is one of the foremost pleasures of life; seeking that pleasure is also how he or she stays alive and keeps growing.

Latter-day puritans might think about copying the infant model. In the 1980s there was a comparative study of the eating habits of some workers in the southwest of France and a group of, to use a serviceable but tellingly passé term, health nuts in California. The French ate enormous amounts of red meat and butter and even drank brandy with their breakfasts. But they enjoyed it. The San Franciscans ate few saturated fats, no meat, and a lot of alfalfa sprouts, and worried constantly about whether they were eating correctly, whether they had absorbed the right balance of vitamins and nutrients. They were careful to take supplements where they thought necessary. The incidence of heart disease among the Californians was much higher than among the southwestern French. It was concluded (I can only believe the scientists in question were French) that a major contributing factor was the anxiety that accompanied the Americans' eating. Since that study, some scientists have made other claims about the health-giving properties of red wine. The discrepancy between the sort of diet some Americans feel is a sinful and self-destructive preparation for cardiac arrest and the low incidence of heart disease in France has since become known as the French Paradox.

I believe that food should never be thought of as mere fuel. Nor should it be venerated on the one hand, feared on the other. Turning such a life-giving pleasure into a joyless, guilt-ridden, and anxiety-provoking but necessary exercise is verging on the criminal. But more—and especially where children are concerned—it is almost bound to be counterproductive.

You can never, alas, ensure good health. But you can learn to enjoy good eating. I'm not sure you can teach it, but you can encourage. If you want children to develop their own taste—and for food other than burgers and pizza—they need to be given good food. I distrust, however, those who have stringent rules about which food is good and which not. The only way to judge whether food is good or not is by tasting it, by eating it. If a child likes pizza and burgers, then it is pointless telling him or her that pizza and burgers are not good to eat. (Anyway, they are.)

There is a lot of fear accompanying judgments about packaged and junk foods. And underneath it all, the fear seems not to be so much about what they will do to the child but about what they will say about the parent. Too often what passes for love of food is, at best, fashion-consciousness, at worst, snobbery. Just as snobbery is in some sense about social insecurity, so food snobbery is really an indication of how frightened and insecure people are about food. They feel that they need to be told what they should like because they have never learned to trust their own palates. This is why it is crucial to eat well, eat passionately, as a child. Love of food should be something we take in with our mother's milk, not a complicated body of knowledge amassed from food magazines in our twenties and thirties. What's good to eat isn't an orthodoxy. But if we don't eat well young, we don't have much to build on. Foundations are everything.

When I was pregnant with my first child, I met the French obstetrician Michel Odent at a party. Of course, during a first pregnancy you are obsessed with it all, and we spoke about babies for as long as I could keep him talking. He told me that one of the reasons breast milk was better than formula was that its taste changed all the time. Whatever a woman's been eating informs the flavor of her milk, and so a breast-fed child has a varied diet from the very beginning. That's to say, the baby learns that unpredictability is in the very nature of food, of life— that change and difference, within a secure context, are not frightening but desirable and to be savored. I should admit here that I am a bottle-fed baby who grew up to eat anything. But I certainly ate very little, and that unwillingly, as a child.

M. Odent also told me his research had shown that the children of women who had been instructed to eat fish during pregnancy grew up to adore seafood. I happened to mention this to a friend of mine, who said that when she'd been pregnant she'd had a craving throughout for olives. Her son, from about eighteen months, had shown a marked and otherwise surprising preference for them; they aren't, after all, exactly normal baby fare. Anecdotal evidence is frowned upon by scientists, but I made a point of eating huge amounts of broccoli while pregnant in the hope of having that rare thing, a child who loved vegetables. I don't mind if it's a coincidence or a result of my intake, but my daughter does love broccoli. While pregnant, I also had to have, every day, a bagel with a slice of smoked salmon on it. Maybe that explains my daughter's extravagant, early, and continuing passion for smoked salmon.

What is the result of genetic predisposition, what of upbringing, I don't know, but they're linked. The way we nurture is part of our nature; the environment we create comes out of what and who we are. It is impossible to convey the pleasures of eating, the real voluptuous joy to be gotten from food, if we don't feel that joy ourselves. Eating disorders are passed on from mother to daughter (this is not sexist, just—sadly—true) but, even before we get on to such complexities and difficulties, it becomes obvious that our attitude to food colors our children's attitude to food.

From the beginning, you should expect your child to like the taste of the food you're offering rather than nervously expecting it to cause alarm. Nervousness conveys itself to the child. I don't mean that you should force anything. Of course, all people—children and adults—have their own taste, their own likes and dislikes, and there is no point battling against that. Mostly, though, a child will change, and food given on one day and rejected will be devoured on another day. But that's if you don't push it the first time.

I do think (and given that this is a chapter devoted to the eating practices of the young, I feel justified in rattling this particular cage), that there is a tendency to wean too young in the West. All babies are different and there may well be some who are ready to go on to solid foods at eleven weeks. There is a hopeful theory that babies will sleep longer once they have solid food and not just milk in their tummies. But giving babies solid food before their digestions can take it is more likely to make them miserable. By the time my daughter was three months old, I was being made to feel that I was in some way negligent for failing to offer her solid food (although she was gaining weight well and showed no signs of dissatisfaction with her diet). I then decided to try some baby rice and a little puréed something. She wasn't interested, so I waited until she seemed ready for it. This happened to be at about four-and-three-quarter months. It worked—I offered, she ate. She remains what people call a good eater.

Both my children are growing up in a household where food plays a central part. They see me cooking, see me eating. Food is thus part of the whole fabric of their lives, not just the constituent parts of mealtimes. I accept that when they go to school we will have to enter a less permissive, more picky stage of eating. But I believe that if you give babies and small children the right foundation, if they see you eat with pleasure and eat pleasurably with you, then, at the end of all the faddishness, they will return to familial normality, if that's not a contradiction in terms. There shouldn't be too much veneration, too much pressure. Let it all just happen. Don't look for trouble.

This brings me to dairy and gluten and the whole, very contemporary, issue of food intolerances. I don't believe in them. Of course allergies exist but, on the whole, allergies manifest themselves radically: you know if you're allergic to some food or other because you are ill, suddenly and as a direct result of having eaten something. The symptoms are incontestably presented. The general malaise that food intolerances are supposed to bring about is much more suspicious. I can't help thinking that adults who are keen to ascribe any number of symptoms—tiredness, lack of energy and enthusiasm—to food intolerance might be better advised to look to their own increasing age for a cause for this insidious drying-up of zip, pep, and go.

Babies, I admit, don't have the same sort of mechanisms in place (although children certainly can learn very young to use food, or rather the withholding of eating it, as part of the parent-child power struggle—but this is not really a food issue, although you can turn it into one). But we, on behalf of our babies, fuss too much about the wrong things. Our fanatical attention to our children's intake, our obsessive worrying about what terrible things some food can do to them, and our almost primitive belief in the magical properties of other near-voodoo foods, might be doing our children more harm than any of the foodstuffs in question. To live in fear of some food-borne catastrophe is going to be exhausting as well as unhelpful, both day to day and at a more profound psychological level. I should own up here, I suppose, that I did wait until I happened to be in the doctor's office with my children before giving them a peanut-butter sandwich for the first time. Although statistically I knew that chances of either of them having some fatal nut allergy were remote, I allowed myself to give in to overprotective maternal neurosis. I am not immune on this score. I worry intermittently about pesticides and shrink from providing adulterated food of indeterminate or covert origin. But I try to resist the notion that children need to be protected from the evils of wheat, milk, sugar, and fat.

Because as adults we want—at some time or other—to eat as much as possible for as little caloric spend as possible, many parents think the same virtues hold for their children. This couldn't be further from the truth. No child under the age of five should be given skimmed or low-fat milk. They certainly shouldn't be afraid of big bad fats. They should eat fruit, vegetables, cereals—of course—but don't fill them up with whole-wheat pasta and brown rice and don't weight their diet toward the bulky, the burlap weave, and the stomach-bloating. Children don't have a huge capacity, but they need lots of fuel. In other words, they need food that ounce for ounce is heavily stoked in calories. They eat and run, so you want to make sure that what they eat keeps them going for as long as possible. (Which is why I, nearly every day, thank God for pasta, without which I would be hard-pressed to find food that is maintaining, full of everything that is considered these days dietetically virtuous, and a useful vehicle for high-fat, calorie-boosting sauces and cheese.) Muesli malnutrition, the term that doctors apply to the low-fat starvation diet on which many well-meaning, affluent parents keep their children, is a tellingly growing concern.

Of course, it doesn't follow that the higher the fat and the lower the fiber in a child's diet, the better. Even diehard opponents of food faddists and anti-fattists have to accept that huge amounts of saturated fats, day in and day out, are on the whole unwise. But I believe that animal fats in moderation are good and, in occasional excess, unharmful. (And we know that some other fats, such as olive oil, are positively beneficial.) I think it's more important, anyway, to make sure every day that children eat fruit and vegetables, even if they accompany foods that have been fried or sauced with butter. It's what's missing from a diet that makes the crucial difference.

What you feed your child will go toward forming lifetime habits. It makes sense now not to stoke up trouble for them later. Much as I detest that specious smug and superstitious demarcation between "healthy" and "unhealthy" food, I accept that there is such a thing as a healthy diet. Be vigilant, but not obsessive.

For the first months of solid food—which in truth is hardly solid—you are just giving babies slops and purées and beginning the process of giving them food that resembles the food you eat yourself. And you absolutely have to stop yourself minding about the mess; in the first days I wiped my daughter's mouth after each spoonful, but I soon stopped. I had to. You have to learn to live with spilled food and stained clothes or you'll never teach your children to relax around food.

I am not a pediatrician or a nutritionist and, given the fanatical leanings of most parents, I am almost bound to be a deficient teacher. When we had the builders in, I took out a subscription to *Interiors* and *House and Gardens;* when I was pregnant, I spent sofa-bound evenings reading through parent-and-baby magazines. We are all child hobbyists now, we late-spawning parents of the consumer age, so I take it for granted that somewhere, some if not all of you will have a book on the subject of babies' and children's food, complete with timetables, graphs, nutritional indices, and medical advice. If not, trust me, they are widely available. But here, just in case, is a weaning timetable.

BABY-WEANING CHART

Do not add salt to your baby's food until he or she is 1 year old or over.

4–5 months	SEMI-LIQUID PURÉES OF: apple, pear, banana, papaya, carrot, cauliflower, potato, zucchini, squash, green beans, sweet potatoes
5–6 months	dried fruit, peach, kiwi fruit, apricot, plum, melon, avocado, peas, tomato, spinach, celery, leek, sweet pepper
6 months	chicken, dairy products, parsnip, foods containing gluten
6–7 months	MINCED OR MASHED FOODS, WHICH CAN INCLUDE: citrus fruit, berries, mango, corn
6–12 months	other meats
8–9 months	CHUNKIER TEXTURES, WHICH CAN NOW INCLUDE: split peas, butter beans, lentils, eggs, fish
over 2 years	shellfish

SOLIDS

Many parents start infants off with baby rice. I understand the reasoning—that it is midway between milk and solid food—but in practice it didn't work for my children. One of the fascinating things about how babies and small children eat is that they regulate their intake themselves—they eat as much as they need; if they eat less one day or for several days, they will make up for the deficit in calories later. Whenever I added baby rice to fruit or vegetable purées, my babies would eat as much as they felt they needed, as if what they were eating was just fruit or vegetables. They couldn't, it seemed, detect the rice. For when the grain swelled in their stomachs later, it transpired that they had eaten too much; consequently, and efficiently, they vomited the excess up. This isn't harmful, but I felt it unhelpful to interfere with the fine calibration of their digestive systems.

So for those with small babies who are about to start eating solids, I advise some fresh, cooked, cooled, puréed pear (peeled, obviously) as a first food. I used to cook it by putting chunks of the fruit in a container in the microwave for a few minutes. Bananas, briefly microwaved, then mashed with milk—breast or formula—are also a good first food. The microwave is very good for cooking most fruits. (Vegetables are better steamed or boiled, I think, as microwaved vegetables have a spooky texture.) Of all fruits, both my children liked papaya best.

PEAR

BANANAS

PAPAYA

I'd cut them in half, scoop out the seeds, and then blitz them briefly in the microwave. The smell of them, thus nuked, is sickly sweet, almost to the emetic point of putrefaction, or so it seemed to me after pulping too many of these honeyed and puce fruits, but children love the sweet, soft, aromatic flesh.

But ordinary fruit and vegetables are just as good. Variety is important, but a baby's diet doesn't have to include one of every foodstuff known to man. Remember that for a baby, all foods are new; stewed apple is just as exotic as steamed papaya.

For my first child I went into food processing overdrive, filling the freezer with as many different purées and pulped meals as possible. If you're going to peel, cook, and purée some carrots, you may as well do it once and have enough in the freezer for the month's meals ahead. Apart from anything else, the amount a baby eats is really tiny; even one carrot makes enough for quite a few meals. The only reason I relaxed (rather than abandoned) my bulk preparations of food with my second child was that I was cooking anyway for one child, so fiddling about with an extra bit of fruit or vegetable or handful of baby pasta at each mealtime didn't seem much trouble.

You do need, however, to be able to feed small babies promptly. If you can prepare baby food in advance, freeze it, and then microwave when needed, you reduce the time you are subjected to outraged, hunger-crazed screaming. But the practical advantage is the least of it. If you slave away cooking from scratch, trying to create some perfect morsel for your baby's edification, you will inevitably take it much harder when she spits it out in disgust or wipes it all over the walls. It isn't wise to put so much emotional pressure on either yourself or your children at mealtimes. If you slave and then freeze the product of your stove-bound slavery, the memory of the effort will inevitably recede and you won't take rejection so badly. This goes for feeding older children, too.

PASTINA

Once a baby has got used to solid food, knows what it's for, and enjoys eating it, baby pasta—pastina—is a useful way of making meals. It takes a few seconds to cook (I tended to cook it in milk, defrosted packages of expressed breast milk when they were very little and whole cow's milk once they were past six months) and all you need to do is toss it in some butter and grated Parmesan. If the baby in question is younger than six months, then you might feel happier adding nothing more, but otherwise use pastina in vegetable purées, too. It's very fine (or the smallest size is) but the grains retain their separateness—it doesn't become a gluey mass. I rather love it as well and, I think, as far as possible, you should try to give your babies food that you could bear to eat too. This is one of the reasons I cannot bring myself to serve up much bottled baby food. I just feel it must constitute the worst sort of culinary education. I am not neurotically and intolerantly bound to the preciously homemade, however; I always kept a supply of Beech-Nut baby foods on hand and often give myself up to the cool but welcoming embrace of the supermarket fridge case.

Indeed, Beech-Nut packages a fine-ground barley meal that I find preferable to baby rice. I gave it to my children for breakfast for ages, before they moved on to Weetabix, a shredded wheat cereal now available in America, and then to proper oatmeal (funnily enough, the baby oats that Beech-Nut also does weren't as popular). I mixed the barley meal with milk (first breast, then cow's) or sometimes fresh orange juice diluted with water, especially if either of them had a cold.

BARLEY MEAL

OATMEAL

I used to freeze baby purée in ice-cube trays. Just empty the thickly colored frozen cubes into plastic bags, label, tie up, and throw back in the freezer. I can't advise labeling these too strongly. Every time I thought I couldn't possibly forget what this luridly colored food was, I ended up being mystified at some later date and would defrost apricots when I was after carrots. The brain does go in the aftermath of childbirth—better accept that now.

I quite like pottering about kitchens, so made up quite a few different foods, but you soon realize that more than five or six can be superfluous; babies inevitably favor certain ones over others and you, as inevitably, choose to defrost the favored. After the first month or so of plain fruits and vegetables, I got into the habit of creating certain mixtures, and they're useful ones. The compound I was most pleased with was a mush of spinach and corn—the spinach, with its metallic, almost bitter hit, is sweetened, and somewhat deslimed by the corn. Another—broccoli and carrot—also works well. Though broccoli has a definite sweetness of its own, it also has a cabbagy mustiness that babies, and adults, can warm to less. Carrots intensify the sweetness and seem to neutralize the otherwise enduring Brassica-family brackishness. You will create a sludge of particularly unattractive khaki, but your baby will be able to live with that. When my babies were beyond purées, they ate the broccoli florets whole, a small green tree clasped in each fat pink fist.

SPINACH
AND CORN

BROCCOLI
AND CARROT

I started off in fear of salt; indeed, medical advice is that you shouldn't add it to food for a child under 1 year (now I let my children pour rivers of soy over their noodles, but there's nothing like having more than one child for easing one's principles, dietary or otherwise). I did succumb, however, to salted canned spinach, but drained it and processed it with drained unsalted canned corn, in about equal measures, before freezing it in cubes. You can, of course, use fresh vegetables, not frozen, or buy organic canned stuff from the health store, which won't have salt added.

I didn't add sugar to any food I gave my daughter and didn't get into the habit of giving her desserts or cookies either, and she isn't interested in eating them much now. My son, who has the advantage in this respect of being the second child, loves cake and anything sugary. But maybe (she said a trifle defensively) this isn't entirely because I have relaxed, giving him foods that normally I might not have fed to a baby, but because they have very different palates to start off with.

And that can't be underestimated. Neither I nor my children like baby rice. Your child might adore it. Babies have their own tastes, and to try to change them by force is as idiotic as the once-accepted practice of making left-handed children write with their right hands. Respond to your child but, at the same time, encourage him or her to experiment, to recognize, to enjoy.

One way to encourage your child is to give him or her a small taste of certain foods gradually. I wanted my children to enjoy eating spinach, so I tried to find ways of insinuating spinach into their diet without actually giving them, until they were older, a whole iron-resonant plate of the stuff. I therefore get for my freezer little packs of puréed spinach frozen in lots of tiny spheres, which I defrost one sphere at a time to stir into some other purée or foodstuff. These spheres exist throughout Europe and you might badger (gently) your supermarket to carry them. In the meantime, you could cook large amounts of spinach, drain, chop it in a processor, then freeze it in ice-cube trays. Defrost and add to food as I do. That way, your child will get used to the taste of spinach and will therefore like it. Children respond to the familiar, the known. Just don't make a big thing about it; don't let children know you expect them not to like something before they actually eat it, or show your surprise if they happen to love it.

Pasta sauce, most often pesto, ground meat, cheesy mashed potatoes, omelet or frittata, puréed peas, cheese sauce—you don't need me to list all the baby foods into which you can stir a cube of thawed and warmed spinach, but, trust me, it is invaluable later when your child is eating meals rather than slops. But do it before he has reached the stage of looking out suspiciously for green bits.

LIVER   Liver is another food that everyone presumes children will have to be forced to eat against their will. I never found this, but it may be that I am irredeemably extravagant because I fed my children calves' liver and carefully de-biled chicken livers rather than the vile, fibrous, bitter livers I was given at school. People who would never think of asking how much something costs before they eat it themselves get twitchy about expensive tastes in their young. Whenever I gave my children smoked salmon I was mocked by friends, as if I was making them wear tutus and speak French to one another in the manner of that rich-kid stunt in *High Society*. But children love smoked salmon, which is a very useful meal to bear in mind for hungry, fractious children kept waiting for an inevitably late lunch by an equally fractious parent after a Saturday morning spent shopping at the supermarket. After all, it's bad enough having to take the food out of the car into the house and then out of the bags into the cupboards. To have to cook any of it would be the final straw. Cut open instead a plastic-wrapped package of smoked salmon, butter some bread, if you must, and grate a few carrots, if you can. (It's worth knowing, in this regard, that most children seem to like frozen peas, as they are, unthawed, to eat from their own little bowls set out in front of them. It's not wise to let very small children eat these chokingly unyielding vegetable beads, but vigilance is a better route than dietary censorship.)

Giving children real food, the sort of food we'd eat ourselves, is important. It's why the French eat well, and the Italians: their children are not fobbed off with lesser ingredients and different meals in the erroneous belief that good food or expensive items are wasted on them. I'm not saying that you must bankrupt yourself to provide your angels with luxuries and *bonnes bouches,* but simply that they should not eat worse than you do. If I grate fresh Parmesan onto my pasta, why should I insist that theirs come ready-grated, bitterly musty, smelling of old socks and trapped in a plastic-lidded drum?

This does not mean that everything your child eats you will want to eat. One of my infant son's favorite meals was chicken liver puréed with soaked dried apricots. I should not choose to lunch on that. But I added the dried apricots to counter the potentially constipating effects of the liver. Deep within me I must have a fixation with digestive habits; I always feel that the balance between what nannies always used to refer to as the "binding" and "loosening" effects of foods has to be maintained. For example, I serve poached egg for supper on top of a bowl of corn.

I threw together the apricots and liver in the first place to use up a liver from a chicken I was roasting; real cooking, I can't help feeling, always starts from leftovers. Thus I concocted the following recipe—I say recipe, but it isn't really anything as precise. For a start, quantities are hard to gauge at any time, but for children, whose ages and appetites vary, it's even harder. But when my son was seven months old, I'd make up a batch of this and figure it would make 2–3 portions for him. You need a chicken liver (about 2 ounces), which you fry gently in butter, and purée made from dried apricots. I figure about 1 tablespoon of purée per liver. Just soak some dried apricots in hot water from a just-boiled kettleful for an hour or so, then boil till soft, drain, and purée. Most apricots are labeled as not needing any soaking, but I figure they do. Take a slice of dry or stale bread and soak it in some milk until saturated. Squeeze it out and add it to the liver and apricots and blend. Chicken liver, fried in butter as above, and blended with an equal weight of chicken breast poached in milk is another idea; use as much of the poaching liquid as you need to get to the texture you want. If you leave it thick, you can spread it onto toast-and-butter fingers. When I wanted the puréed liver as a bowl-bound meal—with or without baby pasta—I sometimes stirred in some puréed carrot, too.

QUICK MEALS

What helps most is having a cache of food you can throw together easily. So you must get stocked up first. You don't need me to tell you to keep a constant supply of canned tuna (which I detest) in the house, but I remind you simply because this is a good way to give children something sustaining to eat. I know people go on about added salt and sugar to canned foods children like, but I can't get worked up about it. It makes sense to watch for salt when they're tiny. I never salted any cooking water—of pasta, vegetables, anything—or added salt later, until my children were four years and eighteen months respectively. Then I decided that, if I wanted them to eat like us, it was inconsistent to refuse to allow them to season their food like us.

BEANS AND OTHER LEGUMES

Children seem to like all legumes. Canned chickpeas, cannellini, pinto, any bean you want, are worth keeping around for them, and if you do mind about salt, then buy canned organic ones without salt added. Just stir some cooked chopped bacon into any of them or some shrimp or fish into the cannellini. Shrimp and beans happens to be an actual contemporary Italian reworking—*i ricchi e i poveri* as it's known—of the traditional *tonno e fagioli;* indeed, tuna, drained, mixed in with a can of beans, and bound with a few drops of good olive oil is another meal worth bearing in mind, as canned tuna seems ideally suited to childish palates. Trout fillets, just poached, then roughly chopped and added to cannellini—or Pink Fish and Beans—are a particular favorite in my household, as my daughter is going through a deeply pink stage that shows no signs of abating. You could use smoked fillets if you want to avoid any cooking whatsoever, or substitute smoked mackerel; this is something of a radical substitution—the taste is much stronger, the texture much oilier—but can be successful.

PASTA

Pasta is another obvious staple, as are Asian noodles. I live near a Thai shop, so buy bagfuls of fettucine-thick, egg-yellow-and-paler thread-thin noodles (which need a minute's cooking) and fresh rice sticks, which don't need to be cooked at all—you just steep them for 5–10 minutes in boiling water. (It doesn't hurt to keep some cooked, cold-water-spritzed, and drained egg noodles in a covered bowl in the fridge, either.) Any of these, with some soy sauce (as I say, I'm not salt-sensitive) lightly sprinkled over, are among the lowest-effort meals I can think of. Supermarkets sell various forms of Asian noodles now, so you don't need access to exotically stocked, stall-sized shops, shelves piled with dried shrimp and sour pastes. But going to specialty stores makes shopping so pleasurable, and it's cheaper. Sometimes I make small bowls of vaguely Japanese soup: stock, some chopped greens, manageable lengths of noodle. This, for my daughter, signals special food, partly because it's food I make for myself (see pages 382–384) and partly because it has seemed a treat ever since I took her to a Japanese restaurant and she ordered noodle soup and was given chopsticks to eat it with. She couldn't really manage them, except singly as a kind of load-bearing punt, and I ended up feeding her, ferrying food, noodle by fat noodle, from bowl to hungry open mouth like a mother bird feeding her gaping-beaked young with worms.

For ordinary pasta, keep bottled tomato sauce on hand and containers of pesto, both good quality. Pesto might not sound like children's food, but they like much stronger flavors than adults give them credit for. But don't buy phony cut-price versions. How are children ever going to know how to eat well if they've been reared on inferior ingredients or ersatz foods? I don't mean—and I can't stress this enough—you must always provide them with comestibles shipped over from Peck or Fauchon, but don't pretend that an inauthentic article is the real thing. By all means cook rice and stir in peas and corn—just don't call it risotto. I speak as someone who gives her children canned ravioli as a special weekend treat when I feel too tired even to put a pan of water on to boil, so I'm not claiming rarefied or superior status. But I don't pretend it's the real thing or that the difference doesn't matter.

COUSCOUS

Just as children love pasta, so they seem to love couscous. This is even easier. Put some quick-cooking couscous in a bowl and pour over some boiling water (about ⅔ cup water for ½ cup couscous). Leave, covered, for about 10 minutes. That's it. Stir in some soft butter and give it to them to eat.

That's the basic, baldest method. Mostly I tend to bolster couscous with vegetables and use stock rather than water; my regular standby involves chopping 1 carrot in the baby processor until it is in tiny cubes and shards, and then boiling it for 2 minutes in a saucepan of bubbling water to which I have added 1 vegetable bouillon cube for every 2 cups of water. I then shake in some couscous, bring it all back to the boil, take the pan off the heat, and cover, leaving it for about 10 minutes. You can fork in some olive oil or butter, as you wish, but I think you do need some fat; small children find it easier to eat when the grains are sticking together rather than fluffily and otherwise desirably separate. You are not making couscous a Moroccan would be proud of, I admit, but nor are you setting out to. If you want to be really brazenly out of context, you can use frozen peas and corn in place of the carrot. Drained, canned chickpeas are the easiest option. Consider cracked wheat also; my daughter loves tabbouleh (see page 236) as well, astringent and onion-spicy as I make it.

POTATOES

Mashed potatoes is a good way to fill up a child. The easiest way to do this is the extravagant one. In other words, don't peel, boil, then mash the potatoes, but bake the potatoes instead. Bake them (½–1 per child, about 60 minutes in a 400°F oven), eat the skin yourself (young children don't seem to cope with this) sprinkled with a good pelt of coarse salt, crunch on crunch, as you fork some butter through the fluffy-cooked flesh in a bowl for your child.

As children get older they seem to prefer the potato kept separate from other things on the plate, but up to the age of two they accept various things to make the mashed, baked potato pulp into entire, distinct meals. Add more or less milk, depending on age. Obviously, the nubblier purées are not suitable for gummy-mouthed babies. Some of the ingredients I used may sound unappealing, but they didn't appear so to my children, so may not to yours. You can add chopped ham, minced meat, strips of chicken, or crunchy vegetables to the side.

When the mashed potato is still at its hottest—don't pour in the milk to thin WITH CHEESE it first—grate in whatever cheese you want. I started off, when my children were babies, with Gruyère and then went on to Cheddar or Parmesan or a mixture of both. Fork potato and cheese vehemently together until the fine strands of cheese start to melt. (I find a hand-held Mouli cheese grater, with drum and handle, the easiest way of doing this, but then I hate those knuckle-shaving punctured metal box graters.) Then stir in milk or milk and butter to make the mixture more liquid. If you want to boost the caloric value of this meal, add a dollop of mascarpone (or cream, of course). I sometimes beat in a raw egg yolk for this reason, too, but I am confident about the healthfulness of my eggs (see page xx). I know the accepted wisdom is that babies and small children shouldn't be given uncooked eggs to eat, but it is not a wisdom I have accepted.

WITH PESTO

From a very young age, both my children loved pesto and ate anything with it in. I add about 1 tablespoon to the flesh of each potato (½ tablespoon per child) and beat it in till smoothly amalgamated. Add 1 tablespoon or so more oil. If you're being echt, which could mean being fancy, you should use Ligurian olive oil to dovetail, culinarily speaking, with the pesto. I do happen to keep this in the house and because it is milder than Tuscan oil, with less of the throat-hitting pepperiness, it is probably more instantly palatable for small children anyway. Sometimes I mix in a bit of quick-thawed and cooked finely chopped spinach; go cautiously with the pesto and spinach, but you can add more than the amount I've suggested if it turns out your children like this purée even stronger and greener. I'm not sure I'd try this on children before they've eaten pesto on pasta, not because I think they may not like the taste (I've not met one who doesn't) but because all children have an inbuilt caution about mixtures.

WITH EGG

If you don't like the idea of introducing raw egg (and I would recommend always using eggs that are checked for salmonella, anyway), you can just soft-boil or poach 1–2 eggs, stir in the oily yolk, and then the finely chopped white. If you're worried about albumen, hard-boil the eggs and then push the dense globes of yolk through a sieve onto the potato, and think of this, archly, as mashed potato mimosa. Add milk as required and butter as desired.

WITH VEGETABLE PURÉE

A few gloopy tablespoons of puréed butternut squash, orange-fleshed sweet potato, or carrot stirred into the potato will make a good orange bowl of mashed potatoes for babies; for older children, you could grate over some Cheddar and shove the purée under a grill for a minute until scorched and almost crunchy. Substitute puréed corn, if your child doesn't mind a few rough bits, and whole corn kernels if they are beyond even gravelly purées. You could use peas (frozen peas, cooked, then puréed with a knob of butter and a tablespoon of Parmesan are wonderful with potatoes, whether you're a child or not), but I'd avoid other grassier green vegetables here. In all cases, consider a dollop of mascarpone for ballast and perhaps the merest, sheerest grating of fresh nutmeg.

WITH
TOMATO
I don't like tomato purée—I find it invasively metallic; everything to which it's added tastes instantly, however fresh, however lovingly homemade, as if it had come out of the tinniest of tins. This, Anna del Conte tells me reprovingly, is because I don't cook the purée long enough; it needs slow, insistent simmering before that front-of-tongue dried-blood taste subsides and the flavor builds to fill the whole mouth with sweet and actual tomatoishness. This makes sense, and I take the point and will act on it from now on, with sauces and stews—but with this kind of cooking for children, which isn't really meant to be cooking, I am not proposing to tend any pan for devoted hours. You have a choice: you can use canned purée made both more gentle and more liquid by the addition of a little warm milk, or a good-quality tomato sauce, strained or not as you wish. And do not hesitate—consider your constituency here—to add a good squeeze of tomato ketchup. Add grated cheese or mascarpone if you want to provide more fuel or some protein.

WITH PEANUT
BUTTER
Peanut butter should be smooth, of course. Yes, I know peanut butter and potato mixed sounds disgusting and, to be frank, even I, the greediest person alive, sitting vulture-like and fork in hand, impatient to snatch the food out of my babies' mouths, manage not to pick when they're eating this. The point is that children like it (and some grownups do too, I've found) and it gets in extra calories and protein at the same time. I have been known—don't gag—to stir in a little coconut cream dissolved in warm milk and this went down very well. It's the sweetness, I suppose, and the fact that we all do seem to have an innate, inbuilt capacity to appreciate fat. Once I've gone this far, though, there's nothing to stop me throwing in a few corn kernels, too.

WITH TAHINI
As long as you don't use too much, children seem to love pungent, soft-clay tahini, diluted with a little milk or olive oil and stirred into the potato.

WITH GARLIC
Children love garlic. Bake the potato as advised on page 418 (I like potatoes really cooked: one grain of unyielding crystalline flesh and they're ruined for me) and, 10 minutes or so in, take a whole head of garlic, lop off the top so the cloves are revealed in cross section, place on a square of foil, pour over a little oil, and wrap up the garlic so that you have a baggy but tightly crimped parcel. Cook for about 50 minutes, then take out and let stand in its foil. When you mash the potato, unwrap the garlic package and squeeze in the sweet, pulpy cloves. Whip with a fork to incorporate smoothly and add butter, milk, or cream to make the sort of purée you want. Heaven.

WITH FISH
You can use tuna or salmon; with the salmon, make sure you've removed any

lingering bones or slimy strips of oil-immersed skin. Add anything else you think would enhance—tomato sauce, mayonnaise, corn. And, with this, you're really halfway to fishcakes (see page 442).

OTHER EASILY-THROWN-TOGETHER MEALS

If you hate the very idea of cooking, no one's stopping you from opening packages or buying ready-prepared meals. And if you're worried about salt and sugar and other additives, you'll probably be able to find more virtuous though not necessarily more palatable precooked meals at health stores. You don't want to foist your hysteria at the stove onto your offspring. Nor do you, on the other hand, want to make a cult out of cooking everything yourself, so that your children either become afraid of any alien meal or develop a terrible longing for microwaved junk food. We all know about the thrill of the illicit. Besides, it's worth keeping a stash of ready-made meals on the grounds alone that it will make your life easier. But low-level cooking needn't feel too demanding. The following suggestions occupy a culinary territory somewhere between the ideas above and the full-blown recipes below.

RICE

Rice is, in my household, just as popular as pasta and couscous. It's popular with me, too, as I've got an electric rice cooker and it is therefore one of my hands-free options. Naturally I am not presuming your possession of such a machine, but basmati rice, cooked in a pot on the stove, is relatively low-effort. Providing you're giving the children a moderately balanced diet as it is, you don't need to add much to rice, though by all means throw in chopped meat or something that makes you feel this is more of a traditionally complete meal, if you want. I have entirely corrupted my children by letting them see how I eat my rice, which is doused in soy, so this is now how they require theirs. There's a tradeoff: I happen to eat my soy-browned rice with steamed or boiled broccoli and so this is, without fuss, introduced as part of the deal.

My children enjoy rice with diced carrot, peas, and corn, in any combination that can be bought in bags from any supermarket, even if the mixture makes me shiver. If you want, you can make a one-egg omelet in a nonstick pan and then cut it into shreds and stir this into the rice. And while we're edging toward it, I should mention that any leftover plain cooked rice languishing in the fridge can

ONE-EGG OMELET

be turned into fried rice, which always goes down well. Put some vegetable oil in a relatively deep-sided frying pan or a wok and, when it's hot (with a wok you should heat the pan before pouring in the oil), stir in 2 peeled, sliced, or chopped garlic cloves and 1 finely sliced scallion, if your children's digestion will take them, and stir-fry for a minute or so. Add some butter to the pan. Now cook some very, very, finely chopped carrot. Then add some sliced button mushrooms and cook—pushing and prodding with your wooden spoon or spatula—for about 5 minutes. Add cold cooked rice and push around the pan for a bit longer. Cook a one-egg omelet in a nonstick pan separately, cut it into shreds, and then stir it into the rice. Turn into bowls. My children like coriander, so I sometimes add

that. And throwing in some cooked peeled shrimp is, as far as my children are concerned, always a good move. In fact, just plain rice and shrimp is a good fall-back Saturday lunch.

I also make an unfussy rice and tomato soup (for myself, too, sometimes, especially when I'm trying to balance out my characteristic gluttony) by diluting a good, bought tomato sauce with water, adding a handful or so of basmati rice, and cooking until the rice is tender, 8–10 minutes. With children it makes more sense to leave the soup fairly solid, but you can add water from a boiled kettle toward the end of the cooking time if you want a thinner soup rather than liquid tomato-rice stew. Grate Parmesan on top and eat—with bibs.

GYPSY TOAST

This is the same thing as French toast. Bread, preferably stale, is soaked in egg beaten up with a bit of milk and then fried in butter. Even though I don't generally go in for making smiley faces and funny shapes out of food, as we're all supposed to do to lure a child to eat, I do cut out shapes of bread before soaking them (I normally use a star-shaped biscuit cutter for this, and I've got some otherwise unforgivably dinky aspic cutters, mini-hearts, diamonds, spades, and so forth, with which I stamp out shapes from bought packages of thinly sliced Gruyère). The golden stars do look beautiful—until they're bloodied by the required shake of tomato ketchup. My children are not particularly keen on ketchup (as I say, they're still preschool), but here they consider it obligatory. I make gypsy toast for a late weekend breakfast or for supper, after bath and just before bedtime, to keep them sleeping longer in the morning, so that the occasional late breakfast is a possibility.

    Mimi Sheraton, in her wonderful memoir-cum-cookbook, *From My Mother's Kitchen,* says that the best French toast is made from slightly stale challah. She's right, but away from New York you might have to substitute brioche. But whatever you have at hand is just fine. Egg-soaked, butter-fried bread is marvelous with either maple syrup (and bacon, too, both of which I rather love) or sprinkled with sugar and cinnamon. Cinnamon toast—that's to say, ordinary toast—made with sliced white bread and spread with a paste made by beating unsalted butter with sugar and cinnamon—is tear-prickingly comforting.

POUSSIN

A poussin is about the right size for two children with leftovers or three children without, and has the advantage of not needing any effort to cook. Just smear with butter or garlic-infused oil and sprinkle with salt or soy (or neither) before putting in a 375°F oven for about 45 minutes. Or throw in whole shallots and cloves of garlic, as on page 8.

LAMB CHOPS

Chops seem such old-fashioned food now, but they cook quickly and can be eaten in fingers. If you've got time and aren't sure how tender the lamb is, marinate it for an hour or more in the juice of 1 orange and 1 tablespoon olive oil with 1 teaspoon red currant jelly. Preheat the broiler, line a baking pan with foil, and cook the chops for a few minutes each side. I don't specify how many minutes because it depends on how well done you want it. In my view, it's never too soon to get a child used to pink lamb and blue beef. Green beans, also eaten with fingers, are good alongside.

GARLIC MUSHROOMS

Simply cook chopped garlic in oil or butter or a mixture and add finely sliced mushrooms. Or use a package of ready-sliced mixed mushrooms. If I'm in a hurry or have run out of garlic, I just add some of my store-bought garlic-infused oil to butter and cook the sliced mushrooms in it. If I'm rich in dried porcini, I soak and finely chop them and then throw them in, reserving the strained liquid. Even if I'm cooking for children, I like to add a slug of white wine, vermouth, or sherry, too. You can stop there, so that the mushrooms have a sparse, syrupy-buttery juice clinging to them. Serve with some buttered, toasted plastic bread or buttered, toasted English muffin to the side, but you could pile the mushrooms on top of either, or pour the mixture on pasta, plain rice, or mashed potatoes. Alternatively, after adding the whoosh of alcohol, let it bubble away till the alcohol's cooked off and the liquid reduced, and then stir in a good few tablespoons of crème fraîche or heavy cream and let that bubble away until the mushrooms are submerged in a thick, buff-colored creamy sauce.

QUAILS' EGGS AND NEW POTATOES

It's not surprising that children like miniature food. Quails' eggs are fiddly to peel, but my children fall upon them as if they were sweets. I buy a dozen for the two of them but am going to have to think of increasing rations to keep up with demand. I like to balance the effects certain foods have on the digestive system, as confessed earlier, so serving boiled or steamed new potatoes (little waxy-fleshed pebbles) alongside to form a routine culinary partnership makes me feel better about the egg-bolting.

Put the eggs in a small saucepan, cover with cold water, bring to the boil, and cook for 4 minutes. Immerse in cold water and leave to cool for 1 minute, then peel. The eggs are slightly easier to peel if you roll them, rather heavy-handedly so that the shell cracks, against the sink's draining board.

If I've got time (it does take longer than boiling) I steam the potatoes; it makes peeling them easier and, even if the skin's meant to be healthy, my children won't eat it; they either hand the unpeeled potato imperiously to me to peel for them or just spit out the offending skin. I sometimes cook some carrot sticks to go with them, a few straight lines to add to the arrangement and because I feel the presence of extra vegetables is a good thing. I have never told my children they're not supposed to like vegetables and they haven't yet worked it out for themselves, so the introduction of carrots is well received.

And while we're on the subject, even children who won't countenance vegetables seem to like corn on the cob with melted butter. You can buy mini-sized ones (that's to say, normal ones halved) in bags, frozen, which are useful to have around. They cook from frozen.

CORN ON THE COB

GARLIC-FRIED POTATOES

I can see that potatoes might not constitute a meal in themselves, but the fat in which they are fried adds enough calories to overrule any hesitation on this score. Chop up garlic and give it a few minutes, stirring, in the hot fat before adding and sautéeing some sliced, cooked, and cooled potatoes. Try cooking them in lard; they taste wonderful and crisp up gloriously. Alternatively, leave out the garlic and just sauté the potatoes in garlic-infused oil. I used to give the children either eggs or a slice of ham with these potatoes, but as it was the potatoes they liked, I gave up on an accompaniment, except for some crunchy green vegetables.

GARLIC ROAST POTATOES

If your children are old enough to understand about skins and will suck the sweet roast garlic flesh from the unpeeled cloves and leave the skins on the side of the plate, I wouldn't bother to peel them. Unpeeled, the garlic steams inside its skin and grows softer and sweeter; peeled, the taste can be stronger and, if you're not careful, bitter. But just remember (if peeling) to parboil the garlic. It's not a big deal, especially as it makes the cloves easy to peel. Preheat the oven to 400°F. If you're using unpeeled cloves, then just scatter a few cloves (about 6 per child, but then I'm always hovering about for leftovers) in a baking dish. Chop up (don't bother to peel; when the potatoes are roasted, children don't seem to mind the skin) some new potatoes into small dice and throw into the pan, too. Pour over some olive oil and mix it all about with your hands to make sure everything's glistening and covered. Sprinkle with salt if your principles allow and roast for about 45 minutes or until cooked and golden. If you're going to peel the garlic, put the unpeeled cloves in a saucepan, cover with cold water, bring to the boil, and boil for 5 minutes. Turn into a colander and run the cold tap over it, and them, and then just slip the skins off and proceed as above.

You can give your children these alone, or with roast chicken or poussin, but we often eat them with fried or poached eggs and some thickly buttered white bread, with fruit after.

Perhaps here is the place to note that, as far as children are concerned, you can never have too many seedless white grapes. Fresh pear, ripe, honeyed, juicy, peeled, and cut into chunks, is the everyday favorite in my household; mangoes, similarly dealt with, but with the stone to gnaw on after, are a special treat, with the status of ice cream.

FRITTATA

A frittata is the Italian version of a Spanish omelette, a fat disc of just-cooked egg, with additions, though not too many of them. I use a blini pan (see page 461), which makes a one-egg frittata that's perfect for one child (or indeed one adult). To make a zucchini frittata, heat the broiler before you start. On the stove, melt a tiny knob of butter in the blini pan, sauté ½ small zucchini cut into small dice for 1 minute or so, then pour in an egg beaten with 1 scant tablespoon grated Parmesan and a grinding of pepper. Cook for a few minutes until the bottom is set and then place under the broiler till cooked. Turn out onto a plate. Peas are also a regular filling, as are chopped leftover cooked potatoes. Any tiny, otherwise unusable, leftover piece of smoked salmon can be usefully dispatched here.

PEAS, POTATOES, SMOKED SALMON

COD AND PEAS

You don't need, obviously, to do this as an amalgam; you can simply broil, roast, or fry the cod and serve peas alongside. This recipe, though, requires nothing more complicated than standing shaking a frying pan for a few minutes. Put some butter and a drop of oil in a pan and fry in it 2 peeled cloves of garlic until they're golden brown. Then chuck them away; you want just a suggestive garlic whiff. Then add some frozen peas, young ones if possible, and if you've had time to thaw them earlier, so much the quicker. Turn the peas in the garlicky butter, add 1 tablespoon or so of vermouth or white wine (or water with a squeeze of lemon juice in it if you prefer; any alcohol will, however, burn off), and when they're soft, taste for seasoning, then add some cod fillet cut into bite-sized pieces. You can dredge the cod in a little seasoned cornmeal first if you prefer, but just as often I leave it as it is. Turn in the pan with the peas and after 2 minutes it should be cooked through. This makes a good sauce—more of a topping, really—for pasta, too. You can use trout in place of cod, wonderful and pink against the vivid Bemelmans green of the peas. This is a good way of trying out various species of fish to see how they go down. Be wary of bones. Safer to stick with fillets, and still look closely to see no bones linger.

TROUT

CHICKEN STRIPS

This is easy. Get a skinned, boned chicken breast and cut it into strips. Then marinate it in yogurt made liquid with milk (or you could use buttermilk) and 1 tablespoon honey or brown sugar stirred in; 1 teaspoon soy can be added, too, if you want. An hour's steeping will do, but you can prepare the marinade at breakfast-time for lunch or even the night before if it helps.

YOGURT AND HONEY

Take the chicken out of the marinade and wipe dry with a paper towel. Fry quickly in olive oil, or butter with a drop of oil, in a hot frying pan. Carrot batons, broccoli, or green beans—whatever you want, but it should have crunch—go well with the chicken. It's worth bothering with the marinade, as children seem to find a lot of meat too fibrous and difficult to swallow if it hasn't been tenderized. And you can vary the marinade as you wish, adding or substituting oil, lemon juice, peanut butter, maple syrup, and so on (see the drumsticks recipe on page 441, too). It's useful to keep yogurt or buttermilk, as both make even the driest meats sweetly tender (see page 315).

RATHER MORE ORGANIZED COOKING FOR YOUNG CHILDREN

If the above recipe suggestions delineate the upper limits of the amount of cooking you feel comfortable doing for your children, then stop here. Of course, I see that faffing about making pastry for children who are just as happy eating burgers might seem just one effort too far. But to that I'd say three things. First, children really do seem to like food such as pies. Second, part of learning about food is being around its preparation, and often helping with it (and more on that later). And, third, perhaps most importantly, everything that follows is real food, the sort of food you will want to eat with your children, and to invite other adults to eat, too.

Of course, children can eat from any of the other recipes throughout the book, but these lay the foundations and delineate the best—neither fussy nor bland—sort of family food.

MACARONI AND CHEESE

You may wonder why I include, indeed start off with, a totally un-Italian pasta recipe, now that we are wholly won over to the authentic Mediterranean way of doing things. I suppose it is nostalgia that makes me feel the need to preserve this wholly old-fashioned nursery staple; I worry sometimes that food like this will disappear. And it does have a certain period authenticity—if no other sort.

If you're to make it properly, observe the proprieties. Use macaroni—those little elbow shapes—rather than penne, and don't substitute any cheese for Cheddar. (If I've only got some corner-store horror of fake tasteless Cheddar, I add a pinch of mustard powder or cayenne.) What we are not trying to create here is some baked pasta with taleggio, however delicious it may be. A bit of grated Parmesan, mixed in with the bread crumbs to be sprinkled on top before going under the broiler, could, however, be accommodated.

2 ounces elbow macaroni

1 tablespoon unsalted butter

1 tablespoon Italian 00 or all-purpose
   flour

pinch English mustard powder or
   cayenne pepper (optional)

1 cup milk

2 ounces Cheddar, grated

salt and freshly milled black pepper

1–2 tablespoons bread crumbs

As the macaroni will take about 15 minutes to cook, first put on a saucepan of water to boil. Then turn on the broiler to let it get good and hot for the browning later. Butter a gratin dish or couple of little (½-cup capacity) casseroles. When the water boils, salt it and throw in the macaroni.

Meanwhile, put the butter in a saucepan on medium heat and, when it's melted, stir in the flour and cook, stirring, for a few minutes. Add the mustard powder or cayenne, if you like. Off the heat, pour in the milk, beating constantly. Usually, I warm the milk in the microwave in a plastic measuring cup, but you can use cold milk. Cook the sauce for about 5 minutes, stirring all the while; then, just before the macaroni's due to come out of the boiling water, take the sauce off the heat and stir in the cheese—keeping 1 tablespoon or so back—and keep stirring. Drain the macaroni thoroughly. Add to the cheese sauce. Taste and season with the salt and pepper. Pour or spoon into the dish or dishes, then sprinkle with 1 tablespoon bread crumbs per dish and the remaining cheese. Brown under the broiler, but remember to let it stand and cool for a bit before giving it to the children, especially if you've made them their own little individual ones. You can fill and freeze the pots and then just sprinkle them with cheese and bread-crumbs before reheating in a moderate oven.

HAM OR ALFREDO SAUCE

You can add chopped ham to this, and I often do; just as often, for a quick lunch, I cook ordinary short pasta and buy alfredo sauce (stocked in containers in supermarket cold cases) to which I add some chopped ham and perhaps a bit of grated Parmesan. Chopped cooked bacon is delicious in regular macaroni and cheese. But if you are frying a little bacon first, then add 1 tablespoon or so

MINCED ONION

minced onion, too, and stir in both together, and be sure, as you decant, to scrape out the pan well.

COD

Sometimes I change direction, but not shape, and leave out the cheese, but add cooked, flaked cod or other white fish instead. And I might toss in some

PEAS

peas, too.

CAULIFLOWER CHEESE

Naturally, cheese sauce can be used to cover a cooked head of small cauli-flower for that British nursery classic, cauliflower cheese. I have found, though, that the only way my children will eat cauliflower is coated in egg and bread crumbs when cooked and cooled, and fried, preferably with garlic.

COTTAGE PIE AND SHEPHERD'S PIE

Whenever British people over a certain age talk about shepherd's pie, which is made with lamb—as opposed to cottage pie, which uses beef—they point out reprovingly that it should contain meat that is already cooked. Of course, they're right. It's just that we don't go in for large roasts and hunks of meat so much now, so we don't tend to have the leftovers to mince. But do you know what? It's better with fresh, raw, ground meat. Still, the leftover-meat version is useful and good enough. And the filling by itself makes a wonderful sauce for pasta.

I do sometimes mince leftover lamb or beef if the bits that linger in the fridge are too well cooked to be eaten pleasurably cold, and, as I've said, I use the filling often as a pasta sauce. (The recipe below makes enough sauce for about 8 ounces uncooked pasta; figure 1–2 ounces per child portion.) Relatively small amounts of leftovers make enough pie filling for a few children.

WITH COOKED MEAT

First off, let me say none of the quantities is sensitive; use what you have. Remember to give the meat a good strong basis of flavor (with onions or shallots and garlic, plus carrot for sweetness, and herbs such as finely chopped rosemary, marjoram, or thyme), and to cook it in such a way—on a low heat and with liquid—that it mellows rather than drying out even more. I throw in some flour before adding liquid; this is to help thicken the sauce, to blend the dryish fibers of meat with the liquid it's cooking in. A bit of chopped liver would do much the same trick, as would fresh bread crumbs.

Use whichever fat goes best with the meat; I'd use olive oil for lamb, beef dripping for beef; I sometimes make the dish with leftover duck, for which I use duck fat (which my children particularly love, though what should this be called— pond pie?). But oil or butter, or a combination of both, is always fine. Bacon fat, if you've got it, gives real depth, or you could always just add a slice or two of bacon to the food processor as you chop the baseline seasoning of vegetables.

I often use shallots in place of onions, as I like the softer flavoring of shallots but don't necessarily want the fiddliness of peeling two or three times over. You can mince the meat by hand or use the shredding disc in a food processor, or grind it, as my mother did.

What follows is not so much a recipe as a suggestion, a reminder not to throw away even small amounts of meat that might be languishing, post–dinner party or –weekend lunch, in the back of your untended fridge.

1½ pounds potatoes, peeled and cut
  into chunks

6 tablespoons (¾ stick) unsweetened
  butter, plus more, if desired,
  for topping

¼ cup milk, plus more, if needed

FOR THE FILLING

1 tablespoon fat (see headnote), plus
  more, if needed

few sprigs parsley, minced

1 large shallot or small onion, minced

1 fat garlic clove

½ celery stalk, peeled and minced

1 small to medium carrot, peeled and
  minced

about ½ cup minced leftover cooked
  meat

1 scant tablespoon all-purpose flour or
  2 tablespoons fresh bread crumbs

1–1¼ cups canned chopped or ground
  tomatoes in tomato purée, as
  needed

⅓ cup milk, plus more, if desired

2 tablespoons heavy cream (optional)

salt and freshly milled black pepper

1 tablespoon unsalted butter, plus
  more, if desired, for topping

2 tablespoons red lentils (optional and
  if needed)

To make the topping, put the potatoes into a large saucepan of cold, salted water. Bring to a boil and cook till soft enough to mash easily, 25–45 minutes. Drain and put the potatoes back in the pan over the heat to dry off, about a minute. Put the potatoes through a ricer and then beat in the butter and milk, adding more milk, if necessary; remember, you want a stiff mash to top the meat, not a liquified purée. Set aside.

For the filling, put the fat in a medium heavy-bottomed frying pan and, when it's hot, add the parsley, shallot, garlic, celery, and carrot. Cook on a gentle heat for a good 10–20 minutes until soft but not browned. Remember to check especially that the carrot is cooked; as the meat is already cooked, it won't need that long in the pan and you don't want the carrots to be crunchy.

When the vegetables are ready, add the meat. If the mixture looks as if it needs it, add another tablespoon of whatever fat you're using before putting the meat in. Stir the meat into the sweet, taste-bolstering vegetables and sprinkle over the flour or bread crumbs, making sure to stir that well in, too. Add the tomatoes, just 1 cup at first, adding more if you think the sauce needs more liquid. Pour in the milk, too, stirring as you do so. Cook on a low heat for about 10 more minutes, or fewer if all the flavors, when you taste, are coming together smoothly. If you want a creamier sauce, add the cream or more milk. When the sauce is off the heat, season to taste with the salt and pepper and stir in the butter.

If you want to thicken the sauce further and can be bothered, cook the lentils until mushy, drain, and stir into the meat to add bulk and body (these add fiber—desirable—and flavor); baked beans (without much of their sauce) will perform the same function.

Pour the filling into 3 small oval pie dishes, measuring 5 inches at their longest point and of about 1-cup capacity, or similar receptacles, and top with the potatoes. If you want the top crispy, dot with butter and put it under a hot broiler for a few minutes. Each dish feeds 1–2 children; you can freeze any portions you're not using immediately.

I tend to make cottage pie rather more often than shepherd's pie, but then I buy my—organic—beef from a good butcher and get it freshly ground (as it must be for this version). I wouldn't want to buy any meat that had been lying under film and the lights in a supermarket. I like to know the source of meat and I instinctively shrink from getting meat from anyone except a butcher.

The quantities as specified make enough filling for about 2 small oval dishes or one larger one, measuring about 10 inches at its longest point. If I'm cooking a batch in advance, I freeze it without the potato in bags for quick defrosting. As often as not, the children eat it then with rice rather than as a pie with potatoes—and, if you want to use it to sauce pasta, add some milk on reheating.

1 pound potatoes, peeled and cut into chunks	¼ pound button mushrooms, sliced thinly (optional)
3 tablespoons milk, plus more, if needed	8 ounces ground beef or lamb
4 tablespoons (½ stick) unsweetened butter, plus more, if desired	1 tablespoon all-purpose flour
1 medium onion, cut into rough chunks	¼ cup Marsala or apple juice
1 medium carrot, peeled and cut into rough chunks	1 cup canned tomatoes, drained
1 garlic clove, chopped roughly	1 teaspoon soy sauce or Worcestershire sauce
½ celery stalk, cut into rough chunks	salt and freshly milled black pepper
2 tablespoons oil	¼ cup grated Cheddar (optional)

Put the potatoes into a large saucepan filled with cold, salted water. Bring to the boil and cook till soft enough to mash easily, 25–45 minutes. Drain them and put them back in the pan over the heat for 1 minute to dry off. Push the potatoes through a ricer and then beat in the milk and butter; add more milk if you wish but remember you want a stiff mash to top the meat, not a near-liquid purée. Set aside.

Put the onion, carrot, garlic clove, and celery into a food processor and pulse to chop finely (or do this by hand). Heat the oil in a medium frying pan with a sturdy bottom and, preferably, a lid and stir in the vegetables. Cook for a good 10 minutes until soft, then add the mushrooms, if using. You may want to add a knob of butter at this stage, too. After 2 minutes, add the meat, pushing and breaking it up with a wooden spoon or spatula. You want it to unclump and lose its pinkness. Sprinkle over the flour and stir well, then add the Marsala or apple juice (most houses with small children seem to have apple juice in the fridge), then the tomatoes and soy or Worcestershire sauce. Stir well, cover, and let simmer for 20 minutes. Uncover, prod, season with the salt and pepper, and cook for about another 10 minutes, by which time the meat should be cooked and not too liquid. You can thicken using the methods suggested in the recipe for already-cooked ground meat above, but the chances are you'll need such strategies less here.

Put into the dishes and top with potato. If you want the top crispy, dot with butter and put it under a hot broiler—sprinkling on grated cheese first, if you like—for a few minutes.

VEAL, LIVER, AND BACON PIE

Although this recipe includes liver, I have yet to find a child (even one who would never own up to eating liver) who didn't like it. This quantity makes enough to fill 2 little oval pie-dishes 5½ inches at their longest point and 2½ inches deep (this is about the right size for an older child or adult; smaller children can share one and you can freeze the other—or, if you're wise, eat it yourself). If you are opposed to veal, then this pie is a double insult, as it also contains calves' liver. Not all calves, thank God, are kept in confinement; I suggest you talk to your butcher about his veal—but if you have objections, please turn over a few pages.

You could grind the meats yourself—in a food processor if you wish, as you want a gentle mush. But I buy the meat from my butcher and ask him to grind veal scallops and liver together.

I have specified heavy cream because it's what I had in the fridge (left over, as it happens, from the Marsala muscovado custard on page 330). Light cream would be fine, too.

I think you do need canned petits pois here; that gray-green, sugary softness, just on the verge of evoking the cooking at a dusty-carpeted residential hotel, is precisely what's required. Frozen young peas wouldn't be catastrophic, just not quite of a piece. But just use what you have at hand.

2 medium potatoes, about ¾ pound
    total, peeled and cut into chunks

salt

1 small carrot, peeled and chopped
    roughly

1 garlic clove, peeled and chopped
    roughly

½ onion, chopped roughly

2 slices bacon, chopped coarsely

½ stalk celery, cut into rough chunks

3 tablespoons unsweetened butter, plus
    more, if desired, for topping

1 2-ounce veal scallop, ground

2 ounces calves' liver, ground

1 tablespoon all-purpose flour

good pinch ground cinnamon

2 bay leaves

1 cup canned whole tomatoes

¼ cup canned petits pois, drained

5 tablespoons heavy cream

2 tablespoons freshly grated Parmesan,
    plus more, if desired

whole nutmeg

salt and freshly milled black pepper,
    if needed

Put the potatoes into a large saucepan filled with cold water, bring to the boil, and, when boiling, add salt. The potatoes will probably need about 30 minutes, so bear that in mind as you get on with everything else.

Put the carrot, garlic, onion, bacon, and celery into a food processor and process until you have a finely minced mess: your *batutto* or *sofritto*.

Put 1 tablespoon of the butter into a frying pan and, when it's melted, add the chopped vegetables and cook on a gentle but not indolent heat until more than softened; you want them cooked and mushy. Ten minutes should do it, but just keep testing. By the time they are soft enough, you will probably find they've absorbed all the fat, so put another tablespoon of butter into the pan. If not ground together, combine the veal and liver, add to the pan, and give a good stir. Add the flour and stir in well, then add the cinnamon, bay leaves, tomatoes, and peas and give another good stir. Cook over a low heat for about 5 minutes until the meats have lost their rawness, stirring and prodding with your wooden spoon every now and again. Add 3 tablespoons of the cream and cook gently for another 5 minutes or so. Remove from the heat while you mash the potatoes.

Drain the potatoes when you're sure they're cooked enough. And don't be impatient: mashed potatoes made with even minimally undercooked potatoes can cause instant, but justifiable, depression. Mash them (I push the potatoes through my ricer) and return to a hot, dry saucepan. Stir well, adding the remaining butter and cream and the Parmesan. Grate over, too, some nutmeg, and taste to see if you need salt and pepper. The potato shouldn't be too slurpy.

Divide the meat mixture between bowls and cover with potato. This doesn't make a thick layer of potato for the top, but I think it's better like this. It looks stingy until you start eating, and then it tastes just right.

You could dot with butter, grate over some more Parmesan, and blitz under a grill, although as small children don't like furiously hot food I tend not to bother. But if you're freezing one, or just keeping it in the fridge to be reheated later, you might as well sprinkle with cheese and a few shavings or gobbets of butter just before putting it into a 375°F oven for about 20 minutes.

BEEF AND BEANS WITH PASTA

1 medium onion	1 quart beef stock, homemade or
1 garlic clove	prepared with bouillon cubes
1 medium carrot	1 can (14.5 ounces) chopped tomatoes
½ celery stalk, chopped roughly	2 tablespoons red wine (optional)
2 tablespoons olive oil	8 ounces small macaroni, preferably
8 ounces ground beef	gnocchetti sardi or ditalini
½–1 can (15 ounces) red kidney beans,	salt and freshly milled black pepper
drained, as desired	chunk Parmesan

This is all you do: put the onion, garlic, carrot, and celery in the processor and pulse for a few seconds until you have a finely chopped orangey-jade mess. (If I'm chopping finely by hand I might, out of laziness or time pressure, not bother with the carrot or celery.) Cook the vegetables in the oil in a medium-large saucepan for 5 minutes or so, until soft but not brown, and then add the beef and turn it in the hot pan, pushing it and breaking it up with a wooden spoon, until browned. Add the drained beans—just half the can if you don't want too many of them. Add the stock, tomatoes, and wine, if using. Don't put the liquid in all at once; add it bit by bit and stir. Bring to the boil, add the macaroni, and cook for about 15 minutes or until tender. Much of the liquid should have evaporated or been absorbed and what you'll have is a thick, busy stew of a soup. Taste and season with the salt and pepper, grate some Parmesan over, and let the eaters grate some more themselves.

If we're partaking of this with the children (and it comfortably makes enough bowlfuls for the four of us), I pour over mine some fierce and glowingly orange chili oil.

MEATBALLS IN TOMATO SAUCE

I think it's the smallness of it all, the walnut-sized balls of meat in sauce, that children like, but they also find the texture of ground meat more digestible than even the tiniest strips of the minced kind.

Because making meatballs is more fiddly than preparing shepherd's pie (but only marginally—no potatoes to peel, remember), I tend to do a lot and then freeze them in little bags of 4 apiece. If I want to cut corners, I don't do all that chopping and gentle frying for the sauce (though mince the vegetables together in the processor for this); I just use canned tomatoes and simmer them for a while with the chopped carrot, as below, but without the onion and with the celery stalk and garlic cloves left whole. I retrieve the bits along with the bay leaves once the tomato and vegetables are cooked, and I give them only 10 minutes simmering before immersing the meatballs. And if you can't bear the idea of pre-cooking the onion to go in the meatballs, just leave it out.

FOR THE MEATBALLS

1 medium onion, minced

salt

1 tablespoon vegetable oil

4 slices stale white bread, crusts
    removed, broken into pieces

1 cup milk

2¼ pounds ground beef

2 beaten eggs

¼ cup grated Parmesan

1 heaping tablespoon chopped parsley

freshly milled black pepper

FOR THE SAUCE

2 tablespoons olive oil

1 tablespoon unsalted butter

1 medium onion, minced

2 garlic cloves, minced

1 medium carrot, peeled and minced

1 celery stalk, minced

2 tablespoons red wine or apple juice

3 cans (14.5 ounces each) whole
    tomatoes with their juice

3 bay leaves

salt and freshly milled black pepper

1 cup milk

_____

all-purpose flour

1 tablespoon oil, plus more, if needed

For the meatballs, sauté the onion, sprinkled with salt, for about 10 minutes in the oil. When it's cooked, remove to a plate and set aside. In the meantime, cover the bread with the milk in a dish and leave for about 10 minutes or until soft.

Put the beef into a large bowl. Drain the bread by squeezing in your hands and add with the beaten eggs, the Parmesan, the cooked onion, the parsley, and some salt and pepper. Mix well, but gently, with your hands, or get the children to do so. Reserve.

Meanwhile, get on with the sauce. In a large saucepan or flameproof dish (I use a rectangular cast-iron affair that goes across 2 burners), combine the oil and butter with the onion, garlic, carrot, and celery. Cook the onion mixture until it becomes a soft, sweet stew and then add wine or apple juice and 2½ cans of the tomatoes with their juice. Push the tomatoes around until they break up, then add the bay leaves and season with salt and pepper. Cook for about 20 minutes, add the milk, then cook for a further 10 minutes, by which time everything should be thick and sweetly tomatoey.

Spread a large surface with the flour and have 2 large plates ready. Using your hands, form the meat mixture into small balls, about the size of a walnut. Then turn each ball in the flour and place on the plates. I make about 46 meatballs with this amount.

Heat the tablespoon of oil in a nonstick frying pan (you will probably have to add more oil as you go) and brown the meatballs in it. I fit in about 11 a time and as each batch cooks put the meatballs into the pan with the sauce. When you've done them all, throw the remaining ½ can tomatoes into the pan in which you've been browning the meatballs and then put the contents on top of the meatballs and sauce. Cook in the sauce for 20–30 minutes. You can test the odd one to see whether they're cooked through. Because my big, low cast-iron pot has a lid, I cook them covered, but it doesn't really matter. Remove the bay leaves if you feel like it, and serve.

We always eat these with rice.

DUCK
MEATBALLS

I make meatballs out of anything, usually halving or quartering the basic recipe above. When I make duck meatballs, I use duck breasts, and just one will do. Because they're often sold in packs of two, I sometimes broil one for myself for supper and use what remains for the children. I strip the fat off and render it down to fry the onion and meatballs in. I chop the meat roughly and put it in the processor to grind, then mix it by hand with some very finely chopped orange zest, a good pinch of cinnamon, an egg, and a slice of bread, as above, but soaked here in yogurt made runny with milk (or buttermilk—either makes the fat-stripped meat more tender when it's thus ground). I often use a canned tomato sauce mixed with some canned tomatoes to which I've added a good pinch of cinnamon (or I cook it with a short cinnamon stick, which I remove later), another good pinch of ground ginger, and, if I've got some in the cupboard, some gorgeous red-golden saffron.

HAM AND
TURKEY

And after Christmas one year, I made some meatballs that were too moussey for adults but that the children (and their friends) were very keen on, out of leftover ham and turkey chopped in the processor and bound with some sausage meat—that's to say, the meat from some good butcher's sausages.

SPECIAL
MEATBALLS

But my favorite meatballs are a Judeo-Italianified variant. I use 1 pound each veal and beef, 2 eggs, and 1 onion, as above, and add some marjoram to the parsley. I use slightly less bread—3 slices—and add about 2 ounces chicken livers, pulped in the processor. Continue as above. These are fabulous—light in texture, smokily delicate in flavor, and what I cook when I've got masses of children and their parents coming for lunch. The sauce is good if you throw in some marjoram with the onions and use Marsala, generously, in place of wine. And sometimes I process one of the cans of tomatoes with another 2 ounces of chicken livers. In my notebook, these go by the name of Special Meatballs, and rightly so.

CLOVE-HOT CHILI CON CARNE

In my experience, children like much stronger tastes than adults assume. When I make a chili con carne for them—well, I'm a child of the seventies, what do you expect?—I use spices—cloves in particular—to infuse it with heat rather than chili. I love it, too.

If you don't want to soak and cook dried beans, by all means use canned ones and add them 15 minutes before the end. I often soak beans at night and cook them at breakfast-time, letting them cool in their cooking liquid for the rest of the morning.

And if you don't want to use porcini, use button mushrooms, about 4 ounces sautéed in 2 tablespoons oil and added to the chili at the end of its cooking time, or no mushrooms at all. But what I do recommend, if not using the porcini, is that you track down some Italian-imported porcini-flavored bouillon cubes and add ½ cup stock made from them when you put in the tomatoes.

FOR THE BEANS

⅔ cup dried pinto beans, soaked
   overnight

3 garlic cloves, minced

1 celery stalk

3 dried porcini

1 medium onion stuck with 2 cloves

1 tablespoon olive oil

½ ounce dried porcini

2 tablespoons olive oil

2 medium carrots, peeled and minced

2 medium onions, minced

3 garlic cloves, minced

1 celery stalk, minced

1 dried red chili pepper

1 pound ground beef

½ teaspoon cinnamon

½ teaspoon cloves

1 can (14.5 ounces) whole tomatoes,
   with their juice

2 tablespoons bottled barbecue sauce

2 tablespoons dark brown sugar

Drain the soaked beans and combine in a saucepan with the garlic, celery, porcini, onion, and oil. Add fresh water to cover generously and simmer over medium heat, covered, until well flavored, about 1 hour. Drain.

Meanwhile, for the rest, cover the porcini with hot water and set aside to soften. Heat the oil in a frying pan, add the vegetables and dried pepper, and cook for about 10 minutes or until soft. Remove the pepper (my daughter, when she was barely three, liked it hotter by having the chili pepper minced with the vegetables in the processor, but go cautiously). Add the meat and the spices, and turn and push about in the pan before pouring in the tomatoes and the barbecue sauce. Add the softened porcini. Strain and add their soaking water, pouring slowly so the gravelly, grainy bits don't gush in too. Stir in the brown sugar and the drained beans and simmer for 1 hour or so.

DUCK LIVER SAUCE

I suppose it's because it was dinned into me when I was a child, but I can't help thinking it incontrovertibly a Good Thing when children eat liver. Duck livers are sweeter and moussier than chicken livers, and so more child-friendly. Sometimes, when I buy a couple of ducks to roast, I use the livers either with leftover meat (in the unlikely event there is any) or some specially bought breast, diced small, to make a chunkier, meatier pasta sauce than the one that follows. For this you'd need to buy duck livers especially, I should think.

I used muscat for this because I had some—dark and Australian—left over in the fridge, but Marsala would do fine—and, if you don't like putting alcohol in children's food, substitute apple juice.

Serve the sauce on penne or tagliatelle—or rice.

1 small onion, chopped roughly	3 tablespoons oil for frying
1 medium carrot, peeled and chopped roughly	10 ounces duck livers (about 4)
1 ounce pancetta or bacon, chopped coarsely	¼ cup muscat wine, Marsala, or apple juice
2 garlic cloves, peeled and chopped roughly	1 tablespoon hoisin sauce
	2 tablespoons tomato purée
	½ can (14:5 ounces) chopped tomatoes

Put the onion, carrot, pancetta, and garlic in a processor and blitz, or mince by hand. Heat 2 tablespoons of the oil in a deep frying pan and add the chopped mix. Cook on a medium to low heat until softened, about 10 minutes. Add the remaining oil and livers and cook, turning often, until browned but still pink inside. Add the muscat, the hoisin sauce, and the tomato purée. Cook for another minute or so and then put in a food processor and give a couple of turns so that it is chopped but not mushy. Put back in the pan, add the tomatoes, and, when warmed through, season with the salt and pepper.

PASTA SAUCE WITH SAUSAGE

As children seem to love sausages, you should try making a pasta sauce with them (see page 434 for the recipe, which is for the shepherd's pie filling, to be used as a sauce). The sausages you need for this are sweet Italian ones. I use 4 sausages (about 8 ounces) in place of the ground beef—in other words, substitute weight for weight. Remove the casings and prod and push about the pan much as you do the beef, only more emphatically, to break the meat up satisfactorily. A tablespoon or so of cream or milk toward the end binds the flavors and textures of the sauce smoothly and harmoniously together.

CHICKEN PATTIES

These pale and miniature burgers take little time, require little effort, and are always, at my house at least, rapturously received. To simplify matters even further, you could always substitute about 10 ounces ground turkey (relatively easy to come by these days) in place of the chicken thighs; in which case use hands rather than machinery to combine everything. If you want, you can make, cook, cool, and then freeze the patties, to be reheated quickly whenever you need a failsafe child-friendly meal at short notice. If you're nervous about any child's reproachful sensitivity about green bits (although I've never had any complaints, even from vegetable-phobic children), then just leave out the parsley.

handful parsley leaves	2 best-quality pork sausages
3 tablespoons bread crumbs	whole nutmeg
4 boned and skinned chicken thighs, cut into rough chunks	2 tablespoons oil, for frying

Put the parsley into the food processor and give a good blitz. If your bread crumbs (see page 22 for directions as to how to make them) are on the dry side, put them in with the parsley; if they're soft, wait. Add the chicken thigh meat and process until very finely chopped. Squeeze the sausage meat out of the casings into the food processor, along with the bread crumbs, if not already added, and a good grating of fresh nutmeg. Process to combine and then, after dampening your hands, form into small rounds, about the size of a large walnut, and squish slightly to make small but bulging discs; you should get about 15 out of this amount.

Preheat the oven to 400°F. Heat the oil in a heavy-bottomed frying pan. Fry the patties for a couple of minutes on either side just to brown them and then transfer them to a baking dish. Bake for about 30 minutes or until golden without, cooked through, with no pinkness within.

CHICKEN PIE

When I first made this chicken pie—with some leftover meat, light and dark, from chicken roasted earlier in the week—I was going to top it with mashed potatoes, but then it occurred to me that it would be less effort and take less time just to make a little disc of pastry. You can bake the pie immediately or, if like me, you find it more convenient, prepare and hold it to be baked later.

The process for making the sauce that coats the chicken is explored in detail on page 19. Just a reminder: make sure the bouillon cube's a good one.

FOR THE PASTRY

½ cup Italian 00 or all-purpose flour

3 tablespoons unsalted butter or butter and vegetable shortening mixed, cold and diced

1 egg yolk, beaten with a teaspoon of water and a pinch of salt

1 tablespoon unsalted butter

½ chicken bouillon cube

1 tablespoon Italian 00 or all-purpose flour

1¼ cups milk, plus more, for wash

1 cup frozen peas or corn kernels or a mixture of both

1½ cups cooked cold chicken, shredded or chunked

salt and freshly milled black pepper

whole nutmeg (optional)

Using the ingredients listed, make the pastry as directed on page 38 and put it in the fridge. Preheat the oven to 375°F.

For the chicken, melt the butter and ½ bouillon cube in a saucepan, prodding the bouillon cube to help it break up and dissolve. Stir in the flour and cook the manila-colored paste for a minute or so, stirring with your wooden spoon. Off the heat, gradually pour in the milk, stirring, if not actually beating, all the while. When all is smoothly incorporated, return to heat and cook for about 10 minutes.

Meanwhile, cook the peas and/or corn. When the sauce is cooked, add the vegetables and the chicken to it, season with the salt and pepper and a scant grating of nutmeg, if you like—and then turn into a buttered dish or dishes. I make this generally in one pie, in an oval stoneware dish with an 1-quart capacity.

If you're not going to bake the pie right away, let the filling cool before covering it with pastry; in any case, roll out the pastry, dampen the edges of the dish, and fit on the pastry lid, cutting off excess and prinking round the edges as you like. Cut a few slashes to let steam escape. The pastry will sit somewhat on the filling. It makes the lid's underside—but only the underside—just a big soggy. This, for me, is the best part.

Brush with the milk and bake for 25–45 minutes, depending on, among other things, whether the filling's cold or not, or until the pastry is golden and the filling hot.

You can always cover the pie loosely with a bit of foil if the pastry looks like it's browning too soon.

A pie this size will feed 4–6 children, but my children and I can polish it off in one go. Last time, both of them had third helpings. I think it's the savory saltiness of the white sauce that they especially love.

MARINATED CHICKEN DRUMSTICKS

When other children are coming to eat, I sometimes marinate chicken drumsticks. It would be foolish to be too rigid about the marinade. I might mix 1 teaspoon grainy mustard, 1 tablespoon honey, 2 crushed garlic cloves, and some minced onion in a glass of white wine or apple juice made slightly more acerbic with a squirt of lemon juice. You could use the marinade for the char siu (page 399—and indeed, do the char siu itself). And I once made a marinade that, although it made me wince as I did it, consisted of creamed coconut dissolved in pineapple juice, a dollop of peanut butter, 1 teaspoon soy, and some brown sugar. The children loved it. If I want to do just 4 drumsticks in a hurry, that's to say, for the next day's lunch—and with stuff I've got routinely in the fridge or cupboard, the marinade is as follows: ½ cup apple juice, ½ cup plain yogurt, 1 tablespoon honey, the same of soy sauce, and 1 garlic clove, minced. But, normally, I tend to leave the drumsticks marinating in the fridge for some time—24 hours, say.

Arrange the drumsticks on a rack in a roasting pan and bake at 400°F for 35–40 minutes and then at 325°F for another 20–25 minutes or until cooked through. Easily made, easily eaten.

You can freeze a few drumsticks at a time in their marinade (I use freezer bags rather than containers) and later remove them portion by portion.

MUSHROOM RISOTTO

Really, risotto does not entail terrific drudgery; I don't know why people think it does. It means you've got to stand by the stove stirring for about 20 minutes, but I find it rather calming. You can pull up a chair and get one of your children to take over. That's how they'll learn to cook; it's certainly how I did. (Remember, though, to watch them carefully, in case of accidents, but try not to nag.)

And, also, because you won't be worrying as much about how the risotto will turn out, whether it will be too gummy or too mushy or whatever, no doubt it'll be perfect.

I use dried mushrooms from the cupboard to save shopping, but you can add, or substitute, fresh ones. As for the stock, I like to use Italian porcini-flavor boullion cubes supplemented with strained mushroom-soaking water.

2 tablespoons unsalted butter, plus
    more, if using fresh mushrooms
    (see below)
1 tablespoon olive oil
1 small onion or 1 large shallot, minced
½ ounce dried porcini, soaked for
    20 minutes in warm water to soften,
    liquid strained and reserved, and/or
    4 ounces fresh mushrooms,
    sliced thinly

1 cup arborio rice
¼ cup white wine or vermouth or
    Marsala (optional)
about 3 cups stock made with porcini
    bouillon cubes or chicken or
    vegetable stock
2–3 tablespoons grated Parmesan, plus
    more, for serving
2–3 tablespoons chopped parsley

In a heavy-bottomed, wide saucepan heat 1 tablespoon of the butter and the oil and cook the onion in the mixture for a few minutes. Chop the soaked porcini, if using; add and stir for another minute. Stir in the rice and toss and turn well in the pan so that every grain is covered and gleaming with the cooking fats. Throw in the wine if you're using it—and if you're not, this is not the place to substitute apple juice—and let it bubble away until some is evaporated, the rest absorbed.

Put the mushroom-soaking liquid, if using porcinis, in a large measuring cup and add the hot stock to make 3 cups; otherwise, use 3 cups of stock. Return to the saucepan and keep it simmering slowly. Stir a ladleful of the hot stock into the rice and keep stirring until the liquid's absorbed. Carry on in this vein for about 20 minutes. If using fresh mushrooms, add them, sautéed first in little butter, at this stage. You may not need all the stock, you may need more than the specified amount and have to add hot water at the end; bear that in mind.

When the rice is creamy and tender with just a bit of bite within, take it off the heat and beat in the remaining butter and the Parmesan. When I make risotto for grownups, I sprinkle over the parsley myself, but for children I put it on a saucer near them on the table and let them do it. It seems to make them like it. And put more Parmesan and the grater there as well.

SALMON FISHCAKES

You can make variations of this recipe, either substituting canned tuna or crab meat or adding peas or corn or chopped scallions, but it stands as a useful blueprint. I find it easier to make the fishcakes in advance, store them in the freezer, and then cook from frozen. (See below for the method.) Bought matzo meal is better than bought bread crumbs.

⅔ cup canned drained salmon

¾ cup cold mashed potatoes (about
  1 floury potato)

1 tablespoon grated Parmesan

good pinch paprika

chopped zest of ¼ lemon (optional)

1 egg beaten with 1 teaspoon milk

3 tablespoons all-purpose flour

3 tablespoons dried bread crumbs or
  matzo meal

vegetable oil, for frying

In a bowl combine the salmon, potatoes, Parmesan, paprika, lemon zest, if using, and half the beaten egg mixture. Using your hands, form the mixture into balls about the size of walnuts and then flatten them slightly to make fat little discs. Dredge them in the flour, then dip them in the remaining egg and then in the bread crumbs or matzo meal. Let rest for 15 minutes in the fridge on a plate or tray lined with plastic film. Put about ¼ inch of the oil into a frying pan, add the cakes, and fry for a minute or so each side until golden. Remove to paper towels to drain. Serve. Enough for 4 children.

If you're making the fishcakes in advance and then freezing them, this is how you work it. Line a couple of small baking sheets with plastic film and arrange the dredged fishcakes on them. Cover with another sheet of film and put in the freezer for at least 1 hour. You want them hard. If you want to keep them in the freezer for a long time, just bag them up once they're set and completely hard.

When you want to cook them, preheat the oven to 250°F and line 2 baking sheets with a double thickness of paper towels. Pour some vegetable oil into a frying pan and heat.

Take the fishcakes out of the freezer, release them from their plastic wrapping, and dredge them first in more flour, dip them in the egg mixture, and cover them in the matzo meal or bread crumbs. Fry them for 2 minutes on each side or until golden, and then put on paper-towel-lined sheets and into the oven. After 20–30 minutes, the fishcakes will be warmed through and ready to eat, but you can leave them there for 2 hours or so without worrying.

You can fry them from frozen like this without worrying; because they're so little they'll reheat in the middle before the surfaces burn. And I sometimes dredge them in flour before freezing and fry like that—no egg, no matzo meal. The benefit of frying and then oven-cooking is that you can do it in advance (which often is the only way one can cook for children).

We also make something we call greencakes, which are like fishcakes only the part of the fish is played by a variety of vegetables, chiefly broccoli and peas (though including nongreen vegetables such as carrots). Cook and mash the vegetables roughly before making them into little balls and proceeding as above. GREENCAKES

SOUP

Children tend to like homemade soup, which has an advantage, beyond the obvious one, over canned, as it can be thicker and is therefore easier for them to spoon from bowl to mouth. When I'm feeling laid-back about mess and spillage, I make pea soup (see page 162), which can be cooked impromptu. A good bean and pasta soup has to be planned ahead, but it doesn't take great military organization to put beans in to soak before you go to bed and to boil them for 45 minutes the next morning before you go to work.

In the evening, fry up the usual onion-carrot-celery mixture, with some chopped bacon or pancetta if wished; add the drained beans, some stock, a can of tomatoes, and a potato, peeled and diced finely. Cook for about 45 minutes. Add some ditalini or other soup pasta for the last 12 minutes. Sprinkle with Parmesan and eat.

As all children seem to like both pasta and beans, cook this when other children are coming over. You can do it all in advance, bar the pasta, so it can be on the table in 20 minutes.

DESSERTS

You may have noticed that there are no recipes for desserts here. It's because we don't go in for them. There's always fruit, though, and some ice cream. And, of course, I seem to spend my life stocking up with multipacks of mini-yogurts and fruit-flavored ice pops.

AN EXCEPTION: CHILDREN'S CHOCOLATE MOUSSE

I do sometimes make dessert when friends and their children come round for lunch and what I'm providing for the adults is too bitter, too rich, too alcoholic, or otherwise unappealing for the children, or I just want to make something that will bludgeon them sweetly into sugar-absorbed silence. And actually, I like this much more than those dark, coffee-sharp, elegant adult versions; so, I find, does just about everyone else. You may want to make up double quantities.

4 ounces Valhrona Lacte or other really good milk chocolate with 40 percent cocoa solids	1 tablespoon golden syrup 2 eggs, separated

In the top of a double boiler over hot water, put the chocolate, broken into pieces, with 1½ tablespoons water and the golden syrup. When you have a smooth, melted brown puddle in the pan, remove from the heat. Whisk the egg whites until you have a stiff snow; it'll make it easier if you wipe round the bowl with the cut surface of a halved lemon before you start. Leave them for the moment and beat the egg yolks, one by one, into the still-warm chocolate mixture. Then take a dollop of egg whites and briskly, brutally even, stir them into the egg-yolky chocolate. This just makes it easier to fold in the remaining egg whites, which you should now do firmly but gently with a metal spoon.

Decant into a bowl and leave in the fridge for a good 6 hours before eating. I generally make this the previous day, or at least the night before. This makes enough for 4 small children, but I can't promise they won't want to eat more.

Generally, I always bear in mind the advice of Penelope Leach—Britain's childcare expert—never to use sweets as reward or solace. Chocolate is food and must be treated as such, normalized, given as part of lunch or supper. You don't want to make the main course at lunch seem like a vile duty that the child has got to wade through, nor do you want to signal that sweet food is the only comforting, treat-like food, the balm for life's ills, unless you actually want to make your child unbalanced around food later. All eating should be a natural pleasure, not just dessert-eating. Still, this is easier said than done, and my method of child-rearing often seems to be one long pattern of bribe-threat-bribe-threat.

I believe in asking children what they want to eat and in not making them sit at the table for hours, if that's what it takes, until they clear their plates. Children have likes and dislikes just as grownups do, and there is no reason why they shouldn't be respected. And yet, and yet. It's useful to learn to eat everything, especially when away from home; it doesn't help children to turn them into picky little brats. You've got to find a middle path. If you teach your children that if they make a fuss they will be indulged, they will just make more of a fuss more of the time. You have to put up with an amount of screaming and to remember that if a child goes without food for one meal, even two, he or she won't starve.

So, even though you should not tell children that if they eat up those horrible vegetables they will be allowed some lovely dessert, neither should you give them any dessert if they won't eat any of their main course. (All this, of course, is so much easier said than done.) I wouldn't want to make a child clear his or her plate for the sake of it, but I'm always enchanted when it's done voluntarily. Remember that a power struggle about food is one that your child will always win and that turning the lunch table into a battleground is asking for grief. When I was young, I was so often made, to the point of torture, to eat up every cold, congealing thing on my plate, that I now can't help but finish up everything in sight, on my plate or other people's. This might be a polite party trick, but it doesn't make for a serene life or stable weight.

The more that children are encouraged to help with the cooking, the less likely they are to become picky eaters. I don't say there's a magic formula to ensure they're never faddy or fussy or hampered by bizarre prejudice, but you will improve your chances of having children who enjoy food if they are part of the enjoyable process of making it. Most children like eating what they cook and are proud of doing it.

My own early memories are of wobbling on a wooden chair pushed up against the stove, stirring my mother's white sauce. I often cook one-handed, with my daughter on a chair stirring or inspecting and my still-just-baby son on my left hip, licking a wooden spoon or doing a bit of stirring with it himself. My daughter, age three, would come into the kitchen and say, "Lovely! Garlic!" when she smelled the cooking, or detected by the smell that a chicken had been put in the oven or some pea pods were being simmered into a stock. That's not genius, but a feeling for and interest in food—much more important.

Doing ordinary, everyday, real cooking with children is more to the point than making any amount of chocolate Rice Krispie Treats. If you want to cook with your children, let them help cook lunch. There's something so companionable about actually cooking with your child rather than just letting him or her play with food as a toy. But of course there are times when it's nice to cook something specially, not for lunch or because you're cooking it anyway. Try to let your children do as much as possible. The results don't have to be perfect; the point of the exercise is the process.

CHEESE STARS

If you haven't got a star cutter, do not even begin to worry. You could just as easily use a floured glass to cut out small rounds. But I find anything made out of stars beautiful, and my children do, too; I like as well the evocation of the cheese straws of my childhood—which these, in effect, are anyway.

If you use a 1½-inch star cutter and roll out the dough to the bitter end—clumping together, reflouring, rerolling till more or less every last cheesy scrap is used up—you should get about 28 stars out of this.

½ cup all-purpose flour

½ teaspoon baking powder

pinch salt

pinch cayenne

2 tablespoons (¼ stick) unsalted butter, softened

⅔ cup finely grated orange Cheddar

¼ cup freshly grated Parmesan

Preheat the oven to 400°F. Mix all the ingredients together in a bowl. Just using hands is most fun for children, but a food processor (let them ceremoniously press the on-button) is fine if you prefer it. You shouldn't need any liquid to bind this. When it first comes together (at least in the processor) it looks crumbly, but after a few kneads it comes together smoothly. What I tend to do is divide the finished orange-glowing dough in two, then keep one in the fridge wrapped in plastic film while I roll out the other. I do this partly because I've only got enough pans to bake half the dough at a time. But from the dough's point of view, it is fine without leaving it to rest in fridge. Dust a surface with flour, roll out neither very thick nor very thin—about ½ inch if you were to measure, I suspect—then cut out the stars. Put them on nonstick or greased or lined baking sheets and bake until beginning to puff on top yet hard underneath, about 10 minutes. Look after 8. The stars continue to crisp up while they're cooling on a rack.

DIGESTIVE BISCUITS

As you will be required to eat whatever's cooked, you may as well try to make sure it's something you like. Although it might seem crazy to make digestive biscuits at home, I rather like them—a case of life imitating artifice. I'm not a great cookie buyer, simply because I'm not a great cookie eater, but when I get the urge for one of these sandy, oaty, wheaty biscuits, which are a cross between cookie and cracker, I brightly, in the manner of a dangly-earringed children's television presenter, suggest we make them.

Spelt flour is available in health stores and from baking ingredients suppliers. Please don't give in to the temptation to use all butter in place of the shortening and butter specified. The biscuits don't work without the shortening; they don't taste like digestives. This makes about 23 biscuits.

½ cup old-fashioned rolled oats

1½ cups spelt flour

½ teaspoon salt

1 teaspoon baking powder

2 tablespoons demerara sugar

¼ cup lard or white vegetable
    shortening, cold and cut into
    ½-inch dice

2 tablespoons unsalted butter, cold and
    cut in ½-inch dice

about ⅓ cup milk

Preheat the oven to 400°F.

Place the oats in a food processor and pulse to make the flakes finer in size. Put the oats, flour, salt, baking powder, and sugar in a bowl and, using your hands, mix well.

Add the diced cold shortening and rub in, using your fingertips or a freestanding mixer. When the shortening is about half rubbed in, add the butter. When all is rubbed in and you have a floury, bread-crumby texture, add cold milk slowly and cautiously, by the scant tablespoon, until the mixture begins to cohere into a firm dough.

Flour a cold surface—and I use plain flour, not spelt, here—and roll the dough out, but not too thinly, about ¼ inch. Make the biscuits using a 2½-inch round cutter—this makes about 23 of them, I repeat—and place on a nonstick baking sheet (I prick the center, in clumsy imitation of those produced by a venerable British brand with the tines of a fork) and bake for 10–15 minutes. When ready, the biscuits should be golden with faintly browning edges. Watch out because they can quickly overcook, turning dusty and slightly bitter.

Transfer to a couple of wire racks: store in an airtight tin when you're done.

FAIRY CAKES

I haven't got a heart of stone; I do realize that children sometimes like making children's food. If we're going to have tea with friends who have children the same ages as ours, we sometimes make a batch of these British-traditional, simply iced, and cherry-topped cupcakes in the morning to take with us. They go down well with the nostalgia-minded parents; the children just pick off or lick off the icing.

I use a processor, but if you want to make the fairy cakes by hand, cream the butter and sugar, then add the beaten eggs and flour in alternate tablespoons. Use milk to bind, as usual, and you won't need the extra baking powder.

1 cup all-purpose flour	2 eggs
pinch salt	1–2 teaspoons pure vanilla extract,
8 tablespoons (1 stick) unsalted butter,	if not using vanilla sugar
very soft	1 teaspoon baking powder
½ cup superfine sugar or vanilla sugar	2 tablespoons milk

Preheat oven to 400°F.

Line a 12-cavity muffin pan with paper liners. Put all the cake ingredients except the milk in the processor and pulse furiously. Then pour in the milk and process again till you have a smooth, flowing cake batter. Then, using a spoon and a rubber spatula, fill the muffin cups with the batter. Bake for 15–20 minutes or until golden around the edges, and cool on a wire rack.

When properly cool, make the icing. You can make an ordinary glacé icing—that's to say 2 cups of confectioners' sugar mixed with 3 tablespoons of milk—or you can make thicker, stiffer royal icing, whipped up from 3 cups confectioners' sugar, 2 egg whites (observe the cautions for raw eggs, see page xx), and 1 teaspoon lemon juice.

Dye as you wish—we run through the full gamut of pink ranging from ballet pink through Pepto-Bismol to all-out Barbie, depending on the intensity of our mood and heavy-handedness with the bottle of coloring.

When the icing is still wet, let your child place a maraschino cherry in the center of each. You can make double the amount in mini-fairy cakes if you prefer (and then, when topping them, remember to slice each cherry in half); just use a mini-muffin pan.

JAM TARTS

Another old-fashioned British nursery delicacy, which in truth I can't remember ever having at home when I was a child but am drawn to for the same sentimental reason my own children are—it evokes not the real but the super-real, the world of picture books and nursery rhymes. So you could say that we have a literary taste for them.

Because children like little things, we make these in mini-tartlet pans. (Though if you find any tiny heart-shaped pans, you will be able to create very girl-friendly pastries.) The pastry rolls out easily—the acid of the yogurt or buttermilk makes it tenderly cohesive—so let them practice. And use cheap jam, the sort without one iota of fruit in it. It saves having to strain it before spooning it into the pastry cases.

I cup Italian 00 or all-purpose flour

4 tablespoons (½ stick) unsalted butter, cold, cut into ½-inch dice

5 tablespoons buttermilk or

   3 tablespoons yogurt with

   2 tablespoons of ice water and

   a pinch of salt

12 teaspoons strawberry jam

1½ teaspoons water

Put the flour in a bowl with the butter and let stand in the freezer for 10 minutes. Process the two until crumbly, add the buttermilk or diluted yogurt, and process again. If it's not beginning to form a dough, add some more ice water, teaspoon by teaspoon, with the machine running. When the dough is just beginning to come together, remove from the processor, form into a fat disc, and wrap in plastic film and leave in the fridge for 20 minutes.

Preheat oven to 425°F.

Roll out the pastry and, with a 2½-inch crinkly cutter, stamp out 24 little circles. Press the pastry circles into the tartlet pan cavities (if you've got only one such pan, divide the dough in two and make one batch up after another) and put back in the fridge while you heat the jam in a saucepan with the water until a syrup liquid. Put about ½ teaspoon of jam into each tart and bake for about 15 minutes or until the pastry is cooked through.

PERIWINKLES

This recipe, which we were shown by an American girl who stayed with us for a while and whose mom used to make these for her, is a way of using up pastry scraps.

You need cinnamon, brown sugar, and honey—and scraps. On each tidied-up, oblonged-off strip of pastry, you—or your children—pour some honey, then sprinkle over cinnamon and brown sugar and roll up, like a jelly roll. With a sharp knife and a firm hand, cut across into slices about 2 inches thick. Place them, lying down, so you can see the sweet cinnamon spirals, on a lined cookie sheet and bake for about 15 minutes in a 400°F oven. You can cook your grownup pie first and then pop in the scraps when the oven's free, adjusting the heat accordingly.

PARTY FOOD

I am unhelpfully obsessive about children's parties; by that I mean I like to cook all the food myself. It gives me pleasure—it feels important. I say "unhelpfully" because I am not as well organized as I am obsessed, so I am inevitably exhausted by the time I have to face 20 overexcited, screaming children.

I have now got wise to the general setup, though, and there are some things you should know before you get started in this game. My comments concern themselves with small children.

1. They will be too excited to eat much. Concentrate on one or two star items—the cake, some special cookies.

2. Your child will be more interested in the cake's icing than in the texture or taste of the layer itself. Reserve your energies; make an all-in-one Victoria sponge (page 24), flavored or colored as required. And buy roll-out marzipan and roll-out or canned icing.

3. Build a party repertoire for yourself. I now do the same cookies party after party, but change their shape and their icing. I do the same sandwiches, provide the same cocktail sausages or franks, and buy the same sort of chips. The routine is reassuring to your children (just like the same old Christmas tree decorations coming out year after year) and helpful for you. Add to this repertoire—and see below—but keep it to provide a solid foundation.

4. Don't try to please other parents. The party is for your child.

5. Don't get agitated about the amount of sugar, food color, salt, cream, or butter. This is not the time.

Here are some ideas.

HALLOWEEN PARTY

- Chocolate cake with green marzipan and orange icing. Put black-hatted witch on top.

- Cookies (see page 453) shaped like pumpkins and decorated correspondingly; others to look like cobwebs.

- Jam tarts (by request; the jam to denote blood), recipe on page 449.

- Monster's eyeballs: just use a melon-baller (for once! useful!) to scoop out a green- or yellow-fleshed melon.

- Cocktail sausages or franks. You can't have too many. For 20 children and 12 or so adults, I make 200. You get about 30 to the round. Roast the sausages in pans in a 350°F oven for 40–50 minutes; grill or broil franks for about 3 minutes per side.

- Sandwiches; pesto-filled (for the green color).

- Violently orange cheese-flavored corn-worm crisps.

- Candy apples.

A GIRL'S FOURTH BIRTHDAY PARTY

- Pink-colored sponge cake, flavored with strawberry flavoring, pink icing, with a Barbie sitting on the corner of the cake. (Beware: fire hazard.)

- Cookies, see page 453, but stamped out with cutter in the shape of a 4, covered with bright pink glacé icing, with sprinkles strewn over when wet.

- Dozens of pink meringues (see page 17 for recipe, adding pink food coloring in final whisk and squeezed through rosette nozzle to make flower shapes about 1½ inches in diameter).

- Cocktail sausages or franks, see above.

- Fairy cakes (page 448).

- Orange cheese-flavored corn-worm crisps.

A BOY'S SECOND BIRTHDAY PARTY

- Plain sponge cake, iced white, with animals clumsily made out of dyed, bought fondant icing and marzipan, to form a circle around the edge. To tell the truth, I cannot ice, but I took the precaution of marrying someone who can.

- Cookies as above and recipe below, chocolate version, with grated zest of an orange added to the cookie mixture, and stamped out with a cutter in the shape, unsurprisingly, of a figure 2. Iced yellow, made with icing sugar, orange juice, and—no sleep tonight—yellow coloring, and sprinkles strewn on top.

- Lemon tarts, following recipe for Jam Tarts (see page 449) but substituting bought lemon curd in place of the jam. You need neither to heat the lemon curd nor add water to it before spooning it into the little tart cases.

- Cheese Stars, following recipe above, but doubling the ingredient amounts.

- Cocktail sausages or franks, see above.

- Several bowls of stalked seedless white grapes.

- Orange cheese-flavored corn-worm crisps.

THE CAKE

This is the children's cake I make, easily, year after year. For a single large cake, use a 10-inch springform pan, greased and lined with baking parchment.

¼ cups all-purpose flour	I teaspoon vanilla extract
2 teaspoons baking powder	5 eggs
pinch salt	2 tablespoons milk
I½ cups superfine sugar	
I¼ cups (2½ sticks) unsalted butter, very soft	

Mix everything together in the processor. (To make a chocolate cake, add 2 tablespoons cocoa powder mixed to a paste with 2 tablespoons boiling water. For a pink cake, add pink food coloring and use strawberry icing.) Pour into the pan and bake in a 400°F oven for 20 minutes, reduce the heat to 350°, and continue to bake another 40–50 minutes or until the cake begins to pull away from the sides of the pan. You may need to cover loosely with foil or greaseproof paper to stop it burning at the end. Allow the cake to sit on a rack in its pan for 10 minutes, then turn it out, domed side down, so its weight flattens what will be the base and you have a nice flat bottom to present to the world and provide a smooth base for the icing.

Because of the sheer volume of ingredients (and lack of air in a cake when you mix it in a processor), this cake doesn't rise much. You could, therefore, also make it in the old-fashioned way, either by hand or with a mixer, creaming the butter and sugar, adding the eggs and flour, and thus beating a lot of air into the batter. Further, you can do the cake mixture in two layer-cake pans, or you can make two full cakes, one after the other, to create a super-layer cake, particularly welcome when there are 20 or more children to feed. For a pink birthday cake I did this and stuck the cakes together with strawberry buttercream because I felt a tall, more frou-frou-looking creation fitted the particular bill. (For the icing I used 3 cups of that compellingly vile strawberry-flavored confectioners' sugar you can get now and 10 tablespoons butter, blended.) But in fact the cake, though it looked wonderful, didn't cut very well. You might decide, after all, that you can live with a not-very-high cake.

On the whole, that last is the wisest way of approaching it. As I said earlier, the birthday girl or boy is going to be far more interested in looking at and eating the icing. And the all-in-one processor method (see page 25, too) is easier, especially when you're up against time—as you inevitably will be. D. W. Winnicott, the distinguished pediatrician and analyst, wrote about being a "good-enough mother"; be satisfied with baking a good-enough cake.

For a chocolate cake—if I may backtrack—I make my own marzipan out of pistachios, but I now see that for what it is: an act of madness. Use ordinary store-bought marzipan and dye it green, or you can buy colored marzipan. You can use black food coloring, available from baking goods suppliers, for coloring a marzipan witch's hat or similarly sparky design. For the animals, let fancy, imagination, or competence be your guide.

THE COOKIES

This is the recipe I always use (it makes good Christmas tree decorations, too, if you have those special cutters and remember to make a hole at the top before baking them). It's rather like a gingerbread, only not as hot, and you can leave out the cinnamon if you like. Some fresh nutmeg grated in works well for a gentler spiciness. The dough rolls out easily. The cookies are not frangible when cooked and take icing well. Children seem to like them, as they eat the whole cookie rather than just licking off the icing.

If you want to make them chocolate-flavored, use 2¼ cups flour and ¼ cup unsweetened cocoa.

2½ cups all-purpose flour	½ cup light muscovado sugar or light
pinch salt	brown sugar
1 teaspoon baking powder	2 eggs
1 teaspoon powdered cinnamon	2 tablespoons golden syrup
(optional) or nutmeg (see headnote)	
8 tablespoons (1 stick) unsalted butter,	
diced	

Sift the flour, salt, and baking powder into a bowl. Add the cinnamon or nutmeg if using. Rub in the butter, then stir in the sugar. With a fork, stir 1 egg into the golden syrup and add to the mixture, beating well. I like doing this by hand (or with a freestanding mixer), especially if I'm making it with the children, but you can just do it in the processor, mixing all but the last two ingredients and then pouring those together down the feed tube. If needed, add the second, beaten, egg a teaspoonful at a time.

When the dough's come together, form into 2 discs and put 1, covered in plastic film or in a freezer bag, in the fridge while you get started on the first. Preheat the oven to 325°F.

Now, this dough is fairly sticky at first and there is a good reason for this—so that you can get a maximum amount of cookies, it needs to be able to absorb quite a lot of flour without becoming too dry. Be prepared to flour the surface, the dough, and the rolling pin well, and bear in mind that the dough will get smoother as you roll and re-roll. Not a shred need be wasted. Anyway, this isn't a difficult procedure, as you'll see.

Roll out to about ¼-inch thick and cut the cookies out as you wish, reclumping, rerolling, and recutting all leftovers till you have no dough left. You may find it easier to leave some leftovers from the first disc of dough and then add them to the leftovers from the second—in effect, giving yourself three discs to roll out in total.

The cookies take 12–20 minutes to cook. They're golden brown anyway, so you can't tell when they're cooked exactly by color. You don't want them to burn, so keep an eye on the edges and prod them with your fingertips occasionally—they shouldn't have any feeling of uncooked dough about them, but neither should they be rigid; they will harden as they cool. Don't get anxious about this—as long as they're not soft to the point of rawness, they should be fine.

Let cool on a rack and, if you want, leave in an airtight tin until you want to ice them. I find this makes on average 60 cookies, but naturally it depends on the shape and size of the cutters. (I don't go in for novelty-shaped or ostentatiously childish food as a rule, but I do have a huge supply of cookie cutters in just about every form available: geometric, animals, modes of transport; all fads and fancies covered. And when I was rootling about a party shop with a specialty cake-decoration wing, I found that one of the pieces in the cutting set sold for fashioning sweet peas out of icing is the perfect shape for stamping out pumpkins.)

GLACÉ ICING

To make glacé icing for these, mix 2½ cups confectioners' sugar with about 3 tablespoons boiling water and drops of food coloring strewn with sprinkles—don't ask me how many.

FISH SANDWICHES

Fish sandwiches are much loved by children. If you want to make them, then just mix some mayonnaise, the bottled stuff, with some canned salmon. But I have come to the conclusion that sandwiches are primarily there to placate the parents; they act as a nutritional sop, making the grownups feel better about all the sweet stuff that the children are really eating—it thus looks like a proper meal, not the full-on sugar orgy it is. So I wouldn't bother to do plateful upon plateful. But make sure you remove all crusts and, just this once, whatever your normal aesthetic, cut them into little triangles. Sometimes the proprieties have to be respected; a children's party is no place for restraint or minimalist chic. Just provide what your child enjoys, what he or she dreams of, and you will enjoy it too.

GLOSSARY

BOUILLON CUBES AND COMMERCIAL STOCKS. Most everyone knows what bouillon cubes are—chicken, meat, or vegetable stock (this includes porcini stock) in dehydrated and compressed form. It is important to remember, however, that not all bouillon cubes are created equal. Some produce stock of good flavor, others a chemical-tasting or overly salty brew. Always taste the stock made from a particular brand of bouillon cube before adding it to a recipe. (The cubes are rehydrated with boiling water, usually in the proportion of 1 cube to 2 cups water.) A wide range of alternative commercial stocks exists, from canned supermarket items to frozen or carton-packed, to be used as is or reconstituted, as instructed on their packages. These often yield stocks of flavor superior to that produced by bouillon cubes and should be investigated.

CAPERS. The sun-dried flower buds of a bush native to Asia and the Mediterranean, these add piquancy to a wide range of dishes. They vary in size from sub-pea to as large as your little fingernail. They are available preserved in vinegar or salt; though salt-packed capers are harder to find, it's worth seeking them out, as their flavor is deeper and their texture less squishy than the vinegar-packed kinds. All capers should be rinsed well under running water before using; the salt-packed also should be steeped in cold water for at least five minutes.

CHESTNUTS. Grown throughout the world, chestnuts are notoriously bothersome to shell and, once you've done that, you confront their bitter inner skins, which must be removed also. That's why I rely on ready-prepared canned or bottled whole chestnuts. Packed cooked, dry or in water, these may be used interchangeably in the recipes. I also use canned unsweetened chestnut purée; do not confuse this with the sweetened variety, which is not suitable for savory dishes.

CREAM, CLOTTED. The British cream repertoire is much more diverse than the American and includes this thick, extraordinarily buttery type. Widely available in American specialty food stores, imported clotted cream (sometimes labeled Devonshire cream) comes in glass jars. The cream is taken from the top of fresh, unpasteurized cream when it is gently heated and then allowed to cool.

DASHI-NO-MOTO. This is the umbrella term for Japanese instant dashi, the basic stock of Japanese cooking. It comes in two forms, granulated and liquid, and I call for both at one time or another. The granulated kind, often labeled hon-dashi ("true dashi"), is made from dried ground bonito and other seasonings and is prepared, generally, in the proportion of 1 level teaspoon to 4 cups simmering water—but always see the recipe I use it in for exact quantity information. Liquid dashi-no-moto, which is sometimes labeled "seasoning sauce" or katsuo dashi, is also made with bonito and seasonings; follow the instructions in the recipe for using it. Please be aware that both products almost invariably contain monosodium glutamate (MSG); those allergic or adverse to the substance might wish to prepare and freeze their own dashi, a simple process (see any Japanese cookbook). In a pinch, a concentrated chicken stock could be substituted for dashi-no-moto, but the flavor of the dish using it will, obviously, differ from that intended.

DUCK, MALLARD. A richly flavored wild duck, mallards make wonderful eating. Unless you are a hunter, however, or know someone who is and is willing to share a wild-duck catch, you will have to rely on commercial mallard distribution (see Sources). These farmed mallards are available seasonally from October through February and, unlike domestic duck varieties, are rather small—2 to 2½ pounds each.

FLOUR, ITALIAN 00 (FARINA DOPIA ZERO). I'm a great fan of this low-protein flour (about 3 grams for every 4 ounces, as opposed to 8 to 14 grams of all-purpose flour for the same amount). Because it is softer than regular flours—contains less gluten and therefore produces less elastic doughs when worked—it yields tender cakes and pastries and velvety sauces. (You can, however, substitute all-purpose flour for it with fine results.) Incidentally, the 00 indicates the degree of sifting for bran and grain that the flour has undergone, according to Italian flour-production standards; 00 is the finest sift, 0 slightly coarser, and on through 1 and 2, the coarsest flour designation.

FLOUR, SPELT. Spelt is a cereal grain native to Southern Europe, where it has been cultivated since ancient times. The flour made from it has a mellow nutty flavor and is slightly higher in protein than flours made from wheat. Many people who find ordinary wheat flours difficult to tolerate have no problem digesting baked goods made with spelt flour, even though it contains gluten.

GELATIN, LEAF. This is the only kind of gelatin I have luck with and I refuse to use any other type. I am, however, willing to admit that for other people, the granulated kind is more convenient and produces, under their care, completely satisfactory results. I therefore offer the option of using the latter in all the recipes calling for gelatin; the usual conversion is 6 sheets equals 1 package (¼ ounce) of granulated gelatin—enough to gel 2 cups of liquid—but see each recipe that requires the sheets for specific conversion quantities. Leaf gelatin is available in packages of thin, transparent sheets, usually imported, and needs a little longer soaking to soften it for use than the granulated kind.

GROUSE. The Glorious Twelfth—August 12th—is what the British call the much-anticipated opening day of their grouse-hunting season, which ends on December 31st. That such acknowledgment exists gives some idea of the British love of grouse, a true game bird with darker and more flavorful meat than that of partridge, its close cousin. In the States the birds are commercially available, imported, in the fall (see Sources) and run to about a pound each. Though expensive, they are a royal treat and worth seeking out. In lieu of grouse, however, use poussin or Cornish hen; these possess, obviously, a different, much milder flavor than grouse, but will work nicely in the recipes designed for grouse.

MUSCAT WINE. The muscat grape produces both dry and sweet wines with varying degrees of alcohol in them, but it is the sweet I refer to and use for a number of the recipes. Of these sweet wines, two stand out: Moscata d'Asti and Muscat de Baumes de Venise. The former is a delicately sweet, slightly effervescent wine from Italy's Piedmont region; the latter, from the southern Rhône valley in France, is golden, rich, and luscious. But any muscat wine of good quality—taste before adding!—can be used, which group includes a number of good California dessert wines.

OIL, GARLIC-INFUSED. This and other flavored oils are now widely available in supermarkets. Some gastro-purists turn up their delicate noses at such innovations, but they can be a boon to the time-starved or ordinarily exhausted cook. And as with all produce, standards vary. Sample to settle on a brand you like.

POMEGRANATE MOLASSES. Used by cooks from the Mediterranean to the Caucasus, this tangy syrup, made usually from the fruit only with the addition of lemon juice, has a rich, molasses-like flavor. In addition to the purposes to which I put it, it can be used for glazing grilled food, in a salad dressing, and to give depth of flavor to a variety of dishes.

SUET. A British cookery mainstay, though not as common as it once was, suet is, unglamorously, the solid white fat found around the kidneys and loins of beef, sheep, and other animals. It produces pie crusts and pastries that are wonderfully delicate and I urge you to try it. Having said this, you will need a sympathetic butcher to provide you with suet, which needs to be ground or chopped finely before using. In Britain, suet is sold commercially, most famously under the Atora label, but I'm not certain that I entirely trust these products: where has the suet come from, I ask myself, and how healthy are the animals who have given it? (Atora also markets "vegetable suet," and this can be used without compunction.) The choice to use these undeniably convenient products is, however, up to you (see Sources).

SUGAR, DEMERARA. This large-crystal, toffee-colored sugar is from the Demerara area of Guyana. Because of its crunchy texture it makes a perfect topping for muffins, cakes, cookies, and other desserts; it has been long used in Europe, also, as a coffee sweetener.

SUGAR, GOLDEN CASTER. Actually beige in color, this unrefined sugar from Mauritius has very fine crystals. I use it in baking, but it is also lovely sprinkled over fruit and other desserts, or used to sweeten drinks.

SUGAR, MUSCOVADO. I predict that once tasted, this richly flavorful sugar, long favored in Britain, will replace in popularity the traditional brown sugars to which most American cooks are accustomed. Muscovado (or Barbados) sugar is available in both light and dark styles. The light muscovado is relatively fine-grained, moderately rich in natural molasses (which gives both the light and dark sugars their color and flavor), and can be used whenever light brown sugar is called for. It has a wonderfully fudgy depth and flavor. Because of its greater molasses content, dark muscovado is more fully flavored than the light and stickier in texture. It evokes the aroma and taste of gingerbread. Store both kinds as you would regular brown sugar, in tightly sealed plastic bags or airtight containers.

SYRUP, GOLDEN. The English dote on this sweetener, which is also known as light treacle. First produced during the last World War as a honey substitute and made from evaporated sugar-cane juice, golden syrup has a deep, rich flavor unlike that of any other syrup. It is widely available in American supermarkets—the favored brand is Lyle's—and is used in baking or as a topping. Note that cookbooks often advise you to substitute light corn syrup for golden syrup; the latter has little of the sweetening power, not to mention flavor of the former—keep this in mind!

YEAST, COMPRESSED FRESH. I favor compressed yeast, which comes in small (0.06-ounce) cakes, for its handling pleasure and the sense of continuity with age-old baking traditions it provides. It can be used in my recipes without proofing; just add it to the dry ingredients and go. Because fresh yeast is extremely perishable, however, always check package expiration dates before you buy and use it promptly, within two weeks of purchase. You can find it in refrigerated cases of many supermarkets; store it similarly.

Sources

Balducci's
  424 Sixth Avenue
  New York, NY 10011
  212 673-2600 or 800 225-3822
  Italian products, including porcini bouillon cubes, pandoro, and savoiardi; also Italian 00 flour

Bangkok Market
  104 Mosco Street
  New York, NY 10013
  212 349-1979
  Thai products, including tom yam and pork bouillon cubes

Bel Canto Fancy Foods Ltd.
  57-01 49th Place
  Maspeth, NY 11378
  718 417-8323 or 718 497-3888
  Italian 00 flour

Bridge Kitchenware Corp.
  214 East 52nd Street
  New York, NY 10022
  212 838-1901 or 212 838-6746
  www.bridgekitchenware.com
  kitchen equipment, including blini pans

Chelsea Market Basket
  75 Ninth Avenue
  New York, NY 10111
  888 727-7887
  Cottage Delight mayonnaise and other products

D'Artagnan, Inc.
  280 Wilson Avenue
  Newark, NJ 07105
  800 DARTAGN or 973 344-0565
  www.dartagnan.com
  grouse, mallard ducks

Dean & DeLuca
  560 Broadway
  New York, NY 10012
  800 999-0306 or 212 226-6800
  www.dean-deluca.com
  English cheeses; Italian products, including salt-packed capers, canned cranberry (borlotti) beans, and spaghetti di farro; also pomegranate molasses

Harrington's of Vermont, Inc.
  210 East Main Street
  Richmond, VT 05477
  800 434-4444
  www.haringtonham.stores.yahoo.com
  slab bacon and other smoked meats

India Tree Gourmet Spices and Specialties
  4240 Gilman Place West #B
  Seattle, WA 98199
  800 369-4848
  muscovado sugar

Katagiri
   254 East 59th Street
   New York, NY 10022
   212 752-4197

   *Japanese products, including
   noodles, dried seaweeds, and dashi-
   no-moto*

King Arthur Flour
   PO Box 876
   Norwich, VT 05055-0876
   800 827-6836
   www.kingarthurflour.com

   *baking goods and equipment of all
   kinds, including Cook-Eze baking
   liners*

Myers of Keswick
   634 Hudson Street
   212 691-4194
   New York, NY 10014

   *English products, including Atora
   suet and Christmas pudding*

Simpson & Vale, Inc.
   3 Quarry Road
   Brookfield, CT 06804
   800 282-8327

   caster sugar

Williams Sonoma
   PO Box 7456
   San Francisco, CA 94120
   800 541-2233
   www.williams-sonoma.com

   *English Christmas pudding and
   other food products*

BIBLIOGRAPHY

Books referred to in the preceding pages are listed below. British and Australian publications can be ordered from Books for Cooks, London, at 171 221 1992 (phone) or www.booksforcooks.com.

Allen, Darina. *Irish Traditional Cooking.* Trafalgar Square, 1998.

Alexander, Stephanie. *The Cook's Companion.* Viking Australia, 1996.

Bhumchitr, Vatcharin. *Vatch's Southeast Asian Cookbook.* St. Martin's Press, 1997.

Borrel, Anne, Alain Senderens, and Jean-Bernard Naudin. *Dining with Proust.* Ebury, 1992.

Boxer, Arabella. *The Herb Book.* Thunder Bay Press, 1996.

———. *Book of English Food: A Rediscovery of British Food from before the War.* Hodder & Stoughton, 1991.

———. *Garden Cookbook.* Merehurst, 1995.

Collister, Linda, and Anthony Blake. *The Baking Book.* Smithmark, 1996.

Corriher, Shirley O. *Cookwise.* Morrow, 1997.

Conte, Anna del. *Classic Food of Northern Italy.* Trafalgar Square, 1999.

———. *Entertaining All'Italiana.* Bantam Press, 1991.

Costa, Margaret. *Four Seasons Cookery Book.* Grub Street, 1996.

Craddock, Fanny, and Johnnie Craddock. *Coping with Christmas.* Fontana, 1968.

Crawford Poole, Shona. *Iced Delights.* Conran Octopus, 1986.

Croft-Cooke, Rupert. *English Cooking: A New Approach.* W. H. Allen, 1960.

David, Elizabeth. *French Provincial Cooking.* Penguin, 1999.

Freud, Clement. *The Gourmet's Tour of Great Britain and Ireland.* Bullfinch, 1989.

Gayler, Paul. *A Passion for Cheese.* St. Martin's Press, 1998.

Gold, Rozanne. *Recipes 1-2-3.* Viking Press, 1996.

Green, Henrietta. *Food Lovers' Guide to Great Britain.* BBC Books, 1994.

Grigson, Jane. *English Food.* Ebury, 1992.

———. *Fruit Book.* Michael Joseph, 1982.

Hazan, Marcella. *Marcella's Italian Kitchen.* Knopf, 1986.

Hopkinson, Simon, with Lindsay Bareham. *Roast Chicken and Other Stories*. Ebury, 1994.

Kafka, Barbara. *Roasting*. Morrow, 1995.

———. *Microwave Gourmet*. Morrow, 1987.

King, Rani, and Chandra Khan. *Tiger Lily: Flavours of the Orient*. Piatkus, 1996.

Kreitzman, Sue. *Lowfat Vegetarian Cookbook*. Crossing Press, 1996.

Little, Alastair, and Richard Whittington. *Keep It Simple*. Conran Octopus, 1993.

Lowinsky, Ruth. *More Lovely Food*. The Nonesuch Press, 1935.

MacMillan, Norma. *In a Shaker Kitchen*. Pavilion, 1995.

Morris, Nicki, ed. *The Women Chefs of Britain*. Absolute Press, 1990.

Palmer, Leonie. *Noosa Cook Book*. The Blue Group, 1996.

Patten, Marguerite. *Classic British Dishes*. Bloomsbury, 1994.

Richfield, Patricia. *Japanese Vegetarian Cooking*. Crossing Press, 1996.

Roden, Claudia. *The Book of Jewish Food*. Knopf, 1996.

———. *A New Book of Middle Eastern Food*. Viking, 1985.

Ross, Rory. *Gastrodrome Cookbook*. Pavilion, 1995.

Rushdie, Sameen. *Indian Cookery*. Century, 1988.

Saleh, Nada. *Fragrance of the Earth: Lebanese Home Cooking*. International Specialized Book Service, 1997.

Saunders, Steven. *Short Cuts*. Trans-Atlantic Publications, 1998.

Sheraton, Mimi. *From My Mother's Kitchen*. HarperCollins, 1991.

Slater, Nigel. *Real Cooking*. Michael Joseph, 1997.

Taruschio, Franco, and Ann Taruschio. *Leaves from the Walnut Tree Inn*. Pavilion, 1993.

Thomas, Anna. *From Anna's Kitchen: Plain and Fancy Vegetarian Menus*. Penguin, 1996.

Wells, Patricia. *At Home in Provence*. Scribner, 1996.

Whittington, Richard, with Martin Webb. *Quaglino's: The Cookbook*. Overlook Press, 1997.

Willan, Ann. *Real Food: Fifty Years of Good Eating*. Macmillan, 1988.

Wolfert, Paula. *The Cooking of the Eastern Mediterranean*. HarperCollins, 1994.

ACKNOWLEDGMENTS

I'd like to thank all those whose recipes I've used or adapted in this book. They are mentioned by name in the text and listed in the bibliography. I'd like also to thank John Armit, and Alexandra Shulman, editor of *Vogue*, where some of these recipes started off, as did my life as a cookery writer, and Rebecca Willis, my editor there.

Thanks, too, to everyone who worked on the book at Chatto & Windus, especially Penny, Hoare, Caz Hildebrand, and Eugenie Boyd, for whose steadying calm I am particularly grateful; as I am also to Jonathan Burnham, to my agent, Ed Victor, and to Arthur Boehm, for the forbearance, intelligence, and wit he brought to bear on the American edition. Inés Alfillé double-checked recipes for me with serenity and efficiency, a rare combination. It's also important for me to express my appreciation of my butcher, David Lidgate; my greengrocer's Michanicou Brothers (and David) as well as Macken & Collins; and my fishmonger's, Chalmers & Gray.

Deepest thanks to Paul Golding, on whose judgment and friendship I have relied throughout; to Lucy Heller, Olivia Lichtenstein, Reggie Nadelson, Justine Picardie, and Tracey Scoffield; and to Sharon Raeburn and Cheryl Robertson, without whom I could not have written this book.

To John, whose idea this book was and whose title it is, who has remained so encouraging despite being cruelly unable to eat the food. I can't say thank you enough. You know.

For invaluable help in the preparation of the American edition of this book, the editor wishes to thank Nick Malgieri for sharing his compendious culinary knowledge; Cara Tannenbaum, for her diligent recipe testing and sweet friendship; and Jenny Scott, for her astute attention to so many queries, and for companionship, too. Thanks also to Miriam Brickman, to Judy Gingold—just because—and to Helen Rogan and Alfred Gingold. To Nigella Lawson, a poem, as yet uncomposed, on the delight of shared effort, and deep appreciation for her kind friendship.

INDEX

Vegetarian recipes are marked by a black diamond, and assume the use (which may mean substitution) of vegetable fat and stock. A red circle signals those recipes that take 30 minutes or less from first move to the plate in front of you.